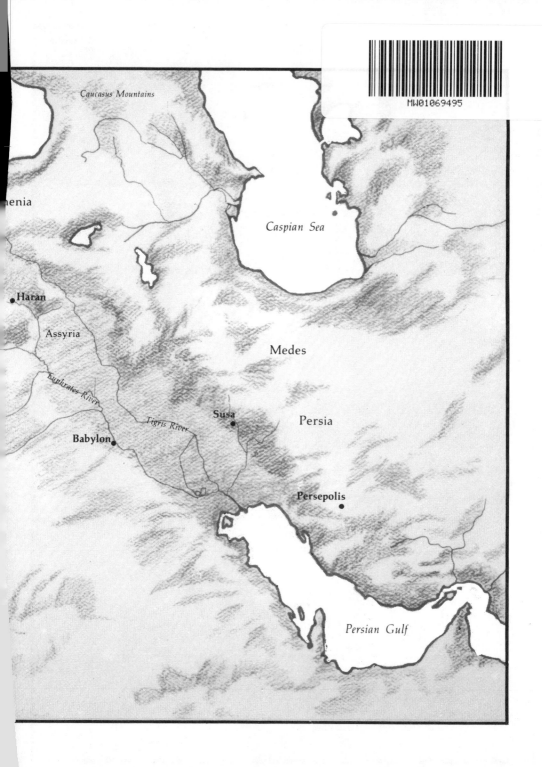

Caucasus Mountains

...enia

Caspian Sea

Haran

Assyria

Medes

Euphrates River

Tigris River

Susa

Persia

Babylon

Persepolis

Persian Gulf

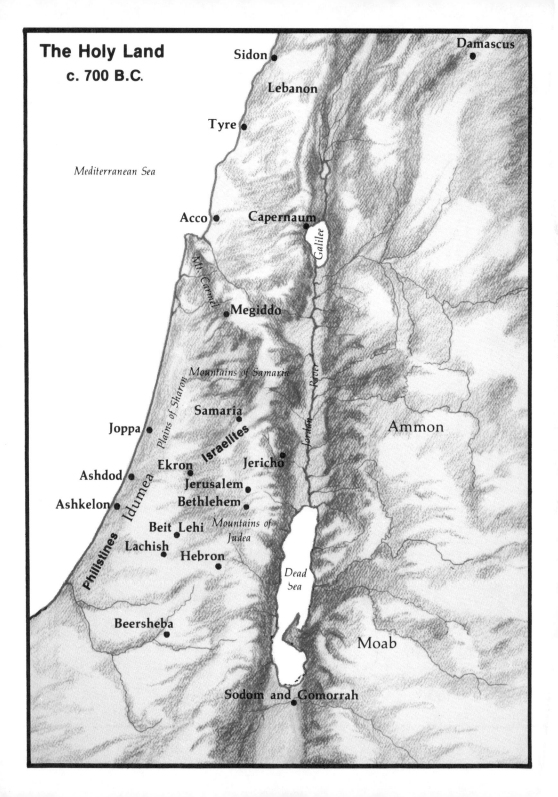

ISAIAH SPEAKS TO MODERN TIMES

W. Cleon Skousen

The Ensign Publishing Company
Salt Lake City, Utah
1984

First printing, November 1984 (2M)
Second printing, June 1985 (5M)
Third printing, August 1988 (3M)
2nd Edition, first printing, February 1993
2nd Edition, second printing, January 1996
2nd Edition, third printing, March 2000

ISBN 0-910558-25-6

The Ensign Publishing Company
Salt Lake City, Utah

Distributed by:
Sounds of Zion
9298 S. 500 W. Sandy, Utah 84070

Contents

Preface

This book has been written on the assumption that the great scripture of Isaiah can become exciting reading for the serious student of the Bible.

It is further appreciated that there are two ways to study Isaiah. One way is to study his writings topically. The second way is to carefully study the original text verse by verse. In this book we have done both.

Part I is designed to cover the life and writings of Isaiah as they unfold chronologically and deal with each topic in a separate discussion.

Part II of this book is a verse by verse commentary on the entire book of Isaiah.

Throughout this work an attempt has been made to bring together some of the finest work of many scholars both past and present. It will be appreciated that a rather phenomenal new interest in the study of Isaiah has been generated in recent years. Perhaps that is because some of his prophecies are being fulfilled all around us in our own day while others are on the verge of being fulfilled.

Certainly it was no idle gesture on the part of the Savior when he told the Saints in America nearly 2,000 years ago, "Search these things diligently; for great are the words of Isaiah" (3 Nephi 23:1).

In the writings of Isaiah we get the sweep of prophetic history over a period of nearly 2,700 years. Most of the recent books on Isaiah have emphasized the application of much of his prophetic insight to the events of our own day. Here are some of the recent books by LDS authors:

Elder Mark E. Petersen caught the impact of Isaiah's writings as they apply to modern times when he wrote his delightful book, *"Isaiah for Today"* (Salt Lake City: Deseret Book Company, 1981).

Professor Monte S. Nyman of Brigham Young University produced a monumental work of careful research and correlation between the writings of Isaiah and the clarification which modern prophets have provided for many of the more obscure passages (Bookcraft: Salt Lake City, 1980).

An exceptionally productive analysis of Isaiah by Dr. L. Lamar Adams, using computerized techniques, positively established that the entire book was written by one writer and not three or more as most of the Biblical scholars of the day have speculated. This book also contains the English text for the Ascension of Isaiah which is now accepted by many as an authentic writing of Isaiah that should have been included in the canon of scripture. Dr. Adams' book is called *The Living Message of Isaiah* (Salt Lake City: Deseret Book Company, 1981).

Many new insights and deeper levels of appreciation will be gained from *Isaiah, Prophet, Seer, and Poet* by Victor L. Ludlow. Dr. Ludlow was appointed as a Church commissioner's research fellow to make this book a singular contribution in Church literature (Salt Lake City: Deseret Book Company, 1982).

A fascinating new translation of Isaiah by Avraham Gileadi was published by the Hebraeus Press in 1982. It is called *The Apocalyptic Book of Isaiah.* Valuable explanatory notes under the title "An Apocalyptic Key" will be found at the conclusion of the Isaiah text.

Another very interesting study of the great prophet was published by Loren D. Martin under the title *Isaiah, An Ensign to the Nations* (Salt Lake City: Valiant Publications, 1982). This book is very easy to read and contains many significant contributions to provide a better understanding of the Isaiah text.

In an earlier study, Dr. Sidney B. Sperry wrote a book entitled *The Voice of Israel's Prophets,* approximately one-third of which was devoted to Isaiah. Dr. Sperry was the inspiration for many of us who began a careful study of Isaiah many years ago. This book was published by Deseret Book Company of Salt Lake City in 1961.

To all of those who have devoted so many years of their lives to make the ancient text of Isaiah a living witness of God's monumental designs for the latter days, I am deeply grateful.

I am also deeply appreciative of my wife and the members of our family who have helped in so many ways to bring the research and writing of this present book to final fruition.

A careful scrutiny of both the text and documentation was undertaken by W. Glen Fairclough, Jr. and Andrew M. Allison. The painstaking typesetting was done by Kenneth E. Neff, Jean Marshall, and Patrick Neff. The cover design is by William Kuhre. Andrew Allison also prepared the comprehensive topical index, and the printing was under the direction of Harold Skousen. Bryan Neville coordinated the project.

To all of these and many other friends who participated either directly or indirectly in helping to finish this publication, I express my heartfelt thanks.

W. Cleon Skousen

Part I

ISAIAH

THE MAN WHO SAW
2,700 YEARS
OF FUTURE HISTORY

Chapter 1

THE PROPHETIC ROLE
OF ISAIAH

This is the incredible story of a remarkable man who lived during the last half of the eighth century B.C. and who recorded the important details of human history for the next 2,700 years. He left us the longest prophetic book in the entire canon of the Bible, yet there are indications that he knew a great deal more than he ever told.[1]

SEVERAL PROPHETS SAW THE FUTURE HISTORY
OF THE WORLD

This was not the first time the Lord had pulled aside the mammoth curtain of the future, but it seems to have been the first time the Lord allowed so much of it to be put in writing for the general public. Adam, for example, saw a history of the world, but no details are given.[2] Enoch also saw the panorama of the future,

---

1. This will become obvious when we study Nephi's commentary on Isaiah.

2. D&C 107:56. Verse 57 says, "These things were all written in the Book of Enoch, and are to be testified of in due time." As yet, we do not have the full text of this scriptural treasure.

but he described only highlights such as the Great Flood,[3] the Crucifixion,[4] the Resurrection,[5] and the Second Coming of Christ.[6] Shortly after the Tower of Babel epoch, the brother of Jared (Mahonri Moriancumer) saw the history of the world from the Creation to the end of the Millennium, but this was hidden up in the sealed portion of the plates of Mormon. The Lord said it was not to be revealed until a time of righteousness finally prevailed upon the earth.[7]

Only Nephi, the magnificent Book of Mormon prophet, was allowed to record and disseminate anywhere near the number of details concerning the future as did Isaiah. Other prophets saw portions of the future and recorded them; nevertheless, it remained for Isaiah to dip deeply into practically every aspect of the colorful spectrum of the coming centuries. In fact, excluding Nephi, the prophet Isaiah recorded for public distribution specific reference to more historical highlights of the future than practically all the other prophets combined.

WHY IS ISAIAH SO DIFFICULT TO READ?

The rich and colorful eloquence of Isaiah makes his writings a brilliant literary treasure, but when it comes to the reader's comprehension of his book, authorities agree that the record of Isaiah is one of the most difficult books in the entire Bible. Why is this so?

In the first place, Isaiah, like all of the prophets, was under certain divine restrictions. For instance, it is obvious that Isaiah deliberately obscured the full meaning in many of his writings. The Lord cannot reveal certain details concerning the future to many of his children without debilitating their free agency and thereby destroying the

---

3. Moses 7:48–51.
4. Moses 7:54–56.
5. Moses 7:56–59.
6. Moses 7:60–67.
7. Ether 4:4–7; 3:25–28; 2 Nephi 27:8.

learning process of the second estate. However, to his righteous servants who can endure it, he disseminates this knowledge either obscurely or in parable form, and then gives them a "key" to unlock the full meaning. Jesus emphasized that this frustrating obscurity is by heavenly design. It is intended to give knowledge to those it will help, but withhold it from those it will hurt. Here is the way he explained it to his disciples: "Unto you it is given to know the mysteries of the kingdom of God: but to others in parables; that seeing they might not see, and hearing they might not understand."[8]

This careful discrimination—giving to man only the quantity and quality of spiritual food he is capable of digesting—is repeatedly emphasized by Paul. Said he: "For every one that useth milk is unskilful [as yet] in the word of righteousness: for he is a babe [in the kingdom]. But strong meat belongeth to them that are of full age, even those who by reason of use have their senses exercised to discern both good and evil."[9] When Paul was writing to the new converts in Corinth, he had no compunction about telling them they were still "babes in Christ," capable of receiving nothing but the milk of the Gospel. Said he: "And I, brethren, could not speak unto you as unto spiritual [mature Saints], but as unto carnal, even as unto babes in Christ. I have fed you with milk, and not with meat: for hitherto ye were not able to bear it, neither yet now are ye able."[10]

Therefore, many of the writings of Isaiah were deliberately made obscure for those who are "not able to bear it." As we shall see in Nephi's commentary, Isaiah's writings require a "key" in order to be fully comprehended. The reader will immediately appreciate the priceless value of this key as we study Isaiah in detail. Were it not for modern revelation, we would be as much in the dark on Isaiah as everyone else.

---

8. Luke 8:10.
9. Hebrews 5:13-14.
10. 1 Corinthians 3:1-2.

THE POETIC TEMPERAMENT OF ISAIAH

A second factor which makes Isaiah difficult to read is his poetic treatment of what he saw. Such an approach was the natural expression of his unusually brilliant mind, which is reflected both in his literary style and in his presentation of the subject matter. Isaiah's mind was quick, sensitive, and scintillating. Apparently his mental muscles flexed themselves by perpetually leaping about with lightning speed. While this was merely an intellectual exercise in psychological gymnastics for Isaiah, his humble readers are confronted with a continuous series of fantastic strides forward, backward, skyward, and sideways. This is because Isaiah takes the poet's approach, sweeping excitedly and impressionistically through the heights and depths of his visions, rather than methodically recording each phase of the revelation the way most prophets have done. Isaiah, when describing a problem relevant to his own time, will frequently (without the slightest warning to his readers) skip to a discussion of an identical problem which he knew would arise in the latter days.

And, just to make it more of a riddle for the uninitiated, Isaiah deliberately identified the enemies of God in the latter days by names, nationalities, and geographical locations of his own day! Hence, the terms Assyria, Babylon, Edom, and Idumea—which were familiar in Isaiah's time—were used extensively to identify the wicked and rebellious nations that Isaiah knew would arise in our time.

Furthermore, the modern reader gets the impression that while Isaiah knew it was his duty to warn his own generation, he would 10,000 times rather have spent all his energy writing about the great day of God's triumph at the time of the Second Coming of Christ. Thus, his writings whirl from verse to verse in tantalizing dizziness, touching a point of historical reality in his own day, and then leaping joyously down the corridor of time to 2,700 years in the future. This is another reason the book of Isaiah requires more than the average amount of careful, prayerful analysis in order for us to understand what he is talking about.

ISAIAH'S LITERARY SKILL

A third factor which makes Isaiah a challenging writer is his extremely advanced skill in the art of literary expression. Isaiah was no rustic bumpkin who just happened to be handy when the Lord needed a spokesman. Apparently, he was reared in Jerusalem and spent his entire life attempting to refine his capacity to serve the Lord. The available text implies that he told the sneering skeptics of his own day that they dared not reject his words as being those of an ignorant numbskull, nor excuse themselves from recognizing the Lord's servant on the grounds that he appeared to be a hermit, mystic, or oddball denizen of the desert. He was one of their own, a city prophet, with all the advantages of education and refinement that Judah's civilization could bestow upon him. Cried he: "The Lord...hath made my mouth like a sharp sword...and made me a polished shaft."[11] Then he added, "The Lord God hath given me the tongue of the learned, that I should know how to speak a word in season to him that is weary."[12]

Nephi verifies that the people of Jerusalem were sufficiently "learned" that Isaiah's sermons did not go over their heads.[13] Nevertheless, it is Isaiah's "tongue of the learned" that makes his complex eloquence additionally difficult when translated into a modern language. In fact, Nephi tells us that within 200 years after Isaiah's time, a branch of his own people were complaining that Isaiah's writings were already too difficult for them to comprehend. Nephi therefore had to interpret Isaiah for them.[14] This brings us to the most valuable commentary on the book of Isaiah that has come into man's possession during our day.

---

11. Isaiah 49:1–2.
12. Isaiah 50:4.
13. 2 Nephi 25:5.
14. 2 Nephi 25:1.

NEPHI WRITES THE ONLY PROPHETIC COMMENTARY ON ISAIAH IN EXISTENCE

By way of background we should mention that around 600 B.C., when Lehi and his colony left Jerusalem for the long, treacherous migration to the Western Hemisphere, they brought along with them the precious brass plates which contained the Hebrew canon of scripture, including the writings of Isaiah. Apparently it was only after their settlement in America that they found time to scrutinize these scriptures more closely. Naturally, they turned to Isaiah, whose writings, along with those of Jeremiah, were among the most recently recorded revelations from God.

But, as we have already noted, the study of Isaiah turned out to be a baffling mirage of elusive complexity for them. That is why they turned to Nephi and asked him to interpret this scripture for them. Nephi responded enthusiastically, for we learn that **Nephi had seen most if not all of the same revelations Isaiah had seen.**[15] Nephi therefore told the people that he would explain Isaiah "according to the spirit [of prophecy] which is **in me;** wherefore I shall prophesy **according to the plainness** which hath been with me from the time that I came out from Jerusalem with my father; for behold, my soul **delighteth in plainness** unto my people, that they may learn."[16]

Nephi prefaced his commentary by saying, "Isaiah spake many things which were hard for many of my people to understand; for they know not concerning the manner of prophesying among the Jews."[17] Then Nephi said he intended to address his commentary on Isaiah to all Israel, both ancient and modern. Said he: "Wherefore, hearken, O my people, which are of the house of Israel, and give ear unto my words; for because the words of Isaiah are not plain unto

---

15. Even before this time, Nephi had referred to his revelations in general terms (see 1 Nephi, chapters 11 to 14), but as he proceeds to explain Isaiah it is obvious that he had received broad and penetrating insights into the most intimate details of the period with which Isaiah seemed the most concerned.

16. 2 Nephi 25:4.

17. 2 Nephi 25:1.

you, nevertheless **they are plain unto all those that are filled with the spirit of prophecy.** . . . Yea, and my soul delighteth in the words of Isaiah, for I came out from Jerusalem, and mine eyes hath beheld the things of the Jews, and I know that the Jews **do understand** the things of the prophets, and **there is none other people that understand** the things which were spoken unto the Jews like unto them, save it be that **they are taught after the manner of the things of the Jews.**"[18]

Nephi then identified his own prophecies, which he was about to relate "in great plainness," as being identical with those given by Isaiah. He said men will recognize their fulfillment when they come to pass in the last days.[19] "Wherefore, they are of worth unto the children of men, and he that supposeth that they are not, unto them will I speak particularly, and confine the words unto [matters involving] mine own people; for I know that they shall be of great worth unto them in the last days; for in that day shall they understand them; wherefore, for their good have I written them."[20]

Nephi then proceeded to unfold his many brilliant and illuminating comments on the book of Isaiah. In doing so, he bluntly stated, "I proceed with mine own prophecy, according to my plainness; in the which **I know that no man can err.**"[21]

THE BOOK OF MORMON SETTLES THE QUESTION AS TO WHETHER THE BOOK OF ISAIAH WAS WRITTEN BY ONE AUTHOR OR SEVERAL

There is no doubt that the book of Isaiah has been one of the casualties of modern scholasticism. Certain biblical "authorities" have undertaken the task of shredding and fragmenting it until it

18. 2 Nephi 25:4–5.
19. 2 Nephi 25:7.
20. 2 Nephi 25:8.
21. 2 Nephi 25:7.

would seem to be a heap of literary shambles rather than a unified pillar of prophecy, exhortation, and faith as Isaiah intended.[22]

Many of the objections to the book in its present form center around the contention that Isaiah just could not have anticipated all of these spectacular events so far in the future. These self-appointed critics thereupon commenced to perform surgery on the text to accommodate this theory. They made an internal analysis of the book itself and lopped off everything they considered to be non-Isaiah text. The results of all this secular cynicism, with its abstracting and subtracting, has been to destroy confidence in practically the entire prophetic panorama that Isaiah left us as a legacy for mankind.

The late Dr. Sidney B. Sperry of Brigham Young University classified this entire school of Isaiah critics into two groups—the moderates and the radicals. The moderates claim that out of 66 chapters in Isaiah, 44 were not written by Isaiah. The radicals go further. They say that out of 1,292 verses in this book, Isaiah wrote only 262! Fortunately, there are many competent Bible scholars whom Dr. Sperry quoted who see far more evidence of unity in the book of Isaiah than the critics can produce to prove disunity.

Nevertheless, it is commonplace today for Bible commentaries to go along with the moderates and accept only chapters 1 to 39 as being written by the prophet Isaiah. They attribute chapters 40 to 55 to a second author, and chapters 56 to 66 to yet a third.

For those who have ears to hear and are not precluded by prejudice from hearing it, the Book of Mormon has a unique and satisfying answer to this whole problem. Since the Isaiah text on the brass plates was recorded sometime before 600 B.C., it seems highly significant that the contents of our present Isaiah in the Bible are almost identical with the wide samplings quoted in the Book of

---

22. For a discussion of this fragmenting of Isaiah, see Sidney B. Sperry, *The Old Testament Prophets* (Salt Lake City: Deseret Sunday School Union, 1965), chapters 15 and 16.

Mormon. Dr. Sperry pointed out that the Nephite records contain fully quoted texts from the following chapters of Isaiah:

ISAIAH	BOOK OF MORMON
Chapters 2–14	2 Nephi, chapters 12–24
Chapter 29	2 Nephi, chapter 27
Chapters 48 and 49	1 Nephi, chapters 20 and 21
Chapters 50 and 51	2 Nephi, chapters 7 and 8
Chapter 52	3 Nephi, chapter 20
Chapter 53	Mosiah, chapter 14
Chapter 54	3 Nephi, chapter 22
Chapter 55:1	2 Nephi 26:25

The last ten chapters of Isaiah include much that is treated in earlier chapters, so there is a consistency in prophetic subject matter and theology between the last ten chapters and those cited above.

This unity and accuracy of Isaiah received the full endorsement of the resurrected Christ. Speaking to the Saints living in the Western Hemisphere around A.D. 34, he declared: "And now, behold, I say unto you, that ye ought to search these things. Yea, a commandment I give unto you that ye search these things diligently; **for great are the words of Isaiah.** For surely he spake as touching all things concerning my people which are of the house of Israel; therefore it must needs be that he must speak also to the Gentiles. And all things that he spake have been and shall be, even according to the words which he spake."[23]

From this we conclude that the samplings from the writings of Isaiah in the Book of Mormon, which were recorded before 600 B.C., prove the original unity of this book. Furthermore, the fact that the Savior endorsed the version of Isaiah which was then in the hands of the Saints living on the American continents gives unprecedented credence to our own version because it is essentially the same.

---

23. 3 Nephi 23:1–3.

Chapter 2

ISAIAH, THE MAN

Let us get better acquainted with Isaiah as an individual and also review the turbulent times in which he lived.

From Isaiah 6:1 we learn that this prophet was receiving revelations and was apparently well into his calling as a servant of the Lord by the time King Uzziah died of leprosy around 739 B.C. We presume, therefore, that he was probably born around 780 B.C., but there is nothing specific concerning his nativity.[1] The Bible simply describes him as the "son of Amoz" without elaborating on it. We know he was married and had a son named Shear-jashub (meaning "the remnant shall return") and a son named Maher-shalal-hash-baz (meaning "spoil speedeth, prey hastens"). The names of both sons were given by revelation as prophetic symbols.[2] It is interesting that

---

1. This is deducted from the fact that Isaiah had a son old enough to accompany him on an assignment in approximately 735 B.C. (Isaiah 7:3).

2. See Isaiah 8:3 as a basis for this conclusion. Isaiah himself said, "Behold, I and the children whom the Lord hath given me are for signs and for wonders in Israel *from the Lord of hosts*" (Isaiah 8:18).

Isaiah's wife was a noble woman of deep spirituality who held the distinction of being called a "prophetess."[3]

So far as we can tell, the ministry of Isaiah lasted at least 48 years.[4] It may have lasted considerably longer. In any event, we can safely say that Isaiah was alive and constituted a powerful religious force around Jerusalem during practically all of the last half of the eighth century before Christ (750 to 700 B.C.).

THE HUMILITY AND RESOLUTION OF ISAIAH

Isaiah was a man of the most profound humility. He attributed every commendable talent he possessed to the goodness of God. Understandably, however, his nonbelieving audiences interpreted this professed humility to be the most blatant kind of pride and boasting. For Isaiah to present himself as "a servant of God" and proclaim that his visions, eloquence, and political insights all came from heaven, was counted almost as blasphemous as the humble testimony of another who came 750 years later and said he was the Son of God.

Nevertheless, Isaiah dared not do less than testify humbly concerning what he had seen, what he had been told, and how he had happened to get involved in the strenuous business of receiving a "prophetic calling." He wanted people to understand that sometimes a man "has to do what he has to do" simply because God has given him the tremendous responsibility of performing a certain mission.

It goes without saying, of course, that Isaiah **could** have rejected the calling, but not without jeopardizing his salvation, which he did not intend to do. Therefore he pressed forward and, in the most resolute manifestation of his own humility, testified that he was merely trying to do what God had required at his hand. Said he: "Hearken, ye people, from far; The Lord hath called me from the

---

3. Isaiah 8:3.

4. Adam Clarke, *The Holy Bible...with a Commentary and Critical Notes,* 6 vols. (Nashville: Abingdon, n.d.), 4:17.

womb; from the bowels of my mother hath he made mention of my name. And he hath made my mouth like a sharp sword; in the shadow of his hand hath he hid me...and said unto me, Thou art my servant, O soldier of God,[5] in whom I will be glorified."[6]

ISAIAH RECEIVES THE MOST DIFFICULT OF ALL PROPHETIC ASSIGNMENTS

Isaiah was much like Noah, Abraham, Jeremiah, and Mormon. He was called to bear down in pure testimony against a people whom he already knew would reject his message. There are few callings in the Priesthood more desperately discouraging than this kind. It is hard enough when there is a chance that one will see the fruits of his labor, but what happens when it becomes repugnantly apparent that there are not going to be any fruits? This is what happened to Isaiah. "Then I said, I have laboured in vain, I have spent my strength for nought, and in vain: yet surely my judgment is with the Lord, and my work with my God."[7]

In chapter 50 we learn why he had become so thoroughly discouraged. Like the Christ who would follow him, Isaiah was subjected to all of the bitter abuse that the apostates who were then in power could heap upon him. Nevertheless, he says, "I was not rebellious, neither turned away....I gave my back to the smiters, and my cheeks to them that plucked off the hair [of my beard]: I hid not my face from shame and spitting."[8]

---

5. In the King James text of Isaiah 49:3, the phrase "soldier of God" is translated as a proper name, "Israel." But since the salutation is addressed to Isaiah, it is believed it should have been translated in its literal sense as a title rather than as a name. This rendition removes the confusion.

6. Isaiah 49:1–3. This passage is correctly interpreted by authorities as referring not only to Isaiah but also to the Christ. It would be a mistake to say that it applied exclusively to the Christ and not to Isaiah. Verse 4 seems to make it very clear that this section of scripture is being addressed to Isaiah personally, since this particular detail does not fit the Messiah's life at all.

7. Isaiah 49:4.

8. Isaiah 50:5–6.

And the Lord assured Isaiah that his labor was not in vain. He was told that even though Israel would not be gathered to the Lord in his day, nonetheless Isaiah would be "glorious in the eyes of the Lord"[9] because he had fought a good fight and had done the work of the Lord valiantly.

THE IMPORTANCE OF ISAIAH'S WRITINGS

Among other things, Isaiah had the calling of proclaiming the good news of Israel's gathering and redemption in the last days. The Lord said he would give Isaiah a message which would be "a light to the Gentiles."[10] Christ is the "light to . . . the Gentiles,"[11] and Isaiah was given the privilege of being the one to prophetically announce for the first time (as far as available scriptures show) that in the latter days the Gospel would first spring forth among the **Gentiles.** So Isaiah was allowed to announce this great promise of hope and encouragement as a "light to the Gentiles." The Lord also told Isaiah his writings would be like a "covenant" of hope for Israel in the latter days whereby they would know that they would eventually reoccupy their "desolate heritages."[12] Like prisoners of captivity they would be liberated and gathered back to their homelands.[13]

With such promises ringing in his heart, Isaiah sang out his psalm of triumph: "For the Lord God will help me; therefore shall I not be confounded: therefore have I set my face like a flint, and I know that I shall not be ashamed."[14]

Because he knew his prophecies would cover nearly all of the remainder of the second estate, he was most anxious that the people record his promises so that as the centuries passed by, men would know that Isaiah had spoken the truth. Said he, "Now go, write it

---

9. Isaiah 49:5.
10. Isaiah 42:6; 49:6.
11. Luke 2:32.
12. Isaiah 49:8.
13. Isaiah 49:9-13.
14. Isaiah 50:7.

before them in a table, and note it in a book, that it may be for the time to come for ever and ever."[15]

Apparently somebody who belonged to the house of Joseph took this instruction seriously and recorded the full text of Isaiah's words in the family canon of scripture which is known to us as the "brass plates."[16] This sacred record came into the hands of a military leader named Laban. After the prophet Lehi had obtained this scriptural treasure from Laban, he brought it to America.[17]

ISAIAH SEES A VISION OF THE LORD

Isaiah appears to have lived in the middle or lower city of Jerusalem,[18] and nearly all of his prophetic activities appear to have centered around the capital of Judah.

It was approximately 739 B.C., the year King Uzziah died, that Isaiah said, "I saw also the Lord sitting upon a throne, high and lifted up, and his train filled the temple."[19] Whether he was actually in the temple or seeing a vision of it, we are not certain. In any event, Isaiah was frightened by the glorious vision of the Lord and his heavenly hosts. He cried out, "Woe is me! for I am undone; because I am a man of unclean lips, and I dwell in the midst of a people of unclean lips: for mine eyes have seen the King, the Lord of hosts."[20] Immediately, one of the Lord's attendants (called a seraphim, or angel of consuming glory)[21] took a coal from the golden altar of incense (the only altar with fire inside the temple), touched it to

---

15. Isaiah 30:8.

16. See 1 Nephi 3:3. That these plates were the family scripture of the house of Joseph is made plain in the Book of Mormon: "And Laban also was a descendant of Joseph, wherefore he *and his fathers* had kept the records." (1 Nephi 5:16; emphasis added.)

17. 1 Nephi 4:38; Alma 37:3–5.

18. 2 Kings 20:4. Note that the text says middle "court." An alternate translation of this word is "city."

19. Isaiah 6:1. Nephi verifies this testimony and says, "...he [Isaiah] verily saw my Redeemer, even as I have seen him" (2 Nephi 11:2).

20. Isaiah 6:5.

21. Clarke, *Commentary*, 4:51.

Isaiah's lips, and said, "Lo, this hath touched thy lips: and thine iniquity is taken away, and thy sin is purged."[22]

Isaiah then heard the Lord saying to his hosts, "Whom shall I send, and who will go for us?"[23] From these words the prophet could not tell exactly where the messenger was to go or what message he was to deliver, but this was of no consequence to this humble man. If the Lord needed an ambassador, Isaiah stood ready. Therefore, he volunteered for the assignment. Said he, "Here am I; send me."[24]

ISAIAH RECEIVES HIS CALLING

The Lord accepted Isaiah and told him to go forth and make a proclamation. Said the Lord: "Go, and tell this people, Hear ye indeed, but understand not; and see ye indeed, but perceive not. Make the heart of this people fat, and make their ears heavy, and shut their eyes; lest they see with their eyes, and hear with their ears, and understand with their heart, and convert, and be healed."[25]

This strange passage makes it sound as though the Lord was deliberately stultifying his people so they would not be converted and saved from the conquest and dispersion which lay ahead. Dr. Adam Clarke believes the Hebrew idiom would be better rendered as follows: "Ye certainly hear, but do not understand; ye certainly see, but do not acknowledge. Seeing this is the case, make the heart of this people fat—declare it to be stupid and senseless; and remove from them the means of salvation, which they have so long abused."[26]

Based on what Isaiah subsequently said to the people, this version would appear to be the more accurate one.

---

22. Isaiah 6:7. The touching of a live coal to Isaiah's lips would suggest that this whole account is the description of a vision rather than a physical experience.

23. Isaiah 6:8.

24. Ibid.

25. Isaiah 6:9–10.

26. Clarke, *Commentary*, 4:50.

Isaiah then asked the Lord how long Israel and Judah would be spiritually blind, spiritually deaf, and spiritually fat-hearted. The Lord replied: "Until the cities be wasted without [an] inhabitant, and the houses without man, and the land be utterly desolate, and the Lord have removed men far away, and there be a great forsaking in the midst of the land."[27]

Then the Lord told Isaiah that in spite of this there would be a "tenth" or remnant that would be left from the dispersion. These would be "the holy seed," which would have in them the "substance" of survival, and their descendants would return to the lands of Israel's inheritance in the due time of the Lord.[28]

ISAIAH'S ENCOUNTER WITH A FAT-HEARTED KING

Three or four years after the above vision, the Syrians and the northern Ten Tribes prepared to attack Jerusalem. By this time the king of Judah was Ahaz, grandson of Uzziah. For the sake of the few righteous among the people of Judah, the Lord sent Isaiah to meet this apostate monarch. The conference took place "at the end of the conduit of the upper pool in the highway of the fuller's field."[29]

The Lord told Isaiah to take his eldest son with him,[30] and tell the king to rely upon the Lord and all would be well. The king was to be told not to form alliances with heathen nations or get all heated up for war because if he obeyed God's counsel, the war being planned against Judah would never take place. To give confidence to the renegade king, Isaiah was even authorized to tell King Ahaz that he could test the prophet's integrity by asking for some great sign as proof that God was indeed behind the promise. However, the king declined. In fact, he ignored the advice of the prophet altogether. He armed the tribe of Judah, made an alliance with the Assyrians, and

---

27. Isaiah 6:11–12.
28. Isaiah 6:13.
29. Isaiah 7:3.
30. Ibid.

immediately suffered a devastating defeat at the hands of Syria and the northern Ten Tribes of Israel.

ISAIAH ITEMIZES THE SINS OF ISRAEL

It will be recalled that Isaiah's ministry was well on its way by 739 B.C., and therefore we know he was proclaiming his message of pleading and warning for more than 20 years before the northern Ten Tribes fell in 721 B.C. All during that time he was denouncing the violence, immorality, and criminal dishonesty of these rebellious children of Israel, predicting what would happen if they did not repent.

When it came to excoriating and peeling off the hides of the apostate Israelites, none of the prophets was more specific or articulate than Isaiah. Note, for example, his denunciation of the widespread problem of alcoholism: "Woe to the crown of pride, to the drunkards of Ephraim, whose glorious beauty is a fading flower.... The priest and the prophet[31] have erred through strong drink, they are swallowed up of wine, they are out of the way through strong drink; they err in vision, they stumble in judgment. For all tables are full of vomit and filthiness, so that there is no place clean."[32]

Sorrowfully, Isaiah exclaimed, "Ah sinful nation, a people laden with iniquity, a seed of evildoers, children that are corrupters: they have forsaken the Lord, they have provoked the Holy One of Israel unto anger, they are gone away backward."[33]

In all Israel he tried to find some level of society or some corner in the nation where righteousness still prevailed, but, he said, "the whole head is sick, and the whole heart faint. From the sole of the foot even unto the head there is no soundness in it; but wounds, and

---

31. The heathen priests of Baal were called "prophets" in Israel, although "false prophets" would have been more apt (1 Kings 18:22).

32. Isaiah 28:1, 7-8.

33. Isaiah 1:4.

bruises, and putrifying sores."[34] He accused the leaders of beating the people to pieces,[35] grinding the faces of the poor,[36] taking away their land,[37] and indulging in pomp, pride, and agnosticism.[38] In addition, they had turned the world upside down by destroying all moral standards and the means of measuring excellence. He said they called "evil good, and good evil," they put "darkness for light, and light for darkness;...bitter for sweet, and sweet for bitter!"[39] He said even the widows and orphans had been corrupted.[40] The great display of temporary prosperity had given many of the people a sense of security, but Isaiah said it was a mirage which would fade away. He said the people had "multiplied the nation" with their conquests but not "increased the joy."[41] Instead of genuine, wholesome happiness which comes from righteousness, the people were living in a drunken dream world. Cried Isaiah: "Woe unto them that rise up early in the morning, that they may follow strong drink; that continue until night, till wine inflame them! And the harp, and the viol, and tabret, and pipe, and wine, are in their feasts: but they regard not the work of the Lord, neither consider the operation of his hands."[42]

THE WOMEN OF ISRAEL

A particularly sharp and cutting barb was aimed by Isaiah at the female population of Israel.

"The daughters of Zion are haughty and walk with stretched forth necks and wanton eyes, walking and mincing as they go, and

---

34. Isaiah 1:5-6.
35. Isaiah 3:15.
36. Ibid.
37. Isaiah 5:8.
38. Isaiah 5:14, 18-23.
39. Isaiah 5:20.
40. Isaiah 9:17.
41. Isaiah 9:3.
42. Isaiah 5:11-12.

making a tinkling with their feet: therefore the Lord will smite with a scab the crown of the head of the daughters of Zion. . . . In that day the Lord will take away the bravery of their tinkling ornaments about their feet, and their cauls, and their round tires like the moon, the chains, and the bracelets, and the mufflers, the bonnets, and the ornaments of the legs, and the headbands, and the tablets, and the earrings, the [finger] rings, and the nose jewels, the changeable suits of apparel, and the mantles, and the wimples, and the crisping pins, the glasses, and the fine linen, and the hoods, and the vails. And it shall come to pass, that instead of sweet smell there shall be stink; and instead of a girdle a rent; and instead of well set hair baldness; and instead of a stomacher a girding or sackcloth; and burning instead of beauty."[43]

It would be interesting to know how the debutantes of Samaria (not to mention their mothers) reacted to a shin-barking sermon like that one!

THE ISRAELITES ACCUSED OF IGNORING COVENANTS MADE AT BAPTISM

From the earliest times, the Lord had emphasized the importance of baptism and the necessity of keeping the covenants made at the time this sacred ordinance is performed. In chapter 48 of the book of Isaiah, the Lord restates his great controversy with Israel. One of the more prominent charges is the fact that Israel had taken oaths in the name of the Lord and made covenants through baptism, but had afterwards broken them.

Joseph Smith's translation of this verse in the Book of Mormon is more correct than the King James Version, and we shall therefore use it to present the Lord's point of view on this problem. Significant words which appear only in the Book of Mormon version are emphasized:

---

43. Isaiah 3:16–24.

"Hearken and hear this, O house of Jacob, who are called by the name of Israel, and are come forth out of the waters of Judah, **or out of the waters of baptism,** who swear by the name of the Lord, and make mention of the God of Israel, yet they swear not in truth nor in righteousness. Nevertheless, they call themselves of the holy city, **but they do not** stay themselves upon the God of Israel, who is the Lord of Hosts; yea, the Lord of Hosts is his name."[44]

The Lord states in this same chapter that he has always told Israel what he intended to do long in advance, "lest thou shouldest say, Mine idol hath done them, and my graven image, and my molten image, hath commanded them."[45] Through Isaiah he now puts Israel on notice that a whole debacle of calamity is about to be unleashed upon the people because of their stubborn, perverted, and diabolical wickedness.

ISAIAH PREDICTS THE FALL OF ISRAEL

Isaiah was well acquainted with the haughty sneers which these egotistical sychophants focused on him whenever he had tried to get them to abandon their swill-barrel lives. Said he, "Woe unto them that are wise in their own eyes, and prudent in their own sight!"[46] Then, looking into the immediate future, he spoke as though the events were happening right before his eyes. Said he, "Your country is desolate, your cities are burned with fire: your land, strangers devour it in your presence, and it is desolate."[47] All that the prudent and the wise of Israel had believed to be impossible would suddenly sweep in on them like a flood.[48] It would wipe out most of them in a single day, particularly the leaders.[49] No foreign aid or alliance could

---

44. 1 Nephi 20:1-2; Isaiah 48:1-2.

45. Isaiah 48:5.

46. Isaiah 5:21.

47. Isaiah 1:7.

48. Isaiah 8:7-8.

49. Isaiah 9:14.

possibly save them.[50] Those who resisted (and were put under siege) would eat their own dead.[51]

Quoting the Lord further, Isaiah said: "Upon the land of my people shall come up thorns and briers; yea, upon all the houses of joy in the joyous city: because the palaces shall be forsaken; the multitude of the city shall be left [gone]; the forts and towers shall be for dens for ever, a joy of wild asses, a pasture of flocks."[52]

Isaiah made no attempt to hide the identity of the nation which would bring about this destruction. He quoted the Lord, who had said: "O Assyrian, the rod of mine anger, and the staff in their hand is mine indignation. I will send him against an hypocritical nation, and against the people of my wrath will I give him a charge, to take the spoil, and to take the prey, and to tread them down like the mire of the streets."[53]

In that hour "shall Ephraim be broken, that it be not a people."[54] "Ephraim" was often used to signify the northern Ten Tribes.

The terrifying king of Assyria who performed this task of obliterating the last vestiges of the Ten Tribes in 721 B.C. was Sargon II, brother of Shalmaneser V. Among the ruins of Sargon's magnificent palace at Khorsabad were found these engraved words: "At the beginning of my rule, in the very first year I reigned...I set siege to and conquered Samaria [the capital of Israel]."[55]

Isaiah himself lived to see all of this come to pass. He witnessed the Ten Tribes, which Jeroboam had set up in 922 B.C., come to their inglorious demise 201 years later. Of course, Sargon II gloried in what he had accomplished, but he had no idea that this victory would have never occurred had not the Lord stepped aside and

---

50. Isaiah 8:9-10, 12.

51. Isaiah 9:20.

52. Isaiah 32:13-14.

53. Isaiah 10:5-6.

54. Isaiah 7:8.

55. Nelson Beecher Keyes, *Story of the Bible World* (Pleasantville, N.Y.: Reader's Digest Association, 1962), p. 83.

allowed it. Sargon therefore gave credit to Assur, his heathen deity, and boasted in the strength of his own mighty arm as well as the heroism of his massive host of soldiers encased in their brass armor. Had he consulted with Isaiah, he would have learned that in little more than a century Assyria would be drowning in her own blood, and the Assyrian city of Nineveh would disintegrate into a multitude of huge, brown mud mounds. Isaiah knew all about it. He had seen it in vision.

THE STATE OF AFFAIRS IN JUDAH

Isaiah, of course, maintained his headquarters in Jerusalem, not in the precincts of the beleaguered Samaria, capital of the northern Ten Tribes. While Isaiah's troubled mind had been dwelling upon the ravaging conquest going on in Israel, a much more pleasant development was taking place in Jerusalem. In fact, some six years[56] before the fall of Israel, Jerusalem had seen the demise of the wicked and apostate King Ahaz. The throne had been taken over by his son, Hezekiah, who turned out to be one of the most notable cases in history of an unusually righteous son coming from the home and environment of an extremely wicked father. If all the facts were known, we might discover that much of the credit for this righteous son belonged to the careful tutoring of his mother, but of this we are not sure. Certainly someone deserves a lot of credit. The Bible says that Hezekiah replaced his father, Ahaz, and immediately initiated a universal reform with a crash program to restore the true worship of God. Any physical object which Hezekiah found the people worshipping he immediately ordered destroyed. This included one of the most sacred relics handed down from the days of Moses—the famous "brazen serpent." Hezekiah discovered the people offering incense to it, so he commanded that it be broken to pieces.[57]

There was such a contrast between Hezekiah and his father that the scripture is glowing in its praise of the new king. The Bible says:

---

56. 2 Kings 18:10–11.
57. 2 Kings 18:4.

"And he did that which was right in the sight of the Lord, according to all that David his father [forefather] did. He removed the high places, and brake the images, and cut down the groves....He trusted in the Lord God of Israel; so that after him was none like him among all the kings of Judah, nor any that were before him."[58] This is high praise indeed.

HEZEKIAH REPAIRS, SANCTIFIES, AND REDEDICATES THE TEMPLE

To Isaiah, the coming of Hezekiah must have seemed almost too good to be true. From the cold, wretched days of apostasy and persecution under Ahaz, Judah suddenly emerged into the warm springtime of a glorious rebirth.

Barely were the coronation ceremonies over before the 25-year-old Hezekiah began "in the first month" to repair the temple so that its doors could be opened once more to the regular worship of Jehovah.[59] During the years of neglect under Ahaz, the sacred precincts of the house of the Lord had become cluttered with rubble. But no more so than the lives of the people, including the priests. Therefore, as soon as the temple was repaired, Hezekiah began the most extensive program of repentance, reformation, and sanctification the land had known in several generations. He called the apostate and lazy Levites into a conference and said unto them:

"Hear me, ye Levites, sanctify now yourselves, and sanctify the house of the Lord God of your fathers, and carry forth the filthiness out of the holy place. For our fathers have trespassed, and done that which was evil in the eyes of the Lord our God....Also they have shut up the doors of the porch [of the temple], and put out the lamps, and have not burned incense nor offered burnt offerings....Wherefore the wrath of the Lord was upon Judah....Our fathers have fallen by the sword, and our sons and

---

58. 2 Kings 18:3-5.
59. 2 Chronicles 29:1-3.

our daughters and our wives are in captivity for this. Now it is in mine heart to make a covenant with the Lord God of Israel, that his fierce wrath may turn away from us."[60]

Then he made a direct appeal to these custodians of the lesser Priesthood: "My sons, be not now negligent: for the Lord hath chosen you to stand before him, to serve him, and that ye should minister unto him."[61] A certain percentage of these Levites responded to the call, but we gain the impression from later statements that it was only the more valiant who responded, and therefore a minority of the tribe.[62]

The scripture continues: "And they gathered their brethren, and sanctified themselves, and came, according to the commandment of the king.... And the priests[63] went into the inner part of the house of the Lord, to cleanse it, and brought out all the uncleanness that they found in the temple of the Lord into the court of the house of the Lord. And the Levites took it, to carry it out abroad into the brook Kidron."[64]

Once everything had been cleaned up, the priests prepared for the rededication of the temple. They followed the same procedure as that which was used at the original dedication. This ritual required eight days of extremely laborious and precise procedure.[65] On the eighth day Hezekiah came with all "the rulers of the city" and had the priests make a special sacrifice as an atonement for the

---

60. 2 Chronicles 29:5-10.

61. 2 Chronicles 29:11.

62. Both scriptural and secular history clearly demonstrate that in a time of crisis, those who respond to the need of the hour have nearly always constituted merely a valiant minority. It seems to be a sociopolitical rule of life as well as a spiritual phenomenon.

63. The priests were those Levites who were direct descendants of Aaron. The remainder of the Levites held offices comparable to teacher and deacon today. Only the priests could go inside the temple.

64. 2 Chronicles 29:15-16. Note that the Levites could only help dispose of the rubbish after it was brought out of the temple by the priests.

65. 2 Chronicles 29:17. For a more detailed description of this procedure, see W. Cleon Skousen, *The Fourth Thousand Years* (Salt Lake City: Bookcraft, 1966), chapter 9. The original dedication of Solomon's Temple is also discussed therein.

wickedness of the whole people, "for the king commanded that the burnt offering and the sin offering should be made for all Israel."[66]

Then the king had the choirs and orchestras assemble themselves. All the people "sang praises with gladness, and they bowed their heads and worshipped."[67] In fact, from the time that the burning of the sacrifice commenced until it was completely consumed, "the singers sang, and the trumpeters sounded."[68] It was a most glorious time of rejoicing.

Then the king invited the people to bring forth their burnt offerings, peace offerings, and oblations just as Solomon had done at the first dedication.[69] But there were immediate complications. As the people brought forth 70 bullocks, 100 rams, and 200 lambs, **there were not enough worthy priests to take care of the offering.** This was not really a great many animals compared to the original dedication, but it was too many for the number of worthy priests. The scripture says, "The priests were too few, so that they could not flay all the burnt offerings: wherefore their brethren the Levites did help them, till the work was ended, and **until the other priests had sanctified themselves: for the Levites were more upright in heart to sanctify themselves than the priests."[70]**

Years before, when the former king Ahaz had closed the temple in order to initiate heathen practices, it had left the sons of Aaron (the priests) and the Levites with practically nothing to do. In one generation they had gone back into secular life and lost themselves in the mundane affairs of the people. It was therefore quite a revolutionary undertaking to have them all called on missions to

---

66. 2 Chronicles 29:24.

67. 2 Chronicles 29:27, 30.

68. 2 Chronicles 29:28.

69. 2 Chronicles 29:31-33.

70. 2 Chronicles 29:34. Whenever there were not enough priests, the Levites were asked to help with the arduous work of skinning, cleaning, and washing the sacrificial animals. It is in this same spirit that deacons and teachers assist the priests today.

once more function in their Priesthood offices. As we shall see, this calling caught the sons of Aaron (the priests) especially off guard. The scripture says "the thing was done suddenly."[71]

HEZEKIAH'S GREAT FEAST OF THE PASSOVER

Since the rededication of the temple took place in the first month of the year, it came into Hezekiah's heart to immediately prepare the people for the great Feast of the Passover, which was always supposed to be celebrated in the second month. However, the Bible says "they had not done it of a long time,"[72] and it gives the following reasons why: "For they could not keep it at that time [in the former days], **because the priests had not sanctified themselves sufficiently,** neither had the people gathered themselves together to Jerusalem."[73]

Hezekiah was so enthusiastic about the possibility of restoring the Passover to its former prominence as the principal feast of the year that he sent invitations to every part of ancient Israel. Not only were letters on royal parchment dispatched to all sections of Judah, but he ventured to invite any fragments of the other tribes that might be found "from Beer-sheba [in the south] even to Dan [in the north]."[74] His invitation was specifically designed to appeal to those who were remnants of the other tribes. It must be kept in mind that these events happened just before the fall of Samaria, but several years following the conquest of northern and eastern Israel by Assyria. Hezekiah's appeal was therefore to King Hoshea and the remnants around the capital city of Samaria. He wrote:

"Ye children of Israel, turn again unto the Lord God of Abraham, Isaac, and Israel, and he will return to the **remnant of you, that are escaped out of the hand of the kings of Assyria.** And be not like your fathers, and like your brethren, which trespassed against the Lord

---

71. 2 Chronicles 29:36.
72. 2 Chronicles 30:5.
73. 2 Chronicles 30:3.
74. 2 Chronicles 30:5.

God of their fathers, who therefore gave them up to desolation, as ye see."[75]

Since Hezekiah knew that King Hoshea of Israel and most of the "remnants" were practicing heathens, his appeal focused primarily on one of their most sensitive sentiments—their concern for their loved ones in captivity. He therefore said, "Now be ye not stiffnecked, as your fathers were, but yield yourselves unto the Lord, and enter into his sanctuary.... **For if ye turn again unto the Lord,** [then] **your brethren and your children shall find compassion before them** [the Assyrians] **that lead them captive,** so that they shall come again into this land: for the Lord your God is gracious and merciful, and will not turn away his face from you, **if ye return unto him.**"[76]

As might have been expected, when Hezekiah's messengers delivered these invitations to King Hoshea and to the few remaining fragments of the apostate northern tribes, "they laughed them to scorn, and mocked them."[77] But the effort was not entirely in vain. The scripture says a "divers" few heeded the call, "humbled themselves, and came to Jerusalem." There they found that the people of Judah had come together in a mammoth congregation. They were united with "one heart to do the commandment of the king...by the word of the Lord."[78]

"Then they killed the passover on the fourteenth day of the second month: **and the priests and the Levites were ashamed, and sanctified themselves....** "[79] We interpret this to mean that many who had been holding back came forward to perform their duties, for the scripture continues: "And they stood in their place after their manner, according to the law of Moses...."[80]

75. 2 Chronicles 30:6–7.
76. 2 Chronicles 30:8–9.
77. 2 Chronicles 30:10.
78. 2 Chronicles 30:11–12.
79. 2 Chronicles 30:15.
80. 2 Chronicles 30:16.

It will be recalled that the first Passover was eaten the night before the children of Israel fled out of Egypt. At the time of the exodus, they were also compelled to eat unleavened bread because they had to bake their dough without having time to leaven it. This is why the Feast of Unleavened Bread was supposed to be celebrated each year for a period of seven days, commencing with the Feast of the Passover. Hezekiah ordered that this be done. However, the scripture says that the people who assembled in Jerusalem on this notable occasion had such a magnificent time of rejoicing during the first seven days that "the whole assembly took counsel to keep [or celebrate] other seven days."[81] So altogether, they were united in celebrating this great occasion of feasting and covenant making for a period of approximately half a month.

There was such a large number of new converts who swarmed in upon the priests during this conference that Hezekiah was fearful lest some small technicalities might have been overlooked in the mass sanctification of so many people. He was also concerned lest the exact procedure might not have been followed by all of the people in connection with the Passover. Hezekiah therefore made a special appeal to the Lord to overlook any small irregularities which might have occurred. He prayed, "[May] the good Lord pardon every one that prepareth his heart to seek God, the Lord God of his fathers, though he be not cleansed according to the purification of the sanctuary."[82] The Lord had emphasized to his prophets from earliest times that the main part of a sacrifice was in the heart or in the attitude of the individual making the offering. Technicalities are incidental. Therefore, "the Lord hearkened to Hezekiah, and healed the people."[83]

The scripture concludes, "And all the congregation of Judah, with the priests and the Levites, and all the congregation that came out of

---

81. 2 Chronicles 30:23.
82. 2 Chronicles 30:18-19.
83. 2 Chronicles 30:20.

Israel, and the strangers [non-Israelite converts] that came out of the land of Israel, and that dwelt in Judah, rejoiced. So there was great joy in Jerusalem: for since the time of Solomon the son of David king of Israel there was not the like in Jerusalem."[84]

One final note should be mentioned concerning the generosity of Hezekiah during this period of public feasting and celebrating. Much of it was made possible because King Hezekiah, like Solomon before him, was willing to contribute thousands of sheep and cattle to feed the people. His princes also joined in this manifestation of generosity so that altogether the people had 2,000 bullocks and 17,000 sheep to feed upon during this gigantic general conference in Jerusalem.[85]

THE FRUITS OF RIGHTEOUSNESS

Once the people had followed their king back into the channels of righteous living, it was only a short time before the fruits of prosperity began to manifest themselves.

The king set the example by offering to contribute all of the sacrificial animals necessary for feast days and for the temple services each night and morning.[86] He then "commanded the people that dwelt in Jerusalem to give the portion of the priests and the Levites, **that they might be encouraged in** [administering] **the law of the Lord.**"[87]

As a result of this appeal, the people began paying their tithes, and they brought the abundance of their "firstfruits" into the house of the Lord as required by the law of Moses.[88]

Within a month such great "heaps" of grain and other supplies began to accumulate in the courts of the temple that Hezekiah

---

84. 2 Chronicles 30:25-26.

85. 2 Chronicles 30:24.

86. 2 Chronicles 31:3.

87. 2 Chronicles 31:4.

88. 2 Chronicles 31:5.

ordered "chambers" to be prepared so that these supplies might be safely stored.[89]

It is hard to believe that all of this revitalization of righteousness in Judah was going on right while Samaria and the remnants of the Ten Tribes were in the last throes of their dissipated apostasy. It was just two or three years after the dedication of the temple in Jerusalem that Assyrian officers arrived in the northern kingdom and placed the king of Samaria under arrest. A short time later the army of Assyria arrived to place the city under siege. The siege extended over a period of time, and when Hezekiah was in the sixth year of his reign the northern capital of the Ten Tribes crumbled in defeat.[90] It will be recalled that the conquest of the northern tribes was completed under Sargon II. It was only a matter of eight years until his famous Assyrian son, Sennacherib, was back in Palestine threatening to do the same thing to Judah!

THE ASSAULT OF ASSYRIA ON JUDAH

The scripture says that it was in the fourteenth year of the reign of Hezekiah that the thousands of Assyrian infantry and charioteers arrived in Palestine. Their main objective was Egypt, but Sennacherib was taking everything in his sweep to be certain there would be no resistance on his flank or in the rear. Judah was on his eastern flank. Since the main battle between Assyria and Egypt was expected to be fought on the plains of Palestine, Sennacherib's campaign commenced by destroying 46 cities of Judah and then laying siege to Lachish, a city lying almost directly west of Hebron.

It is interesting that although King Ahaz, Hezekiah's father, had paid tribute to Assyria, Hezekiah refused. Sennacherib promptly dispatched some of his troops against Judah's military outposts and "fenced cities," with devastating results.[91] Hezekiah immediately

---

89. 2 Chronicles 31:7-11.
90. 2 Kings 18:10.
91. 2 Kings 18:13.

prepared for the siege of Jerusalem which appeared inevitable. It was expected to occur just as soon as the Assyrians had completed their siege of Lachish. Hezekiah "set captains of war over the people, and gathered them together to him in the street of the gate of the city, and spake comfortably to them, saying, Be strong and courageous, be not afraid nor dismayed for the king of Assyria, nor for all the multitude that is with him: for there be more with us than with him: with him is an arm of flesh; but with us is the Lord our God to help us, and to fight our battles."[92]

HEZEKIAH'S TUNNEL

Hezekiah cut a new channel in the limestone rock that allowed water from the famous Gihon Spring to run inside the city, and had the old entrance blocked off from the outside.[93] Said he, "Why should the kings of Assyria come, and find much water?"[94] Hezekiah also put the people to work rebuilding the great wall, and then he constructed a defensive wall beyond it.[95] He strengthened the fortress of Millo just in case there had to be a last stand.[96] Then he settled back to examine his position. This would have been a good time for him to have sent for Isaiah, but apparently he did not. As he considered all the factors involved, Hezekiah suddenly realized he was subjecting his people to an impossible task. No doubt his spies brought in daily reports of the strength and deployment of the enemy's troops, and Hezekiah knew that once the Assyrians had finished with Lachish they could rush up to flatten Jerusalem. In a moment of realistic panic, he apparently forgot his own courageous words to his troops and sent this humble petition to Sennacherib at

---

92. 2 Chronicles 32:6–8.
93. 2 Chronicles 32:30..
94. 2 Chronicles 32:4.
95. 2 Chronicles 32:5.
96. Ibid..

Lachish: "I have offended; return from [being against] me: that which thou puttest on me will I bear."[97]

This was the kind of talk Sennacherib liked. He promptly assessed Judah with a tribute of 300 talents of silver and 30 talents of gold.[98] Hezekiah knew this was a terrible price to pay for peace, but he determined to pay it even if he had to strip the kingdom of all its wealth to achieve it. And this is literally what happened. The scripture says, "And Hezekiah gave him all the silver that was found in the house of the Lord, and in the treasures of the king's house." But it was still not enough. In order to meet the assessment, Hezekiah had to "cut off the gold from the doors of the temple of the Lord, and from the pillars which Hezekiah king of Judah had overlaid."[99] All this was then sent to the king of Assyria. However, the treacherous Assyrians still refused to take off the pressure.

In fact, having impoverished Judah, Sennacherib tried to antagonize and subvert the people of Jerusalem against their king.

THE ASSYRIANS ATTEMPT TO PROVOKE AN INSURRECTION AGAINST HEZEKIAH

Although the king of Assyria was deeply involved with his siege at Lachish, he released "a great host"[100] and sent them with a delegation to parley with the people of Judah. The Assyrian delegates took up a position by "the conduit of the upper pool, which is in the highway of the fuller's field."[101] From this spot they could be seen and heard by all the people standing on top of the nearby city wall. However, Hezekiah was anxious to create a truly diplomatic atmosphere while negotiating with the Assyrians. Therefore, he did not have his delegates shout down from the wall, but sent them out

---

97. 2 Kings 18:14.
98. Ibid.
99. 2 Kings 18:15–16.
100. 2 Kings 18:17.
101. Ibid.

into the public space where the Assyrian nobles were waiting.[102] But
it was soon apparent that there was nothing to negotiate. The
Assyrians were rude, bellicose, and vindictive.

Hezekiah's representatives were embarrassed by the blatant
demands of the Assyrians, and, like typical diplomats, they feared
lest the people of Judah would realize how serious things had
become. They therefore said to the Assyrians, "Speak, I pray thee, to
thy servants **in the Syrian language** [Aramaic]; **for we understand
it: and talk not with us in the Jews' language** [which can be
understood] in the ears of the people that are on the wall."[103]

The disdainful Assyrians not only ignored the request but began
shouting "with a loud voice"[104] so that the people on the wall might
hear even better. Previously, they had accused the people of Judah of
being a secret ally of Egypt, since they had not been willing to fight
with Assyria.[105] Now, however, they made a direct attack on King
Hezekiah himself. The Assyrian spokesman cried out: "Hear the
word of the great king, the king of Assyria.... Let not Hezekiah
deceive you: for he shall not be able to deliver you out of his
[Sennacherib's] hand: Neither let Hezekiah make you trust in the
Lord, saying, The Lord will surely deliver us, and this city shall not
be delivered into the hand of the king of Assyria."[106] Then followed
an extremely significant statement. Said he: "Make an agreement
with me by a present, and come out to me [away from your king],
and then eat ye every man of his own vine,... **until I come and take
you away to a land like your own land, a land of corn and
wine,**... that ye may live, and not die: and hearken not unto
Hezekiah, when he persuadeth you, saying, The Lord will deliver
us."[107]

---

102. 2 Kings 18:18.
103. 2 Kings 18:26.
104. 2 Kings 18:28.
105. 2 Kings 18:21; Isaiah 36:6.
106. 2 Kings 18:28-30.
107. 2 Kings 18:31-32.

Obviously Sennacherib was planning to eventually haul the people of Judah back to Assyria, precisely the way his father, Sargon II, had hauled off the Ten Tribes!

This was enough for the delegates from Jerusalem. They rushed back into the city, tore their fine robes as a token of distress, and went in to report to the king. But Hezekiah was not one whit less distressed than they were. He tore his own clothes, put on sackcloth, and went to the temple.[108] It was not until he had been reduced to this abject level of complete desperation that he finally thought of sending for Isaiah. It was obvious that the material fortifications on which Hezekiah had been instinctively relying were not enough. If God would not save them, nothing would.

THE LORD TESTS THE FAITH OF HEZEKIAH

The king's servants dressed themselves in sackcloth and went as a large delegation to see Isaiah. It is amazing that some contact had not been made with this great spiritual leader long before. Isaiah heard their plea, and then bluntly told them: "Say ye to your master, Thus saith the Lord, Be not afraid of the words which thou hast heard, with which the servants of the king of Assyria have blasphemed me. **Behold, I will send a blast upon him, and he shall hear a rumour, and shall return to his own land; and I will cause him to fall by the sword in his own land.**"[109]

It was a fantastic promise, almost unbelievable in its fullest implications, but there it was. Hezekiah found the strength to rely upon it, and therefore apparently sent the Assyrian delegates away without any satisfaction whatever.[110]

But barely had Hezekiah received what he thought was going to be certain relief from Assyria's monstrous threat when a whole new

---

108. 2 Kings 19:1.

109. 2 Kings 19:6–7.

110. The fact that "the great host" was not used by the delegates to immediately attack Jerusalem would indicate that the Assyrians were not anxious to become involved militarily until after the termination of the siege of Lachish.

cloud of catastrophe settled down upon him. As far as we can tell, it was right at this juncture that Hezekiah came down with a deadly illness caused by a lethal infection or abscess in his body.[111] He became so ill that he asked Isaiah to visit him and disclose what his expectations might be. Isaiah had bitter news for the king. Said he, "Set thine house in order; for thou shalt die, and not live."[112] Even under normal circumstances this would have come as a terrible shock to the king, but in view of the national crisis sweeping down on Judah it seemed completely irrational that the Lord would take him just now.

As soon as Isaiah left the room, Hezekiah turned his face to the wall and sobbed out a special pleading to the Lord. "I beseech thee, O Lord, remember now how I have walked before thee in truth and with a perfect heart, and have done that which is good in thy sight. And Hezekiah wept sore."[113]

By this time, Isaiah was just leaving the middle court of the palace.[114] Suddenly the Spirit stopped him and said: "Turn again, and tell Hezekiah the captain of my people, Thus saith the Lord, the God of David thy father [forefather], I have heard thy prayer, I have seen thy tears: behold, I will heal thee: on the third day thou shalt go up unto the house of the Lord. **And I will add unto thy days fifteen years; and I will deliver thee and this city out of the hand of the king of Assyria;** and I will defend this city for mine own sake, and for my servant David's sake."[115]

Isaiah returned to the palace with this magnificent news. However, lest the healing of the king be taken too much for granted,

111. Although the compiler of 2 Kings put this incident in the next chapter, it obviously happened before the fall of Sennacherib's army, as evidenced by 2 Kings 20:6. We are therefore inserting it in our account where it appears to belong chronologically.

112. 2 Kings 20:1.

113. 2 Kings 20:3. Hezekiah afterwards wrote down just how he felt on this tragic occasion. See Isaiah 38:9-20.

114. 2 Kings 20:4. An alternate translation indicates that this may have been the middle of "the city."

115. 2 Kings 20:5-6.

Isaiah determined to require something at the hands of the king's servant. Just as Naaman, the leper, had been required to dip in the Jordan seven times, so now Isaiah required that a poultice of figs be spread over the king's abscess.[116]

But when King Hezekiah heard all that Isaiah had to say, it soon became apparent that he was not taking any part of this message for granted. These prophecies were all so thrilling to contemplate that he did not dare believe them! Perhaps Isaiah was just trying to make him feel good in his last hours. The king therefore begged for some kind of confirmation, saying, "What shall be the sign that the Lord will heal me, and that I shall go up into the house of the Lord the third day?"[117]

Isaiah could have said, "Be still and wait patiently on the Lord," but the Spirit apparently authorized Isaiah to demonstrate to Hezekiah that the power of God was behind his words. The prophet therefore referred to the famous sundial which had been built by Ahaz, the father of Hezekiah, and asked, "Shall the shadow [on the dial] go forward ten degrees, or go back ten degrees?"[118]

This was a rather fantastic proposition since the changing of the shadow on the dial would apparently involve some dramatic change in the working relationship between the earth and the sun, and Hezekiah so interpreted it. Said he, "It is a light thing for the shadow to go down ten degrees [since that would only involve a speeding up of existing processes]:... but let the shadow **return backward** ten degrees."[119]

The scripture continues, "And Isaiah the prophet cried unto the Lord: and he brought the shadow ten degrees backward, by which it had gone down in the dial of Ahaz."[120] It was a phenomenal miracle and must have impressed the king deeply, not only because of its

---

116. 2 Kings 20:7.
117. 2 Kings 20:8.
118. 2 Kings 20:9.
119. 2 Kings 20:10.
120. 2 Kings 20:11.

spectacular implications but also by giving comfort to his tormented mind. Someday the Lord will no doubt reveal whether this was done by direct intervention in the mechanics of stellar dynamics or whether he achieved it by the more simple and direct device of manipulating the rays of light and thereby causing the shadow to be shifted backward. Whatever the explanation, Hezekiah knew it required the power of the Almighty to achieve it, and that was enough.

KING HEZEKIAH RECEIVES A FRIGHTENING ULTIMATUM

Shortly after Hezekiah had gone through the above experience and recovered his health, something occurred which was enough to send him back to his sickbed. It was a letter from Sennacherib, king of the Assyrians.

Sennacherib had just learned that Tirhakah,[121] king of Ethiopia, was heading north with a fresh army. To the Assyrians, this meant that the quarrel with Judah must be resolved immediately lest Hezekiah be tempted to join the Egyptian-Ethiopian alliance. The rough letter which Sennacherib sent to Hezekiah was recognized by the king of Judah as a frightening ultimatum. In spite of the previous assurances of the Lord, this latest communication created a whole new state of emergency. The Assyrian letter told Hezekiah how the fighting men from Nineveh had utterly and ruthlessly destroyed all who refused to collaborate. "And shalt thou be delivered?" the king asked sarcastically in his letter to Hezekiah.

Hezekiah took the letter and hurried to the temple, where he spread it out "before the Lord."[122] Then he prayed fervently, "O Lord God of Israel, . . . bow down thine ear and hear   Of a truth, Lord, the kings of Assyria have destroyed the nations and their

---

121. Commentators describe Tirhakah as "an Ethiopian who was at first the general and then the successor of the Egyptian king, Shabako. He was contemporary not only with Sennacherib, but with his two successors Essarhaddon and Asshurbanipal." (J.R. Dummelow, ed., *A Commentary on the Holy Bible* [New York: Macmillan Publishing Co., 1949], entry under 2 Kings 19:9.)

122. 2 Kings 19:14.

lands. . . . Now therefore, O Lord our God, I beseech thee, save thou us out of his hand, that all the kingdoms of the earth may know that thou art the Lord God, even thou only."[123]

The Lord answered the king through his chosen spokesman, Isaiah. In this revelation the Lord itemized the offenses of the Assyrians and then concluded by saying: "Therefore thus saith the Lord concerning the king of Assyria, He shall not come into this city, nor shoot an arrow there, nor come before it with shield, nor cast a bank against it. By the way that he came [along the coast], by the same shall he return, and shall not come into this city, saith the Lord."[124]

THE DESTRUCTION OF THE ASSYRIAN ARMY

The Bible declares that the destruction of the Assyrian army came about that very night. The catastrophe came in the form of a "blast" against the Assyrian hosts. If the record is accurate, this involved the massive annihilation of 185,000 soldiers! Even if a cipher has been added, as some authorities attribute to certain statistics in the Bible, it was still a frightening loss. Whether the "blast" was by plague or by storm we are not told. The Bible simply says, "And it came to pass **that night,** that the angel of the Lord went out, and smote in the camp of the Assyrians an hundred fourscore and five thousand: and when they [the survivors] arose early in the morning, behold, they were all dead corpses."[125]

Sennacherib forgot all about attacking Judah. And he certainly was not going to stay around to be trapped by the powerful Ethiopian-Egyptian forces moving up from the south. We do not know whether he even dared stay long enough to dispose of his dead. The record says he departed abruptly for Nineveh with all that remained of his once great army, and he never returned. Nevertheless, the shadow of Isaiah's prophecy followed him to his

---

123. 2 Kings 19:15–19.
124. 2 Kings 19:32–33.
125. 2 Kings 19:35.

Tigris capital. The Lord had not only said that Sennacherib would be compelled to return home, but that after he arrived there he would be murdered.

The fulfillment of this dark prediction took place many years later. While the king was in his chapel praying to his idol, two men crept up behind him unawares. They were actually two of the king's sons. For reasons history has not completely disclosed, they had come to assassinate their father. In an instant they struck him down with their swords, and then fled for their lives to Armenia, the country located just north of Assyria.[126] A third son, named Esar-haddon, promptly seized the throne[127] and became the new king of Assyria around 680 B.C.

THE BABYLONIANS SEEK AN ALLIANCE WITH JUDAH

Now we must go back to a significant event which occurred right after Sennacherib fled out of Palestine following the destruction of the major segment of his army. Shortly after Judah's miraculous escape from what could have been an Assyrian massacre, a delegation arrived from Babylon. These dignitaries had come to congratulate the king of Judah and compliment him for his recent recovery from a well-nigh fatal sickness.[128] The Babylonian monarch had considered this visit so important that he had sent his own son as the leader of the delegation, and in his hand was a substantial gift.

We need to remind ourselves that Babylon was at this time a vassal of Assyria, but her king was secretly building up alliances against Assyria. It is very likely, therefore, that this visit by the crown prince of Babylon had highly significant political overtones. The text would indicate that there were overtures of an alliance by the Babylonians since the scripture says, "And Hezekiah **hearkened unto them,** and shewed them all the house of his precious things,

---

126. 2 Kings 19:37.
127. Ibid.
128. Isaiah 39:1.

the silver, and the gold, and the spices, and the precious ointment, and all the house of his armour, and all that was found in his treasures: there was nothing in his house, nor in all his dominion, that Hezekiah shewed them not."[129]

This would suggest that the Babylonians wanted an assurance from Hezekiah that the Jews could sustain an army if there was a new war. But we immediately wonder where Hezekiah obtained this new royal treasure. Apparently the Assyrians (who had previously stripped Judah of all her wealth as a tribute) were compelled to abandon most of it when they began their hasty retreat. From such spoils Judah could have enriched herself once more. This is the only way to account for the fact that Hezekiah had such an abundance of treasure to display to the Babylonians during their visit.

The above scenario would indicate that Hezekiah had not yet learned that alliances with pagan nations were repugnant to the Lord. Hezekiah did not realize it, but he had just made a serious mistake. These greedy Babylonians never forgot the treasures they saw in Jerusalem when the king took them on a tour of his palace.

ISAIAH'S LAST APPEARANCE IN THE BIBLE

The scripture says that the Babylonians had scarcely departed when Isaiah came striding into the king's presence. He asked, "What said these men? and from whence came they unto thee?"[130] Isaiah was full of questions. When Hezekiah said they were from Babylon, Isaiah inquired further, "What have they seen in thine house?"[131] Hezekiah replied, "There is nothing among my treasures that I have not shewed them."[132] That was just what Isaiah feared he might say. Things were just as serious as the Spirit had apparently been telling him. Isaiah therefore declared to Hezekiah, "Behold, the days come,

---

129. 2 Kings 20:13.
130. 2 Kings 20:14.
131. 2 Kings 20:15.
132. Ibid.

that all that is in thine house, and that which thy fathers have laid up in store unto this day, shall be carried into Babylon: nothing shall be left, saith the Lord."[133] Then he added a more sinister note by saying, "And of thy sons [descendants] that shall issue from thee, which thou shalt beget, shall they [the Babylonians] take away; and they shall be eunuchs in the palace of the king of Babylon."[134]

What could a man do with a devastating prophecy like that hanging over his head? Hezekiah could have gone into a state of despondency, but he finally decided that since this captivity was scheduled for his posterity and was some distance in the future, he would spend the rest of his life making conditions as favorable as possible.

So the scripture says that during the final years of his reign, "Hezekiah had exceeding much riches and honour: and he made himself treasuries for silver, and for gold, and for precious stones, and for spices, and for shields, and for all manner of pleasant jewels; storehouses also for the increase of corn, and wine, and oil; and stalls for all manner of beasts, and cotes for flocks. Moreover he provided him cities, and possessions of flocks and herds in abundance: for God had given him substance very much."[135]

Thus the reign of Hezekiah finally came to a close. After his 15 years of extended life were finally consumed, "Hezekiah slept with his fathers, and they buried him in the chiefest of the sepulchres of the sons of David: and all Judah and the inhabitants of Jerusalem did him honour at his death. And Manasseh his son reigned in his stead."[136]

This transfer of the throne from Hezekiah to Manasseh is believed to have occurred about 696 B.C.

---

133. 2 Kings 20:17.
134. 2 Kings 20:18.
135. 2 Chronicles 32:27–29.
136. 2 Chronicles 32:33.

THE END OF ISAIAH'S MINISTRY

Sometime during these latter years of Hezekiah's reign, the great prophet Isaiah passed from the scene of recorded history. He was indeed one of the most singular personalities in the Bible. He held the Melchizedek Priesthood,[137] and from all we can tell he was never involved in any of the administrative functions of the lesser Priesthood. His entire adult life appears to have been devoted exclusively to teaching, preaching, and writing up the panoramic visions which were revealed to him with such amazing frequency. He was the Lord's official spokesman to several of Judah's kings, and appears to have maintained an active public ministry during more than half a century.

He wrote practically nothing about himself. Even the four historical chapters (36, 37, 38, and 39) which pertain to the events of his days are believed by most scholars to have been borrowed and inserted from 2 Kings.[138] The language is almost identical.[139] It is thought that some well-meaning scribe included them so that readers would have at least a part of Isaiah's fascinating story incorporated in his own writings. Other than these four chapters, we must still depend upon 2 Kings and 2 Chronicles for most of what is known about Isaiah today.

DID ISAIAH DIE A MARTYR?

Although the Bible account does not speak of Isaiah after the reign of King Hezekiah, both Jewish and Christian tradition tell us

---

137. This is based on the statement of Joseph Smith that "all the prophets [of Israel] had the Melchizedek Priesthood and were ordained by God himself." (Joseph Smith, *Teachings of the Prophet Joseph Smith,* sel. Joseph Fielding Smith [Salt Lake City: Deseret Book Company, 1938], pp. 180–81).

138. Sperry, *Old Testament Prophets,* pp. 73–74.

139. It must not be overlooked that Isaiah might have written these chapters and that later they were borrowed and incorporated in 2 Kings. This possibility is strongly hinted in 2 Chronicles 32:32. However, the reader will find no difficulty in observing that these four chapters are sharply different in style from the rest of Isaiah.

that Isaiah lived long enough to encounter the wrath of Judah's most depraved and wicked king, Manasseh.

It seems almost incomprehensible that Manasseh should have turned out to be such an abominable scoundrel when he was the son of the righteous king, Hezekiah. Nevertheless, this is what occurred. Manasseh reigned from 696 to 642 B.C. and followed the lecherous practices of his wicked grandfather, King Ahaz, instead of his father, Hezekiah. Manasseh restored the worship of the fertility gods, Baal and Ashtoreth.[140] He revived the heathen practice of human sacrifice by burning and sacrificing children in the valley of Hinnom.[141] He even sacrificed his own son.[142] He killed any who got in his way or opposed his debaucheries. The scripture says, "Moreover Manasseh shed innocent blood very much, till he had filled Jerusalem from one end to another."[143]

Under these reprehensible circumstances, it might very well have been that Isaiah was indeed a martyr just as the traditions of both the Jews and Christians claim he was.[144] It is stated that King Manasseh had Isaiah shoved into the hollow trunk of a tree and sawn asunder with a wooden saw.[145]

---

140. 2 Chronicles 33:2–4.

141. 2 Chronicles 33:6.

142. 2 Kings 21:6.

143. 2 Kings 21:16.

144. Flavius Josephus, *Josephus: Complete Works*, trans. William Whiston (Grand Rapids, Mich.: Kregel Publications, 1960), Antiquities of the Jews, 10:3.

145. Justin Martyr, "Dialogue with Trypho," in *A Select Library of Nicene and Post-Nicene Fathers of the Christian Church*, Second series, 14 vols. (Grand Rapids, Mich.: Wm. B. Eerdman's Publishing Co., 1952), 1:259.

Chapter 3

ISAIAH'S PROPHECIES
CONCERNING THE FALL
OF THE ANCIENT KINGDOMS

As mentioned in the preface, it is of great assistance in gaining an appreciation of the scope and quality of Isaiah's prophecies to study his writings topic by topic as well as verse by verse.

In this chapter we will present some of the major themes or topics that Isaiah covered in his recorded visions concerning the destiny of the mighty kingdoms which caused mankind to tremble in terror because of their violent conquests in ancient times. He also saw what would happen to the Jews.

THE FALL OF ASSYRIA

Although he never lived to see it, Isaiah knew that the downfall of the mighty Assyrian empire was imminent. Even while Isaiah was predicting that it would be Assyria which would carry off the northern tribes and make a vassal of Judah, he was also announcing the Lord's coming revenge upon Assyria. Through Isaiah the Lord said: "I will punish the fruit of the stout heart of the king of Assyria, and the glory of his high looks. For he saith, By the strength of my hand I have done it, and by my wisdom; for I am prudent.... "[1] The Lord went on to declare that none of the Assyrian conquests would have come to pass had he not stepped aside and permitted them. One day, however, he said the rich fields and possessions of Assyria would be swept away and her cities would become a total desolation.[2]

Actually, during the years immediately following the ministry of Isaiah, Assyria became more powerful than ever before. Sennacherib's son, named Esarhaddon, conquered Egypt in 671 B.C., and his son, who was named Ashurbanipal, completely devastated all opposition by 640 B.C. In fact, the manifest might of Nineveh's tyrants might be said to have reached its zenith at that time. A religious cynic could have certainly poked fun at Isaiah's prophecies during these years. Nevertheless, Assyria's days were numbered. Within 30 more years she was virtually annihilated as a nation. In 612 B.C., "a force made up of Medes, Babylonians and their allies fell upon Nineveh, the fabulous Assyrian capital. While it was under siege the Tigris flooded and carried away parts of its walls, rendering it indefensible. The city was laid waste with such thoroughness that for ages it was completely lost sight of and became something of a myth."[3]

But something equally devastating was awaiting the wicked populace of Judah.

THE FALL OF JUDAH

As we shall see later, Judah succeeded in surviving as a nation for over a century after the capture of the Ten Tribes, and this was achieved in spite of violent military pressure and badgering by the Assyrians. Nevertheless, Isaiah knew that it would not be the Assyrians who would destroy Judah and carry her people away. It

---

1. Isaiah 10:12–13.
2. Isaiah 10:16–19.
3. Keyes, *Story of the Bible World*, p. 89.

would be the Babylonians. We recall the words which Isaiah declared to King Hezekiah: "Hear the word of the Lord. Behold, the days come, that all that is in thine house, and that which thy fathers have laid up in store unto this day, shall be carried into Babylon: nothing shall be left, saith the Lord."[4]

Addressing himself to the city of Jerusalem in her hour of total depravity, Isaiah said: "How is the faithful city become an harlot! it was full of judgment; righteousness lodged in it; but now murderers. Thy silver is become dross, thy wine mixed with water: thy princes are rebellious, and companions of thieves: every one loveth gifts, and followeth after rewards: they judge [consider] not the fatherless, neither doth the cause of the widow come unto them."[5]

Isaiah saw Judah's day of siege and famine,[6] he saw the "people robbed and spoiled...snared in holes...hid in prison houses."[7] Just prior to their collapse he saw that no one would wish to govern. He said, "A man shall take hold of his brother...saying, Thou hast clothing, be thou our ruler, **and let this ruin be under thy hand** [for correction]." But he would refuse, saying, "I will not be a binder up;[8] for in my house is neither bread nor clothing: make me not a ruler of the people."[9] When evil men have corrupted a country, it becomes well-nigh impossible to get even good men to take office.

Isaiah accused Judah of making a covenant with hell in order to escape the wrath which was coming.[10] Nevertheless, he said the people of Judah would find their bed too short and their covers too

---

4. 2 Kings 20:16–17.

5. Isaiah 1:21–23.

6. Isaiah 1:30–31.

7. Isaiah 42:22.

8. The standard version says "an healer," but the alternate translation, "a binder up," appears more appropriate.

9. Isaiah 3:6–7.

10. Isaiah 28:14–15.

narrow.[11] He said the conquest of Judah would be so terrible it would be a vexation to read about it, let alone endure it.[12] It would come suddenly, unexpectedly, like a flood from a bursting dam.[13]

Isaiah said Judah had been told from the beginning what to expect, but except for brief periods of repentance, she had taken no heed.[14] He called them "children of transgression," who were guilty of "enflaming yourselves with idols [in connection with fertility worship] under every green tree, slaying the children in the valleys under the clifts of the rocks."[15] They reveled in false prophets and deliberately demanded lies of them, saying, "Prophesy not unto us right things, speak unto us smooth things, prophesy deceits."[16] They refused to hear the Gospel or teachings concerning the Messiah, but cried out, "Get you out of the way, turn aside out of the path, **cause the Holy One of Israel to cease from before us.**"[17]

Isaiah anticipated the warnings of Jeremiah by a full century. He told the people of Judah that their attempt to escape the wrath of Babylon by forming an alliance with Egypt would be a catastrophic political trap.[18] "Woe to the rebellious children, saith the Lord, that take counsel, but not of me;...that...strengthen themselves in the strength of Pharaoh, and...trust in the shadow of Egypt! Therefore shall the strength of Pharaoh be your shame, and the trust in the shadow of Egypt your confusion.... For the Egyptians shall help in vain, and to no purpose: therefore have I cried concerning this, **Their strength is to sit still.**"[19]

---

11. Isaiah 28:20.
12. Isaiah 28:19.
13. Isaiah 30:13–15.
14. Isaiah 48:3–8.
15. Isaiah 57:4–5.
16. Isaiah 30:10.
17. Isaiah 30:11.
18. Isaiah 30:1–7.
19. Ibid.

And "sit still" is all the Egyptians ever did. By 600 B.C., approximately 100 years after Isaiah's ministry, the rulers of Judah rejected the warnings of both Isaiah and Jeremiah by entering into a sticky alliance with Egypt. This amounted to an open defiance of the Lord. It was also a signal of defiance to the rulers of Babylon and was aggravated by Judah's refusal to pay any further tribute to Babylon.

From this distance, the historical circumstances make the alliance appear so absurd as to border on stupidity. When the Babylonians declared war, the last king of Judah learned to his abject sorrow that the strength of the Egyptians was indeed "to sit still." In 587 B.C., the city of Jerusalem was literally levelled to the ground. Its temple and buildings were burned. The king of Judah was dragged off to the Babylonian camp, where he was forced to watch each of his sons butchered. Then both his eyes were blinded. These were the terrible scenes envisioned by Isaiah, and from which he struggled for half a century to help the people of Judah escape through repentance. But they would not.

THE FALL OF BABYLON

Isaiah also had a message for Babylon. Here was a people who had descended from those ancient rebels who built the Tower of Babel, and who had remained in this area after the general dispersion. In fact, the city of Babylon had been built and destroyed in regular cycles extending back to the first generations after the Flood. Sometimes she had ruled over Assyria, but more recently Assyria had ruled over her. Then, in 612 B.C., Babylon combined with the Medes to destroy Nineveh, and immediately rose to the position of supremacy in the entire Mesopotamian region.

It was under King Nebuchadnezzar that Babylon was completely rebuilt. (The fabulous hanging gardens constructed during this time were to become one of the seven wonders of the ancient world.) One hundred years before this came to pass, Isaiah was talking about it. He also foresaw the wickedness of Babylon in her hour of power. In chapters 13, 14, and 47, Isaiah sets forth the Lord's great controversy with this mighty Babylon of the future.

The Lord said that not only would Babylon be excessively wicked, but she would inflict a terrible punishment on Judah.[20] The Lord said the Babylonians would revel in extreme cruelty, particularly against the aged.[21] Therefore, Isaiah said the Lord would avenge himself on the Babylonians because they did not have the common sense or decency to restrain themselves from these atrocities.

To that future generation of Babylonians, Isaiah declared: "Therefore hear now this, thou that art given to pleasures, that dwellest carelessly, that sayeth in thine heart, I am, and none else [exist] beside me; I shall not sit as a widow, neither shall I know the loss of children: but [on the contrary] these two things shall come to thee in a moment in one day, the loss of children, and widowhood.... Thy wisdom and thy knowledge, it hath perverted thee.... Therefore shall evil come upon thee; thou shalt not know from whence it riseth: and ... thou shalt not be able to put it off: and desolation shall come upon thee suddenly."[22]

Looking upon that future day in vision, Isaiah cried, "Come down, and sit in the dust, O virgin daughter of Babylon, sit on the ground: there is no throne...."[23] He said, "Thou shalt no more be called, The lady of kingdoms."[24] He rebuked Babylon for her "enchantments" and "multitude of ... sorceries." Said he to the people of that day, "Let now the astrologers, the stargazers, the monthly prognosticators, stand up, and save thee from these things that shall come upon thee."[25]

---

20. Isaiah 47:5–6.
21. Ibid.
22. Isaiah 47:8–11.
23. Isaiah 47:1.
24. Isaiah 47:5.
25. Isaiah 47:12–13.

Isaiah left no question as to the extent of their calamity. "Every one that is found shall be thrust through; and every one that is joined unto them shall fall by the sword. Their children also shall be dashed to pieces before their eyes; their houses shall be spoiled, and their wives ravished.... Their bows also shall dash the young men to pieces; and they shall have no pity on the fruit of the womb; their eye shall not spare children."[26]

And just as Babylon would leave Nineveh a mound of desolated ruins, so it eventually would be with Babylon. It would be as desolate as Sodom and Gomorrah. Isaiah declared, "And Babylon, the glory of kingdoms, the beauty of the Chaldees' excellency, shall be as when God overthrew Sodom and Gomorrah. It shall never be inhabited, neither shall it be dwelt in from generation to generation.... But wild beasts of the desert shall lie there; and their houses shall be full of doleful creatures; and owls shall dwell there, and satyrs shall dance there. And the wild beasts of the islands shall cry in their desolate houses, and dragons in their pleasant palaces...."[27]

Isaiah even told the future rulers of Babylon who was going to do all of this: "Behold, I will stir up the Medes against them, which shall not regard silver; and as for gold, they shall not delight in it."[28] In other words, no amount of bribery will induce them to desist. The Medes will go through them like a tornado of destruction. Isaiah also knew that Elam, or Persia, would be joined with the Medes in attacking Babylon.[29] The whole terrible scene was shown to him. He

---

26. Isaiah 13:15–18. Both Herodotus and Xenophon mention that the Persians and Medes used long bows. Xenophon says they were three cubits long, or somewhere around five feet. This is also the period when we begin to hear of steel bows. Nephi had one (1 Nephi 16:18). "A bow of steel" is mentioned in Psalms 18:34 and in Job 20:24. Dr. Clarke suggests that the superiority of the Medes and Persians may also have resulted from this advanced type of weapon. See Clarke, *Commentary,* 4:79.

27. Isaiah 13:19–22.

28. Isaiah 13:17.

29. Isaiah 21:2.

wrote, "I was bowed down at the hearing of it; I was dismayed at the seeing of it."[30]

What he was seeing took place in 539 B.C. The Medes and Persians besieged Babylon and then dug a deep trench which circumnavigated the entire city. One night they turned the Euphrates River into this trench. Before the Babylonians knew what was happening, the attacking troops were able to enter the city through the dry bed of the river which ran beneath the massive city walls. It was ingenious military strategy. Babylon fell like overripe fruit and never rose again.

Isaiah likened the fall of the king of Babylon to the fall of Lucifer after the War in Heaven. He gave the following as a comfort to the Jews and others who would be captives of the Babylonians at the time of her fall:

"And it shall come to pass in the day that the Lord shall give thee rest from thy sorrow, and from thy fear, and from the hard bondage wherein thou wast made to serve, that thou shalt take up this proverb against the king of Babylon, and say, How hath the oppressor ceased! the golden city ceased! The Lord hath broken the staff of the wicked, and sceptre of the rulers. He who smote the people in wrath with a continual stroke, he that ruled the nations in anger, is persecuted, and none hindereth. The whole earth is at rest, and is quiet: they break forth into singing. . . . How art thou fallen from heaven, O Lucifer, son of the morning! how art thou cut down to the ground, which didst weaken the nations! For thou hast said in thine heart, **I will ascend into heaven, I will exalt my throne above the stars of God: I will sit also upon the mount of the congregation, in the sides of the north: I will ascend above the heights of the clouds; I will be like the most High.** Yet thou shalt be brought down to hell, to the sides of the pit."[31]

---

30. Isaiah 21:3.
31. Isaiah 14:3–7, 12–15.

ISAIAH KNEW THE CONQUEROR OF BABYLON
WOULD BE CYRUS

Isaiah said that the military genius who would succeed in leading the Medes and Persians in their conquest of Babylon would be named Cyrus. The first several verses of chapter 45 are addressed to this noble pagan approximately 200 years before he came to power.

Here they are: "Thus saith the Lord to his anointed, to Cyrus, whose right hand I have holden, to subdue nations before him; and I will loose the loins of kings, to open before him the two leaved [double] gates; and the gates shall not be shut; I will go before thee, and make the crooked places straight: I will break in pieces the gates of brass, and cut in sunder the bars of iron: and I will give thee the treasures of darkness, and hidden riches of secret places, that thou mayest know that I, the Lord, which **call thee by thy name, am the God of Israel.** For Jacob my servant's sake, and Israel mine elect, I have even called thee by thy name: I have surnamed thee, **though thou hast not known me.** I am the Lord, and there is none else, there is no God beside me: I girded thee, though thou hast not known me."[32]

Certain modern scholars have felt that it was impossible for Isaiah to predict the rise of Cyrus (and even anticipate his name!) almost two centuries ahead of time.[33] They refuse to believe it. In reality, although many of these skeptics are professional ministers, they are

---

32. Isaiah 45:1–5.

33. See *The Interpreter's Bible*, 12 vols. (New York: Abingdon Press, n.d.), 5:383. Professor James Muilenburg rejects the capacity of Isaiah to see beyond his own day. This is why he and others of the same school insist that chapters 40 to 66 of Isaiah must have been written by some other person at a later date. Professor Muilenburg wrote, "Attempts to show that chapters 40 to 66 are the projection of the prophet's vision into the distant future have led to the most tortuous kind of reasoning and are at variance with the whole nature of Hebrew prophecy where the oracles, however predictive in character, *are always related to concerns and issues of the times in which the prophet is living.*" Jesus and the apostles clearly repudiate Professor Muilenburg's thesis when they state that some of these very chapters were fulfilled clear up to their time! (See Matthew 3:3; 4:14–16; 8:17; 12:17–21; 13:14; Luke 3:4; 4:17; John 1:23; 12:38–39.)

rejecting the power of God to reveal the distant future to his servants. They are denying the divine gift of prophecy.[34]

Actually, the naming of individuals long before they were born has occurred in a number of cases. For example:

Moses was known by name to Joseph, son of Jacob, at least 65 years before he was born.[35]

Aaron was also known to Joseph by name at least 65 years before he was born.[36]

Mary was known by name 100 years before she was born.[37]

John the Beloved was known by name 550 years before he was born.[38]

Joseph Smith was known by name around 3,450 years before he was born.[39] So was his father.[40]

It certainly was nothing unusual for Isaiah to be able to speak prophetically of Cyrus.

Cyrus was a remarkable man. Though a pagan, he had a deep respect for basic human values, comparable in many ways with those who have been trained in the discipline of the Gospel. Among the cruel and vicious heathen tyrants of the ancient world, Cyrus stands out like a pillar of light. For example, his defeat of the Babylonian capital was brilliant, ingenious, and totally successful. But note what happened: "To the astonishment of the conquered, there was no mass slaughter of the inhabitants, no herd of unfortunate people marched away into captivity. Even the gods of Babylon were left undisturbed. With great tolerance, Cyrus allowed life to proceed without violent alteration, in marked contrast to the

---

34. See Sperry, *The Old Testament Prophets,* chapter 16.

35. 2 Nephi 3:10.

36. Joseph Smith Translation, Genesis 50:35.

37. Mosiah 3:8; Alma 7:10.

38. 1 Nephi 14:27.

39. 2 Nephi 3:6, 15.

40. Ibid.

ways the Assyrians and the Babylonians themselves had practiced toward conquered peoples. His vision of empire was completely different from that of others, for Cyrus hoped for a commonwealth of self-governing dominions, under the beneficent control of a clement emperor. Trade and the advantages of peace throughout the world were to be enjoyed by all."[41]

It was under later rulers that the predictions of Isaiah concerning the devastation of Babylon found their final fulfillment. As the Lord had said, he raised up Cyrus, the benevolent pagan, to help the remnant of Jacob return to Jerusalem, but after him there came others, first Persian and then Greek, who finally left the majestic, massive monument of mighty Babylon in a heap of rubble and ruins.

ISAIAH'S HISTORICAL PERSPECTIVE

We have seen enough of Isaiah's prophetic powers to appreciate that the Lord did indeed share with this one man a virtual mountain of prophetic knowledge. In this summary, we have passed over the equally impressive and accurate predictions of Isaiah concerning Egypt,[42] Moab,[43] Phoenicia (Tyre and Sidon),[44] and Syria.[45] All of these prophecies were literally fulfilled.

Now we shall see how much Isaiah knew concerning the birth, ministry, death, and resurrection of Jesus Christ.

---

41. Keyes, *Story of the Bible World,* pp. 97–98.
42. Isaiah, chapter 19.
43. Isaiah, chapters 15 and 16.
44. Isaiah, chapter 23.
45. Isaiah, chapter 17.

Chapter 4

ISAIAH WRITES CONCERNING THE FIRST COMING OF CHRIST

There is nothing of greater importance in the writings of Isaiah than the first and second comings of Christ. In this chapter we will present his insights concerning the first coming. Isaiah knew what extreme measures the Lord would be compelled to employ so that the Jews would still be a national entity when the time came for Christ to be born among them. Giving the law of carnal commandments to Moses was one of these devices of desperation which the Lord used to prepare the Jews for the first coming of the Messiah.

ISAIAH EXPLAINS WHY THE CARNAL COMMANDMENTS WERE IMPORTANT TO BRING JUDAH TO CHRIST

In order to appreciate what Isaiah has to say about the law of carnal commandments, it is important to realize that Moses actually received two different canons of law. He first received the Ten Commandments, the law of the covenant, and the law of liberty, which have always been a permanent part of the gospel.[1] It was only

---

1. For a detailed discussion of this subject, see W. Cleon Skousen, *The Third Thousand Years* (Salt Lake City: Bookcraft, 1964), chapters 14 and 15.

after the open rebellion of Israel and the golden calf incident that the Lord saddled the people with the mass of additional ritual and sacrifices ordinarily referred to as the "law of Moses" or the "law of carnal commandments."

Paul points out that these were "added because of transgressions"[2] and did not typify the procedures which the Lord really desired for his people. They were merely a "schoolmaster" to teach the people the rhythm of obedience. In other words, they were a temporary emergency measure to keep the people from exploding to the four winds until after they had brought forth the Christ. Paul says they were laws "which stood only in meats and drinks, and divers washings, and carnal ordinances, imposed on them until the time of reformation [the coming of Christ]."[3]

All of this was thoroughly understood by Isaiah. He therefore told the people of his own day (whom he compared to the exterminated cities of Sodom and Gomorrah) that their multitudinous sacrifices contained no intrinsic virtue whatever. He wanted them to know that the carnal commandments were merely teaching devices and did not accomplish one iota of good unless they were accompanied by repentance and a firm resolve to obey God's commandments. Quoting the Lord's own words, he proclaimed:

"To what purpose is the multitude of your sacrifices unto me? saith the Lord: I am full of the burnt offerings of rams, and the fat of fed beasts; and I delight not in the blood of bullocks, or of lambs, or of he goats.... Bring no more vain oblations; incense is an abomination unto me; the new moons and sabbaths, the calling of assemblies. I cannot [endure them].... Your new moons and your appointed feasts my soul hateth: they are a trouble unto me; I am weary to bear them. And when ye spread forth your hands, I will hide mine eyes from you: yea, when ye make many prayers, I will not hear: **your hands are full of blood.**"[4]

---

2. Galatians 3:19.

3. Hebrews 9:10.

4. Isaiah 1:10–15.

MAKING RITUAL MEANINGFUL

Of course, the Lord himself had set up all these procedures, sacrifices, assemblies, and ceremonies, but when they were performed as "vain oblations" without being accompanied by repentance and obedience, God hated them all. As Paul later said, they were a schoolmaster to bring Israel to Christ.[5] If they didn't bring Israel to Christ, then all this bleeding, burning, praying, and pontificating were nothing more than a meaningless hodgepodge of ritualistic rigmarole. It was taking the name of the Lord their God in vain. It was much to-do about nothing. Therefore, through Isaiah, the Lord cried out to his people:

"Wash you, make you clean; put away the evil of your doings from before mine eyes; cease to do evil; learn to do well; seek judgment, relieve the oppressed, judge the fatherless, plead for the widow. **Come now, and let us reason together,** saith the Lord: **though your sins be as scarlet, they shall be as white as snow; though they be red like crimson, they shall be as** [white as] **wool. If ye be willing and obedient, ye shall eat the good of the land."[6]

It is interesting that Isaiah's prophetic contemporaries—Amos,[7] Hosea,[8] and Micah[9]—were preaching exactly this same doctrine, but none so completely and eloquently as Isaiah.

Over in the Western Hemisphere a few generations later, the great prophet Nephi said to his people, "Ye must keep the perfor-

---

5. Galatians 3:24.

6. Isaiah 1:16-19.

7. Amos 5:21-24. "I hate, I despise your feast days, and I will not smell in your solemn assemblies.... *But let judgment run down as waters, and righteousness as a mighty stream.*"

8. Hosea 6:6. "For I desired mercy, and not sacrifice; and the knowledge of God more than burnt offerings."

9. Micah 6:6-8. "Wherewith shall I come before the Lord, and bow myself before the high God? shall I come before him with burnt offerings, with calves of a year old? Will the Lord be pleased with thousands of rams, or with ten thousands of rivers of oil? shall I give my firstborn for my transgression, the fruit of my body for the sin of my soul? He hath shewed thee, O man, what is good; and *what doth the Lord require of thee, but to do justly, and to love mercy, and to walk humbly with thy God?*"

mances and ordinances of God until the law shall be fulfilled which was given unto Moses."[10] He left no doubt as to the reason. Said he:

"And, notwithstanding we believe in Christ, we keep the law of Moses, and look forward with steadfastness unto Christ, until the law shall be fulfilled. For, for this end was the law given; wherefore **the law hath become dead unto us,** and we are made alive in Christ because of our faith; **yet we keep the law because of the commandments.**

"And we talk of Christ, we rejoice in Christ, we preach of Christ, we prophesy of Christ, and we write according to our prophecies, that our children may know to what source they may look for a remission of their sins.

"Wherefore, we speak concerning the law that our children may know the deadness of the law; and they, by knowing the deadness of the law, may look forward unto that life which is in Christ, and **know for what end the law was given.** And after the law is fulfilled in Christ, that they need not harden their hearts against him **when the law ought to be done away.**"[11]

This is a significant scripture. It verifies that Nephi, living 600 years before Christ, knew that someday the "schoolmaster law" would be "done away." It would have fulfilled its purpose. This schoolmaster law was eliminated after Jesus was resurrected.

The members of the Church were given the higher law in both Palestine and the Western Hemisphere. As Nephi anticipated this coming transition he urged the people not to harden their hearts. Then, in verse 28, he continued: "Wherefore, I have spoken plainly unto you, that ye cannot misunderstand. And the words which I have spoken shall stand as a testimony against you; for they are sufficient to teach any man the right way; **for the right way is to believe in Christ and deny him not; for by denying him ye also deny the prophets and the law.**"

---

10. 2 Nephi 25:30.
11. 2 Nephi 25:24–27.

Thus spoke the prophet Nephi around 550 years before Christ was born. And 200 years before that, Isaiah was preaching the same doctrine to the Israelites.

HOW MUCH DID ISAIAH KNOW ABOUT JESUS CHRIST?

Isaiah had a remarkably intimate knowledge concerning the life and mission of Jesus Christ.

For example, one of the most beloved Old Testament scriptures referring to the Christ is Isaiah's famous statement: "For unto us a child is born, unto us a son is given: and the government shall be upon his shoulder: and his name shall be called Wonderful, Counsellor, The mighty God, The everlasting Father, The Prince of Peace."[12]

Isaiah, like Nephi[13] and Alma,[14] knew that the Savior would be born of a virgin.[15] The Revised Version of the Bible changes the word "virgin" to read "a young woman," but this will not do. The translators of the Septuagint (the most ancient Greek version) understood the word to mean "virgin," and Matthew quoted it for the purpose of demonstrating that this miraculous birth of a child by a virgin had been fulfilled in Jesus.[16] It will be recalled that Isaiah made this prophecy as a "sign" to King Ahaz to prove his prophetic integrity.[17] The only thing which made the prophecy a unique and significant "sign" was the fact that a **virgin** would bear a child. To simply say that "a young woman" would bear a child would be a perfectly normal thing and would carry no distinction whatever as a "sign." Thanks to the Book of Mormon, we now have an independ-

---

12. Isaiah 9:6.

13. 1 Nephi 11:13. Note that Nephi knew from an open vision that the virgin would be "exceedingly fair" and that Nazareth would be her home.

14. Alma 7:10. Note also that Alma was able to reveal what the virgin's name would be, the English translation of which is "Mary." King Benjamin gave the same information in Mosiah 3:8.

15. Isaiah 7:14.

16. Matthew 1:23.

17. Isaiah 7:11-14.

dent scripture which corroborates the fact that "virgin" is the correct word.[18]

Isaiah also said that this special child, born of a virgin, would be identified as "Immanuel,"[19] which means "God is with us."[20] John specifically speaks of Jesus in this sense,[21] and early Christian writers often referred to the Savior as "Immanuel."[22]

Isaiah knew that Jesus would be a direct descendant of Jesse, the father of King David. However, until modern revelation clarified it, the reference was somewhat obscure. Isaiah simply refers to the "stem of Jesse"[23] incidental to his discussion of a "rod" and a "branch" and a "root."[24] After the Gospel was restored, the question was asked concerning the identity of the "stem of Jesse." The answer came as follows: "Verily thus saith the Lord: It is Christ."[25] Isaiah therefore knew whereof he spoke when he called the Savior a stem or descendant of Jesse.

JOHN THE BAPTIST

Isaiah knew that the ministry of the Savior would be preceded by that of John the Baptist. Isaiah is the source for the scripture which speaks of "the voice of him that crieth in the wilderness, Prepare ye the way of the Lord, make straight in the desert a highway for our

---

18. 1 Nephi 11:13, 15, 18. Note especially Alma 7:10: "And behold, he shall be born of Mary, at [the land of] Jerusalem which is the land of our forefathers, *she being a virgin*, a precious and chosen vessel, who shall be overshadowed and conceive by the power of the Holy Ghost, and bring forth a son, yea, even the Son of God."

19. Isaiah 7:14.

20. F.N. Peloubet, ed., *Peloubet's Bible Dictionary* (Philadelphia: Universal Book and Bible House, 1947), s.v. "Immanuel."

21. John 1:14.

22. Peloubet, *Bible Dictionary*, s.v. "Immanuel."

23. Isaiah 11:1.

24. Isaiah 11:1, 10.

25. D&C 113:2.

God."[26] Both Matthew and John verify that it was John the Baptist whom Isaiah had in mind.[27]

Isaiah knew that during the Savior's ministry, he would reside in the territory originally occupied by the tribes of Zebulun and Naphtali, and that his message of Gospel light would spring from there.[28] Here again, the Bible reference in our modern version of Isaiah is somewhat obscure, but Matthew quotes it in a much clearer form and says it was fulfilled when Jesus began his ministry in Capernaum.[29]

ISAIAH'S MESSIANIC CHAPTER

All of chapter 53 in the book of Isaiah is about Jesus Christ. Isaiah says he will "grow up" before God as a "tender plant" and as a root sprouting up out of dry ground.[30] Surprisingly, however, Isaiah says the Savior would not be particularly handsome nor striking in size and appearance. As though he were looking at Jesus in mortality at that very moment, Isaiah wrote, "He hath no form nor comeliness; and when we shall see him, there is no beauty that we should desire him."[31]

Isaiah also saw how Jesus would be treated. "He is despised and rejected of men; a man of sorrows, and acquainted with grief: and we hid as it were our faces from him; he was despised, and we esteemed him not."[32]

Continuing as though he were watching a vision of Christ's ministry, Isaiah could not help exclaiming:

"Surely he hath borne our griefs, and carried our sorrows: yet we did esteem him stricken, smitten of God, and afflicted. But he was

---

26. Isaiah 40:3.
27. Matthew 3:3; John 1:23.
28. Isaiah 9:1–2.
29. Matthew 4:12–16.
30. Isaiah 53:2.
31. Ibid.
32. Isaiah 53:3.

wounded for our transgressions, he was bruised for our iniquities: the chastisement of our peace was upon him; and with his stripes we are healed."[33]

When Isaiah uses the word "we," he is speaking of the whole human race. He says, "All we like sheep have gone astray; we have turned every one to his own way; and the Lord [the Father] hath laid on him [the Son] the iniquity of us all."[34]

Speaking of the illegal trial and execution of Jesus, Isaiah comments: "He was oppressed, and he was afflicted, yet he opened not his mouth: he is brought as a lamb to the slaughter, and as a sheep before her shearers is dumb, so he openeth not his mouth.[35] He was taken from prison[36] and from judgment:[37] and who shall declare his generation? for he was cut off out of the land of the living:[38] for the transgression of my people was he stricken.[39] And he made his grave with the wicked,[40] and with the rich in his

---

33. Isaiah 53:4-5.

34. Isaiah 53:6.

35. At his trial, false witnesses were used against Jesus. When they brought their charges, Jesus would not even dignify them with a comment or reply. The High Priest tried to force him to say something about these charges, but "Jesus held his peace" (Matthew 26:63). Finally, the High Priest cried out, "I adjure thee by the living God, that thou tell us whether thou be the Christ, the Son of God." This was not a charge but a question; therefore, Jesus condescended to reply. Said he: "Thou hast said [meaning 'it is so']: nevertheless I say unto you, Hereafter shall ye see the Son of man sitting on the right hand of power, and coming in the clouds of heaven." (Matthew 26:63-64.)

36. Jesus was in a state of incarceration from the time of his arrest until he was "taken from prison" to be crucified.

37. Pilate gave a judgment which would have set Jesus free, but he was taken from that judgment "when Pilate saw that he could prevail nothing" (Matthew 27:24) and turned Jesus over to the Roman guard for execution.

38. Jesus was "cut out of the land of the living" before the natural termination of his life.

39. The Septuagint says "smitten to death" (Clarke, *Commentary*, 4:205).

40. His burial place was near the base of the hill of execution, where bodies of criminals were no doubt interred (John 19:41-42).

death;[41] because he had done no violence, neither was any deceit in his mouth."[42]

Isaiah knew that the suffering and tribulation of the Savior involved a problem of infinite and profound significance and that by divine necessity his cruel death was an "offering for sin,"[43] which would "justify many; for he shall bear their iniquities."[44] Isaiah was also aware that after this terrible ordeal Jesus would receive a great reward, and then he would "see his seed."[45]

Isaiah closes by quoting the declaration of the Father: "Therefore will I divide him a portion with the great, and he shall divide the spoil with the strong; because he hath poured out his soul unto death: and he was numbered with the transgressors; and he bare the sin of many, and made intercession for the transgressors."[46]

ISAIAH KNEW JEHOVAH WAS THE COMING MESSIAH

No writer of the Old Testament is as clear as Isaiah in addressing the great Jehovah of the Old Testament as the coming Messiah, the Savior and Redeemer of all mankind. Many people forget that the God of the Old Testament is the same as the God of the New Testament. The Almighty Father, Elohim, did his great work in both ages through his Son. The name of the Son in the Old Testament

---

41. Jesus was fortunate in that "a rich man of Arimathaea, named Joseph...went to Pilate, and begged the body of Jesus" (Matthew 27:57-58). This same scripture says Joseph was a disciple of Jesus and that he laid the body "in his own new tomb, which he had hewn out in the rock: and he rolled a great stone to the door of the sepulchre, and departed" (Matthew 27:60.) We learn from John that "in the place where he was crucified there was a garden; and in the garden a new sepulchre, where was never man yet laid. There laid they Jesus." (John 19:41-42.) No doubt this tomb was at the foot of Golgotha, the place of the skull, where Jesus was crucified. (John 19:17-18.)

42. Isaiah 53:7-9.

43. Isaiah 53:10.

44. Isaiah 53:11. Anyone desiring to pursue the thrilling ramifications of the Atonement is referred to the discussion entitled "Why Was the Atonement Necessary?" found in W. Cleon Skousen, *The First 2,000 Years* (Salt Lake City: Bookcraft, 1953), pp. 352-62.

45. Isaiah 53:10.

46. Isaiah 53:12.

was Jehovah, but after his eternal spirit was born into mortality he became known as Jesus Christ. This is what John was talking about when he said that the Word which was with God [the Father] from the beginning was none other than the Savior: "And the Word was made flesh, and dwelt among us, (and we beheld his glory, the glory as of **the only begotten of the Father,) full of grace and truth.**"[47]

But even recognizing this to be so, certain passages in the patriarchal writings are confusing because they imply that it is the Father, Elohim, who is talking instead of Jehovah, his Son. Take, for example, the revelation to Moses. Moses saw a vision of God's vast creation and then asked how it had all been done. The divine personage with whom he was talking "face to face"[48] replied, "By the word of my power, have I created them, which is **mine Only Begotten Son,** who is full of grace and truth."[49] Certainly this sounds like the Father talking.

It turns out that the key to this problem is found in the fact that heavenly messengers, including Jehovah, often deliver a message in the first person so that there will be no mistake in the mind of the listener as to its source. Therefore, it would be perfectly correct for Moses to say that the Father told him his creations were by his Only Begotten Son. But if Moses testified that it was the Father who appeared before him and gave him this message, it would be an error.

This kind of erroneous conclusion was reached by John the Beloved on the Isle of Patmos. A glorious being appeared before him, and after he showed John great visions of the future, John concluded that this personage standing in glory before him was none other than the Savior. He therefore bowed down to worship him, but the heavenly messenger was horrified and said to him, "See thou do it

---

47. John 1:14.
48. Moses 1:31.
49. Moses 1:32.

not: for I am thy fellowservant, and **of thy brethren the prophets,** and of them which keep the sayings of this book: worship God."[50]

This was the second time John had become confused and tried to worship this glorious personage.[51] After John was restrained the second time, the angel who had described himself as one of the prophets started delivering his message in the first person. One can easily see why John kept getting the idea that this was his glorified friend and master. Listen to this amazing statement by the angel right after he had rebuked John the second time: "Behold, I come quickly; and my reward is with me, to give every man according as his work shall be. I am Alpha and Omega, the beginning and the end, the first and the last."[52] No person in his right mind who has had any experience with God's work would mistake the full implications of this statement. These are clearly the words of Jesus Christ, and they fit no one else! However, it was not Jesus Christ who was standing before John reciting these words of Jesus. This is what the angel was trying to make clear to John. The angel was simply delivering a message from Jesus, but doing it in the first person.

ISAIAH CALLS JEHOVAH THE REDEEMER AND THE SAVIOR

Now it will be more readily appreciated why Isaiah constantly addressed Jehovah in the Old Testament as his Redeemer and Savior. Even though Jehovah sometimes spoke as though he were the Father, Isaiah knew it was the Son, Jehovah, the coming Redeemer of Israel, who was delivering the Father's message in the first person. Twelve different times Isaiah refers to Jehovah as the Redeemer,[53] and on eight occasions he identifies him as the Savior.[54]

---

50. Revelation 22:9.

51. The first occasion is referred to in Revelation 19:10.

52. Revelation 22:12-13. Note that in talking to Isaiah the Lord also used this final phrase: "Hearken unto me, O Jacob...I am he; I am the first, I also am the last" (Isaiah 48:12).

53. Isaiah 41:14; 43:14; 44:6; 44:24; 47:4; 48:17; 49:7; 54:5; 54:8; 59:20; 60:16; 63:16.

54. Isaiah 19:20; 43:3; 43:11; 45:15; 45:21; 49:26; 60:16; 63:8.

Notice such clear-cut statements as these, which demonstrate Isaiah's knowledge that he was dealing with the future Jesus Christ:

"I, even I, am the Lord; and beside me there is no saviour." (Isaiah 43:11.)

"...O God of Israel, the Saviour." (Isaiah 45:15.)

"I the Lord am thy Saviour and thy Redeemer." (Isaiah 49:26; 60:16.)

"And the Redeemer shall come to Zion." (Isaiah 59:20.)

"Thus saith the Lord, thy redeemer, and he that formed thee from the womb,..." (Isaiah 44:24.)

Of course, it would be legitimate to inquire whether Isaiah may not have been using the words "Redeemer" and "Savior" in their political sense rather than in a religious sense. It could be argued that ultimately the Lord was going to be their savior from political captivity and their redeemer from further exploitation and conquest. Isaiah, however, left no doubt as to his true meaning. He had seen the Savior,[55] and Nephi later verified it.[56] Isaiah wanted it understood that he was talking about the very Redeemer who "was wounded for our transgressions, he was bruised for our iniquities:...and with his stripes we are healed."[57] He said he was talking about the Man of Sorrows who "poured out his soul unto death" as an "offering for sin."[58] Even Paul could not have been plainer!

After the death and resurrection of the Savior, his disciples were anxious that Jesus be recognized and appreciated as the Jehovah of the Old Testament. We have already cited John's declaration that "the Word" had been made flesh and "dwelt among us." Jesus himself made emphatic reference to his former status on a number of occasions. At the Last Supper he prayed, "And now, O Father,

---

55. Isaiah 6:1, 5.

56. 2 Nephi 11:2.

57. Isaiah 53:5.

58. Isaiah 53:10-12.

glorify thou me with thine own self with the glory which I had with thee before the world was."[59] Later he prayed, "Father, I will that they also, whom thou hast given me, be with me where I am; that they may behold my glory,...for thou lovedst me before the foundation of the world."[60] Even to the apostate Pharisees Jesus boldly declared, "Verily, verily, I say unto you, Before Abraham was, I am."[61]

Early Christian writers emphasized the role Jesus had formerly occupied as the Jehovah of the Old Testament. In his *Church History,* Eusebius called his second chapter, "Summary View of the Pre-existence and Divinity of Our Saviour and Lord Jesus Christ." In paragraph 8 of his fourth chapter Eusebuis says, "But they [the prophets] also clearly knew the very Christ of God; for it has already been shown that he appeared unto Abraham, that he imparted revelations to Isaac, and he talked with Jacob, that he held converse with Moses and with the prophets that came after." This, of course, has reference to the days when he was revealed to the patriarchs and prophets as Jehovah. But, as we have seen in our study of Isaiah, he and other great prophets were well aware that this glorious being who ministered to them was the Messiah, the coming Jesus Christ.

ISAIAH ANTICIPATES CHRIST'S MISSIONARY WORK AMONG THE DEAD

In one extremely choice passage, Isaiah deals with a perplexing problem which has tantalized the minds of men down through the ages: What happens to the wicked when they die?

Glorious hope has always been held out for the righteous and obedient, but what about the wicked? Doesn't God offer any hope for them? The Greeks pondered this question as though it were something of the most profound significance. So did the

---

59. John 17:5.
60. John 17:24.
61. John 8:58.

Babylonians and Egyptians. The last "book" or chapter of Plato's *Republic* deals almost exclusively with the status of the wicked after this life. But Isaiah knew far more about this question than Plato, even though he wrote less.

Isaiah's reference to this question is raised in connection with his description of events which will occur at the time of the Second Coming. This discussion involves the entire twenty-fourth chapter. He describes how the earth will "reel to and fro like a drunkard,"[62] and how the destruction of mankind will be so universal that it will leave the planet virtually "emptied"[63] and "few men left."[64]

But what happens to all of these? What happens to the kings, the "high ones,"[65] as well as to the hosts of common people who are thus destroyed for their wickedness? Isaiah had the answer. Said he, "And they shall be gathered together, as prisoners are gathered in the pit [dungeon[66]], and shall be shut up in the prison, **and after many days shall they be visited.**"[67]

We learn from another scripture that the wicked who were destroyed at the time of the Great Flood were also held in such a prison until they could be visited.[68] David knew that his spirit would spend some time in this prison because of his disobedience.[69] Alma was told by an angel that this is where all of the unrighteous go, and their condition is exactly what one would expect in a vast assembly of habitually violent and reprobate people.[70] Undoubtedly this is the very condition which helps humble them and prepare them to welcome the messengers of the Gospel when they finally come. In

---

62. Isaiah 24:20.
63. Isaiah 24:3.
64. Isaiah 24:6.
65. Isaiah 24:21.
66. An alternate translation of the word "pit."
67. Isaiah 24:22.
68. 1 Peter 3:19-20.
69. Psalms 16:9-10.
70. Alma 40:14.

fact, this is probably the very reason why they are left in this state for "many days" before relief is offered to them. They must develop eyes that can see and ears that can hear before they are visited.

Isaiah knew that it would be the Savior who would initiate the program of teaching the Gospel to the dead. Isaiah recorded that an important part of the Savior's role as "a light [to] the Gentiles" would be his visit to these rebellious souls in their spirit world prison in order "to open the blind eyes, to bring out the prisoners from the prison, and them that sit in darkness out of the prison house."[71] In other words, he would seek to have them accept the Gospel, discontinue their rebellion against God, and agree to embrace the great plan of salvation designed for man's eternal joy and progression.

It is interesting that when Jesus came to earth and commenced his ministry among men, he quoted Isaiah to show that he knew his mission included the preaching of the Gospel to both the living and the dead. Standing up in the synagogue of his own hometown in Nazareth, Jesus read this passage from the book of Isaiah:

"The Spirit of the Lord God is upon me; because the Lord hath anointed me to preach good tidings unto the meek; he hath sent me to bind up the brokenhearted, **to proclaim liberty to the captives, and the opening of the prison to them that are bound;** to proclaim the acceptable year of the Lord...."[72]

When Jesus had read this passage to the people, he told them he had come to fulfill it.[73] He first preached the Gospel to the living, but after he had been crucified his disembodied spirit crossed over into the spirit world. There he found the righteous in a state of

---

71. Isaiah 42:6-7.

72. Isaiah 61:1-2. Note that the Isaiah text is clearer concerning the preaching of the Gospel to those in prison than the briefer version given in Luke 4:18-19.

73. Luke 4:21.

supreme happiness and joyful activity,[74] while the unrighteous were being held back in a place of confinement or imprisonment (which is what "damnation" means) until they could be taught to behave in some degree or other like sons and daughters of God.[75]

As Jesus entered the spirit world, the time for his preaching to the dead had arrived. Peter says: "For Christ . . . being put to death in the flesh, but quickened by the Spirit: by which also he went and preached unto the spirits in prison."[76] Apparently as of that time (around A.D. 33), the vast majority of those who made up the inhabitants of the spirit world prison were the massive throngs who had been destroyed at the time of the Great Flood. Peter therefore makes special reference to them,[77] thereby implying that in spite of the many millions of wicked humans who had died since the Flood, nevertheless the great hosts who populated the earth in the days of Noah and were drowned in the Flood still constituted the dominant population in the spirit world prison when Christ first visited there.

And these had waited "many days" indeed—over 2,300 years! Surely they must have been almost frantic with anticipation as they waited with voracious appetites for the meat of the Gospel. And excitement must have run equally high among the righteous Saints as Jesus organized his Priesthood and prepared to launch the gigantic project of preaching his message of liberty and hope to the dead.[78] The news of their coming must have been electrifying. What

---

74. Alma 40:12. Jesus sought to demonstrate the separation of the righteous from the wicked and their respective circumstances in the spirit world when he related the parable of Lazarus and the rich man (Luke 16:19–31).

75. The degree of their response determines the degree of glory they will receive (D&C, section 76).

76. 1 Peter 3:18–19.

77. 1 Peter 3:20.

78. The mammoth undertaking which was necessary to preach the Gospel to the dead has been described by a modern prophet, Joseph F. Smith: "And as I wondered, my eyes were opened, and my understanding quickened, and I perceived that the Lord went not in person among the wicked and the disobedient who had rejected the truth, to teach them; but behold, from among the righteous, he organized his forces and appointed messengers,

an acclamation of thanksgiving and rejoicing must have echoed through the dismal darkness of that awful hell-milieu as the cry passed in all directions, "They are coming! They are coming!"

Peter said, "For for this cause was the gospel preached also to them that are dead, that they might be judged according to men in the flesh, but live according to God in the spirit."[79] This, then, was the glorious event the prophet Isaiah had promised.

---

clothed with power and authority, and commissioned them to go forth and carry the light of the gospel to them that were in darkness, even to all the spirits of men; and thus was the gospel preached to the dead. And the chosen messengers went forth to declare the acceptable day of the Lord and proclaim liberty to the captives who were bound, even unto all who would repent of their sins and receive the gospel. Thus was the gospel preached to those who had died in their sins, without a knowledge of the truth, or in transgression, having rejected the prophets. These were taught faith in God, repentance from sin, vicarious baptism for the remission of sins, the gift of the Holy Ghost by the laying on of hands, and all other principles of the gospel that were necessary for them to know in order to qualify themselves that they might be judged according to men in the flesh, but live according to God in the spirit." (D&C 138:29-34.)

79. 1 Peter 4:6.

Chapter 5

ISAIAH WRITES
ABOUT AMERICA

To appreciate the extent of Isaiah's knowledge concerning America, we rely heavily upon the supplementary material furnished by Nephi, the great prophet of the Book of Mormon. As we have already mentioned, Isaiah's writings were brought to the Western Hemisphere by migrating Israelites in the sixth century B.C., and comprised an important part of their scripture. When these people had difficulty understanding Isaiah, they had the supreme good fortune to be living at the same time as Nephi, who appears to have seen just about everything Isaiah had seen. He therefore wrote his commentary on Isaiah with this opening declaration:

"Wherefore, hearken, O my people, which are of the house of Israel, and give ear unto my words; for because the words of Isaiah are not plain unto you, nevertheless they are plain unto all those that are filled with the spirit of prophecy. But I give unto you a prophecy, **according to the spirit which is in me;** wherefore I shall prophesy according to the plainness which hath been with me from the time I came out from Jerusalem with my father.... [Therefore] I proceed with mine own prophecy, according to my plainness; in the which I know that no man can err; nevertheless, in the days that the prophecies of Isaiah shall be fulfilled men shall know of a surety...when they shall come to pass."[1]

Because Nephi had such a depth of understanding concerning the things which Isaiah saw, we will include his inspired writings right along with those of Isaiah. But even with this help, it is important to appreciate how difficult it was for these ancient servants of the Lord to describe what they saw. Consider, for example, the great upheaval of events which have occurred during the past three centuries. Imagine the difficulty of trying to describe these events without being able to use any specific names, places, or dates most of the time. The task of a prophet is not an easy one. Nevertheless, Nephi was confident that when these great events transpired, no honest student would have any difficulty recognizing what he and Isaiah were trying to describe.

PROPHECIES CONCERNING AMERICA

The whole vista of early American history was anticipated by Isaiah and Nephi, and its most significant and dramatic epochs were carefully chronicled centuries before they happened. Other prophets also furnished additional details. For example, Nephi's father knew as early as 600 B.C. that the American continent would be kept hidden for many centuries through the specific design of the Lord. Said he, "And behold, it is wisdom that this land should be kept as yet from the knowledge of other nations; for behold, **many nations would overrun the land, that there would be no place for an inheritance.**"[2]

He said America was being saved to become a wellspring of liberty in the latter days. "Wherefore, this land is consecrated unto him whom [the Lord] shall bring. And if it so be that they shall serve him

---

1. 2 Nephi 25:4, 7.
2. 2 Nephi 1:8.

according to the commandments which he hath given, **it shall be a land of liberty unto them;** wherefore, they shall never be brought down unto captivity; if so, **it shall be because of iniquity;** for if iniquity shall abound cursed shall be the land for their sakes, but unto the righteous it shall be blessed forever."[3]

Isaiah spent a whole chapter describing a land "shadowing [literally 'buzzing'] with wings," which he said was far away "beyond the rivers of Ethiopia."[4] (How else would you tell the people of 700 B.C. about a great land west of their westernmost boundaries?) Isaiah knew a great work would be done in this distant land. He said here is where the Lord would take his rest.[5] It would be the land from which he would send forth swift messengers to gather his people who had been "scattered and peeled."[6] It would be the place where the name of the Lord of Hosts could be found, for it would be the latter-day "mount Zion."[7]

Therefore, Isaiah said, "all ye inhabitants of the world, and dwellers on the earth, **see ye** [pay attention], **when he lifteth up an ensign on the mountains; and when he bloweth a trumpet, hear ye.**"[8]

DISCOVERY AND EARLY SETTLEMENT OF AMERICA

In anticipation of this great work which the Lord would do in America, Nephi described his prophetic vision concerning the discovery and settling of the Western Hemisphere. He saw Columbus and wrote, "I beheld the Spirit of God, that it came down and wrought upon the man;[9] and he went forth upon the many

---

3. 2 Nephi 1:7.
4. Isaiah 18:1.
5. Isaiah 18:4.
6. Isaiah 18:7.
7. Ibid.
8. Isaiah 18:3.
9. One of the foremost authorities on Columbus was the late Dr. Samuel Eliot Morison of Harvard University. He summarized what all biographers of Columbus say concerning his faith in God: "Men may doubt this, but there can be no doubt that the faith of Columbus was

waters."[10] He knew that when Columbus reached the Americas he would find a native people whom Nephi identified as being primarily the descendants of his two brothers, Laman and Lemuel.[11]

In treating the history of the Western Hemisphere we often say that the fifteenth and sixteenth centuries belonged to the Spanish, the seventeenth century belonged to the French, and the eighteenth century belonged to the English. Nephi saw these multitudes of Gentiles sweeping across the continent.[12] He saw the millions of natives whom he knew to be apostate Israelites fleeing before them and being smitten on every hand, even though they greatly outnumbered the newcomers.[13] Nevertheless, he saw that in spite of this devastating conquest of the land by these Gentiles, they would not annihilate the native peoples completely.[14]

With this kind of background, it will be readily seen why Nephi became such a capable commentator on Isaiah's writings concerning America. In addition to the above, Nephi knew that many of the Gentiles who would migrate to America would be motivated by religious ideals,[15] and that they would come forth from the land of the mother Gentiles in order to escape "out of captivity."[16] He said

---

genuine and sincere, and that his frequent communion with forces unseen was a vital element in his achievement. It gave him confidence in his destiny, assurance that his performance would be equal to the promise of his name. This conviction that God destined him to be an instrument for spreading the faith was far more potent than the desire to win glory, wealth and worldly honors, to which he was certainly far from indifferent." (Samuel E. Morison, *Admiral of the Ocean Sea*, 2 vols. [Boston: Little, Brown and Company, 1942], 1:42.)

When Columbus wrote his report concerning the settlement of the New World, he expressed the hope that none but devout Christians would emigrate as settlers, "since this was the end and the beginning of the enterprise, that it should be for the enhancement and glory of the Christian religion, nor should anyone who is not a good Christian come to these parts." (Ibid., p. 271.)

10. 1 Nephi 13:12.
11. Ibid.
12. 1 Nephi 13:13–14.
13. 1 Nephi 13:14.
14. 1 Nephi 13:30–31.
15. 1 Nephi 13:13.
16. 1 Nephi 13:16.

that they would be "white, and exceedingly fair and beautiful," and that they would "prosper and obtain the land [from the natives] for their inheritance."[17]

Nephi saw the United States' war for independence in the late 1700s and the revolutionary wars for independence in the Latin American countries during the 1800s. He said: "I beheld that their mother Gentiles were gathered together upon the waters, and upon the land also, to battle against them. **And I beheld that the power of God was with them,** and also that the wrath of God was upon all those that were gathered together against them to battle."[18] Nephi predicted the outcome of these mighty struggles, saying, "I, Nephi, beheld that the Gentiles that had gone out of captivity [from Europe] were **delivered by the power of God out of the hands of all other nations.**"[19]

The determination of the early American settlers to live the lives of practicing Christians brought some rather amazing blessings. Here is but one historical example.

In October of 1746, the French assembled the largest fleet ever to be sighted from American soil and headed for Boston to avenge their defeat at Louisburg. Because there was no hope of matching the fleet either in cannon fire or manpower, the governor assembled what men and resources he could and called for a day of universal fasting and prayer. The late biographer Catherine Drinker Bowen related what happened thus:

"Everywhere men observed it, thronging to the churches.

In Boston the Reverend Thomas Prince, from the high pulpit of the Old South Meeting-house, prayed before hundreds. The morning was clear and calm, people had walked to church through sunshine. 'Deliver us from our enemy!' the minister implored. 'Send Thy tempest, Lord, upon the waters to the eastward! Raise Thy

---

17. 1 Nephi 13:15.
18. 1 Nephi 13:17–18.
19. 1 Nephi 13:19.

right hand. Scatter the ships of our tormentors and drive them hence. Sink their proud frigates beneath the power of Thy winds!'

"He had scarcely pronounced the words when the sun was gone and the morning darkened. All the church was in a shadow. A wind shrieked round the walls, sudden, violent, hammering at the windows with a giant hand. No man was in the steeple—afterward the sexton swore it—yet the great bell struck twice, a wild, uneven sound. Thomas Prince paused in his prayer, both arms raised. 'We hear Thy voice, O Lord!' he thundered triumphantly. 'We hear it! Thy breath is upon the waters to the eastward, even upon the deep. Thy bell tolls for the death of our enemies!' He bowed his head; when he looked up, tears streamed down his face. 'Thine be the glory, Lord. Amen and amen!'...

"All the Province heard of this prayer and this answering tempest. Governor [William] Shirley sent a sloop, the *Rising Sun*, northward for news.... But she brought news so good it was miraculous—if one could believe it.... The whole fleet was nearly lost, the men very sick with scurvy or some pestilential fever. Their great admiral, the Duc d'Anville, was dead.

"A week later the news was confirmed by other vessels entering Boston from the northeastward. D'Anville was indeed dead; it was said he had poisoned himself in grief and despair when he saw his men dying round him. Two thousand were already buried, four thousand were sick, and not above a thousand of the land forces remained on their fleet. Vice-Admiral d'Estournelle had run himself through the heart with his sword. The few remaining ships, half-manned, were limping off to the southwestward, headed it was thought for the West Indies.

"Pestilence, storm and sudden death—how directly and with what extraordinary vigor the Lord had answered New England prayers!

"The country fell on its knees.... A paper with d'Anville's orders had been found, instructing him to take Cape Breton Island, then proceed to Boston—'lay that Town in Ashes and destroy all he could upon the Coast of North America; then proceed to the West Indies and distress the Islands.'"[20]

Had the French armada succeeded in burning Boston, New York, Philadelphia, and Charleston, the history of early America might have been changed completely.

THE BIBLE, A FREE PEOPLE, AND THE RESTORATION OF THE GOSPEL

Nephi knew that the Bible, which is "a record of the Jews," would be "of great worth unto the Gentiles," and the foundation of the Gentile culture in America.[21]

With what appears to have been a specific reference to the United States, Nephi described a Gentile nation which would prosper in the promised land of America until it had "been lifted up by the power of God above all other nations."[22] Nephi said that among these Gentiles the Lord would commence his "marvellous work and a wonder," spoken of by Isaiah.[23] According to Nephi, the Lord said, "I will be merciful unto the Gentiles in that day, insomuch that I will bring forth unto them, in mine own power, **much of my gospel,** which shall be plain and precious, saith the Lamb."[24]

Nephi knew that in connection with this great restoration of the Gospel in our times, the Lord would raise up a choice prophet. Isaiah was also aware of the mission of this latter-day seer.

JOSEPH SMITH IN PROPHECY

It would appear from everything we have available that some 2,500 years before he was born, Joseph Smith was the man Isaiah had in mind when he wrote about the "root of Jesse" in the eleventh

---

20. Catherine Drinker Bowen, *John Adams and the American Revolution*, (New York: Grosset & Dunlap, 1950), pp. 10-11.

21. 1 Nephi 13:23.

22. 1 Nephi 13:30.

23. Isaiah 29:14.

24. 1 Nephi 13:34.

chapter of his book. Isaiah quoted the Lord as saying, "And in that day there shall be a root of Jesse, which shall stand for an ensign of the people; **to it shall the Gentiles seek:** and his rest [message of peace and salvation] shall be glorious." He then went on to say that in connection with the raising up of this servant "the Lord shall set his hand again the second time to recover the remnant of his people.... And he shall set up an ensign for the nations, and shall assemble the outcasts of Israel, and gather together the dispersed of Judah from the four corners of the earth."[25]

It was Joseph Smith who was given this precise responsibility when the "keys of the gathering of Israel" were conferred upon him and Oliver Cowdery on April 3, 1836.[26]

Joseph Smith was asked who this "root of Jesse" was, and he gave a most interesting but impersonal reply. Perhaps it would be more accurate to describe it as an extremely modest reply. In any event, this is what he said: "Behold, thus saith the Lord, it is a descendant of Jesse, as well as of Joseph, unto whom **rightly belongs the priesthood, and the keys of the kingdom, for an ensign, and for the gathering of my people in the last days.**"[27]

To identify this person, all one needs to do is ask this question: "Who was it in this dispensation who received the Priesthood, the keys of the kingdom, and finally, the keys of the gathering?" If we are correct in concluding that only Joseph Smith fits these specifications, then it becomes obvious why Moroni recited this entire chapter of Isaiah to the 17-year-old Joseph Smith when he came to announce that the Lord's great latter-day program was about to commence.[28] Moroni told Joseph that the things mentioned in this chapter of Isaiah were about to be fulfilled,[29] and of course if

---

25. Isaiah 11:10–12.

26. D&C 110:11.

27. D&C 113:6.

28. Joseph Smith—History 1:40.

29. Ibid.

Joseph was the Lord's instrument to bring it about, Moroni would have a most significant reason in quoting this chapter to him.

Other prophets also talked about the latter-day seer. For example, Joseph, who was sold into Egypt, knew that the prophet of the latter days would be a namesake as well as his own descendant.[30] He said the father of this latter-day prophet would also be named Joseph.[31] Note that Joseph who was sold into Egypt was proud that Joseph Smith would be one of his lineage. Isaiah was also proud that the latter-day prophet would be of Jewish lineage! Isaiah wanted to emphasize that this great servant of the Lord in our times would carry in his veins the same pure blood of Judah as that which flowed in the veins of King David and Jesus. Therefore, Isaiah called him "a root of Jesse." Jesse, of course, was David's father, a Jew from Bethlehem, who was also the ancestor of Mary, mother of Christ.[32]

Now, if Joseph Smith is indeed the "root of Jesse" spoken of by Isaiah, could he also be an Ephraimite? According to the modern revelation quoted above, the answer is yes. The Lord said the "root of Jesse" would be "a descendant of Jesse, **as well as of Joseph....**" When the genealogy of Joseph Smith is finally tabulated, we will no doubt discover that in him the two great houses of Judah (through Jesse) and Joseph (through Ephraim) have been brought together in symbolic harmony. We say "symbolic" since this very same chapter of Isaiah says that in the latter days when the "root of Jesse" will raise up an ensign for the people, "Ephraim shall not envy Judah, and Judah shall not vex Ephraim" anymore.[33] How appropriate, therefore, that the blood lines of these former antagonists should be blended together in this great prophet who was ordained to proclaim the message of the Restoration in the latter days and commence the

---

30. 2 Nephi 3:15.

31. Ibid.

32. Luke 3:23–32. It should be noted that this is believed to have been the ancestral line of *both* Mary and Joseph, but of course Jesus would have partaken of it only through his mother.

33. Isaiah 11:13.

gathering of Israel which would bring about the reconciliation of these two great peoples.

ISAIAH ADDRESSES HIMSELF TO THE ISRAELITES
IN AMERICA

Isaiah, more than any other prophet, addressed himself on a number of occasions to the "isles of the sea." Nephi's brother Jacob said that this referred particularly to the Israelites in America: "For the Lord has made the sea our path, and we are upon an isle of the sea."[34] From the point of view of the Eurasian land mass, the Western Hemisphere could be looked upon as a vast continental island. At least we know that both Isaiah and the Nephites so considered it.

Isaiah invited those great Israelite explorers who had gone down to the sea in ships and become inhabitants of the isles to join him in a new song. He wrote, "Sing unto the Lord a new song, and his praise from the end of the earth, ye that go down to the sea, and all that is therein; the isles, and the inhabitants thereof."[35] He knew that the American Israelites and those on other "isles" would be cut off from the Lord during a long period of apostasy, but he said that God would raise up his servant to "bring forth judgment to the Gentiles." Therefore, he said, "the isles shall wait for his law."[36]

Isaiah frequently made reference to these distant "isles." He began his great 49th chapter, which speaks of the latter-day redemption of Israel, with these words: "Listen, O isles, unto me; and hearken, ye people, from far...."[37] Later, the Lord referred to the same period and said, "Hearken unto me, my people.... My righteousness is near; my salvation is gone forth, and mine arms shall judge the

---

34. 2 Nephi 10:20.
35. Isaiah 42:10.
36. Isaiah 42:1, 4.
37. Isaiah 49:1.

people; **the isles shall wait upon me, and on mine arm shall they trust."**[38]

What were the people on the "isles" waiting for? Isaiah devoted a whole chapter to the redemption of the Israelites on the continental isle of America, and because he was talking about Nephi's own people, that inspired servant of the Lord could not resist devoting several chapters to this part of Isaiah's writings.[39] This, of course, is a scriptural treasure chest for the modern student of Isaiah.

By placing the Isaiah text on one side of the page and the pertinent passages of Nephi's commentary on the other side, we get a whole new insight into the extent of Isaiah's knowledge concerning both ancient and modern America. He knew about the fall of the Lamanite-Nephite civilization through apostasy. He knew of the occupation of the American continent by the Gentiles. And he knew an amazing quantity of detailed information about the coming forth of the Book of Mormon. A careful reading of the following parallel scriptures will prove most profitable.

ISAIAH AND NEPHI ON THE COMING FORTH OF THE BOOK OF MORMON

ISAIAH, Chapter 29

1. Woe to Ariel, to Ariel, the city where David dwelt! add ye year to year; let them kill sacrifices.

2. Yet I will distress Ariel, and there shall be heaviness and sorrow: and it shall be unto me as Ariel.

2 NEPHI, Chapter 25

9. And as one generation hath been destroyed among the Jews because of iniquity, even so have they been destroyed from generation to generation according to their iniquities; and never hath any of them been destroyed save it were foretold them by the prophets of the Lord.

10. Wherefore, it hath been told them concerning the destruction which should come upon them, immediately after my father left Jerusalem; nevertheless, they hardened their hearts; and according to my prophecy they have been destroyed, save it

---

38. Isaiah 51:4-5.
39. 2 Nephi, chapters 25, 26, and 27.
40. Isaiah 29:1-2.

be those which are carried away captive into Babylon.

11. And now this I speak because of the spirit which is in me. And notwithstanding they have been carried away they shall return again, and possess the land of Jerusalem; wherefore, they shall be restored again to the land of their inheritance.

12. But, behold, they shall have wars, and rumors of wars; and when the day cometh that the Only Begotten of the Father, yea, even the Father of heaven and of earth, shall manifest himself unto them in the flesh, behold, they will reject him, because of their iniquities, and the hardness of their hearts, and the stiffness of their necks.

13. Behold, they will crucify him; and after he is laid in a sepulchre for the space of three days he shall rise from the dead, with healing in his wings; and all those who shall believe on his name shall be saved in the kingdom of God. Wherefore, my soul delighteth to prophesy concerning him, for I have seen his day, and my heart doth magnify his holy name.

14. And behold it shall come to pass that after the Messiah hath risen from the dead, and hath manifested himself unto his people, unto as many as will believe on his name, behold, Jerusalem shall be destroyed again; for wo unto them that fight against God and the people of his church.

15. Wherefore, the Jews shall be scattered among all nations; yea, and also Babylon shall be destroyed; wherefore, the Jews shall be scattered by other nations.

3. And I will camp against thee round about, and will lay siege against thee with a mount, and I will raise forts against thee.

2 NEPHI, Chapter 26

14. But behold, I prophesy unto you concerning the last days; concerning the days when the Lord God shall bring these things forth unto the children of men.

15. After my seed and the seed of my brethren shall have dwindled in unbelief, and shall have been smitten by the Gentiles; yea, after the Lord God shall have camped

4. And thou shalt be brought down, and shalt speak out of the ground, and thy speech shall be low out of the dust, and thy voice shall be, as of one that hath a familiar spirit, out of the ground, and thy speech shall whisper out of the dust.

5. Moreover the multitude of thy strangers shall be like small dust, and the multitude of the terrible ones shall be as chaff that passeth away: yea, it shall be at an instant suddenly.

6. Thou shalt be visited of the Lord of hosts with thunder, and with earthquake, and great noise, with storm and tempest, and the flame of devouring fire.

against them round about, and shall have laid siege against them with a mount, and raised forts against them; and after they shall have been brought down low in the dust, even that they are not, yet the words of the righteous shall be written, and the prayers of the faithful shall be heard, and all those who have dwindled in unbelief shall not be forgotten.

16. For those who shall be destroyed shall speak unto them out of the ground, and their speech shall be low out of the dust, and their voice shall be as one that hath a familiar spirit; for the Lord God will give unto him power, that he may whisper concerning them, even as it were out of the ground; and their speech shall whisper out of the dust.

17. For thus saith the Lord God: They shall write the things which shall be done among them, and they shall be written and sealed up in a book, and those who have dwindled in unbelief shall not have them, for they seek to destroy the things of God.

18. Wherefore, as those who have been destroyed have been destroyed speedily; and the multitude of their terrible ones shall be as chaff that passeth away—yea, thus saith the Lord God: It shall be at an instant, suddenly—

19. And it shall come to pass, that those who have dwindled in unbelief shall be smitten by the hand of the Gentiles.

2 NEPHI, Chapter 27

1. But, behold, in the last days, or in the days of the Gentiles—yea, behold all the nations of the Gentiles and also the Jews, both those who shall come upon this land and those who shall be upon other lands, yea, even upon all the lands of the earth, behold, they will be drunken with iniquity and all manner of abominations—

2. And when that day shall come they shall be visited of the Lord of Hosts, with thunder and with earthquake, and with a

great noise, and with storm, and with tempest, and with the flame of devouring fire.

7. And the multitude of all the nations that fight against Ariel, even all that fight against her and her munition, and that distress her, shall be as a dream of a night vision.

8. It shall even be as when an hungry man dreameth, and, behold, he eateth; but he awaketh, and his soul is empty: or as when a thirsty man dreameth, and, behold, he drinketh; but he awaketh, and, behold, he is faint, and his soul hath appetite: so shall the multitude of all the nations be, that fight against mount Zion.

9. Stay yourselves, and wonder; cry ye out, and cry: they are drunken, but not with wine; they stagger, but not with strong drink.

10. For the Lord hath poured out upon you the spirit of deep sleep, and hath closed your eyes: the prophets and your rulers, the seers hath he covered.

11. And the vision of all is become unto you as the words of a book...

...that is sealed,...

3. And all the nations that fight against Zion, and that distress her, shall be as a dream of a night vision; yea, it shall be unto them, even as unto a hungry man which dreameth, and behold he eateth but he awaketh and his soul is empty; or like unto a thirsty man which dreameth, and behold he drinketh but he awaketh and behold he is faint, and his soul hath appetite; yea, even so shall the multitude of all the nations be that fight against Mount Zion.

4. For behold, all ye that doeth iniquity, stay yourselves and wonder, for ye shall cry out, and cry; yea, ye shall be drunken but not with wine, ye shall stagger but not with strong drink.

5. For behold, the Lord hath poured out upon you the spirit of deep sleep. For behold, ye have closed your eyes, and ye have rejected the prophets; and your rulers, and the seers hath he covered because of your iniquity.

6. And it shall come to pass that the Lord God shall bring forth unto you the words of a book, and they shall be the words of them which have slumbered.

7. And behold the book shall be sealed; and in the book shall be a revelation from God, from the beginning of the world to the ending thereof.

8. Wherefore, because of the things which are sealed up, the things which are sealed shall not be delivered in the day of the wickedness and abominations of the people. Wherefore the book shall be kept from them.

9. But the book shall be delivered unto a man, and he shall deliver the words of the book, which are the words of those who have slumbered in the dust, and he shall deliver these words unto another;

10. But the words which are sealed he shall not deliver, neither shall he deliver the book. For the book shall be sealed by the power of God, and the revelation which was sealed shall be kept in the book until the own due time of the Lord, that they may come forth; for behold, they reveal all things from the foundation of the world unto the end thereof.

11. And the day cometh that the words of the book which were sealed shall be read upon the house tops; and they shall be read by the power of Christ; and all things shall be revealed unto the children of men which ever have been among the children of men, and which ever will be even unto the end of the earth.

12. Wherefore, at that day when the book shall be delivered unto the man of whom I have spoken, the book shall be hid from the eyes of the world, that the eyes of none shall behold it save it be that three witnesses shall behold it, by the power of God, besides him to whom the book shall be delivered; and they shall testify to the truth of the book and the things therein.

13. And there is none other which shall view it, save it be a few according to the will of God, to bear testimony of his word unto the children of men; for the Lord God hath said that the words of the faithful should speak as if it were from the dead.

14. Wherefore, the Lord God will proceed to bring forth the words of the book; and in the mouth of as many witnesses as seemeth him good will he establish his word; and wo be unto him that rejecteth the word of God!

...which men deliver to one that is learned, saying, Read this, I pray thee:...

15. But behold, it shall come to pass that the Lord God shall say unto him to whom he shall deliver the book: Take these words which are not sealed and deliver them to another, that he may show them unto the learned, saying: Read this, I pray thee. And the learned shall say: Bring hither the book, and I will read them.

...and he saith, I cannot; for it is sealed:

12. And the book is delivered to him that is not learned, saying, Read this, I pray thee: and he saith, I am not learned.

16. And now, because of the glory of the world and to get gain will they say this, and not for the glory of God.

17. And the man shall say: I cannot bring the book, for it is sealed.

18. Then shall the learned say: I cannot read it.

19. Wherefore it shall come to pass, that the Lord God will deliver again the book and the words thereof to him that is not learned; and the man that is not learned shall say: I am not learned.

20. Then shall the Lord God say unto him: The learned shall not read them, for they have rejected them, and I am able to do mine own work; wherefore thou shalt read the words which I shall give unto thee.

21. Touch not the things which are sealed, for I will bring them forth in mine own due time; for I will show unto the children of men that I am able to do mine own work.

22. Wherefore, when thou hast read the words which I have commanded thee, and obtained the witnesses which I have promised unto thee, then shalt thou seal up the book again, and hide it up unto me, that I may preserve the words which thou hast not read, until I shall see fit in mine own wisdom to reveal all things unto the children of men.

23. For behold, I am God; and I am a God of miracles; and I will show unto the world that I am the same yesterday, today, and forever; and I work not among the children of men save it be according to their faith.

24. And again it shall come to pass that the Lord shall say unto him that shall read the words that shall be delivered him:

25. Forasmuch as this people draw near unto me with their mouth, and with their lips do honor me, but have removed their hearts far from me, and their fear towards me is taught by the precepts of men—

26. Therefore, I will proceed to do a marvelous work among this people, yea, a marvelous work and a wonder, for the wisdom of their wise and learned shall

13. Wherefore the Lord said, Forasmuch as this people draw near me with their mouth, and with their lips do honour me, but have removed their heart far from me, and their fear toward me is taught by the precept of men:

14. Therefore, behold, I will proceed to do a marvellous work among this people, even a marvellous work and a wonder: for the wisdom of their wise men shall perish, and the understanding of their prudent men shall be hid.

15. Woe unto them that seek deep to hide their counsel from the Lord, and their works are in the dark, and they say, Who seeth us? and who knoweth us?

16. Surely your turning of things upside down shall be esteemed as the potter's clay: for shall the work say of him that made it, He made me not? or shall the thing framed say of him that framed it, He had no understanding?

17. Is it not yet a very little while, and Lebanon shall be turned into a fruitful field, and the fruitful field shall be esteemed as a forest?

18. And in that day shall the deaf hear the words of the book, and the eyes of the blind shall see out of obscurity, and out of darkness.

19. The meek also shall increase their joy in the Lord, and the poor among men shall rejoice in the Holy One of Israel.

20. For the terrible one is brought to nought, and the scorner is consumed, and all that watch for iniquity are cut off:

21. That make a man an offender for a word, and lay a snare for him that reproveth in the gate, and turn aside the just for a thing of nought.

22. Therefore thus saith the Lord, who redeemed Abraham, concerning the house of Jacob, Jacob shall not now be ashamed, neither shall his face now wax pale.

23. But when he seeth his children, the work of mine hands, in the midst of him, they shall sanctify my name, and sanctify the Holy One of Jacob, and shall fear the God of Israel.

24. They also that erred in spirit shall come to understanding, and they that murmured shall learn doctrine.

perish, and the understanding of their prudent shall be hid.

27. And wo unto them that seek deep to hide their counsel from the Lord! And their works are in the dark; and they say: Who seeth us, and who knoweth us? And they also say: Surely, your turning of things upside down shall be esteemed as the potter's clay. But behold, I will show unto them, saith the Lord of Hosts, that I know all their works. For shall the work say of him that made it, he made me not? Or shall the thing framed say of him that framed it, he had no understanding?

28. But behold, saith the Lord of Hosts: I will show unto the children of men that it is yet a very little while and Lebanon shall be turned into a fruitful field; and the fruitful field shall be esteemed as a forest.

29. And in that day shall the deaf hear the words of the book, and the eyes of the blind shall see out of obscurity and out of darkness.

30. And the meek also shall increase, and their joy shall be in the Lord, and the poor among men shall rejoice in the Holy One of Israel.

31. For assuredly as the Lord liveth they shall see that the terrible one is brought to naught, and the scorner is consumed, and all that watch for iniquity are cut off;

32. And they that make a man an offender for a word, and lay a snare for him that reproveth in the gate, and turn aside the just for a thing of naught.

33. Therefore, thus saith the Lord, who redeemed Abraham, concerning the house of Jacob: Jacob shall not now be ashamed, neither shall his face now wax pale.

34. But when he seeth his children, the work of my hands, in the midst of him, they shall sanctify my name, and sanctify the Holy One of Jacob, and shall fear the God of Israel.

35. They also that erred in spirit shall come to understanding, and they that murmured shall learn doctrine.

TWENTY PROPHECIES IN THESE TEXTS HAVE
ALREADY BEEN FULFILLED

It is astonishing that the prophecies of Isaiah in the eighth century B.C., and the parallel prophecies of Nephi in the sixth century B.C., should have been so completely, literally, and immaculately fulfilled in the nineteenth century A.D. A careful analysis of the above texts will disclose at least 20 separate conditions which had to be met in order to make these prophecies come true. Between Isaiah and Nephi we find the following:

1. People originating in Jerusalem were to become a corrupted and afflicted segment of humanity who would go into a deep sleep of apostasy.[40]

In his commentary Nephi said this applied to all the people from Jerusalem, but especially to his own people who came to the Western Hemisphere in the sixth century B.C. and whom Isaiah particularly had in mind. These people were the so-called Indian aborigines who numbered in the millions when the New World was first discovered by Europeans. That they had apostatized and lost what was once a magnificent civilization is borne out by the gigantic ruins which can still be seen.

2. Both Isaiah and Nephi said these people would record their history, and through this history these people would "speak out of the ground, and...whisper out of the dust," and it would have a "familiar spirit."[41]

This was fulfilled when the plates of Mormon were taken from the stone box buried on the side of Hill Cumorah.

3. They said this history of the ancient American Israelites would go forth to the world in the form of a book.[42]

This commenced with the publication of the Book of Mormon in

---

40. Isaiah 29:1-2.
41. Isaiah 29:4; 2 Nephi 26:16-17.
42. Isaiah 29:11; 2 Nephi 27:6.

1830. It has since been translated and published in every major language and a number of minor ones.

4. They said part of this record would be sealed, and that this portion would contain a prophetic revelation of human history from the beginning to the end.[43]

A substantial portion of the plates was sealed.[44] Joseph Smith was allowed to translate only the unsealed portion. The sealed portion contained the revelation given to the brother of Jared (Mahonri Moriancumer). Concerning this revelation Moroni said, "Behold, I have written upon these plates the very things which the brother of Jared saw; and there never were greater things made manifest than those which were made manifest unto the brother of Jared."[45]

5. The time for the coming forth of this record was described as being "the last days" when both "the Gentiles and also the Jews...will be drunken with iniquity and all manner of abominations."[46]

The Lord has verified that the age in which we now live is indeed the last days.[47] It is in this age that the Book of Mormon has come forth, just as Isaiah and Nephi said it would. It caught the world in a state of rebellion against God, with agnosticism, cynicism, immorality, crime, violence, and war characterizing the cultural pattern throughout most of the world.

6. The book (or set of plates) was to be delivered into the hands of a man who was not learned.[48]

Many years after Joseph Smith had been martyred, a statement was obtained from his wife, Emma, concerning her recollection of

---

43. Isaiah 29:11; 2 Nephi 27:7–10.

44. George Q. Cannon, *Life of Joseph Smith the Prophet* (Salt Lake City: Deseret News Press, 1907), p. 23.

45. Ether 4:4.

46. 2 Nephi 27:1; Isaiah 29:9–10.

47. D&C 1:4; 27:6; 29:1-26; 39:11.

48. Isaiah 29:12; 2 Nephi 27:19.

those earlier days. Commenting on the inability of Joseph Smith to have produced a volume like the Book of Mormon, she said: "Joseph Smith [as a young man] . . . could neither write nor dictate a coherent and well-worded letter, let alone dictate a book like the Book of Mormon, and though I was an active participant in the scenes that transpired, was present during the translation of the plates, and had cognizance of things as they transpired, it is marvelous to me—a marvel and a wonder—as much as to anyone else."[49]

In bearing her testimony of the Book of Mormon, she said: "My belief is that the Book of Mormon is of divine authenticity—I have not the slightest doubt of it. . . . When acting as his scribe, your father [she was being interrogated by her son] would dictate to me hour after hour; and when returning after meals, or interruptions, he would at once begin where he had left off, without either seeing the manuscript or having any portion of it read to him. This was an unusual thing for him to do. It would have been improbable that a learned man could do this, and for one so ignorant and unlearned as he was, it was simply impossible."[50]

7. Nephi said this unlearned man would not give the actual book to anyone (which Isaiah's more general statement implies), but that he would take the "words which are not sealed" and deliver them to a second man who would then present these words to the learned for examination.[51]

This second man turned out to be a well-to-do citizen farmer from Palmyra named Martin Harris. Joseph Smith was instructed by the Lord to make a facsimile of some of the characters on the plates and have some of the learned men in New York City determine if they could translate them. Joseph made two facsimiles. One he translated, the other he did not.[52] Martin Harris took both of these

49. Quoted in Preston Nibley, *The Witnesses of the Book of Mormon* (Salt Lake City: Stevens and Wallis, 1946), pp. 28–29.

50. Ibid.

51. 2 Nephi 27:10, 15; Isaiah 29:11.

52. *History of the Church*, 1:19.

to New York to find the most eminent linguists of ancient languages to examine them and read "the words" if possible.

8. Both Nephi and Isaiah said that the words of the book[53] would be delivered to some learned or scholarly man for examination.[54]

This "learned man" turned out to be Professor Charles Anthon of Columbia College, now Columbia University. The facsimiles and translation were also shown to Dr. Samuel L. Mitchill.[55] Here is what occurred according to Martin Harris: "I went to the city of New York, and presented the characters which had been translated, with the translation thereof, to Professor Charles Anthon, a gentleman celebrated for his literary attainments. Professor Anthon stated that the translation was correct, more so than any he had before seen translated from the Egyptian.[56] I then showed him those which were not yet translated, and he said that they were Egyptian, Chaldaic, Assyric, and Arabic; and he said they were true characters. He gave me a certificate, certifying to the people of Palmyra that they were true characters, and that the translation of such of them as had been translated was also correct. I took the certificate and put it into my pocket, and was just leaving the house, when Mr. Anthon called me back, and asked me how the young man found out that there were gold plates in the place where he found them. I answered that an angel of God had revealed it unto him.

---

53. Isaiah says "the book," but "*words* of the book" would be more accurate, as indicated in 2 Nephi 27:10, 15.

54. Isaiah 29:11; 2 Nephi 27:15.

55. Stanley B. Kimball, "The Anthon Transcript: People, Primary Sources, and Problems" *Brigham Young University Studies,* vol. x, no. 3 (Spring 1970), p. 334.

56. If Martin Harris was completely accurate in quoting the professor, then Dr. Anthon was extending himself professionally. As R.C. Webb says in his book, *Joseph Smith as a Translator,* page 4: "It is difficult to understand how Professor Anthon could have stated that the translation was correct from the fact that, at that time (1828), the science of Egyptology, or the knowledge of the Egyptian language, had not advanced sufficiently to warrant the supposition that he, or any other scholar, could read a given inscription off-hand. In addition, so far as it is known, Anthon had not devoted sufficient attention to the subject to enable him to give authoritative utterance to such a verdict."

"He then said to me, 'Let me see that certificate.' I accordingly took it out of my pocket and gave it to him, when he took it and tore it to pieces, saying, that there was no such thing now as ministering of angels, and that if I would bring the plates to him, he would translate them. I informed him that part of the plates were sealed, and that I was forbidden to bring them. He replied, 'I cannot read a sealed book.' I left him and went to Dr. Mitch[i]ll, who sanctioned what Professor Anthon had said respecting both the characters and the translation."[57]

9. Nephi said the learned man would say, "Bring hither the book, and I will read them [the words of the book]."[58]

As we have seen in the above statement of Martin Harris, Professor Charles Anthon said to him "that there was no such thing now as ministering of angels, and that if I would bring the plates to him, he would translate them."

10. Nephi said this statement would be made to get fame and money rather than because of his anxiety to help in the work of the Lord.[59]

Dr. Anthon's unfortunate role in these important events was a source of great embarrassment to him in later years. This would tend to verify the statement of Nephi that his motives were not entirely sincere. For example, he wrote a letter to E.D. Howe on February 17, 1834, verifying the visit of Martin Harris but ridiculing the claim that he had given Mr. Harris a certificate vouching for the accuracy of the translation or the authenticity of the writings. Said Professor Anthon, "He [Martin Harris] requested an opinion from me in writing, which, of course, I declined to give, and he then took his leave, taking his paper with him."[60] Seven years later, on April 3,

---

57. *History of the Church,* 1:20.

58. 2 Nephi 27:15.

59. 2 Nephi 27:16.

60. E.D. Howe, *Mormonism Unveiled* (Painesville, Ohio, 1834), chapter 18; quoted in William E. Berrett and Alma P. Burton, eds., *Readings in L.D.S. Church History,* 3 vols. (Salt Lake City: Deseret Book Company, 1953), 1:46.

1841, Professor Anthon wrote a letter to the Rev. Dr. T. W. Coit in which he said, "He requested me to give him my opinion in writing about the paper which he had shown me. **I did so without hesitation,** partly for the man's sake, and partly to let the individual 'behind the curtain' see that the trick was discovered. **The import of what I wrote was, as far as I can now recollect, simply this,** that the marks in the paper appeared to be merely an imitation of various alphabetical characters, and had, in my opinion, no meaning at all connected with them."[61] At that point the duplicity of Dr. Anthon becomes fully evident as he verifies the very thing which he had formerly denied, all of which lends great credence to the simple and direct statement of Martin Harris as to what really happened.

At the time of the above visit, neither Martin Harris nor Joseph Smith was aware that the Book of Mormon contained a commentary on chapter 29 of Isaiah, or that it impugned the motives of Dr. Anthon. In later years, when Professor Anthon was told that he had been identified as the "learned" scholar in Isaiah 29:11, he was intellectually horrified. Martin Harris became aware of this when he made a special trip to New York a second time to personally present a copy of the newly published Book of Mormon to him. Professor Anthon would not even allow Martin Harris to leave a copy in the house![62]

11. Both Isaiah and Nephi said that this learned man would declare that he could not read a "sealed" book.[63]

Nephi described in considerable detail the circumstances which would lead to this strange statement.[64] In the above quotation Martin Harris says, "He then said to me, 'Let me see that certificate.' I accordingly took it out of my pocket and gave it to him, when he took it and tore it to pieces, saying, that there was no such thing

---

61. Ibid., p. 49.
62. Ibid.
63. Isaiah 29:11; 2 Nephi 27:17-18.
64. 2 Nephi 27:7-18.

now as ministering of angels, and that if I would bring the plates to him, he would translate them. I informed him that part of the plates were sealed, and that I was forbidden to bring them. He replied, 'I cannot read a sealed book.'"

12. Both Isaiah and Nephi verified that the unlearned man who was given the "book" would have the gift and power of God to read or translate it.[65]

Once Joseph Smith had learned how to use the Urim and Thummim, and once he had procured Oliver Cowdery to write down the translation, Joseph Smith was able to translate the Book of Mormon at the phenomenal rate of nearly 5,000 words per day.[66] No doubt he could have gone even faster, but apparently that was about as rapid as the scribe could write it down. The frantic haste of the scribe is indicated in the original manuscript by the frequent lack of punctuation and sometimes of capitalization. These defects had to be corrected later.

13. Both Isaiah and Nephi indicated that the sacred record of the Israelites in the New World would not be allowed to go forth to the public, but, as Isaiah says, "in that day shall the deaf hear the words of the book."[67]

Nephi is much more explicit in explaining why the original record would not be placed on public exhibition. He said that because it

---

65. Isaiah 29:12, 14, 18 (also 2 Nephi 27:19-20). The verses in Isaiah are somewhat obscure and must be read carefully. Note that when the man says "I am not learned," the Lord says he will "do a marvelous work" which will cause the wisdom of the wise to perish, and, in verse 18, he says the words of the book will be sent forth. All of this implies that the man who is "not learned" will translate the book through the power of God. Nephi verifies that this is a correct deduction (2 Nephi 27:20).

66. Joseph Smith worked from April 7, 1829, to the latter part of June, 1829, to translate the entire Book of Mormon (except for a few pages which were done earlier). A closer examination of Joseph Smith's history shows that this prodigious task was accomplished in approximately 65 working days. The manuscript is on foolscap sheets, 8 x 13 inches, with approximately 647 words to a page. Joseph covered enough material each day to fill an average of seven pages, which is an average of 4,615 words per day. (See Arch S. Reynolds, *How Did Joseph Smith Translate?* [Springville, Utah: pamphlet published by the author, 1940] pp. 26-27.)

67. Isaiah 29:18; 2 Nephi 27:12.

included the "sealed" section containing the sacred revelation of world history which the Lord intended to disclose at a later time, the record was to be kept "hid from the eyes of the world," and none should see it save those to whom the unlearned man was told to show it.[68]

Joseph Smith verified that even before he received custody of the record, he was strenuously cautioned against showing it to anyone unless commanded by the Lord. He wrote: "Again, he [Moroni] told me, that when I got those plates of which he had spoken—for the time that they should be obtained was not yet fulfilled—I should not show them to any person; neither the breastplate with the Urim and Thummim; only to those to whom I should be commanded to show them; if I did I should be destroyed."[69]

14. Nephi knew that there would be three special witnesses who would be permitted to see the sacred record.[70]

The three witnesses were Oliver Cowdery, David Whitmer, and Martin Harris. They saw Moroni, they saw the sacred record, and, in addition, they saw the breastplate, the sword of Laban, the Urim and Thummim, and the Liahona or "director" which led Lehi and his family safely to America after crossing Arabia and the Pacific Ocean in the sixth century B.C.[71]

15. Nephi knew the three witnesses would not only see the sacred records, but they would issue a declaration to the world in which they would "testify to the truth of the book and the things therein."[72]

This statement is set forth in the front of the Book of Mormon. Even though each of these men subsequently had difficulty keeping up with the pressures and responsibilities involved in setting up the

---

68. 2 Nephi 27:12–14, 21–22.
69. Joseph Smith—History 1:42.
70. 2 Nephi 27:12.
71. See *History of the Church*, 1:52–55.
72. 2 Nephi 27:12.

latter-day kingdom, none ever wavered in the slightest degree in substantiating the integrity of this statement.[73]

16. Nephi knew there would be a "few" others who would see the sacred record in addition to the three witnesses. Said he, "And there is none other which shall view it, save it be a few according to the will of God."[74]

These "few" included the eight witnesses who were allowed to see and handle the plates prior to the time they were returned to the custody and safekeeping of Moroni.[75] They were not allowed to see anything else. The joint statement of these witnesses is also found in the front of the Book of Mormon.

17. Both Isaiah and Nephi predicted that the reason the Lord would elect to do his great work through an "unlearned" man in the latter days was because "this people draw near me with their mouth, and with their lips do honour me, but have removed their heart far from me, and their fear toward me is taught by the precept of men."[76]

The Lord verified that these circumstances existed in 1820. When Joseph Smith received the First Vision in the spring of that year, it so frightened him that at first he could not even speak. However, as he later wrote, "No sooner, therefore, did I get possession of myself, so as to be able to speak, than I asked the Personages who stood above me in the light, which of all the sects was right ... and which I should join. I was answered that I must join none of them, for they were all wrong; and the Personage who addressed me said that all their creeds were an abomination in his sight; that those professors were all corrupt; that: 'they draw near to me with their lips, but their hearts are far from me, they teach for doctrines the

---

73. See Francis W. Kirkham, *A New Witness for Christ in America,* rev. ed., 2 vols. (Salt Lake City: n.p., 1963-67), 1:247-55.

74. 2 Nephi 27:13.

75. *History of the Church,* 1:57–58.

76. Isaiah 29:13; 2 Nephi 27:24–25.

commandments of men, having a form of godliness, but they deny the power thereof.'"[77] This is precisely what Isaiah and Nephi had predicted.

18. Both Isaiah and Nephi knew that in connection with the coming forth of the Book of Mormon the Lord would commence to do "a marvellous work among this people, even a marvellous work and a wonder: for the wisdom of their wise men shall perish, and the understanding of their prudent men shall be hid."[78]

Not only was the "unlearned" Joseph Smith given the power to translate the "reformed Egyptian" of the plates of Mormon, but he translated the writings of Abraham which were brought out of the Egyptian catacombs with eleven mummies in the early 1820s by Antonio Lebolo.[79] Joseph Smith was given a continuous flow of revelations for the modern-day Saints which fill a whole volume.[80] He was given a missing chapter of the Bible describing how Moses happened to write Genesis.[81] By revelation he was given the English version of a lost manuscript written by John the Beloved while on the Isle of Patmos.[82] He received and recorded a vision concerning the different degrees of glory in heaven which Paul felt reluctant to disclose.[83] He received the correct procedures and prayers for administering the ordinances of baptism and the sacrament.[84] He was given the Aaronic Priesthood and later the Melchizedek Priesthood.[85] He was taught how to construct temples, and the

---

77. Joseph Smith—History 1:18-19.
78. Isaiah 29:14; 2 Nephi 27:26.
79. See the book of Abraham.
80. This is called the Doctrine and Covenants.
81. Moses, chapter 1.
82. D&C, section 7.
83. D&C, section 76; 2 Corinthians 12:2-5.
84. D&C 20:73, 77-79.
85. D&C, section 13 and 27:12. The latter scripture makes reference to the ordination, but it had occurred sometime earlier.

proper ordinances to be performed in them.[86] He was shown how to organize and establish the true Church of Jesus Christ upon the earth.[87] He was told what the duties were among all the various ranks of officeholders in the kingdom.[88] Under his administration the marvelous gifts of the Spirit were restored and enjoyed.[89]

Indeed, was not all of this truly a "marvelous work and a wonder?" It has been an astonishing enigma to the world's wise and prudent ever since it first began!

19. Isaiah and Nephi both knew that when the history of the Israelites of the Western Hemisphere went forth, many who had been both deaf and blind to the truthfulness of the Gospel would begin to respond.[90]

Since the restoration of the Gospel, several million Israelites have been gathered into the Gospel net. No single influence has had a greater missionary appeal in convincing men and women that God has spoken again than the Book of Mormon. It is a book which the Lord has promised to endorse by the power of the Holy Ghost to all who will read it prayerfully and earnestly.[91] Thousands upon thousands can now testify that they whose eyes were blind are now able to see out of obscurity and darkness.

20. Isaiah and Nephi knew that the great and marvelous work which God would do among men in the latter days would be of particular significance to the poor and cause them to rejoice "in the Holy One of Israel."[92]

---

86. During his lifetime, Joseph Smith had two temples built (Kirtland and Nauvoo, the latter completed shortly after his death) and had sites dedicated at Independence and Far West for two more. (See N. B. Lundwall, *Temples of the Most High* [Salt Lake City: Bookcraft, 1966], chapters 1, 2, 12, and 13.)

87. Joseph Smith saw a vision of the complete organizational structure of the Church.

88. See, as examples, D&C, sections 20 and 107.

89. An excellent example of these powers being exhibited was at the dedication of the Kirtland Temple. See *History of the Church*, 2:428.

90. Isaiah 29:18; 2 Nephi 27:29.

91. Moroni 10:4.

92. Isaiah 29:19; 2 Nephi 27:30.

In one of the early revelations to the Church, the Lord said, "And the poor and the meek shall have the gospel preached unto them, and they shall be looking forth for the time of my coming, for it is nigh at hand."[93] At a time when churches were characterized by heavy assessments, extravagant vestments, pompous buildings, and exploitation of the lowly, God restored his kingdom specifically designed to make the Gospel free to all men. It was like the return of the fresh, generous spirit of Paul when he said, "What is my reward then? Verily that, when I preach the gospel, I may make the gospel of Christ without charge, that I abuse not my power in the gospel."[94]

Thus we conclude one of the most significant chapters in the entire book of Isaiah. It reflected some of the most important work the Lord would do in the latter days. Note that Nephi thought it was so important that he devoted the largest segment of his entire commentary to this one chapter. Joseph Smith must have been astonished as he went through this material and recognized how many details had been fulfilled during his own administration. That the Lord revealed this information as far back as 700 B.C. shows how important he considered it to be!

---

93. D&C 35:15.
94. 1 Corinthians 9:18.

Chapter 6

ISAIAH'S PROPHECIES CONCERNING MODERN TIMES

Now we turn to those prophecies of Isaiah which extend from the immediate present to the distant future. First, however, let us make an observation concerning certain patterns in prophecy.

As each of the ancient prophets scanned the prophetic visions of the future, they must have been astonished as well as impressed by the fact that history tends to continually repeat itself. This is true for individuals as well as nations. Therefore, Isaiah, David, Moses, Jeremiah, Ezekiel, and a number of other scriptural writers often wrote their prophecies in such a way that their readers could apply them to a variety of situations, times, and places, **and be correct in all of them!**

MANY PROPHECIES ARE FULFILLED MORE THAN ONCE

We have already seen a number of cases in which Isaiah described his own experiences as being a type of the Savior's persecution and suffering which would come 700 years later.[1] David did the same thing.[2]

Isaiah followed the same pattern when he made his declarations concerning the isles of the sea. Nephi and his brother Jacob said these statements included the Israelites in the Western Hemisphere.[3] However, they were both quick to point out that there are Israelites scattered in other parts of the earth, and therefore Isaiah's words would apply to them also.[4]

Isaiah promised that in connection with the great latter-day gathering of Israel, the desert would "blossom as a rose." Here again we have multiple applications. The promise will be fulfilled when the Ten Tribes come down from the north to overflow the land, but it is already being fulfilled in the valleys of the Rockies and on the barren slopes and plains of Palestine. Micah and Isaiah both promised that the house of the Lord would be built in the tops of the mountains. This has already been fulfilled in the tops of the American mountains and will soon be duplicated when a great temple is built in the tops of the mountains of Israel. The gathering of Israel is taking place in America and also in the land of Judah. The Saints of God will be persecuted by the wicked in both places. They will be rescued by the Lord in both places. These are just a few examples of the pattern of "multiple fulfillments" which runs through many prophecies found in the scriptures.

As we have previously noted, Isaiah's prophecies which were fulfilled in the past actually covered a tremendous sweep. The same can be said of his prophecies dealing with the future. It is not our purpose here to provide an exhaustive discussion of all of them, but merely to present their scope. By this means we can appreciate the reason why Jesus told the American Israelites that Isaiah was one of

---

1. Isaiah 50:5-6; 49:1-3.
2. Psalm 22 is a typical example.
3. 1 Nephi 22:4-6; 2 Nephi 10:20-21.
4. Ibid.

the great writers of scripture who deserved careful and diligent analysis. He said: "And now, behold, I say unto you, that ye ought to search these things. Yea, a **commandment** I give unto you that ye search these things diligently; **for great are the words of Isaiah.**"[5]

ISAIAH SPEAKS OF THE TWO GREAT "ZIONS" OF THE LATTER DAYS

One of the most significant terms in scriptural literature is the word "Zion." Isaiah used the word frequently. The Lord said the city of Enoch was first called "Zion" because "they were of one heart and one mind, and dwelt in righteousness; and there was no poor among them."[6] In modern times the Lord has said, "Let Zion rejoice, for this is Zion—THE PURE IN HEART."[7] Joseph Smith said both North and South America were intended by the Lord as "Zion."[8] The ancient prophets often referred to Jerusalem, especially Mount Moriah, as "Zion."[9]

Isaiah knew that in the latter days there would be a Zion in America and a Zion in Palestine. When he addressed both of them together, he often distinguished one from the other by calling America "Zion" and Palestine "Jerusalem." Here are several typical examples:

"O Zion, that bringest good tidings, **get thee up into the high mountain** [the American Rockies, to which the modern Church was led, are about three times higher than the mountains of Judea]; O Jerusalem, that bringest good tidings, lift up thy voice with strength."[10]

---

5. 3 Nephi 23:1.
6. Moses 7:18.
7. D&C 97:21.
8. Smith, *Teachings,* p. 362.
9. 2 Samuel 5:6-7; 1 Kings 8:1.
10. Isaiah 40:9.

"For out of Zion shall go forth the law, and the word of the Lord from Jerusalem."[11]

"Awake, awake; put on thy strength, O Zion; put on thy beautiful garments, O Jerusalem, the holy city."[12]

"For Zion's sake will I not hold my peace, and for Jerusalem's sake I will not rest, until the righteousness thereof go forth as brightness."[13]

"Princes shall be afraid of the ensign, saith the Lord, whose fire is in Zion, and his furnace in Jerusalem."[14]

These are sufficient to show Isaiah's knowledge of and concern for the two great centers of divine administration in the last days. As noted above, however, when he spoke of these two places together, Isaiah frequently used "Zion" for God's work in America and "Jerusalem" to designate the Lord's center of activity in Judea. Nevertheless, when we understand that "Zion" is a condition as well as a place, we can better appreciate why Isaiah would also call Jerusalem a "Zion" on occasion. In one place he specifically talked about the people who "shall dwell in Zion at Jerusalem."[15]

As for the Zion in America, we have already seen that Isaiah was well aware that there was a country far off "beyond the rivers of Ethiopia" from which would go forth swift messengers to gather the Israelites which were once so strong, but by the latter days had become "trodden down, . . . scattered and peeled."[16] He said these people would commence to gather and bring their presents to "the

---

11. Isaiah 2:3.
12. Isaiah 52:1.
13. Isaiah 62:1.
14. Isaiah 31:9.
15. Isaiah 30:19.
16. Isaiah 18:1-7. Zephaniah helps identify America as the land "beyond the rivers of Ethiopia" by pointing out that it is from this land that the "daughter of my dispersed" (the children of Israel) shall come to bring their offering in the last days (Zephaniah 3:10).

place of the name of the Lord of hosts, the mount Zion."[17] Isaiah admonished the whole world to listen when the latter-day trumpet blows and the ensign is set up "on the mountains" of this land.[18]

The Lord's purpose in setting up a "Zion" is to provide a haven of safety for the righteous. Therefore Isaiah said, "He that walketh righteously...shall dwell on high: his place of defence shall be the munitions of rocks: bread shall be given him; his waters shall be sure."[19] Ultimately, this will apply to both Zions.

THE GREAT GATHERING

Isaiah knew that once the trumpet had sounded and the missionaries had gone forth to convert the righteous, they would flock to Zion in America. He also knew there would be a great gathering of the Jews to Jerusalem. Said he: "And it shall come to pass in that day, that the Lord shall set his hand again the second time to recover the remnant of his people.... And he shall set up an ensign for the nations, and shall assemble the **outcasts** of Israel, and gather together the **dispersed** of Judah from the four corners of the earth."[20]

Isaiah said that between the righteous Jews and the righteous descendants of Joseph there would no longer be the antagonism which existed in ancient times. He wrote: "The envy also of Ephraim shall depart, and the adversaries of Judah shall be cut off: **Ephraim shall not envy Judah, and Judah shall not vex Ephraim.**"[21]

The prophet saw that it would be a long time (over 2,500 years for the Israelites and 1,800 years for the Jews!) before they would get the call to rally and return again. Isaiah wanted the people to know this postponement or delay was all part of the plan: "And therefore will the Lord wait, that he may be gracious unto you, and therefore

---

17. Isaiah 18:7.
18. Isaiah 18:3.
19. Isaiah 33:15–16.
20. Isaiah 11:11–12.
21. Isaiah 11:13.

will he be exalted, that he may have mercy upon you: for the Lord is a God of judgment: **blessed are all they that wait for him.**"[22]

Isaiah described a number of details concerning the gathering which are of special interest to those of us who are responsible for bringing it about. What foreign missionary, for example, could not appreciate Isaiah's declaration that "with stammering lips and another tongue will he speak to this people."[23] The Lord knew it would not be easy to overcome centuries of apostasy and ignorance. In order to "teach knowledge" and help them "understand doctrine," Isaiah said they would have to learn "precept upon precept; line upon line,...here a little, and there a little."[24]

Although Isaiah knew the call to the righteous would be worldwide, he declared that there would be a severe screening in gathering out the righteous. He wrote, "Ye shall be gathered one by one, O ye children of Israel."[25]

THE RETURN OF THE LOST TEN TRIBES

As soon as the foundation of the kingdom can be established by this extremely careful screening process, Isaiah indicated that great multitudes would suddenly flow into the Church through the arrival of the lost Ten Tribes. Note that Isaiah specifically called these tribes "outcasts," whereas the Jews were called "dispersed." Parley P. Pratt suggested that there is some deep significance behind the distinction in these two words.[26] From whence will the multitude of the Ten Tribes come? It will be from that mysterious place to which they have been cast out, the location of which is not known at the present time. But we do know that it will take a stupendous miracle to get them to America. Isaiah said, "And there shall be an highway for the remnant of his people, which shall be

---

22. Isaiah 30:18.

23. Isaiah 28:11.

24. Isaiah 28:10.

25. Isaiah 27:12.

26. Parley P. Pratt, *A Voice of Warning* (Salt Lake City: Deseret News Press, 1936), p. 30.

left, from Assyria [the last place the Ten Tribes were seen]; like as it was to Israel in the day that he came up out of the land of Egypt."[27]

Of course, the highway by which the Israelites came up out of Egypt was a most exciting thoroughfare, associated with a continuous series of miracles which included the division of the Red Sea. Apparently the great transmission belt by which the Ten Tribes will return can be expected to be even more amazing. A modern scripture gives us some idea of its gargantuan proportions. Said the Lord: "And they who are in the north countries shall come in remembrance before the Lord; and **their prophets**[28] **shall hear his voice** [divine commands], **and shall no longer stay themselves; and they shall smite the rocks, and the ice shall flow down at their presence. And an highway shall be cast up in the midst of the great deep.** Their enemies shall become a prey unto them, and in the barren deserts there shall come forth pools of living water.... And they shall bring forth their rich treasures unto the children of Ephraim, my servants. And the boundaries of the everlasting hills shall tremble at their presence. And there shall they fall down and be crowned with glory, even in Zion, by the hands of the servants of the Lord, even the children of Ephraim."[29]

It is clear from this passage that the Ten Tribes will come as a great multitude from the north (the direction toward which they disappeared); that the highway or means of returning will appear in the midst of "the great deep" (which could be either space or water); that neither the ice cap of the Arctic nor the mighty battlements of intervening mountains will deter them. They will overcome any

---

27. Isaiah 11:16.

28. In June 1831, Joseph Smith said that John the Revelator was already working among the lost Ten Tribes. See *History of the Church,* 1:176.

29. D&C 133:26–32. This spectacular event will be so marvelous that Jeremiah says: "Therefore, behold, the days come, saith the Lord, that they shall no more say, The Lord liveth, which brought up the children of Israel out of the land of Egypt; but, The Lord liveth, which brought up and which led the seed of the house of Israel out of the north country, and from all countries whither I had driven them; and they shall dwell in their own land." (Jeremiah 23:7–8.)

man-made opposition that stands in their way, and they will come down the spine of the American continent to the modern headquarters of God's Priesthood, where they can enter the holy temples of the Lord and receive their sacred endowments from the Ephraimite Saints who possess the keys to these great blessings.[30]

When will the Ten Tribes come? Perhaps the Savior gave the best clue when he was visiting the Saints in the Western Hemisphere shortly after his resurrection. He said the New Jerusalem would be built on this, the American continent,[31] that the Savior himself would make his appearance there,[32] "**and then** shall the work of the Father commence ... among all the dispersed of my people, yea, **even the tribes which have been lost,** which the Father hath led away out of Jerusalem."[33] So it would seem quite clear that the New Jerusalem must be built before the Ten Tribes return.

As this mammoth host marches down toward the city of Zion, or the New Jerusalem, Isaiah described what it would be like: "They shall not hunger nor thirst; neither shall the heat nor sun smite them: for he that hath mercy on them shall lead them, even by the springs of water shall he guide them. And I will make all my mountains a way, and my highways shall be exalted. Behold, these shall come from far."[34]

After they have arrived, the sudden impact of this population explosion will be so great that the Ephraimite Saints will hardly

---

30. Wilford Woodruff stated: "Again, here are the ten tribes of Israel, we know nothing about them only what the Lord has said by His Prophets. There are Prophets among them, and by and by they will come along, and they will smite the rocks, and the mountains of ice will flow down at their presence, and a highway will be cast up before them, and they will come to Zion, receive their endowments, and be crowned under the hands of the children of Ephraim. . . . They will receive their blessings and endowments, from under the children of Ephraim, who are the first fruits of the kingdom of God in this dispensation, and the men will have to be ordained and receive their Priesthood and endowments in the land of Zion, according to the revelations of God." (*Journal of Discourses*, 4:231–32.)

31. 3 Nephi 21:23–24.

32. 3 Nephi 21:25.

33. 3 Nephi 21:26.

34. Isaiah 49:10–12.

know what to do with them. Isaiah said, "For thou shalt break forth on the right hand and on the left; and thy seed shall inherit the Gentiles, and make the desolate cities to be inhabited."[35] He indicates that the Ten Tribes will be even a greater host than the members of the Church, "for more are the children of the desolate than the children of the married wife, saith the Lord."[36]

The Lord will bless the desolate land and all the surrounding territory. Isaiah wrote: "The wilderness and the solitary place shall be glad for them; and the desert shall rejoice, and blossom as the rose...for in the wilderness shall waters break out, and streams in the desert. And the parched ground shall become a pool, and the thirsty land springs of water: in the habitation of dragons [lizards, etc.], where each lay, shall be grass with reeds and rushes."[37] Isaiah saw that this wonderful blessing was by heavenly intervention. Said he: "For the Lord shall comfort Zion: he will comfort all her waste places; and he will make her wilderness like Eden, and her desert like the garden of the Lord; joy and gladness shall be found therein, thanksgiving, and the voice of melody."[38]

The surging crowds of newcomers will be carefully organized into orderly patterns that will spread out in all directions from the center at New Jerusalem. Isaiah proclaimed: "Enlarge the place of thy tent, and let them stretch forth the curtains of thine habitations: spare not, lengthen thy cords, and strengthen thy stakes; for thou shalt break forth on the right hand and on the left; and thy seed shall inherit the Gentiles, and make the desolate cities to be inhabited."[39]

Eventually, when world conditions will permit it, these great hosts will joyfully move on to Palestine where they will be given a permanent inheritance and help the Jews build up a mighty

---

35. Isaiah 54:3.

36. Isaiah 54:1.

37. Isaiah 35:1, 6-7.

38. Isaiah 51:3.

39. Isaiah 54:2-3. Verse 3 is repeated here, although previously quoted, so that the reader can better appreciate its full intent.

kingdom. Ezekiel was especially impressed with this great day when the Lord would "take the children of Israel...and bring them into their own land: and I will make them one nation," saith the Lord, "in the land **upon the mountains of Israel;** and one king shall be king to them all: and they shall be no more two nations, neither shall they be divided into two kingdoms any more at all.... And David my servant shall be king over them."[40] And just as John the Revelator will have been instrumental in bringing these hosts of Israel to the American Zion[41] for their Priesthood endowments, so also will he no doubt have an important responsibility in leading them back to the land of their original inheritance. According to modern revelation, this is the meaning of the little book which John was required to eat, as mentioned in the tenth chapter of Revelation: "It was a mission, and an ordinance, for him to gather the tribes of Israel."[42]

It is interesting to note that when the Ten Tribes return to Old Jerusalem, they will take along with them any of the tribe of Joseph who wish to go. Even though America is the inheritance of Joseph,[43] Ezekiel said there will be "a portion for Manasseh"[44] and "a portion for Ephraim"[45] when the permanent tribal inheritances are set up in Palestine.

Isaiah saw how marvelous it would be in Jerusalem when her temple had been rebuilt and all of the vast multitudes of Israel had been given their inheritances around her. He wrote, "Thine eyes shall see Jerusalem a quiet habitation, a tabernacle that shall not be

---

40. Ezekiel 37:21-24.

41. See *History of the Church,* 1:176.

42. D&C 77:14.

43. Orson Pratt said that "we are inheriting a land that was given to the remnant of Joseph, and God has said that we must be remembered with them [the Lamanites] in the possession of this land." (*Journal of Discourses,* 12:322; see also 1 Nephi 13:30.)

44. Ezekiel 48:4.

45. Ezekiel 48:5.

taken down; not one of the stakes thereof shall ever be removed, neither shall any of the cords thereof be broken."[46]

THE BUILDING OF THE NEW JERUSALEM IN AMERICA

Let us now go back and take a closer look at the great city of Zion, the New Jerusalem, which is to be built on the American continents in these latter days.

Chapter 54 of Isaiah is devoted to the great gathering of Israel in the Americas and the setting up of her magnificent capital. Jesus put this chapter in its proper context when he visited the Western Hemisphere after his resurrection. The Savior said that he would first bring the Gentiles to inhabit this continent, "for it is wisdom in the Father that they should be established in this land, and be set up as a free people by the power of the Father."[47]

Then he said the Gospel would be restored among them: "For thus it behooveth the Father that it [the restored Gospel] should come forth from the Gentiles, that he may show forth his power unto the Gentiles, for this cause that the Gentiles, if they will not harden their hearts, that they may repent and come unto me and be baptized in my name."[48]

To accomplish this, Jesus said the Father would raise up an inspired servant in our day even though many would not believe him: "There shall be among them those who will not believe it [the Gospel message], although a man shall declare it unto them."[49] Therefore the Lord's servant "shall be marred because of them. Yet I will heal him, for I will show unto them that my wisdom is greater than the cunning of the devil."[50]

---

46. Isaiah 33:20.
47. 3 Nephi 21:4.
48. 3 Nephi 21:6.
49. 3 Nephi 21:9.
50. 3 Nephi 21:10.

At this point Jesus said the Gentiles would have to make a tremendous decision either to support the work of the Lord or be swept from the land. If they should elect to fight the work of God, Jesus told them how terrible the consequences would be.[51] On the other hand, the Lord said, "If they will repent and hearken unto my words, and harden not their hearts, . . . **they shall assist my people,** the remnant of Jacob, and also as many of the house of Israel as shall come, **that they may build a city, which shall be called the New Jerusalem.** And then shall they assist my people that they may be gathered in, who are scattered upon all the face of the land, in unto the New Jerusalem."[52] In order to emphasize that it would be a place of great beauty, power and glory, Jesus declared: "And **then** shall that which is written [by Isaiah] come to pass."[53] He then went directly into the 54th chapter of Isaiah and quoted that portion of scripture in its entirety.

What did Isaiah have to say about this great New Jerusalem which is to be built in America? It will be noted that much that we have already said about the assembling of the Ten Tribes at the New Jerusalem was taken from this same chapter. In addition, Isaiah received the following from the Lord concerning the New Jerusalem and its people:

"Behold, I will lay thy stones with fair colors, and lay thy foundations with sapphires. And I will make thy windows of agates, and thy gates of carbuncles,[54] and all thy borders of pleasant stones. And all thy children shall be taught of the Lord; and great shall be the peace of thy children. In righteousness shalt thou be established; thou shalt be far from oppression for thou shalt not fear, and from terror for it shall not come near thee. . . . No weapon that is formed

---

51. 3 Nephi 21:12–21.

52. 2 Nephi 21:22–24.

53. 3 Nephi 22:1.

54. "Any of certain deep-red gems, especially a garnet with a smooth convex surface." (*Webster's New World Dictionary,* s.v. "carbuncle.")

against thee shall prosper; and every tongue that shall revile against thee in judgment thou shalt condemn. This is the heritage of the servants of the Lord, and their righteousness is of me, saith the Lord."[55]

So wrote Isaiah concerning America's future city of Zion or New Jerusalem.

THE GATHERING OF THE JEWS
AND THE REBUILDING OF OLD JERUSALEM

Isaiah also was aware that during the same general period the Lord was performing his great labor in America, he would be fulfilling his promises concerning the gathering of the Jews and the rebuilding of Old Jerusalem.

Chapter 40 of Isaiah is the prophet's triumphant song of hope for Judah and Jerusalem. Isaiah's vision swept from the beginning of the city's restoration right on through to her glory in the Millennium. Then he cried: "Comfort ye, comfort ye my people, saith your God. Speak ye comfortably to Jerusalem, and cry unto her, that her warfare is accomplished, that her iniquity is pardoned: for she hath received of the Lord's hand double for all her sins. . . . O Jerusalem, that bringest good tidings, lift up thy voice with strength; lift it up, be not afraid; say unto the cities of Judah, **Behold your God!**"[56]

Actually, there will have to be many years of preparation before the Jews finally behold their God, but that time will come. The first task of the Jews has been to establish a homeland in Palestine. Several generations have already passed and the work is still in progress.

A MODERN APOSTLE DEDICATES THE LAND OF JERUSALEM

The Lord's official program for the gathering of the Jews to Palestine was launched on October 24, 1841, when Orson Hyde, a

---

55. 3 Nephi 22:11–17; Isaiah 54:11–17.

56. Isaiah 40:1–9.

modern Apostle of the restored Church, stood on the brow of the Mount of Olives and poured forth his heart in a prayer which ended with the dedication of that land for the return of the Jews. For over four centuries Palestine had been under the rule of the Ottoman Turks, and it had become a land of total desolation, just as the prophets had predicted. It had become the graveyard of a grandeur which had sunk into oblivion. Its terrain no longer boasted beautiful gardens, vineyards, or fat flocks. Only barren, ragged rocks protruded from its mountains and hillsides, while the fields and valleys lay largely neglected. From Dan to Beersheba nothing but the most primitive agricultural arts were being employed by the local Bedouins.

An important part of the prayer of Orson Hyde, as he petitioned heaven from the Mount of Olives, was as follows: "Grant, therefore, O Lord, in the name of thy well-beloved Son, Jesus Christ, to remove the barrenness and sterility of this land, and let springs of living water break forth to water its thirsty soil. Let the vine and olive produce in their strength, and the fig tree bloom and flourish. Let the land become abundantly fruitful and possessed by its rightful heirs;...let thy great kindness conquer and subdue the unbelief of thy people. Do thou take from them their stony heart, and give them a heart of flesh.... Incline them to gather in upon this land according to thy word. Let them come like clouds and like doves to their windows. Let the large ships of the nations bring them from the distant isles; and let kings become their nursing fathers, and queens with motherly fondness wipe the tear of sorrow from their eye."[57]

THE SECOND DEDICATION

In 1873, George A. Smith was sent by Brigham Young to rededicate the land and pray fervently that the work of the Lord

---

57. Joseph Fielding Smith, *Essentials in Church History* (Salt Lake City: Deseret Book Company, 1974), pp. 312–13.

might be expedited.[58] As of that time it is estimated that isolated pockets of Jews sprinkled among the Arab population amounted to no more than 12,000 to 15,000. However, within five years two significant movements were established to encourage additional Jewish migration. One, called the "Lovers of Zion," was set up among the Russian Jews. The other, primarily among Polish and Romanian Jews, was called the Bilu. This name was abbreviated from the Hebrew words meaning "House of Jacob, let us go!" These two groups initiated the first wave of migration to Palestine, which is referred to as the First *Aliyah*. They settled approximately 25,000 immigrants between 1882 and 1902.

THEODOR HERZL

Meanwhile, in 1897, the first conference of the World Zionist Organization was held in Basel, Switzerland. Its founder was Dr. Theodor Herzl, a Jewish journalist and lawyer from Vienna who had been shocked by the anti-Jewish sentiment in France during the famous Dreyfus trial. He had therefore written a dissertation in 1896 called *The Jewish State*. He felt the Jews must shortly gather together or suffer severe persecution. His idea was to create a Jewish homeland in Palestine through diplomatic negotiation with the Turkish government and by purchase of the land from Arab landholders. This first Zionist congress discussed the erection of a Hebrew University in Jerusalem; the creation of a Jewish national fund; the establishment of a Jewish world bank in London to finance colonization; the design for a blue and white flag; and the adoption of a national anthem for their country which did not yet exist.

In 1903, as Herzl had feared, a terroristic and brutal persecution of the Jews broke out in Russia. In Kiskinev of Bessarabia, the Jewish dead were piled in the streets like cordwood. Herzl literally worked himself to death going from one world capital to another seeking support for his new Jewish state. He suddenly died July 3,

---

58. B.H. Roberts, *A Comprehensive History of the Church*, 5:474–75.

1904, at the age of 44, and today lies buried on a peak overlooking Jerusalem which is named after him.

By 1904 a new wave of migration, called the Second Aliyah, had begun. About 40,000 more Jews, mostly young people, migrated between 1904 and 1914. These young people called themselves Halutzim, meaning "pioneers." Among them was a frail, earnest lad from western Russia named David Green. When he began writing articles in the newspapers and magazines he took the name of David Ben-Gurion ("Son of the Young Lion"). Another lad was Chaim Weizmann, from a background similar to that of the Green boy. Later, David Ben-Gurion became the first prime minister of Israel. Chaim Weizmann became its first president.

In 1917 the British succeeded in capturing Palestine from the Turkish Empire. England was afterwards given a mandate over Palestine by the League of Nations. It was also in 1917 that the British issued the famous Balfour Declaration which made it possible for Jews to begin migrating to Palestine more freely. This brought about the Third Aliyah, and about 34,000 additional Jews entered Palestine between 1919 and 1923.

FLIGHT OF THE JEWS

The Nazi terror against the Jews resulted in two migrations: one to Palestine, where the Jewish population soon reached over two million; and the other to the United States, where the immigrants joined with the indigenous Jewish population to become the largest concentration of the children of Judah in the entire world. The Jews in the United States then became the principal source of outside financial support for the Jews in Palestine. It was this combination of dedicated Jewish nation-builders in Palestine and the liberal financial support of the Jews in America that made much of Israel's success possible.

Back in 1879 Wilford Woodruff had written from the St. George Temple, "I wish in this testimony to say that the time is not far distant when the rich men among the Jews will be called upon to use their abundant wealth to gather the dispersed of Judah, and purchase the ancient dwelling places of their fathers in and about Jerusalem, and rebuild the holy city and temple."[59]

THE CREATION OF MODERN ISRAEL

By the commencement of World War II, the British, who had been given the responsibility of maintaining peace between Moslems and Jews, virtually terminated Jewish migration. After the war, however, the Jews insisted that since they had fought with the Allies, there now should be no question whatever as to their right to have a homeland of their own where the masses of refugees from Europe could find a haven. However, British policies against extensive migration continued in force and left the Jews with the conviction that they were being betrayed. As a result, the Jewish antagonism and reprisals grew so heated that the British finally became anxious to rid themselves of the whole problem. The matter came up in the United Nations for settlement, and there it was voted to create a separate state of Israel and a separate Arab state, and to keep Jerusalem an open city. Therefore, as soon as the British forces withdrew, the Jewish leaders of Israel proclaimed themselves a free and independent republic with equal representation in the legislature, according to population, of both Jews and Arabs. This occurred May 14–15, 1948.

However, several Arab nations refused to accept the United Nations partition. These joined together and attacked Israel on May 15, 1948. A fierce engagement resulted which, for a few frantic weeks, threatened to sweep the Jews into the Mediterranean. However, the Israeli forces finally held firm, and a permanent truce was established in July 1949.

THE BUILDING OF A TEMPLE IN JERUSALEM

The rebuilding of the temple in Jerusalem is a very sensitive matter with the Moslems since they have their own beautiful shrine

---

59. Matthias F. Cowley, *Wilford Woodruff* (Salt Lake City: Bookcraft, 1964), p. 509.

called the "Dome of the Rock" covering the spot where the Jewish temple is believed to have stood. The Moslems say this is the spot from which Mohammed ascended into heaven to receive the Islamic religion, so they feel this place is just as sacred to them as it is to the Jews. Many of us who have close friends in both camps wish with all our hearts that some ameliorating circumstance could avoid future conflict, and that eventually the sacred sentiments of both peoples could be happily accommodated. Unfortunately, however, whole armies have risen and fallen over the issue of who shall govern Jerusalem. The Lord has decreed that he, rather than men, must move forward with his program, which will be a blessing to Moslems and Jews alike—in fact, to the whole world. It requires that a temple be built in Jerusalem.

It was Micah who first talked about the fact that "in the last days it shall come to pass, that the mountain of the house of the Lord shall be established in the top of the mountains."[60] This has seemed to refer to the temple in the mountains of the American Zion, but Isaiah quoted this same passage as applying to Jerusalem and Judah as well. In fact he specifically described it as "the word that Isaiah the son of Amoz saw **concerning Judah and Jerusalem**."[61]

A modern prophet also received revelations concerning these events and wrote: "Judah must return, Jerusalem must be rebuilt, and the temple, and water come out from under the temple, and the waters of the Dead Sea be healed. It will take some time to rebuild the walls of the city and the temple,... and all this must be done before the Son of Man will make His appearance."[62]

THE VISION OF EZEKIEL

It was Ezekiel who wrote more about the rebuilding of a temple in Jerusalem than any other prophet. He had a vision of it and was

---

60. Micah 4:1.
61. Isaiah 2:1.
62. *History of the Church,* 5:337.

allowed to walk through its rooms and courts, measuring them as he went.[63] There are enough details in the book of Ezekiel for a modern architect to draw up the entire plan for the temple at Jerusalem without any further revelation.

Ezekiel mentioned the fact that during his vision he was led around to the east gate of the temple, and noted a substantial stream which "issued out from under the threshold of the house eastward: for the forefront of the house stood toward the east, and the waters came down from under the right side of the house, at the south side of the altar."[64] The famous Gihon spring is just below this location, so there is good reason to believe there is considerable water in this mountain. Recently more than a dozen springs have already begun to gush forth. These have been capped, lest they undermine the structures on the temple mount.

According to Ezekiel's prophecy, the water of this temple river will flow into the brook Kidron and down toward the Dead Sea. Ezekiel said he saw that the river would increase in size and volume as it proceeded toward the Arabah Ghor wherein the Dead Sea is cradled. He saw that the sea had an outlet toward the greater sea, presumably the Red Sea at Aqaba, and that as a result the waters of the Dead Sea would be healed. In his vision Ezekiel said he perceived that the Dead Sea had become a fresh-water lake with great schools of fish swimming about.[65] Only the surrounding marshes will remain salty.[66] Anyone who has seen the Dead Sea and tasted its extremely bitter, acrid water can appreciate what a miracle it would take to bring about such a change.

BOTH ARABS AND JEWS EVENTUALLY TO BE UNITED AS GOD'S PEOPLE

Chapter 19 of Isaiah contains an exciting prediction. It states that

---

63. Ezekiel, chapters 40 and 47.
64. Ezekiel 47:1.
65. Ezekiel 47:10–11.

eventually both the Arabs and the Jews will accept the restored Gospel and become God's own people.

The Lord promised Abraham that his oldest son, Ishmael, would "multiply...exceedingly; twelve princes shall he beget, and I will make him a great nation."[66] Commenting on this scripture, Dr. Adam Clarke wrote, "From Ishmael proceeded the various tribes of the Arabs." He then quoted Bishop Newton, who wrote, "These are the only people besides the Jews who have subsisted as a distinct people from the beginning, and in some respects they very much resemble each other:

"1. The Arabs, as well as the Jews, are descended from Abraham, and both boast of their descent from the father of the faithful.

"2. The Arabs, as well as the Jews, are circumcised, and both profess to have derived this ceremony from Abraham.

"3. The Arabs, as well as the Jews, had originally *twelve patriarchs,* who were their princes or governors.

"4. The Arabs, as well as the Jews, marry among themselves, and in their own tribes."[67]

The Lord promised Abraham that eventually his seed would inherit all of the territory from the Euphrates to Egypt.[68] Today, the Arabic people occupy all of these ancient territories including Assyria, Lebanon, Syria, Moab (modern Jordan), and Egypt. Israel is occupied by both Arabs and Jews. So Abraham's seed are already in these lands, just as the Lord promised nearly 4,000 years ago.

Isaiah was fully aware that there would be some conflict between the Arab inhabitants of Egypt and the Jewish inhabitants of Israel,[69] but he also saw that one day this conflict would cease. He wrote, "And the Lord shall be known to Egypt, and the Egyptians shall

---

66. Genesis 17:20.
67. Clarke, *Commentary,* 1:116.
68. Genesis 15:18.
69. Isaiah 19:17.

know the Lord in that day, and shall do sacrifice and oblation; yea, they shall vow a vow unto the Lord, and perform it."[70]

Isaiah then pointed out that the same thing will happen in other regions where the Arabs, or seed of Abraham, are located. He wrote: "In that day shall there be a highway out of Egypt to Assyria, . . . and the Egyptians shall serve [the Lord] with the Assyrians. In that day shall Israel be the third with Egypt and with Assyria, even a blessing in the midst of the land: whom the Lord of hosts shall bless, saying, Blessed be **Egypt** my people, and **Assyria** the work of my hands, and **Israel** mine inheritance."[71]

Isaiah talked about the day when there shall "be an altar to the Lord in the midst of the land of Egypt, and a pillar at the border thereof to the Lord. And it shall be for a sign and for a witness unto the Lord of hosts in the land of Egypt."[72]

Apparently this will happen just about the time the Jews, Egyptians, and other Arab nations receive the Gospel. What a day of reconciliation that will be!

RESTRUCTURING THE SURFACE OF THE EARTH

During the period just prior to the millennial era, there will be great physical changes on the face of the entire planet. Isaiah saw the great mountain ranges, and even the high hills, "melting" down to a more moderate level. He saw the deep canyons and valleys being filled with debris or raised up so that the entire surface of the earth would become a broad vista of gently rolling hills. Said he, "Every valley shall be exalted, and every mountain and hill shall be made low: and the crooked shall be made straight, and the rough places plain."[73]

---

70. Isaiah 19:22.
71. Isaiah 19:23–25.
72. Isaiah 19:19–20.
73. Isaiah 40:4.

A modern revelation adds these important details: "And [the Lord] shall utter his voice...as the voice of a great thunder, which shall break down the mountains, and the valleys shall not be found. He shall command the great deep, and it shall be driven back into the north countries, and the islands shall become one land; and the land of Jerusalem and the land of Zion shall be turned back into their own place, and the earth shall be like as it was in the days before it was divided."[74]

This suggests that the continents, which were divided in the days of Peleg,[75] will join back together, and that a great body of land will come up out of the Pacific so as to force the sea back toward the poles and make the plateau of habitable terrain above sea level into a mighty continent of "one land." It almost sounds as though this vast continental plateau will then extend practically around the whole earth.

THE RIGHTEOUS TO BE PROTECTED
WHILE THE EARTH IS BEING CLEANSED

During the cleansing of the earth and the cataclysmic changes which will occur before the Millennium, the righteous will pass through two stages. The first stage is having them assemble in Zion, which Joseph Smith described as the Western Hemisphere.[76] There they will be safe while the "fire wars" (which would seem to imply nuclear wars) will rage among the wicked.[77]

Through Isaiah the Lord spoke of this first stage, when the righteous will gather to Zion, and said: "Come, my people, enter thou into thy chambers, and shut thy doors about thee: hide thyself as it were for a little moment, until the indignation be overpast. For, behold, the Lord cometh out of his place to punish the inhabitants of

---

74. D&C 133:21-24.

75. Genesis 10:25.

76. Smith, *Teachings*, p. 362.

77. Joel, chapter 2.

the earth for their iniquity: the earth also shall disclose her blood, and shall no more cover her slain."[78]

A modern revelation refers to the same events as those which were seen by Isaiah: "And it shall come to pass among the wicked, that every man that will not take his sword against his neighbor must needs flee unto Zion [the Western Hemisphere] for safety. And there shall be gathered unto it out of every nation under heaven; and it shall be the only people that shall not be at war one with another."[79]

So, just as Isaiah had explained it in his writings, the righteous will hide themselves away in Zion for a little season while war rages among the rebellious nations and the wicked slay the wicked.

Eventually, however, the Lord will be ready for the restructuring of the surface of the earth and the return of this planet to the region of Kolob near the center of the galaxy (see pages 136-37). At this point the protection of the righteous will require them to receive a very special blessing which we call the second stage. Because of the catastrophic changes which will be unleashed on the earth, the destruction of human life will be of devastating proportions. In fact, Isaiah said there will be "few men left."[80] The Lord will therefore perform a great miracle for the righteous so they will not be destroyed. A modern revelation describes it this way: "And the saints that are upon the earth, who are alive, shall be quickened and be caught up to meet him."[81] Paul referred to this same secondary stage and said, "Then we which are alive and remain shall be caught up."[82]

Although there will be "few men left" following the cleansing and restructuring of the earth, those "few" will have a fantastic story to tell. As we have already noted, they will witness tumultuous

---

78. Isaiah 26:20-21.
79. D&C 45:68-69.
80. Isaiah 24:6.
81. D&C 88:96.
82. 1 Thessalonians 4:17.

earthquakes, the reuniting of the continents, the driving back of the seas, the melting down of the mountains and the exalting of canyons and valleys. They will witness the earth beginning to stagger in its orbit around the sun. Finally, they will be engulfed in temporary darkness as the earth leaves its gravitational moorings in our present solar system and heads back toward Kolob with the speed of a "chased roe" (see pages 136-37).

Not everyone will be able to endure the terrorizing trauma of that experience. A modern revelation says: "And all things shall be in commotion; and surely, **men's hearts shall fail them;** for fear shall come upon all people."[83]

THE SECOND COMING

Isaiah identifies the Second Coming of the Savior as occurring in the final stages of the cleansing of the earth. A modern revelation catalogs the sequence of events which will occur just before the opening of the seventh seal, and the opening of the seventh seal is what precedes the Second Coming.[84] Section 88 of the Doctrine and Covenants says that as the final hour for the Second Coming approaches, the following manifestations will occur:

"The earth shall tremble and reel to and fro" (verse 87).
"The sun shall hide his face" (verse 87).
"The moon shall be bathed in blood" (verse 87).
"The stars...shall cast themselves down" (verse 87).
"Earthquakes...shall cause groanings" (verse 89).
"Men...shall not be able to stand" (verse 89).
"The voice of thunderings" (verse 90).
"The voice of lightnings" (verse 90).
"The voice of tempests" (verse 90).
"The waves of the sea heaving themselves beyond their bounds" (verse 90).

83. D&C 88:91.
84. Revelation 8:1.

"All things shall be in commotion" (verse 91).

"Men's hearts shall fail them" (verse 91).

"Fear shall come upon all people" (verse 91).

"Angels shall fly through the midst of heaven,...saying: Prepare ye,...the judgment of our God is come..." (verse 92).

"...The Bridegroom cometh; go ye out to meet him" (verse 92).

"There shall appear a great sign in heaven" (verse 93).

"That great church, the mother of abominations,...is the tares of the earth" (verse 94).

"She is bound in bundles;...ready to be burned" (verse 94).

"There shall be silence in heaven for the space of half an hour" (verse 95).

"Immediately after shall the curtain of heaven be unfolded" (verse 95).

"And the face of the Lord shall be unveiled" (verse 95).

"The Saints...who are alive, shall be...caught up to meet him" (verse 96).

Then comes the terrible conflagration of consuming fire which Isaiah said will make the wicked seem like so much "stubble" because "the fire shall burn them."[85] Malachi spoke of this event in similar words, saying: "For, behold, the day cometh, that shall burn as an oven; and all the proud, yea, and all that do wickedly, shall be stubble: and the day that cometh shall burn them up, saith the Lord of hosts, that it shall leave them neither root nor branch."[86] Paul said, "The Lord Jesus Christ shall be revealed from heaven with his mighty angels, in flaming fire taking vengeance on them that know not God, and that obey not the gospel of our Lord Jesus Christ."[87]

The Lord indicates that this great cleansing will first begin among the wicked who have endeavored to corrupt the restored Church.

---

85. Isaiah 47:14.

86. Malachi 4:1.

87. 2 Thessalonians 1:7-8.

He says: "Behold, vengeance cometh speedily upon the inhabitants of the earth, a day of wrath, a day of **burning,** a day of desolation, of weeping, of mourning, and of lamentation; and as a whirlwind it shall come upon all the face of the earth, saith the Lord. And **upon my house shall it begin,** and from my house shall it go forth, saith the Lord; first among those among you, saith the Lord, who have professed to know my name and have not known me, and have blasphemed against me in the midst of my house, saith the Lord."[88]

However, Isaiah saw that this will be a time of monumental blessings for the righteous. They will not only be rescued from the conflagration of fire, but they will be greatly blessed as the earth moves into its paradisiacal glory and the millennial reign begins. He wrote: "In that day shall the branch of the Lord be beautiful and glorious, and the fruit of the earth shall be excellent and comely for them that are **escaped of Israel.** And it shall come to pass, that **he that is left in Zion, and he that remaineth in Jerusalem** [after the burning, when the quickened Saints have returned to the earth], shall be called holy,... when the Lord shall have washed away the filth of the daughters of Zion, and shall have purged the blood of Jerusalem... by the spirit of judgment, and **by the spirit of burning."**[89]

THE RIGHTEOUS DEAD ARE RESURRECTED

Isaiah saw that it would be at the time of the Second Coming that the righteous dead would come forth as a glorious multitude of resurrected beings. The Lord says this will occur when "the face of the Lord shall be unveiled.... And they who have slept in their graves shall come forth, for their graves shall be opened; and they also shall be caught up to meet him in the midst of the pillar of heaven—they are Christ's, the first fruits, they who shall descend

---

88. D&C 112:24-26.
89. Isaiah 4:2-4.

with him first, and they who are on the earth and in their graves, who are first caught up to meet him."[90]

Isaiah described this great event in similar phraseology: "And he will destroy...the vail that is spread over all nations." Then he added: "Thy dead men shall live, together with **my dead body** shall they arise. Awake and sing, ye that dwell in dust: for...the earth shall cast out the dead."[91]

When the smoke and fury have cleared away and the "quickened" Saints have returned to the earth to resume their earthly mission, the Savior will call for a great feast in Jerusalem. Not only will the Saints be present, but the illustrious dead of all ages will participate. The revelation says: "Wherefore, marvel not, for the hour cometh that I will drink of the fruit of the vine with you on the earth, and with Moroni,...Elias,...John [the Baptist] the son of Zacharias,... Elijah,...Joseph and Jacob, and Isaac, and Abraham,...Michael, or Adam,...and also with Peter, and James, and John,...and also **with all those whom my Father hath given me out of the world.**"[92]

This will be a vast and glorious occasion. In Isaiah's song of joy over the magnificence of the Second Advent (all of chapter 25), he declared: "And in this mountain shall the Lord of hosts make unto all people a feast of fat things, a feast of wines on the lees, of fat things full of marrow, of wines on the lees well refined."[93]

He described the thrilling reaction of the great throng which will attend in these words: "And it shall be said in that day, Lo, this is our God; we have waited for him, and he will save us: this is the Lord; we have waited for him, we will be glad and rejoice in his salvation."[94]

---

90. D&C 88:95-98.
91. Isaiah 25:7; 26:19.
92. D&C 27:5-14.
93. Isaiah 25:6.
94. Isaiah 25:9.

Isaiah had many other beautiful and powerful sentiments to express concerning the Second Coming, but these will be sufficient to catch the breadth of his vision and the depth of his understanding concerning this sacred subject. He is also one of the foremost scriptural authorities on the subject of the Millennium.

RELOCATING THE EARTH

The planet on which we dwell has had a far different history than many of us might have supposed. As Brigham Young said: "When the earth was framed and brought into existence and man was placed upon it, it was near the throne of our Father in heaven. And . . . when man fell, the earth fell into space, and took up its abode in this planetary system, and the sun became our light. . . . This is the glory the earth came from, and when it is glorified **it will return again unto the presence of the Father.**"[95]

Abraham was also shown that prior to the Fall, the earth was operating on a time schedule controlled by Kolob at the center of our galaxy, where each revolution is 1,000 of our years. This would imply that it did not acquire its present rate of rotation until after the Fall.[96]

Isaiah knew that before the earth is restored to its paradisiacal glory (for the millennial reign), it must be shaken free from its present planetary system and returned to the region of its creation. He said, "The earth shall reel to and fro like a drunkard."[97] Then "the earth shall remove out of her place."[98] As this planet hurtles through space to return to the vicinity of Kolob, Isaiah likened it to "a chased roe."[99] (A roe is a small deer which is famous for its great speed.) Once the earth has "fallen" inward toward the center of our

---

95. *Journal of Discourses,* 17:143.
96. Abraham 5:13; 3:4.
97. Isaiah 24:20.
98. Isaiah 13:13.
99. Isaiah 13:14.

galaxy, Isaiah said she would never "rise" or return again to the outer portion of the galaxy where our solar system is located.[100]

The earth is presently around 30,000 light years out and away from Kolob, the center of our galaxy. This would mean that in order for our planet to race back toward Kolob in a reasonable time, the earth would have to travel faster than the speed of light. Isaiah said the people who survive the cleansing of the earth and actually witness this terrifying event will see the star system with which they are familiar literally "dissolved, and the heavens shall be rolled together as a scroll."[101] Because the earth will be traveling at an incredible speed back toward Kolob, it will look as though the stars are falling from heaven when the earth sweeps past them.[102]

In the vicinity of Kolob there will be no need for the sun or the moon. There will be a perpetual light without either the sun or the moon being associated with the earth any longer.[103]

THE MILLENNIUM

The Millennium is a perfect theme for a poetic temperament, and therefore it is ideally suited to the interests and tastes of Isaiah. This theme will be found in his opening chapters, in his last chapter, and scattered all the way in between. His philosophic contemplation of the magnificence of the millennial vision led him to exclaim, "For since the beginning of the world men have not heard, nor perceived by the ear, neither hath the eye seen, O God, beside thee, what he hath prepared for him that waiteth for him."[104] A short time later he recorded the word of the Lord as follows: "The former troubles are forgotten, ... they are hid from mine eyes. For, behold, I create new heavens and a new earth: and the former shall not be remembered,

---

100. Isaiah 24:20.
101. Isaiah 34:4.
102. Isaiah 34:4; D&C 29:14; 34:9; 45:42; 88:87.
103. Isaiah 60:19–20; 24:23.
104. Isaiah 64:4.

nor come into mind. But be ye glad and rejoice for ever in that which I create: for, behold, I create Jerusalem a rejoicing, and her people a joy."[105]

PHYSICAL CHANGES IN THE MILLENNIAL EARTH

He said that during this period the earth will bring forth its strength. Great forests will grow up in the wilderness.[106] Rivers and springs will change deserts and wastelands into meadows and farmland.[107] Noxious weeds, briars, and thorns will give way to groves, orchards, and profitable plant life.[108]

The physical and chemical nature of the earth will also be quickened. As mentioned above, the change will be so great that the Lord speaks of it as "a new earth" and says there will be so little to remind one of the deficient and fallen sphere which we now inhabit that it "shall not be remembered, nor come into mind."[109]

The refinement of the earth at that time will be so marked that the planet is described as being "transfigured." When the Apostles were together on the Mount of Transfiguration they were shown the vision of it, and not at any time since then has the full account of its glory been revealed.[110]

NO DEATH FOR THE RIGHTEOUS

Not only will the earth be transfigured, but among the righteous even human life will function on a more perfect and efficient scale than at any time since the Fall of Adam. In both Isaiah and modern revelation one of the most singular prophecies in all holy writ is recorded. Speaking of the time of the Millennium, it says, "And there shall be no sorrow because there is no death."[111] The

---

105. Isaiah 65:16–18.
106. Isaiah 41:19.
107. Isaiah 35:7.
108. Isaiah 55:13.
109. Isaiah 65:17.
110. D&C 63:21.
111. D&C 101:29; Isaiah 65:20; D&C 63:51.

implications of this promise are tremendous. Such a condition would require strict self-discipline among all human beings and a sufficiently strong control over natural phenomena and secular circumstances so that there would be no accidents, no disease, no infant mortality, no senile old age, and no congenital deformities. Such a condition would change many things in our mode of existence—no funerals, no cemeteries, no mortuaries, no insurance companies.

In saying that there will be no death, however, the Lord does not mean that people living during the Millennium will be immortal. He goes on to explain that this promise simply means that among the righteous there will be no lengthy separation of the body from the spirit—no consignment of the body to the grave.[112] Isaiah said men will live until they are 100 years old,[113] in the full strength of the antediluvian patriarchs; then they will be changed in the twinkling of an eye from mortal to resurrected beings.[114] Such persons will be "caught up" and their rest will be glorious.[115]

Nor does the Lord imply that this blessed promise of "no death" applies to everyone. It applies only to the righteous and obedient. During at least the early part of the Millennium, there will be many who will survive the great destruction who are not members of Christ's kingdom. These will have the opportunity to hear the Gospel and join the Church if they so desire.[116] If they do not, however, but choose to remain in their sins, Isaiah clearly indicated that the sorrows of death will descend upon them even as now.[117]

The scripture also indicates that among the righteous there will be no juvenile crime, no disobedient or disrespectful youth. For, says

---

112. D&C 101:30–31; 63:51.
113. Isaiah 65:20.
114. D&C 63:51.
115. D&C 101:31.
116. D&C 77:11.
117. Isaiah 65:20.

the Lord, "their children shall grow up without sin unto salvation."[118] In the same place he states that the Saints will "multiply and wax strong." It is highly possible that with the cessation of war, the eradication of infant mortality, the increase of the human life span to 100 years, and the marked increase in the arable land area, the number of individuals who will populate the earth during the 1,000 years of the millennial reign will total more than all those who have lived on the earth during the past 6,000 years.

ENMITY OF ANIMALS WILL CEASE

Another of the rather startling predictions of changes which will come during the Millennium is the prophecy that animals will lose their enmity one toward another. Isaiah twice described this phenomenon and definitely made it clear that "the wolf also shall dwell with the lamb, and the leopard shall lie down with the kid; and the calf and the young lion and the fatling together."[119]

He went even further and predicted that the animal species which have formerly been classified as carnivorous, because of their dependence on flesh from other animals, will thereafter become herbivorous so that they can exist upon plant life rather than meat. "The lion shall eat straw like the bullock: and dust shall be the serpent's meat. They shall not hurt nor destroy in all my holy mountain, saith the Lord."[120] In another place he again referred to this biological change: "The lion shall eat straw like the ox."[121]

Not only will enmity between members of the animal kingdom disappear, but fear and enmity between men and animals will likewise cease. Referring to it, Isaiah said: "And the sucking child shall play on the hole of the asp, and the weaned child shall put his

---

118. D&C 45:58.
119. Isaiah 11:6–9; 65:25; Hosea 2:18.
120. Isaiah 65:25.
121. Isaiah 11:7.

hand on the cockatrice' den. They shall not hurt nor destroy in all my holy mountain."[122]

NO MORE WAR

Predatory enmity between individuals will also be eliminated. For centuries political scientists have dreamed of the unprecedented progress which mankind could make if their investments of money, energy, and materials could be directed exclusively toward peaceful pursuits. In the Millennium this will occur. Speaking of the relationships between individuals and nations, Isaiah said, "They shall beat their swords into plowshares, and their spears into pruninghooks: nation shall not lift up sword against nation, neither shall they learn war any more."[123]

Under such favorable circumstances the Saints of Israel will thrive and grow. Isaiah said, "He shall cause them that come of Jacob to take root: Israel shall blossom and bud, and fill the face of the world with fruit."[124] This will cause the people of Israel in that day to say to the Lord, "Thou hast increased the nation, O Lord, thou hast increased the nation: thou art glorified: thou hadst removed it far [extended it] unto all the ends of the earth."[125]

NO MORE AGNOSTICS OR ATHEISTS

There will be no agnostics or atheists in those days. Isaiah said, "The earth shall be full of the knowledge of the Lord, as the waters cover the sea."[126]

Nor will the Saints have as much difficulty rising to the spiritual level where they can communicate with the Lord. Isaiah was told by the Lord "that before they call, I will answer; and while they are yet speaking, I will hear."[127]

---

122. Isaiah 11:8–9.
123. Isaiah 2:4.
124. Isaiah 27:6.
125. Isaiah 26:15.
126. Isaiah 11:9.
127. Isaiah 65:24.

Human relations will be on the highest level. Not only will there be peace and prosperity, but all will have the security of their own inheritances, and "none shall want her mate."[128] Malachi added to this by saying children will be raised up as carefully as calves in a stall.[129] No wonder Isaiah surveyed this great era of the future and said, "Then judgment shall dwell in the wilderness, and righteousness remain in the fruitful field. And **the work of righteousness shall be peace; and the effect of righteousness quietness and assurance for ever.** And my people shall dwell in a peaceable habitation, and in sure dwellings, and in quiet resting places."[130]

Thus we come to the end of our visit with the great prophet Isaiah. Surely we can confirm the pronouncement of Jesus when he said, **"Great are the words of Isaiah!"**[131]

In the second part of this study we will consider the words of Isaiah verse by verse.

---

128. Isaiah 34:16.
129. Malachi 4:2.
130. Isaiah 32:16-18.
131. 3 Nephi 23:1.

Part II

A Verse by Verse
Commentary on
The Book of Isaiah

Isaiah, Chapter 1

1. The vision of Isaiah the son of Amoz, which he saw concerning Judah and Jerusalem, in the days of Uzziah, Jotham, Ahaz, and Hezekiah, kings of Judah.

This first verse was the original title to the book of Isaiah. It was written by one of the ancient scribes, possibly Ezra, who compiled the Old Testament around 450 B.C.

Isaiah's father was Amoz, whose identity is not positively established, but Peloubet says rabbinical tradition has it that Amoz was the brother of Amaziah, king of Judah from 796 to 766 B.C.

Isaiah's revelations came during the reign of four kings of Judah. The first was Uzziah, son of Amaziah, who governed Judah from about 766 B.C. to 739 B.C., when he died of leprosy. If rabbinical tradition is correct, this would make Isaiah the cousin of King Uzziah. The second king of Judah under whom Isaiah prophesied was Jotham, son of Uzziah, who died around 735 B.C. Ahaz, Jotham's son, then took over the throne and was one of the most wicked kings Judah ever had. However, he died in 727 B.C. and was succeeded by his son, Hezekiah, who ruled until 696 B.C. He was one of the best kings Judah ever had.

All of these kings have a place in Isaiah's writings.

2. Hear, O heavens, and give ear, O earth: for the LORD hath spoken, I have nourished and brought up children, and they have rebelled against me.

The first chapter of Isaiah is an overview or introduction, and may have been given in the later years rather than at the beginning of his ministry. Much of this chapter is a lamentation of God over his ungrateful children, especially those who were his "chosen people," blessed above all other nations. When we consider the ten amazing plagues which the Lord imposed on Egypt so that Pharaoh would release the Israelites, and when we recall the dividing of the Red Sea, the revelations at Sinai, the miracles in the wilderness, the miraculous manna which fed Israel for 40 years, the dividing of the river Jordan, the conquest of the Canaanites—all these events make it especially appropriate for God to say he had indeed "nourished" his children and yet they had "rebelled" against him.

3. The ox knoweth his owner, and the ass his master's crib: but Israel doth not know, my people doth not consider.

Even dumb animals are more faithful to their masters than Israel had been to the Lord.

4. Ah sinful nation, a people laden with iniquity, a seed of evildoers, children that are corrupters: they have forsaken the LORD, they have provoked the Holy One of Israel unto anger, they are gone away backward.

It is a terrible thing when a whole nation is wicked. Even a righteous people will have an occasional rebel among them, but here the whole people, as a nation, were burdened down with wickedness. Each generation provided the seed for more evil to pass on to the next generation. The Lord found himself nourishing and raising up children who were corrupters of everything beautiful and decent. Even the Lord could not help but be disgusted and provoked to anger when he saw this entire nation rushing headlong toward a catastrophic calamity which Isaiah had already seen in vision.

5. Why should ye be stricken any more? ye will revolt more and more: the whole head is sick, and the whole heart faint.

Isaiah could not help but wonder why they wanted to invite more punishment and affliction when they had already suffered bitterly because of their wickedness in the past. Nevertheless, he knew what they were going to do—God had already shown it to him. They would go right ahead in their stubborn stupidity, revolting against God. They were a nation of sick mentalities, and their hearts lacked the courage to repent and ask the Lord to forgive them.

6. From the sole of the foot even unto the head there is no soundness in it; but wounds, and bruises, and putrifying sores: they have not been closed, neither bound up, neither mollified with ointment.

For their past wickedness they had already been literally beaten to a pulp. Speaking of the nation of Israel as a body, Isaiah said the head, which should have been providing righteous leadership, was covered with wounds, bruises, and "putrifying sores." And nothing was being done to bandage the wounds or soothe and anoint the running infections.

7. Your country is desolate, your cities are burned with fire: your land, strangers devour it in your presence, and it is desolate, as overthrown by strangers.

Isaiah knew from his visions what would happen when the Assyrians, led by Sennacherib, would come in 701 B.C. and methodically slaughter, burn, rape, loot, and devastate the whole country. No nation in ancient times was so totally brutal and destructive as the Assyrians.

8. And the daughter of Zion is left as a cottage in a vineyard, as a lodge in a garden of cucumbers, as a besieged city.

He had foreseen the people of Jerusalem (daughters of Mount Zion) huddled together in their besieged city which was no more secure than the temporary shacks of the farmers who labored in the vineyards and gardens.

9. Except the LORD of hosts had left unto us a very small remnant, we should have been as Sodom, and we should have been like unto Gomorrah.

Isaiah had seen that the coming destruction would be so complete that if it were not for a very small remnant (literally "a little part"), the whole people would be as completely annihilated as Sodom and Gomorrah. Those two cities had been destroyed by the wrath of God's fire from heaven some 1,200 years earlier.

10. Hear the word of the LORD, ye rulers of Sodom; give ear unto the law of our God, ye people of Gomorrah.

Because of all Isaiah knew about the future, he had an urgent errand to perform and a frightening message to deliver to this wayward people. He declared that what he was about to say was directly from the Lord, and knowing of the whirlwind of violent destruction they were going to suffer because of their disdain for the Lord's law, he could not resist calling them "Sodom" and "Gomorrah"!

11. To what purpose is the multitude of your sacrifices unto me? saith the LORD: I am full of the burnt offerings of rams, and the fat of fed beasts; and I delight not in the blood of bullocks, or of lambs, or of he goats.

Isaiah says the Lord wants this wicked people to know that elaborate ceremonies, even the ones God himself had designated as teaching devices, are no substitute for moral obedience. The sacrifices were initiated as a reminder of the coming death and suffering of the very Son of God, by which all mankind can gain forgiveness of their sins if they will repent. But what a mockery it is for wicked men and women to go through all these elaborate rituals when their own personal lives are an abomination! It makes the sacrifices which they offer totally abhorrent to God. He asks to what purpose are all their sacrifices. Under the circumstances, they are meaningless. God has no delight or satisfaction in them whatever.

12. When ye come to appear before me, who hath required this at your hand, to tread my courts?

The Lord wants to know whoever suggested that these sacrifices were required or even desirable when performed with unclean hands and wicked hearts.

13. Bring no more vain oblations; incense is an abomination unto me; the new moons and sabbaths, the calling of assemblies, I can not away with; it is iniquity, even the solemn meeting.

14. Your new moons and your appointed feasts my soul hateth: they are a trouble unto me; I am weary to bear them.

Now comes the commandment: Immediately cease and desist from this hypocritical and VAIN ritual of meaningless sacrifices! Their pilgrimages at the time of the new moon or beginning of the month, as well as their special conferences and so-called sacred feast days, are a burden to the Lord. He is disgusted to even look down and see what they are doing. The whole wretched fiasco of wickedness makes him weary to even consider what is happening.

15. And when ye spread forth your hands, I will hide mine eyes from you: yea, when ye make many prayers, I will not hear: your hands are full of blood.

What is worse, they come with outspread palms (hands) and many pious prayers. God knows that those very hands have helped destroy human life and commit the most heinous crimes. Those praying hands are "full of blood"!

16. Wash you, make you clean; put away the evil of your doings from before mine eyes; cease to do evil;

The Lord wants the people to cleanse themselves. He wants them to "wash" themselves in the holy ordinance of baptism. If they have already been baptized, then they should perform the sacramental washing and anointing associated with the ceremonies of the Aaronic Priesthood. But let not these be VAIN oblations. The people must put away the evil and terrible abominations which the all-seeing eyes of God are continually beholding. All this ugly evil must stop.

17. Learn to do well; seek judgment, relieve the oppressed, judge the fatherless, plead for the widow.

The Lord wishes that for once in their lives, they would "learn" about the good and decent things of life. They should seek to perform acts of justice and to right the wrongs which are being continually inflicted upon the weak and the helpless, the widows and the orphans. The Lord wants them to relieve the oppressed and help them begin to enjoy the better things of life.

18. Come now, and let us reason together, saith the LORD: though your sins be as scarlet, they shall be as white as snow; though they be red like crimson, they shall be as wool.

Now comes the Lord's plea: he begs them to come together and think seriously about what they are doing to themselves. God is not anxious to destroy and avenge himself on his wicked children. He longs, he yearns, to bless them. Therefore, even at this late hour, he will make them a marvelous promise. Even though their sins were as red as scarlet, they will be made white as the driven snow. Even though their offenses were so serious that they thought there was no hope of forgiveness, he assures them that their record can be made as white as washed wool.

19. If ye be willing and obedient, ye shall eat the good of the land:

All they have to do is be "willing" to respect the commands of God and be obedient to his guidance. If they will just do these simple things, they will be blessed beyond all expectations and shall "eat the good of the land." Approximately 300 years earlier, the Lord had said something similar in a vision to King Solomon.

The Lord had said, "If my people, which are called by my name, shall humble themselves, and pray, and seek my face, and turn from their wicked ways; then will I hear from heaven, AND WILL FORGIVE THEIR SIN, AND WILL HEAL THEIR LAND" (2 Chronicles 7:14; emphasis added).

20. But if ye refuse and rebel, ye shall be devoured with the sword: for the mouth of the LORD hath spoken it.

But a loving Father must warn them of the alternative: it will be death to rebels if they do not repent. Isaiah assures them that this is not any vindictive pronouncement of his own, but "the Lord hath spoken it."

21. How is the faithful city become an harlot! it was full of judgment; righteousness lodged in it; but now murderers.

Having delivered his message with its promise and its warning, Isaiah cannot help but comment on the way things have changed in his beautiful city of Jerusalem. What was once the headquarters of righteousness and the capital city of God's kings and priests has prostituted itself for riches and riotous living. Once it was full of justice and righteousness; now it had become the headquarters for murderers!

22. Thy silver is become dross, thy wine mixed with water:

Her silver and other riches will become like the "dross" that is skimmed off and thrown away because it has no value. Her strength might be compared to rich wine that has been diluted with water until it is insipid and tasteless.

23. Thy princes are rebellious, and companions of thieves: every one loveth gifts, and followeth after rewards: they judge not the fatherless, neither doth the cause of the widow come unto them.

Even her princes, who are supposed to lead and inspire the people, have turned against God and have conspired with thieves to rob the people and share their loot. The people are always looking for a bribe or "gifts" and special "under the table" rewards for everything they do. This means the poor, the widows, and the orphans suffer, because they cannot "buy" such favors, let alone the necessities of life.

24. Therefore saith the Lord, the LORD of hosts, the mighty One of Israel, Ah, I will ease me of mine adversaries, and avenge me of mine enemies:

Having itemized the wretched wickedness of the people for the second time, Isaiah proceeds to deliver the Lord's message a second time. The prophet declares that the Lord told him he would soon be relieved of all this unrighteousness in the Holy City of Jerusalem, and satisfy the demands of justice against those who have polluted its precincts.

25. And I will turn my hand upon thee, and purely purge away thy dross, and take away all thy tin:

The Lord will turn against the people of Jerusalem and skim them off into oblivion like "dross." Thus he will remove the "tin," or cheap alloy, which has been contaminating the precious metal of God's chosen people.

26. And I will restore thy judges as at the first, and thy counsellors as at the beginning: afterward thou shalt be called, The city of righteousness, the faithful city.

Isaiah is now looking down the corridors of time to the day of the Millennium. He sees the millennial Jerusalem with righteous judges and leaders (or counselors) like the great patriarchs in the beginning, when Adam and his righteous posterity, such as Enoch, established a Zion society of purity and righteousness.

27. Zion shall be redeemed with judgment, and her converts with righteousness.

Isaiah assures his disdainful listeners that even though Israel might be a most wicked people in their day, eventually there would be a great redemption in Zion that would convert those who came to see it. They would long to enjoy its peace and righteousness.

28. And the destruction of the transgressors and of the sinners shall be together, and they that forsake the LORD shall be consumed.

Isaiah also saw the great conflagration which nearly all of the prophets mention in connection with the cleansing of the earth just before the Millennium. Isaiah beheld that the transgressors of the law of God and those who reveled in sin would all be destroyed together. He also saw that the members of God's Church who had forsaken the Lord would be "consumed."

29. For they shall be ashamed of the oaks which ye have desired, and ye shall be confounded for the gardens that ye have chosen.

He foresaw that when God comes out of his hiding place and makes bare his arm in judgment against the wicked, those who worshipped idols in the groves of oaks will be ashamed of their idolatry. Those who sought out the gardens of luxury where the licentious rites of the fertility cults were practiced will be "confounded." As they are caught up in the swirling turmoil of God's judgment, they will know how guilty they are.

30. For ye shall be as an oak whose leaf fadeth, and as a garden that hath no water.

In that hour the wicked will be like the grove of oaks where they worshipped idols. They will both fade away. Likewise, the "gardens of love" will die from lack of water, and those who reveled there will die because they lack the water of everlasting life.

31. And the strong shall be as tow, and the maker of it as a spark, and they shall both burn together, and none shall quench them.

Those who seemed so mighty in the day of wickedness will be like a tuft of inflammable material (tow), and those who built them up will be the spark to light the tinder. They shall all burn together, and none will be able to prevent it.

Isaiah, Chapter 2

1. The word that Isaiah the son of Amoz saw concerning Judah and Jerusalem.

This first verse is the title to the chapter, rather than part of the prophet's declaration. Note that this is what Isaiah "saw."

2. And it shall come to pass in the last days, that the mountain of the LORD's house shall be established in the top of the mountains, and shall be exalted above the hills; and all nations shall flow unto it.

Once Isaiah started talking about the Millennium, it was a subject he was reluctant to abandon. In the vision, his eyes must have dwelt longingly on the "last days," when the hopes of Israel would be finally fulfilled. The Lord's House (a holy temple) would be built in the tops of the mountains, and people from all parts of the world would "flow unto it" because nowhere else could they receive what they were seeking. This great prophecy has already been literally fulfilled in Zion and will be duplicated in its fulfillment when the Lord's temple is finally built in Jerusalem.

3. And many people shall go and say, Come ye, and let us go up to the mountain of the LORD, to the house of the God of Jacob; and he will teach us of his ways, and we will walk in his paths: for out of Zion shall go forth the law, and the word of the LORD from Jerusalem.

Now Isaiah discloses specifically why the people of all nations would gravitate to the mountain of the Lord (headquarters of the Church) and to his holy temple which would be built there. He says they would come to be taught the ways of God and learn how to walk in his paths. Then Isaiah makes an interesting comment that "out of Zion" (America) would "go forth the law," and the "word of the Lord from Jerusalem."

Already the Lord has raised up "wise men" who were inspired to set down those basic principles of law and good government which will be used under a theocracy during the Millennium. At the present time they are adaptable to premillennial needs and are designed "for the rights and protection of all flesh, according to just and holy principles; that every man may act in doctrine and principle pertaining to futurity, according to the moral agency which I have given unto him.... Therefore, it is not right that any man should be in bondage one to another. And for this purpose have I established the Constitution of this land, by the hands of wise men whom I raised up unto this very purpose." (D&C 101:77-80.)

Modern prophets have indicated that these principles of constitutional law should now go forth to other nations because the Lord says this is the system of divinely inspired law specifically designed to protect the principles of freedom "in maintaining rights and privileges, [which belong] to all mankind" (D&C 98:5).

When the Idaho Falls Temple was dedicated, President George Albert Smith declared in his prayer:

"We thank Thee that Thou hast revealed to us that those who gave us our Constitutional form of government were men wise in Thy sight and that Thou didst raise them up for the very purpose of putting forth that sacred document [i.e., the Constitution]....

"We pray that kings and rulers and the peoples of all nations under heaven may be persuaded of the blessings enjoyed by the people of this land by reason of their freedom under Thy guidance and be constrained to adopt similar governmental systems, thus to fulfill the ancient prophecy of Isaiah that 'out of Zion shall go forth the law, and the word of the Lord from Jerusalem.'" (N.B. Lundwall, comp., *Temples of the Most High*, rev. and enl. [Salt Lake City: Bookcraft, 1966], pp. 188-89.)

4. And he shall judge among the nations, and shall rebuke many people: and they shall beat their swords into plowshares, and their spears

Isaiah is about to make it vividly clear that the judgments of God will be very severe when he comes to rebuke the wicked nations and cleanse the earth. Nevertheless, Isaiah saw that those who did survive the great

into pruninghooks: nation shall not lift up sword against nation, neither shall they learn war any more.

debacle of destruction would indeed beat their swords into plowshares, and their spears of war into the orchard keeper's pruning hooks. Isaiah saw that not a single nation would try to invade or conquer another nation during this millennial period. In fact, the arts of defense and war would not even be taught anymore.

5. O house of Jacob, come ye, and let us walk in the light of the LORD.

Half of this verse is missing from the King James translation. The brass plates, from which the Isaiah text in the Book of Mormon was transcribed around 600 B.C., had this additional phrase: "yea, come, for ye have all gone astray, every one to his wicked ways" (2 Nephi 12:5).

6. Therefore thou hast forsaken thy people the house of Jacob, because they be replenished from the east, and are soothsayers like the Philistines, and they please themselves in the children of strangers.

There are also several words missing from this verse, making the meaning less clear. The Book of Mormon version from the brass plates restores the correct text and shows that Isaiah is interjecting his own commentary at this point. He declares, "Therefore, O LORD, thou hast forsaken thy people, the house of Jacob, because they be replenished from the east [with the teachings of false mystics], and HEARKEN UNTO soothsayers like the Philistines, and they please themselves in the children of strangers" (2 Nephi 12:6; emphasis added).

When the Lord is trying to build a more refined culture with a higher quality of life, it is displeasing to him that his chosen people find pleasure in the coarse, ribald, and riotous living of strangers who belong to a lower culture.

7. Their land also is full of silver and gold, neither is there any end of their treasures; their land is also full

The people of Israel in the days of Isaiah were prospering in their wickedness. It seemed ironical to contemplate the apostate condition of the Lord's people in

horses, neither is there any end of their chariots:

Isaiah's day (around 750 B.C.) in the light of what would happen to Israel during the great millennial reign. Isaiah saw the Israel of his own day reveling in riches, with silver in abundance and chariots and horses without number.

8. Their land also is full of idols; they worship the work of their own hands, that which their own fingers have made:

What was particularly abhorrent to God was the abomination of idol worship in the land. Idolatry was invariably accompanied by adultery and fornication, which were an inseparable part of the ancient fertility cults.

9. And the mean man boweth down, and the great man humbleth himself: therefore forgive them not.

This verse does not make sense in the King James Version because the two most important words are left out. The brass plates correctly recorded it as follows: "And the mean [lowly or common] man boweth NOT down, and the great man humbleth himself NOT, therefore, forgive him not" (2 Nephi 12:9; emphasis added).

10. Enter into the rock, and hide thee in the dust, for fear of the LORD, and for the glory of his majesty.

Now Isaiah darts back to the premillennial day of judgment when the proud and disdainful Israelites who have rejected the message of the restored Gospel, and also the Gentiles (the Philistines of the latter days), will be smitten by the sudden appearance of God's glory and majesty when he comes in judgment.

There are four words missing from this verse which originally clarified the fact that God's great judgment in the latter days is specifically directed against those who have corrupted themselves. The four missing words were, "O ye wicked ones" (2 Nephi 12:10). This was Isaiah's identification of those who were about to get the treatment!

11. The lofty looks of man shall be humbled, and the haughtiness of men shall be bowed down, and the LORD alone shall be exalted in that day.

Isaiah saw the day when every knee would bow and every tongue confess that Jesus is the Christ. A modern revelation indicates that this will be all the more remarkable because this sudden manifestation of humility will be displayed by the people of a telestial lifestyle who have seriously gloried in their role as rebellious reprobates (see D&C 76:98–110). In the hour of premillennial judgment, "the Lord alone shall be exalted."

12. For the day of the LORD of hosts shall be upon every one that is proud and lofty, and upon every one that is lifted up; and he shall be brought low:

Here Isaiah wants to emphasize the universal application of God's judgment. Once again we turn to the brass plates for a more perfect rendition: "For the day of the Lord of Hosts SOON COMETH UPON ALL NATIONS, yea, upon every one; yea, upon the proud and lofty, and upon every one who is lifted up, and he shall be brought low" (2 Nephi 12:12; emphasis added).

13. And upon all the cedars of Lebanon, that are high and lifted up, and upon all the oaks of Bashan,

To emphasize how the high and mighty will be brought low, Isaiah says in the brass plates version, YEA, AND THE DAY OF THE LORD SHALL COME upon all the cedars of Lebanon, for they are high and lifted up; and upon all the oaks of Bashan" (2 Nephi 12:13; emphasis added). The oak forest of Bashan was located east of the Jordan River. This is the forest where Absalom, the rebellious son of King David, got his hair entangled in the branches of a tree while trying to escape and was killed by Joab (see 2 Samuel 18:9–14).

14. And upon all the high mountains, and upon all the hills that are lifted up,

The King James Version leaves out a significant part of this verse which is given in the brass plates. They contained the statement that this terrible destruction would not only come upon the high hills and mountains, but also "upon all the nations which are lifted up, and upon every people" (2 Nephi 12:14).

In this verse, Isaiah wants the people to know what he had seen. He could scarcely believe it himself as he saw the high mountains and hills brought down. Both ancient and modern scripture verify the literal reality of the things Isaiah is talking about. John the Revelator said a great earthquake would roar through the earth with a violence that had never before been known (see Revelation 16:18). Ezekiel said, "The mountains shall be thrown down, and the steep places shall fall, and every wall shall fall to the ground" (Ezekiel 38:20). Jeremiah saw the crust of the whole earth roll and quake:

"I beheld the earth, and, lo, it was without form, and void; and the heavens, and they had no light. I beheld the mountains, and, lo, they trembled, and all the hills moved lightly. . . . I beheld, and, lo, the fruitful place was a wilderness, and all the cities thereof were broken down AT THE PRESENCE OF THE LORD." (Jeremiah 4:23–26; emphasis added.) This will also be the time when "he shall command the great deep, and it shall be driven back into the north countries, and the islands shall become one land" (D&C 133:23).

No wonder the Lord said in a modern revelation: "For after your testimony cometh the testimony of earthquakes, that shall cause groanings in the midst of her, and men shall fall upon the ground and shall not be able to stand. And also cometh the testimony of the voice of thunderings, and the voice of lightnings, and the voice of tempests, and the voice of the waves of the sea heaving themselves beyond their bounds. And all things shall be in commotion; and surely, men's hearts shall fail them; for fear shall come upon all people." (D&C 88:89–91.)

The earth itself shall begin to stagger in its orbit about the firmament, and the sun and the stars will refuse to shine (see D&C 34:9).

15. And upon every high tower, and upon every fenced wall,

In view of everything Isaiah and other prophets have said about these coming events, it almost goes without saying that they would have a tremendously devastating impact "upon every high tower, and upon every fenced wall."

16. And upon all the ships of Tarshish, and upon all pleasant pictures.

These events will have an equally destructive impact on ships at sea. Isaiah uses the term "ships of Tarshish" because they were the largest trans-Mediterranean ships in his day. They had three decks and were used to transport tin from Tarshish (probably Tartessus), an ancient Phoenician city in southern Spain (See William Smith, *A Dictionary of the Bible*, Rev. ed. [Grand Rapids, Mich.: Zondervan Publishing House, 1948], p. 674).

In this verse "pleasant pictures" means "pleasant scenery." This verse also contains a remarkable demonstration of the integrity of the brass plates. In the Greek or Septuagint version, there is a phrase that is not in the Hebrew version; and the Hebrew version has a phrase that is not in the Greek. But the Book of Mormon version taken from the brass plates has both of them! (See 2 Nephi 12:16; also Sidney B. Sperry, *The Voice of Israel's Prophets* [Salt Lake City: Deseret Book Company, 1961], pp. 90-91.)

17. And the loftiness of man shall be bowed down, and the haughtiness of men shall be made low: and the LORD alone shall be exalted in that day.

Isaiah repeats in this verse precisely what he had tried to emphasize in verse 11—namely, that pride goeth before a fall, and that there will be a severe humbling of all the proud and egocentric people when the Savior makes bare his mighty arm. Again Isaiah says that after the dust has cleared away, "the Lord alone shall be exalted."

18. And the idols he shall utterly abolish.

The idolatrous works of men's hands will be destroyed just as completely in the latter days as they were in Isaiah's day.

19. And they shall go into the holes of the rocks, and into the caves of the earth, for fear of the LORD, and for the glory of his majesty, when he ariseth to shake terribly the earth.

The display of God's power will be so frightening that the wicked will run and hide themselves in the holes of the rocks and in the caves of the earth when they see the terrible quaking which will destroy everything in sight.

20. In that day a man shall cast his idols of silver, and his idols of gold, which they made each one for himself to worship, to the moles and to the bats;

They will remove their idols from their temples and take their treasures of gold and silver from their secret hiding places. All these will be buried in the earth, which is the habitation of moles, or piled up in caves, which are the habitations of bats.

21. To go into the clefts of the rocks, and into the tops of the ragged rocks, for fear of the LORD, and for the glory of his majesty, when he ariseth to shake terribly the earth.

Apparently the turmoil will be so terrible and universal that the wicked will instinctively flee to the highest crags and cliffs hoping to find security.

22. Cease ye from man, whose breath is in his nostrils: for wherein is he to be accounted of?

The wicked have always entered into compacts and alliances designed to protect them in their frauds, crimes, or secret machinations. Isaiah warns that such man-made citadels of security will mean nothing in the hour of God's judgment. Men are all susceptible to being swept away at any moment. Mankind is never more than a breath away from death, and therefore any institution of security which depends upon man can also disappear in an instant. The only sound security is living so that we can enjoy the eternal blessings and security of a loving Heavenly Father. That is the point Isaiah is making as he concludes this great chapter concerning the "last days" and the coming of the Lord to cleanse the earth from wickedness.

---

1. For, behold, the Lord, the LORD of hosts, doth take away from Jerusalem and from Judah the stay and the staff, the whole stay of bread, and the whole stay of water,

In this chapter Isaiah commences a series of prophecies which were to be literally fulfilled on at least three separate occasions—in 587 B.C., when Jerusalem would be destroyed by the Babylonians; in A.D. 70, when Jerusalem would be destroyed by the Romans; and in the latter days at the great battle of Armageddon, when Jerusalem will be under siege for 3½ years. On each of these occasions, the suffering and death of the people would be caused by the lack of food and water.

2. The mighty man, and the man of war, the judge, and the prophet, and the prudent, and the ancient,

In a time of crisis it is a great affliction to be without any kind of reliable leadership. The Lord wanted the Jews to know that, because of their wickedness, in their hour of severe distress they would find themselves without political leaders, without military leaders, without judges, without prophets, and without men of wisdom from whom to seek guidance.

3. The captain of fifty, and the honourable man, and the counsellor, and the cunning artificer, and the eloquent orator.

The captains of 50, upon whom the people usually depended for policing the city, will be missing. The most distinguished and honorable men will also disappear from the scene. There won't even be clever mechanics, architects, artists, or other skilled workers to perform their usual services.

4. And I will give children to be their princes, and babes shall rule over them.

For many years the people will have "children" ruling over them. This passage may be referring to the period when the Gentiles would rule over them. Gentiles were often described in derision as "dogs," "stones," "infantile," or "children." (See Monte S. Nyman, *"Great Are the Words of Isaiah"* [Salt Lake City: Bookcraft, 1980], pp. 34–35.) For nearly 2,500 years, the Jews were governed almost continually by the "children of the Gentiles."

5. And the people shall be oppressed, every one by another, and every one by his neighbour: the child shall behave himself proudly against the ancient, and the base against the honourable.

In a time of crisis when the people lack sound leadership, there is a tendency for the whole culture to collapse. The people begin to oppress one another. Cheating and deception become a way of life, even between neighbors. Children become arrogant toward their elders, and those who have served the people in the past, and have been honored in the community, are no longer respected.

6. When a man shall take hold of his brother of the house of his father, saying, Thou hast clothing, be thou our ruler, and let this ruin be under thy hand:

Isaiah also saw in his vision that during these days of crisis, it would be extremely difficult to get anyone to serve in public office. Even within families, one brother would pressure another brother, urging him, because he was well off, to be willing to rule and NOT let the ruin of the people continue while he was their ruler. (The word "not" is missing from the King James Version, but is quoted correctly from the brass plates by Nephi in 2 Nephi 13:6.)

7. In that day shall he swear, saying, I will not be an healer; for in my house is neither bread nor clothing: make me not a ruler of the people.

But Isaiah saw that the brother would argue back, claiming that he was poverty-stricken and in no position to take on the governing of the people as a "healer" of the nations.

8. For Jerusalem is ruined, and Judah is fallen: because their tongue and their doings are against the LORD, to provoke the eyes of his glory.

The prevailing circumstances would confirm the brother's hopeless feeling. The beautiful city of Jerusalem would be in ruins, and Judah herself would be a conquered people. Furthermore, the apostate condition of the people would be so chronic that the justice of God would require him to withhold blessings from them.

9. The shew of their countenance doth witness against them; and they declare their sin as Sodom, they hid it not. Woe unto their soul! for they have rewarded evil unto themselves.

Now Isaiah describes the wickedness of the people. He says that even the countenances of the people would witness against them. This was not merely because of dissipated living, but their very faces would reveal that they were indulging in homosexuality, the abomination of Sodom. The King James Version says their faces would "witness against them" so that they "hide it not." But the brass plates version is even more emphatic, saying "they CANNOT hide it" (2 Nephi 13:9; emphasis added). This would imply that their faces would bear the marks of disease or otherwise reflect the evidence of their sins of sexual depravity, for which Sodom and Gomorrah had been literally consumed with fire because of God's wrath. It should be mentioned that in ancient times, those who participated in degenerate sexual fertility rites, sacramental intoxication, and the taking of hallucination-producing drugs from exotic plants usually identified themselves with peculiar hair styles, bizarre beards, and decorative embellishments, including marks in the flesh. All these the Lord strictly forbade (see Leviticus 19:27–28). Certainly these aspects of their countenances would witness against them.

10. Say ye to the righteous, that it shall be well with him: for they shall eat the fruit of their doings.

But in the midst of all these terrible circumstances, the Lord has a special message for the few righteous. They are assured that God has not forsaken them, and that they shall enjoy the good fruits of their righteous lives. No matter how extensive or intensive their trials might be, in the end they will be able to sing, as the Saints of the latter days did as they crossed the plains, "all is well, all is well."

11. Woe unto the wicked! it shall be ill with him: for the reward of his hands shall be given him.

Nevertheless, there is no such respite for the wicked. The punishments coming to them will be fixed in their dimensions, and certain in their fulfillment. As Paul would later express it, "Be not deceived; God is not mocked: for whatsoever a man soweth, that shall he also reap" (Galatians 6:7).

12. As for my people, children are their oppressors, and women rule over them. O my people, they which lead thee cause thee to err, and destroy the way of thy paths.

The sweeping vision of Isaiah's perspective led him to lament that, instead of being governed by the Priesthood, they would be oppressed by children (probably meaning the children of the Gentiles, whom the Jews called "children" in derision), and women would rule over them. Isaiah saw that this leadership would cause the Jews to err through wickedness and turn away from God's plan for happy living that is contained in the original Gospel as taught by the prophets.

13. The LORD standeth up to plead, and standeth to judge the people.

Often people think that their evil ways must not be too sinful because they continue to prosper, but Isaiah says they can be assured that eventually the Almighty will reveal his wrath as he stands forth to "plead" (the Hebrew word means "to contend") and judge his people.

14. The LORD will enter into judgment with the ancients of his people, and the princes

The judgment of the Lord will be particularly harsh against the apostate elders or "ancients" of the people who have combined with the political rulers and princ-

thereof: for ye have eaten up the vineyard; the spoil of the poor is in your houses.

es to exploit the nation and steal, by taxes or by fraud, the essentials of life from the impoverished people.

15. What mean ye that ye beat my people to pieces, and grind the faces of the poor? saith the Lord GOD of hosts.

Isaiah quotes the Lord's challenge which will be thrown down like a gauntlet in the day of judgment: How can they justify the terrible crimes they have committed against the people of God, crushing and beating them to pieces, virtually grinding the faces of the poor into the dirt?

16. Moreover, the LORD saith, Because the daughters of Zion are haughty, and walk with stretched forth necks and wanton eyes, walking and mincing as they go, and making a tinkling with their feet:

This is one of the rare passages in scripture where women are singled out for their contribution to the debaucheries of a fallen nation. Usually only the guilt of the wicked men is mentioned, but here Isaiah says the women will have had much to do with promoting evil in that day. Notice that Isaiah is addressing the "daughters of Zion." The city of Jerusalem was built on Mount Moriah, which is often referred to as Mount Zion. However, Isaiah also uses "Zion" as a general term referring to America. So he could be referring to the daughters of Zion in both places. The Lord, through Isaiah, calls these women "haughty" who no longer provoke their menfolk to righteousness. They walk about with stretched-forth necks and wanton eyes. With an air of affectation, they prance along with mincing steps, making a tinkling sound with their feet so as to attract attention.

17. Therefore the Lord will smite with a scab the crown of the head of the daughters of Zion, and the LORD will discover their secret parts.

Isaiah saw that in the hour of judgment, the beautiful, well-groomed hairdos of these haughty women would be replaced by a scab on the crown of their heads. God's judgment would also "discover their secret parts," which is a Hebrew idiom meaning they would be subjected to the indignity of being stripped naked and held up to the leering gaze of their captors. A similar reference is found in Nahum 3:5–6: "...I will shew the nations thy nakedness...and will set thee as a gazingstock."

18. In that day the Lord will take away the bravery of their tinkling ornaments about their feet, and their cauls, and their round tires like the moon,

Isaiah said that in the day of God's judgment, these proud and haughty women could be assured that their sense of "bravery" and arrogance would be shattered. No longer would they be high-minded with all their tinkling ornaments, their cauls (embroidered shawls or head coverings), and their round tires (ornaments or headdresses) like the moon.

19. The chains, and the bracelets, and the mufflers,

20. The bonnets, and the ornaments of the legs, and the headbands, and the tablets, and the earrings,

21. The rings, and nose jewels,

22. The changeable suits of apparel, and the mantles, and the wimples, and the crisping pins,

23. The glasses, and the fine linen, and the hoods, and the vails.

In these verses, Isaiah gives an elaborate list of the clothing, ornaments, and decorations which represent the sophistication of the age in which he lived. These include 18 specific items: chains, bracelets, mufflers, bonnets, leg ornaments, headbands, tablets, earrings, rings, nose jewels, changeable suits of apparel, mantles, wimples, crisping pins, glasses [transparent garments], fine linen, hoods, and veils.

24. And it shall come to pass, that instead of sweet smell there shall be stink; and instead of a girdle a rent; and instead of well set hair

As in all ages, the generous use of perfume was a matter of greatest importance among the feminine elite. However, Isaiah saw that in the days of coming disaster, which these women would help bring upon

baldness; and instead of a stomacher, a girding of sackcloth; and burning instead of beauty.

themselves, there would be no sweet perfumes to delight the senses, but only the odor of death and decay. There would be no stylish girdle, but women would cover themselves with torn remnants. Their hair styling would be replaced by baldness, and instead of beautiful dresses and skirts they would be girded about with sackcloth. Their faces would no longer be fair and beautiful, but would reflect the burning of wind and sun as they labored and wandered about in their distressed condition.

25. Thy men shall fall by the sword, and thy mighty in the war.

At this point the vision of Isaiah is definitely pointed toward the latter days and the great last cleansing of the earth prior to the Millennium. This is specifically referred to in verse 5 of the next chapter, being a continuation of the present one. Isaiah saw hosts of men hewn down and destroyed in such great numbers that, as we shall see in the next chapter, there would be few men left.

26. And her gates shall lament and mourn; and she being desolate shall sit upon the ground.

Isaiah compares the once mighty city of Jerusalem to a woman who has lost everything and can only sit by the wayside in mourning and total desolation.

Isaiah, Chapter 4

INTRODUCTION:

In the previous chapter, Isaiah described the wickedness of the Lord's people and the consequences of their sins. We now know that these prophecies have been fulfilled a number of times in the past, but their ultimate and most literal fulfillment is still in the future. The great last war against the Jews is often referred to as the battle of Armageddon (see Revelation 16:16). As Peloubet points out, this means "the hill or city of Meggido." This is the ancient fortress city overlooking the Esdraelon Valley where many of the most critical battles in world history have been fought. It is from this site that prophecy says a powerful coalition of Gentile nations will sweep down on Judah in the latter days and lay siege to Jerusalem for 3½ years (see Revelation 11:2; Daniel 7:25).

Two great prophets of God will use the power of the Priesthood to hold back the attacking hosts during this period, but finally the Lord will allow them to be killed, and half of the city of Jerusalem will be ravished and conquered. Then, just as Gog and his hosts of Magog (Gentiles) are about to sweep in upon the rest of the city, these two prophets will be raised up from the dead and the Savior will appear on the Mount of Olives to rescue his people in a great display of power (see Revelation 11:3-13; D&C 45:48).

At the first opportunity, the Jews will gather round their Messiah in great rejoicing. Apparently he will "withhold his glory," as resurrected beings are able to do when they wish (see Hebrews 13:2), and the Jews will look upon him as a mortal being until someone notices the evidence of deep wounds in his hands and in his feet. They will then ask him the meaning of these, and he will tell them that these are the wounds "with which I was wounded in the house of my friends" (Zechariah 13:6; see also D&C 45:51-53).

For the first time the people will realize that their Messiah really did come among their ancestors and was rejected, just as Isaiah had clearly predicted in chapter 53 of his inspired writings. Then all the people will mourn for 30 days. After the Jews have cleansed the land, the survivors will enjoy a glorious period of peace and prosperity which Isaiah is about to describe.

1. And in that day seven women shall take hold of one man, saying, We will eat our own bread, and wear our own apparel: only let us be called by thy name, to take away our reproach.

This verse is out of place. Since chapter 4 is a continuation of chapter 3, the matter is not of any great significance, but it should be observed that in the Hebrew Bible, as well as in the Joseph Smith Translation, this verse comes at the conclusion of chapter 3 to demonstrate how few men will survive the great last battle of the Jews.

Notice that the women in this verse consider it a "reproach" not to be married and have children. In periods of rebellion and unrighteousness some women want to avoid the blessings of motherhood and the joys of raising up a happy family. They say they want to be "liberated" from any such obligations. But Isaiah says that when the great wars of the latter days have destroyed millions of men, the surviving women will offer to support themselves and enter into a plurality of wives if they can have a husband and a family. Of course, the Lord forbids a plurality of wives unless it is under the patriarchal order of the Priesthood. The Lord has declared that the patriarchal order of plural marriage is specifically designed to provide superior homes for the special spirits which the Lord needs to have trained and brought up for the performance of gigantic tasks of building God's kingdom in the earth. The Lord's position is set forth by the Nephite prophet Jacob, who said: "Hearken to the word of the Lord: For there shall not any man among you have save it be one wife; and concubines he shall have none; for I, the Lord God, delight in the chastity of women.... If I will, saith the Lord of Hosts, raise up seed UNTO ME, I will COMMAND MY PEOPLE; otherwise they shall hearken unto these things." (Jacob 2:27–28, 30; emphasis added.)

2. In that day shall the branch of the LORD be beautiful and glorious, and the fruit of the earth shall be excellent and comely for them that are escaped of Israel.

Isaiah seems to be looking at the great changes which will result from the cleansing of the earth preparatory to the launching of the long-awaited Millennium. First of all, he says the "branch of the Lord" will be beautiful and glorious. This, of course, is after its cleansing and purging. The branch is believed to refer to the children of Joseph whom Jacob said would be like a fruitful vine by a well whose branches would run over the wall of the great seas and come to America (see Genesis 49:22). The prophet Lehi commented on the fulfillment of this blessing after he, a descendant of Joseph, had come to America with his family shortly after 600 B.C. Said he: "Wherefore, Joseph [who was sold into Egypt] truly saw our day. And he obtained a promise of the Lord, that out of the fruit of his loins the Lord God would raise up a righteous BRANCH unto the house of Israel; not the Messiah, but a branch which was to be broken off." (2 Nephi 3:5; emphasis added.) Isaiah saw that in the latter days this people would be purged, and then they would be beautiful and glorious. Furthermore, he saw that the earth would bring forth its fruits in great abundance for all those who "escaped of Israel." This could mean "Israel" in general terms, or it might have specific reference to the escaping hosts of the returning Ten Tribes.

3. And it shall come to pass, that he that is left in Zion, and he that remaineth in Jerusalem, shall be called holy, even every one that is written among the living in Jerusalem:

This verse has some ominous implications. Isaiah indicates that the great destruction that will sweep over the earth will be so universal that the only ones who are "left" in Zion (America) and "remain" in Jerusalem shall be called "holy." In fact, these are probably the ones seen by Paul (1 Thessalonians 4:17) who were "caught up" so they would not be destroyed during the great burning. This is described in greater detail in Doctrine and Covenants 88:88-98. This would suggest that these righteous ones are temporarily transfigured so that they can be caught up during the great destruction and then return with the Savior to occupy the earth after it has been cleansed by fire. In Doctrine and Covenants 101:24-25, the Lord describes this cleansing by fire as follows: "And every corruptible thing, both of man, or of the beasts of the field, or of the fowls of the heavens, or of the fish of the sea, that dwells upon all the face of the earth, shall be consumed; and also that of element shall melt with fervent heat; and all things shall become new, that my knowledge and glory may dwell upon all the earth."

No wonder Isaiah would later say, "Therefore hath the curse devoured the earth, and they that dwell therein are desolate: therefore the inhabitants of the earth are burned, and few men left" (Isaiah 24:6). The Lord indicates that only half of the Church will be worthy to be saved from this great destruction (see Matthew 25:1-12). In the Doctrine and Covenants the Lord says: "I have sworn in my wrath, and decreed wars upon the face of the earth, and the wicked shall slay the wicked, and fear shall come upon every man; AND THE SAINTS ALSO SHALL HARDLY ESCAPE; nevertheless, I, the Lord, am with them, and will come down in heaven from the presence of my Father and consume the wicked with unquenchable fire.... And until that hour there will be foolish virgins among the wise; and at that hour cometh an entire separation of the righteous and the wicked; and in that day will I send mine angels to pluck out the wicked and cast them into unquenchable fire." (D&C 63:33–34, 54; emphasis added.)

The prophets make it clear that this "unquenchable fire" is not a poetic reference to suffering in the spirit world, but is describing a consuming of the wicked "in the flesh." As Malachi wrote,"For, behold, the day cometh, that shall burn as an oven; and all the proud, yea, and all that do wickedly, shall be stubble: and the day that cometh shall burn them up, saith the Lord of hosts, that it shall leave them neither root nor branch" (Malachi 4:1). In a modern revelation the Lord emphasizes the need for faithfulness among the Saints, especially in paying their tithes to support the work of the kingdom. He said this law was given "to prepare them [the modern Saints] against the day of vengeance and burning" (D&C 85:3). And then the Lord says, "for he that is tithed shall not be burned at his coming" (D&C 64:23).

4. When the LORD shall have washed away the filth of the daughters of Zion, and shall have purged the blood of Jerusalem from the midst thereof by the spirit of judgment, and by the spirit of burning.

Notice how Isaiah continually refers to Zion (America) and Jerusalem (the land of the Jews) together so that the reader will know that the great destruction will occur in both places. Throughout his writings he combines his observations of BOTH Zion and Jerusalem—America and Judah. In this verse he states that the daughters of Zion (women of the Church in America, primarily) will have been purged of their "filth," and the "spirit of judgment" and the "spirit of burning" will have purged the blood of those who have survived in Jerusalem.

5. And the LORD will create upon every dwelling place of mount Zion, and upon her assemblies, a cloud and

Once the glory and power of God have been revealed to all flesh, a marvelous manifestation of God's presence will be enjoyed in Zion just as it was when Moses

smoke by day, and the shining of a flaming fire by night: for upon all the glory shall be a defence.

and the children of Israel were coming out of Egypt. Isaiah says the Lord will create over every dwelling place in the entire region of Mount Zion a "cloud and smoke" by day and the shining of a pillar of fire by night. This is not a new phenomenon. The same thing was done for Israel when Moses brought them up out of Egypt (see Exodus 13:21). Two words are missing from the modern Bible which were in the plates of brass. The last phrase of this verse should read, "for upon all the glory OF ZION shall be a defence" (2 Nephi 14:5; emphasis added).

6. And there shall be a tabernacle for a shadow in the daytime from the heat, and for a place of refuge, and for a covert from storm and from rain.

In this verse we encounter a statement that possibly means a great deal more than appears on the surface. It states that there will be a tabernacle for a shadow (or shade) in the daytime so as to be a protection against the heat, and it will also be a refuge and a protection from storms and rains. It has been thought by some that prior to the Great Flood there was a protective mantle over the earth that allowed dew to settle on the plant life but provided protection from the sun so that there was not the constant evaporation and rainfall cycle as we know it today. If this were true, there would not have been the phenomenon of the rainbow until after this mantle was taken away following the Flood. The appearance of the rainbow after the Flood seems to have been a new phenomenon that the Lord used as a sign of God's covenant with Noah that the earth would never be totally submerged in water again (see Genesis 9:8-17). Of course, should this mantle or "tabernacle" be restored at the beginning of the Millennium, the phenomenon of the rainbow would once more disappear. We are not certain that this is the meaning of this passage, but such a possibility is implied from the following words of Joseph Smith: "I have asked of the Lord concerning His coming; and while asking the Lord, He gave a sign and said, 'In the days of Noah I set a bow in the heavens as a sign and token that in any year that the bow should be seen the Lord would not come; but there should be seed time and harvest during that year: but whenever you see the bow withdrawn, it shall be a token that there shall be famine, pestilence, and great distress among the nations, and that the coming of the Messiah is not far distant.'" (*History of the Church*, 6:254.) On another occasion the Prophet said: "The Lord hath set the bow in the cloud for a sign that while it shall be seen, seed time and harvest, summer and winter shall not fail; but when it shall disappear, woe to that generation, for behold the end cometh quickly." (*History of the Church*, 5:402.)

These citations would indicate that the great terrestrial disturbances just prior to the Second Coming will be during a time when the rainbow will not be seen. This may be due to the fact that the Lord will have thrown a mantle over Zion (or perhaps the whole earth) to protect it from the storms of snow and rain which are the result of the evaporation-rain cycle. With this mantle, the earth would be like a gardener's greenhouse, and the verdure of the planet would spring forth in strength, watered by the moisture of gentle dews rather than violent storms.

Isaiah, Chapter 5

INTRODUCTION:

At this point Isaiah introduces the famous parable of the vineyard. This is a very abbreviated version of what was probably a rather detailed parable in the Hebrew scriptures depicting the history of Israel. The economy of Israel was based on three industries: the culture of grapes, the culture of olives, and the raising of livestock (sheep, goats, and cattle). The Lord and his prophets used these familiar occupations in their parables. The most detailed parable depicting the history of Israel is the allegory of the tame and wild olive trees recorded by Zenos on the brass plates and copied into the Book of Mormon (Jacob, chapter 5). Paul talks about this parable in Romans 11:17-24, and Jesus used the symbolism of the vineyard of olives and grapes in several of his parables. He also frequently used parables involving sheep and goats.

To appreciate our Heavenly Father's point of view, we have to remind ourselves that in the premortal existence, the second estate had to be carefully preplanned in terms of the limited leadership available. Even in the premortal existence, this precious group of leaders was called "Israel"—which means "soldiers of God," or those who overcome with God (see Bruce R. McConkie, *Mormon Doctrine*, 2d ed. [Salt Lake City: Bookcraft, 1966], p. 389). In Deuteronomy 32:7-9, Israel is described as the "Lord's portion" on whom he depends for leadership among the less valiant multitudes from the premortal existence who must be guided through the pitfalls of the second estate here on earth. From about 1800 B.C., the children of this choice seed were ushered onto the earth through Jacob and his descendants (see Deuteronomy 32:9). Jacob's name was changed to "Israel" because through him the valiant spirits (the "soldiers of God" from the premortal existence) would come into the earth (see Genesis 32:28). The Father's plan for his earthly children depends largely on the descendants of Jacob being able to remain true to their calling.

Thus we come to Isaiah's song which the Father sings to his beloved Son concerning a beautiful vineyard. Verse 7 tells us that the vineyard is a representation of Israel, and his "pleasant plant" is Judah.

1. Now will I sing to my wellbeloved a song of my beloved touching his vineyard. My wellbeloved hath a vineyard in a very fruitful hill:

We note that this vineyard has been given by the Father to his beloved Son, and that it was located in a very choice place which is described as a "fruitful hill." As we proceed we learn that the Lord is talking about the land of Judah. The fruitful hill probably has reference to Jerusalem and the surrounding hills of Judea.

2. And he fenced it, and gathered out the stones thereof, and planted it with the choicest vine, and built a tower in the midst of it, and also made a winepress therein: and he looked that it should bring forth grapes, and it brought forth wild grapes.

Everything had been done to make this vineyard a success. It had been cultivated, nurtured, fenced, and planted with the choicest of vines. Verse 7 tells us that the choice vine refers to the children of Judah who were among the Lord's chosen leaders in the premortal existence. The tower that the Lord built for his vineyard is believed to refer to Solomon's temple. The winepress might refer to the ordinances of the temple in which those who had brought forth good fruits consecrated themselves to the Lord. Of course, the Lord expected this extensive investment in time and effort to bring forth a very high quality of fruit, but to his amazement it had produced only a variety of "wild grapes" which were often bitter and virtually useless for pressing into wine.

3. And now, O inhabitants of Jerusalem, and men of Judah, judge, I pray you, betwixt me and my vineyard.

The Father's beloved Son therefore calls upon the inhabitants of Jerusalem and the men of Judah to give an accounting of themselves. The Lord is about to pass judgment on this vineyard, and he wonders what they will have to say for themselves and their corrupted stewardship.

4. What could have been done more to my vineyard, that I have not done in it? wherefore, when I looked that it should bring forth grapes, brought it forth wild grapes?

He had done everything possible to make it a success. In fact, he challenges these reprobate heirs of the vineyard to name anything more which he might have done. Under such circumstances, how could it be imagined that instead of choice fruit he would get a harvest of bitter, wild grapes (translated in some texts as "poisonous berries")?

5. And now go to; I will tell you what I will do to my vineyard: I will take away the hedge thereof, and it shall be eaten up; and break down the wall thereof, and it shall be trodden down:

It is obvious that the Lord has been betrayed, and so he tells these "inhabitants of Jerusalem and men of Judah" to be gone. The Lord in his disappointment declares that he will not labor over this vineyard any longer. He is going to tear down everything—the hedge, the wall, and even the tower or temple would be destroyed. The whole vineyard was to be trodden down. This occurred in 587 B.C.

6. And I will lay it waste: it shall not be pruned, nor digged; but there shall come up briers and thorns: I will also command the clouds that they rain no rain upon it.

The Lord intends to let this entire vineyard go back to desert. It will then be a desolate waste, with nothing growing in it but briars and thorns. Neither will it be cultivated with other crops. Even the seasonal rains will no longer come to water it.

7. For the vineyard of the LORD of hosts is the house of Israel, and the men of Judah his pleasant plant: and he looked for judgment,

Here begins the interpretation of this parable. The vineyard represents Israel, the Lord's chosen people. The choice plant, from which he was expecting so much, represents Judah, the tribe which was supposed

but behold oppression; for righteousness, but behold a cry.

to provide valiant leadership. Instead of good government and justice, the Lord can hear only cries of oppression; instead of the joyful fruits of righteousness, the Lord can hear only weeping.

8. Woe unto them that join house to house, that lay field to field, till there be no place, that they may be placed alone in the midst of the earth!

The governors of the people will be engaged in getting control over all the land and houses, so that without their permission no one can find a place to have a house or a field to cultivate. These wicked, greedy men will be trying to set up a monopoly so that they can be in charge of everything. With dictatorial authority, they will stand alone in the midst of the earth.

Apparently some ancient copier or scribe added the words "that lay field to field." This phrase was not included on the brass plates (2 Nephi 15:8).

Dr. Monte S. Nyman of Brigham Young University has pointed out that this verse has even greater significance when it is realized that when God's people are gathered together they must set up a society of Zion, just as Enoch did (see Nyman, *"Great Are the Words of Isaiah,"* p. 44). This can be done only when the people are free to practice the laws of consecration and stewardship (see D&C 78:1-7). However, consecration and stewardship involve individual initiative and the private ownership of property (see D&C 42:30-32; 51:1-5; 78:14). A Zion society cannot be established where the leaders have monopolized the ownership or control of all the means of production, dictating to everyone what he can own and what he must do for a living. In modern economic philosophy, this is called socialism. In its more brutal forms it is called communism, nazism, or fascism. These philosophies have been a great affliction to all those who have had to live under their highly centralized and oppressive dictatorships (see Nyman, *"Great Are the Words of Isaiah,"* p. 44).

9. In mine ears said the LORD of hosts, Of a truth many houses shall be desolate, even great and fair, without inhabitant.

The Lord assures the leaders of Judah and Jerusalem that all this expensive property they have been acquiring is going to be leveled into rubble. The whole region will be desolate and without inhabitants.

10. Yea, ten acres of vineyard shall yield one bath, and the seed of an homer shall yield an ephah.

Furthermore, the agricultural production will be so meager that ten acres of vineyard will produce only one bath (eight and one-half gallons) of wine, and the seed of a homer (equal to ten baths) planted by a farmer will produce only an ephah (the dry weight of a single bath). In other words, the harvest will be only one-tenth of the seed which the farmer originally planted!

11. Woe unto them that rise up early in the morning, that they may follow strong drink; that continue until night, till wine inflame them!

The Lord is greatly offended that the people he has blessed and prospered have not only apostatized, but have become a generation of drunkards. They have become chronic alcoholics who can hardly wait to arise in the morning to start drinking, and they continue imbibing throughout the day, until by nightfall they have become roaring drunk. Their minds are inflamed and their thoughts are in a stupor.

12. And the harp, and the viol, the tabret, and pipe, and wine, are in their feasts: but they regard not the work of the LORD, neither consider the operation of his hands.

They are continually running after entertainment. They clamor after food, wine, music, and the bright spots designed for dissipated indulgences. The Lord accuses them of deliberately neglecting their assignment as his chosen leaders. They are paying no attention to the duties connected with the great work God has called them to perform for the good of themselves and the rest of humanity.

13. Therefore my people are gone into captivity, because they have no knowledge: and their honourable men

As a result of their neglect, a flood of desolating destruction will sweep over the people of the Lord. It turned out that Israel (the northern Ten Tribes) was

are famished, and their multitude dried up with thirst.

taken into captivity under the Assyrians around 721 B.C., and Judah was desolated and captured by the Babylonians in 587 B.C. Isaiah indicated earlier that he had seen all this in vision. It was terrible. Because the leaders of the people (their so-called honorable men) would not listen to the prophets, they would be left to their own ignorance, concocting plans for themselves based on the philosophies of men. They would be vessels without content, helplessly thrashing about in the midst of a national crisis. They would find themselves "famished" for lack of knowledge, and the people dying of thirst because they had never been given the living water of their Savior.

14. Therefore hell hath enlarged herself, and opened her mouth without measure: and their glory, and their multitude, and their pomp, and he that rejoiceth, shall descend into it.

What would be the result of this apostasy, arrogance, and wickedness? Quite simply, HELL WILL HAVE ENLARGED HERSELF by gaining such a great host of captives from among the ranks of those choice "soldiers of God" who had been foreordained to be the Lord's leaders. Isaiah saw that during their days of lecherous power, these "chosen people" would be lifted up in pride and be disdainful of God. Nevertheless, under Satan's destructive but victorious onslaught, they would go down with all their pride and pretense into the abyss of Lucifer's dominion.

This reminds us of the words of Rudyard Kipling:

> The tumult and the shouting dies,
> The captains and the kings depart;
> Still stands thine ancient sacrifice,
> An humble and a contrite heart,
> Lord God of Hosts, be with us yet,
> Lest we forget, lest we forget!
> Far-called, our navies melt away,
> On dune and headland sinks the fire;
> Lo, all our pomp of yesterday

Is one with Nineveh and Tyre!
Judge of the nations, spare us yet,
Lest we forget, lest we forget!
("God of Our Fathers, Known of Old,"
Hymns, no. 76.)

15. And the mean man shall be brought down, and the mighty man shall be humbled, and the eyes of the lofty shall be humbled:

Isaiah knew the coming devastation would cause the "mean man" (man of low estate) to be brought down. The mighty men of Israel would also be greatly humbled.

16. But the LORD of hosts shall be exalted in judgment, and God that is holy shall be sanctified in righteousness.

The Lord wanted to assure his obstinate and wicked children (who had been given a chosen calling in the premortal existence) that their apostasy and captivity would not deter him in his plan to promote righteousness across the face of the earth. Isaiah had seen the great day of the Lord's triumph when evil would be expelled from the hearts of men. Isaiah knew that eventually the Lord's work would be sanctified in righteousness.

17. Then shall the lambs feed after their manner, and the waste places of the fat ones shall strangers eat.

Isaiah saw that after the wicked had been led out of the Lord's choice vineyard and taken into captivity, the whole land would become a feeding ground for sheep and goats. He saw that the vineyards and estates of the wealthy (the fat ones) would become the residence of aliens and strangers.

18. Woe unto them that draw iniquity with cords of vanity, and sin as it were with a cart rope:

Isaiah pronounces a "woe" upon all who carry their iniquities around as though they were a treasure load which they pull after them by the cords of their own vanity. A woe is also pronounced upon those who drag sin behind them as though they were attached to it with a cart rope.

19. That say, Let him make speed, and hasten his work, that we may see it: and let the counsel of the Holy One of Israel draw nigh and come, that we may know it!

These are the kind of people who taunt the Lord to hasten his work so that their eyes might behold the fulfillment of his glorious promises. In spite of their wickedness, they demand revelations so that the counsel of the Holy One of Israel will be made known unto them.

20. Woe unto them that call evil good, and good evil; that put darkness for light, and light for darkness; that put bitter for sweet, and sweet for bitter!

Now a woe is pronounced on those who are so wicked that they see everything in its opposite dimension. They call evil good, and good evil. They put darkness for light, and light for darkness. They put bitter for sweet, and denounce sweet as bitter. Such was the degenerate state of humanity in the days of Noah, in the days of Sodom and Gomorrah, in the days of ancient Israel, and now in our own day. It seems almost incomprehensible that modern scholars would be rushing up and down the land, preaching that we must do away with moral principles and the code of "right" and "wrong." They claim that their approach will liberate the human spirit and bring peace to the world. Sound mental health is promised if we can just do away with all our concepts of good and evil.

Consider, for example, the words of the late Dr. G. Brock Chisholm, the first director general of the World Mental Health Organization. He charged that religion and morality are the principal causes of war, crime, and hate, saying:

"The only lowest common denominator of all civilizations and the only psychological force capable of producing these perversions [war, crime, hate, etc.] is MORALITY, the concept of right and wrong....

"For many generations we have bowed our necks to the yoke of the conviction of sin. We have swallowed all manner of poisonous certainties fed us by our parents, our Sunday and day school teachers, our politicians, our priests, our newspapers and others with a vested interest in controlling us....

"The re-interpretation and eventually eradication of the concept of right and wrong which has been the basis of child training, the substitution of intelligent and rational thinking for faith in the certainties of the old people, these are the belated objectives of practically all effective psychotherapy....

"The suggestion that we should stop teaching children moralities and rights and wrongs and instead protect their original intellectual integrity has of course to be met by an outcry of heretic or iconoclast.... We all recognize these reactions as those of the immature, the inferior, the guilty, which are not found in the mature, integrated personality. Freedom from moralities means freedom to observe, to think and behave sensibly, to the advantage of the person and the group, free from outmoded types of loyalties and from the magic fears of our ancestors....

"There is something to be said for taking charge of our own destiny, for gently putting aside the mistaken old ways of our elders if that is possible. If it cannot be done gently, it may have to be done roughly or even violently—that has happened before." ("The Reestablishment of Peacetime Society," *Psychiatry* 9, no. 1 [February 1946].)

A philosophy called secular humanism follows this same line of thinking. Secular humanism has gained a foothold in higher education, in the National Council of Churches, and in much of the media. Corliss Lamont, a secular humanist who has written much on the subject, defends the precepts set forth in the *Humanist Manifesto I* and the *Humanist Manifesto II*. The creed of secular humanism includes the following precepts:

1. There is no God.
2. There are no divine or fixed principles of morality.

3. Man has no divine destiny.
4. Man has no soul.
5. Man is an animal.
6. There is no life beyond this one.
7. There is no divine judgment after this life.

21. Woe unto them that are wise in their own eyes, and prudent in their own sight!

The Lord pronounces a woe on all those who are so arrogantly wise in their own eyes and so vainly prudent in their own sight.

22. Woe unto them that are mighty to drink wine, and men of strength to mingle strong drink:

The Lord also pronounces a woe on those who pride themselves in being great consumers of wine and boast of gorging themselves on strong drink.

23. Which justify the wicked for reward, and take away the righteousness of the righteous from him!

These same people aspire to high places in the courts, in certain churches, and in the media, where they can justify the wicked "for reward"! At the same time, they use their high offices to rob the righteous of their just dues.

24. Therefore as the fire devoureth the stubble, and the flame consumeth the chaff, so their root shall be as rottenness, and their blossom shall go up as dust: because they have cast away the law of the LORD of hosts, and despised the word of the Holy One of Israel.

This verse emphasizes the total futility of following any other course than that which a loving Heavenly Father has worked out for the earthly happiness and eternal welfare of his children. Those who take the route of "no morality," drunkenness, and depravity, and those who try to cheat, steal, defraud, and lie their way into high places, will end up as stubble and chaff— consumed by fire. Their end is like the root of a plant eaten up with rottenness, or like wilting blossoms that fade and crumble into dust. But this terrible fate would never have happened to these people if they had not cast away the law of the Lord and despised the word of the "Holy One of Israel," who is identified in the scriptures as Jesus Christ (see 2 Nephi 1:10).

25. Therefore is the anger of the LORD kindled against his people, and he hath stretched forth his hand against them, and hath smitten them: and the hills did tremble, and their carcases were torn in the midst of the streets. For all this his anger is not turned away, but his hand is stretched out still.

When men go braying off into the wilderness, defiantly sinning against knowledge, the Lord becomes angry. He therefore stretches forth his hand to hold back the Priesthood forces beyond the veil who are assigned to protect the children of the covenant. This leaves the Lord's apostate "chosen" people exposed to the onslaught of their enemies. Of course, this happens only when the wickedness of God's covenant people prevents a just and loving Heavenly Father from blessing them. That is why his protective mantle is removed on such occasions and the vengeance of satanical forces is able to sweep in with such violence that the very hills tremble. The carcasses of the proud and prosperous Israelites are torn and left lying in the streets. Yet this is not the only affliction Israel must endure. Isaiah saw that the suffering of Israel would continue for centuries before the Lord's anger would be turned away. Then he would commence his "marvelous work and a wonder" in the latter days.

26. And he will lift up an ensign to the nations from far, and will hiss unto them from the end of the earth: and, behold, they shall come with speed swiftly:

All through the prophetic warnings of Isaiah, the Lord sprinkles in passages of hope which refer to the day when the Lord will finally raise up an ensign which will send forth a signal to the Israelites in distant nations that they should begin gathering home. We read in this verse that the Lord will "hiss" or signal unto Israel from the ends of the earth so that they can gather quickly, before it is too late. This probably has reference to the great last gathering of the Saints just before the Second Coming. It will be recalled that the initial gathering of the Saints began very slowly, with great suffering and much stumbling. Those who gathered in the beginning established themselves at the center stakes. They then sent forth missionaries to establish stakes all over the world. Only at the last moment will the Lord "hiss," or signal the Saints, saying, "Gather to the center stakes of Zion!" (See D&C 88:84-85.)

27. None shall be weary nor stumble among them; none shall slumber nor sleep; neither shall the girdle of their loins be loosed, nor the latchet of their shoes be broken:

This verse makes it sound as though the great last gathering will be by jet travel! People will reach Zion without having to "slumber" or even undress along the way. They will come with such facility that not even the latchets of their shoes will be broken or become unfastened.

28. Whose arrows are sharp, and all their bows bent, their horses' hoofs shall be counted like flint, and their wheels like a whirlwind:

They will also come in massive strength. No nation will be able to frustrate the gathering hosts of Israel in the latter days. The ancient prophets were shown some of the modern modes of travel as well as many types of modern weapons. However, they found it impossible to adequately describe them. They had to refer to symbols with which the people in their own day were familiar. This is why Isaiah tried to portray these scenes which passed before his eyes with words that would be meaningful to his own people. If you were Isaiah, and you saw a vision of people pointing long instruments that struck down enemies with deadly accuracy, would it not be appropriate to say their "arrows were sharp"? And would not this vision of modern weapons suggest that they were using powerfully bent bows which launched their missiles with unbelievable rapidity and accuracy? And what about the modern vehicles of war which men ride upon? Do they not seem to go charging along with sparks and smoke trailing behind them like horses with hooves of flint? Of course, Isaiah makes it clear that these men of the latter days were not literally riding on horses, but in vehicles with wheels spinning like a whirlwind.

29. Their roaring shall be like a lion, they shall roar like young lions: yea, they shall roar, and lay hold of the prey, and shall carry it away safe, and none shall deliver it.

Isaiah says the thundering noise they made was like the roaring of lions, and that it was impossible to resist them. They carried away captives without serious hindrance, and no one could liberate them. Such will be the irresistible power of Israel when they return. It is believed this particular prophecy will be fulfilled when the lost Ten Tribes return from the north. They will be opposed by the Gentile nations and will have to come down with "sparks" and "smoke" and "wheels like the whirlwind." In a modern revelation the Lord says: "And they who are in the north countries shall come in remembrance before the Lord; and their prophets shall hear his voice [hissing a warning to gather], and shall no longer stay themselves; and they shall smite the rocks, and the ice shall flow down at their presence. And an highway shall be cast up in the midst of the great deep. THEIR ENEMIES SHALL BECOME A PREY UNTO THEM." (D&C 133:26–28; emphasis added.)

30. And in that day they shall roar against them like the roaring of the sea: and if one look unto the land, behold darkness and sorrow, and the light is darkened in the heavens thereof.

The whole land will be a vista of darkness and sorrow for those who fight against the Lord. Even the heavens will be darkened against them.

Isaiah, Chapter 6

INTRODUCTION:

Isaiah is now going to tell us how he happened to receive his calling as a prophet. It is interesting that Jeremiah tells about his prophetic calling in the very first chapter of his writings, whereas Isaiah works it into his sixth chapter. He may very well have borne verbal witness to this sacred experience when he felt it was appropriate, but he seems to have refrained from recording the details of this great vision until he was well into his mission. A modern prophet, Joseph Smith, did the same thing. He told his family and close friends who were early converts to the Church about the First Vision (which occurred in 1820) and the revelations which followed it; however, he did not record the full and relevant details of these sacred experiences until he began to prepare the text for the history of the Church. (See Milton V. Backman, Jr., *Joseph Smith's First Vision: Confirming Evidences and Contemporary Accounts*, 2d ed., rev. and enl. [Salt Lake City: Bookcraft, 1980], chapter 5.)

1. In the year that king Uzziah died I saw also the Lord sitting upon a throne, high and lifted up, and his train filled the temple.

Isaiah fixes the date of his calling as having occurred in the year that Uzziah, king of Judah, died. This was around 739 B.C. Uzziah, who became king when he was only 16 years old, was a fairly righteous ruler. He governed Judah for 52 years (see 2 Kings 15:2). During his reign, the kingdom of Judah prospered to a greater extent than at any time since the reign of King Solomon. However, at the height of his career, Uzziah longed to go before the Lord and participate in the

offering of incense as the priests did. When he undertook to do so, he met with resistance from the high
priest and 80 of his Levitical associates on the grounds
that Uzziah did not have the Priesthood authority to
serve at the altar of incense. Uzziah ignored their pro-
testations, and went right ahead with his incense offering. In the middle of the ceremony, the Lord suddenly
struck Uzziah with leprosy. Only then did Uzziah realize what a wicked thing he had done. He remained
under quarantine for the rest of his life. Jotham, his
young son, had to be the regent until his father passed
away around 739 B.C. (see 2 Chronicles 26:16-23).
Except for this incident, King Uzziah is referred to by
the Lord as a righteous king (see 2 Chronicles 27:2).

So it was in the year that Uzziah died—around 739
B.C.—that Isaiah had the great vision in which he was
called to be a prophet. Isaiah says that in this glorious
vision he saw the Lord (in this case Jehovah, rather
than the Father) surrounded by a tremendous "train"
of followers.

2. Above it stood the sera-
phims: each one had six
wings; with twain he cov-
ered his face, and with
twain he covered his feet,
and with twain he did fly.

Ordinarily we think of God as being worshipped and
attended by only the righteous Saints. However, Isaiah
saw that the worshippers included a host of seraphim.
This word is a collective noun and refers to "the fiery
or glorified ones." Ezekiel called them "living creatures," representing man, the lion, the ox, and the
eagle. All were glorified, radiant beings, praising the
Lord and ministering to him (see Ezekiel 10:8-22). John
the Revelator saw what appears to be the same vision
as Isaiah and Ezekiel (see Revelation 4:2-11). He
describes the same four creatures mentioned by
Ezekiel—a man, a lion, an eagle, and a calf (Ezekiel 1:10
says "ox"). The Prophet Joseph Smith inquired of the
Lord concerning the meaning of these four creatures,
and he learned that they signified the various estates

which different types of creatures enjoy in the "paradise of God." They were to show the "happiness of man, and of beasts, and of creeping things, and of the fowls of the air" (D&C 77:2).

All of these living things enjoy the glory and felicity which have been prepared for them in their resurrected and exalted estate. Collectively, these glorified creatures who surround the throne of God are called "seraphim" or "cherubim." In other words, the Lord surrounds himself with glorified creatures of every kind which he has made. Ezekiel calls them by the name of "cherubim" (Ezekiel, chapter 10), while Isaiah calls them "seraphim." We note that not only man, but all of the "living creatures" are described as having wings and eyes that see both before and behind (see Revelation 4:6–8). Joseph Smith asked the meaning of these wings and eyes and was told that they were symbolic of the powers of exalted beings of all kinds: "Their eyes are a representation of light and knowledge; and their wings are a representation of power, to move, to act, etc." (D&C 77:4).

3. And one cried unto another, and said, Holy, holy, holy, is the LORD of hosts: the whole earth is full of his glory.

Note that all forms of animal life in their exalted state are able to articulate their praises to the Lord (see Revelation 4:8).

The glory of God which emanates from his throne and fills the earth is difficult for the prophets to describe. The vision of the Lord's throne always seems to be projected at a time when there is a heavenly conference, with hundreds of millions of the Lord's seraphic hosts surrounding him in rejoicing and worship. A huge halo of multicolored light encircles the throne of God, which John calls a "rainbow" that is "like unto an emerald" (Revelation 4:3). There are also great manifestations of light and sound, which various prophets have described as thunder, lightning, great voices, and the rushing of mighty waters.

4. And the posts of the door moved at the voice of him that cried, and the house was filled with smoke.

In Isaiah's vision, the sound of those who sang out their praises was so great that the mighty pillars at the entrance of the temple vibrated and moved. Isaiah also noted that the temple was filled with "smoke." Throughout Old Testament history the Lord comes in a "cloud of darkness," then shows himself in brilliant glory. This occurred frequently when Moses was leading the Israelites out of Egypt (see, for example, Exodus 19:18; 40:34). In fact, Isaiah seems to have seen in vision the same spectacular phenomenon that Solomon and the children of Israel experienced in the bright light of day at the time the temple of Solomon was dedicated (see 2 Chronicles 5:13–14). A cloud of darkness filled the temple, and then it became a radiant medium of glory as the Lord appeared (see 1 Kings 8:10–12). No doubt the "smoke" Isaiah saw filling the temple is the "cloud" referred to by the other prophets.

5. Then said I, Woe is me! for I am undone; because I am a man of unclean lips, and I dwell in the midst of a people of unclean lips: for mine eyes have seen the King, the LORD of hosts.

At this point, Isaiah suddenly decided he had seen enough. He thought that his unworthiness made it extremely dangerous for him to be in this holy place and in the presence of the Lord. The King James Version says that Isaiah felt he was "undone," but the original Hebrew word means "cut off," or destroyed. Isaiah was truly frightened. He considered himself far from worthy to be in the presence of the Lord God Jehovah. He described himself as being a person of "unclean lips." Everyone, in a moment of reckless indifference, is likely to utter things which are later regretted. Isaiah apparently felt there were occasions when he had done this. In fact, he dwelt in the midst of a whole people who were guilty of indiscretion and "unclean lips."

6. Then flew one of the seraphims unto me, having a

It seems as though the seraphim was able to read Isaiah's mind and sense the terror that had seized him.

live coal in his hand, which he had taken with the tongs from off the altar:

One of them "flew," or moved through the air, toward him. This seraphim seems to have been a glorified human being, for he picked up a hot coal from the altar of incense (the only altar inside the temple) and brought it in his "hand" to Isaiah.

7. And he laid it upon my mouth, and said, Lo, this hath touched thy lips; and thine iniquity is taken away, and thy sin purged.

To Isaiah's further dismay, the seraphim placed the "live" coal directly on his mouth. Isaiah no doubt expected to be terribly seared and struck with burning pain, but he was not. The "live" coal neither burned him nor hurt him. The seraphim pronounced Isaiah sacramentally clean and said that his sins, whatever they were, had been "purged," or blotted out. He was now clean before the Lord.

8. Also I heard the voice of the Lord, saying, Whom shall I send, and who will go for us? Then said I, Here am I; send me.

Isaiah had barely completed this frightening experience when he heard the Lord speaking to the whole multitude. The Lord invited this huge conference to nominate someone to go forth as a representative of the heavenly Priesthood to proclaim a special message to the people. Isaiah was so excited by everything that had happened that he did not even wait to be nominated. Almost impetuously he cried out, "Here am I; send me!" It is this quality of enthusiastic spirit which the Lord loves, for it is typical of a valiant son of God.

9. And he said, Go, and tell this people, Hear ye indeed, but understand not; and see ye indeed, but perceive not.

This passage is very confusing in the Old Testament text, but it becomes clearer in the Book of Mormon version taken from the brass plates. From this source we learn that Isaiah originally wrote this passage as follows: "And he said: Go and tell this people—Hear ye indeed, but they understood not; and see ye indeed, but they perceived not" (2 Nephi 16:9). This version clearly indicates that the people would hear what Isaiah had to say in his message from the Lord, but they would refuse to embrace it or even try to understand it. They would also see what was happening all around them as Isaiah warned against the evils of their day, but they would not catch the significance of these onrushing events and therefore would fail to "perceive" the terrible consequences of their profligate ways. This is precisely what is happening today.

10. Make the heart of this people fat, and make their ears heavy, and shut their eyes; lest they see with their eyes, and hear with their ears, and understand with their heart, and convert, and be healed.

This passage is given in the Book of Mormon almost exactly as it appears here, so it is presumably correct. Nevertheless, it could be misunderstood if we interpret it to mean that the Lord is going to make the hearts of the people "fat" so they won't be converted and allow the Lord to heal them. Paul quoted this passage as he understood it in the following words: "For the heart of this people is waxed gross, and their ears are dull of hearing, and their eyes have they closed; lest they should see with their eyes, and hear with their ears, and understand with their heart, and should be converted, and I should heal them" (Acts 28:27). In other words, the people do not want to be converted. They revel in their wickedness and don't want to understand or perceive what the Lord is trying to tell them. When Christ was on the earth, he declared that it was because of the wickedness and anxiety of the people not to be converted that he spoke to them in parables. Pouring sacred Gospel truths upon a wicked and unrepentant people would be "casting pearls," and merely add to their condemnation. Therefore, Jesus said, "For this people's heart is waxed gross, and their ears are dull of hearing, and their eyes they have closed; lest at any time they should see with their eyes, and hear with their ears, and should understand with their heart, and should be converted, and I should heal them" (Matthew 13:15).

Just before Jesus quoted this passage, his disciples had asked him: "Why speakest thou unto them [the wicked unbelievers] in parables? He answered and said unto them, Because it is given unto you to know the mysteries of the kingdom of heaven, but to them it is not given.... Therefore speak I to them in parables." (Matthew 13:10–11, 13.) So this is the key to this passage. The wicked will receive a call to repent and be taught with parables. But unless they do repent, the mysteries of the kingdom of heaven will be kept from them.

11. Then said I, Lord, how long? And he answered, Until the cities be wasted without inhabitant, and the houses without man, and the land be utterly desolate,

The wording of this verse would suggest that Isaiah had been shown a panoramic vision of the calamities that were about to fall on the people. It would further imply that he had been shown the terrible destruction of Jerusalem which would occur in 587 B.C. And perhaps he also saw the capture of the northern Ten Tribes by Assyria which was to occur approximately 18 years after Isaiah received his calling. Whatever he saw, it caused him to plead with the Lord and ask him "how long" this terrible affliction was to be endured by the people before God could bless them again. Notice that the desolation of the land was to be complete. The cities were to be depopulated. In fact, when this prophecy was fulfilled there were only a few shepherds left to tend their scanty flocks. The cities were truly wasted and "without inhabitant."

12. And the LORD have removed men far away, and there be a great forsaking in the midst of the land.

The Lord also wanted Isaiah to know that the people were not going to remain in the vicinity of their inheritance. They were going to be dragged "far away," and their land would be abandoned or forsaken without anyone to claim or own it.

13. But yet in it shall be a tenth, and it shall return, and shall be eaten: as a teil tree, and as an oak, whose substance is in them, when they cast their leaves: so the holy seed shall be the substance thereof.

Here again we have a better version of this verse in the Book of Mormon. It reads, "But yet THERE shall be a tenth, and THEY shall return, and shall be eaten, as a teil-tree, and as an oak whose substance is in them when they cast their leaves; so the holy seed shall be the substance thereof" (2 Nephi 16:13; emphasis added).

We assume that this verse has special reference to the Jews, since only a tenth of those who were taken captive were allowed to return. Those who did return could be likened to a teil tree which had been defoliated by goats and sheep browsing upon it. It is interesting that a teil tree is an evergreen that sprouts up new shoots even from an old stump which has been cut down. The Lord also compares the returning remnant to an oak which has cast its leaves yet still has the strength within it to survive. That strength is the "holy seed" which will yet restore life to God's chosen people.

As a final note, we might mention that another reason we think the present verse is referring only to the Jews is because the lost Ten Tribes will not return as a "tenth," but as a great host which will have greatly multiplied (see Isaiah 54:1-3).

INTRODUCTION:

Now we come to the famous "virgin birth" chapter of Isaiah which is quoted so often at Christmas time. It should be noted, however, that the events related in this chapter occurred a considerable number of years after Isaiah's calling described in the last chapter. Here, then, is the historical setting for chapter 7:

Isaiah's calling occurred in the year that the great King Uzziah died of leprosy—around 739 B.C. Uzziah's son, Jotham, was a righteous king who ruled over the Jews until around 734 B.C. But when Jotham died, his unrighteous son Ahaz ascended the throne. Ahaz ruled from 734 to 727 B.C. This king apostatized completely. He eventually embraced the heathen cult of the Canaanites and "burnt his children in the fire, after the abominations of the heathen" (2 Chronicles 28:3). But before he had degenerated that far, the events in this chapter took place.

It seems that an international crisis had occurred when the terrible Assyrian hosts began moving out from Nineveh to place all the nations of the west under their tribute. To avoid a massacre and the cruel blood-bath for which the Assyrians were famous, some nations volunteered to pay tribute without being conquered. This included the king of Israel (the northern Ten Tribes), who was named Menahem. After he died his son was going to continue to pay tribute, but he was assassinated by Pekah, the captain of the guard. Pekah then became king of Israel. Pekah refused to pay tribute to the Assyrians. In fact, he wrote a letter to

King Ahaz of Judah and to King Rezin of Syria, who lived in Damascus, urging that they join a federation to fight the Assyrians. Rezin agreed, but Ahaz of Judah would not. Ahaz said he would rather pay tribute. So Pekah, the king of Israel, and Rezin, the king of Syria, decided to attack Judah and force Ahaz to join their alliance. It was under the gloom of this pending assault that the events in this chapter occurred.

1. And it came to pass in the days of Ahaz the son of Jotham, the son of Uzziah, king of Judah, that Rezin the king of Syria, and Pekah the son of Remaliah, king of Israel, went up toward Jerusalem to war against it, but could not prevail against it.

From this verse we learn that there had already been a preliminary attack against Jerusalem by the Israelite-Syrian forces under King Pekah and King Rezin.

2. And it was told the house of David, saying, Syria is confederate with Ephraim. And his heart was moved, and the heart of his people, as the trees of the wood are moved with the wind.

It is apparent that when the Jews learned they were about to be attacked again, they knew that this time they would be facing the combined forces of both Israel and Syria. This caused the people to tremble in fear. Isaiah says the hearts of the people of Judah were like trees "moved with the wind."

3. Then said the LORD unto Isaiah, Go forth now to meet Ahaz, thou, and Shear-jashub thy son, at the end of the conduit of the upper pool in the highway of the fuller's field;

At this point, Isaiah receives his errand from the Lord. He is instructed to take his son with him and wait for King Ahaz, who often came to the conduit of the upper pool located along the highway leading to the fuller's field. We think this son was born to Isaiah shortly after the prophet received his calling. The name Shear-jashub means "the remnant shall return," and this was the promise that the Lord had made to Isaiah at the time of his calling (see Isaiah 6:13).

The conduit or tunnel that carried water from the city's only water source, called Gihon Spring, still exists and is located just outside of what used to be the city wall. This made the city very vulnerable in time of siege. The king might have come to this upper pool of Gihon Spring to consider the means by which the city could be defended. But with his heart filled with apostasy and his mind muddled with anxiety over the imminent attack of a huge army from the north, Ahaz would certainly not be in a mood to feel sympathetic to what Isaiah was about to tell him.

4. And say unto him, Take heed, and be quiet; fear not, neither be fainthearted for the two tails of these smoking firebrands, for the fierce anger of Rezin with Syria, and of the son of Remaliah.

The message that the Lord wanted Isaiah to deliver must have sounded like pure insanity to the king. Isaiah was to tell King Ahaz that the Lord wanted him not to arm, but to "be quiet." He was told to be neither afraid nor fainthearted toward the enemy from the north. In essence, Isaiah was telling Ahaz to abandon his plans to arm the Jews and prepare a defense. Isaiah was also instructed to assure Ahaz that he had nothing to fear from these two kings from the north. The Lord compared their threat to the "tails of...smoking firebrands." A firebrand is a burning piece of wood, or a torch. When it has served its purpose and burned out, it becomes nothing but a "smoking firebrand" with little trails of smoke rising from its spent ashes. The Lord knew that both Ephraim (or the Ten Tribes under Ephraim) and Syria were soon to be conquered by the Assyrians, and that if Judah would simply "be quiet" and not provoke these northern enemies, their threatened attack on Judah would be aborted because they themselves would be under attack from Assyria.

5. Because Syria, Ephraim, and the son of Remaliah,

Isaiah was also instructed to tell King Ahaz that the Lord was well aware how Syria and the northern Ten

have taken evil counsel
against thee, saying,

Tribes had conspired together to attack Judah. He recognized and appreciated the anxiety of King Ahaz.
Nevertheless, the king was urged to refrain from
arming.

6. Let us go up against Judah,
and vex it, and let us make
a breach therein for us, and
set a king in the midst of it,
even the son of Tabeal:

The Lord even disclosed the plans of the enemy. He
said they intended to "make a breach" in Judah's
defenses and put a man of their own choosing on the
throne. This would be a "son of Tabeal." Tabeal is
described as "a man whose son went with the armies of
Pekah, the king of Israel, and Rezin of Damascus, when
they invaded Judah in the time of Ahaz" (Francis
Nathan Peloubet, *Peloubet's Bible Dictionary* [Philadelphia:
The John C. Winston Company, 1925], p. 659). The
idea was to set up the son of Tabeal as a puppet king if
Judah was conquered.

7. Thus saith the Lord GOD,
It shall not stand, neither
shall it come to pass.

Isaiah was authorized by the Lord to tell King Ahaz
that he could be assured that the plans of these kings
would not come to pass if they were not provoked. This
promise came directly from the Lord, therefore Ahaz
could depend upon it.

8. For the head of Syria is
Damascus, and the head of
Damascus is Rezin; and
within threescore and five
years shall Ephraim be
broken, that it be not a
people.

Isaiah was also instructed to tell Ahaz that King
Rezin of Syria would not have the northern Ten Tribes
as a partner much longer, because within 15 years the
people of Ephraim (the Ten Tribes under Ephraim)
would no longer be a nation. As it turned out, the Ten
Tribes were virtually wiped out in 721 B.C. by Assyria.
In 669 B.C. King Esarhaddon of Assyria returned again
and not only mopped up whatever Israelites were left,
but brought in heathen immigrants to intermarry with
them. As a result, these people were no longer referred
to as Israelites, but as Samaritans. The Jews despised
these Samaritans and considered them half-breeds
(half Israelite and half pagan foreigners or Gentiles).

9. And the head of Ephraim is Samaria, and the head of Samaria is Remaliah's son. If ye will not believe, surely ye shall not be established.

Isaiah was then instructed to warn Ahaz that if he did not believe this warning and heed the Lord's advice, then he himself would not be "established."

10. Moreover the LORD spake again unto Ahaz, saying,

11. Ask thee a sign of the LORD thy God; ask it either in the depth, or in the height above.

To further assure Ahaz that this message came directly from the Lord, Isaiah was authorized to invite Ahaz to call for a sign that would demonstrate to his apostate and unbelieving mind that this message was from God. Ordinarily signs are not given to the wicked, but only to the righteous (see D&C 63:9). However, in this case the Lord knew that unless Ahaz listened to this warning, the kings of Israel and Syria would be immediately provoked into attacking Judah, and many of the righteous as well as the wicked would be lost. For the sake of the Lord's people, Ahaz was invited to ask for a sign. It is rather amazing how far the Lord was willing to go with Ahaz. He was invited to ask for a sign "in the depth, or in the height above." The Revised Standard Version of the Bible puts it even more clearly by stating that Ahaz could call for a sign "deep as Sheol [the spirit world] or high as heaven."

12. But Ahaz said, I will not ask, neither will I tempt the LORD.

Of course, Ahaz considered himself a practical politician who did not need or intend to take the advice of a spiritual adviser like Isaiah. He not only did not believe in the Priesthood or the prophets of Jehovah, but he was not about to test Isaiah's credentials by having some miraculous sign manifested that might dissuade him from his firm resolve to arm the nation. To excuse himself from accepting the Lord's challenge and asking for a sign, Ahaz (apparently remembering what is written in Deuteronomy 6:16) said, "I will not ask, neither will I tempt the Lord." This was like saying, "I am not going to ask for a sign; for did not the Lord himself declare that we should not tempt God by asking for signs?"

13. And he said, Hear ye now, O house of David; Is it a small thing for you to weary men, but will ye weary my God also?

Isaiah was disgusted. King Ahaz was of the house of David, which had the assignment of providing the nation with righteous leadership. Isaiah therefore addressed the king as "house of David," and accused him not only of making the people weary with his presumptuous impositions, but of making God weary as well.

14. Therefore the Lord himself shall give you a sign; Behold, a virgin shall conceive, and bear a son, and shall call his name Immanuel.

Whether Ahaz liked it or not, Isaiah proceeded to give him a sign from the Lord. He told Ahaz about a marvelous miracle that would be a sign unto the entire house of David. Isaiah declared that a "virgin" would conceive without ever having known a man, and that she would bear a son whose name would be called "Immanuel," meaning "God is with us" (James Hastings, ed., *Dictionary of the Bible*, rev. ed. [New York: Charles Scribner's Sons, 1963], s.v. "Immanuel").

Many modern theologians have protested the use of the word "virgin" and have tried to replace it with a phrase such as "a young woman of marriageable age" (see Hastings, *Dictionary of the Bible*, rev. ed., s.v. "Immanuel" and "Virgin"). They will not accept the miracle of a virgin conceiving and bearing a son. They would rather believe that Mary was simply a young woman who conceived a child out of wedlock. They even suggest that the miracle of the virgin birth was invented to cover up her shame. But we need only to stop and think for a moment how ridiculous this would have sounded to King Ahaz. What kind of "sign" would it have been if Isaiah had said, "Behold, a young woman of marriageable age shall conceive and bring forth a son." What kind of a miracle would that have been? The brass plates, as transcribed in the Book of Mormon, use the word "virgin," and so does the Septuagint version, which is the oldest Greek translation of the Old Testament. The Book of Mormon refers to the mother of the Savior as a virgin six different times (see 1 Nephi 11:13, 15, 18, 20; 2 Nephi 17:14; Alma 7:10).

15. Butter and honey shall he eat, that he may know to refuse the evil, and choose the good.

Isaiah said this sacred child, Immanuel, would eat the butter or "curd" as well as the honey and other common fare of men in the flesh, that he might know how to refuse that which is evil and choose that which is good. The "butter" and "honey" are simply Hebrew symbols of the common lot and frailties of all mankind in the flesh. It is like saying that we must all eat the bread of mortality in order to learn the difference between good and evil. It is interesting that Jesus was the only mortal man who ever lived through this life and was able to learn the difference between good and evil without committing any sin (see D&C 45:4).

16. For before the child shall know to refuse the evil, and choose the good, the land that thou abhorrest shall be forsaken of both her kings.

Isaiah knew that King Ahaz was one of those apostate minds among God's chosen people who would hear without understanding and see without actually perceiving. Isaiah therefore told Ahaz a solid truth, even though he knew the wicked ruler would have no comprehension of what he was talking about. Isaiah said that before this wonderful Immanuel had matured sufficiently to know good from evil, the land to the north which Ahaz feared so greatly would be forsaken by both the rulers of Israel and the rulers of Syria.

17. The LORD shall bring upon thee, and upon thy people,

The Lord had a prophecy of woe for Judah which would be fulfilled long before the coming of Immanuel.

and upon thy father's house, days that have not come, from the day that Ephraim departed from Judah; even the king of Assyria.

Isaiah says that there would be an attack on Judah which would be worse than anything that had happened to the house of David since the northern Ten Tribes separated from Judah and Levi around 922 B.C. Isaiah was referring to the total desolation which would come to this whole territory in 701 B.C. when Sennacherib, the king of Assyria, would sweep down and spread blood and terror throughout the land. Certain sections of Judah would never be rebuilt again.

18. And it shall come to pass in that day, that the LORD shall hiss for the fly that is in the uttermost part of the rivers of Egypt, and for the bee that is in the land of Assyria.

Isaiah likened the armies of Egypt, which would be involved in this conflict, to the stinging fly from that land. Anyone who has been to Egypt cannot help but appreciate the accuracy of this metaphor. The hosts of Assyria who would be bent on conquering Egypt are likened unto the bee of Assyria, which must have been somewhat like the modern "killer" bee.

19. And they shall come, and shall rest all of them in the desolate valleys, and in the holes of the rocks, and upon all thorns, and upon all bushes.

Isaiah said the invading hosts of these enemies would infest the land like a plague. They would occupy the desolate valleys, the holes in the rocks, the briars and the bushes. There would be no place where the people could flee or hide.

20. In the same day shall the Lord shave with a razor that is hired, namely, by them beyond the river, by the king of Assyria, the head, and the hair of the feet: and it shall also consume the beard.

After Ahaz turned down Isaiah's advice, he went straight to the temple, stripped it of all its precious ornaments, and sent them to the king of Assyria as a bribe to induce him to immediately attack Syria and the northern Ten Tribes before they attacked Judah. In this verse Isaiah is assuring Ahaz that although the Assyrians were like a "razor that is hired" (hired by Ahaz, in fact!), they would nevertheless turn around and shave Judah.

21. And it shall come to pass in that day, that a man shall nourish a young cow, and two sheep;

The Lord said the land would be so completely stripped of its population and resources that any man who was left would be fortunate to have a cow and two sheep.

22. And it shall come to pass, for the abundance of milk that they shall give he shall eat butter: for butter and honey shall every one eat that is left in the land.

People would be reduced to the most meager fare. Instead of enjoying an abundance of milk, they would have to thrive on butter (better rendered as "curds") and honey. This is all that would be available for those who would be "left in the land."

23. And it shall come to pass in that day, that every place shall be, where there were a thousand vines at a thousand silverlings, it shall even be for briers and thorns.

Isaiah said that this rich area of luxurious vineyards and gardens would be desolated. Where once there were thousands of vines worth thousands of "silverlings" (Persian silver coins), there would be nothing but briars and thorns.

24. With arrows and with bows shall men come thither; because all the land shall become briers and thorns.

This whole territory would be used by hunters, who would come among the briars and bushes with bows and arrows to seek game.

25. And on all hills that shall be digged with the mattock, there shall not come thither the fear of briers and thorns: but it shall be for the sending forth of oxen, and for the treading of lesser cattle.

The luxurious, terraced hills, which were so carefully cultivated and weeded to keep out thorns and briars, would no longer be used for the vine or the tree. These hills would all be occupied by oxen, sheep, and goats.

INTRODUCTION:

In the previous chapter, Isaiah had given the wicked King Ahaz a "sign" by saying that a virgin would conceive and bring forth a son. Of course, this was to be fulfilled far in the future. No doubt Isaiah had hoped that King Ahaz would accept the Lord's invitation and ask for some marvelous sign which would be persuasive to both the king and the people, but Ahaz had refused. So, in desperation, Isaiah had decided to relate to Ahaz one of the greatest signs God would ever give to the human family. That would be the conception and bringing forth of a son by a "virgin." This went right over the head of Ahaz. Nevertheless, it gave Isaiah an opportunity to get the prophecy recorded. It also gave him a second opportunity to stress the prophetic promise of the Lord that Judah's two terrible enemies—Syria and the northern Ten Tribes—would soon be conquered by the Assyrians.

To further emphasize this second prophecy concerning the fall of Syria and the northern Ten Tribes, the Lord gave Isaiah a sign which would be fulfilled in the IMMEDIATE future and which would leave King Ahaz without any excuse.

1. Moreover the LORD said unto me, Take thee a great roll, and write in it with a man's pen concerning Maher-shalal-hash-baz.

It would appear that shortly after Isaiah returned from conversing with King Ahaz, the Lord told the prophet to procure a great "roll" and write on it concerning another son who would be born to Isaiah. The "great roll" may very well have been a huge parchment (rolled on a stick), upon which Isaiah was recording all of the revelations he received from the Lord. There would have been no reason for the Lord to have instructed Isaiah to inscribe this rather short revelation on a great roll or book unless it were part of many other writings. Notice that the Lord did not want this prophecy recorded on a slate with a stencil, which would be temporary and easily destroyed. He wanted it officially recorded in the great scroll of official scripture, written with permanent ink and inscribed by a pen. It is interesting that Isaiah already had a son with a prophetic name—Shear-jashub (meaning "the remnant shall return"). But here the Lord promised Isaiah a second son, whose name will mean "to speed to the spoil, he hasteneth the prey."

2. And I took unto me faithful witnesses to record, Uriah the priest, and Zechariah the son of Jeberechiah.

It was the custom of false prophets in that day to wait until some great event had occurred, and then claim that they had prophesied it some time earlier. They would bring forth a document to prove the prophecy had been recorded, but the matter would have actually been written down AFTER the event occurred. Many of the people were aware of these tricks used by false prophets, so Isaiah did not want the people to have any excuse for rejecting his prophecy by claiming it was written down after his son was born. He therefore selected two "faithful witnesses" whom the people would accept for their integrity and reliability. Notice that one was Uriah the priest. The other was Zechariah, who was undoubtedly a prominent person of equal dignity and acceptability.

3. And I went unto the prophetess; and she conceived, and bare a son. Then said the LORD to me, Call his

The wife of Isaiah was a very spiritual and wonderful woman who was known among the people as a "prophetess." Isaiah wanted it understood that he had

Isaiah, Chapter 8   211

name Maher-shalal-hash-baz.

recorded the Lord's promise concerning the conception and birth of this new son even before they had united together in their connubial relationship. Notice that when the son was born, the Lord repeated his instruction that the child should be given a name directly related to the historical events which were about to take place. The name "Maher-shalal-hash-baz" referred to the fact that the Lord was going to hasten the time when Syria and the northern Ten Tribes would be despoiled and their lands conquered.

4. For before the child shall have knowledge to cry, My father, and my mother, the riches of Damascus and the spoil of Samaria shall be taken away before the king of Assyria.

Here the prophet spells out precisely what is about to happen. Before his new son will be able to say "my father and my mother," the riches of Damascus (the capital of Syria) and the spoils of Samaria (the capital of the northern Ten Tribes) will be captured and taken away by the king of Assyria. This prophecy contains some rather terrible implications. The Assyrians were famous for the merciless ferocity which always accompanied their conquests. Their military policy was to terrorize the people by torturing their leaders in public exhibitions. Sometimes these leaders would be dismembered, or skinned alive, or slowly burned, or subjected to the so-called living death, which consisted of cutting off successive portions of the body over a long period of time. This is what Isaiah is predicting will happen to the wicked people of Syria and Ephraim (the northern Ten Tribes).

5. The LORD spake also unto me again, saying,

6. Forasmuch as this people refuseth the waters of Shiloah that go softly, and rejoice in Rezin and Remaliah's son;

In these verses, and in verse 7, the Lord compares the coming events to two famous streams of water with which the people were familiar. The first was the soft flowing stream of Shiloah, or Siloah, which came from Gihon Spring, the only perennial spring in Jerusalem. It flowed from beneath the lower suburb of Jerusalem called the city of David. These precious waters passed along a conduit to the king's garden, where they emptied into a pool at the foot of the stairway used by the people to obtain their water each day (see Nehemiah 3:15; John 9:6-7). The Lord says the people of Israel had rejected the waters of Shiloah "that go softly," probably referring to the quiet, long-suffering persuasion of the Lord. Instead of listening to the Lord, they had rejoiced in the king of Damascus and the apostate king of the northern Ten Tribes.

7. Now therefore, behold, the Lord bringeth up upon them the waters of the river, strong and many, even the king of Assyria, and all his glory: and he shall come up over all his channels, and go over all his banks:

In this verse the Lord speaks of a second famous river to illustrate the immediate events of history. This time he refers to "the waters of the river, strong and many." This river is the mighty Euphrates (see Jeremiah 46:6-7) over which the Assyrian hosts will come like a tidal wave of ferocious destruction that cannot be channeled away or headed off but will overflow in all directions.

8. And he shall pass through Judah; he shall overflow and go over, he shall reach even to the neck; and the stretching out of his wings shall fill the breadth of thy land, O Immanuel.

Not only will Syria and the northern Ten Tribes be drowned in the Assyrian bloodbath, but Judah also will be penetrated by the hosts of Assyria. In fact, the Assyrians will overflow the land and pass through it to the land beyond. It is interesting that this prophecy does not say that Judah will be drowned in the flood of Assyrian fury, but it says she will be submerged "to the neck." The flanks of regiments, or "wings," of the Assyrian hosts will encompass the entire land where Immanuel is to be born. The word "Immanuel" means "God is with us" (Hastings, *Dictionary of the Bible*, rev. ed., s.v. "Immanuel"). Notice that in speaking of Judah, Isaiah calls it "thy land, O Immanuel."

The literal fulfillment of the prophecies in these verses began with the Assyrian conquest of the Syrians and the northern Ten Tribes around 721 B.C. This occurred under Shalmaneser V and his son, Sargon II. At that time the Assyrians did not invade Judah, and no doubt many of the people of Jerusalem rejoiced to see that at least one of Isaiah's prophecies would not be fulfilled. But their rejoicing was premature. A few years after Sargon II obliterated the Ephraimite capital of Samaria and carried the remnants of the northern Ten Tribes to Assyria, Sargon's son, Sennacherib, came crashing down on Judah like a hungry desert lion. He desolated many of the foremost cities of Judah so completely that many of them were never entirely rebuilt. Today the ruins of Lachish and Lehi still bear mute testimony to the terrible siege of 701 B.C. which left them in a pile of rubble.

It is possible that the prophet Lehi was a descendant of those who were driven from the city of Lehi when it was destroyed. We know that Lehi had his caravan business somewhere "down" from Jerusalem at a place where he kept all of his gold and silver and which was called his "land of...inheritance" (1 Nephi 3:16). If the city of Lehi which was destroyed completely in 701 B.C. was indeed the prophet Lehi's family home, it is understandable why he would maintain merely his flocks and caravan in the area of these ruins while actually maintaining the family home within the security of the great walled city of Jerusalem. Note that Lehi "dwelt at Jerusalem in all his days" (1 Nephi 1:4), even though he maintained his caravan business, along with his gold and silver, "down" at his land of inheritance (1 Nephi 3:22).

9. Associate yourselves, O ye people, and ye shall be broken in pieces; and give ear, all ye of far countries: gird yourselves, and ye

It will be recalled that Syria and the northern Ten Tribes were going to attack Judah because they wanted to force King Ahaz to confederate with them and resist the Assyrian campaign of conquest. It was because

shall be broken in pieces; gird yourselves, and ye shall be broken in pieces.

Ahaz refused to join them that the two northern kingdoms contemplated attacking Judah. Now Isaiah gives these wicked and apostate nations the final word of the Lord. He declares that no amount of treaties, alliances, or associating and confederating together is going to save them. In the absence of repentance, they are doomed. No matter how they "gird" themselves with arms and defense weapons, they will be broken to pieces.

10. Take counsel together, and it shall come to nought; speak the word, and it shall not stand: for God is with us.

Furthermore, Isaiah says it will do them no good to attempt concocting a variety of clever plans. All of these will fail. Isaiah assures his listeners that "God is with us," meaning that he is with Isaiah and those few who believed him. Isaiah knew that the prophetic words which the Lord had given him would be completely vindicated with the passing of time.

11. For the LORD spake thus to me with a strong hand, and instructed me that I should not walk in the way of this people, saying,

Isaiah wants his listeners to know that his errand from the Lord was not given to him in soft whispers, but was spoken to him "with a strong hand." Isaiah was not only instructed to warn the people, but he was specifically instructed NOT to walk in the paths or after the manner of the people. He was to deliver the Lord's message no matter how controversial or unpopular it might prove to be.

12. Say ye not, A confederacy, to all them to whom this people shall say, A confederacy; neither fear ye their fear, nor be afraid.

It would have been very popular for Isaiah to have encouraged the leaders of Syria and the northern Ten Tribes to form a confederacy with the surrounding nations, because that is what they wanted to do. But the Lord tells Isaiah that when he sees the violent anger of these leaders because of what Isaiah would tell them, he was not to be intimidated by them or become frightened. The Lord is simply telling the prophet to trust in his Heavenly Father and everything would work out exactly as the Lord had promised.

13. Sanctify the LORD of hosts himself; and let him be your fear, and let him be your dread.

Isaiah's task was to "sanctify" the Lord and the great calling he had received. Obviously, if he truly honored and loved the Lord, it would be the Lord alone whom he would fear to offend.

14. And he shall be for a sanctuary; but for a stone of stumbling and for a rock of offence to both the houses of Israel, for a gin and for a snare to the inhabitants of Jerusalem.

Isaiah is assured that the Lord will always be his fortress of security or sanctuary. But the Lord will be a stone of stumbling and a rock of offense on which the two houses of Israel (the northern Ten Tribes and Judah) will be broken. The Lord will be a "gin" and a "snare" to the inhabitants of Jerusalem. A gin is a trap for catching birds or small animals. It was held up by a stick with a snare attached to capture the prey.

15. And many among them shall stumble, and fall, and be broken, and be snared, and be taken.

Isaiah assures his listeners that this is precisely what is going to happen to many of them. They will stumble and fall right into the trap which has been prepared for them by the Assyrians.

16. Bind up the testimony, seal the law among my disciples.

Isaiah, meanwhile, had a double task to perform. He was to bind up the law and the testimony against those who utterly rejected the Lord's warning and refused to heed the prophetic declarations which Isaiah had so clearly pronounced. As the Lord said to his servants in modern times: "And in whatsoever house ye enter, and they receive you not, ye shall depart speedily from that house, and shake off the dust of your feet as a testimony against them.... And know this, that in the day

of judgment you shall be judges of that house, and condemn them; and it shall be more tolerable for the heathen in the day of judgment, than for that house."
(D&C 75:20–22.) Of course, all those who accepted the
message of salvation were to be counted as disciples.
They were to be sealed up unto eternal life in
accordance with the laws and ordinances of the
Priesthood. These blessings, obviously, are dependent
upon the people faithfully "enduring to the end," and
not sliding back into their wicked ways of the past.

17. **And I will wait upon the LORD, that hideth his face from the house of Jacob, and I will look for him.**

Isaiah commits himself to patiently wait upon the
Lord, even though the Lord had completely hidden
himself from the people because of their wickedness.
Isaiah says he will look for the Lord and seek him out.

18. **Behold, I and the children whom the LORD hath given me are for signs and for wonders in Israel from the LORD of hosts, which dwelleth in mount Zion.**

Had the people only realized who Isaiah was, they
could have obtained the will of the Lord through this
great prophet standing in their midst. Isaiah declared
that both he and his sons (with their prophetic names)
are proof to the people that the powers and wonders of
God are in their midst.

19. **And when they shall say unto you, Seek unto them that have familiar spirits, and unto wizards that peep and that mutter: should not a people seek unto their God? for the living to the dead?**

In a time of apostasy when there is no revelation and
the people are frightened by war or some other emergency, they desperately feel the need for divine help
and guidance. Nevertheless, since they are without
revelation because of their wickedness, they often do
just what King Saul did. They seek out someone who
has "familiar spirits." Just before his great last battle,
King Saul could get nothing from heaven, neither
through a prophet, a priest, nor the Urim and Thummim. He therefore went to the witch of Endor to see if
she could reach the prophet Samuel, who had recently

died (see 1 Samuel, chapter 28). What she reached was a familiar spirit who pretended he was Samuel the prophet. There was much "peeping" and "muttering" as the familiar spirit gave Saul a message through the medium. Isaiah says the people should not go to those who peep and mutter, but they should seek out God. If they repent, God will pour out revelations upon them and give them the guidance they need.

20. To the law and to the testimony: if they speak not according to this word, it is because there is no light in them.

This passage is a warning to the people of God in all ages. Here Isaiah says that if any come along peeping and muttering and claiming to have revelations, the Lord's disciples can test the validity of their sayings by comparing them with the things the Lord has already revealed. This is why it is so important to study the scriptures regularly. God's revelations are the means by which we can test the words of any new teachers or pretended prophets.

21. And they shall pass through it, hardly bestead and hungry: and it shall come to pass, that when they shall be hungry, they shall fret themselves, and curse their king and their God, and look upward.

False prophets bring nothing but anguish to the people. In them there is no hope and certainly no promise. They pretend to feed the mind with knowledge, and the spirit with enlightenment, but the disciples of soothsayers and wizards are always left hungry and unsatisfied. In their frustration they tend to blame their predicament on those who preside over them. They curse the king and even God while pretending to look up to them.

22. And they shall look unto the earth; and behold trouble and darkness, dimness of anguish; and they shall be driven to darkness.

The false prophets and their disciples look across the world and see nothing but trouble and darkness. They wander through life in a miasma of anguish and confusion, while their frustration seems to drive them ever deeper into a state of darkness and despair.

Isaiah, Chapter 9

INTRODUCTION:

In chapter 7, verse 14, Isaiah introduced the theme of a child being born of a virgin. Isaiah said the child would be named Immanuel, which means "God is with us." He wanted it clearly understood that this child would be the long-awaited Messiah.

In this chapter, Isaiah relates more about the coming Messiah. For one thing, he knew that most of the Savior's ministry would be in Galilee. But he also knew about some of the traumatic events that would transpire in Galilee long before the Messiah ministered there. The Lord had shown Isaiah that in his own lifetime the territory of Galilee and the surrounding region occupied by the northern Ten Tribes were going to be devastated by an Assyrian holocaust. The Ten Tribes would be slaughtered, their cities burned, and the remnant carried off to Assyria, never to return.

Because the Messiah's ministry and the Assyrian holocaust were both going to take place in Galilee, Isaiah incorporates both of these events in the same chapter. The first few verses are much more meaningful if we first remind ourselves of the basic historical facts connected with the Assyrian war against the smaller nations along the coast of the Mediterranean. This campaign was in preparation for Assyria's ultimate objective—the conquest of Egypt.

We have already learned that when Syria and the northern Ten Tribes saw Assyria getting ready for her campaign in the west, they confederated together to oppose the Assyrian king Tiglath-pileser III, and they

wanted Judah to join them. However, King Ahaz of
Judah refused their request. The other two nations
therefore attacked Judah to force her to join them.
They were just getting ready to attack a second time
when the Lord sent Isaiah to King Ahaz to tell him to
"be quiet." Ahaz did not accept this message from the
Lord. Instead, he stripped the temple of all its precious
decorations of gold, silver, and precious stones in order
to bribe Tiglath-pileser into attacking Syria and the
northern Ten Tribes, thus diverting them from attacking Judah. Tiglath-pileser accepted the bribe, but did
not immediately attack as Ahaz had requested (see 2
Chronicles 28:21). Consequently, Judah was attacked
again by her northern enemies and lost around 300,000
of her people.

Not until 734 B.C. did Tiglath-pileser finally move
across the Euphrates River to launch his campaign in
the west. First he attacked Damascus, the capital of
Syria. King Rezin was brutally slain. The noblemen
were impaled on stakes, the women were ravished, and
the city was ransacked. After that, Tiglath-pileser
charged down upon the terrified Ten Tribes. He first
attacked the tribal territories of Zebulun and Naphtali
in the region of Galilee. However, this first attack came
"lightly" compared to a later attack when the Assyrians
literally devastated the territory of western Galilee
preparatory to proceeding toward the Red Sea and
their ultimate objective—Egypt.

1. Nevertheless the dimness
shall not be such as was in
her vexation, when at the
first he lightly afflicted the
land of Zebulun and the
land of Naphtali, and afterward did more grievously
afflict her by the way of the

In this first verse, Isaiah continues his reference to
the "dimness" and "darkness" engulfing the people,
which represents the cloud of apostasy discussed in the
previous chapter. In this chapter Isaiah will discuss the
spiritual dimness which he knew would prevail when
the Savior came to minister on earth (verse 2). But in

sea, beyond Jordan, in Galilee of the nations.

this first verse he wants us to understand that the dimness was far more dark and terrible during the latter part of the eighth century B.C. when the Assyrians demolished the northern Ten Tribes.

We have already pointed out that Tiglath-pileser, in the initial Assyrian assault around Galilee, "lightly afflicted the land." But later, his armies came back and absolutely devastated the region. There was a widespread slaughter of the people and burning of cities. Many of the survivors were captured and hauled off to Assyria.

Notice that this second attack was incidental to the Assyrian campaign toward the "sea." The King James Version leaves out the word "Red," but the Book of Mormon says "Red Sea" (2 Nephi 19:1), which clearly emphasizes that the conquest of Syria and the Ten Tribes was merely incidental to reaching the main target, Egypt.

2. The people that walked in darkness have seen a great light: they that dwell in the land of the shadow of death, upon them hath the light shined.

Now Isaiah wants the reader to know that in this very region, where the people were so severely defeated by the hosts of Assyria, a later generation would inhabit this area. They also would be walking in darkness. But suddenly there would appear among them a "great light," and even though the people would be living under the "shadow of death" (Roman rule), the great new light would shine upon them. Matthew quotes the first two verses of this chapter and states that Isaiah was referring to the coming of Christ (Matthew 4:15-16). It is interesting that Jesus spent the greater part of his ministry in the territories of Zebulun and Naphtali, which were located in the region of Galilee. It turned out just as Isaiah said it would.

We should point out that in this verse, and the five verses which follow, Isaiah seems to be viewing the vast expanse of history from the birth of the Savior down to the millennial reign of Christ. He knew the Savior would eventually establish his royal domain over the entire planet and that the enemies of his people would be destroyed. These verses are more meaningful if this is kept in mind.

3. Thou hast multiplied the nation, and not increased the joy: they joy before thee according to the joy in harvest, and as men rejoice when they divide the spoil.

Isaiah saw that when this great light would be manifest among the people, the population would have mutiplied again. Furthermore, the people would have occasion to greatly increase their joy when this "great light" came among them. In the King James Version this verse states that the people would NOT increase their joy, but the Book of Mormon gives the correct rendition. In fact, the King James translators inserted a marginal note indicating there was some question about the word "not." The Revised Standard Version leaves out the "not" just as the Book of Mormon did nearly a century earlier. The word "not" obviously contradicts the next two phrases, which say that the joy of the people will be so exuberant that it will be similar to the happiness which always accompanies the gathering in of the harvest, or the happiness of those occasions when the booty is about to be distributed after a long, hard-fought campaign for victory.

4. For thou hast broken the yoke of his burden, and the staff of his shoulder, the rod of his oppressor, as in the day of Midian.

Now the vision clearly emphasizes the time of triumph in the latter days. The Lord will break off the yoke of burden that was imposed upon his people for so long, and there will no longer be the staff or rod of an oppressor beating Israel across the shoulder. The King James Version adds the phrase "as in the days of Midian." This refers to Judges 7:19-23, when the Midianites came 120,000 strong to oppress the Israelites and Gideon was able, with the help of the

Lord, to rout them with only 300 men. This was such a dramatic event that some ancient scribe apparently added this phrase to the original text for emphasis. It is not included in the Book of Mormon.

5. For every battle of the warrior is with confused noise, and garments rolled in blood; but this shall be with burning and fuel of fire.

This will be a time when those who come to fight against God's people will ultimately be defeated. It will be a time of war, bloodshed, and much destruction, but the Lord's people will finally prevail. This will be accomplished through the consuming conflagration of "fire." All of the prophets refer repeatedly to the element of fire as being a universal characteristic of the great wars in the latter days (see, for example, Joel 2:3-5). The Lord will also use fire to cleanse the earth (see Joel 2:30; Malachi 4:1).

6. For unto us a child is born, unto us a son is given: and the government shall be upon his shoulder: and his name shall be called Wonderful, Counsellor, The mighty God, The everlasting Father, The Prince of Peace.

Now comes the beloved scripture which is quoted so often at Christmas time. Notice that Isaiah's acclamation of messianic praise extends from the birth of the Savior clear up to that magnificent moment of triumph at the beginning of the Millennium when he becomes Lord of Lords and King of Kings. At that time he will be called "Wonderful," which means "of the greatest excellence." He will also be called "Counselor," which is most appropriate since he has served in that capacity at the right hand of the Eternal Father ever since our premortal estate. He will also be called "The Mighty God," which is a status he achieved in the pre-earth life as a member of the First Presidency of heaven. The word "God" means the ultimate in goodness and perfection, and is most appropriate for the Savior since he achieved both. Isaiah says he will also be acclaimed as "The Everlasting Father." Jesus is a "father" in three ways. He is the father or creator of the heavens and the earth. He is the father of our salvation through his atoning sacrifice. He is also the father of the faithful, calling himself the husband of the Church, and speaking of its members as his "sons and daughters" (D&C 25:1). Jesus is also called "The Prince of Peace." This appears to be a most sacred and singular title which is associated with the holy Priesthood. It was attributed to Melchizedek (Alma 13:18) and sought after by Abraham (Abraham 1:2).

7. Of the increase of his government and peace there shall be no end, upon the throne of David, and upon his kingdom, to order it, and to establish it with judgment and with justice from henceforth even for ever. The zeal of the LORD of hosts will perform this.

In the kingdom of God there is no such thing as a plateau of static or fixed existence. It is a kingdom of progression, improvement, refinement, expansion, and numerical increase. Isaiah saw that the Savior's dominions during and after the Millennium were of this eternally expanding variety. The Savior will administer his dominions in justice and equity—something rarely found in this mortal life—and he will conduct the affairs of his kingdom with wisdom and good judgment. Mankind instinctively longs for this kind of existence, but cannot find it during earth life. Isaiah assures us that the "zeal" or determination of the Lord is to perform all these things which he has promised.

It is interesting that in the Book of Mormon version of this verse, the word "his" is missing from the phrase "his government" (2 Nephi 19:7). However, Joseph Smith did include it in his translation of the Bible, so we assume that the absence of this word in the Book of Mormon text was due to a copier's error.

8. The Lord sent a word unto Jacob, and it hath lighted upon Israel.

Now Isaiah turns back to his own day. He says the Lord has sent forth his word of warning unto all the tribes of Jacob, and it is about to be fulfilled on Israel (the northern Ten Tribes). Notice that the King James Version says "a" word, but the Book of Mormon version says "his" word. This is how we know that it signifies a word of warning from the Lord.

9. And all the people shall know, even Ephraim and the inhabitant of Samaria, that say in the pride and stoutness of heart,

10. The bricks are fallen down, but we will build with hewn stones: the sycomores are cut down, but we will change them into cedars.

The principal sin of the northern Ten Tribes was pride. They were disdainful of the prophets' warnings of any attack from any quarter. They rationalized that even if their cities were torn down, they would build better ones. And even if their houses of bricks were demolished, they would replace them with beautiful structures of stone. They said that if their enemies should cut down their sycamores of pithy, soft wood, they would replace them with tough, beautiful cedar trees, a much finer wood.

11. Therefore the LORD shall set up the adversaries of Rezin against him, and join his enemies together;

12. The Syrians before, and the Philistines behind; and they shall devour Israel with open mouth. For all this his anger is not turned away, but his hand is stretched out still.

But all of this pride and planning will fail to save the Ten Tribes. Isaiah outlines what would happen. First of all, the enemy of Rezin would sweep down upon him. Rezin was king of Syria, and his enemy, as we have previously mentioned, was Assyria. Isaiah is saying that Assyria would overthrow Rezin and then unite the conquered Syrians with the conquered Philistines to sweep into Israel with such overwhelming velocity that she would be swallowed up in one gulp. But even after all of this, Isaiah says, the Lord's anger would not be turned away. Nevertheless, his hand would remain outstretched by way of invitation to reform and repent.

13. For the people turneth not unto him that smiteth them, neither do they seek the LORD of hosts.

In this awful crisis Isaiah says the stricken Israelites will have no place to turn. Certainly they could not look upon their conquerors as being any source of deliverance, nor would they repent and turn back to the Lord.

14. Therefore the LORD will cut off from Israel head and tail, branch and rush, in one day.

This is why the Lord is determined to let both the head and the tail of Israel (the high and the low) be cut off in a single day.

15. The ancient and honourable, he is the head; and the prophet that teacheth lies, he is the tail.

The leaders whom the Lord blames more than anyone else for this calamity are the "ancient and honorable." This would be the ruling aristocracy of the people. However, the Book of Mormon does not include "and honourable" in its text. Some ancient scribe may have added this as a personal embellishment. The Lord also identifies those who are at the bottom of the heap insofar as blame for the degenerate apostasy of the people is concerned. These are the false prophets who teach lies. The Lord identifies them as the tail.

16. For the leaders of this people cause them to err; and they that are led of them are destroyed.

The Lord puts the major blame for the apostasy and corruption squarely on the shoulders of these two sets of leaders. They have deliberately caused the people to err, both in judgment and in their corrupt manner of life. Because of this wickedness the people will be destroyed, but the leaders must bear most of the blame as far as the Lord is concerned.

17. Therefore the Lord shall have no joy in their young men, neither shall have mercy on their fatherless and widows: for every one is an hypocrite and an evildoer, and every mouth speaketh folly. For all this his anger is not turned away, but his hand is stretched out still.

Not only have the adults been corrupted, but the Lord cannot even find joy in the upcoming generation of youth. The same must be said of the orphan and the widow, who ordinarily would be the objects of deepest compassion. These also have become hypocrites and evildoers. Their conversation is foul with folly. It is for these things that the Lord is allowing the wrath of destruction to sweep down upon them.

18. For wickedness burneth as the fire: it shall devour the briers and thorns, and shall kindle in the thickets of the forest, and they shall mount up like the lifting up of smoke.

All of this wickedness will be consumed by the fire and sword of the Assyrians. It will sweep through the cities and hamlets, humble cottages and rich palaces. Every forest, every vineyard, every thicket and briar patch of this wicked population will be lifted up from the face of the land like a pillar of ascending smoke.

19. Through the wrath of the LORD of hosts is the land darkened, and the people shall be as the fuel of the fire: no man shall spare his brother.

In the fury of this great destruction the people will turn on one another. They will consume one another. No man will spare the family of another, not even his brother. The consuming destruction will leave the land barren and desolate.

20. And he shall snatch on the right hand, and be hungry; and he shall eat on the left hand, and they shall not be satisfied: they shall eat every man the flesh of his own arm:

During a time of siege the people will begin stealing from others for the necessities of life, but this will not save them because the scarcity of food will be so extreme. In desperation the people will begin consuming their own dead, especially their children who are nearly always the first to die in a time of famine. This is what it means when it says that "they shall eat every man the flesh of his own arm," meaning his son or his daughter. Josephus, the Jewish historian, says this literally came to pass.

21. Manasseh, Ephraim; and Ephraim, Manasseh: and they together shall be against Judah. For all this his anger is not turned away, but his hand is stretched out still.

The tribe of Joseph had been the leaders of the northern Ten Tribes ever since they broke away from Judah around 922 B.C. However, during this coming crisis the Lord said the tribe of Joseph would no longer be united. Ephraim would fight against Manasseh, and Manasseh against Ephraim. They would become so enraged with each other that nothing would unite them except their common hatred of Judah. Therefore, they would combine their mutual strength to avenge themselves on Judah. Isaiah knew that his readers might think that with such calamities pouring down upon them, the Israelites would come to their senses and turn back to the Lord. However, Isaiah had already seen in vision that they would not, even though the hand of the Lord would be stretched out still. He would beckon them to return, but Isaiah saw that they would rush headlong toward their own destruction.

Isaiah, Chapter 10

INTRODUCTION:

All that Isaiah predicted in the previous chapters concerning the fall of the Ten Tribes came to pass. Now we come to the chapter in which Isaiah gives the same warning to the Jews. To fix these events in our minds, here is the historical background which will help us understand this chapter:

As we mentioned in the beginning of the last chapter, Tiglath-pileser III conquered Damascus and then struck the Israelites "lightly" around the borders of Zebulun and Naphtali (Isaiah 9:1). He then extended the campaign into Trans-Jordan (east of the Jordan river). This campaign ended around 732 B.C. However, his main target was Egypt, and so he marched his hosts along the coast, conquering both Arabs and Philistines as he went. But he had barely made it to the gates of Egypt when he died in 727 B.C. He was replaced by his son, Shalmaneser V. This change in leadership shook the kingdom, and many of the tributaries stopped sending in their money, including the king of what was left of the Ten Tribes of Israel. Shalmaneser therefore laid siege to Samaria, the capital of the northern Ten Tribes. This time the Assyrians did not attack "lightly"!

The siege lasted three years and must have reduced the people to a terrible state of suffering, as Isaiah had predicted. However, just before the collapse of Israel, Shalmaneser died, or was assassinated, in 722 B.C. The Bible says the throne was taken over by Sargon II, who ruled Assyria from 722 to 705 B.C. For many years historians claimed Sargon II was a mythical Bible character who never existed, but in 1843 Paul Emile Botta uncovered his palace north of Nineveh. On one of the walls were inscribed these words: "At the beginning of my rule . . . I set siege to and conquered Samaria [capital of the northern Ten Tribes]. . . . I carried away into captivity 27,290 persons who lived there." Thus the words of Isaiah were literally fulfilled concerning the fall of the Ten Tribes and their being led away into captivity.

Now it was only a question of time until Assyria would decide to take Judah. Isaiah was still the main prophet, but both Assyria and Judah were ruled by new kings. Ahaz, the wicked king of Judah, had died in 727 B.C., and his righteous son Hezekiah had ascended the throne. In Assyria, the wicked king Sargon II had died in 705 B.C. and his ambitious son, Sennacherib, had taken over. Many of the tributaries stopped making payments to young Sennacherib of Assyria, so he set out with sword in hand to punish the kingdoms which had defected.

These were terrifying days as Sennacherib swept along the coast leaving fire, blood, and desolation in his wake. The Jews realized they were in very serious trouble. They had not followed the example of their righteous king, Hezekiah, but had reveled in the wickedness of his father, King Ahaz. So in this chapter Isaiah is going to warn the people of Judah that the Lord will allow Assyria to humble them. As it turned out, Sennacherib conquered every fortified city of Judah (46 of them!), and he would have taken Jerusalem had it not been for the sudden intervention of the Lord, who struck down 185,000 soldiers of the Assyrian troops in a single night (2 Kings 19:35). But that is getting ahead of our story. Let us see what Isaiah had to say to the people when Sennacherib first appeared on the scene.

1. Woe unto them that decree unrighteous decrees, and that write grievousness which they have prescribed;

Isaiah wants the priests and judges of the people to know that God has prepared a rod for those who write unjust laws and proclaim unrighteous decrees. This has been a well-nigh universal offense of the ruling elite in every nation of every age. It is one of the major problems facing the nations of the world today—the decrees of unrighteous judges.

2. To turn aside the needy from judgment, and to take away the right from the poor of my people, that widows may be their prey, and that they may rob the fatherless!

Just as in our own day, the principal offense is taking advantage of the weak—the widows and orphans.

3. And what will ye do in the day of visitation, and in the desolation which shall come from far? to whom will ye flee for help? and where will ye leave your glory?

But the Lord wants Isaiah to ask these wicked judges and bureaucrats a question. What are they going to do in the coming crisis when destruction descends on them by an enemy who has come from afar? What good will their ill-gotten wealth be to them in that threatening situation? To whom will they flee for help? And since there is going to be a universal destruction of the wicked, to whom will they leave the glory of their inheritance?

4. Without me they shall bow down under the prisoners, and they shall fall under the slain. For all this his anger is not turned away, but his hand is stretched out still.

The people of Judah are warned that since they have forsaken God, the people will find themselves pressed in among the many prisoners or smothered under the piles of the slain. Even then the Lord assures them he will not be able to turn back his anger because they will still refuse to be humble and repentant. Nevertheless, his outstretched hand will continue to be extended toward them.

5. O Assyrian, the rod of mine anger, and the staff in their hand is mine indignation.

Now the Lord salutes the king who is to inflict this punishment on Judah. He calls him an Assyrian. At last the nationality of the coming conqueror is clearly identified. The Lord says that this force of vengeance sweeping down on the unrighteous people of Judah will serve as God's rod of anger and the staff of his indignation.

6. I will send him against an hypocritical nation, and against the people of my wrath will I give him a charge, to take the spoil, and to take the prey, and to tread them down like the mire of the streets.

Whenever the Lord withdraws his protection from a people, they are exposed to the destructive force of their enemies and their evil ambitions. This would be the situation with the coming of Sennacherib. By allowing apostate Judah to be exposed to the Assyrian assault (which God could have easily prevented, and did so when the people deserved it), Sennacherib became, in a sense, the rod of God's anger against a hypocritical people who had been originally designated to be a light to the rest of the world. And because God's protection would be withdrawn from Judah, Sennacherib would be allowed to take spoil and tread the people down like mire in the street.

7. Howbeit he meaneth not so, neither doth his heart think so; but it is in his heart to destroy and cut off nations not a few.

Of course, the Lord knew that Sennacherib had no intention of accomplishing GOD'S purposes. The intent of his heart would be to destroy, desolate, and cut off many nations which would lie in his path. He would do it for what he thought were his own purposes.

8. For he saith, Are not my princes altogether kings?

The Lord said Sennacherib would come forth boasting that his exploits and conquests had been so numerous that he was able to have all the princes of his realm designated kings and rulers over vassal kingdoms which had been brought under Assyrian rule.

9. Is not Calno as Carchemish? is not Hamath as Arpad? is not Samaria as Damascus?

The Lord revealed that Sennacherib would boast about the cities which the Assyrians had conquered in the past. The six which are named were all taken by previous rulers such as Tiglath-pileser, Shalmaneser, or Sargon. The city of Calno in lower Babylon was conquered in 738 B.C. The city of Carchemish on the west bank of the Euphrates River was captured in 717 B.C. The city of Hamath, a former Hivite capital on the Orontes River, was captured in 720 B.C. The city of Arpad, near Hamath, was taken back in 740 B.C. The city of Samaria, the capital of the northern Ten Tribes of Israel, fell in 721 B.C. Finally, Damascus, the capital of Syria, fell in 732 B.C. This demonstrates that Isaiah wrote this chapter after the fall of both Syria and Israel and just before the attack on Judah. This is how we are able to identify the "Assyrian" in this chapter as Sennacherib, even though he is not named.

10. As my hand hath found the kingdoms of the idols, and whose graven images did excel them of Jerusalem and of Samaria;

11. Shall I not, as I have done unto Samaria and her idols, so do to Jerusalem and her idols?

The Lord revealed that Sennacherib would reason within himself that since Assyria had already conquered nations with idols or gods who were considered to be far more numerous and powerful than those of either Samaria or Jerusalem, and since Samaria had already fallen, what was to prevent Assyria from overcoming the idols or gods of Jerusalem? Surely if he had conquered the gods of a strong nation, what was to prevent him from overcoming the gods of a weak one like Judah?

12. Wherefore it shall come to pass, that when the Lord hath performed his whole work upon mount Zion and on Jerusalem, I will punish

The Lord concluded this whole discussion by saying that after the Assyrian king had been allowed to do all that God intended as a punishment against Mount Zion (the temple mount, usually called Mount Moriah), the fruit of the stout heart of the king of Assyria, and the glory of his high looks.

and also against Jerusalem, then the Lord would punish the stout heart of Sennacherib and humble the "glory of his high looks."

13. For he saith, By the strength of my hand I have done it, and by my wisdom; for I am prudent: and I have removed the bounds of the people, and have robbed their treasures, and I have put down the inhabitants like a valiant man:

Of course, Sennacherib would think all of his conquests were accomplished by his own hand and by his own wisdom. He would contemplate with great satisfaction how he had rearranged the boundaries of nations, robbed them of their treasures, and subjugated their people because he was such a great and valiant warrior.

14. And my hand hath found as a nest the riches of the people: and as one gathereth eggs that are left, have I gathered all the earth; and there was none that moved the wing, or opened the mouth, or peeped.

He would recall how he had searched through every conquered country and found the sanctuaries or nests where the rulers had hidden their riches. He would gather these treasures all together from every nation, much as one would gather eggs from helpless chickens which allow themselves to be looted without moving a wing, clucking in protest, or making a peep.

15. Shall the axe boast itself against him that heweth therewith? or shall the saw magnify itself against him that shaketh it? as if the rod should shake itself against them that lift it up, or as if the staff should lift up itself, as if it were no wood.

But there were some basic questions to ask this proud Assyrian. Was not Sennacherib like an axe boasting against the axeman, or a saw magnifying itself above the carpenter who worked with it, or a rod shaking itself against the man who carried it, or a staff asserting itself to be more than plain wood?

16. Therefore shall the Lord, the Lord of hosts, send among his fat ones leanness; and under his glory he shall

Now Isaiah was allowed to pronounce an ominous prophecy against Assyria. Verily, the time is coming when that wicked and cruel nation will no longer be fat

kindle a burning like the burning of a fire.

and rich but will display a scrawny and lean figure because the glory of that nation will go up in flames when it is decisively conquered by another nation.

17. And the light of Israel shall be for a fire, and his Holy One for a flame: and it shall burn and devour his thorns and his briers in one day;

Isaiah declared that just as God had allowed Assyria to triumph for a while, so he will, in his own due time, decide when she is ripe in her wickedness to be consumed by the torch of conquest. He said that when that happens, it will come suddenly; like the burning of dry, crackling thorns which are consumed quickly. It will be done by the "light of Israel," which is the Lord.

18. And shall consume the glory of his forest, and of his fruitful field, both soul and body: and they shall be as when a standardbearer fainteth.

The Lord reveals that the destruction of Assyria will consume the glory of her forests and decimate the beauty of her fruitful and productive fields. The shocking thing will be the fact that Assyria, as a nation, will be completely destroyed. She will become extinct. It will be as though the standard-bearer of the nation had suddenly fainted and disappeared in the heat of the battle.

19. And the rest of the trees of his forest shall be few, that a child may write them.

Now the vision of Isaiah sweeps down the corridors of time and, as he contemplates the latter days (the time factor is established in the next three verses), he predicts that the vestiges of the Assyrian people will be so few in number that a child will be able to write them. In other words, for all practical purposes the mighty nation of Assyria will be extinct.

20. And it shall come to pass in that day, that the remnant of Israel, and such as are escaped of the house of

Isaiah also saw that by the latter days the remnant of Israel and all those who had escaped from the house of Jacob will no longer be subject to their original captors,

Jacob, shall no more again stay upon him that smote them; but shall stay upon the LORD, the Holy One of Israel, in truth.

but will be ready to stay upon the Lord with a total commitment to the truth.

21. The remnant shall return, even the remnant of Jacob, unto the mighty God.

It was almost unbelievable that it would take so long to bring the stubborn chosen people of the Lord to their senses, but Isaiah did indeed behold that in due time the "remnant of Jacob" would actually return to the Almighty God whom they had forsaken.

22. For though thy people Israel be as the sand of the sea, yet a remnant of them shall return: the consumption decreed shall overflow with righteousness.

23. For the Lord GOD of hosts shall make a consumption, even determined, in the midst of all the land.

When that day finally comes to pass, Isaiah declared that the people of Israel will have become so numerous that Jacob's descendants will be as the countless sands of the sea. He also hints that out of these many millions of heirs to the latter-day kingdom, only a "remnant" will elect to return. After that, God's great "consumption" or cleansing will take place so that the earth can overflow with righteousness. This verse explains why the missionaries cannot convert all of the blood of Israel even where it is known to exist. Nevertheless, a choice remnant has been responding, and this is the bulwark of the Church which the Lord will preserve (if they are valiant) against the day when he intends to cleanse the earth and set up a righteous dominion at the beginning of the Millennium.

24. Therefore thus saith the Lord GOD of hosts, O my people that dwellest in Zion, be not afraid of the Assyrian: he shall smite thee with a rod, and shall lift up his staff against thee, after the manner of Egypt.

Meanwhile, the Lord had a message of comfort for the people of Mount Zion in Isaiah's day. They were told not to fear the Assyrian. Though he would smite them with his rod for a season, even as the Egyptians did in the days of Israel's captivity, nevertheless, in a little while Judah could be assured that the indignation

25. For yet a very little while, and the indignation shall cease, and mine anger in their destruction.

of this enemy would cease because God's anger against Assyria would cause her to be utterly destroyed.

26. And the LORD of hosts shall stir up a scourge for him according to the slaughter of Midian at the rock of Oreb: and as his rod was upon the sea, so shall he lift it up after the manner of Egypt.

The Lord declared that he had a scourge in store for Assyria. It came in less than a century. Assyria was obliterated as a nation by the Babylonians. The Lord said it would be like the slaughter of the Midianites. This apparently has reference to Gideon and his 300 men who followed the instructions of the Lord and routed 120,000 Midianites from the land around 1300 B.C.

This was one of the most famous battles in the history of Israel, and it ended when the Midianite princes were captured and slain (see Judges 7:25).

Notice also that the rod (actually Priesthood power) which was lifted up by Moses to divide the Red Sea, as Israel came up out of Egypt, will apparently be used to smite the rocks in the latter days on behalf of the returning Ten Tribes. This is described by the Lord in a modern revelation when he said:

"And the Lord, even the Savior, shall stand in the midst of his people, and shall reign over all flesh. And they who are in the north countries shall come in remembrance before the Lord; and their prophets shall hear his voice, and shall no longer stay themselves; and they shall smite the rocks, and the ice shall flow down at their presence. And an HIGHWAY SHALL BE CAST UP IN THE MIDST OF THE GREAT DEEP. Their enemies shall become a prey unto them." (D&C 133:25-28.)

Isaiah later refers to this great event in chapter 11, verse 16. We might also mention that in Jeremiah 16:14-15 it says that the great miracle of the highway raised up for Israel in the latter days will be so marvelous that people won't even mention the dividing of the Red Sea anymore.

27. And it shall come to pass in that day, that his burden shall be taken away from off thy shoulder, and his yoke from off thy neck, and the yoke shall be destroyed because of the anointing.

In the latter days the Gentile element will impose a burden on the shoulders of Israel just as the Assyrians did in ancient times. The "Assyrian" symbol is therefore used by Isaiah even for the latter days, when a similar political power will be exercised over Israel by the Gentiles. Isaiah assures the Israelites of the latter days that this Gentile or Assyrian yoke will be lifted from off their necks and the burden of affliction imposed upon them shall be taken away. Then we have the tremendously significant statement that this will be done because of the "anointing." This refers to the foreordination in the premortal existence of those who had earned the privilege of coming into the earth as "Israelites." This was described by Moses as follows:

"Ask thy father, and he will shew thee; thy elders, and they will tell thee.

"When the most High divided to the nations their inheritance, when he separated the sons of Adam, HE SET THE BOUNDS OF THE PEOPLE ACCORDING TO THE NUMBER OF THE CHILDREN OF ISRAEL [which were yet to be born but had already been numbered and anointed]." (Deuteronomy 32:7-8; emphasis added.)

Paul also referred to this anointing or foreordination in the premortal existence when he said:

"And we know that all things work together for good to them that love God, to them who are the called according to his purpose.

"For whom he did foreknow, he also did predestinate [foreordain]. . . .

"Moreover whom he did predestinate, THEM HE ALSO CALLED: and whom he called, them he also justified: and whom he justified, them he also glorified." (Romans 8:28-30.)

The Nephite prophet Alma taught the same doctrine with even greater clarity when he described how the valiant in the premortal existence were "called and prepared."

"Being called and prepared from the foundation of the world according to the foreknowledge of God, on account of their exceeding faith and good works; in the first place being left to choose good or evil; therefore they having chosen good, and exercising exceedingly great faith, are called with a holy calling, yea, with that holy calling which was prepared with, and according to, a preparatory redemption for such" (Alma 13:3).

28. He is come to Aiath, he is passed to Migron; at Michmash he hath laid up his carriages:

29. They are gone over the passage: they have taken up their lodging at Geba; Ramah is afraid; Gibeah of Saul is fled.

30. Lift up thy voice, O daughter of Gallim: cause it to be heard unto Laish, O poor Anathoth.

31. Madmenah is removed; the inhabitants of Gebim gather themselves to flee.

32. As yet shall he remain at Nob that day: he shall shake his hand against the mount of the daughter of Zion, the hill of Jerusalem.

In these verses Isaiah sees all of the famous cities in ancient Israel occupied by the hosts of the Lord in the latter days.

33. Behold, the Lord, the LORD of hosts, shall lop the bough with terror: and the high ones of stature shall be

So those who had been anointed as Israelites from before the foundation of the world will finally come into their own and occupy all those cities which were

hewn down, and the haughty shall be humbled.

lost anciently to the Assyrians. Isaiah declared that in the day of the Lord's power he will lop off the bough of those who stood tall in defiance against him. These high ones will be hewn down and the haughty will be humbled.

34. And he shall cut down the thickets of the forest with iron, and Lebanon shall fall by a mighty one.

Prophecies connected with the Second Coming indicate that there will be a massive destruction as the "wicked slay the wicked" with their weapons of iron. The Lord will also use his mighty power to complete the cleansing of the earth preparatory to the ushering in of the Millennium.

INTRODUCTION:

Now we come to another chapter which relates to our own day. It describes the Savior's servants who were to be raised up in modern times to prepare the earth for the ushering in of the Millennium. You will note that this chapter presents four symbols which refer to certain persons who will do a great work in modern times. However, no one could possibly guess their identity without a "key." Part of that key is given in a modern revelation (D&C 113), and therefore this chapter has become much more comprehensible since the Gospel was restored.

1. And there shall come forth a rod out of the stem of Jesse, and a Branch shall grow out of his roots:

Note that in this very first verse, Isaiah makes reference to all four of these persons who will be leaders in doing the Lord's work in the latter days:

1. The stem of Jesse
2. The rod
3. The Branch
4. The root

According to the Doctrine and Covenants, section 113, here is the identification of these individuals:

1. THE STEM OF JESSE: "Verily, thus saith the Lord: It is Christ" (D&C 113:2).

2. THE ROD WHICH COMES OUT OF THE STEM OF JESSE: "Behold, thus saith the Lord: It is a SERVANT in the hands of Christ, who is partly a descendant of Jesse as well as of Ephraim, or of the house of Joseph, on whom there is laid much power" (D&C 113:4). One is

almost tempted to assume that this refers to Joseph Smith, but his calling is more clearly identified with "the root," which we will discuss in a moment. The Lord's description of the rod is not sufficient for us to positively identify the person he had in mind as yet, but we will no doubt be able to recognize him when he fulfills this assignment. It is interesting that in some scriptures Jesus refers to the "rod of his mouth" (for example, see Isaiah 11:4; D&C 19:15), but section 113 of the Doctrine and Covenants clearly identifies the person to whom Isaiah is referring as a SERVANT of Christ.

3. THE BRANCH GROWING OUT OF THE ROOTS OF JESSE: This "Branch" is identified a number of times in the Old Testament as a great leader who will be raised up among the Jews. In fact, so much is told about the work he will do that we should have no difficulty recognizing him when he finally comes on the scene. This "Branch" is described by Jeremiah as a righteous king who will rule over the Jews in the latter days (Jeremiah 23:5). Joseph Smith was aware that his name would be David (see *History of the Church*, 6:253). Concerning this "Branch" named David, Ezekiel says: "And I will set up one shepherd over them [the Jews who are gathered to Jerusalem in the latter days], and he shall feed them, even my servant David; he shall feed them, and he shall be their shepherd. And I the Lord will be their God, and my servant David a prince among them." (Ezekiel 34:23–24; see also chapter 46.)

Zechariah knew of this choice servant of God and said: "Behold the man whose name is The BRANCH; and he shall grow up out of his place, and HE SHALL BUILD THE TEMPLE OF THE LORD: even he shall build the temple of the Lord; and he shall bear the glory, and shall sit and rule upon his throne; and he shall be a priest upon his throne." (Zechariah 6:12–13.)

The administration of this outstanding leader will apparently last a long time and will extend over to the time when the Ten Tribes—who will first gather in America to receive their blessings (D&C 133:26-32)—are led back to Palestine to become one nation with the Jews, "and they shall be no more two nations, neither shall they be divided into two kingdoms any more at all.... And David my servant shall be king over them." (Ezekiel 37:22-24.) This would suggest that this Branch or Prince David will not only build the temple in Jerusalem, but will still be in charge of affairs when Jesus makes his appearance following the great battle of Armageddon.

4. THE ROOT OF JESSE WHICH WILL STAND FOR AN ENSIGN TO THE PEOPLE IN THE LATTER DAYS: We will discuss the identity of this individual when we come to verse 10 of this chapter.

2. And the Spirit of the LORD shall rest upon him, the spirit of wisdom and understanding, the spirit of counsel and might, the spirit of knowledge and of the fear of the LORD;

Notice that in the first verse Isaiah is talking about the leaders who would be a rod, or a branch, or a root growing out of the "stem of Jesse" which is Jesus Christ. Therefore, "the stem" or the Savior is the main subject of not only the first verse, but all of the first FIVE verses. So this second verse is saying that when the Savior or "stem of Jesse" comes to the earth (first to minister and later to rule), he will have the Spirit of the Lord resting upon him. This will be manifest in his exceptional wisdom and understanding of all things. He will also exhibit the spirit of a wise counselor and a person of mighty strength in governing the people. He will not only possess great knowledge but will be humble before the Lord, his Heavenly Father.

3. And shall make him of quick understanding in the fear of the LORD: and he shall not judge after the

The Savior will possess a quick understanding in carrying out the will of the Father. He will not judge man on the basis of appearances—that which can be seen by

sight of his eyes, neither reprove after the hearing of his ears:

the eye or heard with the ears—for he will perceive in the heart the actual intent of every person who comes before the bar of judgment.

4. But with righteousness shall he judge the poor, and reprove with equity for the meek of the earth: and he shall smite the earth with the rod of his mouth, and with the breath of his lips shall he slay the wicked.

That is why he will know how to judge or minister to the poor in righteousness. He will be the defender and advocate for the meek of the earth (those who become as a "little child" and accept baptism; see 3 Nephi 11:37-38). Concerning the wicked it says that he will merely have to speak the word and the elements will respond to consume the wicked with fire or otherwise slay them.

5. And righteousness shall be the girdle of his loins, and faithfulness the girdle of his reins.

The Savior's entire administration will be so completely just and efficient that men will think of him as wearing a mantle or girdle of righteousness. He will fulfill every promise made in the scripture concerning him, and he will be looked upon as one who is girded about the "reins" (waist) with the very ultimate in "faithfulness."

6. The wolf also shall dwell with the lamb, and the leopard shall lie down with the kid; and the calf and the young lion and the fatling together; and a little child shall lead them.

This verse clearly identifies the present chapter as portraying events of the latter days and the ushering in of the great Millennium. Isaiah longed for that day of complete triumph by the Lord. He had seen it in vision and knew that the present cold and dreary world with its predatory animals, briars and noxious weeds, would be sublimated and become a different kind of habitation for man. He saw that the Millennium will be an amazing epoch when the wolf will dwell peacefully with the lamb; the leopard will lie down with the young goat; even the lion will be harmless as it is led along with a young calf by a little child.

7. And the cow and the bear shall feed; their young ones shall lie down together: and the lion shall eat straw like the ox.

The whole earth will be a scene of harmonious peace. The cow and the bear will occupy the same meadow peacefully together. The bear's cubs and the cow's calves will lie down together. And even more fantastic will be the transition of carnivorous animals (which presently survive by slaying and eating other animals) into herbivorous creatures which will thrive on plants alone! Thus the lion will be seen eating straw and grass like an ox.

8. And the sucking child shall play on the hole of the asp, and the weaned child shall put his hand on the cockatrice' den.

Not only animal life will be safe in its millennial environment, but so will the people. The suckling infant will play around the hole of the poisonous asp, which was greatly feared by the people in Isaiah's day because of its lethal bite. (Cleopatra is said to have committed suicide by being bitten by an asp.) Older children will have no fear as they probe about the den of the cockatrice (large poisonous serpent).

9. They shall not hurt nor destroy in all my holy mountain: for the earth shall be full of the knowledge of the LORD, as the waters cover the sea.

It is amazing to contemplate, but Isaiah assures us that in those days there will be no crime, no war, no cheating, stealing, robbing, or ravishing. In fact, the Lord says people and animals "shall not hurt or destroy in all my holy mountain."

The modern prophet of the restoration, Joseph Smith, had the following comments on verses 6 to 9:

"Men must become harmless before the brute creation, and when men lose their vicious dispositions and cease to destroy the animal race, the lion and the lamb can dwell together, and the sucking child can play with the serpent in safety." (Smith, *Teachings*, p. 71.)

On another occasion he said:

"Friendship is one of the grand fundamental principles of 'Mormonism'; [it is designed] to revolutionize and civilize the world, and cause wars and contentions to cease and men to become friends and brothers. Even the wolf and the lamb shall dwell together; the leopard shall lie down with the kid, the calf, the young lion and the fatling; and a little child shall lead them; the bear and the cow shall lie down together, and the sucking child shall play on the hole of the asp, and the weaned child shall play on the cockatrice's den; and they shall not hurt or destroy in all my holy mountain, saith the Lord of hosts." (Smith, *Teachings*, p. 316.)

It is interesting that there will be no atheists or agnostics during the Millennium. Isaiah says that the whole earth will be filled with a knowledge of the Lord, even as the waters cover the sea. The unveiling of the spirit world so that all mankind can see the Lord at once is referred to in a modern revelation as follows: "And there shall be silence in heaven for the space of half an hour; and immediately after shall the curtain of heaven be unfolded, as a scroll is unfolded after it is rolled up, and THE FACE OF THE LORD SHALL BE UNVEILED. ... EVERY KNEE SHALL BOW, AND EVERY TONGUE SHALL CONFESS." (D&C 88:95, 104.)

No wonder there will be neither atheists nor agnostics! Jeremiah said: "And they shall teach no more every man his neighbour, and every man his brother, saying, Know the Lord: for they shall all know me, from the least of them unto the greatest of them" (Jeremiah 31:34).

The Millennium will be almost like heaven on earth. As Isaiah had said earlier, "they shall beat their swords into plowshares, and their spears into pruninghooks: nation shall not lift up sword against nation, neither shall they learn war any more" (Isaiah 2:4).

The Lord will once again restore the pure language of Adam (Zephaniah 3:9). The history of the world will be revealed (D&C 88:108–10). The Lord will reveal how the world was created (D&C 101:33-34). The righteous will not die and be buried in graves, but will be changed in the twinkling of an eye (D&C 101:29-31). Science and astronomy will be taught by revelation (D&C 121:28-31). The whole human family will bow in humble recognition of the divinity and governing power of Jesus Christ (Isaiah 45:23; Romans 14:11; Philippians 2:10-11).

10. And in that day there shall be a root of Jesse, which shall stand for an ensign of the people; to it shall the Gentiles seek: and his rest shall be glorious.

Now Isaiah makes it clear that in the latter days the Lord will provide his own special Priesthood leadership as he prepares the world for his Second Coming. Isaiah saw that the Lord would raise up a "root of Jesse" who would lift up a mighty ensign to all nations. He saw that as the remnant of Israel gathered about this ensign, the world would learn that this was the core around which the Lord would establish his reign of righteousness. Notice that this ensign would attract the "Gentiles" of the latter days. It is interesting that practically all of the Gentiles who joined the Church turned out to be descendants of ancient Israel (primarily from the tribe of Joseph), although their bloodline from that ancient people had been mixed with that of the Gentiles, and even thought of themselves as Gentiles.

One cannot help but wonder who the "root of Jesse" might be. We note that, whoever he is, the next two verses indicate that his assignment will be to raise up a banner or ensign for the Lord which will result in the great gathering of the remnant of the Israelites, and these will once more be designated as the Lord's people.

Joseph Smith was once asked who this "root of Jesse" might be, and it turned out that he had already inquired about it. The Lord said: "Behold, thus saith the Lord, it is a descendant of Jesse, as well as of Joseph, unto whom rightly belongs the priesthood, and the keys of the kingdom, for an ensign, and for the gathering of my people in the last days" (D&C 113:6).

To identify this person, one merely needs to ask: "Who was it in this dispensation who received the Priesthood, the keys of the kingdom, and finally, the keys of the gathering?" We know this is precisely what happened to Joseph Smith. The Priesthood began to be restored May 15, 1829, and the keys of the kingdom as well as the higher Priesthood were restored by Peter, James, and John (D&C 13; 27:12–13). The keys of the gathering were restored by Moses (D&C 110:11).

Perhaps this is why Moroni recited this entire chapter of Isaiah to the 17-year-old Joseph Smith when he first came to announce that the Lord's great latter-day program was about to commence (Joseph Smith—History 1:40).

Moroni told Joseph Smith that the things mentioned in this chapter of Isaiah were about to be fulfilled. Since Joseph was the Lord's chosen instrument to initiate this marvelous dispensation of the fulness of times, it was particularly significant that Moroni would recite this entire chapter of Isaiah to the youthful prophet who was being raised up to do the work. But notice that when the members of the Church asked Joseph Smith who the "root of Jesse" was, he simply identified THE WORK which this person would do. He never boasted of his own role but went right ahead working out his mission with "fear and trembling."

It will be observed that the Lord's reference to the "root of Jesse" in the Doctrine and Covenants has some very interesting implications. The Lord said: "it is a descendant of Jesse, as well as of Joseph"(D&C 113:6). This would mean that the prophet of the latter days would be a descendant of the same Jewish line as King David and the Savior. And his other bloodline would be that of Joseph who was sold into Egypt.

11. And it shall come to pass in that day, that the Lord shall set his hand again the second time to recover the remnant of his people, which shall be left, from Assyria, and from Egypt, and from Pathros, and from Cush, and from Elam, and from Shinar, and from Hamath, and from the islands of the sea.

Isaiah now makes specific reference to God's great premillennial program to recover the remnant of his people. Isaiah names all of the countries known to the people of his day so that they would know this would be a worldwide gathering. Here are the countries and their location:

1. Assyria—the northern territory between the Tigris and the Euphrates rivers with its capital at Nineveh.
2. Egypt—the lower kingdom of the Nile with its capital at Memphis (near modern Cairo).
3. Pathros—The upper kingdom of Egypt with its capital at Thebes (about 400 miles south of Cairo).
4. Cush—the Hamitic people who eventually concentrated in the territory of the Sudan along the upper Nile.
5. Elam—a territory named after a son of Shem which comprised the heartland of modern Iran or Persia. Its capital was Susa.
6. Shinar—the great alluvial plain between the lower Tigris and Euphrates rivers which became known as Babylonia.
7. Hamath—the territory north of Syria leading up toward Asia Minor. The capital city of Hamath was located on the Orontes River and was originally settled by the descendants of Ham.

12. And he shall set up an ensign for the nations, and shall assemble the outcasts of Israel, and gather together the dispersed of Judah from the four corners of the earth.

Isaiah says the Lord will establish an "ensign" or central place to which the outcasts of Israel can gather as well as the dispersed of Judah. Notice that the Ten Tribes are described as "outcasts," whereas the Jews are described as "dispersed" among the nations. This differentiation is often made throughout the scriptures. This would indicate that wherever the Ten

Tribes are located, they are intact as a people and not "dispersed" to the four corners of the earth as are the Jews.

13. The envy also of Ephraim shall depart, and the adversaries of Judah shall be cut off: Ephraim shall not envy Judah, and Judah shall not vex Ephraim.

In Isaiah's day a vitriolic hatred existed between the leaders of Israel, the Ephraimites, and the Jews. However, in the latter days, Isaiah predicted that the gathering Ephraimites and the gathering Jews would cooperate together to fulfill the Lord's purposes. Ephraim would no longer envy Judah, and Judah would no longer vex Ephraim. Both of these people must be prepared for tremendous responsibilities as the Lord begins to establish his government back on earth. The Jews must gather and rebuild the ancient city of Jerusalem in Israel. The Ephraimites and children of Manasseh (the two branches of the tribe of Joseph) must build the NEW Jerusalem which will be on the American continent (see 3 Nephi 20:22; 21:23).

To accomplish God's purposes, a converting and cleansing must take place among both Ephraimites and Jews. Because the Ephraimites were the first to be drawn out from among the Gentiles and receive the restored Gospel, they have a great responsibility toward the Jews. From time to time there are waves of anti-Semitism (hatred of the Jews) in various parts of the world. The modern prophets have warned that the children of Joseph have the task of sharing the Gospel with the children of Judah, and therefore there is no place for sentiments of anti-Semitism in The Church of Jesus Christ of Latter-day Saints. Nevertheless, this antagonism sometimes surfaced among many people. In 1921 a wave of anti-Semitism was sweeping through the United States as the result of a spurious document called the *Protocols of the Learned Elders of Zion*. (For the history of this document see W. Cleon Skousen, *Fantastic Victory*, appendix.) In April conference of that year, President Heber J. Grant spoke to the membership of the Church on this subject and said:

"Some of you may be familiar with the agitation that is going on at the present time, in the publications, against the Jewish people. There should be no ill-will, and I am sure there is none in the heart of any true Latter-day Saint, toward the Jewish people. By the authority of the Holy Priesthood of God that has again been restored to the earth, and by the ministration under the direction of the Prophet of God, Apostles of the Lord Jesus Christ have been to the Holy Land and have dedicated that country for the return of the Jews. And we believe that in the due time of the Lord they shall be in the favor of God again. Let no Latter-day Saint be guilty of taking any part in any crusade against these people. I believe in no other part of the world is there as good a feeling in the hearts of mankind towards the Jewish people as among the Latter-day Saints." (Heber J. Grant, in *Improvement Era,* June 1921, p. 747.)

14. But they shall fly upon the shoulders of the Philistines toward the west; they shall spoil them of the east together: they shall lay their hand upon Edom and Moab; and the children of Ammon shall obey them.

To ancient Israel the Philistines represented the Gentiles (Sidney B. Sperry, *Book of Mormon Compendium* [Salt Lake City: Bookcraft, 1968], p. 228). However, in Isaiah 49:22-23, Isaiah does not use "Philistines" as a symbol but comes right out and says it will be the "Gentiles" of the latter days who would help the remnants of Israel gather together and defend themselves against their enemies. From the time the Balfour Declaration was signed by the English Gentiles in 1917 (allowing the Jews to return to Palestine) to the present, the people of Israel have received abundant assistance from the Gentile nations in order to survive. In times of war they have literally flown on the shoulders or wings of the "Philistines" in order to preserve themselves.

The territory to be occupied by the tribe of Judah in the latter days is not large, but it will include the three territories east and south of Judah which were once conquered by David. They were anciently known as Edom (the Arabah valley south of the Dead Sea), Moab (which is east of the Dead Sea), and Ammon (which is east of the Jordan River). It is interesting that the Jews have never occupied any of these territories except by purchase or as a defensive measure when they were attacked. Notice that as they occupy any of the territory designated in this verse they immediately establish a policy of equality for both Jews and non-Jews so long as they keep the peace. Notice also that the modern state of Israel has conquered the Sinai twice and given it back both times. It is not part of their permanent inheritance. As we shall see in Isaiah, chapter 19, the day will come when all the Arabs of these territories, including Egypt, will be members of the Savior's church and will dwell peaceably with Judah as part of God's people (see Isaiah 19:19-25).

15. And the LORD shall utterly destroy the tongue of the Egyptian sea; and with his mighty wind shall he shake his hand over the river, and shall smite it in the seven streams, and make men go over dryshod.

In that great day when the power of God is manifest on behalf of his people, the Lord will utterly destroy the tongue of the Egyptian Sea. The "Egyptian Sea" is thought to refer to the Red Sea and the "tongue" to refer to the Suez Gulf. However, the exact meaning is obscure.

The Lord will also smite a certain river and smite it in the seven streams so that men can pass over dry-shod. Some have thought this refers to the Nile, which divides into a number of streams as it moves out across the delta toward the Mediterranean Sea. However, this river is the lifeblood of Egypt, and if it were to dry up it would be catastrophic. Four thousand miles of the Nile Valley would go back to the desert in a single year unless there were rainfall to replace it. We should also keep in mind that the scriptures often refer to the Euphrates as "the river," and some have thought this passage has reference to that mighty waterway. Actually, we do not know for certain. We need a key from the Lord.

16. And there shall be an highway for the remnant of his people, which shall be left, from Assyria; like as it was to Israel in the day that he came up out of the land of Egypt.

In this verse Isaiah says that when the time comes for the gathering of the Israelites "which shall be left from Assyria" (the Ten Tribes who disappeared after being taken to Assyria), the Lord will raise up a miraculous "highway" for their return. In a modern revelation, as we have pointed out earlier, the Lord comments on this event in the following words:

"And they who are in the north countries shall come in remembrance before the Lord; and their prophets shall hear his voice, and shall no longer stay themselves; and they shall smite the rocks, and the ice shall flow down at their presence. AND AN HIGHWAY SHALL BE CAST UP IN THE MIDST OF THE GREAT DEEP. Their enemies shall become a prey unto them, and in the barren deserts there shall come forth pools of living water.... And they shall bring forth their rich treasures unto the children of Ephraim, my servants. And the boundaries of the everlasting hills shall tremble at their presence. And there shall they fall down and be crowned with glory, even in Zion, by the hands of the servants of the Lord, even the children of Ephraim." (D&C 133:26–32; emphasis added.)

This will be such an amazing development that it will make past miracles look small by comparison. Jeremiah emphasized this when he said:

"Therefore, behold, the days come, saith the Lord, that they shall no more say, The Lord liveth, which brought up the children of Israel out of the land of Egypt;

"But, The Lord liveth, which brought up and which led the seed of the house of Israel out of the north country, and from all countries whither I had driven them; and they shall dwell in their own land." (Jeremiah 23:7–8.)

Isaiah, Chapter 12

INTRODUCTION:

This brief chapter is the song of Israel following her redemption. The miraculous manner in which God's chosen remnant will be converted, gathered, cleansed, and magnified in the latter days will be a marvelous thing to behold.

1. And in that day thou shalt say, O LORD, I will praise thee: though thou wast angry with me, thine anger is turned away, and thou comfortedst me.

In this first verse Isaiah says that there will come a time when the rebellious Israelites will praise the name of God with all their hearts. They will have had enough experience through the centuries to know that when they have been wicked, God has exhibited genuine anger toward them. When they have repented, his anger has been turned away. In the latter days the people of Israel will be comforted and rejoice in their Redeemer.

2. Behold, God is my salvation; I will trust, and not be a-fraid: for the LORD JEHO-VAH is my strength and my song; he also is become my salvation.

One of the purposes of earth life is to learn for time and all eternity that there is only one loving Heavenly Father to whom mankind can look for salvation, and that is through his Only Begotten Son, Jesus Christ. All through the Old Testament the divine spirit personality (who later would be born to Mary) was known as Jehovah. Some churches teach that Jehovah is our Heavenly Father, but Isaiah and all the prophets down through the ages knew that Jehovah was actually the name of the Savior before he came into mortality. That is why Isaiah comes right out a number of times and calls him the Redeemer. In this verse Isaiah declares that Jehovah is "my strength and my song," even "my salvation."

3. Therefore with joy shall ye draw water out of the wells of salvation.

Isaiah knew that eventually all Israel would acknowledge that the great Jehovah, even Jesus Christ, is their salvation. With the greatest of joy, those who are worthy will drink of the living water from the well of salvation which the Savior has provided through his sacrifice. This is the living water Jesus would later talk about when he visited with the woman at Jacob's well in Samaria (John 4:6–14). The Gospel of salvation is sometimes called the "water of life" (Revelation 21:6).

4. And in that day shall ye say, Praise the LORD, call upon his name, declare his doings among the people, make mention that his name is exalted.

It will be in the latter days that the gathered hosts of Israel will praise the Lord and call upon his name. They will have learned that the beginning of repentance and the turning away from stubborn apostasy starts with humble prayers, and calling upon God to forgive and guide his wayward children. No longer will they be atheistic or agnostic, or seek to hold God in derision. No longer will they be humanistic or "man centered" in seeking happiness and the true meaning of life. Finally, they will acknowlege the Lord as the Supreme and Exalted One.

5. Sing unto the LORD; for he hath done excellent things: this is known in all the earth.

That day will be such a period of glorious exultation that the people of Israel will declare to one another: "Sing unto the Lord." They will acknowledge that he has done "excellent" and unbelievably great things for all mankind. And who can deny it? By the time the Lord has consummated his work in fully establishing the great epoch of the Millennium, the physical and spiritual manifestations of his astonishing powers will be known throughout the whole earth.

6. Cry out and shout, thou inhabitant of Zion: for great is the Holy One of Israel in the midst of thee.

The people of Israel will be so moved by these great events that they will "cry out and shout" in exalted joy. No longer will the Savior be hidden in eternity, but he will minister among them. He will be in their midst and "among the people."

Isaiah, Chapter 13

INTRODUCTION:

Isaiah is famous for his predictions concerning the rise and fall of nations. From history we learn that every one of his prophecies relating to ancient nations was literally fulfilled. We can assume that his predictions concerning modern nations and modern times also will be literally fulfilled.

In chapters 13 to 23, Isaiah discusses the rise and fall of nine different nations. Chapters 13 and 14 are devoted to Babylon.

As we go through these chapters, we need to keep in mind that Isaiah's prophetic vision swept from the time of these ancient nations right on down to our modern era. He saw the same thing happening to the wicked of our day as that which he had seen happening to the wicked in ancient times. He therefore addresses himself to the wicked and the righteous of both ages. He warns the wicked and commends the righteous. When any prophet writes about events which will be fulfilled or duplicated several different times, we call such writings "multiple-fulfillment prophecies." The writings of Isaiah are characterized by many "multiple-fulfillment prophecies."

In modern times the Lord has helped us to identify many of these multiple-fulfillment prophecies by quoting Isaiah and applying his words to the destruction of the wicked in the latter days as well as in ancient times. As we go through these next few chapters, you will see that Isaiah himself was conscious of the fact that his words would be fulfilled more than once.

Now, before discussing Isaiah's prophecies concerning the events leading to the fall of Babylon, let us briefly trace the history of that famous nation. Babylon became the dominant political and military power in the world when she completely destroyed the Assyrians in 605 B.C. Most of the building of the Babylonian empire occurred under King Nebuchadnezzar. Incidental to his conquests along the Mediterranean, he conquered the Jews. He tried to be kind to them, but the Jewish kings continually rebelled, so Nebuchadnezzar came in 587 B.C. and completely demolished Jerusalem. He destroyed the beautiful temple of Solomon and carried off to Babylon those Jews who were not slain or scattered during the siege. Babylon would have probably kept the Jews in captivity forever, but she became so wicked that her power over the surrounding nations lasted only until 539 B.C. That was the year the Medes and Persians came sweeping down from the mountains and high plateaus to the east and conquered Babylon in a single night. They were led by Cyrus, whom Isaiah identified by name around 175 years before Cyrus was born (see Isaiah 44:28; 45:1). After Babylon was overthrown, Cyrus allowed the Jews to return to Jerusalem in 538 B.C.

1. The burden of Babylon, which Isaiah the son of Amoz did see.	Notice that the pending fall of Babylon was not merely whispered to Isaiah by the Spirit. He was allowed to "see" it in open vision nearly 200 years before it occurred.
2. Lift ye up a banner upon the high mountain, exalt the voice unto them, shake the hand, that they may go into the gates of the nobles.	This verse is addressed to Cyrus and the hosts of Medes and Persians whom Cyrus would assemble in the highlands east of the Tigris River. They were to raise up the banner and descend on the nobles of

Babylon. It is interesting that in the Joseph Smith Translation it says "MY banner," suggesting that Cyrus is representing the rod of God's wrath as he goes forth to conquer Babylon. We should also note that the Hebrew word for "banner" is also translated as "ensign" (Isaiah 11:10) and "standard" (Isaiah 62:10).

In the latter days the Lord's banner is raised up, but for a different purpose. It is to lead God's people out of Babylon or the wickedness of the world. Here is how the Lord says it in modern times: "Go ye out of Babylon; gather ye out from among the nations, from the four winds, from one end of heaven to the other.... Go ye forth unto the land of Zion.... And let them who be of Judah flee unto Jerusalem, unto the mountains of the Lord's house. Go ye out from among the nations, even FROM BABYLON, from the midst of wickedness, WHICH IS SPIRITUAL BABYLON." (D&C 133:7–14; emphasis added.)

3. I have commanded my sanctified ones, I have also called my mighty ones for mine anger, even them that rejoice in my highness.

The "sanctified ones" are those whom God will bless. In ancient times these were Cyrus and his Medes and Persians, who were blessed in putting down the wickedness of Babylon. In the latter days it will be the leaders of the gathering hosts of Israel.

The last part of this verse has been mutilated. It is impossible to derive the true meaning from the King James Version. The correct version is in the brass plates which says, "for mine anger IS NOT UPON them that rejoice in my highness" (2 Nephi 23:3; emphasis added). This is a great compliment to Cyrus because he was reared among pagans and never did hear the full message of the Gospel. Nevertheless, the Lord assures him that he will be blessed because he, in his limited way, honored God.

4. The noise of a multitude in the mountains, like as of a great people; a tumultuous noise of the kingdoms of nations gathered together: the LORD of hosts mustereth the host of the battle.

The hosts of Cyrus were tremendous, consisting of many tribes and nations. The same will be true of modern Israel, particularly when the Ten Tribes come down from the north. They will be resisted by the wicked. The scripture says: "And they who are in the north countries shall come in remembrance before the Lord; and their prophets shall hear his voice, and shall no longer stay themselves; and they shall smite the rocks, and the ice shall flow down at their presence. And an highway shall be cast up in the midst of the great deep. THEIR ENEMIES SHALL BECOME A PREY UNTO THEM.... And they shall bring forth their rich treasures unto the children of Ephraim, my servants. ...And there shall they fall down and be crowned with glory, even in Zion, by the hands of the servants of the Lord, even the children of Ephraim." (D&C 133:26–32; emphasis added.)

5. They come from a far country, from the end of heaven, even the LORD, and the weapons of his indignation, to destroy the whole land.

Just as Isaiah saw a great host being mustered for battle in the days of Cyrus, so it would be in the latter days.

The nations which were allied with Cyrus came from the very outskirts of civilization. Some came from the Caspian Sea coasts, some from northeast Persia, and some from beyond. They came by the tens of thousands to display the Lord's indignation against the wickedness of Babylon.

In the latter days when the Ten Tribes come down they will be such a host that "the boundaries of the everlasting hills shall tremble at their presence" (D&C 133:31). The wicked will fall before them as they come down to receive their blessings "in Zion" (D&C 133:28, 32).

6. Howl ye; for the day of the LORD is at hand; it shall come as a destruction from the Almighty.

At this point, and continuing through the next ten verses, Isaiah is addressing himself almost exclusively to the wicked of the latter days. It applies in some ways to the fall of ancient Babylon, but is far more applicable to the fall of "spiritual Babylon" just before the ushering in of the Millennium. Notice Isaiah's reference to the "destruction from the Almighty." In the days of ancient Babylon, the destruction was through the instrumentality of Cyrus and his hosts. In the latter days, the Lord has made it clear that he will be directly involved himself.

7. Therefore shall all hands be faint, and every man's heart shall melt:

Neither the Lord nor Isaiah wished to leave any doubt as to the terrifying trauma which will sweep over the wicked on both of these occasions. In the days of the Babylonians it was the terror of the Persian sword, but the Lord has said that in the latter days it will not only be the terror of war, but the very elements will be in convulsions. The Lord says, "And all things shall be in commotion; and surely, men's hearts shall fail them; for fear shall come upon all people" (D&C 88:91).

8. And they shall be afraid: pangs and sorrows shall take hold of them; they shall be in pain as a woman that travaileth: they shall be amazed one at another; their faces shall be as flames.

The fear in the faces of the people will be like the anguish of a woman in travail. Sorrow shall be throughout the land as great afflictions assail the wicked on every side. We get some idea of the unprecedented amount of massive destruction to Babylon in the latter days when the Lord describes the events which will cause men's hearts to fail them. The modern revelation says:

"But, behold, I say unto you that before this great day [of the Millennium] shall come the sun shall be darkened, and the moon shall be turned into blood, and the stars shall fall from heaven, and there shall be greater signs in heaven above and in the earth beneath; . . . and there shall be a great hailstorm sent forth to destroy the crops of the earth. . . . I the Lord God will send forth flies upon the face of the earth, which shall take hold of the inhabitants thereof, and shall eat their flesh, and shall cause maggots to come in upon them; . . . and their flesh shall fall from off their bones, and their eyes from their sockets." (D&C 29:14–19.)

The Lord goes on to say that many will be destroyed by "devouring fire" (D&C 29:21), and Isaiah says they shall be amazed at one another for their faces "shall be as flames."

As these references to the coming calamities continue, notice that Isaiah is referring more and more to the latter days and the destruction of the "world" (verse 11 of this chapter), not just the destruction of the nation of Babylon.

9. **Behold, the day of the LORD cometh, cruel both with wrath and fierce anger, to lay the land desolate: and he shall destroy the sinners thereof out of it.**

Notice in this verse that specific reference is made to the "day of the Lord," which has always referred to the latter days. Isaiah knew from the vision he had seen that these latter days would come upon the people with such violence that the lands of the wicked would become totally desolate as their unrighteous inhabitants were wiped off the face of the globe.

10. **For the stars of heaven and the constellations thereof shall not give their light: the sun shall be darkened in his going forth, and the moon shall not cause her light to shine.**

Here is the passage which clearly indicates what Isaiah has been talking about ever since verse 6. He is speaking of the premillennial period when the sun will be darkened and the moon and stars cannot be seen. In fact, as we shall see in verse 13, the earth itself will be removed out of her place. All of these things relate to the last days as described by the Lord in the Doctrine and Covenants. "And it shall be a great day AT THE TIME OF MY COMING, for all nations shall tremble. But BEFORE that great day shall come, the SUN SHALL BE DARKENED, and the moon be turned into blood; and the stars shall refuse their shining, AND SOME SHALL FALL, and great destructions await the wicked" (D&C 34:8-9). In another revelation the Lord says, "Wherefore, be not deceived, but continue in steadfastness, looking forth for the heavens to be shaken, and the earth to tremble and to reel to and fro as a drunken man" (D&C 49:23; emphasis added).

11. And I will punish the world for their evil, and the wicked for their iniquity; and I will cause the arrogancy of the proud to cease, and will lay low the haughtiness of the terrible.

Isaiah provides further evidence in this verse that he is discussing the fall of wicked Babylon IN THE LATTER DAYS. He says it will be a time when the Lord will punish THE WHOLE WORLD for its iniquity. It will be a time of final reckoning when the arrogance of the proud will cease. The haughtiness of the "terrible" will be brought low. The overwhelming trauma of those days will humble the most vicious dictator, the mighty men of warmongering nations, and all of those who terrorize the community or region which they dominate. All these will fall in the day of God's vengeance.

12. I will make a man more precious than fine gold; even a man than the golden wedge of Ophir.

To survive in a day of such universal destruction will indeed make the life of any person who survives more precious than fine gold. The gold of Ophir was so fine that Solomon had his merchant ships import it to Israel. Ophir is believed to have been in southern Arabia, but some scholars think it might have been in India or Africa.

13. Therefore I will shake the heavens, and the earth shall remove out of her place, in the wrath of the LORD of hosts, and in the day of his fierce anger.

Certainly this verse has some astonishing implications. Nothing is more disturbing to mankind than to have the elements suddenly go out of control. It does not matter whether it is a hurricane, an earthquake, a tornado, or a terrible storm at sea. The human heart is seized with fearful anxiety when the environment or elements comprising our earthly home go into convulsions. Anything experienced by mankind in the past will be negligible compared to the terrors which will seize the hearts of men in the latter days just before the Second Coming of Christ.

The Lord warns us that the very heavens will be shaken. There will be a violent revolution in the galaxy to which the earth belongs. In fact, the earth will be removed out of its orbit in the present solar system and given a new location. It shall "remove" out of its "place." This will not be the first time the earth has been shifted about in its galactic position. Brigham Young said: "When the earth was framed and brought into existence and man was placed upon it, it was near the throne of our Father in heaven. And when man fell . . . the earth fell into space, and took up its abode in this planetary system, and the sun became our light. . . . This is the glory the earth came from, and when it is glorified IT WILL RETURN AGAIN UNTO THE PRESENCE OF THE FATHER." (Brigham Young, in *Journal of Discourses*, 17:143; emphasis added.) President John Taylor also spoke of the earth prior to its fall, and said it was "first organized, near the planet Kolob" (John Taylor, "Origin, Object, and Destiny of Women," in *Mormon,* 29 Aug. 1857, p. 2). Abraham was shown that prior to the fall the earth was operating on a time schedule controlled by Kolob, "which . . . is set nigh unto the throne of God" (Abraham 3:9). It did not acquire its present rate of rotation until after the Fall (see Abraham 5:13).

But at the time of Christ's coming it will apparently be the intention of the Lord to return the earth to its original environment. To do this quickly would require that the earth be returned to Kolob faster than the speed of light. Such a phenomenon would seem to fit the words of the Lord in this verse. He said he would shake the heavens, and the earth would remove out of her place. Of course the earth's present place is about 30,000 light years out from the center of our galaxy. To pull the earth back toward Kolob in a very short time would give the appearance of all the stars falling from heaven as earth went rushing by.

14. And it shall be as the chased roe, and as a sheep that no man taketh up: they shall every man turn to his own people, and flee every one into his own land.

Now the Lord emphasizes this very point. He says the earth will be as a chased roe (which is famous for its fleetness and tremendous speed). This implies that the planet will not only be moved out of its place, but it will flee back toward Kolob at a fantastic speed. The Lord says the earth will be like an abandoned sheep which no man takes up or claims. For the earth to seem to be running loose through the night sky will be a terrifying experience for those who are then living upon this planet. Many will perish. The hearts of many will fail them because of their terror.

Here is the way the Lord describes these coming events in a modern scripture: "For not many days hence and the earth shall tremble AND REEL TO AND FRO AS A DRUNKEN MAN; and the sun shall hide his face, and shall refuse to give light; and the moon shall be bathed in blood; and the stars shall become exceedingly angry, and shall cast themselves down as a fig that falleth from off a fig-tree." (D&C 88:87; emphasis added.) No doubt this is exactly what it will seem like for all those living on the earth. The planet will be moving too fast for the light of the sun to reach it; in fact, the prophetic writings suggest it will have departed out of our present solar system altogether. The light of the stars will go rushing past, giving the impression that they are falling.

As we have quoted earlier, the Lord goes on to say, "And all things shall be in commotion; and surely, men's hearts shall fail them; for fear shall come upon all people" (D&C 88:91). The Lord says that as this period of commotion commences, every man will hasten to get home to his own people and flee into his own land.

---

15. Every one that is found shall be thrust through; and every one that is joined unto them shall fall by the sword.

Many different scriptures warn us that just prior to the Second Coming there will be a period of fratricidal warfare. The Lord says the proud will be thrust through, and all those who are in confederation with the wicked shall fall by the sword.

---

16. Their children also shall be dashed to pieces before their eyes; their houses shall be spoiled, and their wives ravished.

This is the terrible day of the Apocalypse seen by John the Revelator, when the abomination of desolation will be poured out upon the wicked. Children will be dashed to pieces before the eyes of their parents. No house will be left unviolated or unspoiled. The vicious military forces will go through like a ferocious beast. Not only will children be killed, but their mothers will be ravished. This is the insanity of savage men who engage in desolating, predatory war.

---

17. Behold, I will stir up the Medes against them, which shall not regard silver; and as for gold, they shall not delight in it.

Suddenly, and without the slightest explanation or apology, Isaiah moves back to his own day. Now he is talking about the destruction of ANCIENT Babylon. This is typical of the writings of Isaiah as his eyes sweep back and forth across the panorama of the vision the Lord is showing him. His words therefore require the closest scrutiny. In this verse the Lord specifically identifies the nation which will be in charge of the great confederation which will assemble in the mountains "to the east" preparatory to the launching of the attack on Babylon. The Lord says it will be the Medes. They will be so anxious to conquer Babylon that they cannot be turned aside or bribed with either silver or gold.

The man who led the Medes and the confederation of nearby nations against Babylon turned out to be Cyrus. His mother was the daughter of the king of the Medes, and according to tradition the old king was so cruel to his people that Cyrus rose up and overthrew him. Cyrus was supported by the Persians. He combined the two peoples. He also conquered all of the tributaries of the old Assyrian empire and formed many of them into a confederation before attacking Babylon in 539 B.C. Cyrus was not a cruel or brutal king, but generous with his subjects and wise in his administration of their affairs. The Lord therefore blessed him with success in putting down the wickedness of Babylon. It was not Cyrus, but subsequent Persian kings, who fulfilled Isaiah's prophecies concerning the total devastation of Babylon.

18. Their bows also shall dash the young men to pieces; and they shall have no pity on the fruit of the womb; their eye shall not spare children.

19. And Babylon, the glory of kingdoms, the beauty of the Chaldees' excellency, shall be as when God overthrew Sodom and Gomorrah.

Before the Persians had finished with Babylon (long after Cyrus), the youth of Babylon were indeed dashed to pieces. Neither did the Persians spare the fruit of the womb (meaning expectant mothers). The beauty and excellency of Babylon became like the ruins of Sodom and Gomorrah.

20. It shall never be inhabited, neither shall it be dwelt in from generation to generation: neither shall the Arabian pitch tent there; neither shall the shepherds make their fold there.

Isaiah predicted that after its fall the ancient city of Babylon would not be inhabited again from generation to generation. Not even the bedouin Arabs would dare to pitch their tents there, nor would shepherds use it to gather their sheep into folds.

21. But wild beasts of the desert shall lie there; and their houses shall be full of doleful creatures; and owls shall dwell there, and satyrs shall dance there.

Instead, wild beasts of the desert would make the ruins of Babylon their habitation. The rich Babylonian homes would be infested with doleful creatures. Owls would dwell there and satyrs (wild male goats) would dance there.

22. And the wild beasts of the islands shall cry in their desolate houses, and dragons in their pleasant palaces: and her time is near to come, and her days shall not be prolonged.

Isaiah said that the ruins of the once mighty Babylon would be haunted by the cry of wild animals in their desolated houses. There would be no restructuring of the city, but lizards and other creatures of the desert would inhabit their once beautiful palaces and public buildings. Isaiah said all of this would happen in the not-too-distant future because the Lord had determined that the days of Babylon's wickedness were not to be prolonged.

In the original text, Isaiah closed this chapter with a word of comfort to go along with the blistering warning which he had just proclaimed. This closing sentence appears in the brass plates: "FOR I WILL DESTROY HER SPEEDILY; YEA, FOR I WILL BE MERCIFUL UNTO MY PEOPLE [who are righteous], BUT THE WICKED SHALL PERISH." (2 Nephi 23:22; emphasis added.)

Isaiah, Chapter 14

INTRODUCTION:

The century to which Isaiah belonged and the two centuries which followed are all part of the historical panorama which needs to be understood in order to appreciate the details of this great segment of scripture. Here, in capsule form, are the principal events of this period.

1. Around 800 B.C., a quarter of a century before Isaiah was born, the most wicked and cruel nation on earth was the Assyrians with their capital at Nineveh. Jonah was sent to warn that city. He told them that unless they repented they would be destroyed. Amazingly, they did repent and their destruction was temporarily averted. However, after approximately 40 years, they started moving out again, as ruthless as ever.

2. Over a period of several years, from about 735 to 721 B.C., the Assyrians conquered the northern Ten Tribes, finally destroying their capital city of Samaria, and carried off as captives the remnant which had survived. All of this Isaiah not only predicted but saw fulfilled.

3. In 701 B.C., the Assyrians were back to conquer Egypt, but en route they desolated the Palestinian strongholds of Judah. They also would have subjugated Jerusalem had not the Lord suddenly struck down the Assyrian army with a plague which killed 185,000 in one night. The Assyrian king therefore gave up his campaign and returned home. All this happened during the days of Isaiah.

He was an active participant in warning and prophesying concerning these events.

4. During the next 75 years the Babylonians were gradually rising to power. In 612 B.C. they led an attack on Nineveh, the capital of Assyria, and it fell. The Assyrians then tried to regroup, and a showdown battle was fought at Carchemish in 605 B.C. This was one of the most famous battles in history. It completely annihilated Assyria as a nation, and the Babylonians then became the dominant force in the earth for the next 66 years.

5. The Babylonians then set about to bring all of the surrounding countries under their tribute, including the Jews. Nebuchadnezzar was in charge of the Babylonian armies under his father and entered Jerusalem in 606 B.C. to put the people under tribute. He did not destroy the city of Jerusalem but took back a few young Jews to teach them the Babylonian language so they could be administrators for the king. These included Daniel, Shadrach, Meshach, and Abednego.

6. In 601–598 B.C., Nebuchadnezzar made a series of minor assaults on Jerusalem to keep the obstreperous Jewish kings in line and secure a more prompt payment of the tribute. Incidental to these campaigns, the king of Babylon exported from Judah 10,000 of their best artisans to work in Babylon. One of these was Ezekiel, who was later called to be a prophet after five years in captivity.

7. In 587 B.C. Nebuchadnezzar returned to Jerusalem with a huge force. The king of Judah had refused to pay the annual tribute and had entered into an alliance with Egypt. Nebuchadnezzar therefore decided to avenge himself on the city of Jerusalem just as Isaiah had predicted. The temple of Solomon was destroyed, the whole city was depopu-

lated, and the people who survived were carried off to Babylon as captives.

8. Nebuchadnezzar ruled Babylon until 562 B.C. and was then replaced by his son, Amil-Marduk (Evil-merodach of the Bible). After a reign of only two years, Evil-merodach was killed in 560 B.C. by his ambitious brother-in-law, Neriglissor, who was a prominent army officer. Neriglissor ruled until 556 B.C., when he died and was replaced by his young son, Labashi-Marduk. This unfortunate boy lasted only nine months before he was assassinated, and one of the conspirators took over the throne. His name was Nabonidus, and he ruled Babylon until its fall in 539 B.C. During this period the corruption of Babylon was as notorious as the wealth of her fabulous cities. Daniel was the principal prophet in Babylon during these years. In the fourth chapter of Daniel it tells how he went to the king to warn him that he would be insane for a period of seven years. Some ancient scribe inserted the name of the king as being Nebuchadnezzar, but we know from the Dead Sea scrolls and from history that the king who went insane was Nabonidus. It was during his mental illness that a son, Belshazzar, served as regent and was also called "king."

9. During the reign of Nabonidus and his son, Belshazzar, over Babylon, a young man by the name of Cyrus was rising to power just to the east. His father was king of Persia and his grandfather was king of the Medes. Cyrus combined both countries into one and began building a mighty kingdom by conquering many areas which formerly belonged to the Assyrian Empire. He conquered much of Asia Minor in 546 B.C. and then took the rich Greek islands into his empire. In 539 B.C. he met

Nabonidus in the battle of Opis. Nabonidus had only recently recovered from his siege of insanity and fought with Cyrus at Opis, where his Babylonian armies were defeated. However, Nabonidus escaped. Cyrus then turned toward the great city of Babylon. The son of Nabonidus, King Belshazzar, who had occupied the throne during his father's illness and still served as a "king," was having a great feast the night Cyrus decided to attack. It would therefore appear that the "king of Babylon" in the fourteenth chapter of Isaiah is Belshazzar.

10. Belshazzar held a feast for 1,000 of his lords, but in the midst of the celebration a ghostly human hand was seen writing some strange words on the wall. The king was terribly frightened, and when none of his wise men could explain the meaning of the words, his queen suggested that they send for the famous Hebrew prophet, Daniel. Belshazzar was not acquainted with Daniel, but knew him by reputation. Daniel responded and interpreted the message on the wall. He told the king that it said:

"MENE; God hath numbered thy kingdom, and finished it.

"TEKEL; Thou art weighed in the balances, and art found wanting.

"PERES [UPHARSIN]; Thy kingdom is divided, and given to the Medes and Persians." (Daniel 5:26–28.)

Great consternation took over the leaders of Babylon assembled at the feast. That night two of Belshazzar's leading officials murdered him (Adam Clarke, *The Holy Bible...with a Commentary and Critical Notes*, 6 vols. [Nashville: Abingdon, n.d.], 4:586). Meanwhile, a huge contingent of the Persian army built a diversionary channel for the branch of the Euphrates River which flowed under the wall and into the city of Babylon to provide its luxurious fountains and waterways. Once the water of this stream was diverted, it opened up a passage for the Persian troops to enter the city. Before daybreak the city had been taken.

1. **For the LORD will have mercy on Jacob, and will yet choose Israel, and set them in their own land: and the strangers shall be joined with them, and they shall cleave to the house of Jacob.**

It will be recalled that the last verse of chapter 13 has a sentence missing in which the Lord says that "I will be merciful unto my people, but the wicked shall perish" (2 Nephi 23:22). Now the Lord amplifies his assurance to those who are righteous and who remain faithful to the covenant made between Abraham and the Lord. The Lord says he will be merciful to the tribes of Jacob and, in spite of their temporary captivity or persecution, they will be reclaimed by the Lord and identified as his people. This happened to the Jews in 538 B.C., when Cyrus invited them to return to their homeland and rebuild their temple. Isaiah saw that the same thing would happen in the latter days. And not only to the Jews, but to all Israel. They would all be gathered to the lands of their inheritance. It is interesting that each time the Lord has gathered Israel, there have been "strangers" or Gentiles who were anxious to accompany them. This has been true whenever Israel has been righteous and worthy of the Gentiles' admiration. They want to "cleave to the house of Jacob" and be one with Israel.

2. **And the people shall take them, and bring them to their place: and the house of Israel shall possess them in the land of the LORD for servants and handmaids: and they shall take them captives, whose captives they were; and they shall rule over their oppressors.**

The people of Israel will accept these strangers and bring them to their gathering places where they can be together. There will be a change in the governing of the land, and those who formerly oppressed Israel will be governed under the righteous leadership of Israel.

In the original text of this verse there were 18 words which have been left out of the King James Version. The brass plates contained these words and clarified three others: "And the people shall take them and bring them to their place; YEA, FROM FAR UNTO THE ENDS OF THE EARTH; AND THEY SHALL RETURN TO THEIR LANDS [note the plural] OF PROMISE. And the house of Israel shall possess them, and the land of the Lord SHALL BE for servants and handmaids; and they shall take them captives UNTO WHOM they were captives; and they shall rule over their oppressors." (2 Nephi 24:2; emphasis added.)

Note how extensive the gathering will be. Also note that the two lands of promise (Palestine and America) will be exclusively for the servants and handmaids of the Lord. Those who formerly persecuted the people of Israel will now find themselves depending on the children of Israel for the administration of the government in righteousness.

---

3. And it shall come to pass in the day that the LORD shall give thee rest from thy sorrow, and from thy fear, and from the hard bondage wherein thou wast made to serve,

In this verse there is a beautiful promise that the people of Israel will eventually have their day of peace in which there will be no more bitter sorrow, persecution, and fear. No longer will they be in bondage and servitude. They will be free. In the King James Version it is somewhat difficult to fix the time when this promise is to be fulfilled, but in the brass plates it does not say "the day," but in "THAT day" (2 Nephi 24:3; emphasis added). This means the day of the Lord when he will come in power to judge the whole world (Isaiah 13:11).

---

4. That thou shalt take up this proverb against the king of Babylon, and say, How hath the oppressor ceased! the golden city ceased!

There were three notable occasions when this verse was literally fulfilled for the Jews. The first was when they were liberated along with the rest of Israel from captivity and hard bondage under the Egyptians. The second was when they were liberated from the Baby-

5. The LORD hath broken the staff of the wicked, and the sceptre of the rulers.

6. He who smote the people in wrath with a continual stroke, he that ruled the nations in anger, is persecuted, and none hindereth.

lonians by Cyrus and the Persians. The third has been in modern times when powerful dictators such as Adolf Hitler and Benito Mussolini established a policy of slave labor camps for Jews, and said they would eventually exterminate all Jews coming within their power. In each of these instances the terrible desolation hanging over the people was suddenly lifted. It was virtually unbelievable at first. And so it will yet be when the Jews face their Armageddon. After much tribulation, it will suddenly end. As with the fall of ancient Babylon in a single night, so shall it be in the latter days. Their oppressors will dissolve into nothing just as the golden city of the Babylonians ceased to be a threat once the Persians had taken over.

7. The whole earth is at rest, and is quiet: they break forth into singing.

In Isaiah's day it was virtually impossible to comprehend how it could be achieved, but suddenly the whole earth would be at rest. There would be no more killing, ravishing, and enslaving. Everything would be peaceful and quiet. In a spirit of grateful jubilation the people would begin singing their praises to God, who made it all possible.

8. Yea, the fir trees rejoice at thee, and the cedars of Lebanon, saying, Since thou art laid down, no feller is come up against us.

In this verse Isaiah uses a common metaphor of trees to represent vast populations of people. They are like forests of fir trees and the cedars of Lebanon. They will rejoice together, saying that since the cruel and evil kingdom of Babylon has been put down, no feller (one who cuts or fells trees) has come up to molest them.

9. Hell from beneath is moved for thee to meet thee at thy coming: it stirreth up the dead for thee, even all the

As the king of Babylon is murdered and his great golden city conquered, the hosts of hell will gather to look with astonishment on the disembodied spirit of

chief ones of the earth; it hath raised up from their thrones all the kings of the nations.

the mighty ruler who has fallen. Not only will the masses of spirits of the dead rise to meet the former king of Babylon, but all the royal rulers will gather about him in dismay, for this is the mighty king of Babylon who had sent many of them to an early grave.

10. All they shall speak and say unto thee, Art thou also become weak as we? art thou become like unto us?

The rulers of many nations who were conquered by Babylon will look into the countenance of this once mighty master of the Babylonian empire and exclaim: "Art thou also become weak as we? Art thou become like unto us?"

11. Thy pomp is brought down to the grave, and the noise of thy viols: the worm is spread under thee, and the worms cover thee.

It will be difficult for them to believe that this ruthless tyrant whom they thought was invincible has been suddenly shorn of all his pomp and power. His glory has all collapsed into dust in a single night. (See Daniel 5:30–31. Note that Darius is given credit for the conquest of Babylon. This is a scribe's error. Darius came later. It was Cyrus who conquered Babylon the first time.)

No longer will the fallen ruler of Babylon be able to enjoy feasts and listen to the soothing music of the viols in his rich palace. His once proud physique that made him such a strong warrior will be lifeless, food for worms.

12. How art thou fallen from heaven, O Lucifer, son of the morning! how art thou cut down to the ground, which didst weaken the nations!

Suddenly Isaiah realizes how the fall of the evil king of Babylon will be very much like the fall of Satan, that supreme prince of evil. Isaiah and, later, John the Revelator refer to the fall of Lucifer during the premortal existence (see Revelation 12:7–9). His arrogance and pride carried the same spirit of evil, zeal, and ambition as that which will be exhibited by the wicked king of

Babylon. So Isaiah addresses Lucifer to remind him of that terrible day when he made war in heaven and was cast down in abject defeat just as the king of Babylon, Satan's evil servant, will be defeated.

Isaiah calls Lucifer the "son of the morning." This is said to mean that he is one of the "early born spirit children of the Father" (Bruce R. McConkie, *Mormon Doctrine*, 2nd ed., p. 744). The name Lucifer means "lightbearer" or "shining one" (ibid., p. 461). Jesus referred to Lucifer's fall during the premortal existence when he said, "I beheld Satan as lightning fall from heaven" (Luke 10:18). John the Revelator describes how "there was war in heaven: Michael and his angels fought against the dragon. . . . And the great dragon was cast out, that old serpent, called the Devil, and Satan, which deceiveth the whole world: he was cast out into the earth, and his angels were cast out with him." (Revelation 12:7-9.) In view of all this it is easy to appreciate why Isaiah would say of Satan: "How art thou fallen from heaven, O Lucifer, son of the morning! how art thou cut down to the ground, which didst weaken the nations!" During the war in heaven, Satan weakened the ranks of the Father's children to the extent that one-third fell away (D&C 29:36). When he was cast out with his followers into the temporal earth, he was literally "cut down to the ground."

13. For thou hast said in thine heart, I will ascend into heaven, I will exalt my throne above the stars of God: I will sit also upon the mount of the congregation, in the sides of the north:

This verse tells us how serious the war in heaven really was. Satan had said he would ascend into heaven and exalt HIS throne above the "stars" or sons of God. He aspired to rule over the Father's children by sitting on the "mount of the congregation, in the sides of the north." This strange expression acquires more meaning when we read Psalms 48:1-2: "Great is the Lord, and greatly [is he] to be praised in the city of our God IN THE MOUNTAIN of his holiness. . . . The joy of the whole earth, is MOUNT ZION, ON THE SIDES OF THE NORTH, THE CITY OF THE GREAT KING." So now we understand what Isaiah is saying. Lucifer aspired to rule mankind and replace Jehovah as the "great King" who would rule the earth from Mount Zion.

14. I will ascend above the heights of the clouds; I will be like the most High.

In this verse the picture becomes even more clear. Isaiah says Satan wanted to be "like" the Most High or the Father, and ascend above the heights of the clouds or ascend into heaven. When this verse says that Satan wanted to be "like" the Father, it might be assumed that he merely wanted to be coequal with the Father, but this was not the case. In a modern revelation the Lord says Satan actually wanted to take over the "honor" and "power" of being God (D&C 29:36). The Lord makes it clear in this passage that Lucifer's scheme was a terrible and literal "rebellion" against the Father.

Lucifer exhibited a rebellious spirit on more than one occasion. There seem to have been at least two major councils in heaven, and the rebellious spirit of Lucifer was manifested in both of them. One of these councils is described in Abraham 3:23–28. This council was to select a heavenly authority to be in charge of the structuring of the earth. It says that a person "like unto God" (apparently the Father) said, "Whom shall I send?" And a person "like unto the Son of Man" (apparently Jehovah) spoke up and said, "Here am I, send me." Then "another" answered in the same words. The Father said, "I will send the FIRST." The second person then commenced a rebellion or agitation against the one who had been chosen to supervise the project of structuring the earth. He was not cast out at this time. The record simply says, "And the second was angry, AND KEPT NOT HIS FIRST ESTATE; and, at that day, many followed after him" (Abraham 3:28; emphasis added).

Note that in this particular council we have the FIRST one chosen and the SECOND rebelling. Now notice what happens in the council which is described by Moses (Moses 4:1-3).

This second council was for the purpose of adopting the Father's plan of salvation and selecting a redeemer. In this council the FIRST person to speak up and volunteer for the role of redeemer was Satan. In fact, he had a scheme whereby he guaranteed that "one soul shall not be lost." The scripture says he was going to "destroy the agency of man," which means he wanted to save mankind by compelling each person to be good whether he wished to or not. Lucifer thought this was such a great scheme that he demanded the "honor" of being God (D&C 29:36). At this point the scripture says, "But, behold, my Beloved Son, which was my Beloved and Chosen from the beginning [probably referring to the first council], said unto me—Father, thy will be done, and the glory be thine forever" (Moses 4:2).

The Father then says, "Satan rebelled against me, and sought to destroy the agency of man, which I, the Lord God, had given him, and also, that I should give unto him mine own power; by the power of mine Only Begotten, I caused that he should be cast down" (Moses 4:3). Not only did Satan fail to keep his "first estate," but Jude speaks of those who followed Satan and also "kept not their first estate." These were cast out with Satan and "reserved in everlasting chains" until the final judgment (Jude 1:6).

15. Yet thou shalt be brought down to hell, to the sides of the pit.

Therefore, as this verse verifies, Lucifer was brought down to hell. He did not ascend to the "mount of the congregation, in the sides of the north" (Zion), but descended to the "sides of the pit" in hell.

16. They that see thee shall narrowly look upon thee, and consider thee, saying, Is this the man that made the earth to tremble, that did shake kingdoms;

Now Isaiah swings back to the fall of the king of Babylon, who would also fall and go down into the pit of hell, precisely as Satan had done. Isaiah said that when this happens the inhabitants of hell would "narrowly look" (squint) at the king of Babylon and say, "Is this the man that made the earth to tremble" and whose ferocity "did shake kingdoms"?

17. That made the world as a wilderness, and destroyed the cities thereof; that opened not the house of his prisoners?

The king of Babylon had been a violent potentate who made the world a wilderness, and destroyed the cities which each nation had so carefully built. Once he had taken anyone as a prisoner he would never open the doors of freedom to him again.

18. All the kings of the nations, even all of them, lie in glory, every one in his own house.

Of course, it was always the custom when kings died to make them an elaborate, expensively decorated tomb where they could rest in glory and be honored by subsequent generations.

19. But thou art cast out of thy grave like an abominable branch, and as the raiment of those that are slain, thrust through with a sword, that go down to the stones of the pit; as a carcase trodden under feet.

Isaiah declared that this would not happen to the king of Babylon when he died. Isaiah said he would be cast out of his grave like something that was abominable or the garment of someone who had been slain and cast down upon the stones (or bottom) of the pit, which is a mass grave for all those who have been trodden under foot and run over by chariots until they can scarcely be recognized or identified anymore.

20. Thou shalt not be joined with them in burial, because thou hast destroyed thy land, and slain thy peo-

Isaiah says the king of Babylon will not be joined with other kings in their extravagant and elaborate tombs because he has been an enemy to his own people. During his hour of power he will destroy the land and

ple: the seed of evildoers shall never be renowned.

slay the people. And his descendants will not fare any better. The prophet declares that the seed of evildoers will never be renowned.

21. Prepare slaughter for his children for the iniquity of their fathers; that they do not rise, nor possess the land, nor fill the face of the world with cities.

Isaiah declared that the children or descendants of this wicked king would be killed along with their father. This whole dynasty was to come to an end, never again to fill the world with great cities erected after the abominable order of Babylon.

22. For I will rise up against them, saith the LORD of hosts, and cut off from Babylon the name, and remnant, and son, and nephew, saith the LORD.

Isaiah declares that the name of this family will be wiped out. The destruction of this dynasty would include every remnant, even the king's son and his nephew.

23. I will also make it a possession for the bittern, and pools of water: and I will sweep it with the besom of destruction, saith the LORD of hosts.

Isaiah declared that after its fall, the great golden city of Babylon would be possessed by "bittern" (heron-like wading birds with a booming cry) and pools of water would accumulate within the precincts of that once great city. This literally came to pass as the Euphrates River swept into many parts of the city and left stagnant pools inhabited by wild water fowl.

24. The LORD of hosts hath sworn, saying, Surely as I have thought, so shall it come to pass; and as I have purposed, so shall it stand:

The Lord pronounced through Isaiah a solemn certification that whatever he has sworn to do will surely come to pass. Whatever he proposes to accomplish, it shall become a reality and stand forth as a testimony of his power.

25. That I will break the Assyrian in my land, and upon
my mountains tread him
under foot: then shall his
yoke depart from off them,
and his burden depart from
off their shoulders.

The Lord has not only determined to destroy
Babylon in due time, but he has already programmed
the means by which a more immediate threat to Israel
will be eliminated. This was the Assyrian Empire,
which preceded Babylon and was the terror of the
world in Isaiah's day. In this verse the King James
Version says the Lord will "break" the Assyrians, but in
the brass plates it says the Lord will "BRING" the
Assyrians into the promised land (2 Nephi 24:25). This
makes the rest of the verse more sensible. For it says
these Assyrians will pour into the mountains of Israel
and tread them under foot (conquer them). It turned
out that the Assyrians did not storm the mountains of
Judah but only the mountains of Ephraim, where the
Ten Tribes were located. These were trodden under
foot from around 735 to 721 B.C., when the surviving
remnants were carried off to Assyria. There they
remained as virtual captives or hostages until Babylon
came along in 605 B.C. and virtually annihilated the
Assyrian people as a nation. This allowed the Ten
Tribes to escape from their Assyrian captors and flee
northward over the Caucasus Mountains, where they
disappeared and became known as the lost tribes.

26. This is the purpose that is
purposed upon the whole
earth: and this is the hand
that is stretched out upon
all the nations.

All of this is what the Lord is referring to in the latter
part of verse 25 when he says: "THEN [meaning in the
due time of the Lord] shall his [Assyria's] yoke depart
from off them, and his burden depart from off their
shoulders." It is interesting that the lifting of the yoke
of the Assyrians would be by the Babylonians, and then
when the Babylonians had fixed a yoke on the necks of
the Jews, it would be the Persians who would conquer
Babylon and lift the Babylonian yoke from off the
necks of the Jews. Truly, the Lord could certify that as
he had planned it, so these historical events would
surely come to pass!

27. For the LORD of hosts hath purposed, and who shall disannul it? and his hand is stretched out, and who shall turn it back?

This appears to be Isaiah's commentary on the previous verses. Here he is telling of events that will occur during the next two centuries, and he knows that the judgments of God will come upon each wicked nation in its turn. Isaiah leaves the scoffer to answer the question: "Who shall disannul it . . . who shall turn it back?"

Actually, nothing can nullify or turn aside a pronounced judgment of God upon the wicked except repentance. In the days of Jonah, the wicked city of Nineveh had postponed its destruction through repentance, but Isaiah was saying in these verses that this would not be the case during the next two centuries. First Assyria would fall by the hands of the Babylonians, and then Babylon would fall at the hands of the Persians.

28. In the year that king Ahaz died, was this burden.

Isaiah says that these visions and prophecies concerning Babylon and Assyria were given to him in the year that Ahaz, the wicked king of Judah, died (see Isaiah, chapter 7). The date for the death of Ahaz is considered to have been about 728 B.C., just seven years before the Assyrians finally conquered the Ephraimites and the Ten Tribes.

29. Rejoice not thou, whole Palestina, because the rod of him that smote thee is broken: for out of the serpent's root shall come forth a cockatrice, and his fruit shall be a fiery flying serpent.

Isaiah now addresses a few brief comments to the pagan enemies of Israel, the Philistines. They had been conquered by the Jewish armies a few years before under King Uzziah (see 2 Chronicles 26:6). But since the Assyrians were already marauding the Mediterranean coasts and the mountains of Ephraim, the Philistines had asserted their independence. Isaiah warns them not to rejoice over the fact that they have broken the yoke and escaped the tributary which they formerly paid to Jerusalem, because something far worse is about to happen to them. Out of the serpent's root (Satan's evil kingdom) will come a cockatrice (poisonous serpent, which turned out to be the cruel atrocities of Assyria), and the fruit of the future will bring Palestine even more evil, a "flying serpent"!

---

30. And the firstborn of the poor shall feed, and the needy shall lie down in safety: and I will kill thy root with famine, and he shall slay thy remnant.

Isaiah predicted that the rich and wicked people of Palestine would be driven out by famine and that one day this whole land would no longer have even a remnant of the Philistines. Famine and sword would wipe them out. In their place, the poor and needy would dwell safely and cultivate the rich Palestinian plain for their food.

---

31. Howl, O gate; cry, O city; thou, whole Palestina, art dissolved: for there shall come from the north a smoke, and none shall be alone in his appointed times.

Isaiah tells the Philistines to prepare to howl and cry, for they are about to be totally dissolved. A fiery smoke shall come out of the north and consume the whole people. None will be left to attend their "appointed times" or great assemblies.

---

32. What shall one then answer the messengers of the nation? That the LORD hath founded Zion, and the poor of his people shall trust in it.

Isaiah also knew that ultimately the whole Philistine coast would be occupied by a righteous people who would say: "The Lord hath founded Zion, and the poor of his people shall trust in it." The word "Zion" refers to a place and a condition. Modern prophets have been told that the place called Zion is North and South America, to which Isaiah referred frequently in his writings (Smith, *Teachings*, p. 362). However, "Zion" as a condition can be anywhere. As the Lord has declared, "This is Zion—the pure in heart" (D&C 97:21). Isaiah knew that ultimately Palestine would belong to the pure in heart.

Thus we come to the conclusion of Isaiah's great prophecy or "burden" concerning Babylon and the wickedness she represented, both anciently and in our own day.

INTRODUCTION:

Before commencing our discussion of chapter 15, let us get better acquainted with the Moabites, who are the subject of this chapter.

The Moabites were Hebrews. They were descendants of Terah, father of Abraham. Their immediate ancestor was Lot, grandson of Terah and therefore a nephew of Abraham. Lot's father died in the famine at Ur around 2000 B.C., and Terah therefore adopted Lot and his two sisters, Sarai and Milcah. This made Lot Abraham's foster brother and the two girls his foster sisters (see Abraham 2:1-2, 22-25). Abraham married Sarai (later renamed Sarah), and Abraham's brother, Nehor, married Milcah. Abraham took his wife and Lot with him in his travels to Egypt and then to Palestine. Abraham allowed Lot to take his flocks to whatever part of this promised land he desired. Lot chose the rich valley of Sodom and Gomorrah and made his home in the city of Sodom. Around 1950 B.C. Lot was warned by heavenly messengers to flee, and the Lord completely annihilated both Sodom and Gomorrah by fire. Lot's wife lost her life when she failed to follow the instructions of the angelic beings who came to warn them. As a result, only Lot and his two daughters escaped (see Genesis, chapter 19). They first went to the nearby city of Zoar, but this was also a wicked heathen city and so they fled into the nearby mountains to live in a cave (Genesis 19:30).

At this point the two daughters of Lot felt they had a serious problem. They thought their father was the

last in line of the "covenant people" who had not apostatized (this was a year before Isaac was born to Sarah
and Abraham). It must have appeared to them that if
their father Lot left no descendants the line of the covenant people would be lost from off the face of the
earth. The two daughters therefore decided to do a
desperate thing. They determined to have their father
beget children through them. They knew Lot would
never consent to this, so they decided to try to get him
intoxicated and thereby blur his judgment. The scripture tells the rest of the story in Genesis, chapter 19, as
follows:

"And they made their father drink wine that night:
and the firstborn went in, and lay with her father; and
he perceived not when she lay down, nor when she
arose.

"And it came to pass on the morrow, that the firstborn said unto the younger, Behold, I lay yesternight
with my father: let us make him drink wine this night
also; and go thou in, and lie with him, that we may
preserve seed of our father.

"And they made their father drink wine that night
also: and the younger arose, and lay with him; and he
perceived not when she lay down, nor when she arose.

"Thus were both the daughters of Lot with child by
their father.

"And the firstborn bare a son, and called his name
Moab: the same is the father of the Moabites unto this
day.

"And the younger, she also bare a son, and called his
name Ben-ammi: the same is the father of the children
of Ammon unto this day." (Genesis 19:33–38.)

Unfortunately, both the Moabites and the Ammonites apostatized like all the rest of the Hebrews. The
only exceptions were Abraham's direct descendants
through Isaac, and they ended up in slavery making

bricks for the Pharaohs. By the time the Israelites escaped out of Egypt (around 1450 B.C.), the Moabites had become the enemies of both God and Israel. They had their own gods—pagan gods, patrons of sex worship and even human sacrifices. As a result, Moses was not allowed to travel across their country en route to the Jordan Valley, but had to lead the hosts of Israel far to the east. He then followed the Arnon River, the boundary between the Moabites on the south and the Ammonites on the north. From then on, it was one great battle after another until Moses had safely occupied the eastern side of the Jordan Valley.

It was then that the Moabites tried to bribe Balaam, a prophet of the Lord from Syria, to curse Moses. They wanted to induce the God of Israel to forsake Moses so the Israelites could be overcome. Balaam came down three different times to ask God to curse the Israelites, but each time the Lord instructed him to bless the people instead of curse them. Balaam did what he was told, but later rebelled, abandoned his own calling, and went over to the Moabites. He suggested that the Moabites send over their beautiful women to seduce the young soldiers of the Israelites, thereby corrupting them so they would lose God's blessings. The scheme succeeded until the Lord sent a great plague which destroyed 24,000 Israelites before they repented. Moses then led an attack against the Moabites and their allies, destroying many of their cities and slaying their armies. Among the thousands of the dead, the body of Balaam was found.

After the Israelites had taken over the "promised land," fairly friendly relations developed between the Moabites and the Israelites. Around 1150 B.C. a famine developed in Judah, and a man from Bethlehem took his wife and two sons to Moab to survive. One of the sons married a Moabite girl named Ruth. However, the husband of Ruth died, so she moved to Bethlehem as a young widow. There she married Boaz, a well-to-do wheat farmer. They became the great-grandparents of David, hence the ancestors of Christ. When David was in hiding from King Saul, he took his parents to the king of the Moabites for safekeeping. The king of the Moabites welcomed him and allowed David's parents to stay with him for the duration of the war.

Over three centuries later, in the year 726 B.C., the good King Hezekiah ruled over the kingdom of Judah. The Moabites had once more become enemies, and Isaiah was ready to predict the total annihilation of the Moabites as a nation.

1. The burden of Moab. Because in the night Ar of Moab is laid waste, and brought to silence; because in the night Kir of Moab is laid waste, and brought to silence:

Isaiah's "burden" of prophecy concerning the virtual annihilation of the Moabites begins here. The great prophet foresaw that a tremendous destruction would come upon two of their best fortified cities. Both Ar and Kir would go down in a single night. In just a few hours these two great cities would be devastated and their military forces put to silence.

2. He is gone up to Bajith, and to Dibon, the high places, to weep: Moab shall howl over Nebo, and over Medeba: on all their heads shall be baldness, and every beard cut off.

Dr. Adam Clarke states that this verse is not properly translated. In the original Hebrew it is more meaningful. It says that the people will stampede toward their great house of idolatry (Bajith) and their high tower of licentious worship (Dibon) to petition their pagan gods and mourn their calamity. These were two of the "high places" which the prophets continually denounced as an abomination before the Lord. (Clarke, *Commentary*, 4:85.)

This verse also says the people will climb to the heights of Mount Nebo (where Moses was translated) to howl bitterly in sorrow and lamentation. They will do the same at Medeba, possibly another high mountain. In time of mourning or war the heathen nations often had their men shave off the hair of their heads, as well as their beards. Therefore, Isaiah says that in the day of the Moabite destruction the men of that nation will all be in mourning with their heads bald and their beards shaved.

3. In their streets they shall gird themselves with sackcloth: on the tops of their houses, and in their streets, every one shall howl, weeping abundantly.

The destruction will be so sudden and overwhelming that the survivors will go about the streets in the rough, loose-woven sackcloth which signified sorrow and lamentation. Isaiah says that no matter where an observer might go in that day, he will see the people in the streets and on the roofs of their houses crying out in the most wretched desolation.

4. And Heshbon shall cry, and Elealeh: their voice shall be heard even unto Jahaz: therefore the armed soldiers of Moab shall cry out; his life shall be grievous unto him.

The mourning will not only extend throughout the territory south of the Arnon River, but it will extend to the northern area from which the Moabites had been driven by the Amorites. The capital of the Amorite king, Sihon, was HESHBON, which Moses conquered (see Numbers 21:25-26). Another famous city nearby was ELEALEH. Isaiah also mentions JAHAZ, a little further north, where King Sihon made his last stand against Moses and the Israelites (Numbers 21:23-24). Moses did a great favor to the Moabites by liberating all this area from the Amorites, but because of their wickedness, Isaiah saw the day of judgment against the people of Moab when all of these great cities would be in mourning. Their proud soldiers would be so completely humbled that they would weep with the common people. Isaiah said life in that day would be a grief and a pain.

5. My heart shall cry out for Moab; his fugitives shall

Dr. Clarke points out that in the Greek or Septuagint version of Isaiah it does not say "my heart shall cry" but

flee unto Zoar, an heifer of three years old: for by the mounting up of Luhith with weeping shall they go it up; for in the way of Horonaim they shall raise up a cry of destruction.

"HIS heart shall cry" (Clarke, *Commentary*, 4:85). Isaiah saw that many of the people will try to escape by rushing down from the highlands of Moab to the plain below where Sodom and Gomorrah used to be. Those cities, of course, were wiped out more than 1,000 years earlier, but the nearby city of ZOAR will still exist and these fugitives will flee to it. Isaiah says the destruction of Moab will not come in a time of weakness but in her prime, like a heifer three years old. This was a Hebrew metaphor commonly used in a pastoral society. The fugitives will pass over the hill or ascent of LUHITH which is on the way to Zoar. Another sanctuary or stopping place will be HORONAIM, meaning the place of several caverns (ibid.). At all of these places, Isaiah saw the people mourning with "a cry of destruction."

6. For the waters of Nimrim shall be desolate: for the hay is withered away, the grass faileth, there is no green thing.

The plain of Sodom and Gomorrah was always considered a place of relatively luxurious growth. Even after those cities were destroyed the surrounding area remained fertile and attractive. One of its more abundant areas which had meadows of grass and grain was NIMRIM, where there were watering pools for flocks. This is believed to have been just a few miles from Zoar, on the plain of Sodom. Isaiah saw in his vision that this beautiful oasis of the past would be "desolate" in the days of Moab's downfall. The hay would be withered away, the grass gone, and there would be no green thing in sight.

7. Therefore the abundance they have gotten, and that which they have laid up, shall they carry away to the brook of the willows.

Isaiah also saw that the inhabitants of this place, who had stores and reserves from the past, would carry them off and hide them among the willows and undergrowth so that their food and grain would not be seized by the crowds of fugitives surging down from the heights of Moab.

8. For the cry is gone round about the borders of Moab; the howling thereof unto Eglaim, and the howling thereof unto Beer-elim.

The fall of the Moabites to their Assyrian conquerers will cause all the inhabitants on the borders of Moab to become alarmed lest they also become engulfed in the destruction. The mourning and cry of alarm will reach one of the outposts called EGLAIM (two ponds) and another one called BEER-ELIM (meaning "well of heroes").

9. For the waters of Dimon shall be full of blood: for I will bring more upon Dimon, lions upon him that escapeth of Moab, and upon the remnant of the land.

One of the streams running down from the heights of Moab to the Dead Sea was called Dimon. Isaiah saw that the slaughter of the Moabites would be so universal that the waters of this stream would be red with blood. And once the fleeing survivors left the main highways to escape into the mountains and highland ravines, they would find themselves preyed upon by the lions and other predatory animals which were a constant menace in these regions during ancient times.

Isaiah, Chapter 16

INTRODUCTION:

We now continue Isaiah's vision of the destruction of the Moabites by the Assyrians, which he commenced to describe in chapter 15.

1. Send ye the lamb to the ruler of the land from Sela to the wilderness, unto the mount of the daughter of Zion.

In this first verse we wish we had the clear and precise commentary of Nephi to decipher exactly what is intended. The most plausible interpretation seems to be that of Dr. Adam Clarke in his commentary on the Bible (Clarke, *Commentary*, 4:86). He points out that we know from 2 Kings 3:4 that the king of the Moabites was a "sheepmaster," and that whenever the Moabites were subjugated they often paid tribute in lambs by the tens of thousands. Dr. Clarke believes that in this first verse, Isaiah is simply suggesting to the king of the Moabites that he send a tribute of lambs to the king who rules from Sela in the south to Mount Zion, where the temple is located. Sela, which means "rock," is probably Petra, a city south of the Dead Sea. Petra (Greek for "rock") was the ancient capital of the Edomites, ancestors of the Arabs. It was the righteous King Hezekiah, king of Judah, who ruled from Jerusalem southward. Isaiah suggested that the Moabite king might seek asylum from Judah so his people would have a refuge when the Assyrian assault occurred.

2. For it shall be, that, as a wandering bird cast out of

In his vision, Isaiah had seen the fair daughters of the Moabites fleeing across the fords of the river Arnon

the nest, so the daughters of Moab shall be at the fords of Arnon.

like frightened, wandering birds cast out of their nest. Women and children would need refuge in this hour of pending distress. No doubt this was the reason Isaiah had suggested in the previous verse that the king of Moab send a tribute to King Hezekiah of Judah so the Moabites would have an asylum and a refuge to which they could flee.

3. Take counsel, execute judgment; make thy shadow as the night in the midst of the noonday; hide the outcasts; bewray not him that wandereth.

Now Isaiah seems to be addressing himself to the king of Judah and the people on Mount Zion. Dr. Clarke points out that the verb structure of this verse seems to relate back to "Zion," the last word in verse 1 (Clarke, *Commentary,* 4:87). This interpretation fits the text. Isaiah is telling King Hezekiah, who rules over Mount Zion and all the territory down to Sela (Petra), that he should meet with his leaders to take counsel. He should send forth a decree of judgment among the people that the outcasts of Moab are to be hidden from their enemy. (After all, these people are Hebrews and descendants of Lot!) There should be a decree that the people of Judah are not to "bewray" (meaning betray or reveal) the whereabouts of the fugitive Moabites.

4. Let mine outcasts dwell with thee, Moab; be thou a covert to them from the face of the spoiler: for the extortioner is at an end, the spoiler ceaseth, the oppressors are consumed out of the land.

Continuing this same thought, Dr. Clarke says the text should read, "Let the outcasts of Moab sojourn with thee, O Zion" (ibid.). Isaiah is saying that the people of Judah should serve as a cover or protection of the Moabites against the "spoiler." Down through the years the main "spoiler" of the Moabites had been the apostate kings of the northern Ten Tribes of Israel, who had also been the enemies of Judah. This is referred to in 2 Kings 3:4. Isaiah seems to be saying that these "spoilers" who have extorted great wealth from the Moabites are about to be "consumed" or eliminated out of the land. This happened just a short time later when the northern Ten Tribes were conquered and carried off by the Assyrians.

5. And in mercy shall the throne be established: and he shall sit upon it in truth in the tabernacle of David, judging, and seeking judgment, and hasting righteousness.

It seems in this verse that Isaiah is addressing himself to the good King Hezekiah of Judah and commending him for any kindness he might show the Moabites in their hour of distress. Isaiah says that "in mercy" the king's throne will be established. The king of Judah will sit on the throne or in the tabernacle of King David and not only pretend to be the protector of his people and the Moabite refugees, but he will do so "in truth." His reign will be one of "hasting righteousness."

6. We have heard of the pride of Moab; he is very proud: even of his haughtiness, and his pride, and his wrath: but his lies shall not be so.

The merciful asylum which Hezekiah is to offer the Moabites will be considered all the more generous because everybody knows the Moabites have been a repugnantly proud and apostate people. They have been filled with haughtiness and deceit. But when their doom of destruction descends upon them, this pride and deceit will "not be so."

7. Therefore shall Moab howl for Moab, every one shall howl: for the foundations of Kir-hareseth shall ye mourn; surely they are stricken.

In their hour of distress, the people of Moab will "howl" in anguish. The translation says, "for the foundations of Kir-hareseth shall ye mourn." Dr. Clarke says the more ancient manuscripts indicate that this should read, "for the men of Kirhares shall ye mourn" (ibid.). This is verified by Jeremiah, who uses almost the same words in referring to the destruction of the Moabites. He says, "Therefore will I howl for Moab, and I will cry out for Moab; mine heart shall mourn for the men of Kirheres" (Jeremiah 48:31). Both Isaiah and Jeremiah are referring to the destruction of the men at one of the major fortress cities of the Moabites.

8. For the fields of Heshbon languish, and the vine of Sibmah: the lords of the heathen have broken down the principal plants thereof, they are come even unto Jazer, they wandered through the wilderness: her branches are stretched out, they are gone over the sea.

In this verse, Isaiah begins referring to the destruction of some of the Moabite cities which he had previously mentioned in chapter 15. He says the fertile fields of Heshbon (the capital city of King Sihon, conquered by Moses) shall languish from neglect. The same will be true concerning the famous vineyards of Sibmah. These will be broken down by the heathen conquerors. These marauding hosts will sweep up to Jazer of Gilead to the north (see Numbers 32:1). There will be great lamentation over the destruction of these vineyards, for they were among the most famous of all the wine-producing vineyards in the region of the Mediterranean Sea. Branches or shoots of these vines were carried to far countries, even "over the sea" (Clarke, *Commentary*, 4:88).

9. Therefore I will bewail with the weeping of Jazer the vine of Sibmah: I will water thee with my tears, O Heshbon, and Elealeh: for the shouting for thy summer fruits and for thy harvest is fallen.

Isaiah predicted that the destruction of the Moabites would come right at the time of harvest. Dr. Clarke states that the making of the vintage from these famous Moabite vineyards was always celebrated with shouting, singing, and continuous festivities. But when the ferocious Assyrian assault occurred, these summer fruits would be wasted and "fallen."

10. And gladness is taken away, and joy out of the plentiful field; and in the vineyards there shall be no singing, neither shall there be shouting: the treaders shall tread out no wine in their presses; I have made their vintage shouting to cease.

The "gladness" of the people while making their vintage will all be "taken away." There will be no treading of the grapes for the winepresses. The Assyrians will descend on the wicked Moabites almost like a divine judgment. It will cause the "vintage shouting to cease."

11. Wherefore my bowels shall sound like an harp for

Isaiah says that the vision of it caused his "bowels" (meaning his heart or inward feelings) to lament like

Moab, and mine inward parts for Kir-haresh.

the sad composition of a harp. (Jeremiah 48:36 says "pipes.") His "inward parts" also ached for what he saw would happen to the great city of Kir-haresh.

12. And it shall come to pass, when it is seen that Moab is weary on the high place, that he shall come to his sanctuary to pray; but he shall not prevail.

Naturally, the people of Moab will struggle with all their might to overcome the invading enemy, but when they become weary and perceive that they are likely to be defeated, they will hasten to the sanctuary of their pagan gods to plead for help. But it will be in vain. The Moabites will not prevail.

13. This is the word that the LORD hath spoken concerning Moab since that time.

Isaiah says this is all he was shown in the first revelation concerning the destruction of Moab.

14. But now the LORD hath spoken, saying, Within three years, as the years of an hireling, and the glory of Moab shall be contemned, with all that great multitude; and the remnant shall be very small and feeble.

Nevertheless, he was later shown that "within three years" Moab would be destroyed and only a small remnant of the people left. Isaiah says the three years were to be calculated as the "years of an hireling," which is thought to mean that the time was not a general term meaning "several years," but precisely the way a hireling calculates time in a very careful and specific manner. The three years are believed to have commenced with the reign of King Hezekiah around 727 B.C. It was during the three years following the commencement of Hezekiah's reign that the marauding hosts of the Assyrians devastated the whole region except for Judah. All of the territory east of the river Jordan and the Dead Sea was desolated. The Assyrians then besieged Samaria, the capital of the northern Ten Tribes, and finally carried off the remnants of that conquered city in 721 B.C.

It is significant that Isaiah said there would also be a "remnant" left from among the Moabites. These, however, were never carried away as were the Israelites. They returned to their ravaged land and rebuilt it. Around 100 years later, Jeremiah repeated the prophecy of Isaiah concerning Moab because they were about to be destroyed again. However, this time Jeremiah said the Moabites would "be destroyed from being a people" (Jeremiah 48:42). This second destruction occurred when Nebuchadnezzar obliterated the Moabites in 582 B.C., just 5 years after he demolished the great city of Jerusalem and hauled the Jews off to Babylon. From that day to this, the Moabites have ceased to be a people. However, Jeremiah states that in the latter days the Lord's people will "bring again the captivity of Moab" (Jeremiah 48:47). However, this seems to refer to the territory rather than the people.

INTRODUCTION:

This chapter is believed to have been written a few years before chapter 16. Most authorities think it was recorded shortly after chapters 7 and 8 when the wicked King Ahaz had just commenced his reign. (See Clarke, *Commentary*, 4:89.) The first verse indicates that this chapter is devoted to the future of Damascus, but much of it is connected with the Israelites who were confederated with Damascus against Judah. Damascus was the capital of Syria.

1. The burden of Damascus. Behold, Damascus is taken away from being a city, and it shall be a ruinous heap.

In this vision, Isaiah sees Damascus being conquered. In fact, it is totally destroyed so that it is no longer a city but a "ruinous heap." This was fulfilled when Tiglath-pileser came over from Assyria around 734 B.C. The late Nelson Beecher Keyes described what happened:

"Rezin, the king [of Damascus], was slain, the noblemen were impaled upon stakes, the city itself was ransacked, if not burned, and towns and villages in sixteen surrounding districts were leveled. Some eight hundred citizens, probably those of leading families, were led away to servitude." (Keyes, *Story of the Bible World* [Pleasantville, N.Y.: Reader's Digest Association, 1962], p. 83.)

2. The cities of Aroer are forsaken: they shall be for

We are not able to identify the cities of Aroer, but they must have been included in the 16 districts around

flocks, which shall lie down, and none shall make them afraid.

Damascus which were ransacked. There was also a city of Aroer on the Arnon River, but this obviously would not be the one to which Isaiah is referring in this passage. Isaiah says the destruction was so complete that flocks could graze over the area and be herded together at night without any fear of their being disturbed.

3. The fortress also shall cease from Ephraim, and the kingdom from Damascus, and the remnant of Syria: they shall be as the glory of the children of Israel, saith the LORD of hosts.

Now the vision expands to a broader vista to include Samaria, the capital city of the people of Ephraim (Ephraim is often used as a collective name for the northern Ten Tribes). The vision also includes the remainder of Syria, Damascus being the capital. Note that the Syrian territories will suffer the same fate as the "glory of the children of Israel." Of course, the "glory" of the children of Israel was violently pulled down by the Assyrians and many of the people led off to the land of Assyria. Isaiah said the same thing would happen to many of the people in Damascus and the surrounding territory of Syria.

4. And in that day it shall come to pass, that the glory of Jacob shall be made thin, and the fatness of his flesh shall wax lean.

Isaiah verifies what we have just mentioned; namely, the glory of Jacob (or Israel) shall no longer be abundant and affluent, but shall "wax lean."

5. And it shall be as when the harvestman gathereth the corn, and reapeth the ears with his arm; and it shall be as he that gathereth ears in the valley of Rephaim.

When Tiglath-pileser came into this region, he swept away the whole population like a reaper stripping off the heads of corn (wheat) at harvest time. In the Bible, the word "corn" comes from kernel and refers to wheat or similar grains (Peloubet, *Bible Dictionary*, s.v. "Corn"). The "ears" of the corn refer to the heads of this grain. The corn with which modern man is familiar is a crop which seems to have been developed exclusively in

America and was apparently unknown in Asia and Europe before the discovery of America.

In Isaiah's day the word "Rephaim" was used in the same sense that we use "Garden of Eden" to typify an environment of pleasant living and abundance. Rephaim was actually a fertile region near Jerusalem. The crops were so abundant in that area that the reapers did not bother to gather in all the harvest, but left a remnant of the crop in their wake. Isaiah said it would be the same way the Assyrians would sweep off the population of Syria and Israel. They would take nearly all of the people, but there would be a small remnant left behind.

6. Yet gleaning grapes shall be left in it, as the shaking of an olive tree, two or three berries in the top of the uppermost bough, four or five in the outmost fruitful branches thereof, saith the LORD God of Israel.

Isaiah also compares these events with the gleaning of grapes or the shaking of the olive trees. Some of the fruit is left scattered among the vines or on the uppermost branches of the trees.

7. At that day shall a man look to his Maker, and his eyes shall have respect to the Holy One of Israel.

The Assyrian attack will be so violent that it will greatly humble the people. At long last they will cast their eyes upward in humble supplication to their Maker. Once more they will express a renewed respect for the "Holy One of Israel," their redeemer.

8. And he shall not look to the altars, the work of his hands, neither shall respect that which his fingers have made, either the groves, or the images.

The apostate people of these conquered lands will no longer depend upon their altars where their pagan idols stand silent and senseless. Neither will they rejoice anymore in reveling in the lecherous and sensuous ceremonies of sex worship in the "groves." The phallic

symobls and ugly images of the pagan gods will have
become an abomination to them. According to the Jewish *Midrash,* Damascus had 365 streets with the image
of a god in each one of them. A separate ritual of
worship was ordained for one of these idols each day so
that all 365 were worshipped before the end of the
year. Nevertheless, when the Assyrian assault occurs,
Isaiah says these images will be honored no longer.

9. In that day shall his strong
cities be as a forsaken
bough, and an uppermost
branch, which they left because of the children of
Israel: and there shall be
desolation.

Isaiah once more emphasizes that after the fury of
the conquest has passed over the land, the strong cities
of this region will be like the harvested fields of the
Israelites. A remnant will be left. The Israelites had
been told by the Lord to let the poor glean the remnant
of the crop (see Leviticus 19:9–10).

10. Because thou hast forgotten the God of thy salva-
tion, and hast not been
mindful of the rock of thy
strength, therefore shalt
thou plant pleasant plants,
and shalt set it with strange
slips:

11. In the day shalt thou make
thy plant to grow, and in
the morning shalt thou
make thy seed to flourish:
but the harvest shall be a
heap in the day of grief and
of desperate sorrow.

The people will be guilty of offending the God of
their salvation, who is the real rock of their strength.
Prior to the Assyrian conquest, Isaiah saw them cultivating the pleasant transplants of religious culture
from foreign lands. He calls them "strange" slips or
grafts from foreign soil. They will have a corrupting
influence. However, they will become meaningless and
of no value whatsoever when the people are subjected
to the "desperate sorrow" of pillage, rapine, and
conquest.

12. Woe to the multitude of
many people, which make a
noise like the noise of the
seas; and to the rushing of

Beginning with this verse, Isaiah looks further down
the corridor of time and says that the Assyrians also
will have their day of desperate sorrow. He therefore

nations, that make a rushing like the rushing of mighty waters!

pronounces a day of doom for the Assyrians. Isaiah does not call them the Assyrians, of course, but the "multitude of many people" sweeping across the Fertile Crescent like the "noise of the seas" and the boisterous "rushing of nations." The sound of their coming will be like the roar of "mighty waters."

13. The nations shall rush like the rushing of many waters: but God shall rebuke them, and they shall flee far off, and shall be chased as the chaff of the mountains before the wind, and like a rolling thing before the whirlwind.

Nevertheless, the day of doom is coming for these Assyrians. Isaiah saw the day when the Babylonians would sweep in upon their mighty capital city of Nineveh (in 612 B.C.) and the Assyrians would fly like chaff in the wind to the highest mountain retreat. Later, in their total defeat by the Babylonians at Carchemish (605 B.C.) they were virtually annihilated as a nation. They tried to escape by literally scrambling into the mountains like "a rolling thing before the whirlwind."

14. And behold at eveningtide trouble; and before the morning he is not. This is the portion of them that spoil us, and the lot of them that rob us.

Isaiah wanted to assure the people of Israel that while these terrifying Assyrians were a plague of destruction during their eveningtide of trouble, they would all be gone at a future time which he had seen in vision. As he saw the fall of the Assyrians under the swords of the Babylonians he could not help but say, "This is the portion [fate] of them that spoil us, and the lot of them that rob us."

Isaiah, Chapter 18

INTRODUCTION:

For centuries this chapter has been a mystery to Bible scholars. Dr. Adam Clarke says: "This is one of the most obscure prophecies in the whole Book of Isaiah. The *subject* of it, the *end* and *design* of it, the *people* to whom it is addressed, the *history* to which it belongs, the *person* who sends the messengers, and the *nation* to whom the messengers are sent, are all obscure and doubtful." (Clarke, *Commentary*, 4:91–92; emphasis in the original.)

It was not until the Gospel was restored and the Book of Mormon became available that we learned what this chapter is all about. It turned out that this chapter is referring to America. All of the major events portrayed in this chapter are identified in various modern scriptures with the great gathering of the remnant of Jacob to Mount Zion in the last days.

---

1. Woe to the land shadowing with wings, which is beyond the rivers of Ethiopia:

In the first verse Isaiah starts out by saluting a certain distant land. The word "Woe" should be translated "Ho!" It is a form of salutation like the word "Hail" (Clarke, *Commentary*, 4:92).

It is as though Isaiah were saying, "Hail to the land shadowing [the Hebrew word is actually "buzzing"] with wings, which is beyond the rivers of Ethiopia." In the original Hebrew it says "beyond the rivers of Cush." Ethiopia is part of Cush, but Isaiah was talking about the whole area occupied by the dark peoples of Africa, which would be much more extensive than the relatively small kingdom of Ethiopia. Isaiah says he is talking about a land far beyond the upper Nile, the Congo, and all of the rivers inhabited by the blacks, or the people of Cush. In other words, it is a land beyond the continent of Africa. Modern man would know that he is talking about the Western Hemisphere. Isaiah knew that it was a huge continental island surrounded by water. Many of his chapters addressed to "the isles of the sea" are specifically referring to the great continental body surrounded by water that we call America. The Nephite prophet Jacob refers to America as an "isle" when he says, "We have been driven out of the land of our inheritance [Judea]; but we have been led to a better land [America], for the Lord has made the sea our path, and we are upon AN ISLE OF THE SEA" (2 Nephi 10:20; emphasis added).

If Isaiah were shown a vision of modern America, he could literally say it was "buzzing" with wings. How marvelous it must have been to Isaiah to see the wonders of the twentieth century!

2. That sendeth ambassadors by the sea, even in vessels of bulrushes upon the waters, saying, Go, ye swift messengers, to a nation scattered and peeled, to a people terrible from their beginning hitherto; a nation meted out and trodden down, whose land the rivers have spoiled!

This verse should probably begin with the word "He," just as the next verse indicates. It would then read: "He [the Lord] sendeth ambassadors by the sea, even in vessels of bulrushes upon the waters, saying...." The term "vessels of bulrushes" may seem strange to modern man, but not to the people in Isaiah's day. The Egyptians used vessels of bulrushes (or papyrus) because they are light and buoyant. The Norwegian ethnologist Thor Heyerdahl (best known for his 1947 voyage from Peru to eastern Polynesia on a balsa wood raft named *Kon Tiki*), used a papyrus boat named *Ra II* to cross the Atlantic in 1970. Around 600 B.C., the Egyptians are said to have circumnavigated the entire continent of Africa (Herodotus, *History*, 4:42; discussed in Paul Herrmann, *Conquest by Man*, trans.

Michael Bullock [New York: Harper & Brothers, 1954],
pp. 73-76, 79-81). The Egyptian vessels of bulrushes
even in Isaiah's day may have symbolized to the people
a vessel which was light and buoyant and could travel
swiftly over vast areas of water.

We note that these "swift messengers" were to take
their special message to a people located in a land
beyond Africa who were "scattered and peeled." These
people were further identified by Isaiah as having been
"terrible [wicked, ferocious] from their beginning."
They had also been "meted out and trodden down." No
people fits this historical pattern more accurately than
the Lamanites, whose origin and development are
portrayed in exactly these terms throughout the Book
of Mormon. They were "terrible" from the beginning
of their sojourn in the promised land, and except for
brief intervals of repentance (during which God blessed
them abundantly), they were "scattered and peeled,"
"meted out and trodden down" for a thousand years.

Isaiah saw that the lands of these people were spoiled
by their great rivers. All of America's important rivers
overrun their banks during certain seasons. Fringe set-
tlements along the courses of these rivers are wiped
out and spoiled. This is particularly true of the two
greatest rivers in America, the Amazon and the
Mississippi.

3. All ye inhabitants of the world, and dwellers on the earth, see ye, when he lifteth up an ensign on the mountains; and when he bloweth a trumpet, hear ye.

Not only will the people inhabiting America receive
the Lord's important message, but Isaiah calls attention
to the fact that this message is going to all the inhabitants of the world, to all "dwellers on the earth." This
will be at a time when the Lord is lifting up an ensign
on the mountains of Zion (verse 7), and sounding a
trumpet to hear the word of the Lord. Isaiah commands
the people of the whole earth to pay attention to this
important event. He says to modern man that when

these messengers come trumpeting across the earth,
"HEAR YE"!

4. For so the LORD said unto me, I will take my rest, and I will consider in my dwelling place like a clear heat upon herbs, and like a cloud of dew in the heat of harvest.

Isaiah says the Lord discussed this subject with him. He was told that the Lord wanted to prepare a day of rest so that he could make his "dwelling place" in Mount Zion (verse 7). It was going to be a time of abundance and flourishing growth similar to the season of clear and sunny skies when the green herbs thrive the best. At the same time, it will be a day of pleasant and refreshing coolness such as occurs when the dews descend in the heat of harvest time. There is no doubt that this is referring to the Millennium, when the Lord will rest and the earth will become a thoroughly pleasant and abundant place to live.

5. For afore the harvest, when the bud is perfect, and the sour grape is ripening in the flower, he shall both cut off the sprigs with pruning hooks, and take away and cut down the branches.

Isaiah explains that before this millennial era commences, there will be a time of pruning and cutting back of the Lord's vineyard. This is a common practice in vineyard culture so that the strength of the fruit is not lost in the needless growth of wild new sprigs and branches. The Lord's vineyard is the human family, and before the great day of rest can be ushered in, there must be a pruning of the wicked and unproductive branches of the Lord's vineyard so that these will not sap the strength of the righteous, which is the Lord's harvest.

6. They shall be left together unto the fowls of the mountains, and to the beasts of the earth: and the fowls shall summer upon them, and all the beasts of the earth shall winter upon them.

The cleansing and pruning of the Lord's vineyard will result in the destruction of the wicked. Isaiah says they will be left for the predatory birds and beasts of the earth to devour both in summer and in winter.

7. In that time shall the present be brought unto the LORD of hosts of a people scattered and peeled, and from a people terrible from their beginning hitherto; a nation meted out and trodden under foot, whose land the rivers have spoiled, to the place of the name of the LORD of hosts, the mount Zion.

And when the cleansing process is completed, the people in America who were "scattered and peeled," "meted out and trodden down," will bring a beautiful present to the Lord of Hosts at Mount Zion. This is no doubt referring to the time when the converted Lamanites will come in great numbers to help build the New Jerusalem on Mount Zion, which is to be in America (see 3 Nephi 21:22–29; Ether 13:4; Moses 7:62; D&C 84:2–3).

Isaiah, Chapter 19

1. **The burden of Egypt. Behold, the LORD rideth upon a swift cloud, and shall come into Egypt: and the idols of Egypt shall be moved at his presence, and the heart of Egypt shall melt in the midst of it.**

This chapter is devoted to Isaiah's vision concerning the destiny of Egypt. He speaks of it as though it were a "burden" which he must unload onto the prophetic record. As with chapter 18, this vision seems to relate entirely to the latter days. Isaiah says it will be a day when the power of God will come like a cloud of glory sweeping along on the tide of the wind. David uses similar language in describing the power of God in his day (see Psalms 18:10; 104:3). It will be the kind of manifestation that will move the idols of Egypt out of their places and so frighten the people that their pride and idolatry will melt away.

2. **And I will set the Egyptians against the Egyptians: and they shall fight every one against his brother, and every one against his neighbour; city against city, and kingdom against kingdom.**

There will be widespread insurrection and civil strife. Egyptians will fight against Egyptians. Even the members of individual families will be found fighting against each other. The same will be true of neighbors, communities, and cities. Even the provinces (or kingdoms) of the Egyptians will be locked in conflict against each other.

3. **And the spirit of Egypt shall fail in the midst thereof; and I will destroy the counsel thereof: and they shall seek to the idols, and to the charmers, and to them that have familiar spirits, and to the wizards.**

The element of national unity will disintegrate. The officials and advisers to those in charge of the government will be completely unable to cope with the situation. People will flock to their idols and the mystic sanctuaries of those who have familiar spirits or purport to be psychics (wizards).

4. And the Egyptians will I give over into the hand of a cruel lord; and a fierce king shall rule over them, saith the Lord, the LORD of hosts.

As so often happens, Isaiah perceived that in this time of internal strife and confusion, a powerful leader will arise and take over the government of the people. Unfortunately, he will be a ruthless dictator. For approximately 4,000 years of its known history, the people who have occupied the territory of Egypt have always been under various types of autocratic rulers. However, this one in the latter days will be particularly cruel and fierce.

5. And the waters shall fail from the sea, and the river shall be wasted and dried up.

About this time, something will happen which has never occurred before in the recorded history of Egypt. The great river Nile, the life blood of Egypt, will fail. Isaiah says this will be due to the fact that "the waters shall fail from the sea." The great inland sea which constitutes the principal source for the water of the Nile is Lake Victoria. This is the second largest freshwater lake in the world, and the largest lake on the continent of Africa. It covers 26,828 square miles, second only to Lake Superior in North America. It is 3,726 feet above sea level, and the region receives around 75 inches of rain each year. This vast lake spills its excess water over the Ripon Falls at the northern end, and this water is called the White Nile, which flows approximately four thousand miles to empty into the Mediterranean Sea. The Nile has a tributary called the Blue Nile, which flows down from a lake further east in Ethiopia called Lake Tana. If these sources of the Nile suddenly ceased to send their excess waters down the channel of the Nile Valley, it would mean complete and unmitigated disaster for Egypt. Note that it does not merely say that the supply of water would be lower than usual, but that it would be totally "wasted and dried up"!

6. And they shall turn the rivers far away; and the brooks of defence shall be emptied and dried up: the reeds and flags shall wither.

Isaiah seems to have seen that this disaster would be caused by the two rivers "far away"—the White Nile and the Blue Nile—failing to send their usual supply of life-giving water into the main channel of the Nile Valley. He says that even the small brooks which occasionally feed the Nile would be dried up. The reeds and foliage along the banks of the river would all wither and die.

7. The paper reeds by the brooks, by the mouth of the brooks, and every thing sown by the brooks, shall wither, be driven away, and be no more.

From time immemorial, the late summer has brought a rich flood of water down the Nile to sweep gently over its banks and flow out onto the surrounding fields of the valley floor. The deposits of silt have always made these fields so rich that the acreage produces 2½ times as much cotton as a similar amount of acreage in the United States. But when the Nile River fails, all of the crops sown along its banks and among the network of brooks (canals) will "wither, be driven away, and be no more."

8. The fishers also shall mourn, and all they that cast angle into the brooks shall lament, and they that spread nets upon the waters shall languish.

The famous Egyptian fishing industry will be completely destroyed. The fishermen will mourn because of the affliction which has come upon them.

9. Moreover they that work in fine flax, and they that weave networks, shall be confounded.

Furthermore, the processing of linen from flax will be disrupted. Not only will the growing of the flax be impossible, but the weaving of the linen thread into fine tapestries will be terminated.

10. And they shall be broken in the purposes thereof, all that make sluices and ponds for fish.

Every type of industry and every form of commerce will come to a standstill. Those who have fish hatcheries and small ponds for fish will not be able to save them.

11. Surely the princes of Zoan are fools, the counsel of the wise counsellors of Pharaoh is become brutish: how say ye unto Pharaoh, I am the son of the wise, the son of ancient kings?

Isaiah has something to say about the leaders of the nation in that day. He says the princes or aristocratic leaders of "Zoan" will be fools. Zoan was an ancient city of great prominence located on the Tanitic branch of the Nile and called "Tanis" by the Greeks. It literally means "Place of Departure," because it was not far from the harbors leading to the Mediterranean Sea. These leaders of Zoan are described by Isaiah as giving unwise counsel to the "Pharaoh" or ruler of Egypt (Pharaoh is a title, not a proper name). They expect their counsel to be accepted because they will boast of being descendants of the wise men and rulers of Egypt in former times.

12. Where are they? where are thy wise men? and let them tell thee now, and let them know what the LORD of hosts hath purposed upon Egypt.

Isaiah dares these so-called wise men to predict what is going to happen to Egypt. He knows they would not dare to anticipate anything as amazing as the visions of the future which Isaiah has seen.

13. The princes of Zoan are become fools, the princes of Noph are deceived; they have also seduced Egypt, even they that are the stay of the tribes thereof.

The prophet now repeats his denunciation of the ruling class of Zoan, calling them fools. He also denounces the leaders in the other major city of lower Egypt called Noph. This city is better known to most people by its Greek name of Memphis. It was located on the west side of the Nile, just south of the three famous pyramids. If Isaiah were living in our own day, he would probably refer to the city of Cairo, which is across the river. There is where the leaders are today. Nevertheless, we must not dismiss the name "Noph" lightly. This is a famous Egyptian name. George Reynolds wrote: "Its roots are Egyptian; meaning, good, excellent, benevolent.... One of the names given to the god (Osiris), expressive of his attributes, was Nephi or Dnephi,... and the chief city dedicated to him was called N-ph, translated into Hebrew as Noph, in which form it appears in Hosea, Isaiah and Jeremiah; its modern English name is Memphis." (George Reynolds and Janne M. Sjodahl, *Commentary on the Book of Mormon,* ed. Philip C. Reynolds, 7 vols. [Salt Lake City, 1955-61], 1:4.) Note that Isaiah states that the leaders in the city of Noph have been deceived. He says they have also "seduced Egypt" to believe in these deceptions, even the leaders of the foremost families or tribes.

---

14. The LORD hath mingled a perverse spirit in the midst thereof: and they have caused Egypt to err in every work thereof, as a drunken man staggereth in his vomit.

When Isaiah was shown this vision, he saw that in the day when these events would transpire, there would be a particularly perverse spirit among the Egyptian people. Every enterprise they undertook would seem to fail. Isaiah said it reminded him of a drunken man who has regurgitated the burden of his stomach and is floundering around in his own bilious discharge.

---

15. Neither shall there be any work for Egypt, which the head or tail, branch or rush, may do.

Under these circumstances, there will be no undertaking or work which can be commenced with confidence. Neither the high nor the low (the head or the tail), neither the youth nor the child (the branch or the rush—i.e., reed), will engage in any activity of consequence because of the continuous upheaval in the land.

16. In that day shall Egypt be like unto women: and it shall be afraid and fear because of the shaking of the hand of the LORD of hosts, which he shaketh over it.

Egypt is likened unto a frightened woman who sees the hand of the Lord in the terrible things which will be happening to the country.

17. And the land of Judah shall be a terror unto Egypt, every one that maketh mention thereof shall be afraid in himself, because of the counsel of the LORD of hosts, which he hath determined against it.

Now we come to a verse that describes a coming event which has never happened in all of the history of Egypt until our day. It says Judah will be a "terror unto Egypt." In 4,000 years, Judah has never been a threat to Egypt until modern times. Only as Israel came into being in 1948 as a modern nation did Egypt seem compelled to attack Judah. In four successive wars (1948, 1956, 1967, 1973), Egypt attempted to conquer Israel with tremendous odds in her favor, but each time the Israeli forces held off the Egyptians. All four of these wars were called "miracle victories" for Judah. In terms of manpower, equipment, and logistics, many predicted a victory for the Egyptian forces. Military authorities have pointed out that to a certain extent, the advantage of the Israeli forces was psychological. The Egyptians, under good leadership, are great fighters. It was only against Judah that their morale seemed to fade. This has been equally true with Syrian troops, the major ally of Egypt in these four wars. (The 1948, 1956, and 1967 wars are described in W. Cleon Skousen, *Fantastic Victory: Israel's Rendezvous with Destiny* [Salt Lake City: Bookcraft, 1967]. The Yom Kippur war of 1973 is detailed by the former head of Israeli military intelligence, Major General Chaim Herzog, in *War of Atonement: October, 1973* [Boston: Little, Brown and Company, 1975].) Isaiah said the time would come when the very mention of the military successes of Judah would cause consternation in Egypt. Some would begin to feel that the hand of God was in these victories and that the Almighty was favoring Judah over Egypt.

18. In that day shall five cities in the land of Egypt speak the language of Canaan, and swear to the LORD of hosts; one shall be called, The city of destruction.

Now, beginning with this verse, Isaiah presents an entirely different picture. He begins describing a remarkable change in the whole Middle East situation—both politically and culturally. At a certain point in the latter days, Isaiah saw that a more cordial relationship would develop between Judah and Egypt. One cannot help but wonder if this transition began to take place around November 15, 1977, when Anwar Sadat of Egypt was invited to visit Israel and speak to the Knesset (the Israeli parliament). Sadat shocked the entire Arab world by accepting this invitation from Prime Minister Menachem Begin, who had been his enemy for 30 years. Sadat risked his life by ignoring warnings from the leaders of other Arab nations (including the terrorist Palestine Liberation Organization). He visited Israel on November 19, 1977. Two days later he returned to Cairo and millions of cheering Egyptians. All of this signified that the leader of the most populous Arab nation in the world had virtually given diplomatic recognition to the existence of Israel as a nation. This was something no other Arab leader had done.

Isaiah states that the time will come when five cities in Egypt will speak the "language of Canaan." Today the language spoken in the land formerly occupied by the Canaanites is Hebrew. Therefore, if five cities in Egypt will be speaking Hebrew, it would be logical to assume that this will be a time of extensive trade and joint enterprises between these two nations. This is not all. These five cities will all be committed to obey the commandments of the Lord. It says one of these cities will be the metropolis of "Heres" (destruction) or "Cheres" (the sun). Bible scholars are not quite certain about this text. If the correct word is "Cheres" (the sun), this would probably refer to the most famous of ancient Egyptian centers of learning called Heliopolis

(city of the sun), which was located on what is today
the outskirts of Cairo near the international airport.

19. In that day shall there be an altar to the LORD in the midst of the land of Egypt, and a pillar at the border thereof to the LORD.

Not only will these cities be made up primarily of
those who have entered into a covenant with "the Lord
of Hosts," but they will have an altar of worship (which
is nearly always associated with a temple), and there
will be a pillar or a memorial monument on the border
of the land signifying that this territory is occupied by
those who believe in the Lord.

20. And it shall be for a sign and for a witness unto the LORD of hosts in the land of Egypt: for they shall cry unto the LORD because of the oppressors, and he shall send them a saviour, and a great one, and he shall deliver them.

Apparently, these five cities will be subject to great
persecution for a period of time, but they will plead
unto the Lord "because of the oppressors," and in due
time he will send them a savior who will deliver them.
This may be referring to the coming of the Savior after
the great battle of Armageddon. The scriptures say
that the mass conversion of the Jewish people in Israel
will be incidental to the terrible 3½-year war in which a
mighty ruler of the Gentiles called "Gog" will bring a
great host of other nations "out of the north" to launch
an overwhelming attack against the Jewish people.
These marauding hosts will occupy all of Israel and
then lay siege to Jerusalem. The leader of the Jews in
that day will be named David (see Isaiah 55:3-4;
Jeremiah 30:9; Ezekiel 34:23-24; Hosea 3:4-5).
Zechariah speaks of this great leader as THE BRANCH
who will "build the temple of the Lord" (Zechariah
6:12). David will be supported by two prophets with
great Priesthood power. John the Revelator said of
them:

"And I will give power unto my two witnesses.
. . . And if any man will hurt them, fire proceedeth out
of their mouth, and devoureth their enemies. . . . These
have power to shut heaven, that it rain not in the days

of their prophecy: and have power over waters to turn them to blood, and to smite the earth with all plagues, as often as they will." (Revelation 11:3-6.)

The Gentile armies will take half of Jerusalem and come up to the outer courts of the temple, but no further. For three and one-half years they will be held at bay (Revelation 11:1-2). At the end of that period, Gog will succeed in killing the two prophets (Revelation 11:7). Their bodies will lie in the streets 3½ days. Then they will be resurrected and caught up to meet the Lord. Immediately there will be a terrible earthquake and a great destruction of the armies of Gog (Ezekiel 38:18-23). It is interesting that three other nations are involved with the Gentile hosts from the north. These are Persia (called Iran today), Ethiopia, and Libya (Ezekiel 38:3-6). The Mount of Olives will divide, leaving a great canyon through which the surviving Jews can escape (D&C 45:48-50; Zechariah 14:4-5). These Jews will gather about the Messiah, who will apparently be withholding his glory (as resurrected beings can do), and the Jews will say, "What are these wounds in thine hands and in thy feet?" He will reply, "These wounds are the wounds with which I was wounded in the house of my friends. I am he who was lifted up. I am Jesus that was crucified. I am the Son of God." (D&C 45:51-52; Zechariah 13:6.) The scripture says, "And then shall they weep because of their iniquities; then shall they lament because they persecuted their king" (D&C 45:53). The news of these events will sweep through all the surrounding nations so that "many people and strong nations shall come to seek the Lord of hosts in Jerusalem, and to pray before the Lord.... In those days it shall come to pass, that ten men shall take hold out of all languages of the nations, even shall take hold of the skirt of him that is a Jew, saying, We will go with you: for we have heard that God is with you." (Zechariah 8:22-23; Ezekiel 39:21-23.)

21. And the LORD shall be known to Egypt, and the Egyptians shall know the LORD in that day, and shall do sacrifice and oblation; yea, they shall vow a vow unto the LORD, and perform it.

As a result of these events, the Lord shall be known in Egypt and the true Gospel will be taught among the Egyptians. This is probably when the five cities will "speak the language" of the Jews and have "an altar to the Lord." This probably will be the time when they will hear about the Savior who can deliver them. This verse says, "The Lord shall be known to Egypt, and the Egyptians...shall do sacrifice and oblation." These Egyptians will enter into covenants with the Lord and faithfully "perform" them.

22. And the LORD shall smite Egypt: he shall smite and heal it: and they shall return even to the LORD, and he shall be intreated of them, and shall heal them.

Nevertheless, it would appear that Egypt as a nation will still need further chastising before the remainder of the people are willing to follow the example of the more righteous Egyptians. Isaiah saw that Egypt would be smitten with some terrible calamity. Perhaps this is when the great river Nile will fail, and its waters dry up. Apparently this calamity will be sufficient to cause the whole Egyptian nation to humble themselves and plead for the blessings of the Lord. This passage says that the Lord will respond and he "shall heal them." Thus, they will become a converted nation, just as the Jews will have been converted as a nation.

23. In that day shall there be a highway out of Egypt to Assyria, and the Assyrian shall come into Egypt, and the Egyptian into Assyria, and the Egyptians shall serve with the Assyrians.

In this verse we have even more good news. Isaiah saw that there would be a vast network of communications between the people of Assyria and Egypt. It would be like a great highway connecting the inhabitants of Assyria with Egypt so that the Assyrians would go into Egypt and the Egyptians would go into Assyria. The real significance of this is the fact that in our own day, Egypt has been cut off from all of the other Arab nations (the very people who occupy much of what was once the Assyrian Empire). But there will come a day of reconciliation when they shall all begin to intermingle again. Apparently the remarkable element which will bring them into unity will be the Gospel of Jesus Christ. Notice that it says in this verse that "the Egyptians shall serve [the Lord] WITH the Assyrians." The territory of the Assyrian Empire as Isaiah knew it is now inhabited by Jordan, Lebanon, Saudi Arabia, Iraq, and Libya. All of these will become members of God's restored kingdom and worship Jesus Christ with the Egyptians.

---

24. In that day shall Israel be the third with Egypt and with Assyria, even a blessing in the midst of the land:

In that day, the Israelites will intermingle among all these people and will be a great blessing "in the midst of the land."

---

25. Whom the LORD of hosts shall bless, saying, Blessed be Egypt my people, and Assyria the work of my hands, and Israel mine inheritance.

Isaiah closes this chapter with a note of supreme triumph as he quotes the Lord, saying: "Blessed be Egypt my people, and Assyria the work of my hands, and Israel mine inheritance"!

In our own day, who could imagine such an incredible development as that which Isaiah predicted. For centuries, there has been strong hostility between the various Arab nations. And as between the Arabs and the Jews, there have been overwhelming tidal waves of genocidal hatred. It will be truly miraculous when all of the vitriolic hatred and enmity suddenly melt away under the sublimating influence of the Gospel of Jesus Christ. At long last these three great peoples will be united in the bonds of affection and Christian brotherhood. It is interesting to note that all of these people are descendants of Abraham, and when these events transpire the Lord's promise to Abraham will be fulfilled when he said, "Unto thy seed have I given this land, from the river of Egypt unto the great river, the river Euphrates" (Genesis 15:18).

Isaiah, Chapter 20

INTRODUCTION:

Now Isaiah swings all the way back to Egypt in his own day. In this chapter Isaiah describes events which will occur in the immediate future as the terrifying armies of the Assyrians sweep down along the Canaanite plain toward Egypt and Ethiopia. During these campaigns, the Ethiopian armies came up along the eastern coast of the Red Sea to resist the Assyrians in the Sinai and the Negev.

1. In the year that Tartan came unto Ashdod, (when Sargon the king of Assyria sent him,) and fought against Ashdod, and took it;

Isaiah fixes the date of this revelation as having occurred at a different time than the revelation in chapter 19. He states that it was given to him in the year that Tartan attacked Ashdod.

Ashdod, which still exists, was a major city of the Canaanites. Of course, today it has been rebuilt as a city of Israel located along the Mediterranean coast 20 miles south of Tel Aviv. Tartan was one of the principal generals over the armies of Sennacherib, the king of Assyria (see 2 Kings 18:17). He is also believed to have served under Sennacherib's father, Sargon.

It is important to remember that the wars against the nations of the west (Syria, Israel, Judah, Canaan, Egypt, and Ethiopia) extended from around 734 B.C. to 660 B.C., a period of more than 70 years. Isaiah saw most of these wars and predicted the ultimate outcome. We recall that it was Sargon who took over as king of Assyria around 722 B.C. and finished the conquest of Israel (the northern Ten Tribes) in 721 B.C. It was he who carried the remnants of these tribes off to Assyria. Sargon then continued his wars along the Mediterranean until 705 B.C. That was the year he died and was replaced by his son, Sennacherib. A short time before his death, Sargon had sent Tartan down to conquer Ashdod, which he did. Tartan thereafter fought under the new king, Sennacherib. To Isaiah and the people of Judah, the conquest of Ashdod by Tartan would be vividly remembered.

2. At the same time spake the LORD by Isaiah the son of Amoz, saying, Go and loose the sackcloth from off thy loins, and put off thy shoe from thy foot. And he did so, walking naked and barefoot.

About the time this revelation was given, everyone was wondering whether or not Assyria would finally penetrate the powerful nation of Egypt and take it captive just as it had succeeded in doing with all the other nations in the west. To symbolize what was going to happen to Egypt, the Lord told Isaiah to take off the coarse sackcloth clothing which he wore as his outer garments and also to take off his shoes so that he would be barefooted. Dressed only in his undergarments and walking barefoot, Isaiah was told to go among the people predicting what would happen to Egypt.

3. And the LORD said, Like as my servant Isaiah hath walked naked and barefoot three years for a sign and wonder upon Egypt and upon Ethiopia;

4. So shall the king of Assyria lead away the Egyptians prisoners, and the Ethiopians captives, young and old, naked and barefoot, even with their buttocks uncovered, to the shame of Egypt.

The Lord declared that he had instructed Isaiah to go among the people for three years in his underclothing and walking barefoot as a symbol of what would happen to the Egyptians and the Ethiopians when they were taken captive. They would be "led away" naked and barefoot, even with their buttocks uncovered. It would be to the utter shame of the great nation of Egypt when this had come to pass.

In order to appreciate the literal fulfillment of the prophecies in this chapter, we need to trace the highlights of history during this period. Here is the story.

Sargon became the king of Assyria as a usurper in 722 B.C. and ruled until his assassination in 705 B.C. His death is believed to have been instigated by his son, Sennacherib, who ruled Assyria from 705 to 681 B.C. Sennacherib was also assassinated by one or more of his sons. The son who took over the throne of Assyria in 680 B.C. was Esar-haddon, who ruled until 669 B.C. All three of these kings had tried to conquer Egypt, but it was Esarhaddon who was the first to invade Egypt and subdue it. The first attack came in 674 B.C. and the second in 671 B.C. The throne of Egypt at that time was occupied by an Ethiopian named Tirhakah. Esarhaddon forced Tirhakah to give up both Egyptian capitals— Memphis (of lower Egypt) and Thebes (of upper Egypt)—and flee back to his home in Ethiopia (the Sudan of our own day). Thus, Esarhaddon was the first king of Assyria who could call himself the king of both Egypt and Assyria.

It was customary with the Assyrians to haul off many of the people they conquered and carry them back to the prisons which were set up in the Assyrian capital of Nineveh. Prisoners of the Assyrians were treated with the utmost cruelty. When the captured Egyptians and Ethiopians were hauled off to Assyria, they no doubt marched with barely enough food to keep them alive and without any new issue of clothing whatever. Thus, approximately 25 years after Isaiah is believed to have died (around 696 B.C.), these prophecies concerning Egypt were literally fulfilled. Later, they were even further fulfilled under the son of Esarhaddon, whose name was Assurbanipal (668–628 B.C.).

5. And they shall be afraid and ashamed of Ethiopia their expectation, and of Egypt their glory.

Isaiah knew from the revelations he had received that these prisoners would be terribly afraid. Furthermore, the Egyptians would be ashamed of the Ethiopians, the people of Tirhakah, who had made such glowing promises to the Egyptians when they had set him on the throne of Egypt. The Egyptians would also be ashamed of the boasted "glory of Egypt" which had suddenly come to such an inglorious defeat at the hands of the Assyrians.

6. And the inhabitant of this isle shall say in that day, Behold, such is our expectation, whither we flee for help to be delivered from the king of Assyria: and how shall we escape?

Now Isaiah turns to his own people and the inhabitants of "this isle," or the region where Isaiah was living. Isaiah said in that terrible day when Assyria would conquer Egypt, it would be the lament of the Jews that they would not know where they could appeal for help or how they might escape. In the past, Judah had leaned heavily on Egypt for support. Now it would be impossible to expect succor from that quarter any longer.

INTRODUCTION:

In the last chapter we discussed the 70 years of warfare by the Assyrians which eventually culminated in the conquest of Egypt. This struggle left Assyria seriously weakened in spite of her subjugation of Egypt. She was not only depleted of her wealth but also her military manpower. Assyria was therefore very vulnerable to attack during the latter part of the seventh century B.C. The nation which rose up to destroy her was Babylon, her southern neighbor, which had been previously ruled by Assyria and had been forced to pay heavy tribute for many years. Nearly a century after Isaiah's day, Babylon was finally successful in gaining an upper hand, and she conquered the hosts of Assyria in 605 B.C. after a terrible battle at Carchemish (located along the headwaters of the Euphrates River).

Once Assyria was demolished, it was Babylon's hour of power, which lasted until 539 B.C. The Babylonians were great despoilers among all the surrounding nations. They accumulated so much wealth that Babylon was represented as the "head of gold" by Daniel in the vision of the image depicting the future world empires (see Daniel 2:31–38).

The fall of Babylon occurred when Nabonidus was king. However, he had suffered a long period of mental illness so his son, Belshazzar, served as regent or co-king with his father. This is important to remember since it was Belshazzar who was presiding at the great feast in Babylon the night that the nation was suddenly taken over by Cyrus, leader of the Medes and Persians.

The exciting events of that night are described in Daniel, chapter 5. (Note that some ancient scribe erroneously inserted the name of Darius in the last verse. It should read "Cyrus.")

This background is necessary in order to appreciate what Isaiah is describing in this chapter. He tries to describe his feelings as he saw in vision the coming destruction of Babylon.

1. **The burden of the desert of the sea. As whirlwinds in the south pass through; so it cometh from the desert, from a terrible land.**

Isaiah says his message or burden of prophecy in this chapter will relate to that region known as the "desert of the sea." Dr. Adam Clarke points out that this phrase has reference to the vast area of swampland which existed around and below Babylon in ancient times. It extended southward to the sea (Persian Gulf). The area where the Tigris and the Euphrates rivers came together was often flooded. This created a vast wasteland of swamps and marshes which made it appropriate for Isaiah to call it the "desert of the sea." (Clarke, *Commentary*, 4:99.) The land of the "desert of the sea" was Babylon, which is what this chapter of Isaiah is about.

Isaiah saw that the invading forces would roar in on Babylon like the whirlwinds from the southern deserts—something with which Isaiah's listeners were thoroughly familiar. He further says that the conquest is going to come from a "terrible land." This is probably referring to the ferocity of the attack rather than the land itself. However, the land of the Medes and the Persians was located in the highlands and mountains to the east of Babylon, and perhaps its rugged terrain could be described as "terrible" in comparison with the lush, easy living enjoyed in the pleasant plains of Shinar between the two great rivers of the Tigris and the Euphrates (see Genesis 11:2).

2. A grievous vision is declared unto me; the treacherous dealer dealeth treacherously, and the spoiler spoileth. Go up, O Elam: besiege, O Media; all the sighing thereof have I made to cease.

Isaiah now begins to reflect the anguish and "grievousness" which a prophet is required to endure while beholding some of the awful events which are shown in open vision. In referring to the wickedness of the Babylonians, he calls them a treacherous people who were indulging themselves in all kinds of perfidious and deceitful practices. They also had a policy of despoiling all who came within their reach. No wonder they accumulated so much wealth that Babylon was symbolized as the "head of gold" described by Daniel.

Isaiah now speaks to the coalition of two great nations which will punish Babylon. One of these nations is Elam (or Persia), which occupied the region across from the Tigris River and directly east of Babylon. The other nation was the Medes, who occupied the territory further north. The Lord revealed to Isaiah that it would be through the conquest of Babylon by these two nations that the "sighing" or lamentations under Babylonian oppression would finally cease.

3. Therefore are my loins filled with pain: pangs have taken hold upon me, as the pangs of a woman that travaileth: I was bowed down at the hearing of it; I was dismayed at the seeing of it.

In this verse Isaiah again describes his personal reaction to the vision in which he saw the conquest of the Babylonians in 539 B.C. He says the emotional intensity accompanying the vision became so great that it caused his loins and inward parts to cramp with pain similar to that of a woman in childbirth.

Isaiah implies that a description of the fall of Babylon was first given to him by the Lord or one of his angelic ministers, and that afterwards he was allowed to see it in vision.

4. My heart panted, fearfulness affrighted me: the night of my pleasure hath he turned into fear unto me.

Isaiah noted that his heart was pounding in his chest as he observed the vision which the Lord opened up before him. Ordinarily it is a special pleasure to have a communication from the Lord, but Isaiah's pleasure was suddenly turned into a nightmare of dismay as he beheld the horrors of war and bloodshed which would occur in this military conquest.

5. Prepare the table, watch in the watchtower, eat, drink: arise, ye princes, and anoint the shield.

This verse is thought by some authorities to refer to Isaiah's vision of Belshazzar's famous feast the night before the fall of Babylon. It was the occasion when a mysterious hand began writing on the wall. When Daniel was called in to interpret the writing, he said it was a message of doom. The prophet told King Belshazzar that the kingdom would be wrested from him that very night (see Daniel, chapter 5).

Isaiah tells the Babylonians to go ahead preparing their sumptuous tables for eating, drinking, and merrymaking. Nevertheless, he says they had better place a lookout in the watchtower because he foresaw that an alarm would be sounded and every one of them, including their lords and princes, would be required to rise from their tables of festivity and rush for their shields in order to fight for their very lives.

6. For thus hath the Lord said unto me, Go, set a watchman, let him declare what he seeth.

Isaiah said the Lord had told him to place a man on the watchtower overlooking Babylon and have this watchman carefully report all that could be seen.

7. And he saw a chariot with a couple of horsemen, a chariot of asses, and a chariot of camels; and he hearkened diligently with much heed:

In this vision the Medes and Persians are represented by the two great leaders of these nations, Cyrus and Darius. It was Cyrus who conquered Babylon and Darius who came a few years later to despoil her. In this vision they were followed by two chariots, one pulled by asses or mules and the other by camels. These chariots represent the combined forces of the Medes and Persians.

8. And he cried, A lion: My lord, I stand continually upon the watchtower in the daytime, and I am set in my ward whole nights:

This verse says the watchman cries out, "A lion!" However, Bible authorities state that this is a defective translation. Dr. Clarke indicates that certain of the texts give the more correct version, indicating that the word which was translated as "lion" should have been a slightly different Hebrew word which means a person who stands upon a watchtower (Clarke, *Commentary*, 4:100). This verse would then read that the watchman on the tower wants his lord and master to know that he is watching carefully by day and by night. He wishes to report carefully and accurately on everything he sees.

9. And, behold, here cometh a chariot of men, with a couple of horsemen. And he answered and said, Babylon is fallen, is fallen; and all the graven images of her gods he hath broken unto the ground.

Isaiah once more refers back to the symbolism of the chariots and the two horsemen representing Cyrus and Darius. In due time, the watchman on the tower declares that an amazing thing has happened. The great and so-called invincible Babylon has fallen. All of the idols which represented the gods of the Babylonians are smashed and scattered upon the ground.

10. O my threshing, and the corn of my floor: that which I have heard of the LORD of hosts, the God of Israel, have I declared unto you.

After witnessing the scenes of this vision, Isaiah says he feels as though he had been threshed like grain. He says the trauma of seeing these revelations has made him feel like the kernels of wheat (called "corn" in the Bible) which have been flayed from their husks and left scattered about on the threshing room floor. He knows that what he has written may surprise many, but he assures the reader that he has not recorded his own thoughts or speculations. He has carefully recorded exactly what the Lord revealed to him.

11. The burden of Dumah. He calleth to me out of Seir,

Now Isaiah includes in this report the prophecies which were given him concerning Dumah, one of the

Watchman, what of the
night? Watchman, what of
the night?

notable cities of the Ishmaelites or Edomites. The dat-
ing for these events goes back to the time of the Assyrians, nearly 200 years earlier than the events described
in the previous ten verses. To identify these people of
Dumah, let us remind ourselves that they were descendants of Ishmael, the brother of Isaac. Isaac's son
Esau became known as Edom, and he married one of
Ishmael's daughters. Therefore Ishmaelites and Edomites were virtually one people. Many of them lived in
the Arabah Valley, which extends from the Dead Sea to
the Aqaba Gulf of the Red Sea. For this reason they are
often referred to as Arabs or Arabians. One of the
principal mountains of this region is called Mount Seir.

Isaiah was told that within a year (see verse 16) his
prophecy concerning the conquest of the Edomites and
Ishmaelites by the Assyrians would be fulfilled. He
therefore notes in this verse that these people would
call from Mount Seir asking, "Watchman, what of the
night?" This is interpreted to mean that they wished to
know when they will be liberated from their Assyrian
oppressors.

12. The watchman said, The
morning cometh, and also
the night: if ye will enquire,
enquire ye: return, come.

The watchman replies that they will indeed be liberated as the morning light cometh. Nevertheless, their
liberation will in due time be terminated, and they will
be conquered again. This will be like the night returning. The watchman encourages the people to continue
to inquire of him from time to time and take the message of the prophet to the people. Then he wants them
to return again for more information.

13. The burden upon Arabia.
In the forest in Arabia shall
ye lodge, O ye travelling
companies of Dedanim.

Isaiah says his prophecy concerning Arabia includes
the people of Dedan. Dedan was a grandson of Abraham through his third wife, Keturah (see Genesis

25:3). "Dedanim" is the Hebrew plural for Dedan or the people of Dedan. They inhabited the desert regions along with their near relatives, the Ishmaelites and Edomites. All of them together are frequently referred to as Arabians.

14. The inhabitants of the land of Tema brought water to him that was thirsty, they prevented with their bread him that fled.

Isaiah saw that the people of Tema (the southern desert) would bring water and bread to the other Arabians when they fled frantically from the superior forces of the Assyrian hosts.

15. For they fled from the swords, from the drawn sword, and from the bent bow, and from the grievousness of war.

Isaiah saw them fleeing from the mighty warriors of Assyria who would inflict them with the awful "grievousness of war."

16. For thus hath the Lord said unto me, Within a year, according to the years of an hireling, and all the glory of Kedar shall fail:

Isaiah had it revealed to him that "within a year, according to the years of an hireling," all of this would come to pass. The "year of a hireling" is to emphasize that these events will be fulfilled in the period of a year as calculated by a wage earner. It would not be one of the Lord's symbolic years, which may equal as much as 1,000 years (see Abraham 3:4).

17. And the residue of the number of archers, the mighty men of the children of Kedar, shall be diminished: for the LORD God of Israel hath spoken it.

To appreciate the prophecy concerning the fall of Kedar, we must remind ourselves that this name is taken from the second son of Ishmael. The people of Kedar were among the most heroic and valiant members of the Arabian armed forces. Nevertheless, Isaiah saw that they would fail to resist the onslaught of the Assyrians.

We learn from this verse that the children of Kedar will put up a great struggle and suffer many casualties. The number of their mighty archers and fighting men will be greatly reduced. And just in case some might doubt that such a thing could happen to the proud warriors of Kedar, Isaiah assures the reader that this was not his own prognostication. It was the Lord who said it would come to pass.

Isaiah, Chapter 22

INTRODUCTION:

Isaiah now turns to a series of visions concerning Judah and the region around Jerusalem. The setting for the fulfillment of this vision appears to be the historical events connected with the Assyrian campaign against Judah and her allies in 701 B.C.

It will be recalled that the northern Ten Tribes were conquered and the remnants carried off to Assyria in 721 B.C. Assyria's King Sargon also established his power over the Palestinian plain. However, in 705 B.C. Sargon died, and Hezekiah, the king of Judah, promptly instigated a confederated revolt against Assyrian rule in this region. The new king of Assyria was Sargon's son Sennacherib, but there was nothing he could do about Hezekiah's revolt for several years because he had to put down a number of revolts closer to home. However, by 701 B.C. Sennacherib was on the Palestinian plain and ready to deal with the revolt in this area. The Palestinian plain was the pathway to Egypt, which Sennacherib wanted to conquer. He was not about to tolerate any interference from petty kingdoms on either flank. He therefore determined to destroy every city of Judah as well as those on the plain. A total of 46 cities of Judah were finally captured and 200,150 prisoners carried off to Assyria (Hastings, *Dictionary of the Bible*, rev. ed., s.v. "Sennacherib"). Even Jerusalem was seriously threatened before King Hezekiah agreed to pay tribute. Later on, Sennacherib became dissatisfied with Hezekiah's tribute and determined to take Jerusalem after all, but that is another story.

Isaiah knew that it was not the intention of the Lord to have Judah conquered by Sennacherib if the people of Judah would repent and fight valiantly. However, Isaiah was shown in vision that they would not repent, but would carry on with their riotous reveling even when the enemy was at their gates.

1. The burden of the valley of vision. What aileth thee now, that thou art wholly gone up to the housetops?

Isaiah opens this chapter by saying that this is the burden of his prophetic writings concerning "the valley of vision." As the chapter unfolds it becomes apparent that he is referring to the region of Jerusalem, where visions are being continually given to the Lord's prophet.

In this particular vision, Isaiah sees all of the people rushing to their rooftops so they can see what is happening in the streets or out beyond their city walls. It is obviously a time of alarm. Isaiah cannot help asking, "What aileth thee?"

2. Thou that art full of stirs, a tumultuous city, a joyous city: thy slain men are not slain with the sword, nor dead in battle.

Isaiah was astonished that in this terrible day of tumult and threatened disaster there was no evidence that the men of Judah were either courageous or valiant in defending their freedom or their families. Men that should have been willing to be slain rather than be conquered had not been slain. Men who should have gone bravely into battle even at the risk of their lives had not gone into battle. Instead, they were reveling in wickedness and making their habitations a "joyous city" of indulgence and dissipation when their strength should have been spent in fortifying and defending themselves.

3. All thy rulers are fled together, they are bound by

The members of the ruling class—the governors, the counsellors, the judges, and the mayors—had all fled

the archers: all that are found in thee are bound together, which have fled from far.

like cowards. But they would not escape. Isaiah saw that 200,000 Jews would be captured and bound in chains or fetters by the archers or bowmen of the invading host. Even those who had come from afar to enjoy the protection of the walled cities of Judah would be captured and bound.

4. Therefore said I, Look away from me; I will weep bitterly, labour not to comfort me, because of the spoiling of the daughter of my people.

Because Isaiah knew that the scenes before him would literally come to pass in the not-too-distant future, he wept bitterly. And he would not be comforted, especially by those whom he knew would allow the whole nation of Judah to be ravaged by these invading hosts. Isaiah said he could not help but weep bitterly over the "spoiling of the daughter of my people."

5. For it is a day of trouble, and of treading down, and of perplexity by the Lord GOD of hosts in the valley of vision, breaking down the walls, and of crying to the mountains.

Isaiah describes the vision of these tragic days as a time of "trouble." It was to be a season of cruel devastation, of "treading down, and of perplexity" which the Lord would allow Assyria to inflict upon this proud and unrepentant people. Throughout the land the mighty walls of 46 cities would tumble to the ground. Many of the people would be left homeless, hungry, and desperately frightened as they frantically fled "crying to the mountains."

6. And Elam bare the quiver with chariots of men and horsemen, and Kir uncovered the shield.

In this vision Isaiah was impressed by the fact that not only the Assyrians would be attacking Judah, but many of their mercenaries and allies as well. He saw the chariots of the people of Elam (Persia) bearing quivers filled with arrows and spears. He also saw their cavalry of horsemen. Then he saw the shield-bearing soldiers of the infantry from Kir, a principal city of the Medes which was located just north of Elam. Both the

Medes and Persians (or Elamites) had become tributaries of Assyria.

7. And it shall come to pass, that thy choicest valleys shall be full of chariots, and the horsemen shall set themselves in array at the gate.

Because the mountainous terrain of Judah was so rough and difficult to cultivate, the rich valleys were the nation's most precious possessions. In this vision Isaiah saw these valleys filled with war chariots, which would mean that the fields and vineyards would be trampled down and virtually destroyed. He also saw the great congregation of horsemen assembled at "the" gate, apparently referring to the main gate of Jerusalem since this is the site mentioned in the next verse.

8. And he discovered the covering of Judah, and thou didst look in that day to the armour of the house of the forest.

Isaiah saw that the king of Assyria (Sennacherib) would "discover the covering" of Judah. This Hebrew phrase means to expose or make the city of Jerusalem naked and open to the enemy's attack. He saw the people of Jerusalem carting out the armor and weapons from the arsenal which was maintained in the "house of the forest." This was the huge structure built by Solomon from the cedars of Lebanon furnished by King Hyrum. It was therefore called the "house of the forest of Lebanon" (1 Kings 7:2–5).

9. Ye have seen also the breaches of the city of David, that they are many: and ye gathered together the waters of the lower pool.

Isaiah also saw numerous breaches in the wall of "the city of David." This was the area of the city which had previously been the stronghold of the Jebusites, and which David had used as the site for his palaces and military headquarters after he had captured Jerusalem. The breaches in the walls were "many," Isaiah says, which would suggest that the defenses of the "joyous city" had been seriously neglected in the past and would not be able to withstand a formidable attack unless extensive repairs were undertaken. It may have been this very weakness in the defenses of the city which caused Hezekiah to pay tribute to the Assyrians. Later, of course, he grew bolder and temporarily refused to pay the tribute. This confidence may have resulted from substantial strengthening of the city.

10. And ye have numbered the houses of Jerusalem, and the houses have ye broken down to fortify the wall.

Almost as though he were talking to King Hezekiah, Isaiah says, "Ye gathered together the waters of the lower pool." What Hezekiah did was to have a tunnel cut from Gihon Spring (the upper pool) so that the waters could flow down or be "gathered" at the Pool of Siloam (the lower pool). This was designed to keep an adequate quantity of water within the protective walls of Jerusalem.

Isaiah says the king has also taken a survey of the houses of Jerusalem and designated some of those which had been built of stone to be torn down so that the stone could be used to "fortify the wall." This would suggest that the breaches which he mentioned above were from neglect, and King Hezekiah therefore had houses torn down to repair the damage rather than take the time to quarry new rock.

11. Ye made also a ditch between the two walls for the water of the old pool: but ye have not looked unto the maker thereof, neither had respect unto him that fashioned it long ago.

The prophet now refers to the "ditch" (actually a tunnel) which had been dug to carry water from the "old pool," or Gihon Spring, to the new pool known as the Pool of Siloam. However, Isaiah feels the king at this point in his life is not listening to counsel which the Lord has been giving him through Isaiah. The entire idea of a revolt against Assyria (which Hezekiah had promoted) was not the will of the Lord but the strategy of the king. Isaiah is therefore reprimanding the king and telling him in this verse that he has not properly honored the Creator who provided Gihon Spring as a source of water "long ago."

12. And in that day did the Lord GOD of hosts call to weeping, and to mourning, and to baldness, and to girding with sackcloth:

Isaiah saw that in the day when this vision would come to pass there would be weeping and mourning. The people would cut their hair and shave their heads (a common custom in time of mourning), and gird themselves in sackcloth, the apparel of mourning.

13. And behold joy and gladness, slaying oxen, and killing sheep, eating flesh, and drinking wine: let us eat and drink, for to morrow we shall die.

Nevertheless, there would be many who would not mourn, nor would they take the threatened destruction of Judah seriously. They would portray an attitude of "joy and gladness," and go about their affairs with jubilation and smug indifference toward the crisis at hand. Their attitude would be such that they would say: "Let us eat and drink, for tomorrow we shall die."

14. And it was revealed in mine ears by the LORD of hosts, Surely this iniquity shall not be purged from you till ye die, saith the Lord GOD of hosts.

Isaiah was told that this "iniquity" would continue with these people until they did die. In other words, Isaiah was not to expect them to repent, because the Lord had disclosed that they would go right ahead indulging themselves and ultimately reaping the whirlwind of destruction which they deserved.

15. Thus saith the Lord GOD of hosts, Go, get thee unto this treasurer, even unto Shebna, which is over the house, and say,

Now Isaiah gets down to cases. The Lord has revealed that one of the top executives of the king's government is corrupting his station. His name is Shebna. In 2 Kings 18:37, he is described as "a scribe," but Isaiah suggests that he is the king's treasurer as well. Isaiah said the Lord had instructed him to give Shebna a message and a warning.

16. What hast thou here? and whom hast thou here, that thou hast hewed thee out a sepulchre here, as he that heweth him out a sepulchre on high, and that graveth an habitation for himself in a rock?

Isaiah was to confront Shebna and ask him what he thought he was doing. Was he trying to accumulate a vast fortune and build for himself a mighty sepulchre as though he were some person of great distinction and riches?

17. Behold, the LORD will carry thee away with a mighty captivity, and will surely cover thee.

Shebna is to be warned that if he continues his present course he will be carried away captive and the Lord will "cover" him (dispose of him in death). There would be no magnificent sepulchre to honor him.

18. He will surely violently turn and toss thee like a ball into a large country: there shalt thou die, and there the chariots of thy glory shall be the shame of thy lord's house.

Isaiah says the future of Shebna is dark with prophecy if he continues on his present course. He will be treated with violence in a large, foreign country where he will be tossed to and fro. In fact, he will die there. Meanwhile back home, the devices of deception by which he had expected to ride to riches in a chariot of glory will have become a shame in the house of his former master (which was probably Hezekiah, the king).

19. And I will drive thee from thy station, and from thy state shall he pull thee down.

The prophecy is that Shebna will be pulled down from his high and lofty station in the king's government.

20. And it shall come to pass in that day, that I will call my servant Eliakim the son of Hilkiah:

When this occurs, the office of Shebna will be turned over to a more trustworthy servant. It will be Eliakim, the son of Hilkiah. Eliakim means one "whom God raised up." Throughout the rest of this chapter Eliakim is treated by Isaiah as symbolic of the coming Messiah whom God will also raise up.

21. And I will clothe him with thy robe, and strengthen him with thy girdle, and I will commit thy government into his hand: and he shall be a father to the inhabitants of Jerusalem, and to the house of Judah.

In this verse we learn that Shebna must have occupied a position of great trust, more like a prime minister than merely the treasurer. Isaiah says that when Eliakim replaces Shebna, he will wear Shebna's robe of authority and his high office of government will be placed in his hand. The office of prime minister or chief steward of the king is implied by the statement that Eliakim shall "be a father to the inhabitants of Jerusalem, and to the house of Judah." This description also applies to the coming Messiah.

22. And the key of the house of David will I lay upon his shoulder; so he shall open, and none shall shut; and he shall shut, and none shall open.

His authority will be supreme—next to the king himself. He will have the "key" of authority which belongs to the "house of David." That key is the power to rule. This supreme authority gives him the power to open and shut whatsoever he desires, and no person (save the king) can prevent it. In the case of the Messiah, the "key" of authority is the Priesthood.

23. And I will fasten him as a nail in a sure place; and he shall be for a glorious throne to his father's house.

Eliakim is to be firmly fixed in his position like "a nail in a sure place." This implies a secondary nail to secure the first. The first nail is to hold something in place. The nail in the "sure place" is to make it firm and permanently secure. The administration of Eliakim will be a glorious throne or pedestal of honor in his father's house.

24. And they shall hang upon him all the glory of his father's house, the offspring and the issue, all vessels of small quantity, from the vessels of cups, even to all the vessels of flagons.

In fact, the whole clan of his father's house will glory in Eliakim as their major claim to fame. This will include the great and the small. All of his relatives (vessels small and great) will glory in him and bask in the reflected radiance of his fame long after he is dead.

25. In that day, saith the LORD of hosts, shall the nail that is fastened in the sure place be removed, and be cut down, and fall; and the burden that was upon it shall be cut off: for the LORD hath spoken it.

But Isaiah says the time is coming when all of that honor and glory is going to fade away. The nail that was fastened in the sure place will be removed, and all who had depended upon his reputation and high office will find themselves "cut off."

In verses 23 to 25 we observe Isaiah inserting into the text certain phrases of metaphoric language which refer to the crucifixion of the Savior in a very literal sense, and refer to Eliakim in merely a representative sense. "The nail in a sure place" was not a literary metaphor with Jesus, but terribly real. He was first nailed to the cross through his hands, and then spikes were driven through each wrist as "a nail in a sure place." Later, after the Savior was dead, the "nail that is fastened in the sure place" was "removed," and the "burden that was upon it" was lifted down and carried away to a nearby garden where the body of Jesus was washed and placed in a new tomb (see Matthew 27:58–60; John 19:40–42).

Isaiah, Chapter 23

INTRODUCTION:

Since Tyre was the most famous seaport of the ancient world, the entire region (including Zidon or Sidon) was often referred to as the kingdom of "Tyre." The city took its name from the island of rock on which Tyre was originally built. The island is a mile long and nearly a mile wide. It is situated a half-mile from the mainland. It had two elaborate harbors, one at each end of the island. These were both protected from the ravages of the seas by elaborate moles or stone breakwaters to guard its docks and wharves. The merchants and seamen of Tyre established major trading posts around the Mediterranean (such as Cyprus and Carthage), and some were as far away as the Persian Gulf. They had fleets in the Red Sea and circumnavigated the entire continent of Africa around 600 B.C. The people of Tyre spread to the mainland and built a city with strong defenses. However, in time of siege they would usually retreat to the protection of the island.

The "ships of Tarshish" were the large three-decked merchant ships of Tyre which peddled wares all along the Mediterranean coast to Tarshish (probably Tartessus, the ancient Phoenician city in southern Spain). There the boats would be loaded with tin to bring back to the regions of copper mining, where it was mixed with copper to make bronze. Tyre herself produced beautiful items of glassware, and she also exported a famous dye called "crimson" or "purple," which was made from shellfish.

However, her greatest source of wealth was trade. All trade routes from Egypt, Persia, Asia Minor, North Africa, and Spain converged at Tyre. Her sailors maintained elaborate secret charts of currents, the depth of the sea, the seasons of favorable winds, and other advantages not known to the sailors of other nations. Often the ships of Tyre sailed at night so their competitors would not learn the sea lanes which they followed.

In time, Tyre literally became the warehouse of the ancient world. This made it a rich prize for any nation which could raid its treasures. However, Tyre was not easily conquered. This is borne out by the fact that the Assyrian siege against Tyre lasted five years before she fell. The Babylonian siege under Nebuchadnezzar lasted 13 years. Every time the city was invaded, a great slaughter of her people would ensue and much destruction of property would occur. Nevertheless, she would rebuild and rise to power again as soon as her enemies retired from the scene. As one would have suspected of a wealthy pagan culture, Tyre was a center of gross immorality and pagan rites which were strongly denounced by the prophets of Israel.

1. The burden of Tyre. Howl, ye ships of Tarshish; for it is laid waste, so that there is no house, no entering in: from the land of Chittim it is revealed to them.

In this vision, Isaiah saw the great destruction which would come upon Tyre. Isaiah does not identify the conquering nation, but we know from verses 15 to 17 that he is talking about a conquest which would be followed by 70 years of oblivion for Tyre. Jeremiah refers to this same event and says the 70 years of oblivion would take place following the conquest of Tyre by the Babylonians (see Jeremiah 25:9–11). The siege of Tyre began about the same time Jerusalem fell in 586 B.C. However, Tyre did not fall until she had endured the siege for 13 years (586 to 572 B.C.)! (See Hastings, *Dictionary of the Bible*, rev. ed., s.v. "Tyre.")

Once the Babylonians broke through her defenses, they laid the city "waste." Isaiah said the great ships which plied the Mediterranean as far away as Tarshish (an ancient Phoenician city in southern Spain) would find no haven when they returned. There would be no port or "house" for their "entering in." When they stopped off at Chittim (Cyprus), they would be warned that Tyre had been reduced to ruin.

2. Be still, ye inhabitants of the isle; thou whom the merchants of Zidon, that pass over the sea, have replenished.

In this verse Isaiah initiates the theme that the rich merchants and people of Tyre will deserve what is going to happen to them. He tells them to "be still." They cannot justly complain that they had not been blessed. Originally they had been greatly enriched and strengthened when the merchants from Zidon (Sidon) had transferred their businesses to Tyre and thereby "replenished" it with great wealth and resources.

3. And by great waters the seed of Sihor, the harvest of the river, is her revenue; and she is a mart of nations.

Furthermore, the great ships of Tyre had brought back vast stores of grain from the rich valley of the Nile (called Sihor because of its dark, muddy waters). The business operations of Tyre had made her the commercial center for all of the surrounding nations.

4. Be thou ashamed, O Zidon: for the sea hath spoken, even the strength of the sea, saying, I travail not, nor bring forth children, neither do I nourish up young men, nor bring up virgins.

However, Isaiah saw that all these blessings would be lost. The merchants of Zidon who had transferred their operations to Tyre would be humbled and "ashamed." The fortified island of Tyre, which had been called "the strength of the sea," would be virtually depopulated, being unable to raise up a new generation of young men and virgins to populate the island.

5. As at the report concerning Egypt, so shall they be sorely pained at the report of Tyre.

Isaiah perceived that a similar fate would be inflicted on Egypt about this same time. People would be amazed to learn that each of these great centers of wealth and power had been invaded and conquered simultaneously. Isaiah saw that the invasion of Egypt would be associated with the campaign of Nebuchadnezzar to destroy Jerusalem and all the nearby nations which would confederate together to oppose the Babylonians. It turned out that they stopped paying tribute and allied themselves with Egypt. Nebuchnezzar therefore came into the region and reconquered all of them.

6. Pass ye over to Tarshish; howl, ye inhabitants of the isle.

As Isaiah saw what would happen to Tyre, he suggested that the merchants and sailors of that ill-fated city might just as well flee to Tarshish (Tartessus in Spain) for safety. There would be nothing but howling and lamentation in Tyre.

7. Is this your joyous city, whose antiquity is of ancient days? her own feet shall carry her afar off to sojourn.

Isaiah wanted the people of Tyre to realize that they had invited this disaster upon themselves because of their wickedness. They were known throughout the world as a "joyous city," a city of pleasure, revelry, and debauchery such as most port cities become. However, he knew that when this great affliction came upon them, many would no longer consider it a "joyous city," but would hurriedly migrate elsewhere. They would set their feet upon paths which would take them to far-off places to "sojourn."

8. Who hath taken this counsel against Tyre, the crowning city, whose merchants are princes, whose traffickers are the honourable of the earth?

Isaiah asks the people of that future day if they had any idea who had decided to allow this great calamity to come upon them. After all, Tyre was a "crowning city" of great renown whose men of business were counted as the most "honourable" or distinguished merchants of the whole earth.

9. The LORD of hosts hath purposed it, to stain the pride of all glory, and to bring into contempt all the honourable of the earth.

Isaiah declares that the "Lord of hosts," the very God of the earth, had decided it should happen. Isaiah said it would be necessary to "stain the pride" of these high-minded tycoons of wealth and splendor. It was to give them a taste of the "contempt" which they deserved because of the kind of lives they lived.

10. Pass through thy land as a river, O daughter of Tarshish: there is no more strength.

Isaiah challenged the inhabitants of Tyre in that future day to sweep through their great city like a river and see what had happened. Everywhere they would find desolation. This home base for the ships of Tarshish could boast no longer, nor could they revel in their wickedness, for they would be without strength.

11. He stretched out his hand over the sea, he shook the kingdoms: the LORD hath given a commandment against the merchant city, to destroy the strong holds thereof.

Isaiah wanted the people to know that the Lord himself had decreed that many of the proud nations of the earth were to be shaken and humbled. This decree would include the great "merchant city" of Tyre. Its mighty walls would be thrown down and its "strongholds" demolished.

12. And he said, Thou shalt no more rejoice, O thou oppressed virgin, daughter of Zidon: arise, pass over to Chittim; there also shalt thou have no rest.

Isaiah gave God's pronouncement of that day: "Thou shalt no more rejoice." The people who were descendants of those merchants who had transferred their business headquarters from Zidon to Tyre would be forced to flee. But Isaiah warned that it would do them no good to go to nearby Chittim (Cyprus), for that island trade center would also "have no rest." It would feel the destructive power of the enemy's invading host just as severely as Tyre.

13. Behold the land of the Chaldeans; this people was not, till the Assyrian founded it for them that dwell in the wilderness: they set up the towers thereof, they raised up the palaces thereof; and he brought it to ruin.

Isaiah wanted to give them another example of a people who felt the wrath of the Lord because of their wickedness. He reminds them of the Chaldeans in the land of Ur. They were not of much consequence among the nations of the earth until the Assyrians came and built for them great palaces and towers for their defense. Nevertheless, Isaiah pointed out that all of these fine buildings and towers of defense did them no good when they began to taint their social culture with wicked practices. Isaiah said the Lord brought them to ruin, just as he would bring Tyre to ruin for similar reasons.

14. Howl, ye ships of Tarshish: for your strength is laid waste.

This is why Isaiah tells the ship captains and merchants of that future day of destruction to "howl" with grief. Their strength will be "laid waste."

15. And it shall come to pass in that day, that Tyre shall be forgotten seventy years, according to the days of one king: after the end of seventy years shall Tyre sing as an harlot.

16. Take an harp, go about the city, thou harlot that hast been forgotten; make sweet melody, sing many songs, that thou mayest be remembered.

Isaiah predicted that when this great destruction comes upon Tyre, it will leave the great city virtually forgotten and of little consequence to the rest of the world. This will be the situation for 70 years. She will be like a forsaken harlot who has been abandoned. For 70 years she will try to attract attention with new songs of sweet melody in her attempt to remind people of her popularity in the past.

17. And it shall come to pass after the end of seventy years, that the LORD will visit Tyre, and she shall turn to her hire, and shall

Nevertheless, Isaiah saw that after 70 years Tyre would gradually rise to power again. He had to remorsefully predict, however, that the bitter lessons of the past 70 years will have left no lasting impression

commit fornication with all
the kingdoms of the world
upon the face of the earth.

upon her people. They will go back to trade practices with other nations which the Lord denounces as corrupt. Honest trade is the key to prosperity and happiness, but the exploitation of trade involving vice and shrewd practices of deceit are an abomination before the Lord. Isaiah says Tyre will be like a harlot who has returned to her "hire" and will begin committing acts of "fornication" with "all the kingdoms of the world."

18. And her merchandise and her hire shall be holiness to the LORD: it shall not be treasured nor laid up; for her merchandise shall be for them that dwell before the LORD, to eat sufficiently, and for durable clothing.

Isaiah concludes by saying that with the passing of time the wealth of Tyre will pass into the hands of those who will use it for God's purposes. It will no longer be "laid up" in the strongholds of wicked Tyre, but will be "for them that dwell before the Lord, to eat sufficiently, and for durable clothing." Just how and when this was fulfilled, available records do not tell us.

Isaiah, Chapter 24

INTRODUCTION:

God's prophetic timetable is divided into seven periods of one thousand years each. This is the planned duration for the temporal existence of the human family on this planet in its present stage of development (D&C 77:6). The restoration of the Gospel was scheduled for the latter part of the sixth thousand-year period. The Gospel message was then to go to every nation under heaven (Matthew 24: 14; D&C 1:4-7). This is where we are at the present time. In the not-too-distant future the fulness of the Gentiles will reach its windup stage as the Elders of Israel seek mightily to convert as many people as possible before it is too late. Following this phase of prophetic history the Lord will begin preaching his own sermons, and do it in a most impressive way. He says: "For after YOUR testimony cometh the testimony of earthquakes.... the voice of thunderings,... of lightnings,... of tempests,... of the waves of the sea heaving themselves beyond their bounds. And all things shall be in commotion; and surely, men's hearts shall fail them." (D&C 88:88-91; emphasis added.)

According to John the Revelator, all of these monumental convulsions in the earth will come at the close of the sixth-seal epoch. John described the scene as it was revealed to him:

"And, lo, there was a great earthquake; and the sun became black as sackcloth of hair, and the moon became as blood; and the stars of heaven fell unto the earth.... And the heaven departed as a scroll when it is rolled together; and every mountain and island were moved out of their places." (Revelation 6:12-14.)

This is followed by the opening of the seventh seal, which signals the cleansing of the earth preparatory to the ushering in of the Millennium. At first the earth will continue to have violent storms and earthquakes, but the greatest destruction will come from plagues and a terrible war in which FIRE is the principal weapon. Joel's description of this war suggests that the "fire" of that day will be by nuclear weapons with fallout which will prevent the growing of crops (see Joel, chapter 2). All of these revelations indicate that few will survive this terrible onslaught. This may very well be the period when the Saints will be "caught up" to save their lives (see D&C 88:96; 1 Thessalonians 4:17). This will require that they be temporarily transfigured and then be returned to the earth and restored to their normal status after the great destruction in order to continue their temporal lives until the full course of their second estate has transpired.

It is this perspective of the sixth and seventh seals which Isaiah now describes.

1. Behold, the LORD maketh the earth empty, and maketh it waste, and turneth it upside down, and scattereth abroad the inhabitants thereof.

When we consider what the Lord has said he must do to the earth to prepare it for the Millennium, it is no wonder that the prophets who saw it in vision could not help but describe the earth as turned upside down. The mountains must be lowered and the valleys raised (see Isaiah 40.4). The islands and the continents must be joined back into one land (see D&C 133:23-24). The earth has to hurtle back through space toward Kolob (see Isaiah 13:13-14 and notes). Wars, plagues, and desolation by fire must sweep the wicked from off the face of the earth. The earth will indeed be a planet of widespread waste and emptiness immediately after this cleansing process occurs.

2. And it shall be, as with the people, so with the priest; as with the servant, so with his master; as with the maid, so with her mistress; as with the buyer, so with the seller; as with the lender, so with the borrower; as with the taker of usury, so with the giver of usury to him.

Isaiah saw that the destruction of the wicked will be universal. The bankers and businessmen will be no less surprised than their most humble employees. And if they were wicked the destroying angels of God will afflict them whether they were rich or poor, learned or ignorant.

3. The land shall be utterly emptied, and utterly spoiled: for the LORD hath spoken this word.

Isaiah repeats his observation that the "land shall be utterly emptied, and utterly spoiled." He verifies that if the Lord said he will do this, it is a foregone conclusion that it will occur.

4. The earth mourneth and fadeth away, the world languisheth and fadeth away, the haughty people of the earth do languish.

Isaiah tries to convey some of his impressions as he saw this vision of the earth in convulsions and several billion human beings going down to destruction. He could only exclaim: "The earth mourneth and fadeth away, ... the haughty people of the earth do languish," or droop with despair.

5. The earth also is defiled under the inhabitants thereof; because they have transgressed the laws, changed the ordinance, broken the everlasting covenant.

At the same time, Isaiah knew from the vision that a just God could not have endured any longer the flood-tide of depraved debauchery which he saw engulfing mankind throughout the earth in that day. Isaiah saw that every covenant the people had made with God would be deliberately violated. Every holy ordinance revealed by God for the salvation of his children would be corrupted, changed, or disdainfully rejected. Every commitment to God which pertained to the everlasting covenant of the Gospel would be shattered and cast aside.

6. Therefore hath the curse devoured the earth, and they that dwell therein are desolate: therefore the inhabitants of the earth are burned, and few men left.

Isaiah wanted to make it emphatically clear that what would happen to the human race during this terrible winding-up scene was a consuming curse of suffering and death which the people would bring upon themselves. They would debase themselves to such a corrupt and degenerate level that they would invite the wrath of heaven just as millions of people were doing before the Great Flood around 2344 B.C. Jesus referred to this latter-day epoch of defilement when he said: "And as it was in the days of Noe [Noah], so shall it be also in the days of the Son of man. They did eat, they drank, they married wives, they were given in marriage, until the day that Noe entered into the ark, and the flood came, and destroyed them all." (Luke 17:26–27.) Isaiah saw the same thing happening at the time of the Second Coming, except that this time it would not be a destruction by drowning. It would be by fire. Isaiah saw that there would be a holocaust of devouring conflagration which would so completely consume the several billion inhabitants of the defiled and desecrated planet that there would be "FEW MEN LEFT"!

7. The new wine mourneth, the vine languisheth, all the merryhearted do sigh.

8. The mirth of tabrets ceaseth, the noise of them that rejoice endeth, the joy of the harp ceaseth.

Isaiah saw that this would be a day when every aspect of human happiness and reason for rejoicing would be lacking. Ordinarily the people would have great festivals at the time of the grape harvest and the making of the new wine. But Isaiah said there would be no cause for festivals of happiness at the time of harvest in this future day of judgment. Instead of the festival of joy there will be mourning. All the "merryhearted" will be sighing and moaning in depression and grief. The laughter and mirth which have always accompanied these festivals will be absent. There will be no instruments of music to lighten their spirits.

9. They shall not drink wine with a song; strong drink shall be bitter to them that drink it.

There will be no rousing drinking songs as in the past. The wine and distilled alcohol which were formerly thought to be a source of exhilarating stimulation will be bitter to the taste and sour to the stomach.

10. The city of confusion is broken down: every house is shut up, that no man may come in.

Ordinarily people flock to the towns and cities for security in time of danger or for social enjoyment during holidays and celebrations. But the city of this future day will be no harbor for security or recreation. Everything will be in total confusion and broken down. Houses will not be open to visitors. They will be locked up with doors bolted and windows covered. Each family will have so little with which to survive they will not welcome anyone. They will say, "No man may come in!"

11. There is a crying for wine in the streets; all joy is darkened, the mirth of the land is gone.

The languishing, moaning people will long for an escape from the misery of that day. Some will wander about the streets crying out for some wine or similar beverage to slake their alcoholic appetite and dull their senses to the distress they see all about them. No one will be joyful or optimistic. Isaiah looked upon the scene and said, "The mirth of the land is gone."

12. In the city is left desolation, and the gate is smitten with destruction.

Throughout all the wicked nations of the earth there will be the same somber scene of destruction. No city will be a refuge. Each city will be a rubble of desolation. The sources of light and power will be cut off. The garbage will lie about in heaps. There will be no police protection, no fire departments in operation, no hospitals for the sick, no stores piled with food. From the gate or entrance to the city to the full extent of all its suburbs, Isaiah could see nothing but destruction.

13. When thus it shall be in the midst of the land among the people, there shall be as the shaking of an olive tree, and as the gleaning grapes when the vintage is done.

Isaiah says the vision of that future day reminded him of the violent shaking of the olive trees when they are forced to cast off their fruit at harvest time. It even reminded him of the searching for the last vestige of the grapes when the gleaners have stripped every vine and poked under every leaf.

14. They shall lift up their voice, they shall sing for the majesty of the LORD, they shall cry aloud from the sea.

In contrast to all of this desolation among the wicked, Isaiah perceived that in Zion there would be an isolated haven of security from all of this ferocity of war and the consuming conflagration of fire. Isaiah said that among the righteous there would be praise and thanksgiving to the Lord. They would rejoice and salute the majesty of his divine judgment. From their sanctuary of safety beyond the sea, they would cry aloud to the Lord in thanksgiving. As Isaiah says a little later on concerning this period, "And the ransomed of the Lord shall return, and come to Zion with songs and everlasting joy upon their heads: they shall obtain joy and gladness, and sorrow and sighing shall flee away" (Isaiah 35:10).

15. Wherefore glorify ye the LORD in the fires, even the name of the LORD God of Israel in the isles of the sea.

In contemplation of that great day among the righteous, Isaiah glories in their rejoicing and urges them to sing forth their praises. The phrase which says "glorify ye the Lord in the FIRES" is thought by most authorities to be an erroneous translation. Some feel it should be "valleys"; others suggest that the scribe should have said "isles." In either case, we know that Isaiah was looking at the righteous who were secure among the "isles of the sea." It is interesting that the prophets have often referred to the Western Hemisphere by this term, as well as the islands of the Pacific, where so many of the children of Israel have been found. We note that the great prophet Jacob in the Book of Mormon refers to America as "an isle of the sea" (2 Nephi 10:20).

16. From the uttermost part of the earth have we heard songs, even glory to the righteous. But I said, My leanness, my leanness, woe unto me! the treacherous dealers have dealt treacherously; yea, the treacherous dealers have dealt very treacherously.

Isaiah emphasizes that all of this rejoicing which will take place among the righteous during these days of God's judgment will not come from the lands occupied by the wicked, but will come from the "uttermost" part of the earth. From other scriptures previously quoted we know this is referring to the Western Hemisphere, which is among the "isles of the sea." It will enjoy protection from the debacle of devastation which will be poured out in such overflowing quantities upon the lands where the wicked have been gathered in bundles ready to be burned.

Reluctantly, Isaiah turns from the rejoicing in Zion to behold the terrible scene he was viewing earlier. He cries out, "My leanness, my leanness, woe unto me!" Some authorities in Bible translation feel the word "leanness" should be "secret." In other words, Isaiah is lamenting over this great vision of the future which he alone knows. Knowing what awaits the wicked elements of mankind in the latter days is a burden of sorrow to him. As he looks upon them he is particularly distressed with the plundering and looting which will go on among the people. He sees the people dealing treacherously with one another. In fact, he is so disgusted with the sight of it that he repeats with emphasis that they will deal VERY treacherously with one another.

17. Fear, and the pit, and the snare, are upon thee, O inhabitant of the earth.

As Isaiah saw the wicked inhabitants of the earth in that future day scrambling about in terror trying to escape the judgments of God, he likened it to the way wild beasts of the forest are trapped by falling into deep pits or are captured by clever snares. If they are not caught one way, they are snared another. Therefore Isaiah said the "fear" (which hunters induce in their prey with the noise of pounding drums and great shouts) will drive the quarry into the deep pits or the entangling snares of God's inescapable judgments, which shall be poured out upon the fleeing multitudes of depraved humanity.

18. **And it shall come to pass, that he who fleeth from the noise of the fear shall fall into the pit; and he that cometh up out of the midst of the pit shall be taken in the snare: for the windows from on high are open, and the foundations of the earth do shake.**

Isaiah assures the people of that coming day that there will be no way they can escape. The people will be like the beasts which they themselves hunt. The noise and fury of that day will drive them into the pits of an inferno of destruction. And if they somehow escape from that terrifying situation, they will still be snared by something else just as deadly. Isaiah says the heavens will be wide open. All kinds of destruction will pour down from above, while at the same time the earth will provide no security because its very foundations will shake and crumble.

19. **The earth is utterly broken down, the earth is clean dissolved, the earth is moved exceedingly.**

Now Isaiah emphasizes just how terrifying it will be for those living on the earth in that day. In fact, we know from Doctrine and Covenants 88:96 and 1 Thessalonians 4:17 that the righteous will have to be "caught up" by the Lord so they will not be destroyed. Isaiah saw the continental regions of the earth completely broken down so that they seemed to be dissolving before his eyes. The surface of the planet seemed to be heaving itself about with such turbulence that Isaiah says "the earth is moved exceedingly."

20. **The earth shall reel to and fro like a drunkard, and**

Nothing seems to terrify mankind more than the ferocious upheaval of nature which Isaiah describes in

shall be removed like a cottage; and the transgression thereof shall be heavy upon it; and it shall fall, and not rise again.

these next few verses. To have the very planet on which men make their habitation suddenly appear to go out of control will be like an unbelievable nightmare. The earth will begin rolling on her axis, reeling to and fro. The climate will change from summer to winter overnight and then change back again. It will stagger in its orbit about the sun like a drunkard, and then suddenly it will be removed out of its present place in the galaxy and be hurtled back toward Kolob at such a phenomenal speed that the stars will appear to be falling from heaven as the earth sweeps past them. Isaiah speaks of this removal of the cottage or dwelling place of mankind from its present abode in our solar system to a more central location near Kolob as a "fall." He says that once the earth falls inward toward the center of the galaxy it will not "rise" or return again to its present location some 30,000 light years out from Kolob (see notes on Isaiah 13:13–14).

21. And it shall come to pass in that day, that the LORD shall punish the host of the high ones that are on high, and the kings of the earth upon the earth.

The great destruction on the earth incidental to all of these disruptive terrestrial phenomena will be God's just and long-overdue judgment on the wicked who corrupted the earth. He will destroy the dissolute, debauched, and high-minded elite who thought they owned the whole earth, and he will also destroy the kings and rulers who governed the earth as though it were their private domain.

22. And they shall be gathered together, as prisoners are gathered in the pit, and shall be shut up in the prison, and after many days shall they be visited.

The spirits of these wicked people who are destroyed from off the face of the earth will be gathered together in the spirit world, where they will be held in a prison-like place. No doubt those who were atheists will be astounded to see that their spirits are still living entities even though their polluted bodies were destroyed.

They will find themselves continuing their eternal existence, which they thought was a myth. They will have a thousand questions which none in their own company of wicked spirits can answer. Like the millions who died in the Great Flood, they will be held in prison for a season until they can be taught (see 1 Peter 3:18-20). But as with those who died in the Great Flood, so shall it be with the wicked who are destroyed just before the Second Coming; they shall be visited.

23. Then the moon shall be confounded, and the sun ashamed, when the LORD of hosts shall reign in mount Zion, and in Jerusalem, and before his ancients gloriously.

When the earth returns to its original environment near Kolob it will be surrounded by light on every side. No longer will it need the sun or the moon to give warmth or light. In fact, the radiance and beauty of this new environment will make the memory of the moon dim or "confounded" by contrast, and that of the sun "ashamed" by comparison. (See the comment of Orson Pratt concerning this passage in *Journal of Discourses*, 20:12.) Such will be the state of the earth when Christ rules over it during the Millennium.

Perhaps it will be this situation to which the Lord is referring when he says there will be "time no longer" (Revelation 10:6; D&C 84:100). Time on the earth during its first six thousand years of human habitation has been measured by the sun for days, by the moon for months, and again by the sun for years and for seasons. Think what it will be like when there is neither day nor night, winter nor summer, times nor seasons. We may even go back into the prolongation of our existence in terms of God's time, one day of which is as a thousand years of our present time (see 2 Peter 3:8; Abraham 3:4; 5:13). Surely it will seem as though there is "time no longer" as we have known it during the past six thousand years. There will always be mechanical time, or the measuring of our passing existence from one moment to the next, but time in terms of days and nights, months and years, will cease to be when the earth moves back into its original sphere of perpetual light and perpetual summer.

As Isaiah later says: "The sun shall be no more thy light by day; neither for brightness shall the moon give light unto thee.... The sun shall no more go down; neither shall thy moon withdraw itself." (Isaiah 60:19-20.) This same theme occurs in the revelation to John: "And THERE SHALL BE NO NIGHT THERE; and they need no candle, neither light of the sun; for the Lord God giveth them light." (Revelation 22:5; emphasis added.)

Isaiah, Chapter 25

INTRODUCTION:

Now the prophet's vision fastens onto the glorious vista of that day mentioned in the last verse of chapter 24, which Isaiah describes as the day when "the Lord of hosts shall reign in mount Zion, and in Jerusalem, and before his ancients gloriously."

1. O LORD, thou art my God; I will exalt thee, I will praise thy name; for thou hast done wonderful things; thy counsels of old are faithfulness and truth.

Isaiah cannot help but sing out to the Lord in triumph. He exclaims with profound satisfaction what marvelous things he sees the Lord doing to cleanse the earth and prepare it for the millennial reign. Everything the Lord has promised from the days of old, he has faithfully fulfilled. Everything he said would happen turned out to be the truth.

2. For thou hast made of a city an heap; of a defenced city a ruin: a palace of strangers to be no city; it shall never be built.

As Isaiah contemplated the magnificent and mighty cities of the latter days which would be populated by millions and have powerful defenses, he could not help but marvel how God's judgment would reduce them to a "heap" of ruins. He noted that the rich palaces of the very proud (erroneously translated "strangers," according to Adam Clarke; *Commentary*, 4:114) would no longer be a city or habitation for these wicked elitists of the latter days. He saw the skyscraper palaces of the latter days so completely destroyed that they could never be rebuilt.

3. Therefore shall the strong people glorify thee, the city of the terrible nations shall fear thee.

Isaiah saw that in that great day of God's judgment, the righteous who had remained strong in spite of their poverty and persecution would glorify God. On the other hand, the wicked inhabitants of each mighty city of the "terrible nations" would be horror stricken as God's judgment swept down upon them.

4. For thou hast been a strength to the poor, a strength to the needy in his distress, a refuge from the storm, a shadow from the heat, when the blast of the terrible ones is as a storm against the wall.

Isaiah makes it clear in this verse those whom he identifies as "the strong." They are the poor and the needy whom God has raised up in strength because they remained faithful. At a time when the "blast" of the "terrible ones" will pound upon the "needy in distress" like a storm against the wall, God will become their refuge and raise them up from their afflictions to become a strong and powerful people.

5. Thou shalt bring down the noise of strangers, as the heat in a dry place; even the heat with the shadow of a cloud: the branch of the terrible ones shall be brought low.

Isaiah saw that the Lord will bring down the clamor and noise of the very proud (once again erroneously translated "strangers" as in verse 2). The Lord will cause them to wilt like a bough or branch of a green plant when it is exposed to "the heat in a dry place." The next phrase is thought to be defective. In order to fit it into the context and meaning of the rest of the verse it is believed to have been originally written, "the heat WITHOUT the shadow of a cloud."

6. And in this mountain shall the LORD of hosts make unto all people a feast of fat things, a feast of wines on the lees, of fat things full of marrow, of wines on the lees well refined.

The Lord allowed Isaiah to see that in "this mountain" of Moriah where Jerusalem would be rebuilt in the latter days, the Lord of hosts would make a great feast for his people. This no doubt refers to the great feast which the Lord describes in a modern revelation:

"Wherefore, marvel not, for the hour cometh that I will drink of the fruit of the vine with you ON THE

EARTH, and with Moroni, ... and also with Elias, ... and also John the son of Zacharias, ... and also Elijah, ... and also with Joseph and Jacob, and Isaac, and Abraham, ... and also with Michael, or Adam, ... and also with Peter, and James, and John, ... and also with all those whom my Father hath given me out of the world." (D&C 27:5-14; emphasis added.)

The Lord says this magnificent feast of triumph will be a glorious occasion with the finest of food and "wines of the lees well refined." In Isaiah's day the best wine was that which had been allowed to age "in the lees" and then filtered or refined for consumption. There would also be the finest of meats "full of marrow."

What a tremendous occasion this will be when the resurrected patriarchs and prophets of the past will dine with the righteous who have survived the great cleansing of the earth!

7. And he will destroy in this mountain the face of the covering cast over all people, and the vail that is spread over all nations.

Isaiah saw that the great veil which separates the temporal world from the spiritual sphere would be removed or taken away so that all mankind can see the hosts of heaven descend with the Savior as he returns to the earth in glory. In a modern revelation the Lord describes this event as follows: "And there shall be silence in heaven for the space of half an hour; and immediately after shall the curtain of heaven be unfolded, as a scroll is unfolded after it is rolled up, and the face of the Lord shall be unveiled" (D&C 88:95).

8. He will swallow up death in victory; and the Lord GOD will wipe away tears from off all faces; and the rebuke of his people shall he take away from off all the earth: for the LORD hath spoken it.

It will be just prior to the time of this great unveiling that the first resurrection will take place. The Lord has said, "And they who have slept in their graves shall come forth, for their graves shall be opened; and they also shall be caught up to meet him in the midst of the pillar of heaven" (D&C 88:97).

As for the living, the Lord "will wipe away tears from off all faces." The prophecies indicate that just prior to the Second Coming the righteous will undergo bitter persecution and oppression. However, with the coming of the Savior "the rebuke of his people shall he take away from off all the earth." They also shall be "caught up" to meet him (D&C 27:18; 88:96; 101:31).

9. And it shall be said in that day, Lo, this is our God; we have waited for him, and he will save us: this is the LORD; we have waited for him, we will be glad and rejoice in his salvation.

In their moment of liberation from oppression, the righteous will exclaim: "Lo, this is our God; we have waited for him, and he will save us!" The righteous will rejoice mightily that their salvation has come at last.

10. For in this mountain shall the hand of the LORD rest, and Moab shall be trodden down under him, even as straw is trodden down for the dunghill.

Isaiah saw that in this very mountain of Moriah (Jerusalem) where he had performed his great ministry, the Lord would have his refuge of peace and rest. Former enemies, like Moab, would be trodden down and no longer constitute a threat to the righteous.

11. And he shall spread forth his hands in the midst of them, as he that swimmeth spreadeth forth his hands to swim: and he shall bring down their pride together with the spoils of their hands.

The Lord will move in among them as a swimmer plunges into the water and pushes himself forward with mighty strokes. The Lord will bring down the pride of the Moabites or anyone else who seeks to oppress the righteous.

12. And the fortress of the high fort of thy walls shall he bring down, lay low, and bring to the ground, even to the dust.

Those who have built high walls and mighty, fortified cities will find them of no defense against the judgment of the Lord. Their cities and their high walls will be brought down to the ground, even to the dust.

Isaiah, Chapter 26

INTRODUCTION:

This chapter is the song of jubilation which Isaiah was inspired to record as he completed the vision of the redemption of Israel in the latter days.

1. In that day shall this song be sung in the land of Judah; We have a strong city; salvation will God appoint for walls and bulwarks.

The very fact that Jerusalem will be counted the residence of the Lord after he comes to his temple will make it a "strong city" in the eyes of all nations. The salvation which will come with the Savior's appearance among the Jews will be a greater boon to them than stout walls and great bulwarks of defense.

2. Open ye the gates, that the righteous nation which keepeth the truth may enter in.

The Jews will not be the only nation to inhabit Jerusalem. Isaiah saw the day when it will also include the righteous nation of Israel (the northern Ten Tribes), who will come down from the north and, after settling for a time in America, will take up their residence in Jerusalem and its environs. Therefore, Isaiah exclaims: "Open ye the gates, that the righteous nation which keepeth the truth may enter in!"

3. Thou wilt keep him in perfect peace, whose mind is stayed on thee: because he trusteth in thee.

By that time all Israel will know that the Lord gives a sense of perfect peace to men and women who cling to the iron rod of Nephi's vision and keep their minds focused on the Lord and the work he expects the righteous to perform. The righteous learn from experience that they can trust the Lord, who always fulfills his promises.

4. Trust ye in the LORD for ever: for in the LORD JEHOVAH is everlasting strength:

After they have learned this lesson of life, Isaiah urges them to continue trusting in the Lord God Jehovah forever because he is the source of everlasting strength to all mankind.

5. For he bringeth down them that dwell on high; the lofty city, he layeth it low; he layeth it low, even to the ground; he bringeth it even to the dust.

History demonstrates that from the earliest times, the Lord has humbled and brought down into the dust those mighty cities of the ancient empires that were considered invincible.

6. The foot shall tread it down, even the feet of the poor, and the steps of the needy.

In due time those cities were trodden down by the poor and afflicted who had suffered under the ruthless tyranny of those ancient empires.

7. The way of the just is uprightness: thou, most upright, dost weigh the path of the just.

The only people who are considered just in the sight of the Lord are those who are upright. The Lord, who is upright, constantly evaluates his earthly children to see which are on the pathway of obedience and righteousness. These alone are "just" in the sight of the Lord. Notice that in this verse, Isaiah begins his personal psalm of praise to God. Isaiah is addressing his personal praise directly to the Throne of Grace up through verse 19.

8. Yea, in the way of thy judgments, O LORD, have we waited for thee; the desire of our soul is to thy name, and to the remembrance of thee.

Isaiah speaks for the persecuted Saints of all ages and proclaims to the Lord that the righteous have patiently waited for the judgments of the Lord to strike down or humble their enemies. Isaiah says it is the desire of the righteous to endure temptation by constantly keeping in their hearts a remembrance of the Lord, who is the source of all blessings.

9. With my soul have I desired thee in the night; yea, with my spirit within me will I seek thee early: for when thy judgments are in the earth, the inhabitants of the world will learn righteousness.

As Isaiah contemplates the past, he recalls the many nights of depression and despair when he felt his only companion was the Lord. Like thousands of the Father's children, Isaiah had learned to cry before the Lord in the night. Isaiah pledges himself to compel his spirit to rise above the pressures and distractions of the day and seek the Lord early. Isaiah comments on the great visions which he had seen. One thing in particular stood out in his mind: when the judgments of God fall upon the inhabitants of the world, they quickly begin to "learn righteousness."

10. Let favour be shewed to the wicked, yet will he not learn righteousness: in the land of uprightness will he deal unjustly, and will not behold the majesty of the LORD.

However, those who have an evil heart consistently defy the Lord. They do not turn from their wicked ways. Even when they reside in the "land of the righteous," they deal unjustly with their neighbors. They refuse to acknowledge the hand of the Lord in the judgments being poured down upon them.

11. LORD, when thy hand is lifted up, they will not see: but they shall see, and be ashamed for their envy at the people; yea, the fire of thine enemies shall devour them.

Isaiah has observed, furthermore, that when the Lord lifts his hand to show forth his power and make bare his mighty arm, the wicked, at first, will refuse to acknowledge it. But Isaiah has seen what happens to them after death. When the wicked pass beyond the veil they are ashamed of their conduct. They find themselves being consumed in the flames of their own guilt-ridden souls. The terrible suffering of the wicked when they reach the spirit world and realize what great blessings they missed through their rebellion is often described in scripture as being like "fire" and "brimstone." (See 2 Nephi 9:16; Mosiah 3:27; D&C 63:17; 76:36.)

12. LORD, thou wilt ordain peace for us: for thou also hast wrought all our works in us.

But Isaiah, like Alma, knew that the Lord has ordained peace and a state of supreme happiness for those who have endured in righteousness (see Alma 40:12). It is in the righteous that God has "wrought" or achieved his great purposes. This is why Isaiah says, "Thou also hast wrought all our works in us." He gives the Lord credit for the good that the righteous have been motivated to achieve.

13. O LORD our God, other lords beside thee have had dominion over us: but by thee only will we make mention of thy name.

Peering back through the corridors of history, Isaiah recalls how much of the time the people have been under the domination of "lords" other than Jehovah. Often they subjected themselves to false gods whom the people were told to worship. Sometimes their own rulers demanded that they must be worshiped as gods. Isaiah proclaims that "by thee only will we make mention of thy name."

14. They are dead, they shall not live; they are deceased, they shall not rise: therefore hast thou visited and destroyed them, and made all their memory to perish.

Isaiah saw that ultimately all these wicked rulers of the past would be counted as nothing. They would all be dead. Their influence would all be gone. Never again would their presence or power rise up among men. The wrath of God will have visited them in judgment so that they and their empires will have been wiped off the face of the earth. The very memory of them will have perished.

This phenomenon has happened in modern times. The names of violent and vicious dictators who caused nations to tremble in terror are dead. The rising generation can scarcely remember that they ever existed!

15. Thou hast increased the nation, O LORD, thou hast

Meanwhile, Isaiah could see prophetically how God would increase his own nation of Israel in the latter

16. LORD, in trouble have they visited thee, they poured out a prayer when thy chastening was upon them.

17. Like as a woman with child, that draweth near the time of her delivery, is in pain, and crieth out in her pangs; so have we been in thy sight, O LORD.

18. We have been with child, we have been in pain, we have as it were brought forth wind; we have not wrought any deliverance in the earth; neither have the inhabitants of the world fallen.

19. Thy dead men shall live, together with my dead body shall they arise. Awake and sing, ye that dwell in dust:

---

increased the nation: thou art glorified: thou hadst removed it far unto all the ends of the earth.

days. His nation of righteousness will ultimately assemble in Jerusalem and Zion, where the Lord will be glorified. They will be assembled from "the ends of the earth."

Although Israel had been a rebellious and scattered people, in their hour of anguish and repentance they "visited" with the Lord and called upon him in mighty prayer.

In terrible anguish the repentant people of Israel cried out to the Lord, like a woman with child who is about to be delivered.

Isaiah loved to linger on the panoramic vision of the future when the righteous Israelites would be gathered from the ends of the earth. However, at the moment, he had to proclaim a message of warning against the people of his own day. The people in Isaiah's day were so wicked that even though they travailed and cried out in anguish like a woman about to be delivered, they brought forth no child but only stomach gas. For this reason the Lord did not strike down their enemies or bring judgment to the wicked as he had promised to do in the latter days. As a result, many of them will be destroyed.

Nevertheless, Isaiah rejoiced in the coming resurrection of the dead. He knew of the universality of the resurrection. He exclaimed: "Thy dead men shall live,

for thy dew is as the dew of
herbs, and the earth shall
cast out the dead.

together with my dead body shall they arise!" As
though he were speaking to the tens of millions of the
human family who had been hewn down in death
through the past ages, he cried out: "Awake and sing,
ye that dwell in the dust:...the earth shall cast out the
dead."

20. Come, my people, enter
thou into thy chambers,
and shut thy doors about
thee: hide thyself as it were
for a little moment, until
the indignation be over-
past.

Now Isaiah turns from his psalm of praise to admon-
ish the righteous of every age to hide themselves in
time of great trouble because no predatory power of
dictatorship and oppression lasts forever. If the people
have done their best to be prepared against a time of
trouble, they need not fear (see D&C 38:30). Isaiah
says, "Hide thyself as it were for a little moment, until
the indignation be overpast." The people of the Lord
are not to despair or give up hope. They are to wait
with patience "for a little moment," until the holocaust
has passed. (See also Amos 5:13)

21. For, behold, the LORD cometh out of his place to punish the inhabitants of the
earth for their iniquity: the
earth also shall disclose her
blood, and shall no more
cover her slain.

The entire historical record of the past as well as the
vision of the future declares the fact that in every crisis
the Lord eventually provides the means by which the
wicked rulers and inhabitants of the earth are punished
severely for their iniquities.

No matter how the diabolical bands of evil men seek
to hide their crimes of oppression, conquest, criminal-
ity, assassinations, and all their secret strategies by
which they have robbed and shed the blood of their
victims, it will all be disclosed. The earth will no longer
keep these crimes hidden within her. The shallow
graves of those who have been slain will no longer hide
the heinous crimes which these evil men have inflicted
upon their victims.

INTRODUCTION:

This chapter begins almost as though it were a continuation of the psalm in chapter 26. The last verse of chapter 26 refers to the day when the Lord will accomplish his purposes and will come forth "to punish the inhabitants of the earth" who have corrupted the planet with their wickedness.

1. In that day the LORD with his sore and great and strong sword shall punish leviathan the piercing serpent, even leviathan that crooked serpent; and he shall slay the dragon that is in the sea.

This first verse begins by saying "in *that* day" the Lord will punish the great naval power which will spread terror among the nations as it comes in from the sea. It is likened unto the mythical "leviathan," a "crooked serpent" which the Lord intends to annihilate.

2. In that day sing ye unto her, A vineyard of red wine.

Isaiah says it will be appropriate in that day for the people to recite a song praising a choice vineyard which produces the best of red wine. Red wine was considered the most choice kind, and the Lord's vineyard will produce the finest of fruit when the people are righteous. The vineyard represents Israel (see verse 6).

3. I the LORD do keep it; I will water it every moment: lest any hurt it, I will keep it night and day.

The song begins with the Lord declaring that he intends to keep and preserve this choice vineyard. He will watch over it every moment. Nothing will be allowed to hurt it because he will be guarding it night and day.

4. Fury is not in me: who would set the briers and thorns against me in battle? I would go through them, I would burn them together.

It was customary in the psalms of the Jews to have the choirs divide in two parts and dialogue back and forth. In the third verse we have the Lord speaking of his vineyard. Now we have the vineyard's reply sung back by another section of the choir. The vineyard says, "Fury is not in me." This is said by many authorities to be a mistranslation. The word "fury" should be "wall," and the sense of the verse is that the vineyard has no wall to protect it. (See Clarke, *Commentary*, 4:122.) In case of attack, how will the Lord protect the vineyard? Who will protect the vineyard from the undergrowth of briars and thorns which constantly threaten choice vineyards?

The Lord immediately responds that he will go out among these thorns and briars and burn them up. He will rake them in piles so that they can all be burned together.

5. Or let him take hold of my strength, that he may make peace with me; and he shall make peace with me.

The Lord invites Israel to rely on his divine strength and make peace with him by obeying his commandments and doing his will. The Lord predicts that this will ultimately happen. Israel WILL make peace with the Lord.

6. He shall cause them that come of Jacob to take root: Israel shall blossom and bud, and fill the face of the world with fruit.

The choirs then seem to combine at this point to sing out in unison that the Lord will indeed cause Jacob (whose name was changed to Israel; see Genesis 32:28) to take root and flourish. Ultimately, he will spread throughout the whole world, filling the earth with good "fruit."

7. Hath he smitten him, as he smote those that smote

The singers now ask whether the Lord has smitten Israel in the days of her wickedness even as he smote

him? or is he slain according to the slaughter of them that are slain by him?

those who oppressed Israel. Have the Israelites been driven and slain even as the Lord eventually slew their enemies? The answer, obviously, is "yes!"

8. In measure, when it shooteth forth, thou wilt debate with it: he stayeth his rough wind in the day of the east wind.

When wickedness has occurred, God has matched it measure for measure either in debate or by direct confrontation. He has steadied the course of events by matching his own mighty wind against the debilitating and destructive east wind.

9. By this therefore shall the iniquity of Jacob be purged; and this is all the fruit to take away his sin; when he maketh all the stones of the altar as chalkstones that are beaten in sunder, the groves and images shall not stand up.

This has been the means by which the Lord has purged the children of Jacob (Israel) from their sins. Israel has had to endure these punishments because they resulted from their own sins. In the days of their unrighteousness the sacrifices of the people were not acceptable to the Lord (see Isaiah 1:11-15). Their altars were no better than chalkstones which will crumble to powder. The Lord has also determined that the groves and fertility gods which Israel used in connection with her debaucheries will be hewn down and destroyed.

10. Yet the defenced city shall be desolate, and the habitation forsaken, and left like a wilderness: there shall the calf feed, and there shall he lie down, and consume the branches thereof.

There will be no defense against the Lord in his day of judgment. The carefully protected city with its stout walls will collapse and become desolate. The destruction will be so complete that where there was once a bustling city, the calves will feed as though it were a pasture. The Lord will make it a place of rest instead of riotous living.

11. When the boughs thereof are withered, they shall be broken off: the women come, and set them on fire:

The choir sings out its declaration that in the vineyard culture with which they are familiar, the withered boughs are broken off by the women, and after they

for it is a people of no understanding: therefore he that made them will not have mercy on them, and he that formed them will shew them no favour.

have been piled together they are burned. So shall it be with the wicked city in spite of its defenses. This is because the people are "of no understanding." They will not listen to their Creator. Therefore he will not have mercy on them or show them favor, even though he made them.

12. And it shall come to pass in that day, that the LORD shall beat off from the channel of the river unto the stream of Egypt, and ye shall be gathered one by one, O ye children of Israel.

The psalm now refers to something which Isaiah had mentioned earlier. The singers refer to the time when Egypt will be humbled by having the waters of the Nile temporarily cut off (see notes on Isaiah 19:5-10). This will occur at the time the people of Israel are being gathered to Jerusalem.

13. And it shall come to pass in that day, that the great trumpet shall be blown, and they shall come which were ready to perish in the land of Assyria, and the outcasts in the land of Egypt, and shall worship the LORD in the holy mount at Jerusalem.

This will be close to the time when the Arabs from Assyria as well as from Egypt will be converted and go up to Jerusalem to worship along with the Israelites (see notes on Isaiah 19:22-25).

Isaiah, Chapter 28

INTRODUCTION:

When the northern Ten Tribes of Israel broke away from Judah around 922 B.C., the revolt was led by Jeroboam, the leader of the largest tribe—the tribe of Ephraim. This tribe continued to rule the northern Ten Tribes right down to the time when they were attacked by the Assyrians and carried off in 722–21 B.C. It is for this reason that the northern Ten Tribes are often referred to as "Ephraim." Sometimes they are referred to simply as "Israel."

During their 200 years of separation and apostasy, the northern Ten Tribes had strong warnings from such great prophets as Elijah, Elisha, Amos, and Isaiah, but they rejected them all. The Ephraimite leadership was wicked and led the people into lecherous practices of gross immorality. They also persecuted the prophets, and in the days of Ahab and Jezebel they tried to have all of them killed.

In the commentaries on the Bible, there is a long-standing error concerning the identification of the second tribe which stayed behind with Judah after the other tribes were carried away. The commentaries usually say it was the tribe of Benjamin. It is true that part of the tribe of Benjamin remained with Judah, but so did the remnants of several of the tribes. This included some of the Ephraimites and some from the tribe of Manasseh. This explains why it is recorded that as of 600 B.C. we find the families of Lehi, Laban, and Ishmael living in or near Jerusalem. All of these were from the tribe of Joseph through Ephraim and Manasseh.

However, the Bible is very clear as to which of the tribes joined Judah with virtually its ENTIRE population. It was the tribe of Levi.

The Levites were the priests and teachers, and therefore they had not been given a particular territory for their inheritance but were scattered among all the tribes to serve as their teachers and religious leaders. When Jeroboam, the Ephraimite leader, took over the northern Ten Tribes, he began ordaining wicked men from the various tribes as priests. He then began persecuting the Levites so severely that they were compelled to take their families and flee to Judah. Here is what the scripture says:

"And the priests and the Levites that were in ALL ISRAEL resorted to him [Rehoboam, king of Judah] out of all their coasts. For the Levites left their suburbs and their possession, and came to Judah and Jerusalem: for Jeroboam [king of the northern Ten Tribes] and his sons had cast them off from executing the priest's office unto the Lord." (2 Chronicles 11:13–14; emphasis added.)

Today, a family among the Jews who carry the name of "Cohen" (priest) are simply declaring that they belong to the tribe of Levi.

1. Woe to the crown of pride, to the drunkards of Ephraim, whose glorious beauty is a fading flower, which are on the head of the fat valleys of them that are overcome with wine!

Isaiah now proclaims his doomsday message to the northern Ten Tribes under their Ephraimite rulers. For generations they had been tremendously prosperous and affluent because of their trade alliances with Tyre and Sidon. But they had also become notorious for their drunkenness and dissipation. Isaiah had seen in his vision that their beautiful terraces, proud cities, and fruitful valleys would be turned into a desolation. It would inevitably occur because of the reckless, drunken, dissolute people who inhabited this choice land.

2. Behold, the Lord hath a mighty and strong one, which as a tempest of hail and a destroying storm, as a flood of mighty waters overflowing, shall cast down to the earth with the hand.

Isaiah warned that God had prepared a rod, "a mighty and strong one," to smite these wicked children of Israel on whom the Lord had been depending for exemplary leadership among the rest of humanity. His "chosen" people had chosen to apostatize. Therefore a flood of destruction would sweep down upon them from Assyria and smite these wicked people to the earth.

3. The crown of pride, the drunkards of Ephraim, shall be trodden under feet:

The crown of Ephraim was not one of dignity and honor, but a crown of arrogant pride worn by drunken sots. Isaiah said their pride and their crowns would be trodden under foot by the conquering hosts of the Assyrians.

4. And the glorious beauty, which is on the head of the fat valley, shall be a fading flower, and as the hasty fruit before the summer; which when he that looketh upon it seeth, while it is yet in his hand he eateth it up.

It seemed tragic to contemplate that all of the beauty and fruitfulness of this land was about to fade into oblivion. As for the people, they would be devoured by the sword on the spot, like early fruit (mistranslated here as "hasty") which is hungrily devoured as the first fruit of the season. It is interesting that most of the northern Ten Tribes were cut down and destroyed right in their own land. The remnants were carried off to Assyria.

5. In that day shall the LORD of hosts be for a crown of glory, and for a diadem of beauty, unto the residue of his people,

Isaiah (always grateful for the righteous remnant) says the Lord of hosts will be for a crown of glory and a diadem of beauty to the righteous residue of the people. In this case, it would be Judah to whom he would turn with a cornucopia of blessings ready to be poured out upon the people.

6. And for a spirit of judgment to him that sitteth in judgment, and for strength to them that turn the battle to the gate.

He would be ready to give wise and judicious inspiration to those sitting in authority. He would also bless with strength and vigor those in the armed forces embroiled with the enemy at the gates.

7. But they also have erred through wine, and through strong drink are out of the way; the priest and the prophet have erred through strong drink, they are swallowed up of wine, they are out of the way through strong drink; they err in vision, they stumble in judgment.

Tragically, however, Judah was in no position to receive such blessings as a "righteous remnant." Her people were also given to wine-bibbing and drunkenness. They indulged in distilled liquors which were even stronger than wine, making them intoxicated even more quickly. This was not only true of the common people but equally true of the religious leaders. Furthermore, the priests of Levi and the phony "prophets" which had become such a plague in the land were all swallowed up in their wine. They were addle-brained and "out of the way," or irrational in their drunken stupor. They erred in vision and stumbled in judgment.

8. For all tables are full of vomit and filthiness, so that there is no place clean.

Isaiah was revolted and disgusted as he contemplated the condition of the residue of God's people who would be left in the land after the northern Ten Tribes were carried away. Judah and Levi, together with a few fragments of the other tribes, would remain, but Isaiah knew they would be found wallowing in their drunken regurgitation like swine in the mire. Everything about them would turn out to be abject filthiness.

9. Whom shall he teach knowledge? and whom shall he make to understand doctrine? them that are weaned from the milk, and drawn from the breasts.

Under these circumstances, to whom can God turn to give knowledge? Who would be able to understand the beautiful and profound principles of the true Gospel which ought to be passed on from generation to generation? Isaiah answered his own question by saying that it would not be those who are still spiritual infants and must be breast-fed with milk. Instead, it would be those who have matured enough to be weaned from the soft milk diet of babies and who are ready for the meat of the Gospel which is essential to growth and maturity.

10. For precept must be upon precept, precept upon precept; line upon line, line upon line; here a little, and there a little;

It is extremely interesting why this is so. The Lord seldom teaches Gospel principles in the form of essays or extensive dissertations. Instead, he sprinkles the gems of doctrinal truth throughout the scripture like diamonds in a haystack. Therefore, hunting for scriptural treasures can be a fascinating endeavor. It is not the purpose of the Lord to be obscure, but rather to hide from the unprepared mind the brilliant diadems of truth which might blind the delicate faith of the spiritually immature. He therefore tucks morsels of meaty doctrine in among the routine passages of scriptural instruction. The spiritually alert and intellectually mature Gospel student will find the diamonds and appreciate their value. The less mature spirits will feed on the milk and pablum until such time as they are strong enough to digest the deeper doctrines. All of this is portrayed in Isaiah's classic passage, "For precept must be upon precept, ... line upon line; here a little, and there a little."

Paul became disgusted with the members of the Church in his own day because they couldn't get over their milk diet. They would not perfect their knowledge of the Gospel. We therefore read in the Joseph Smith Translation what Paul had to say to the members of the Church who had been converted from Judaism but would not pursue further light and knowledge. He wrote:

"Therefore NOT leaving the principles of the doctrine of Christ, let us go on unto perfection; not laying again [or repeatedly] the foundation of repentance from dead works, and of faith toward God,

"Of the doctrine of baptisms, and of laying on of hands, and of resurrection of the dead, and of eternal judgment." (Joseph Smith Translation, Hebrews 6:1–2; emphasis added.)

In other words, we have gone over the fundamentals many times so there should be no question in anybody's mind about faith, repentance, baptism, bestowing the gift of the Holy Ghost, resurrection, or the final judgment. There are other things to learn if the Saints are to perfect their knowledge and understanding.

11. For with stammering lips and another tongue will he speak to this people.

It saddened Isaiah that he could not speak to these people with all the eloquence of his soul and clearly explain to them the beautiful and profound principles of eternity which God had vouchsafed to him. But he was not allowed to do it. He was required to speak to them with stammering lips and a tongue that was so inarticulate that it seemed as though it belonged to someone else. What a terrible frustration this was for Isaiah. He was extremely skillful in language and wrote his entire book in poetic meter. He was also filled with the visions of heaven, which he longed to tell the people, but he was not allowed to cast pearls.

12. To whom he said, This is the rest wherewith ye may cause the weary to rest; and this is the refreshing: yet they would not hear.

God had already brought his great message to these people and told them how to be relieved of the burden of their sins. He had told them how to be cleansed and refreshed, but they had rejected everything out of hand. This had prevented Isaiah from sharing with them the treasures of knowledge which he was so anxious to deliver to them.

13. But the word of the LORD was unto them precept upon precept, precept upon precept; line upon line, line upon line; here a little, and there a little; that they might go, and fall backward, and be broken, and snared, and taken.

This is why the Lord had required Isaiah to hide the meat of the Gospel in obscure passages so that it could not be discovered unless a spiritually inspired student put it together precept upon precept, line upon line, here a little and there a little. Isaiah knew most of the people would not do this. Therefore, they would "fall backward, and be broken, and snared, and taken." Paul had the same trouble with the Hebrews. Speaking of Christ and the fulness of his Gospel, Paul said:

"Of whom we have many things to say, and hard to be uttered, SEEING YE ARE DULL OF HEARING.

"For when...ye ought to be teachers, ye have need that one teach you again...the first principles...and are become such as have need of milk, and not of strong meat.

"For every one that useth milk is unskilful in the word of righteousness: for he is a babe.

"But strong meat belongeth to them that are of full age, even those who by reason of use have their senses exercised to discern both good and evil." (Hebrews 5:11-14; emphasis added.)

14. Wherefore hear the word of the LORD, ye scornful men, that rule this people which is in Jerusalem.

Now Isaiah specifically identifies those to whom he has been talking since verse 5. He has been delivering a message directly from the Lord to the "scornful men" who rule over Jerusalem.

15. Because ye have said, We have made a covenant with death, and with hell are we at agreement; when the overflowing scourge shall pass through, it shall not come unto us: for we have made lies our refuge, and under falsehood have we hid ourselves:

Isaiah accuses these wicked leaders in Jerusalem of committing themselves to a diabolical covenant with death and hell—in other words, with Satan. They think they are going to escape the desolating scourge of war and pestilence by using lies and subtle deception in evil alliances with the enemies of God and the enemies of God's people.

In modern times these same kinds of evil covenants have been embraced by men who consider themselves extremely clever. They make alliances with the most murderous and evil forces presently preying upon mankind. By joining hands with these sons of death and hell, they somehow think they can escape the devastation which these power-hungry and avaricious leaders of certain warmongering nations intend to pour out upon the whole earth.

16. Therefore thus saith the-Lord GOD, Behold, I lay in Zion for a foundation a stone, a tried stone, a precious corner stone, a sure foundation: he that believeth shall not make haste.

The Lord had a message for these reprobate apostates who were the leaders in Jerusalem. He said all their plotting and planning would come to nought because he was planting in Zion a stone which had been tried and tested. In fact, it would be the cornerstone for the whole foundation of what God was planning to build for all mankind. Isaiah promised that anyone who relied upon this stone and believed in the things it represented would not have to "make haste" or flee in fear.

Notice that Isaiah did not identify the stone. He simply stated the "precept" which these dull-witted apostates were not likely to comprehend or even be curious enough to ask about.

Peter quotes this passage of Isaiah and gives it an interesting rendering. He said, "It is contained in the scripture, Behold, I lay in Sion a chief corner stone, elect, precious: and he that believeth on HIM shall not be CONFOUNDED" (1 Peter 2:6; emphasis added).

Obviously, the stone is Jesus Christ.

Paul quotes this same verse with additional insight. He wrote, "As it is written, Behold, I lay in Sion a stumblingstone and rock of offence: and whosoever believeth on him shall not be ashamed" (Romans 9:33).

Jesus referred to this passage and explained it to the priests and the Pharisees as follows: "And whosoever shall fall on this stone shall be broken: but on whomsoever it shall fall, it will grind him to powder.

"And when the chief priests and Pharisees had heard his parables, they perceived that he spake of them." (Matthew 21:44-45.)

17. Judgment also will I lay to the line, and righteousness to the plummet: and the hail shall sweep away the refuge of lies, and the waters shall overflow the hiding place.

Now comes the Lord's warning to those who think that somehow it will be to their advantage to betray their high offices, deceive the people, and enter into covenants of death with the sons of Satan who are the servants of hell. Covenants of death are the secret oaths of the murder cults which Satan established in the days of Cain. They were also established among the Jaredites, and later among the Gadiantons during the days of the Nephites. The Book of Mormon calls them "secret combinations," and Moroni warned the Gentiles of the latter days that these murder covenants in high places would become the most terrifying and overpowering threat to civilization in modern times. He wrote:

"Wherefore, O ye Gentiles, it is wisdom in God that these things should be shown unto you, that thereby ye may repent of your sins, and suffer not that these murderous combinations shall get above you, which are built up to get power and gain—and the work, yea, even the work of destruction come upon you, yea, even the sword of the justice of the Eternal God shall fall upon you, to your overthrow and destruction if ye shall suffer these things to be.

"Wherefore, the Lord commandeth you, when ye shall see these things come among you that ye shall awake to a sense of your awful situation, because of this secret combination which shall be among you; or wo be unto it, because of the blood of them who have been slain; for they cry from the dust for vengeance upon it, and also upon those who built it up.

"For it cometh to pass that whoso buildeth it up seeketh to overthrow the freedom of all lands, nations, and countries; and it bringeth to pass the destruction of all people, for it is built up by the devil, who is the father of all lies; even that same liar who beguiled our first parents, yea, even that same liar who hath caused man to commit murder from the beginning; who hath hardened the hearts of men that they have murdered the prophets, and stoned them, and cast them out from the beginning.

"Wherefore, I, Moroni, am commanded to write these things that evil may be done away, and that the time may come that Satan may have no power upon the hearts of the children of men, but that they may be persuaded to do good continually, that they may come unto the fountain of all righteousness and be saved." (Ether 8:23–26.)

Isaiah declares that these wicked leaders who enter into such secret combinations will one day know the scalding wrath of the judgment of God. He is going to put judgment on the line so that every act, every lie, every secret machination of wickedness will be exposed for all to see. He is going to sweep away the refuge of their lies, and penetrate the deepest and darkest hiding place to reveal to the whole world how abominable and devilish they have been.

18. And your covenant with death shall be disannulled, and your agreement with hell shall not stand; when the overflowing scourge shall pass through, then ye shall be trodden down by it.

The Lord wanted all of these conspiring men and women to know that nothing can save them, even though they enter into covenants "to murder and get gain," and sit in secret chambers to plot the destruction of entire nations. Their secret covenants, administered by the sons of Satan as death oaths, will not be allowed to prevail forever. They will be disannulled. Their agreements with hell will not stand. The overflowing scourge which always engulfs the wicked at the height of their folly will eventually encompass these evil leaders like a flood of vengeance pouring down from the Almighty.

19. From the time that it goeth forth it shall take you: for morning by morning shall it pass over, by day and by night: and it shall be a vexation only to understand the report.

Once the judgments of God begin pouring out on these evil powers, they will not be turned back. They will surge over them like a roaring sea of retribution both by day and by night. They will be so terrible that people will not want to hear the newscasts telling about them.

20. For the bed is shorter than that a man can stretch himself on it: and the covering narrower than that he can wrap himself in it.

No matter how these former power-people try to arrange it, nothing can be made to fit. Their beds will be too short and their covers too narrow. Only misery and discomfort await them.

21. For the LORD shall rise up as in mount Perazim, he shall be wroth as in the valley of Gibeon, that he may do his work, his strange work; and bring to pass his act, his strange act.

The showing forth of God's power in his day of judgment will be similar to the time when he allowed King David to wreak vengeance on the Philistines at the Mount of Baal-Perazim (see 1 Chronicles 14:11). It will also be similar to the time when the hosts of Joshua slew the armies of the Amorites and the sun was stayed in the heavens by the Lord's miraculous power until the task was completed (see Joshua 10:10–14).

The Lord abhors the terrors which must be inflicted on humanity in consequence of their evil works. Nevertheless, the cleansing of the earth and the elimination of wickedness and satanical secret combinations is necessary before the Lord can introduce his new dispensation of truth and raise up a series of choice generations of righteous human beings on this earth. This is what is beginning to happen in our own day, for the Lord has said, "I design to prepare mine apostles to prune my vineyard for the last time, that I may bring to pass my STRANGE ACT, THAT I MAY POUR OUT MY SPIRIT UPON ALL FLESH" (D&C 95:4; emphasis added).

The Lord's "strange act" is the opening of the heavens, the sending forth of ministering angels, and the restoration of the Gospel in its fulness. It is the "marvelous work and a wonder" referred to by the Lord in Isaiah 29:14. In modern times the Lord is accomplishing this very thing. He says he is doing it "to bring to pass my act, my strange act, and perform my work, my strange work, THAT MEN MAY DISCERN BETWEEN THE RIGHTEOUS AND THE WICKED, saith your God" (D&C 101:95; emphasis added).

22. Now therefore be ye not mockers, lest your bands be made strong: for I have heard from the Lord GOD of hosts a consumption, even determined upon the whole earth.

In this verse Isaiah issues both a warning and a plea. He warns the people to repent of their mockery which they no doubt had heaped upon Isaiah as he tried to tell them about the coming judgments of God. It is almost as though he were pleading with them to come to their senses and recognize the reality of their awful situation. He declares with the utmost soberness and intensity of feeling that he has "heard from the Lord," and the divine computers have already been set in motion for a devastating "consumption" or destruction of the wicked all over the earth.

23. Give ye ear, and hear my voice; hearken, and hear my speech.

Isaiah breaks forth into direct pleading as he says almost on bended knee, "Give ye ear, and hear my voice; hearken, and hear my speech."

24. Doth the plowman plow all day to sow? doth he open and break the clods of his ground?

25. When he hath made plain the face thereof, doth he not cast abroad the fitches, and scatter the cummin, and cast in the principal wheat and the appointed barley and the rie in their place?

In these verses Isaiah is presenting the parable of the farmer who plants certain crops in a special way appropriate to their needs. The Lord does the same in preparing the historical circumstances most likely to get the best results from his fallen and rebellious children. The farmer has to carefully plow and cultivate the land before the seeds are sown. Some seeds like the fitches (a type of pepper plant) can be sprinkled or cast out rather casually. The same is true of a carrot-like plant with aromatic seeds called cumin. But the farmer must be more careful about planting wheat, barley, and rye because the seeds must be covered over slightly in order for them to germinate.

26. For his God doth instruct him to discretion, and doth teach him.

In all of these activities, the Lord has instructed mankind as to the precise manner in which different types of crops must be handled.

27. For the fitches are not threshed with a threshing instrument, neither is a cart wheel turned about upon the cummin; but the fitches are beaten out with a staff, and the cummin with a rod.

28. Bread corn is bruised; because he will not ever be threshing it, nor break it with the wheel of his cart, nor bruise it with his horsemen.

It is also extremely important how each crop is harvested. The flail, the rod, and the hoof of cattle or the wheel are each appropriate to extract the seed from its pod or husk in a certain way. What works with one type of seed will destroy another. It takes great wisdom to know how to deal with each one.

29. This also cometh forth from the LORD of hosts, which is wonderful in counsel, and excellent in working.

The same thing is true pertaining to God's dealing with his children. They are all different and must be treated like different seeds or crops. Truly, as Isaiah says, God is "wonderful in counsel, and excellent in working" out his great purposes for all mankind.

INTRODUCTION:

Isaiah concluded chapter 28 by describing God's great day of judgment and how he would do everything possible to gather out the righteous so that they would be preserved in the latter days. In verse 21 of the last chapter, Isaiah spoke of God's "work" which he would launch in the latter days. It would be a time when he would perform his "strange work; and bring to pass his . . . strange act." In this chapter we are going to get a more detailed account of what this strange work or strange act would be.

Fortunately for the modern student of the scriptures, we have the words of another prophet who saw the same vision and who described it in greater detail than Isaiah. This was the prophet Nephi. Young Nephi learned that his father, Lehi, had seen this great vision, and he asked the Lord to let him see it also (1 Nephi 11:1-3). At a later period, Nephi undertook to explain to his people the words of Isaiah in terms of the vision which he and his father had seen (2 Nephi 25:4-7).

In this chapter we will quote the words of Isaiah and then present the commentary of Nephi as he refers to particular verses. The description of Nephi's vision is in 1 Nephi, chapters 12, 13, and 14. His commentary on Isaiah 29 is in 2 Nephi, chapters 25, 26, and 27.

1. Woe to Ariel, to Ariel, the city where David dwelt! add ye year to year; let them kill sacrifices.

Dr. Adam Clarke wrote that the word "Ariel" means "lion of the Lord." He also pointed out that this name was given to the great altar of the temple. Dr. Clarke said that in this verse Isaiah is referring to Jerusalem, their capital city, rather than the altar. As Isaiah saw approximately 2,700 years of history sweeping before him in vision, he could not help but exclaim concerning Jerusalem and its people: "Woe to Ariel, to Ariel, the city where David dwelt!"

First of all, the Ten Tribes had been cut off from Jerusalem and scattered abroad, and then Isaiah saw the same thing happening to Judah. He knew that no matter where the children of Israel were scattered, they would be persecuted.

Nephi perceived that Isaiah knew about the Israelites who would be in America as well as those who would be scattered upon the islands of the sea and elsewhere. In fact, almost the entire text of Isaiah chapter 29 relates to events in America in the latter days. This becomes apparent as Nephi begins his commentary on Isaiah.

2. Yet I will distress Ariel, and there shall be heaviness and sorrow: and it shall be unto me as Ariel.

Both Isaiah and Nephi saw that no matter how many sacrifices the Israelites offered, they would be "distressed" if their lives were not pure before God. Isaiah had already pointed out that these sacrifices from year to year meant nothing unless they were accompanied by righteous living (see Isaiah 1:11-16). As Isaiah saw the great suffering which would come upon the Israelites, he recorded that the Lord said: "There shall be heaviness and sorrow: and it shall be unto me as Ariel." In other words, it will be a time of sorrow to God even as it is to Israel. The Lord's sorrow will come upon him when he sees the suffering which these wicked children of Jacob will have to endure.

3. And I will camp against thee round about, and will

Beginning with this verse, we learn (thanks to Nephi) that Isaiah is referring to circumstances which lay siege against thee with a mount, and I will raise forts against thee.

would sweep down upon the Israelites in America. The latter days would find this branch of Israel in an apostate condition. Nephi saw that America would be discovered and invaded by great hosts of "Gentiles" from Europe. He wrote: "And it came to pass that I beheld many multitudes of the Gentiles upon the land of promise; and I beheld the wrath of God, that it was upon the seed of my brethren; and they were scattered before the Gentiles and were smitten" (1 Nephi 13:14).

Nephi's "brethren," of course, were the Lamanites who had within them the blood of Ephraim and Manasseh (through Lehi and Ishmael), and also Judah (through the Mulekites). They were Israelites indeed. Concerning their condition in the latter days, Nephi later wrote:

"But behold, I prophesy unto you concerning the last days; . . .

"After my seed and the seed of my brethren shall have dwindled in unbelief, and shall have been smitten by the Gentiles; yea, after the Lord God shall have camped against them round about, and shall have laid siege against them with a mount, and raised forts against them; and after they shall have been brought down low in the dust, even that they are not, yet the words of the righteous shall be written, and the prayers of the faithful shall be heard, and all those who have dwindled in unbelief shall not be forgotten." (2 Nephi 26:14–15.)

We learn from this that Isaiah and Nephi were referring to the day when America would be discovered by the Gentiles of Europe, and men like Hernando Cortez (1485–1547) and Francisco Pizarro (1470–1541) would conquer whole nations of Lamanites with European military forces numbering only hundreds. Just how completely these Lamanites were besieged and decimated with the most excruciating cruelty was described by the noted historian, the late John Fiske:

"Indians were slaughtered by the hundred, burned alive, impaled on sharp sticks, torn to pieces by bloodhounds. In retaliation for the murder of a Spaniard it was thought proper to call up fifty or sixty Indians and chop off their hands. Little children were flung into the water to drown, with less concern than if they had been puppies. In the mingling of sacred ideas with the sheerest devilry there was a grotesqueness fit for the pencil of Dore. Once, 'in honour and reverence of Christ and his twelve Apostles,' they hanged thirteen Indians in a row at such a height that their toes could just touch the ground, and then pricked them to death with their sword-points, taking care not to kill them quickly. At another time, when some old reprobate was broiling half a dozen Indians in a kind of cradle suspended over a slow fire, their shrieks awoke the Spanish captain who in a neighbouring hut was taking his afternoon nap, and he called out testily to the man to despatch those wretches at once, and stop their noise. But this demon, determined not to be baulked of his enjoyment, only gagged the poor creatures. Can it be, says [Bartolome de] Las Casas [a missionary, later called "The Apostle of the Indians," who accompanied Columbus on his third voyage], that I really saw such things, or are they hideous dreams? Alas, they are no dreams; 'all this did I behold with my bodily mortal eyes.'

"This tyranny went on until the effect was like that of a pestilence. The native population rapidly diminished [from 300,000 to 500 in Hispaniola!] until labour grew scarce, and it was found necessary in Hispaniola to send and kidnap Indians from other islands, and to import from Seville negroes that had been caught by the Portuguese in Africa." (John Fiske, *The Discovery of America*, The Historical Writings of John Fiske, 12 vols. [Boston and New York: Houghton Mifflin Company; Cambridge: Riverside Press, 1902], 3:267–68.)

4. And thou shalt be brought down, and shalt speak out of the ground, and thy speech shall be low out of the dust, and thy voice shall be, as of one that hath a familiar spirit, out of the ground, and thy speech shall whisper out of the dust.

Both Nephi and Isaiah saw these abominable practices which would crush the Lamanite population into the dust. Nevertheless, they both recorded that the righteous ancestors of these people who had recorded their history and dealings with God in the days of their righteousness would not be forgotten. Their writings would come forth and speak to modern man like a "voice from the dust." These writings would have a familiar spirit and arouse a compelling attraction to the children of Israel in the latter days. Nephi describes this as follows:

"For those who shall be destroyed shall speak unto them out of the ground, and their speech shall be low out of the dust, and their voice shall be as one that hath a familiar spirit; for the Lord God will give unto him power, that he may whisper concerning them, even as it were out of the ground; and their speech shall whisper out of the dust.

"For thus saith the Lord God: They shall write the things which shall be done among them, and they shall be written and sealed up in a book, and those who have dwindled in unbelief shall not have them, for they seek to destroy the things of God." (2 Nephi 26:16–17.)

Notice that Nephi emphasizes why the apostate Lamanites will not be allowed to possess the sacred record of their ancestors. In their state of spiritual blindness they would have destroyed them.

5. Moreover the multitude of thy strangers shall be like small dust, and the multitude of the terrible ones shall be as chaff that passeth away: yea, it shall be at an instant suddenly.

Both Isaiah and Nephi were impressed with the fact that the destruction and subjugation of these fallen Israelites would be accomplished with amazing rapidity. Furthermore, their mighty warriors who seemed so fierce and strong would be scattered like chaff. It would happen suddenly, almost in an instant.

Nephi explains that this great destruction will be by the Gentiles who come into the land of promise. He says:

"Wherefore, as those who have been destroyed have been destroyed speedily; and the multitude of their terrible ones shall be as chaff that passeth away—yea, thus saith the Lord God: It shall be at an instant, suddenly—

"And it shall come to pass, that those who have dwindled in unbelief shall be smitten by the hand of the Gentiles." (2 Nephi 26:18-19.)

6. Thou shalt be visited of the LORD of hosts with thunder, and with earthquake, and great noise, with storm and tempest, and the flame of devouring fire.

In this verse Isaiah describes the judgments of the Lord which will come upon the earth in the latter days. Nephi is much more specific as to the reason for these terrible judgments. He identifies the people on whom these great catastrophes will fall:

"But, behold, in the last days, or in the days of the Gentiles—yea, behold all the nations of the Gentiles and also the Jews, both those who shall come upon this land [America] and those who shall be upon other lands, yea, even upon all the lands of the earth, behold, they will be drunken with iniquity and all manner of abominations—

"And when that day shall come they shall be visited of the Lord of Hosts, with thunder and with earthquake, and with a great noise, and with storm, and with tempest, and with the flame of devouring fire." (2 Nephi 27:1-2.)

7. And the multitude of all the nations that fight against Ariel, even all that fight against her and her munition, and that distress her,

Isaiah and Nephi both foresaw that mighty enemies would rise up against the Lord's people in the latter days. Notice that Isaiah calls them "Ariel" in verse 7 and "Mount Zion" in verse 8. Nephi quotes Isaiah

shall be as a dream of a night vision.

8. It shall even be as when an hungry man dreameth, and, behold, he eateth; but he awaketh, and his soul is empty: or as when a thirsty man dreameth, and, behold, he drinketh; but he awaketh, and, behold, he is faint, and his soul hath appetite: so shall the multitude of all the nations be, that fight against mount Zion.

almost verbatim but uses the word "Zion" instead of "Ariel."

Both Isaiah and Nephi saw that the Lord would be with his people when their enemies came upon them in the latter days. Nephi spells it out in language very similar to that of Isaiah. He wrote:

"And all the nations that fight against ZION, and that distress her, shall be as a dream of a night vision; yea, it shall be unto them, even as unto a hungry man which dreameth, and behold he eateth [in his dream] but he awaketh and his soul is empty; or like unto a thirsty man which dreameth, and behold he drinketh [in his dream] but he awaketh and behold he is faint, and his soul hath appetite; yea, even so shall the multitude of all the nations be that fight against Mount Zion." (2 Nephi 27:3; emphasis added.)

9. Stay yourselves, and wonder; cry ye out, and cry: they are drunken, but not with wine; they stagger, but not with strong drink.

This verse is addressed to the wicked whom Nephi specifically identified in his commentary on verse 6. To make sure that Isaiah's words would be correctly understood, he wrote, "For behold, ALL YE THAT DOETH INIQUITY, stay yourselves and wonder, for ye shall cry out, and cry; yea, ye shall be drunken but not with wine, ye shall stagger but not with strong drink" (2 Nephi 27:4; emphasis added).

10. For the LORD hath poured out upon you the spirit of deep sleep, and hath closed your eyes: the prophets and your rulers, the seers hath he covered.

In this verse the prophet is speaking of the wicked of all lands, not just America. Nephi had already made this clear (see 2 Nephi 27:1-2), and he also explains why the Lord has allowed the wicked to have their eyes covered and descend into a deep spiritual sleep. He says, "For behold, the Lord hath poured out upon you the spirit of deep sleep. For behold, ye have closed your eyes, and YE HAVE REJECTED THE PROPHETS; and your rulers, and the seers hath he covered because of your iniquity." (2 Nephi 27:5; emphasis added.)

11. And the vision of all is become unto you as the words of a book that is sealed, which men deliver to one that is learned, saying, Read this, I pray thee: and he saith, I cannot; for it is sealed.

Now we come to the meat of the matter. Isaiah refers to the marvelous record or book which is going to come forth in the latter days. This is exciting to Nephi because it is the record of his own people. He therefore has a lot more to say about this book than Isaiah.

Analysis of Nephi's Commentary on Isaiah 29:11

Probably the most extensive commentary in the Book of Mormon on a single verse of scripture is Nephi's illuminating explanation of Isaiah, chapter 29, verse 11. This commentary is contained in 2 Nephi, chapter 27. Each verse will be presented as Nephi wrote it, and this will be followed by the author's observations concerning it.

6. And it shall come to pass that the Lord God shall bring forth unto you the words of a book, and they shall be the words of them which have slumbered.

Both Nephi and Isaiah describe how the Lord will bring forth the words of this book in "that day." The book will contain the writings of those who have slumbered (those who have died), and will come forth in the latter days.

7. And behold the book shall be sealed; and in the book shall be a revelation from God, from the beginning of the world to the ending thereof.

Both Isaiah and Nephi point out that this book would be sealed, although in verse 15 Nephi points out that part of the book would NOT be sealed. As it turned out, approximately two-thirds of the plates of Mormon were sealed (see Orson Pratt in *Journal of Discourses,* 3:347), and the remainder constituted the abridged history of the Nephites which Joseph Smith was allowed to translate. The thing which Nephi wished to emphasize in this present verse is the fact that the "sealed" part of these plates will contain a revelation from God which will present a prophetic history of the world from the beginning to the end.

8. Wherefore, because of the things which are sealed up, the things which are sealed shall not be delivered in the day of the wickedness and abominations of the people. Wherefore the book shall be kept from them.

We are told that the reason part of the book will be sealed is simply because it is not to come forth in a day of wickedness. Nevertheless, the members of the Church who come forth from among the Gentiles do have a promise that they will have a chance to receive the sealed portion of these plates if they fulfill certain conditions. The prophet Moroni (who copied this great prophetic revelation onto the plates of Mormon) received this promise from the Lord:

"For the Lord said unto me: They shall not go forth unto the Gentiles until the day that they shall repent of their iniquity, and become clean before the Lord.

"And in that day that they shall exercise faith in me, saith the Lord, even as the brother of Jared did, that they may become sanctified in me, then will I manifest unto them the things which the brother of Jared saw, even to the unfolding unto them all my revelations, saith Jesus Christ, the Son of God, the Father of the heavens and of the earth, and all things that in them are." (Ether 4:6-7.)

Here, then, is the real reason why the gold plates were returned to Moroni by Joseph Smith after he had finished translating the part of the book which was not sealed. They are to be held in God's custody and preserved until a day when the Saints of the latter days (who come forth from among the Gentiles and are therefore called Gentiles) will be worthy to receive them. A similar promise is made to the members of the Church concerning the large plates of Nephi (see 3 Nephi 26:7–11). Now we continue with 2 Nephi, chapter 27.

> 9. But the book shall be delivered unto a man, and he shall deliver the words of the book, which are the words of those who have slumbered in the dust, and he shall deliver these words unto another;
>
> 10. But the words which are sealed he shall not deliver, neither shall he deliver the book. For the book shall be sealed by the power of God, and the revelation which was sealed shall be kept in the book until the own due time of the Lord, that they may come forth; for behold, they reveal all things from the foundation of the world unto the end thereof.

The so-called book referred to by both Nephi and Isaiah turned out to be the gold plates recorded by Mormon and his son Moroni. Nephi (who is still speaking of the latter days) says that this sacred record would be given to a man (who turned out to be Joseph Smith). He, in turn, would deliver "the words" (not the book!) to another (who turned out to be Martin Harris of Palmyra, New York). Nephi now adds an important clarification which is not in the writings of Isaiah. Nephi says that the words of the record which are sealed will not be delivered to this other man (Martin Harris). Neither will the record itself. What Joseph Smith actually did was copy some of the engravings from the plates onto several pieces of paper so that Martin Harris could show these writings to some of the learned men in New York. (See *History of the Church,* 1:19–20.) It was important that the sacred record not be delivered into other hands, especially the sealed portion. Nephi explains that this part had been sealed by the power of God and was therefore designed to be kept hidden until the "due time" of the Lord. As we have seen from Ether 4:6–7, quoted above, this will not happen until a day of righteousness. Then mankind will have this marvelous revelation which sets forth the prophetic history of the world from its foundation to the end thereof.

> 11. And the day cometh that the words of the book which were sealed shall be read upon the house tops; and they shall be read by the power of Christ; and all things shall be revealed unto the children of men which ever have been among the children of men, and which ever will be even unto the end of the earth.

Nephi, whose vision of the future extended right up to the Second Coming of Christ, promised that eventually the sealed portion of the plates would be revealed to all mankind. In fact, he said it would be "read upon the housetops"! One cannot help wondering if this was Nephi's attempt to describe the means of modern communications. He is quick to point out, however, that this sacred record can be read (or translated) only by the power of Christ. Not only will this record come forth in its completeness, but Nephi says that all things shall be revealed to the children of men in that day, including everything that has ever happened upon the face of the earth. This may have reference to the great revelation described in D&C 88:108–10, where the Lord says he will reveal the "secret acts of men, and the mighty works of God" 1,000 years at a time until the whole history of the world is revealed. (The only people whose secret acts will not be shown at that time will be those who have repented of their sins, entered into the waters of baptism, and who have been justified by the Holy Ghost so that the Atonement has "blotted out" the ugly parts of their lives. On that occasion, how thankful the Saints will be for the first four principles of the Gospel!)

12. Wherefore, at that day when the book shall be delivered unto the man of whom I have spoken, the book shall be hid from the eyes of the world, that the eyes of none shall behold it save it be that three witnesses shall behold it, by the power of God, besides him to whom the book shall be delivered; and they shall testify to the truth of the book and the things therein.

Nephi now reveals the severely restricted circumstances under which Joseph Smith would receive the plates of the Book of Mormon. Nephi knew Joseph Smith would be absolutely forbidden to show these plates to anyone until he was authorized to do so by the Lord. Nephi knew there would be three witnesses who would see the record through a special dispensation of power from God, and that these would afterwards testify to the truthfulness of this book and the things it contained. Reference is made to these same three witnesses in Ether 5:3–4, where it says their words will "stand as a testimony against the world at the last day."

The three men whom God selected for this important assignment turned out to be Oliver Cowdery, age 22, who had served Joseph Smith as his scribe during almost the entire translation process; David Whitmer, age 24, who had been a valiant friend to both Joseph Smith and Oliver Cowdery during the translating process; and Martin Harris, age 46, who had been Joseph Smith's associate and scribe when the translation first began. Through the power of God these three men were allowed to see the Angel Moroni, the gold plates on which Mormon and Moroni had made their record, the breastplate used in connection with the translation, the sword of Laban, the Urim and Thummim, and the Liahona (see D&C 17:1). Joseph Smith was present when these men enjoyed this monumental experience and described what happened (see *History of the Church*, 1:54–57).

Here is the testimony of these three men which stands as a witness to all the world:

Be it known unto all nations, kindreds, tongues, and people, unto whom this work shall come: That we, through the grace of God the Father, and our Lord Jesus Christ, have seen the plates which contain this record, which is a record of the people of Nephi, and also of the Lamanites, their brethren, and also of the people of Jared, who came from the tower of which hath been spoken. And we also know that they have been translated by the gift and power of God, for his voice hath declared it unto us; wherefore we know of a surety that the work is true. And we also testify that we have seen the engravings which are upon the plates; and they have been shown unto us by the power of God, and not of man. And we declare with words of soberness, that an angel of God came down from heaven, and he brought and laid before our eyes, that we beheld and saw the plates, and the engravings thereon; and we know that it is by the grace of God the Father, and our Lord Jesus Christ, that we beheld and bear record that these things are true. And it is marvelous in our eyes. Nevertheless, the voice of the Lord commanded us that we should bear record of it; wherefore, to be obedient unto the commandments of God, we bear testimony of these things. And we know that if we are faithful in

Christ, we shall rid our garments of the blood of all men, and be found spotless before the judgment-seat of Christ, and shall dwell with him eternally in the heavens. And the honor be to the Father, and to the Son, and to the Holy Ghost, which is one God. Amen.

OLIVER COWDERY
DAVID WHITMER
MARTIN HARRIS

The prophet Nephi continues (2 Nephi, chapter 27) as follows:

13. And there is none other which shall view it, save it be a few according to the will of God, to bear testimony of his word unto the children of men; for the Lord God hath said that the words of the faithful should speak as if it were from the dead.

Nephi emphasizes that no others would get to see the sacred record of the Nephite people except a "few" who would have this privilege so that they also could bear witness of the validity of this work. It was important that this work go forth to every nation, kindred, tongue, and people so that the words of the faithful Nephite Saints who had long since passed away might speak, as it were, from the dead. These "few" additional witnesses turned out to be eight men who were allowed to examine the gold plates but did not have the privilege of seeing the Angel Moroni and the sacred artifacts of the Nephite civilization. These eight men bore the following solemn testimony to all mankind:

Be it known unto all nations, kindreds, tongues, and people, unto whom this work shall come: That Joseph Smith, Jun., the translator of this work, has shown unto us the plates of which hath been spoken, which have the appearance of gold; and as many of the leaves as the said Smith has translated we did handle with our hands; and we also saw the engravings thereon, all of which has the appearance of ancient work, and of curious workmanship. And this we bear record with words of soberness, that the said Smith has shown unto us, for we have seen and hefted, and know of a surety that the said Smith has got the plates of which we have spoken. And we give our names unto the world, to witness unto the world that which we have seen. And we lie not, God bearing witness of it.

CHRISTIAN WHITMER   HIRAM PAGE
JACOB WHITMER   JOSEPH SMITH, SEN.
PETER WHITMER, JUN.   HYRUM SMITH
JOHN WHITMER   SAMUEL H. SMITH

OLIVER COWDERY (1806–1850)

Next to Joseph Smith, Oliver Cowdery witnessed more heavenly manifestations in connection with the restoration of the Gospel than any other man.

Born in Wells, Vermont, on October 3, 1806, Oliver Cowdery became acquainted with the Smith family and volunteered to act as scribe while Joseph Smith translated the Book of Mormon.

Shortly thereafter, on May 15, 1829, he was privileged to be with Joseph Smith when they were both given the Aaronic Priesthood by a resurrected being who was known in earth life as John the Baptist. He was also with Joseph Smith when the keys of the kingdom were restored with the Melchizedek Priesthood by Peter, James, and John.

Oliver Cowdery was designated as one of the Three Witnesses to the Book of Mormon and was allowed to examine the gold plates and other Nephite artifacts in the presence of the Angel Moroni during the summer of 1829.

Later, he was with Joseph Smith in the Kirtland Temple on April 3, 1836, when they were allowed to see the Savior and were visited by several of the great prophets of the past—Moses, Elias (Noah), and Elijah.

Oliver Cowdery died March 3, 1850, in Richmond, Missouri.

DAVID WHITMER (1805-1888)

David Whitmer was born January 7, 1805, at a small trading post in Pennsylvania. The family later moved to Fayette, New York, where David became acquainted with Oliver Cowdery. Through him the Whitmer family learned of the Book of Mormon, which was then in the process of being translated. When Joseph Smith encountered difficulty in completing the work because of persecution, David Whitmer drove a wagon approximately 100 miles to bring Joseph Smith and his scribe, Oliver Cowdery, to the Whitmer home in Fayette, New York. It was in the Whitmer home that the work of translation was completed.

David Whitmer was one of the three men described by the prophet Nephi who would be special witnesses to the authenticity of the gold plates on which the Book of Mormon was written. In the summer of 1829, David Whitmer—along with Martin Harris and Oliver Cowdery—was allowed to examine the gold plates in the presence of the Angel Moroni. The testimony of these three men has appeared in the front of every edition of the Book of Mormon since it was published.

David Whitmer died January 25, 1888, at Richmond, Missouri, and one of his last acts was to bear solemn testimony concerning the divine origin and authenticity of the Book of Mormon.

MARTIN HARRIS (1783–1875)

Here is a man who was referred to in scripture more than 2,300 years before he was born. In the fifth century B.C., Nephi wrote: "The Lord God shall say unto him [Joseph Smith] to whom he shall deliver the book: Take these words [copied from the plates or book] which are not sealed and deliver them to ANOTHER, that he may show them unto the learned" (2 Nephi 27:15; emphasis added). It turned out that Martin Harris was the man who received that assignment.

Martin was born in Easttown, Saratoga County, New York, but moved to Palmyra when he was 9 years of age. By 1827 he was about 44 years of age (nearly twice the age of Joseph Smith) and had become highly respected and a well-to-do farmer.

Members of the Smith family had worked for Martin Harris at various times, and he was apparently the first person outside the Smith family to be told of the visitations of Moroni. In 1828, soon after the plates came into the custody of Joseph Smith, arrangements were made to have samples of the characters copied from the gold plates so they could be shown to certain "learned men" in the East. This is how Martin Harris happened to have his famous interview with the noted scholar of classical languages at Columbia College, Professor Charles Anthon.

The most thrilling event in the life of Martin Harris was in the summer of 1829 when he was given the privilege of examining the gold plates in the presence of the Angel Moroni. When it was over he exclaimed: "'Tis enough; 'tis enough; mine eyes have beheld; mine eyes have beheld!"

PROFESSOR CHARLES ANTHON (1787-1867)

This is the brilliant and scholarly gentleman who turned out to be the "one that is learned" spoken of in Isaiah 29:11 and in 2 Nephi 27:15-18. It was to this learned professor that Martin Harris took the characters which had been copied from the plates of the Book of Mormon.

Charles Anthon was professor of classical studies at Columbia College (later Columbia University) for 47 years—1820-1867. In earlier years he attended Columbia as a student and is described as probably the most brilliant scholar ever to attend Columbia College.

The *Dictionary of American Biography* describes Professor Anthon as a prolific writer and editor. During a period of 30 years he edited at least one volume annually. "Each of his text books passed through several editions, and for thirty years ... his influence upon the study of the classics in the United States was probably greater than that of any other one man" (*Dictionary of American Biography*, 1:314). Edgar Allen Poe wrote of Anthon: "If not absolutely the best, he is at least generally considered the best classicist in America" (*The Literati*, New York, 1859, pp. 45-47). *Harper's Weekly* of August 17, 1867, said Professor Anthon was "more widely known in Europe than any other American commentator on classical authors."

Charles Anthon was a bachelor and lived in a wing of Columbia College. It is believed that it was there, in his study, that Martin Harris interviewed him. (The above information was abstracted from "The Anthon Transcript: People, Primary Sources, and Problems," by Professor Stanley B. Kimball of Southern Illinois University, *Brigham Young University Studies*, Spring 1970, pp. 331–32.)

The text of 2 Nephi chapter 27 continues:

14. Wherefore, the Lord God will proceed to bring forth the words of the book; and in the mouth of as many witnesses as seemeth him good will he establish his word; and wo be unto him that rejecteth the word of God!

Nephi knew it was the intention of the Lord to have this book widely distributed among the children of men. He said the Lord would proceed to bring forth the words of the book, and since the truthfulness of the existence of the original record would be certified by so many witnesses, Nephi said, "Wo be unto him that rejecteth the word of God!"

15. But behold, it shall come to pass that the Lord God shall say unto him to whom he shall deliver the book: Take these words which are not sealed and deliver them to another, that he may show them unto the learned, saying: Read this, I pray thee. And the learned shall say: Bring hither the book, and I will read them.

Both Isaiah and Nephi knew that Joseph Smith would be commanded by the Lord to take some of the words "which are not sealed" and deliver them to "another." In Joseph Smith's biography by his mother we find the following: "Joseph began to make arrangements to accomplish the translation of the Record. The first step that he was INSTRUCTED to take in regard to this work was to make a *facsimile* of some of the characters, which were called reformed Egyptian, and to send them to some of the most learned men of this generation and ask them for the translation thereof." (Lucy Mack Smith, *History of Joseph Smith by His Mother*, ed. Preston Nibley [Salt Lake City: Bookcraft, 1958], p. 114; emphasis added, italics in original.)

Actually, Joseph Smith made two "facsimiles" of the characters appearing on the gold plates. One was translated, the other was not (see Roberts, *Comprehensive History of the Church*, 1:100). Some people have been under the impression that these facsimiles were taken by Martin Harris to certain "learned" men in New York in order to convince Harris that the gold plates were genuine and that Joseph Smith had been called of God to translate them. However, such was not the case. As we noted in the quotation above, Joseph Smith followed this procedure because he was INSTRUCTED to do so by the Lord. As we shall see in a moment, the visit with the learned men in New York had a tremendous impression upon the mind of Martin Harris, but that was not the principal reason for his going. This procedure was followed in order to fulfill a commandment of the Lord, which, in turn, fulfilled a prophecy made by Isaiah some 2,500 years earlier and was subsequently verified in a revelation to the prophet Nephi around 600 B.C. It will be noted in verse 15, which we are presently studying, that Nephi says that the Lord would specifically tell Joseph Smith to deliver the "words" to "another" so they could be shown to the learned.

Nephi further states that when the "words" would be shown to the learned man he would be asked to read them and he would say, "Bring hither the book and I will read them." Nephi describes the motivations of both Charles Anthon and Dr. Samuel L. Mitchill, who was later shown the characters copied from the plates:

16. And now, because of the glory of the world and to get gain will they say this, and not for the glory of God.

17. And the man [Martin Harris] shall say: I cannot bring the book, for it is sealed.

18. Then shall the learned say: I cannot read it.

It is rather amazing how literally these three verses were fulfilled. Here is what Martin Harris says happened:

"I went to the city of New York, and presented the characters which had been translated, with the translation thereof, to Professor Charles Anthon, a gentleman celebrated for his literary attainments. Professor Anthon stated that the translation was correct, more so than any he had before seen translated from the Egyptian. I then showed him those which were not yet translated, and he said that they were Egyptian, Chaldaic, [Assyriac], and Arabic; and he said they were true characters. He gave me a certificate, certifying to the people of Palmyra that they were true characters, and that the translation of such of them as had been translated was also correct. I took the certificate and put it into my pocket, and was just leaving the house, when Mr. Anthon called me back, and asked me how the young man found out that there were gold plates in the place where he found them. I answered that an angel of God had revealed it unto him.

"He then said to me, 'Let me see that certificate.' I accordingly took it out of my pocket and gave it to him, when he took it and tore it to pieces, saying, that there was no such thing now as ministering of angels, and that if I would bring the plates to him, HE WOULD TRANSLATE THEM. I informed him that part of the plates were sealed, and that I was forbidden to bring them. He replied, 'I cannot read a sealed book.' I left him and went to Dr. [Mitchill], who sanctioned what Professor Anthon had said respecting both the characters and the translation." (*History of the Church,* 1:20; emphasis added.)

---

12. And the book is delivered to him that is not learned, saying, Read this, I pray thee: and he saith, I am not learned.

Once more we have Nephi commenting extensively on this same theme. This also is taken from 2 Nephi, chapter 27. We will quote Nephi's comments verse by verse with appropriate observations after each one.

Analysis of Nephi's Commentary on Isaiah 29:12

19. Wherefore it shall come to pass, that the Lord God will deliver again the book and the words thereof to him that is not learned; and the man that is not learned shall say: I am not learned.

According to Isaiah and Nephi, the Lord would leave this sacred record in the custody of the man who would be uneducated and unskilled. They knew he would protest, saying, "I am not learned."

To gain some idea of the truly "unlearned" status of Joseph Smith at the age of 23, we quote these words from his wife, Emma Hale Smith, who testified in later years concerning the inability of Joseph Smith to have written the Book of Mormon or even a simple treatise. She said:

"Joseph Smith [as a young man]...could neither write nor dictate a coherent and well-worded letter, let alone dictate a book like the Book of Mormon, and though I was an active participant in the scenes that transpired, was present during the translation of the plates, and had cognizance of things as they transpired, it is marvelous to me—a marvel and a wonder—as much as to anyone else...."

"My belief is that the Book of Mormon is of divine authenticity—I have not the slightest doubt of it. I am satisfied that no man could have dictated the writing of the manuscripts unless he was inspired; for, when [I was] acting as his scribe, your father [she was being interrogated by her son, Joseph Smith III] would dictate to me hour after hour; and when returning after meals, or interruptions, he would at once begin where he had left off, without either seeing the manuscript or having any portion of it read to him. This was a usual thing for him to do. It would have been improbable that a learned man could do this, and FOR ONE SO IGNORANT AND UNLEARNED AS HE WAS, IT WAS SIMPLY IMPOSSIBLE." (Quoted in Preston Nibley, comp., *The Witnesses of the Book of Mormon* [Salt Lake City: Stevens & Wallis, 1946], pp. 28–29; emphasis added.)

> 20. Then shall the Lord God say unto him: The learned shall not read them, for they have rejected them, and I am able to do mine own work; wherefore thou shalt read the words which I shall give unto thee.

The Urim and Thummim was with the gold plates. Through the power of God, the gift of translation was given to Joseph Smith and he was able to use the Urim and Thummim, as did Aaron of old, to receive the necessary revelations to accurately translate the plates. However, the translating procedure was a very strenuous undertaking. The Lord later described the translating procedure to Oliver Cowdery as follows: "But, behold, I say unto you, that you must study it out in your mind; then you must ask me if it be right, and if it is right I will cause that your bosom shall burn within you; therefore, you shall feel that it is right.

"But if it be not right you shall have no such feelings, but you shall have a stupor of thought that shall cause you to forget the thing which is wrong; therefore, you cannot write that which is sacred save it be given you from me." (D&C 9:8–9.)

It is scarcely any wonder that Joseph Smith had such tremendous confidence in this monumental work once the translation was complete. On one occasion he said, "I told the brethren that the Book of Mormon was the most correct of any book on earth, and the keystone of our religion, and a man would get nearer to God by abiding by its precepts, than by any other book" (*History of the Church*, 4:461).

The Lord's instructions to this "unlearned" man, Joseph Smith, continue:

> 21. Touch not the things which are sealed,
> for I will bring them forth in mine own due
> time; for I will show unto the children of men
> that I am able to do mine own work.

It is interesting that both Nephi and Moroni (Ether 5:1) warned Joseph Smith not to allow himself to be tempted to tamper with the sealed part of the sacred record entrusted to him. The last part of the above verse suggests that when the sealed portion of the plates is translated it will be by God's special gift and not by the wisdom of men. Nephi records in the next verse what the Lord wanted Joseph Smith to do with the record when the unsealed portion had been translated:

> 22. Wherefore, when thou hast read the
> words which I have commanded thee, and
> obtained the witnesses which I have promised
> unto thee, then shalt thou seal up the book
> again, and hide it up unto me, that I may
> preserve the words which thou hast not read,
> until I shall see fit in mine own wisdom to reveal
> all things unto the children of men.

When will the "sealed" part of the Book of Mormon come forth? It will be at a very special time when the Lord will have this record translated and broadcast "upon the housetops." It will reveal what will happen right up to "the end of the earth"! Here is what the Lord told Nephi concerning the "sealed" part of the plates:

"And the day cometh that the words of the book which were sealed shall be read upon the house tops; and they shall be read by the power of Christ; and all things shall be revealed unto the children of men which ever have been among the children of men, and which ever will be even unto the end of the earth" (2 Nephi 27:11).

23. For behold, I am God; and I am a God of miracles; and I will show unto the world that I am the same yesterday, today, and forever; and I work not among the children of men save it be according to their faith.

"The Lord is God," and here he bears witness of himself and his power in the universe. The Lord has no difficulty giving an "unlearned" young man the power to translate an ancient record. Men may call such things "miracles" and scoff because they do not possess such power, but the Lord declares. "I work NOT among the children of men save it be according to their faith"!

13. Wherefore the Lord said, Forasmuch as this people draw near me with their mouth, and with their lips do honour me, but have removed their heart far from me, and their fear toward me is taught by the precept of men:

14. Therefore, behold, I will proceed to do a marvellous work among this people, even a marvellous work and a wonder: for the wisdom of their wise men shall perish, and the understanding of their prudent men shall be hid.

Here is Nephi's version of these two verses in 2 Nephi, chapter 27 (emphasis added):

24. And again it shall come to pass that the Lord SHALL SAY UNTO HIM THAT SHALL READ THE WORDS THAT SHALL BE DELIVERED HIM:

25. Forasmuch as this people draw near unto me with their mouth, and with their lips do honor me, but have removed their hearts far from me, and their fear towards me is taught by the precepts of men—

26. Therefore, I will proceed to do a marvelous work among this people, yea, a "marvelous work and a wonder", for the wisdom of their wise and learned shall perish, and the understanding of their prudent shall be hid.

Notice that Nephi identifies the person to whom these verses will be addressed. It will be the unlearned person who is given the sacred record to read.

We observe that the Lord identifies the coming forth of the Book of Mormon as an important part of his "strange act" which would be a "marvelous work and a wonder." It has been especially wonderful in that many worldly theories and philosophies of men have been completely demolished by the remarkable truths disclosed in the Book of Mormon and other modern revelations associated with it.

It all began when Joseph Smith knelt in prayer to ask which church was right. As he recorded:

"I was answered that I must join none of them, for they were all wrong; and the Personage who addressed me said that all their creeds were an abomination in his sight; that those professors were all corrupt; that: "they draw near to me with their lips, but their hearts are far from me, they teach for doctrines the commandments of men, having a form of godliness, but they deny the power thereof" Joseph Smith—History 1:19).

Nevertheless, out among those churches were sincere searchers after truth, including many of the ministers. The restored Gospel was to proclaim the truth—the "good news" of the Restoration. The Lord said to Joseph Smith in 1829: "Contend against no church, save it be the church of the devil" (D&C 18:20). In other words, denounce evil but do not denounce the various denominations or churches. Just tell people the good news of the marvelous and wonderful restoration of the Gospel.

15. Woe unto them that seek deep to hide their counsel from the LORD, and their works are in the dark, and

Now Isaiah pronounces a "woe" upon those who set up secret combinations and conspire to murder and get gain. These are the Gadiantons of every age who "have

they say, Who seeth us?
and who knoweth us?

made a covenant with death, and with hell are...at agreement" (Isaiah 28:15).

The scripture describes how these covenants with death and hell were first introduced:

"And Satan said unto Cain: Swear unto me by thy throat, and if thou tell it thou shalt die; and swear thy brethren by their heads, AND BY THE LIVING GOD, that they tell it not; for if they tell it, THEY SHALL SURELY DIE; and this that thy father may not know it.... And all these things were done in secret. And Cain said: Truly I am Mahan, the master of this great secret, that I MAY MURDER AND GET GAIN. Wherefore Cain was called Master Mahan, and he gloried in his wickedness." (Moses 5:29–31; emphasis added.)

An example of such secret combinations in modern times is the testimony of Joseph Valachi, who exposed and described the American criminal syndicate in testimony before a Senate investigating committee. In a United Press International dispatch dated October 1, 1963, we read:

"Joseph Valachi, underworld informer, described today how he took a blood oath in joining the Cosa Nostra crime syndicate and said his disclosure of the secret rites meant: 'This is my doom!'"

"Valachi gave his description to the Senate investigations subcommittee.

"Valachi said he took an oath to live 'by the gun and the knife and die by the gun and the knife' during an initiation ceremony conducted in an upstate New York hideaway by the boss of his 'family'—Salvatore Maranzano....

"Valachi, reenacting parts of the ceremony before television cameras, said he and two other initiates were taken one by one into a big room where 35 to 40 men were sitting around a long table.

"Valachi said there was a knife and a revolver on the table and Maranzano explained in a Sicilian dialect, 'You live by the gun and the knife.'

"Then, Valachi said, he was given a piece of paper and burned it, passing from hand to hand while repeating in Italian: 'This is the way I burn if I expose this organization.'

"Then those around the table decided by chance [drawing of lots] who his crime 'godfather' would be. His was Joseph Bonanno, who is still one of the top five New York syndicate chiefs, Valachi said.

"Then, he continued, Bonanno pricked his finger to draw blood to indicate brotherhood and solidarity with other members of the 'family.'" (*Seattle Times*, 1 October 1963; a similar account is found in Peter Maas, *The Valachi Papers*, [New York: G.P. Putnam's Sons, 1968], pp. 94–98.)

In modern revelation, the Lord said the location of the Church headquarters was specifically designed to be set up where there would be a refuge. He said, "This [is] in consequence of that which is coming on the earth, and of secret combinations" (D&C 42:64).

Congressional investigations have revealed that secret combinations in modern times are a perfect duplication of those in the past, their purpose being to "murder and get gain." Some of these are underworld conspiracies, some are multinational economic or financial combinations, and some are political secret combinations designed to overthrow nations and enslave millions of human beings.

These are they who "have made a covenant with death, and with hell are . . . at agreement."

16. Surely your turning of things upside down shall be esteemed as the potter's clay: for shall the work say of him that made it, He

Nephi gives this verse as follows: "Surely, your turning of things upside down shall be esteemed as the potter's clay. BUT BEHOLD, I WILL SHOW UNTO THEM, SAITH THE LORD OF HOSTS, THAT I KNOW

made me not? or shall the thing framed say of him that framed it, He had no understanding?

ALL THEIR WORKS. For shall the work say of him that made it, he made me not? Or shall the thing framed say of him that framed it, he had no understanding?" (2 Nephi 27:27; emphasis added.)

The arrogance of man in defying the God of the universe is so irrational and self-destructive that it borders on either abject depravity or outright insanity. We live in a day when men and women say of God, "He made me not!" They behold the universe and say it was done without design or understanding.

17. Is it not yet a very little while, and Lebanon shall be turned into a fruitful field, and the fruitful field shall be esteemed as a forest?

Nephi gives a somewhat fuller text to this verse. He says: "BUT BEHOLD, SAITH THE LORD OF HOSTS: I WILL SHOW UNTO THE CHILDREN OF MEN THAT it is yet a very little while and Lebanon shall be turned into a fruitful field; and the fruitful field shall be esteemed as a forest" (2 Nephi 27:28; emphasis added).

As we see from the next verse, the Lord is saying that "a very little while" after the Book of Mormon is revealed he will fulfill the blessings which are promised for the Lebanon region of the Holy Land. Lebanon is one of the areas which war and famine have denuded of its vegetation and its people. In this verse the Lord is saying that it will not be long after the coming forth of the Book of Mormon that this great restoration in Lebanon (and the regions round about) will begin to take place. This prophecy is presently in the process of being fulfilled.

18. And in that day shall the deaf hear the words of the book, and the eyes of the blind shall see out of obscurity, and out of darkness.

Nephi gives the text of this verse exactly as it is given by Isaiah. It is a declaration that in that day when the Book of Mormon comes forth, the multitudes of humanity who have been deaf to the call of the Lord and blind to an understanding of the Gospel shall suddenly find that they are able to hear the call of the Lord. They find light coming to their minds so that they are able to comprehend what the whole Gospel message is all about. They also begin to understand the scriptures, the inspiring words of the prophets, the meaning of their warnings, and the promises of great blessings which God said he would bestow on all those who respond to the Gospel call of the latter days.

19. The meek also shall increase their joy in the LORD, and the poor among men shall rejoice in the Holy One of Israel.

Nephi's rendition of this verse is slightly different. He says, "AND the meek also shall increase, AND their joy SHALL BE in the Lord, and the poor among men shall rejoice in the Holy One of Israel" (2 Nephi 27:30; emphasis added).

The meek of the earth are those who are quietly trying to mind their own business and serve God and their fellow men the best way they can. They try to avoid contention. They have no ambitions to rule nations or conquer other people. Nevertheless, more often than not these are the very people who are the most abused and exploited by those who seek treasures of riches and worldly power. However, this scripture verifies that when the Gospel is restored, the meek will be reassured by the modern prophets as well as those in the Book of Mormon. Their joy shall increase, Isaiah says, and Nephi confirms it. This great dispensation of new knowledge and Godly power will refresh their souls, strengthen their reliance on their Savior, and cause them to rejoice in the Holy One of Israel.

20. For the terrible one is brought to nought, and the scorner is consumed, and all that watch for iniquity are cut off:

Nephi renders this verse as follows: "FOR ASSUREDLY AS THE LORD LIVETH THEY [the meek] SHALL SEE that the terrible one is brought to naught, and the scorner is consumed, and all that watch for iniquity are cut off" (2 Nephi 27:31; emphasis added).

Down through the centuries, as the meek of the earth have been persecuted, enslaved, betrayed, and sometimes slaughtered, it seemed there was no justice on the earth. Only the "terrible ones" with money and might seemed to succeed. In their haughty and smug self-glorification they scorned the poor and the meek of the earth. But Isaiah and Nephi assure mankind that God will not be mocked. In the day of his power which began with the coming forth of the Book of Mormon, mankind will commence to see the tyrants of the earth brought to their knees and the scorner consumed. Eventually they will see all those whose minds were filthy with evil designs and moral debaucheries cut off from the face of the land.

21. That make a man an offender for a word, and lay a snare for him that reproveth in the gate, and turn aside the just for a thing of nought.

Nephi prefaces this verse with the words "AND THEY" to make certain the reader associates this verse with the one just before. Among those whose works God despises are those nit-pickers who, with devilish delight, latch onto a single word spoken in haste or by inadvertence and use this to discredit a mighty message of truth and salvation. Such are the hecklers at street meetings where the servants of God are seeking to preach the plan of salvation and the great message of the Restoration. They try to cleverly ensnare the young missionary and use some trivia or tiny technicality to discredit or turn aside his message of God's "good news."

22. Therefore thus saith the LORD, who redeemed Abraham, concerning the house of Jacob, Jacob shall not now be ashamed, neither shall his face now wax pale.

Nephi records this verse in the same words as Isaiah. This verse contains the assurance of the Lord that just as he saved Abraham from death on many occasions and thereafter redeemed him in exalted glory, so shall the house of Jacob (the children of Israel) eventually enjoy the confidence of the Lord and no longer be ashamed. In other words, when the great restoration of the Gospel commences with the coming forth of the Book of Mormon, the people who are of the house of Israel and who respond to the Gospel call will no longer need to be downcast and ashamed. Neither will they need to be fearful of the "terrible ones" any longer. They will be able to lift up their heads in joyful hope, and their faces can finally be filled with the glow of confidence and security in the Lord.

23. **But when he seeth his children, the work of mine hands, in the midst of him, they shall sanctify my name, and sanctify the Holy One of Jacob, and shall fear the God of Israel.**

Nephi also records this verse in the same words as Isaiah. It is a declaration that in the latter days when Jacob or Israel suddenly sees the children or sons of God rising in the midst of the people as Priesthood leaders, prophets, apostles, evangelists, and patriarchs, the whole house of Israel will have cause to sanctify the name of the Lord. They will gain a renewed appreciation of his love and concern for them and his nearness to them. They will so respect and love the Lord that they will "fear" to do anything which would offend him.

24. **They also that erred in spirit shall come to understanding, and they that murmured shall learn doctrine.**

Once again Nephi renders this verse in the same words as Isaiah. These two prophets wanted the modern children of Israel to appreciate that the Gospel would be restored so that those who had sincerely erred "in spirit" could gain a correct understanding of Gospel principles. The Restoration in general and the Book of Mormon in particular are for the benefit of those who have complained that they could not understand God and his program for the human family. The great truths which have now been poured out upon humanity in a floodtide of revelation are specifically designed to give every honest heart and every sincere, searching mind God's answers to the most perplexing questions. These answers are his "doctrines," which are a glorious inspiration to all who will take time from their busy lives to study them.

SUMMARY:

Thus we come to the conclusion of one of the most important chapters in the entire book of Isaiah. Let us summarize the facets of prophetic truth contained in this unique segment of scripture.

1. Isaiah foresaw the woes that would befall "Ariel" or the people of Israel.
2. He saw the conquest and destruction of millions of the children of Lehi in America.
3. However, Isaiah knew that their righteous ancestors would write a marvelous scriptural record which would be buried in the earth.
4. He knew that in the last days this record would come forth.
5. He also knew that it would have a "familiar spirit" which would whisper to modern man like a voice from the dust speaking out of the ground.
6. Isaiah said the Lord would rescue his people in the latter days with a great demonstration of power.
7. He saw that all who fought against "Ariel" or Zion would be destroyed.
8. It would all begin with the coming forth of a sacred book.
9. But part of it would be sealed.
10. The words of the ancient book would be delivered to a very learned man, who turned out to be Dr. Charles Anthon of Columbia College, New York.
11. When this man was asked to translate and read the book, Isaiah prophetically announced almost the exact words he would say.
12. Isaiah said the book would be left in the hands of an "unlearned" individual. This turned out to be young Joseph Smith.

13. Isaiah knew that the Lord would use this unlearned young man to bring forth this sacred record in a modern translation through the gift and power of God.

14. He also knew that the Lord would tell this youthful prophet that the professional clerics of that day would be teaching for commandments the doctrines of men, and that they would draw near to him with their lips but their hearts would be far from him. This message was delivered to Joseph Smith during the First Vision, which occurred in the spring of 1820.

15. Isaiah knew that this would be the beginning of God's "strange act" whereby he would do "a marvelous work and a wonder."

16. He knew that this would be the day when the Lord would pour forth a flood of new revelation to expose the fallacies of the "wisdom" of men.

17. Isaiah said the coming forth of the sacred book would be the signal for many other things to start happening. In fact, he knew that "a very little while" after the coming forth of this book, the Lord would undertake the restoration of the Holy Land.

18. It would also be a time when the Lord would commence the cleansing of the earth from the scourge of the "terrible ones" who would be guilty of spreading so much terror and destruction among mankind.

19. When this happened the wicked would be reveling in their iniquities and trying to make the righteous appear foolish because of a single word. Isaiah saw that these conniving twisters of the truth would be "cut off."

20. Eventually, Isaiah said, there would come a time of rejoicing among the children of Israel because they

would feel the closeness of a loving Heavenly Father and the security of seeing him intervene in the affairs of men so that universal justice might spread across the face of the whole earth.

INTRODUCTION:

This chapter is a continuation of chapter 28. Isaiah interjected his marvelous prophecy concerning America and the coming forth of the Book of Mormon in chapter 29, but now he is ready to return to the Lord's denunciation of those "scornful men" who "rule this people which is in Jerusalem" (Isaiah 28:14). These are men who had made a "covenant with death" and the servants of evil in hopes of saving themselves. The Lord had said in chapter 28 that this covenant will be "disannulled, and your agreement with hell shall not stand" (Isaiah 28:18).

1. Woe to the rebellious children, saith the LORD, that take counsel, but not of me; and that cover with a covering, but not of my spirit, that they may add sin to sin:

When the Lord gives counsel on political matters and his people ignore the warning, it is counted as a manifestation of wicked rebellion on the part of his people. In this verse the Lord says these leaders take counsel, but not HIS counsel. In fact, they enter into secret places where they think their conspiracy will be hidden or covered. Nevertheless, the Lord assures them that his spirit is not with them in these wicked, secret counsels. In fact, they use these undercover operations to plot one evil on top of another, thinking it is a great secret hidden from the Lord.

2. That walk to go down into Egypt, and have not asked at my mouth; to strengthen themselves in the strength

The Lord now exposes what they have been secretly doing. They have sent a delegation to Egypt to engage that nation in an alliance with Judah. They want to

of Pharaoh, and to trust in the shadow of Egypt!

combine their strength with Egypt to fight against the terrible Assyrians who will be attacking them. At that moment, the Assyrians were trying to recover from the death of their king (Sargon), which had occurred in 705 B.C. However, Sargon's son, Sennacherib, was already reorganizing the Assyrian government, and rumor had it that he would soon take to the field. The leaders in Jerusalem had correctly anticipated that Sennacherib would attack Judah on his way to Egypt. They were therefore undertaking to set up an alliance with Egypt for mutual protection. But the Lord had a better strategy in mind. He criticized these leaders in Jerusalem for rushing down to Egypt without first seeking counsel from the Lord. Had they asked the Lord, they would have been assured that it was a serious mistake to trust in the "shadow of Egypt." In other words, there was no real military security in an alliance with the Pharaoh. What appeared to be Egyptian military might was nothing but a shadow.

3. Therefore shall the strength of Pharaoh be your shame, and the trust in the shadow of Egypt your confusion.

The Lord warned that their reliance on the strength of Egypt would turn out to be a shame and an embarrassment. There would be no security in an Egyptian alliance, but only confusion and military complications.

4. For his princes were at Zoan, and his ambassadors came to Hanes.

Egypt at this time was under an Ethiopian dynasty of rulers whose capital was several hundred miles up the Nile. Nevertheless, the Ethiopian Pharaoh had sent his princes up as far as Zoan or Tunis, which was not far from the borders of Palestine. He also had ambassadors in middle Egypt at Hanes or Anusis. The proximity of these Ethiopian officials must have made the officials in Jerusalem think that Egypt would resolutely hold firm when the Assyrians came. They were basing their whole strategy on this assumption.

5. They were all ashamed of a people that could not profit them, nor be an help nor profit, but a shame, and also a reproach.

It would appear from this verse that the envoys from Jerusalem would find themselves spurned by the Egyptians, who would say that the tiny kingdom of Judah was of no profit to them. They would consider her a reproach and a hindrance in case of war with the Assyrians.

6. The burden of the beasts of the south: into the land of trouble and anguish, from whence come the young and old lion, the viper and fiery flying serpent, they will carry their riches upon the shoulders of young asses, and their treasures upon the bunches of camels, to a people that shall not profit them.

Isaiah is now given a "burden" or a prophecy to deliver to the rebellious leaders in Jerusalem. He is told to tell them that when they go down into the southern desert to meet the Egyptian envoys, they will take great treasures on their beasts of burden to buy the good will and cooperation of the Egyptians. But it will not profit them. It will be a waste of their wealth.

7. For the Egyptians shall help in vain, and to no purpose: therefore have I cried concerning this, Their strength is to sit still.

The Lord says flatly that the expectation of aid from the Egyptians will be totally in vain and will accomplish no purpose whatsoever. That is why Isaiah, as God's emissary, has been trying to tell them what to do. They are to "sit still" and not make enemies of the Assyrians by entering into an alliance with Egypt. In other words, Sennacherib of Assyria will not have any quarrel with the Jews unless they become an armed threat on his left flank as he marches toward Egypt. If he learns that Judah is an ally of Egypt, he will attack the Jews even before he goes down into Egypt!

8. Now go, write it before them in a table, and note it in a book, that it may be for the time to come for ever and ever:

That is exactly what Sennacherib did in 701 B.C. The Lord anticipated this development and therefore commanded Isaiah to write the Lord's prediction in a book and also in a "table" (a stone tablet?) so that the people would know in the future that the Lord had told them exactly what would happen if they did not listen to his counsel.

9. That this is a rebellious people, lying children, children that will not hear the law of the LORD:

Isaiah was to record that Judah was a "rebellious" people, a deceitful people, who would not hearken to the law of the Lord.

10. Which say to the seers, See not; and to the prophets, Prophesy not unto us right things, speak unto us smooth things, prophesy deceits:

11. Get you out of the way, turn aside out of the path, cause the Holy One of Israel to cease from before us.

In fact, their leaders would not allow the warning of the Lord's prophets to be proclaimed among the people. They wanted to shut the mouths of the Lord's servants from telling them "right things." They commanded them to proclaim "smooth things," even though they were lies. The corrupt leaders wanted the Lord's prophets out of their sight if they were going to preach repentance and proclaim words of warning. They declared that the "Holy One of Israel" should never be mentioned.

12. Wherefore thus saith the Holy One of Israel, Because ye despise this word, and trust in oppression and perverseness, and stay thereon:

13. Therefore this iniquity shall be to you as a breach ready to fall, swelling out in a high wall, whose breaking cometh suddenly at an instant.

Isaiah therefore speaks in the name of the Holy One of Israel and says that since the people despise the words of warning which God has sent unto them, and because they choose to depend upon oppression and wicked conniving, therefore the Lord will count it a breach and a great offense which they have committed against him. The Lord says this offense will bring great judgment upon this people, like a wall that begins to buckle and then unexpectedly collapses. It will happen "suddenly at an instant."

14. And he shall break it as the breaking of the potters'

The threshing of the people will be so severe that it will be like the shattering of a potter's vessel. There

vessel that is broken in pieces; he shall not spare: so that there shall not be found in the bursting of it a sherd to take fire from the hearth, or to take water withal out of the pit.

will not be any pieces big enough to carry fire or ashes out of the hearth. Nor will there be any curved saucer-like portions which can be used to dip out a little water.

15. For thus saith the Lord GOD, the Holy One of Israel; In returning and rest shall ye be saved; in quietness and in confidence shall be your strength: and ye would not.

Isaiah then quotes the Lord as having said that by returning to their cities and remaining quiet they could avoid the coming calamity, but they will not.

16. But ye said, No; for we will flee upon horses; therefore shall ye flee: and, We will ride upon the swift; therefore shall they that pursue you be swift.

Instead, they reason among themselves that if their plans do not work out successfully they can always flee on their horses. In the end, the Lord said that is precisely what they will be forced to do. However, he wanted them to know that those who pursued them would not let them escape. The enemy's horses would be much faster than their own.

17. One thousand shall flee at the rebuke of one; at the rebuke of five shall ye flee: till ye be left as a beacon upon the top of a mountain, and as an ensign on an hill.

The Lord further predicted that they would be in such a panic that a single enemy soldier would cause 1,000 from the house of Judah to flee wildly into the wilderness. Or at the rebuke of 5 they would find themselves charging off as though a whole army were after them. The Lord said this would continue to be the case until these arrogant officials came to their senses and returned to their foreordained role as exemplary leaders of the Lord's people. In that hour they will become as a beacon on top of the mountain or an ensign on a hill.

18. And therefore will the LORD wait, that he may be gracious unto you, and therefore will he be exalted, that he may have mercy upon you: for the LORD is a God of judgment: blessed are all they that wait for him.

Because the Lord knew that eventually this would happen, he has decided to wait until that blessed day when these people of Judah would be worthy of the Lord's special endowments and gracious acceptance. The Lord promised that when that day arrives, the people will be blessed, and they will see that the Lord is a God of mercy. Isaiah exclaimed, "Blessed are all they that wait for him."

19. For the people shall dwell in Zion at Jerusalem: thou shalt weep no more: he will be very gracious unto thee at the voice of thy cry; when he shall hear it, he will answer thee.

The Lord is now talking about the day when the people of God will dwell "in Zion at Jerusalem." There will also be a Zion in America. In fact, Zion is anyplace where the people of God are gathered together and have become a people who are "pure in heart" (see D&C 97:21). The Lord knew that Judah would suffer many generations of hardship before her redemption, but following her redemption the Lord promised the Zion in Jerusalem that she would weep no more. At that time the Lord will be gracious to these repentant disciples. He will answer their prayers and petitions. They will never be scattered or confounded again. As the prophet Nephi said, "And I did rehearse unto them THE WORDS OF ISAIAH, who spake concerning the restoration of the Jews, or of the house of Israel; and after they were restored they should NO MORE BE CONFOUNDED, NEITHER SHOULD THEY BE SCATTERED AGAIN" (1 Nephi 15:20; emphasis added).

20. And though the Lord give you the bread of adversity, and the water of affliction, yet shall not thy teachers be removed into a corner any more, but thine eyes shall see thy teachers:

The Lord assures the people that although they will be required to eat the bread of adversity during their days of apostasy and wade through deep waters of affliction, nevertheless the day will come when the Lord will raise up prophets and teachers in their midst who can be seen and heard again. In a time of wickedness the Lord will send prophets to plead with the people, but only for a specified time. If they refuse to heed the voice of prophetic warning, then the Lord takes these teachers and prophets out of their midst. This has happened many times in the past.

21. And thine ears shall hear a word behind thee, saying, This is the way, walk ye in it, when ye turn to the right hand, and when ye turn to the left.

In the latter days the people will hear the voice of the Lord once more. His servants will be raised up to guide the righteous along a straight path, saying, "This is the way, walk ye in it." The voice of God will come through his prophets to tell the Saints when to turn to the right or to the left. One of the greatest blessings the Lord bestows upon his people is the privilege of having living prophets to guide the people in their personal lives and community affairs.

22. Ye shall defile also the covering of thy graven images of silver, and the ornament of thy molten images of gold: thou shalt cast them away as a menstruous cloth; thou shalt say unto it, Get thee hence.

In that future day Isaiah says the people will be ashamed of their objects of worship and adoration. They will consider the workmanship of their own hands which they had held to be the center of their existence, and will disdainfully spurn it. Suddenly these objects which they had lusted after and worked for all their lives will seem cheap and shoddy. They will say, "Get thee hence!"

23. Then shall he give the rain of thy seed, that thou shalt sow the ground withal; and bread of the increase of the earth, and it shall be fat and plenteous: in that day shall thy cattle feed in large pastures.

The blessings showered upon the Lord's people in that day will include all the bounties of the earth. There will be bounteous crops with regular moisture pouring down from the heavens to facilitate the reaping of good harvests. The cattle will feed in "large pastures."

24. The oxen likewise and the young asses that ear the ground shall eat clean provender, which hath been winnowed with the shovel and with the fan.

Even the domestic animals will no longer have to scrounge among weeds and brush for a few morsels of grass, but they will feed upon clean hay and threshed grain.

25. And there shall be upon every high mountain, and upon every high hill, rivers and streams of waters in the day of the great slaughter, when the towers fall.

Here the Lord says that after the day of judgment and the slaughter of the wicked, there will be an abundance of water, with brooks running down from every mountain and rivers of water stretching out across the fertile plains.

26. Moreover the light of the moon shall be as the light of the sun, and the light of the sun shall be sevenfold, as the light of seven days, in the day that the LORD bindeth up the breach of his people, and healeth the stroke of their wound.

It will be a time when everything will be accentuated with beauty and productivity. The moon will be so bright it will seem like the sun, and the sun will increase its radiant energy sevenfold. This will be the great day of prophecy when God will bind up the breach of his people and instantly heal their wounds.

27. Behold, the name of the LORD cometh from far, burning with his anger, and the burden thereof is heavy: his lips are full of indignation, and his tongue as a devouring fire:

But before all of these marvelous things can occur the earth must be cleansed and the wicked removed. This will be the age of cleansing fire. The people who have been warned for so long without any visible effect will find the burning anger of the Lord overflowing on every side and his lips speaking forth the words of indignation which have been restrained in him for so long. The words of his wrath will go forth like a devouring fire.

28. And his breath, as an overflowing stream, shall reach

This destruction will sweep through the enemies of God's people like an overflowing stream. It will reach to the midst of the neck, to sift the nations with the sieve of vanity: and there shall be a bridle in the jaws of the people, causing them to err.

clear up to their necks, threatening to drown them in its fury. It will sift the nations like a sieve, and all that are filled with vanity shall feel the rod of judgment. The furnace of tribulation will be such an affliction that it will be like a bridle in their jaws, causing them to thresh about in anguish so that an observer will consider that they "err," and behave foolishly.

29. Ye shall have a song, as in the night when a holy solemnity is kept; and gladness of heart, as when one goeth with a pipe to come into the mountain of the LORD, to the mighty One of Israel.

But for the righteous there will be a song of rejoicing and worship. They will feel drawn to new heights as though it were by the music of a flute. They will move toward the high place where the Lord can be found in his temple.

30. And the LORD shall cause his glorious voice to be heard, and shall shew the lighting down of his arm, with the indignation of his anger, and with the flame of a devouring fire, with scattering, and tempest, and hailstones.

The Lord will speak forth so the righteous can hear him. They will actually witness the flames of devouring consumption as the Lord issues his decrees of fiery judgment on the wicked. They will see the elements literally responding to his commands. Fire, tempest, and great hailstones will reap down those who have corrupted God's beautiful planet earth.

31. For through the voice of the LORD shall the Assyrian be beaten down, which smote with a rod.

The setting for all of this is the latter days, so the reference to the Assyrians should have the meaning of "Gentiles," or those who are foreign to the ways of God.

32. And in every place where the grounded staff shall pass, which the LORD shall lay upon him, it shall be

As the Lord completes his work of cleansing, there will be a festival of rejoicing among those who have suffered under wicked oppressors. The place of

with tabrets and harps: and in battles of shaking will he fight with it.

33. For Tophet is ordained of old; yea, for the king it is prepared; he hath made it deep and large: the pile thereof is fire and much wood; the breath of the LORD, like a stream of brimstone, doth kindle it.

Tophet, a heathen headquarters where abominations were practiced, will be prepared for a complete consumption of fiery devastation sent by the Lord.

Isaiah, Chapter 31

INTRODUCTION:

In the previous chapter the prophet had proclaimed the Lord's warning against alliances with Egypt, which was then being ruled by an Ethiopian. The Lord wanted Judah to know that if she remained quiet and did not mobilize her armies under an alliance with Egypt, she would not be attacked by the Assyrians who would soon be marching down to conquer Egypt.

In this chapter the Lord's message to Isaiah continues this theme.

1. Woe to them that go down to Egypt for help; and stay on horses, and trust in chariots, because they are many; and in horsemen, because they are very strong; but they look not unto the Holy One of Israel, neither seek the LORD!

When two mighty military forces are about to engage in open conflict, it is frightening to sit quietly on the sidelines. The natural inclination is to join whichever side seems to have the best chance of winning. Nevertheless, in this verse the Lord specifically warns Judah not to "go down to Egypt for help." Judah is not to rely on Egypt's famous cavalry of war horses and chariots which give the appearance of being such a mighty strength because of their numbers. Judah is warned that she will deeply regret it if she does not listen to "the Holy One of Israel" and abide by his counsel.

2. Yet he also is wise, and will bring evil, and will not call back his words: but will arise against the house of the evildoers, and against

Isaiah warns the people that the Lord is far wiser in judgment than either the general populace or their leaders. God has determined to bring down a flood of evil on the wicked nations of the earth. He will not

the help of them that work iniquity.

recall his decree, and this tide of destruction will fall not only on these wicked nations but upon any who become their allies and seek to become the "help of them that work iniquity."

3. Now the Egyptians are men, and not God; and their horses flesh, and not spirit. When the LORD shall stretch out his hand, both he that helpeth shall fall, and he that is holpen shall fall down, and they all shall fail together.

Sometimes human beings look upon strong armies and their leaders as invincible, almost as though they were godlike in their power and authority. The Lord says this is a grievous error. The Egyptians are merely men, not gods. Their horses are easily destroyed, for they are of mortal flesh and not indestructible spirit. The Lord says he is about to stretch out his hand to destroy these wicked people, and those who are trying to help them will go down in violent destruction at the same time.

4. For thus hath the LORD spoken unto me, Like as the lion and the young lion roaring on his prey, when a multitude of shepherds is called forth against him, he will not be afraid of their voice, nor abase himself for the noise of them: so shall the LORD of hosts come down to fight for mount Zion, and for the hill thereof.

Isaiah says the Lord has made a promise to Judah through his chosen prophet that if they will abide by his counsel, the Lord will protect them. Isaiah likens the power of the Lord with that of a young lion which has such amazing strength and courage when it is famished with hunger. Even in the presence of numerous shepherds with slings and arrows, it will charge into the flock and seize its prey. No amount of noise or threats can turn it aside. Isaiah says that in just such a manner will the Lord "come down to fight for Mount Zion, and for the hill thereof." Mount Zion was a high, fortress-like elevation which guarded the lower "hill" of Mount Moriah. After the temple was built on Mount Moriah it was decided to level Mount Zion so that it could not be used by the enemies of Judah to attack the temple mount from a higher elevation. The original Mount Zion was just south of where the temple esplanade stands today.

5. As birds flying, so will the LORD of hosts defend Jerusalem; defending also he will deliver it; and passing over he will preserve it.

Just as birds hover in the vicinity of their nests and fly menacingly toward anyone who comes near, so the Lord shall defend Jerusalem. Not only will he defend the capital city of Judah, but he will deliver the people from their enemies. It will be like the "passing over" in Egypt when God destroyed the firstborn of the Egyptians but preserved the firstborn of Israel.

6. Turn ye unto him from whom the children of Israel have deeply revolted.

Isaiah pleads with the people of Judah to turn to the mighty Jehovah, against whom the northern Ten Tribes of Israel previously rebelled. Just a little over 20 years earlier the Assyrians swept down on Israel (722–21 B.C.). They massacred thousands of the children of Israel and carried the remainder off into captivity. In 701 B.C. the Assyrian king, Sennacherib, is going to do the same thing to the Jews if they do not repent and hearken to the warning of the Lord.

7. For in that day every man shall cast away his idols of silver, and his idols of gold, which your own hands have made unto you for a sin.

As it turned out, when Sennacherib destroyed 46 cities of the Jews and threatened Jerusalem, the leaders of the people tried to pacify the Assyrian king with vast quantities of gold. We know that the king of the Jews at that time was Hezekiah, and that he not only took all of the silver out of the temple but even cut off the gold from the doors of that sacred building in an effort to pacify the Assyrians with tribute (see 2 Kings 18:15–16). In this verse we have the suggestion that the people will also be required to surrender or "cast away" any of their "idols of silver" and "idols of gold" to meet the requirements of the tribute.

8. Then shall the Assyrian fall with the sword, not of a

But it was not the tribute which stopped the Assyrians. They were not at all deterred by this fabulous

mighty man; and the sword, not of a mean man, shall devour him: but he shall flee from the sword, and his young men shall be discomfited.

collection of wealth. The Assyrians accepted the tribute but proceeded immediately to threaten Jerusalem with an all-out attack (see 2 Kings, chapter 18:17–35). However, the Lord said the Assyrians would "fall." The Lord said they would be killed, but not by the sword of a mighty man or even a mean (or lowly) man. Nevertheless, there would be such a slaughter of the Assyrians that their squadrons of young warriors would be "discomfited." They were actually slain by the sword of the Lord—185,000 of them! Here is the description of that event recorded in 2 Kings 19:35: "And it came to pass that night, that the angel of the Lord went out, and smote in the camp of the Assyrians an hundred fourscore and five thousand: and when they [the king and his young princes] arose early in the morning, behold, they were all dead corpses."

The "sword of the Lord" which struck down this mighty host appears to have been some kind of plague which destroyed most of this army in a single night. Sennacherib's young men were indeed "discomfited."

9. And he shall pass over to his strong hold for fear, and his princes shall be afraid of the ensign, saith the LORD, whose fire is in Zion, and his furnace in Jerusalem.

Isaiah predicted that the king of the Assyrians would immediately flee back to his "stronghold for fear." And this is precisely what happened. The scripture says, "So Sennacherib king of Assyria departed, and went and returned, and dwelt at Nineveh" (2 Kings 19:36).

Isaiah said the Assyrian princes would be terrified by the "ensign" or banner of Zion. They would look upon the destruction from the God of the Jews as a "fire" in Zion or a "furnace" of consuming devastation from Jerusalem.

Isaiah, Chapter 32

INTRODUCTION:

This chapter appears to be completely independent of any particular historical setting in Isaiah's day. It begins and ends with reference to conditions during the Millennium. In between, it refers to the terrible anguish of the people and the desolation of their promised land during the many centuries of wickedness and apostasy.

1. Behold, a king shall reign in righteousness, and princes shall rule in judgment.

During the messianic era or the Millennium, the true king of this earth will reign in righteousness. He will be assisted by princes or men endowed with the royal Priesthood who will rule the people honestly, affectionately, and justly.

2. And a man shall be as an hiding place from the wind, and a covert from the tempest; as rivers of water in a dry place, as the shadow of a great rock in a weary land.

The most precious commodity of any society is the blessing of good leaders. Nations rise and fall in terms of strong or weak leadership. There is nothing more disheartening to the people of a nation than to have judges who do not provide justice, administrators who are wasteful and inefficient, police who are lazy or corrupt, and public officials who are indolent and capricious. However, during the messianic era a man will be chosen for a position of leadership because he is a pillar of integrity and strength, a man of wisdom and good counsel. Such a man is like a shelter from the cruel winds of life. He is like a covering place in a tempest. He also may be likened unto a river or a spring in a dry desert. He might even be compared with a mighty rock which gives shelter to the weary traveler crossing a vast wilderness.

3. And the eyes of them that see shall not be dim, and the ears of them that hear shall hearken.

During the Millennium the people will perceive the goodness of God. When the Lord tells them to behold a certain thing, they will perceive it with clarity. When he speaks to them of righteousness and repentance they will hearken. What a contrast this will be compared to the wicked people in Isaiah's own day. Their eyes refused to see the most obvious facts all about them. Their hearing was so blunted to spiritual truths that Isaiah's words seemed to fall on ears suffering from deafness.

4. The heart also of the rash shall understand knowledge, and the tongue of the stammerers shall be ready to speak plainly.

Isaiah saw that during the Millennium those kinds of people who in his day were impetuous and "rash" would stop and listen to the Lord and his servants. He also saw that those who formerly were very timid or hesitant in their speech would be able to speak with clarity and plainness.

5. The vile person shall be no more called liberal, nor the churl said to be bountiful.

Isaiah also saw that during the messianic reign, the wicked and vile person would no longer be called a good or liberal person. Nor would the selfish and avaricious man be hailed as a generous and bountiful giver of gifts. In other words, each person will see as he is seen, and know as he is known (see D&C 76:94). It is amazing in our own day (as it was in the days of Isaiah) to see how many wicked and conniving men are hailed by the press and the public because of their extravagant and seemingly benevolent gifts to charitable foundations, art galleries, libraries, and sometimes even to the poor. However, a careful study of their lives will reveal that their methods of wringing their wealth from the people are often accompanied by trickery and deceit. Isaiah says that the so-called liberality of such men cannot be approved of God. These men cannot cover up their wickedness with a trickle of charity to a few "good causes." In contrast to such "vile" individuals there are the righteous rich. These are they who acquired their wealth through honest business practices and hard work, but share their wealth liberally, and often anonymously. These are the truly "liberal rich" whom the Lord loves. These are the only kind of rich who will be honored when the Messiah comes.

Note that Isaiah is equally critical of the "churl." Ordinarily we think of a churl as a peasant, but in this verse the original Hebrew word means "a miserly person." This is one of the more technical meanings of the word "churl." In the Millennium a miser will not be honored because of his abundant wealth, because he is not circulating it to do good. His wealth is lying dormant and dead in his money chest. There is nothing "bountiful" about a man who does this.

6. For the vile person will speak villany, and his heart will work iniquity, to practise hypocrisy, and to utter error against the LORD, to make empty the soul of the hungry, and he will cause the drink of the thirsty to fail.

Isaiah says, in effect, that if we obtain all the facts about a "vile" person we will find that he produces fruit which could be expected from a vile tree. He speaks "villainy," and his heart is set upon devices of iniquity. Many of the rich in modern times obtained their wealth by publishing pornographic literature, pushing addictive drugs, and exploiting immorality and vice. Others engaged in fraudulent business schemes. Many of these prey especially on the poor. All such villainy is a crime "against the Lord" and his law. Instead of being a blessing to society, such people are a curse. Their villainy takes from the poor their food and drink. It causes those who trust in them to fail.

7. The instruments also of the churl are evil: he deviseth wicked devices to destroy the poor with lying words, even when the needy speaketh right.

Isaiah says the "churl" or miserly person falls under the same condemnation. The devices by which he obtains and hoards his wealth are to deceive the poor with "get-rich-quick" schemes and other con games that he knows are fraudulent. He gets the poor to open their hearts and their meager pocketbooks by causing them to trust him and enter into contracts which they are led to believe will be mutually beneficial. Then the poor later find they have been betrayed and defrauded. Isaiah says such devices are a special evil because they induce the poor to enter into these schemes in good faith. In other words, the poor "speaketh right" when they participate, but the churl uses "lying words."

8. But the liberal deviseth liberal things; and by liberal things shall he stand.

Isaiah then points out how different it is with a person who is truly generous and liberal. His generosity is not tainted with trickery and deceit. He does not betray the poor, but helps them get out of their poverty. He does not take from them their meager fare, but aids them in acquiring the necessities of life and becoming established in jobs or in a business. In the Millennium such people who are truly "liberal" and wisely generous will stand before the public in their true greatness.

9. Rise up, ye women that are at ease; hear my voice, ye careless daughters; give ear unto my speech.

But that was enough for the moment on the theme of the Millennium. What Isaiah had to cope with were the indolent and idle rich of his own day. He said he wanted the wealthy, idle women to pay particular attention to what he is about to say. He called them "careless daughters" of the land who were wasting away their second estate and needed to repent.

10. Many days and years shall ye be troubled, ye careless

Isaiah had seen in vision that between his own day and the great messianic era of the latter days there

women: for the vintage shall fail, the gathering shall not come.

would be one generation after another engaged in wicked apostasy and violent war, and reveling in the abomination of desolation. He saw that much of this would be due to the carelessness and wickedness of God's chosen people. Isaiah believed the women could be a major influence to prevent this from happening if they felt inclined to do so. He said that if the women continued to be careless in their responsibilities of raising up righteous children and provoking their husbands to good works, the whole land would be cursed. There would be neither food nor drink for the people. The harvest would fail.

11. Tremble, ye women that are at ease; be troubled, ye careless ones: strip you, and make you bare, and gird sackcloth upon your loins.

As Isaiah reflected on the terrifying and ugly scenes which he had seen in vision, he felt compelled to cry out to the idle, careless women of his own day: "Tremble, ye women that are at ease; be troubled, ye careless ones." He was trying to shock them into a realization of the hazardous situation which would soon engulf them. He wanted them to cast aside their gaudy clothes and get to work so they could accomplish their mission in life. Instead of sitting around in their finery, he wanted them to gird on their work clothes of sackcloth and get involved.

12. They shall lament for the teats, for the pleasant fields, for the fruitful vine.

Isaiah emphasized the distress which would come upon them if they did not listen to his words. The milk for their children would fail, the abundance of their crops would disappear, and the fruit of the vine would not come forth.

13. Upon the land of my people shall come up thorns and

Isaiah described what he had seen in vision: "Upon the land of my people shall come up thorns and briers."

briers; yea, upon all the houses of joy in the joyous city:

Not only that, but he had also beheld the sorrow and lamentation of the people. Every household became a place of bitter sorrow instead of joy. Isaiah saw that the whole joyous city of Jerusalem would be turned to mourning and lamentation.

14. Because the palaces shall be forsaken; the multitude of the city shall be left; the forts and towers shall be for dens for ever, a joy of wild asses, a pasture of flocks;

Sometimes the rich think calamity will come only upon the poor, but Isaiah said he saw that the palaces of the rich would be abandoned and forsaken. He also saw that the multitude of the homes of the common people would be abandoned or "left." Even the great forts and towers which were on the Ophel, or the ancient city of David (a suburb of Jerusalem just below the temple mount), would be nothing more than a shelter for wild asses. All the surrounding vineyards and garden places would be nothing more than open grazing fields for goats and sheep.

15. Until the spirit be poured upon us from on high, and the wilderness be a fruitful field, and the fruitful field be counted for a forest.

But Isaiah could endure this part of the vision no longer. He therefore closed this chapter with six verses about the Millennium. He assured the people that after many generations of desolation the Spirit of God would be poured out upon the people and they would return to him so that he could bless them. He promised that in that beautiful era the wilderness of many centuries would become a fruitful field once more. In fact, the production would be so abundant that the fields would seem like "a forest" of thriving vines and orchards.

16. Then judgment shall dwell in the wilderness, and righteousness remain in the fruitful field.

In that day Isaiah saw that the wilderness would be overcome with "judgment," or wise, scientific procedures, and those who cultivated the land would do so in righteousness, which means hard, honest labor. Managers would not try to cheat their workers of their just wages, and workers would give an honest day's labor for the wages they received.

17. And the work of righteousness shall be peace; and the effect of righteousness quietness and assurance for ever.

In this vision the prophet beheld a marvelous vista of future happiness. Isaiah saw that when the people work together in righteousness there is no longer a desire to prey upon one another. Throughout the land there is peace. Everyone enjoys a quiet and peaceful existence with the full assurance that he will not be robbed, cheated, or deceived by those with whom he conducts his affairs.

18. And my people shall dwell in a peaceable habitation, and in sure dwellings, and in quiet resting places;

It is such a great blessing to "dwell in a peaceful habitation" where homes are not invaded nor crimes committed against those who live in them. Homes thereby become "sure dwellings" and are places of peaceful and quiet enjoyment.

19. When it shall hail, coming down on the forest; and the city shall be low in a low place.

In this verse, Isaiah seems to be seeing a city in the latter days which will be situated in a valley. In spite of hail and storm it will be protected. This location does not fit Jerusalem, but a modern apostle, Orson Pratt, believed Isaiah was contemplating the rise of God's people in the land of Zion (America) just prior to the Millennium. He visualizes a conversation with Isaiah, and says:

"Now let us see what Isaiah says about it, for he looked upon it as well as you, if he did live twenty-five hundred years ago. 'The Lord shall comfort Zion, he will make her wilderness like Eden, her desert like the garden of the Lord. Joy and gladness shall be found therein, thanksgiving and the voice of melody.' Indeed! Did you see it, Isaiah, as well as the people that live in our day? Did you see a people go into the desert and offer up thanksgiving and the voice of melody? Did you see that desert and wilderness redeemed from its sterile condition and become like the garden of Eden? 'O yes,' says Isaiah, 'I saw it all, and I left it on record for the benefit of the generation that should live some two or three thousand years after my day.' But Isaiah, are we to understand that the people are to be gathered together in that desert, and that the gathered people are to be instrumental in the hands of God, in redeeming that desert? Yes, Isaiah has told us all this. We will go back to what we read in his thirty-second chapter— 'Until the spirit be poured out upon us from on high, and the wilderness be a fruitful field, and the fruitful field be counted for a forest. Then judgment shall dwell in the wilderness and righteousness remain in the fruitful field.' What fruitful field? Why, the wilderness that will be converted into a fruitful field. 'The work of righteousness shall be peace, and the effect of righteousness, quietness, and assurance forever; and my people shall dwell in peaceable habitations, and in sure dwellings and in quiet resting places.'

"Was that the way we dwelt in Missouri or Illinois? Did we live in quietness and with assurance continually in those States? Oh, no, we were tossed about; as Isaiah says—'tossed to and fro and not comforted.' That was the case with Zion while down in the States, and that was in accordance with a modern revelation, in which, speaking of Zion, the Lord says—'You shall be persecuted from city to city and from synagogue to synagogue, and but few shall stand to receive their inheritance.' But when the time should come for Zion to go up into the wilderness things would be changed; then 'my people shall dwell in peaceable habitations, in sure dwelling places, and in quietness and assurance.'

"Will they have any capital city when they get up into the mountain desert? O, yes. Isaiah says here—'When it shall hail, coming down on the forest, the city shall be low in a low place.' How often have I thought of this since we laid out this great city, twenty-eight years ago! How often have this people reflected in their meditations upon the fulfillment of this prophecy! They have seen, on this eastern range of mountains and on the range of mountains to the west of this valley, snow and storms pelting down with great fury, as though winter in all its rigor and ferocity had overtaken the mountain territory, and at the same time, here, 'low in a low place,' was a city, organized at the very base of these mountains, enjoying all the blessings of a spring temperature, the blessings of a temperature not sufficient to cut off our vegetation. What a contrast! 'When it shall hail, coming down on the forest, the city shall be low in a low place.' That could not be Jerusalem, no such contrast in the land of Palestine round about Jerusalem! It had reference to the latter-day Zion, the Zion of the mountains." (Orson Pratt, in *Journal of Discourses*, 18:148–49.)

20. Blessed are ye that sow beside all waters, that send forth thither the feet of the ox and the ass.

As Isaiah saw the cultivating of luxurious fields and orchards with streams of water and canals to make them flourish, he exclaimed: "Blessed are ye that sow beside all waters, that send forth thither the feet of the ox and the ass." This last phrase undoubtedly has reference to the great ranches and grazing lands which would produce more cattle and domestic animals than perhaps at any time in history.

INTRODUCTION:

Because history tends to continually repeat itself, each of the prophecies in the scriptures must be carefully examined in terms of the specific event to which it refers. This chapter appears to be talking about the events described in 2 Kings, chapters 18 and 19.

After Sennacherib came down from Assyria in 701 B.C., he destroyed 46 cities of the Jews and threatened to demolish Jerusalem. The righteous king of the Jews at that time was Hezekiah, and when he saw what was happening he wrote to Sennacherib (who was then attacking the stronghold of Lachish) and offered to pay the ruthless Assyrian king whatever was necessary to get Sennacherib to depart out of the land. Sennacherib said he wanted 300 talents of silver and 30 talents of gold.

In order to provide this tribute, Hezekiah had to empty his own personal treasury and assemble the articles of precious metal found in the temple. In addition to this he cut off the gold which overlaid the carving on the doors of the temple, and also the gold plating on the two great pillars at the front of the temple. Nevertheless, all of this sacrifice and strenuous effort to pacify the Assyrian ruler was in vain.

After accepting the tribute, Sennacherib sent up a great host to threaten Jerusalem with total desolation. It was only when the Lord intervened and killed 185,000 of Sennacherib's soldiers in a single night that the Assyrian king abandoned his camp and all of the loot he had assembled. He fled in a panic with the remnants of his army back to the stronghold of Nineveh, his Assyrian capital (see 2 Kings 19:35–36).

If these facts are correlated with the words of Isaiah in this chapter, they seem to fit Isaiah's theme with exactness.

1. **Woe to thee that spoilest, and thou wast not spoiled; and dealest treacherously, and they dealt not treacherously with thee! when thou shalt cease to spoil, thou shalt be spoiled; and when thou shalt make an end to deal treacherously, they shall deal treacherously with thee.**

First Isaiah pronounces a "woe" upon the wicked king of Assyria who comes into this peaceful land to sack and loot the cities. The prophet reminds this ruler that no attempt has been made by the people of Judah to despoil his land, therefore the Lord has disclosed that when he finally departs from the land (after ruthlessly despoiling it), he will suddenly find himself despoiled. This undoubtedly refers to the fact that the Lord's plague, which killed 185,000 soldiers of the Assyrian troops in a single night, so completely terrified Sennacherib that he left his camp and all the spoils in it in order to flee back to Nineveh. No doubt the armies of Judah immediately gathered these abandoned spoils of Sennacherib unto themselves. Bible authorities deduct this from the fact that Hezekiah's treasury was overflowing with gold and other kinds of wealth almost immediately after Sennacherib departed (see 2 Kings 20:12–13).

2. **O LORD, be gracious unto us; we have waited for thee: be thou their arm every morning, our salvation also in the time of trouble.**

As Isaiah beheld the vision of the Jews being rescued from the terrifying threat of the Assyrians' assault, he cried out: "O Lord, be gracious unto us; WE HAVE WAITED FOR THEE!" He prayed that the Lord would continue to be the arm of strength for Judah each new day, and that the Lord would continue to rescue the people (at least for the sake of the righteous) in time of great trouble.

3. At the noise of the tumult the people fled; at the lifting up of thyself the nations were scattered.

When Sennacherib came into the land the people fled in all directions, seeking shelter in any available fortified place. However, after God stretched forth his mighty arm and displayed his divine power by striking dead 185,000 Assyrians in a single night, it was the nations which were represented in Sennacherib's powerful army who broke and fled in terror. Even the king departed in a panic, leaving behind him the spoils of this terrible war.

4. And your spoil shall be gathered like the gathering of the caterpiller: as the running to and fro of locusts shall he run upon them.

The spoils left behind by Sennacherib and his army became the Lord's. This allowed the people of righteous King Hezekiah of Judah to go forth and gather these riches together like caterpillars bringing in their food or like locusts devouring these riches that had been left behind. Isaiah saw that "he" (probably referring to King Hezekiah) and the people of Judah would "run upon" these treasures and carry them back up to Jerusalem to put in the king's royal treasury. This is all the more remarkable when it is recalled that previously this treasury had been completely emptied to meet the demands of Sennacherib for tribute. As we pointed out earlier, just a short time after Sennacherib departed, Hezekiah was able to show off to the visiting ambassadors from Babylon a great accumulation of "precious things, the silver, and the gold, and the spices, and the precious ointment, and all the house of his [jewels]" (2 Kings 20:13; read "jewels" for "armour").

5. The LORD is exalted; for he dwelleth on high: he hath filled Zion with judgment and righteousness.

All of these momentous events exalted the Lord in the eyes of the repentant Jews. Mount Zion of Jerusalem was once more a place of honest judgment and righteous living.

6. And wisdom and knowledge shall be the stability of thy times, and strength of salvation: the fear of the LORD is his treasure.

Isaiah makes the declaration that when wisdom, knowledge, and righteous living exist among the people, there is stability throughout these "times." This is the strength in a society which knows its salvation comes from the Lord. In fact, when the people "fear" the Lord and are anxious to be worthy of his blessings, this constitutes the "treasure" of the Lord. These are the conditions which cause rejoicing in heaven and allow the Lord to pour out blessings in abundance upon his people.

7. Behold, their valiant ones shall cry without: the ambassadors of peace shall weep bitterly.

This verse goes back to remind the people of their feelings prior to God's interventions and the destruction of the Assyrian army. He reminds them of their feelings of despondency when their "valiant" armies and their ambassadors found that Sennacherib was not going to keep his word. Sennacherib had accepted the tribute money from the Jews, but then he betrayed his promise and prepared to attack. It caused the ambassadors of peace who had entered into the negotiation between Hezekiah and Sennacherib to "weep bitterly."

8. The highways lie waste, the wayfaring man ceaseth: he hath broken the covenant, he hath despised the cities, he regardeth no man.

Under the desolating threat of an attack by the mighty hosts of Assyria, the highways between the various cities of Judah were useless to them. The business and traveling between the many cities of Judah came to a standstill. No one dared to venture forth. The astonishing message went forth that Sennacherib had "broken the covenant" of peace and showed his complete contempt for the welfare of the inhabited cities of Judah. He had no regard or sense of honor or obligation for any man, not even for King Hezekiah, who had completely fulfilled his covenant by paying the tribute.

9. **The earth mourneth and languisheth: Lebanon is ashamed and hewn down: Sharon is like a wilderness: and Bashan and Carmel shake off their fruits.**

Now the vision of Isaiah stretches down through the centuries as he beholds the great wickedness of the human family from generation to generation. He sees that "the earth mourneth and languisheth." He sees the hundreds of years when the fabulous forests and verdure of Lebanon will be hewn down. He sees that the fertile plains, valleys, and regions east of the Jordan River (Bashan) as well as the famous vineyards on Mount Carmel will produce no fruits.

10. **Now will I rise, saith the LORD; now will I be exalted now will I lift up myself.**

But as Isaiah contemplates the great messianic era (which he loved so much to dwell upon), he quotes the Lord as saying, "Now will I rise,...now will I be exalted; now will I lift up myself."

11. **Ye shall conceive chaff, ye shall bring forth stubble: your breath, as fire, shall devour you.**

Isaiah next addresses himself to the wicked nations of the latter days and says that the offspring of the wicked will be as chaff and without value. Their labors will produce nothing more than stubble, which is the withered stumps of plants that remain after a field has been harvested and burned. In fact, the Lord says the breath or spirit of the people will be like a consuming fire that will destroy them.

12. **And the people shall be as the burnings of lime: as thorns cut up shall they be burned in the fire.**

Isaiah saw that the consuming of the people would make them appear as though they had been burned in a lime pit. The fury of their consumption would be like a blistering conflagration similar to dried thorns which have been cut and piled together. The crackling flames leap toward the sky as though they are pouring forth from a roaring furnace.

13. Hear, ye that are far off, what I have done; and, ye that are near, acknowledge my might.

As in verse 10, Isaiah once more quotes the Lord, who says, "Hear, ye that are far off, what I have done; and, ye that are near, acknowledge my might." The Lord has great ambitions for his children, but he has always had great difficulty in getting them to pay attention to his directions and acknowledge his supremacy as the creator and ruler of the earth. Unless they do acknowledge his leadership and fear the consequences of wickedness and disobedience, he is unable to exalt them. His love for humanity is overwhelming, but the economy of heaven does not allow blessings to be poured out upon the wicked, nor can exaltation be granted to the rebellious. Hence the Lord earnestly urges all mankind to observe his work in the earth and the universal manifestation of his power and might which are displayed continually.

14. The sinners in Zion are afraid; fearfulness hath surprised the hypocrites. Who among us shall dwell with the devouring fire? who among us shall dwell with everlasting burnings?

As Isaiah beheld the vision of the latter days when the power of God's might would be revealed, he observed that the "sinners in Zion [were] afraid." He said a particularly heavy cloud of fearfulness would come over the "hypocrites." The dictionary says that a hypocrite is "a person who pretends to be what he is not; one who pretends to be better than he really is, or pious, virtuous, etc. without really being so." The Lord says that when he comes in glory he will show forth the vision of everything that has ever happened on this earth, one thousand years at a time. The life of each individual will be shown for all to see (D&C 88:108–110) except that which has been blotted out through repentance and the power of the Atonement; (see D&C 88:108–10). What anguish this moment of disclosure will be to the hypocrite who has deceived his family, his friends, and perhaps his church leaders by pretending piety when his personal life was one of wickedness. What a frightening experience it will be when he suddenly realizes that his whole deceitful life is about to be displayed in this vision for all to see!

Now Isaiah challenges the reader to answer a most urgent question. He asks, "Who among us shall dwell with the devouring fire? who among us shall dwell with everlasting burnings?" Until the Gospel was restored this passage was completely obscure. Now, however, we have a passage in a modern revelation which says, "The angels do not reside on a planet like this earth; but they reside in the PRESENCE OF GOD, ON A GLOBE LIKE A SEA OF GLASS AND FIRE, where all things for their glory are manifest, past, present, and future, and are continually before the Lord" (D&C 130:6–7; emphasis added). The Lord then goes on to say that when the earth is sanctified as a residence for those who attain a celestial glory it will also "be made like unto crystal" (D&C 130:9), or, in other words, "a globe like a sea of glass and fire" (D&C 130:7). What Isaiah is therefore asking is simply this: "Who among us is worthy to live in such a divine celestial home, where there will be devouring fire and everlasting burnings?" We might ask ourselves the same question!

15. He that walketh righteously, and speaketh uprightly; he that despiseth the gain of oppressions, that shaketh his hands from holding of bribes, that stoppeth his ears from hearing of blood, and shutteth his eyes from seeing evil;

Isaiah immediately answers his own question by saying that the only type of person who will be able to inherit and endure the glories of the celestial kingdom will be "he that walketh righteously, and speaketh uprightly; he that despiseth the gain of oppressions, that shaketh his hands [or withdraws his hands] from holding of bribes, that stoppeth his ears from hearing of blood [or murder plots by which he might get gain], and shutteth his eyes from seeing evil." Some people lust to see evil. They revel in obscenities and pornographic literature They seek out the part of the city where there are lewd women and various forms of degradation. Unless they repent, none of these will see the glorious kingdom where God dwells.

16. He shall dwell on high: his place of defence shall be the munitions of rocks: bread shall be given him; his waters, shall be sure.

Not only will the person "that walketh righteously, and speaketh uprightly" be blessed in the next world, but he will enjoy special blessings in this life as well. As Isaiah contemplates the last days (which he discusses during the remaining verses of this chapter), he sees that the righteous of the last dispensation will occupy "high" places where they will be protected by the "munitions of rocks," and where they will be secure because they will be blessed with food. Their fields and flocks will have "waters" which "shall be sure."

Now that the Gospel has been restored and the great dispensation of the fulness of times ushered in, we see the headquarters of the Church established in the tops of the Rocky Mountains where there is a security in "the munitions of rocks," and where the precious waters of mountain streams and lakes provide the moisture which makes it a secure place for raising food and flocks.

17. Thine eyes shall see the king in his beauty: they shall behold the land that is very far off.

These righteous followers of God in the latter days will have the marvelous privilege of seeing the "king in his beauty," the Messiah. Isaiah says these are the ones who "see" and inherit that marvelous land which he has beheld and which "is very far off." In Isaiah 18:1, the prophet called this far-distant land of America "the land shadowing with wings, which is beyond the rivers of Ethiopia," or in other words, beyond Africa, the most distant land known to the people in Isaiah's day.

18. Thine heart shall meditate terror. Where is the scribe? where is the receiver? where is he that counted the towers?

The righteous of the latter days will meditate on the terror which is being spread over most of the earth as the abomination of desolation consumes the wicked in what would seem to be nuclear warfare (see Joel, chapter 2), but Isaiah saw the vision of blessed security which will be enjoyed by the righteous in Zion. As he contemplated that day which will come with the redemption of Zion he declared, "Where is the scribe [who tallies the wealth of the people for heavy taxation]? where is the receiver [who gathers up the tribute from conquered peoples]? where is he that counted the towers [the spy of the enemy who determines the defenses of the people in their stronghold]?" (See Clarke, *Commentary*, 4:140.)

19. Thou shalt not see a fierce people, a people of a deeper speech than thou canst perceive; of a stammering tongue, that thou canst not understand.

When Zion is redeemed, Isaiah beheld that there will be no "fierce people" coming into the land as conquerors. Nor will there be alien enemies from distant continents and empires sweeping in upon the righteous with their foreign language which the people of Zion cannot understand.

20. Look upon Zion, the city of our solemnities: thine eyes shall see Jerusalem a quiet habitation, a tabernacle that shall not be taken down; not one of the stakes thereof shall ever be removed, neither shall any of the cords thereof be broken.

Isaiah knew that when the reign of the Messiah is finally established there will be two great capitals, the New Jerusalem in America (which he often calls Zion) and the refurbished Old Jerusalem in Palestine (which is also referred to on occasion as a Zion). In this verse Isaiah invites us to look upon the great Zion of the latter days which he is seeing in vision. It is the great center from which "shall go forth the law" during the Millennium (Isaiah 2:3). The righteous will also see the famous, ancient city of Jerusalem (from which will emanate "the word of the Lord"; Isaiah 2:3). It will no longer be a center of war and plunder, but will be "a quiet habitation," a sanctuary where the tabernacle or temple of the Lord will never be taken down or destroyed again. He also saw that from this time forward none of the "stakes" of the Church would be removed or its "cords" broken, which connect each of them to the headquarters in Zion. It is interesting that Isaiah would have known by revelation that the organizational precincts of the Church in the latter days would be called stakes. He likens these to the tent stakes to which cords are fastened and which anchor and stabilize the canopy or tent of Zion. In one of his songs concerning the latter days, Isaiah cries out, "Enlarge the place of thy tent, and let them stretch forth the curtains of thine habitations: spare not, lengthen thy cords, and strengthen thy STAKES" (Isaiah 54:2; emphasis added). During the great trials and tribulations just preceding the Millennium, the stakes of the Church will perhaps undergo some dislocation and perhaps even an uprooting in some areas. Nevertheless, Isaiah saw that when the reign of the Messiah becomes established, not one of the stakes will thereafter be removed nor its connecting cords to the center stake of Zion broken asunder.

21. But there the glorious LORD will be unto us a place of broad rivers and streams; wherein shall go no galley with oars, neither shall gallant ship pass thereby.

Isaiah saw that the two centers of "Zion" established by the Lord during the Millennium will be places of broad rivers and streams. He saw that "no galley with oars" (warships) nor other "gallant ship" will come by these sacred places to molest the Saints of God.

22. For the LORD is our judge, the LORD is our lawgiver, the LORD is our king; he will save us.

In that blessed day of the future, Isaiah beheld that the supreme judge of the Saints will be the Lord himself. He will also be their great legislator, or lawgiver. He will be the righteous ruler of the people, and he will save them from any predatory enemy who seeks to destroy them. Further, he will be the means by which the righteous will be saved and exalted in the future kingdom of glory.

23. **Thy tacklings are loosed; they could not well strengthen their mast, they could not spread the sail: then is the prey of a great spoil divided; the lame take the prey.**

As Isaiah beheld the foes of the righteous seeking to overthrow them, he saw that their "tacklings [were] loosed." It would be as though their great ropes were hanging loose so that their ship would be impossible to manage. It would be difficult for them to maintain their "mast" or the mainsail in a strong position. Consequently, they would not be able to "spread the sail" and get their venture of conquest going. Their situation would become so hopeless that the weakest of the people of Zion would be able to "take the prey" and divide the "great spoil" which they will capture.

24. **And the inhabitant shall not say, I am sick: the people that dwell therein shall be forgiven their iniquity.**

The people who dwell in the stakes of Zion in that blessed day of the future will not complain of illness because they will enjoy radiant health. They will know they are blessed because they have gained forgiveness for their sins.

INTRODUCTION:

At regular intervals Isaiah returns to the theme of the great day of God's judgment. The vision of it was fascinating to Isaiah and yet horrible to contemplate. Nevertheless, he knew that it would all come to pass some time after the end of the six thousand years of human history (see Revelation, chapter 8).

1. Come near, ye nations, to hear; and hearken, ye people: let the earth hear, and all that is therein; the world, and all things that come forth of it.

God's warning in the last days is not just to Israel, or to Judah, or to any certain nation, but to all nations of the whole earth. What Isaiah saw in vision was so vast that he applied the Lord's warning to the plants, the animals, to mankind, and even to the very planet itself "and all things that come forth of it." The Lord's introduction to his book of revelations in modern times begins with seven verses of universal application similar to this first verse (see D&C 1:1-7).

2. For the indignation of the LORD is upon all nations, and his fury upon all their armies: he hath utterly destroyed them, he hath delivered them to the slaughter.

Isaiah saw that in the latter days when the great abomination of desolation would sweep across the earth, it would engage the armies of every wicked nation in violent turmoil. Joel saw that this great destruction of mankind would involve weapons of fire. Speaking of a day when the coming of the Lord "is nigh at hand," Joel says: "A day of darkness and of gloominess,...a great people and a strong; there hath not been ever the like, neither shall be any more after it, even to the years of many generations. A FIRE

DEVOURETH BEFORE THEM; and behind them a FLAME burneth: the land is as the garden of Eden before them, and behind them a desolate wilderness; yea, and nothing shall escape them." (Joel 2:1-3; emphasis added.) Then Joel goes on to describe these modern armies which fight with fire. As Isaiah saw the vision of it he could not help but exclaim, "For the indignation of the Lord is upon ALL NATIONS, and his fury upon all their armies: he hath utterly destroyed them, he hath delivered them to the slaughter." In Isaiah 4:2-3 he described what a great blessing it would be for the few who would be left alive to enjoy the glorious Millennium which would follow the cleansing of the earth. (see Isaiah 4 2-3). He said there would be a great depopulation of the earth and "few men left." (Isaiah 24:6).

3. Their slain also shall be cast out, and their stink shall come up out of their carcases, and the mountains shall be melted with their blood.

Isaiah knew that not only would the great armies of warring nations destroy one another with fire, but the Lord would also make bare his mighty arm and display his vengeful power in the very elements of the earth. In a later chapter, Isaiah described the changes in the earth's surface that will take place just before the Millennium. He said, "Every valley shall be exalted, and every mountain and hill shall be made low: and the crooked shall be made straight, and the rough places plain" (Isaiah 40:4). No doubt many of those mountains and high places will be covered with the armies of the warring nations, and perhaps with vast numbers of civilians trying to escape from the burning cities on the plains. As the high mountains and hills sink to a more or less common level, Isaiah saw that there would be a terrible destruction of human life. It would be almost as though "the mountains" were "melted with their blood."

4. And all the host of heaven shall be dissolved, and the heavens shall be rolled together as a scroll: and all their hosts shall fall down, as the leaf falleth off from the vine, and as a falling fig from the fig tree.

The convulsions of nature will extend even to the cosmic universe. The sun will be darkened and the moon turned to blood (see Joel 2:31; D&C 88:87). The earth will "tremble and reel to and fro as a drunken man; . . . and the stars shall become exceedingly angry, and shall cast themselves down as a fig that falleth from off a fig tree" (D&C 88:87). No doubt Isaiah is referring to this phenomenon when he describes the "host of heaven" or stars of heaven being "dissolved" and falling from their places in the constellations like leaves falling from a tree. What will actually occur is, that the EARTH "shall remove out of her place" (Isaiah 13:13) and hasten faster than the speed of light back toward Kolob, where the earth was first created. As Brigham Young said: "When the earth was framed and brought into existence and man was placed upon it, it was near the throne of our Father in heaven. And when man fell, . . . the earth fell into space, and took up its abode in this planetary system, and the sun became our light. . . . This is the glory the earth came from, and when it is glorified IT WILL RETURN AGAIN UNTO THE PRESENCE OF THE FATHER." (*Journal of Discourses,* 17:143; emphasis added.) Abraham was also shown that prior to the fall the earth was operating on a time schedule controlled by Kolob, and it did not acquire its present speed of rotating every 24 hours until after the fall (see Abraham 5:13). Not only will the stars seem to be falling as they hurtle past the earth on its way to Kolob, but "the heavens shall be rolled together as a scroll." This is probably referring to the Second Coming, which is described in similar language in a modern revelation where the Lord says that after all the terrible confusion and frightening experiences, "there shall be silence in heaven for the space of half an hour; and immediately after shall the curtain of heaven be unfolded, as a scroll is unfolded after it is rolled up,

AND THE FACE OF THE LORD SHALL BE UNVEILED"
(D&C 88:95; emphasis added). What a glorious
moment that will be!

5. For my sword shall be bathed in heaven: behold, it shall come down upon Idumea, and upon the people of my curse, to judgment.

Meanwhile, Isaiah goes back to the Lord's judgment which will pour down upon the wicked. Even now his mighty sword of vengeance is sweeping through the heavens ready to fall upon the millions of depraved human beings whose wickedness he has endured until the cup of his indignation is nearly overflowing. Isaiah saw that mighty sword of judgment flash down across the whole face of the world. "Idumea" was both a place and a symbol. It is another word for Edom meaning "red" (William Smith, *A Dictionary of the Bible*, rev. ed. [Grand Rapids, Mich: Zondervan Publishing House, 1948], s.v. "Edom, . . . or Idumea"). Esau ("hairy"), who was covered with red hair when he was born (Genesis 25:25), was later called Edom (Genesis 25:30). Esau's descendants occupied the Arabah valley extending from the Dead Sea to the Aqaba Gulf of the Red Sea. They were called Edomites, and because they occupied the Arabah valley and afterwards spread over much of the vast deserts of the region, they were known as the Arabs (of Arabah valley). So Arabah, Edom, or Idumea became a symbol of worldly things or the "Gentile" world. Therefore, when the Lord says his sword "shall come down upon Idumea, and upon the people of my curse, to judgment," he is talking about the wicked of the world in general and of the land of Idumea in particular.

6. The sword of the LORD is filled with blood, it is made fat with fatness, and with the blood of lambs and goats, with the fat of the kidneys of rams: for the

The terrible destruction of the wicked is the price they are required to pay for their multitude of murders, their killing of the prophets who came to warn them, their immorality and depravity which they practiced with wanton abandon. The sacrifice of their

> LORD hath a sacrifice in Bozrah, and a great slaughter in the land of Idumea.

wicked lives is a token of penance for all of the evil they have inflicted on one another. Referring directly to the people in the land of Idumea, the Lord says all their flocks shall be destroyed. The Edomites had never sacrificed to the Lord properly, and therefore Isaiah states that the destruction of all of these flocks in the latter days is like a great sacrifice to the Lord at Bozrah, the fortified capital of Idumea or Edom.

> 7. And the unicorns shall come down with them, and the bullocks with the bulls; and their land shall be soaked with blood, and their dust made fat with fatness.

The Lord speaks of this great destruction as though wild beasts were sweeping down upon the wicked. The "unicorn" is thought by some to mean the one-horned creature in Greek and Roman mythology. However, authorities point out that the unicorn in the Bible had two horns. In fact, these two horns were represented in the blessing given to Joseph as being the two great tribes who would descend from Joseph—Ephraim and Manasseh. (See English translation of original Hebrew of Deuteronomy 33:17 with commentary in Francis Nathan Peloubet, *Peloubet's Bible Dictionary* [Philadelphia: John C. Winston Company, 1925], s.v. "unicorn.")

Modern scholars generally agree that the "unicorn" which appears in the Bible seven times is referring to the ferocious wild ox. The bulls of this breed as well as the young bullocks were of a mean disposition and would attack at the slightest provocation. These animals were very large and are believed to have been the aurochs, which are now extinct. Caesar describes them as "uri" in his day and says: "These uri are scarcely less than elephants in size, but in their nature, color and form are bulls. Great is their strength and great their speed; they spare neither man nor beast when once they have caught sight of them." (*Bell. Gall.* vi. 28, cited by Peloubet.) All of this fits Isaiah's use of the word "unicorn" perfectly.

8. For it is the day of the LORD's vengeance, and the year of recompences for the controversy of Zion.

The Lord is a God of love, but he is also a God of justice. When Jesus was ministering among the Jews he said the debauchery and depravity of the human race just before the day of judgment would be as terrible as it was in the days of Noah (see Matthew 24:37; Luke 17:26; and Joseph Smith—Matthew 1:41). All this wickedness will occur right at the time the Lord is attempting to set up the great sanctuary of "Zion"— [meaning] "the pure in heart" (D&C 97:21). Naturally the wicked will have a great "controversy" against Zion (and the righteous wherever they are found among the wicked). In fact, this will be a time when there will be a great persecution of the Saints of God by the secret combinations of wicked men (see Ether 8:23-25). Therefore "the day of the Lord's vengeance" will be like a "year of recompences" for the flood of persecution which the wicked have inflicted upon the Saints of Zion.

9. And the streams thereof shall be turned into pitch, and the dust thereof into brimstone, and the land thereof shall become burning pitch.

Because the day of the Lord's judgment will be a time of great destruction by fire, it would be natural for the wicked to flee to their sanctuaries where there is water and they can feel safe. However, the Lord says there will be no sanctuaries in that day for these evil multitudes. He says that "the streams thereof shall be turned into pitch [asphalt or tar], and the dust thereof into brimstone, and the land thereof shall become become burning pitch." When the prophet Malachi saw it he said, "For, behold, the day cometh, that shall burn as an oven; and all the proud, yea, and all that do wickedly, shall be stubble: and the day that cometh shall burn them up, saith the Lord of hosts, that it shall leave them neither root nor branch" (Malachi 4:1).

10. It shall not be quenched night nor day; the smoke thereof shall go up for ever: from generation to generation it shall lie waste; none shall pass through it for ever and ever.

All of this will be particularly true in that region which was known to the people of Isaiah's day as Arabah, Edom, or Idumea. It would appear that even during the Millennium this region will remain a desert wilderness to remind humanity of the past wages of sin among its former inhabitants. The Lord says that from generation to generation it will remain "waste." No traveler shall wish to pass through it.

11. But the cormorant and the bittern shall possess it; the owl also and the raven shall dwell in it: and he shall stretch out upon it the line of confusion, and the stones of emptiness.

In fact, its only inhabitants will be the cormorant (hawk) and the bittern (heron) along with the owl and the raven. All across the horizon will be a vista of desolate and broken terrain. Nothing will exist there but "confusion, and the stones of emptiness."

12. They shall call the nobles thereof to the kingdom, but none shall be there, and all her princes shall be nothing.

If anyone goes through this land seeking the former nobles and princes, he will find none. They will all have disappeared.

13. And thorns shall come up in her palaces, nettles and brambles in the fortresses thereof: and it shall be an habitation of dragons, and a court for owls.

Here is one of Isaiah's brilliant, descriptive passages that is so eloquently stated in the original Hebrew. He says there will be weeds, briars, and thorns growing up in the magnificent palaces of wicked Edom. These mighty strongholds of the past will be haunted skeletons of their former grandeur, with nothing but lizards running about their vaulted halls. Instead of ladies in beautiful gowns and courtly nobles walking the marble terraces, there will be nothing but "a court for owls"!

14. The wild beasts of the desert shall also meet with the wild beasts of the island, and the satyr shall cry to his fellow; the screech owl also shall rest there, and find for herself a place of rest.

These ancient citadels which once knew such wealth and grandeur will be nothing more than meeting places for "the wild beasts of the desert" (literally, mountain cats), and "the wild beasts of the island" (thought to mean jackals). The satyr (probably the wild he-goat) will bleat out his call to other satyrs, and the screech owl will make its nest there.

15. There shall the great owl make her nest, and lay, and hatch, and gather under her shadow: there shall the vultures also be gathered, every one with her mate.

The desolated cities of this region will become the permanent habitation of huge owls, and the scavenger of the desert—the vulture—will also be found there with its mate.

16. Seek ye out of the book of the LORD, and read: no one of these shall fail, none shall want her mate: for my mouth it hath commanded, and his spirit it hath gathered them.

17. And he hath cast the lot for them, and his hand hath divided it unto them by line: they shall possess it for ever, from generation to generation shall they dwell therein.

Isaiah urges the reader to search the various scriptures, where he will find that these prophecies are not unique. They have been repeated many times. He has said nothing except that which the Lord has commanded him to say. All of these doleful creatures, which he has described as inhabiting this land, will be brought there by a spirit of gathering from the Lord. And because the rest of the earth will be so fruitful and verdant, this region will be a grim reminder of what happened to the wicked before the Millennium began. Apparently that is why the Lord will want this one territory to remain a wilderness. It will be a historical teaching aid for those who will be born from generation to generation during the Millennium.

Isaiah, Chapter 35

INTRODUCTION:

After reading about the inferno of destruction in chapter 34 (which will accompany God's judgment on the wicked), one cannot help but ask what will happen to the righteous during this period. Fortunately, the Lord intends to prepare certain "holy places" (D&C 45:32; 87:8; 101:22, 64) to which the righteous can flee for protection and thereby escape the calamities which will pour down upon the wicked In chapter 35 Isaiah describes the great gathering of the last days when Zion will be established and a place of refuge provided for those who love God.

1. The wilderness and the solitary place shall be glad for them; and the desert shall rejoice, and blossom as the rose.

We now know from modern scriptures that the Lord intends to fulfill this prophecy in each of the places where the Lord's people will be gathered for safety. It has been fulfilled to an amazing extent in the tops of the Rocky Mountains, where there was frost every month of the year until the Saints began to gather there. Gradually the seasons changed. When water was spread out across the mountain valley floors through canals and irrigation streams, the crops of the people flourished. General Authorities have frequently quoted this verse as being literally fulfilled by the great changes which have taken place as the modern Saints have settled the valleys of the Rockies and the desolate places of the desert regions.

A modern revelation declares that this verse will be literally fulfilled again when the lost Ten Tribes are gathered to America (see D&C 133:26–29).

It will be fulfilled in the same literal sense for the Lamanites as they receive the Gospel and return to the worship of their Savior (see D&C 49:24).

2. It shall blossom abundantly, and rejoice even with joy and singing: the glory of Lebanon shall be given unto it, the excellency of Carmel and Sharon, they shall see the glory of the LORD, and the excellency of our God.

Here Isaiah assures us that the first verse also applies to the region of ancient Palestine that has been dedicated by modern apostles for the return of the Jews. The first dedication was on October 24, 1841, but there have been five subsequent dedications in which the modern Saints have petitioned the Lord to expedite his great work in that land. Today, we see the promises in this verse beginning to be literally fulfilled. The glory of Lebanon was once its mighty forests. Here Isaiah promises that the former glory of Lebanon will be restored. Mount Carmel was the former delight of Elijah and Elisha. It is a mountain range extending from the Mediterranean Sea inland along the southern border of the Jezreel Valley. It has many springs and an abundance of trees, flowers, and small plants. Just a few years ago the plains of Sharon along the Mediterranean coast were swamps. The millions of tons of fine silt which had been washed into the Mediterranean by the Nile River were carried by the tides onto the shores of the beaches of what is today called Israel. This red silt built up huge sand dunes that prevented the streams coming down from the mountains of Judah and Ephraim from draining into the Mediterranean Sea. Consequently, the plains of Sharon became huge swamps. Today, however, they have been drained. Conduits have been cut through the sand dunes to allow the water to escape. As a result, the beautiful plains of Sharon have been restored to their original productivity. This is now one of the richest regions for raising vegetables and citrus fruits in the entire Middle East. Its products are shipped to practically every nation in Europe.

3. Strengthen ye the weak hands, and confirm the feeble knees.

Nevertheless, Isaiah could see from his vision of the latter days that the gathering of the Lord's people, either to Zion in America or to Old Jerusalem in Israel, would be most difficult. For some it would be well-nigh impossible. Therefore, Isaiah cried out to those who seemed to have greater strength, both spiritually and physically: "Strengthen ye the weak hands, and confirm [or sustain] the feeble knees." One of the most significant characteristics of the movement of the Saints from New York to Ohio, from Ohio to Missouri, from Missouri to Illinois, and from Illinois to the Rocky Mountains was the most earnest concern of the leaders of the Church for the welfare of the poor and the weak. During each move tremendous exertions were made by the more able to help those who otherwise would have been left behind.

4. Say to them that are of a fearful heart, Be strong, fear not: behold, your God will come with vengeance, even God with a recompence; he will come and save you.

One of the most frightening things connected with the great persecution of the people of God in the latter days has been the fact that they seemed to have been forsaken by their Heavenly Father. They could not conceive of his allowing such terrible calamities to be heaped upon them. Even the Prophet Joseph Smith became frightened and disheartened while he was in Liberty Jail, and cried out, "O God, where art thou?" (D&C 121:1). The Lord answered: "My son, peace be unto thy soul; thine adversity and thine afflictions shall be but a small moment; and then, if thou endure it well, God shall exalt thee on high; thou shalt triumph over all thy foes" (D&C 121:7-8). It is said that after this revelation, Joseph never faltered again. It was just such things as this that led Isaiah to plead with the people of God in the latter days to help each other, to strengthen each other with the assurance that God would sweep down on the wicked in due time. Isaiah says their enemies will receive a full "recompence" for all the evil they have done to God's people. The Saints can be assured that in the due time of the Lord he will come and save them.

5. Then the eyes of the blind shall be opened, and the ears of the deaf shall be unstopped.

Wherever and whenever the Savior comes into direct contact with the righteous, marvelous things begin to happen. He is a Lord of miracles. The eyes of the blind are made to see, while the ears of the deaf are made to hear. Also, eyes that were spiritually blind are made to perceive and understand that which was formerly a mystery to them. Those who were dull of hearing in a spiritual sense and had no interest in the Gospel, or the good news of the Restoration, suddenly find themselves becoming intensely interested. This has happened whenever the Savior has ministered to the people. It was true in New Testament times. Jesus quoted this verse from Isaiah to prove to the disciples of John that he was indeed the Messiah (see Matthew 11:2-5). He performed similar miracles when he appeared as a glorified, resurrected being among the Nephites (see 3 Nephi 17:5-10).

6. Then shall the lame man leap as an hart, and the tongue of the dumb sing: for in the wilderness shall waters break out, and streams in the desert.

In the latter days, Isaiah saw that great miracles would again occur. The lame man would be healed and leap about in joy as though he were a "hart" (a male deer). He saw that the dumb would be equally blessed so that they would regain their faculty of speech and be able to sing out their praises to God. He saw that there would be many things for which the people would be thankful and joyful. In the wilderness, or desert, there would be gushing springs of living water so that streams would appear in the desert to give nourishment to crops and flocks.

7. And the parched ground shall become a pool, and the thirsty land springs of water: in the habitation of dragons, where each lay, shall be grass with reeds and rushes.

People will be astonished to see how the terrain will change when the Lord begins to bless the desert places. Ancient lake beds and parched, cracked ground will begin to fill up with water as pools and small lakes are formed again. Regions where there once lived only lizards and wild creatures of the desert will be lagoons of precious water where grass, reeds, and rushes will thrive.

8. And an highway shall be there, and a way, and it shall be called The way of holiness; the unclean shall not pass over it; but it shall be for those: the wayfaring men, though fools, shall not err therein.

Now, all that we have described above will be incidental to one of the greatest miracles of all. It will consist of mighty changes on the surface of the earth and a great highway suddenly appearing "in the midst of the great deep" by which the lost tribes can gather to America to receive their blessings at the hands of the children of Ephraim. Isaiah calls this highway "The way of holiness." He emphasizes that no unclean thing can pass over it. This sacred thoroughfare will be exclusively for those who are acceptable to the Lord and are hastening to the temples of Zion to receive their endowments. In a modern revelation the Lord sets forth the details of the time and circumstances when this great miracle will occur. We read:

"He shall command the great deep, and it shall be driven back into the north countries, and the islands shall become one land;

"And the land of Jerusalem and the land of Zion shall be turned back into their own place, and the earth shall be like as it was in the days before it was divided.

"And the Lord, even the Savior, shall stand in the midst of his people, and shall reign over all flesh.

"And they who are in the north countries shall come in remembrance before the Lord; and their prophets shall hear his voice, and shall no longer stay themselves; and they shall smite the rocks, and the ice shall flow down at their presence.

"And an highway shall be cast up in the midst of the great deep.

"Their enemies shall become a prey unto them,

"And in the barren deserts there shall come forth pools of living water; and the parched ground shall no longer be a thirsty land.

"And they shall bring forth their rich treasures unto the children of Ephraim, my servants.

"And the boundaries of the everlasting hills shall tremble at their presence.

"And there shall they fall down and be crowned with glory, even in Zion, by the hands of the servants of the Lord, even the children of Ephraim.

"And they shall be filled with songs of everlasting joy." (D&C 133:23-33.)

It is obvious from this scripture that the rejoining of the continents and the raising up of a mighty highway "in the midst of the great deep" will be an astonishing series of events. Jeremiah said these miraculous occurrences will be so monumental that people will no longer refer to the miracles which occurred when Moses crossed the Red Sea but they will point to the phenomenal events which will have occurred in connection with the return of the lost Ten Tribes from "the land of the north" (Jeremiah 16:14-15).

It will be observed that the highway or "The way of holiness" which God will raise up is described as being "in the midst of the great deep." We would naturally assume that this refers to the ocean seas, but there is a possibility that it might refer to the "great deep" of outer space. At least that possibility should be kept in mind because the Lord told his apostles that he would gather his people not only from every part of the earth but "from one end of heaven to the other" (Joseph

Smith—Matthew 1:37). We also notice that the Lord sometimes refers to the Jews as being "dispersed" among the various nations of the earth, but the lost Ten Tribes as being "outcasts" (Isaiah 11:12; 2 Nephi 21:12). We also hear the prophet of the Lord saying in Isaiah 11:16, "And there shall be an highway for the remnant of his people,... LIKE AS IT WAS TO ISRAEL IN THE DAY THAT HE CAME UP OUT OF THE LAND OF EGYPT" (emphasis added). This might suggest that the highway is going to be raised up in the midst of a great body of water. In either case, we might keep both possibilities in mind as we wait for these mighty events of the future to unfold.

A final note on this subject from Isaiah 35:8 is interesting. Isaiah said "The way of holiness" which God will raise up in the midst of the great deep will be such that even the most weak and foolish who travel it will be able to arrive safely in Zion. Isaiah said that no one will be able to wander off and get lost or "err therein."

9. No lion shall be there, nor any ravenous beast shall go up thereon, it shall not be found there; but the redeemed shall walk there:

This highway will be completely safe to travel. There will be no lion there or any wild beasts to prey upon the people. Nor will there be robbers or thieves. Only those whom the Lord considers "redeemed" will be allowed to "walk there."

10. And the ransomed of the LORD shall return, and come to Zion with songs and everlasting joy upon their heads: they shall obtain joy and gladness, and sorrow and sighing shall flee away.

Isaiah says the triumphant pilgrims who return to Zion on this mighty, miraculous highway will be those whom the Lord has "ransomed" or brought under his Atonement through repentance, baptism, and the confirming spirit of the Holy Ghost.

As one might expect, these pilgrims will sing out their songs of everlasting joy as they troop to Zion. They will bring their "rich treasures" (D&C 133:30), and also their history and scriptures that will describe the ministry of Christ among them nearly 2,000 years ago (see 2 Nephi 29:13-14; 3 Nephi 16:1-3; 17:4).

During a conference of the Church in June 1831, Joseph Smith stated that "John the Revelator was then among the ten tribes of Israel" and was working "to prepare them for their return from their long dispersion" (*History of the Church,* 1:176n).

Isaiah, Chapter 36

INTRODUCTION:

It will be recalled that in 722–21 B.C. the Assyrian armies had conquered the northern Ten Tribes of Israel and carried the remnant off to their own kingdom. Now, in 701 B.C., the son of the man who conquered the Ten Tribes is determined to conquer Judah because she is an ally of Egypt, and the Assyrians did not dare to make their all-out attack on Egypt until Judah had been subdued. The king of Assyria at this time was named SENNACHERIB (pronounced Sen-NACK-er-eeb). As we have mentioned earlier, Sennacherib conquered 46 walled cities of Judah before he prepared to attack the capital city of Jerusalem (see *Interpreter's Bible*, 5:362).

The events in this chapter will also be found in 2 Kings, chapters 18-19, and 2 Chronicles, chapter 32. Because Isaiah chapters 36 to 39 are historical in nature, it is possible that the scribes inserted these chapters in the book of Isaiah because they contain five of Isaiah's great prophecies that were all literally fulfilled. But on the other hand, Isaiah himself wrote a history of the kings during his days (see 2 Chronicles 32:32), and the scribes may have taken these four chapters from Isaiah's own writings to put in 2 Kings and 2 Chronicles. In any event, these chapters refer to Isaiah in the third person as though someone else were writing about Isaiah rather than Isaiah writing about himself. When the Lord reveals all of the writings of Isaiah, along with all of the other scriptural records, we will know for certain the correct source of these four chapters.

1. Now it came to pass in the fourteenth year of king Hezekiah, that Sennacherib king of Assyria came up against all the defenced cities of Judah, and took them.

It is generally agreed that the fourteenth year of Hezekiah's reign was 701 B.C. The terrible devastation of the cities of Judah during this year is described by Sennacherib in his own records (see *Interpreter's Bible,* 5:362).

2. And the king of Assyria sent Rabshakeh from Lachish to Jerusalem unto king Hezekiah with a great army. And he stood by the conduit of the upper pool in the highway of the fuller's field.

One of the most heavily defended cities on the Palestinian plain was Lachish, located about 25 miles southwest of Jerusalem. When this assault was nearly completed, and Sennacherib knew that city was about to fall, he sent his chief envoy (this is the meaning of the title "Rabshakeh") to Jerusalem to try to intimidate the people into forcing the king to surrender so Jerusalem would not be destroyed like all the other cities. Note that the chief envoy did not come with a delegation of dignitaries but with a huge army. This envoy came to the principal meeting place near the entrance to the pool of Gihon Spring. This was just outside the main gates entering into the city of David, which was the most heavily defended part of Jerusalem. There was a mighty stronghold of ancient design at this place called the Millo. From this fortress the high walls extended all around the city.

The "fuller's field" mentioned in this verse was the place near "the upper pool" where cloth was cleaned and whitened. The bleaching process used alkali, urine, and chalk, and the fuller's field was therefore considered an unpleasant place because of the odors associated with it.

3. Then came forth unto him Eliakim, Hilkiah's son, which was over the house, and Shebna the scribe, and Joah, Asaph's son, the recorder.

In some of the older copies of this text it begins by saying, "And they [Rabshakeh and his associates] demanded audience of the king" (see Clarke, *Commentary,* 4:147). However, Hezekiah would not go out to parley with them. Instead, he sent Eliakim, son of Hilkiah, who was the steward over the king's household (2 Kings 18:18). He also sent Shebna, the king's secretary or scribe, and Joah, the king's historian and recorder.

It would appear from verse 3 that the Jewish officials "came forth" to meet the Assyrians just outside the gate to the city. Large concourses of people crowded onto the battlements of the high walls to hear what was being said.

4. And Rabshakeh said unto them, Say ye now to Hezekiah, Thus saith the great king, the king of Assyria, What confidence is this wherein thou trustest?

The Assyrian envoy told the Jewish officials to carry a message to King Hezekiah. They were to ask the king why he should place confidence in his ally, Egypt, when the Assyrians were far too powerful for the Egyptians to effectively intervene in their behalf. The specific reference to Egypt does not appear until verse 6.

5. I say, sayest thou, (but they are but vain words) I have counsel and strength for war: now on whom dost thou trust, that thou rebellest against me?

This verse is more clearly stated in Joseph Smith's translation, which says: "I say, thy words are but vain when thou sayest, I have counsel and strength for war. Now, on whom dost thou trust that thou rebellest against me?" (JST, Isaiah 36:5.)

The purpose of this speech is to introduce a very persuasive and threatening argument. The design of the Assyrian envoy is to convince King Hezekiah that he cannot possibly expect to resist the mighty forces of Assyria by himself. Therefore, on whom does he think he can rely to help him?

6. Lo, thou trustest in the staff of this broken reed, on Egypt; whereon if a man lean, it will go into his hand, and pierce it: so is

The spies of the Assyrians had long since reported to their king that the Jews had been sending ambassadors to Egypt to sign an alliance for their mutual defense. The Assyrian envoy wants to assure the Jews that this

Pharaoh king of Egypt to all that trust in him.

is a vain hope. He disdainfully describes Egypt as a broken reed. He points out that it is well known that any nation that has relied on the Pharaoh of Egypt in the past has been injured. It is like leaning on a fragile reed which, when it breaks, wounds the hand.

7. **But if thou say to me, We trust in the LORD our God: is it not he, whose high places and whose altars Hezekiah hath taken away, and said to Judah and to Jerusalem, Ye shall worship before this altar?**

The Assyrian spies had perhaps also learned that King Hezekiah had greatly strengthened the people by saying, "With him [the king of Assyria] is an arm of flesh; but with us is the Lord our God to help us, and to fight our battles" (2 Chronicles 32:8).

The Assyrian envoy therefore arrogantly declared that if the king had told them to trust in the Lord, they should recall that it was this same Hezekiah who had torn down all of their magnificent pagan altars and ordered them to worship only at the altar of Jehovah in Jerusalem. The shrewd Assyrian was trying to revive the animosities of those apostate Jews who had been required to give up their pagan worship during the cleansing of the land by Hezekiah some time earlier (2 Kings 18:4; 2 Chronicles 30:14). He wanted to remind them that if the Assyrians took over, the people could once more return to their pagan worship with the fertility orgies, drunkenness, and all that went with it.

8. **Now therefore give pledges, I pray thee, to my master the king of Assyria, and I will give thee two thousand horses, if thou be able on thy part to set riders upon them.**
9. **How then wilt thou turn away the face of one captain of the least of my master's servants, and put thy trust on Egypt for chariots and for horsemen?**

The Assyrian envoy said that if the people of Judah would give pledges or hostages to show their good faith, he would deliver to them 2,000 horses, if they could provide riders out of their own people. He lured them on with this generous offer, saying that if he, one of the most humble of the Assyrian king's captains, could do so much for them, how could they think of turning away from such a great power as the Assyrians and relying upon Egypt for chariots and horsemen?

10. And am I now come up without the LORD against this land to destroy it? the LORD said unto me, Go up against this land, and destroy it.

Rabshakeh says the king of Assyria would never have come up to attack Judah if he had not been commanded to do so by "the Lord." Of course, he had been castigating the Lord God Jehovah as weak, so he is not referring to the Lord God of the Jews but to the pagan god of the Assyrians. Pagan leaders often appealed to their gods before going into battle. Their false priests would pretend to have a revelation assuring them of great victories (see 1 Kings 22:5-13; 2 Chronicles 35:20-21).

11. Then said Eliakim and Shebna and Joah unto Rabshakeh, Speak, I pray thee, unto thy servants in the Syrian language; for we understand it: and speak not to us in the Jews' language, in the ears of the people that are on the wall.

It was obvious to the Jewish leaders who had come to parley with the Assyrians that this speech was not directed to them but was designed to stir up the remnant of apostate Jews to rebel against their king. The people had crowded along the top of the city wall and were no doubt straining to catch every word. Therefore the Jewish officials appealed to the Assyrian envoy saying, "Speak, I pray thee, unto thy servants in the SYRIAN language; for we understand it: and speak not to us in the Jews' language, in the ears of the people that are on the wall."

12. But Rabshakeh said, Hath my master sent me to thy master and to thee to speak these words? hath he not sent me to the men that sit upon the wall, that they may eat their own dung, and drink their own piss with you?

Rabshakeh, the Assyrian, could see that his speech had really struck a tender nerve. He therefore poured on the heat with added zeal. He told them that his master, the king of Assyria, had not sent him up to be moderate or respond to requested favors, but to pulverize the Jews. He was to pull these men down from their perches on the high wall and make them eat dirt and drink their own excrement. At this point the Assyrian officer was resorting to gutter talk to impress upon the people how harshly he intended to treat them unless they capitulated.

13. Then Rabshakeh stood, and cried with a loud voice in the Jews' language, and said, Hear ye the words of the great king, the king of Assyria.

Having responded to the Jewish emissaries in the harshest language he could contrive, the Assyrian envoy now shouted at the top of his voice to the Jewish people who were assembled on top of the wall. He shouted in Hebrew so all could understand. He called upon the people to hear the message which he brought to them from the great King Sennacherib.

14. Thus saith the king, Let not Hezekiah deceive you: for he shall not be able to deliver you.

First of all, he said the people should not be deceived by the declaration of King Hezekiah that he would be able to save them. It was impossible.

15. Neither let Hezekiah make you trust in the LORD, saying, The LORD will surely deliver us: this city shall not be delivered into the hand of the king of Assyria.

Furthermore, they should not be persuaded by King Hezekiah that the Lord God Jehovah could save them from being delivered into the hands of King Sennacherib. That also would be impossible.

16. Hearken not to Hezekiah: for thus saith the king of Assyria, Make an agreement with me by a present, and come out to me: and eat ye every one of his vine, and every one of his fig tree, and drink ye every one the waters of his own cistern;

17. Until I come and take you away to a land like your own land, a land of corn and wine, a land of bread and vineyards.

Rabshakeh said that since nothing could save them and resistance would only mean their destruction, the great King Sennacherib had a generous proposal to offer them. All they would have to do would be to submit themselves to Assyrian rule and make a present to King Sennacherib, and then they could all relax and enjoy their homes and farms UNTIL THEY WOULD BE TRANSPORTED TO ASSYRIA! In other words, Sennacherib intended to do the same thing to the Jews that his father Sargon had done to the Ten Tribes of Israel. They were to be taken as captives back to the land of the Assyrians!

18. Beware lest Hezekiah persuade you, saying, The

Now Rabshakeh pointed out some well-known facts of recent history which were intended to terrorize the

LORD will deliver us. Hath any of the gods of the nations delivered his land out of the hand of the king of Assyria?

Jews into surrendering their city without further resistance. The crafty Assyrian first warned them, for the second time, not to believe King Hezekiah if he promised the Lord God Jehovah would save them. For positive proof, Rabshakeh pointed out that not a single tribal god on the face of the land had been able to stand up against Sennacherib and his ferocious legions. He challenged the Jews to name one god who had exhibited sufficient power to resist the Assyrians.

19. Where are the gods of Hamath and Arphad? where are the gods of Sepharvaim? and have they delivered Samaria out of my hand?

Rabshakeh challenged them to consider how important the god of Hamath had been. Hamath was located up on the Orontes River in northwest Syria, and it had been desolated. The same had happened to Arphad, located just a little further north. It, too, had fallen. Even the great city of Sepharvaim, located on the Euphrates above Babylon, had been destroyed. And then, coming closer to home for the clincher, Rabshakeh reminded these children of Jehovah that their God had not saved the northern Ten Tribes of Israel when the Assyrians had captured and destroyed their famous capital city of Samaria.

20. Who are they among all the gods of these lands, that have delivered their land out of my hand, that the LORD should deliver Jerusalem out of my hand?

And so the question which the king of Assyria now put to the Jews was simply this: if they were going to rely on their God to save them, where in all the land had there been a god who could do it? Even their own God, Jehovah, did not save the Israelites. What made them think Jehovah, or any other deity, could save Jerusalem now that Sennacherib was about to besiege it?

21. But they held their peace, and answered him not a

To all of this taunting rhetoric, the Jewish leaders made no reply. Hezekiah had very wisely instructed

**word: for the king's com-
mandment was, saying, An-
swer him not.**

them not to argue with Rabshakeh, but simply to bring
the message of the Assyrian envoy back to the palace
for thoughtful consideration. It must have been frustrating to Rabshakeh as he saw Eliakim and his two
associates withdraw from the parley without answering him a word. Nevertheless, he was an experienced
negotiator. He probably surmised what had happened.
At least he made no attempt to launch an attack on the
city. He was willing to bide his time for a while.

**22. Then came Eliakim, the son
of Hilkiah, that was over
the household, and Shebna
the scribe, and Joah, the
son of Asaph, the recorder,
to Hezekiah with their
clothes rent, and told him
the words of Rabshakeh.**

However, Hezekiah's three emissaries were not as
calm as their silence may have suggested. They were
terrified and filled with consternation. In a state of near
hysteria, they returned to King Hezekiah with their
clothes torn to shreds in order to display their anguish
as they brought him their dreadful report.

1. **And it came to pass, when king Hezekiah heard it, that he rent his clothes, and covered himself with sackcloth, and went into the house of the LORD.**

It would appear that the message that Eliakim and his two associates brought from the Assyrian envoy was far worse than King Hezekiah had expected. The message was virtually an ultimatum that offered no way out. It was surrender or die.

The righteous king of Judah was beside himself. He was helpless. In his anguish he tore his royal clothing. This was a custom among the people when they were overwhelmed with sorrow or indignation. Then he dressed in the most humble apparel —sackcloth—hastened to the temple to plead with the Lord for guidance. Before leaving, however, he did one other thing.

2. **And he sent Eliakim, who was over the household, and Shebna the scribe, and the elders of the priests covered with sackcloth, unto Isaiah the prophet the son of Amoz.**

The king had the deepest love and respect for the Lord's aged prophet, Isaiah. He also wanted Isaiah to plead with the Lord for an answer. Hezekiah therefore instructed Eliakim, Shebna, and ALL THE ELDERS OF THE PRIESTS to dress in sackcloth and together go to ask Isaiah to intervene with the Lord in this time of pending calamity.

3. **And they said unto him, Thus saith Hezekiah, This day is a day of trouble, and of rebuke, and of blasphemy: for the children are come to the birth, and there is not strength to bring forth.**

When this rather large body of the king's servants and the leaders of the Priesthood arrived at the home of Isaiah, they made their plea. They said the Jewish people had certainly come to a time of great trouble and "rebuke" from the Lord for all their past offenses. Nevertheless, they felt the enemies of the Lord's people were even greater offenders. They had actually blasphemed against God and defied him to display his power. They confessed that the Lord's people should avenge this great offense, but they were helpless. They were like a child in its mother's womb who is supposed to come forth, but has not enough strength to perform the great act.

4. It may be the LORD thy God will hear the words of Rabshakeh, whom the king of Assyria his master hath sent to reproach the living God, and will reprove the words which the LORD thy God hath heard: wherefore lift up thy prayer for the remnant that is left.

They suggested to Isaiah that perhaps God had heard the blasphemy which Rabshakeh, the Assyrian, had spoken on behalf of Sennacherib, his pagan master. Perhaps, in spite of the unworthiness of the Jews, the Lord would stretch forth his mighty arm and avenge this great offense against his name. They pleaded with Isaiah, "Lift up thy prayer for the remnant that is left." The Jews were indeed a "remnant" since all of the other Tribes, save the Levites and a few from the other Israelites, had been killed or carried away northward.

5. So the servants of king Hezekiah came to Isaiah.

6. And Isaiah said unto them, Thus shall ye say unto your master, Thus saith the LORD, Be not afraid of the words that thou hast heard, where-with the servants of the king of Assyria have blasphemed me.

It would appear that almost instantly the mind of Isaiah was opened to receive a direct revelation from the Lord. First, Isaiah gave these frightened men a comforting assurance directly from the Lord. He said, "Be not afraid of the words that thou hast heard, wherewith the servants of the king of Assyria have blasphemed me." These few words meant much to the men in this delegation. It told them that the Lord HAD heard the words of the arrogant Assyrian envoy. The Lord did indeed count it a blasphemy against his name. But best of all, he was going to do something about it. The word of the Lord was, "BE NOT AFRAID"!

7. Behold, I will send a blast upon him, and he shall hear

Now we learn what the Lord had in mind. He is going to send a "blast" on King Sennacherib. There is no

a rumour, and return to his own land; and I will cause him to fall by the sword in his own land.

indication of what the "blast" would be, but it is to be so devastating that when the king hears the "rumour" of it (*report* is the more correct word), he will suddenly flee back to his own land. What a welcome message to learn that Jerusalem would be spared! But then Isaiah added another prophecy. He said that when Sennacherib arrived back in Nineveh he would be slain by the sword in his own land. It was virtually unbelievable how quickly circumstances could be so completely reversed! What a blessing to have the Lord for a Savior. And what a blessing to have a prophet who could reveal his will.

8. So Rabshakeh returned, and found the king of Assyria warring against Libnah: for he had heard that he was departed from Lachish.

So Hezekiah apparently decided not to respond to Rabshakeh either yea or nay. When the Assyrian envoy felt he could wait no longer, he returned to report to his king. However, he did not go back to Lachish because he heard that Sennacherib had moved his armies a little further west to Libnah. This was one of the ancient royal cities of the Canaanites. There Sennacherib had joined battle with the Ethiopian pharaoh of Egypt.

9. And he heard say concerning Tirhakah king of Ethiopia, He is come forth to make war with thee. And when he heard it, he sent messengers to Hezekiah, saying,

Tirhakah was the last of three Ethiopian kings who ruled as pharaohs of Egypt in what is called the twenty-fifth dynasty. In accordance with his previous alliance with Judah, he had come up to engage the Assyrians in battle. Surely it was better to confront Sennacherib on the plains of Palestine while he was engaged in conflict with the Jews and other nearby city-states rather than wait until the war was carried down into the precincts of Egypt.

So it was at Libnah that Rabshakeh brought the disquieting report to Sennacherib that the king of the

Jews would not respond to the threat which had been made against him. Sennacherib therefore decided to make one more effort to intimidate the Jews into surrender. He sent a letter containing a final ultimatum to King Hezekiah.

---

10. Thus shall ye speak to Hezekiah king of Judah, saying, Let not thy God, in whom thou trustest, deceive thee, saying, Jerusalem shall not be given into the hand of the king of Assyria.

Actually the message from Sennacherib (set forth in a letter; see verse 14) was recited orally by the Assyrian envoys. We do not know whether this delegation included Rabshakeh or not. The message was nothing more than a repeat of what had been said before, except that this time the Assyrians were asking that the Jews not allow their GOD to deceive them! The message said that even if the Lord God Jehovah promised that he would save Jerusalem, they should not believe it because the city was doomed.

---

11. Behold, thou hast heard what the kings of Assyria have done to all lands by destroying them utterly; and shalt thou be delivered?

Sennacherib wanted to remind Hezekiah of what was already widely known, namely, that the Assyrians had not merely conquered the cities they had targeted for attack, but destroyed them "utterly."

---

12. Have the gods of the nations delivered them which my fathers have destroyed, as Gozan, and Haran, and Rezeph, and the children of Eden which were in Telassar?

13. Where is the king of Hamath, and the king of Arphad, and the king of the city of Sepharvaim, Hena, and Ivah?

In these two verses, Sennacherib's letter names a number of cities he had conquered which were not included in his previous message to the king of Judah. Perhaps he thought Hezekiah would be more impressed with a longer list. For example, there was Gozan, which is believed to have been located on a tributary of the mighty Euphrates River; and there was Haran, to which Abraham had fled after leaving Ur as a young man. It was there that Rebecca was born, also Rachel and Leah. The Assyrians had also conquered and plundered Rezeph, further south toward Palmyra.

Somewhere in between, and west of the Euphrates, is where Telassar is believed to have been located. It was a lush country and its inhabitants were referred to as the "children of Eden." Sennacherib then includes a number of cities mentioned before but adds Hena and Ivah, neither of which can any longer be identified with any particular geographical area.

14. And Hezekiah received the letter from the hand of the messengers, and read it: and Hezekiah went up unto the house of the LORD, and spread it before the LORD.

It is obvious that this letter greatly frightened the king of Judah. Hezekiah had already been promised by Isaiah that he need not fear, but it is apparent from the prayer which is set forth in the following verses that he needed further reassurance. The vicious brutality of the Assyrians was so notorious that it terrorized the people to even think about it. For example, the Assyrians would slay captive leaders by skinning them alive or impaling them on sharp poles. Some they would torture to death in public simply as an example to the rest of the populace. Others would be dismembered a limb at a time, or a joint at a time, and the wound allowed to heal before the next joint was severed. These terrifying thoughts must have been in the mind of Hezekiah as he hastened to the temple to spread Sennacherib's threatening letter before the Lord and pray fervently for protection.

15. And Hezekiah prayed unto the LORD, saying,

16. O LORD of hosts, God of Israel, that dwellest between the cherubims, thou art the God, even thou alone, of all the kingdoms of the earth; thou hast made heaven and earth.

Hezekiah addressed the Lord as the "Lord of hosts, God of Israel, that dwellest between the cherubims." In the Holy of Holies of the temple was the Ark of the Covenant. On the top of the Ark were two angelic beings with outspread wings, symbolizing their power of movement. Between them was the so-called seat of judgment or mercy-seat. It was from this place that the voice of the Lord seemed to emanate when he

17. Incline thine ear, O LORD, and hear; open thine eyes, O LORD, and see: and hear all the words of Sennacherib, which hath sent to reproach the living God.

communicated with the high priest or with one of his prophets who had come before him seeking light and knowledge. Hezekiah spread Sennacherib's letter before the Lord and invited him to consider the blasphemous things it contained.

18. Of a truth, LORD, the kings of Assyria have laid waste all the nations, and their countries,

19. And have cast their gods into the fire: for they were no gods, but the work of men's hands, wood and stone: therefore they have destroyed them.

Hezekiah emphasized the truth of Sennacherib's boast that he had indeed destroyed all of those cities which he had named in his letter, and he had cast their pagan gods into the fire. Hezekiah realized, of course, that they were man-made gods fashioned of wood or stone, and therefore not gods at all; but Sennacherib believed they were gods, and he further believed he had proven himself more powerful than all of them.

20. Now therefore, O LORD our God, save us from his hand, that all the kingdoms of the earth may know that thou art the LORD, even thou only.

Hezekiah pleaded with the Lord to show forth his mighty power and save his people so that the boast of Sennacherib would be silenced forever. He emphasized that if the Lord condescended to do this it would demonstrate to the whole world that the mighty Jehovah is indeed the God of the whole earth.

21. Then Isaiah the son of Amoz sent unto Hezekiah, saying, Thus saith the LORD God of Israel, Whereas thou hast prayed to me against Sennacherib king of Assyria:

It would appear that after Hezekiah had returned to his palace a messenger came with a written revelation which Isaiah had received from the Lord. The message from the Lord said that since Hezekiah had pleaded with the Lord against the designs of Sennacherib, this revelation was what the Lord had to say in response.

22. This is the word which the LORD hath spoken concerning him; The virgin, the daughter of Zion, hath

The Lord pointed out first of all that the great city of Jerusalem, which remained unsullied by the intrusion of the Assyrians, was like a virgin daughter of Zion, or

despised thee, and laughed thee to scorn; the daughter of Jerusalem hath shaken her head at thee.

a daughter of Jerusalem, that had defied Sennacherib and shaken her head at him in scorn.

23. Whom hast thou reproached and blasphemed? and against whom hast thou exalted thy voice, and lifted up thine eyes on high? even against the Holy One of Israel.

Now the Lord challenges Sennacherib. Does he realize whom he has "reproached and blasphemed"? His offense was not against any ordinary pagan god but against the "Holy One of Israel."

24. By thy servants hast thou reproached the LORD, and hast said, By the multitude of my chariots am I come up to the height of the mountains, to the sides of Lebanon; and I will cut down the tall cedars thereof, and the choice fir trees thereof: and I will enter into the height of his border, and the forest of his Carmel.

Sennacherib had sent his servants to speak evil against the Holy One of Israel. Through these emissaries he had also disclosed the extent of his military aspirations. He had intended to go up to the heights of the Lebanese mountains and destroy their famous cedar forests. He had also said he would do the same thing to the forests on Mount Carmel, the favorite mountain retreat of Elijah and Elisha (see 1 Kings 18:20-42; 2 Kings 2:25; 4:25).

25. I have digged, and drunk water; and with the sole of my feet have I dried up all the rivers of the besieged places.

Sennacherib had boasted about digging into the lands between the Euphrates and the Mediterranean. He had drunk deeply of the spoils there. He had trodden down or destroyed the precious sources of water on which these many besieged cities had been dependent.

26. Hast thou not heard long ago, how I have done it; and of ancient times, that I have formed it? now have I

In this revelation the Lord asked the Assyrian king if he had not heard from "long ago" how the Lord formed the earth and everything that embellishes it. He asked

brought it to pass, that thou shouldest be to lay waste defenced cities into ruinous heaps.

whether Sennacherib realized that the Lord had the power to prevent all of those massive conquests which had become such a great source of Assyrian pride.

27. Therefore their inhabitants were of small power, they were dismayed and confounded: they were as the grass of the field, and as the green herb, as the grass on the housetops, and as corn blasted before it be grown up.

The Lord says that those conquests succeeded only because he did not intervene. The inhabitants of these cities were too weak to resist. They were frightened, dismayed, and confounded. Therefore they wilted like tender plants which the drought of a hot summer blasts out of existence before they grow up with sufficient strength to survive.

28. But I know thy abode, and thy going out, and thy coming in, and thy rage against me.

The Lord says that even though he did not intervene, he was well aware of those bloody conquests and was watching every detail of those ugly events. During the second estate divine justice is meted out only in special situations because this is a time of testing to determine how the Father's children will use their free agency. The balancing of the scales of justice usually takes place after the second estate has run its course. Down through history the Lord has often seen opposing nations, EQUALLY WICKED, destroying one another. In such cases he does not intervene. However, a righteous nation is entitled to a special blessing by way of divine intervention, and the Lord declares that the righteous King Hezekiah is about to receive such a blessing. In the past the Lord has watched the pagan Assyrians slaughter other wicked pagans from Nineveh to Libnah. The Lord wants Sennacherib to know that every cruel act he perpetrated was under the continuous scrutiny of heaven.

29. Because thy rage against me, and thy tumult, is come

The Lord now reveals what is about to happen. Because Sennacherib has finally aimed his deadly war

up into mine ears, therefore will I put my hook in thy nose, and my bridle in thy lips, and I will turn thee back by the way by which thou camest.

machine against a righteous people, and has railed against the God of that people, the Lord intends to intervene in a most spectacular way. The Lord wants Sennacherib to know that he is about to have a hook put through his nose and a bridle put between his lips. This symbolized the terrifying circumstances which were about to sweep down on Sennacherib and his Assyrian hosts, causing them to flee back to their own country.

30. **And this shall be a sign unto thee, Ye shall eat this year such as groweth of itself; and the second year that which springeth of the same: and in the third year sow ye, and reap, and plant vineyards, and eat the fruit thereof.**

Of course, the main question in a prophecy that is worded as explicitly as this one is the element of timing. When will all of this take place? The Lord said he would give Hezekiah a sign when Sennacherib would be turned back to his own place. It would be in that year when there would be no planting, followed by a year when the only harvest would be from things which had grown up by themselves, and these two frugal years would then be followed by a third year of normal planting and harvest. This is the description of a jubilee year among the Israelites (see Leviticus, chapter 25). The Lord had told Moses that the land should rest every seventh year, and that after seven sabbatical years (which would make a total of 49 years) there should be a fiftieth year of jubilee when the only harvest would be from seeds which had sprouted by themselves. The year after that would be the normal year of sowing and planting. So Hezekiah was being assured that Judah's relief would come in a year when these three events would take place.

31. **And the remnant that is escaped of the house of Judah shall again take root downward, and bear fruit upward:**

At this point the Lord does an interesting thing. He knew that not only would the Assyrians try to annihilate Jerusalem, but in due time so would the Babylonians. The Lord therefore wanted to record the prophecy that out of these two campaigns to destroy and carry off the people of Judah, a remnant would escape. Not only would they flee successfully out of the land, but they would establish new roots in another place where they would produce a posterity that God could describe as bearing "fruit upward."

32. For out of Jerusalem shall go forth a remnant, and they that escape out of mount Zion: the zeal of the LORD of hosts shall do this.

The Lord wanted to record that this remnant would escape through the intervention or "zeal of the Lord of hosts" from Jerusalem. It also says in the King James Version that they will "escape out of mount Zion," but this is a mistranslation. The Joseph Smith Translation gives us the original text for this verse as follows: "For out of Jerusalem shall go forth a remnant; and they that escape out of Jerusalem SHALL COME UP UPON MOUNT ZION; the zeal of the Lord of hosts shall do this" (JST, Isaiah 37:32; emphasis added).

Here we see a clear distinction between Jerusalem and the Mount Zion of America. The Lord says a special remnant of the Jews will escape from Jerusalem and go to America. Two groups or REMNANTS escaped from the doomed Jerusalem. The first group consisted of the families of Lehi and Ishmael, who were led out of Jerusalem by the Lord in 600 B.C. The second group left at the close of the Babylonian war, which totally destroyed Jerusalem around 587–8 B.C. This group of Jews took the young son of King Zedekiah, named Mulek, and were led by the Lord to America. (The Book of Mormon refers to this remnant in Omni 1:15–16; Mosiah 25:2; Helaman 6:10; 8:21.) They established themselves on the Sidon River and became known as the Mulekites. The Mulekites, in addition to the families of Lehi and Ishmael, are the only remnants which are known to have escaped from Jerusalem and who were led to America by the "zeal of the Lord." All the rest of the Jews were killed or led captive to Babylon.

33. Therefore thus saith the LORD concerning the king of Assyria, He shall not come into this city, nor shoot an arrow there, nor come before it with shields, nor cast a bank against it.

34. By the way that he came, by the same shall he return, and shall not come into this city, saith the LORD.

Having made his point concerning the remnant which would "escape out of mount Zion [Jerusalem]," the Lord now turns back to Sennacherib to repeat the prophecy which Isaiah had been given concerning the Assyrian king (see verse 7). He states that Sennacherib will not only fail in his aspiration to destroy Jerusalem, but he will not even have the opportunity of shooting arrows into it, nor bring up his armed forces against it, nor even dig a siege bank around it. Instead, Sennacherib will suddenly return home. In verse 7 the Lord had already told Isaiah this king would be killed after returning to his own land.

35. For I will defend this city to save it for mine own sake, and for my servant David's sake.

The Lord declared that he intended to defend Jerusalem against the Assyrians. This was because of the number of righteous people in this city who were entitled to this special blessing. This is the meaning of the Lord's statement that he is going to defend the city "for mine own sake." The Lord rejoices in blessing the righteous and does it "for [his] own sake." He also wanted to bless this city for the sake of Hezekiah, who was of the seed of David. Thus we come to the conclusion of the revelation to Isaiah which was delivered to Hezekiah in response to his earlier plea to the Lord in the temple.

36. Then the angel of the LORD went forth, and smote in the camp of the Assyrians a hundred and fourscore and five thousand: and when they arose early in the morning, behold, they were all dead corpses.

At this point the scriptural historian adds a postscript to testify to the literal fulfillment of these prophecies. However, this verse is given more perfectly in the Joseph Smith Translation, which says: "Then the angel of the Lord went forth, and smote in the camp of the Assyrians a hundred and four-score and five thousand

[185,000], and when THEY WHO WERE LEFT AROSE, early in the morning, behold, they were all dead corpses" (JST, Isaiah 37:36; emphasis added).

Note that this great destruction was achieved by one or more of the angelic servants of God (the Priesthood beyond the veil) passing among the sleeping Assyrians and calling their spirits to return to the spirit world.

37. So Sennacherib king of Assyria departed, and went and returned, and dwelt at Nineveh.

38. And it came to pass, as he was worshipping in the house of Nisroch his god, that Adrammelech and Sharezer his sons smote him with the sword; and they escaped into the land of Armenia: and Esar-haddon his son reigned in his stead.

When this terrible destruction of 185,000 Assyrians was completed, the terrified Sennacherib was among those who were "left." Fleeing in a state of virtual panic, he returned to his own land and once more took up his residence at the royal palace in Nineveh. But some time later, when he was worshipping his pagan god, Nisroch, two of his own sons crept up behind him and ran a sword through him. The dying king probably never knew what struck him. These two sons are believed to have been jealous of their brother, whom Sennacherib had designated as his heir. After killing their father they fled to Armenia, or eastern Turkey. The third brother, whose name was Esar-haddon, then took over the throne of Assyria (see also 2 Kings 19:37).

In this chapter five prophecies were literally fulfilled:

1. The people of Jerusalem had no need to fear (verse 6).

2. The Lord would send a blast on the Assyrian armies (verse 7).

3. Sennacherib would flee back to his own land (verses 7 and 34).

4. There he would be slain by the sword (verse 7).

5. The city of Jerusalem would not be attacked with arrows, armed troops, or siege banks (verse 33).

INTRODUCTION:

As we pointed out earlier, chapters 36 to 39 of Isaiah seem to be an historical insert placed in the text by ancient scriptural historians. Having described the great Assyrian war against Judah and the final, successful outcome, these historians now wanted to go back and include a dramatic incident which occurred right in the midst of the devastating attack on Judah which had destroyed 46 cities and even threatened to demolish the capital city of Jerusalem.

We know that the events in this chapter occurred in the fourteenth year of the reign of King Hezekiah, which is calculated to be 701 B.C. Because of severe illness Hezekiah almost died in the fourteenth year of his reign, but he was granted an additional 15 years of life. The scripture states that he reigned a total of 29 years (see 2 Kings 18:2); therefore, if we subtract the 15 years of extended life, it brings us to the fourteenth year of his reign.

We also know from verse 6 in this chapter that the sickness that preyed upon the life of Hezekiah occurred during the threatened attack by Sennacherib and before the loss of his 185,000 troops that caused the Assyrians to flee back to Nineveh.

1. In those days was Hezekiah sick unto death. And Isaiah the prophet the son of Amoz came unto him, and said unto him, Thus saith

What consternation must have filled the heart of King Hezekiah when he became deathly ill right at the time his people needed him most. It was customary for the kings to ask the prophets of their day whether or

the LORD, Set thine house in order: for thou shalt die, and not live.

not they would survive a severe illness (see 2 Kings 1:2-16; 8:7-15), and it is likely that Hezekiah had made such an inquiry of Isaiah. However, whether Hezekiah had asked for it or not, a doomsday message came to the king through Isaiah which said, "Set thine house in order: for thou shalt die."

2. Then Hezekiah turned his face toward the wall, and prayed unto the LORD,

3. And said, Remember now, O LORD, I beseech thee, how I have walked before thee in truth and with a perfect heart, and have done that which is good in thy sight. And Hezekiah wept sore.

As soon as Isaiah had left the room, Hezekiah turned his face to the wall and sobbed out a special pleading to the Lord. Said he, "Remember now, O Lord, I beseech thee, how I have walked before thee in truth and with a perfect heart, and have done that which is good in thy sight." Then the scripture says, "And Hezekiah wept sore."

4. Then came the word of the LORD to Isaiah, saying,

5. Go, and say to Hezekiah, Thus saith the LORD, the God of David thy father, I have heard thy prayer, I have seen thy tears: behold, I will add unto thy days fifteen years.

In 2 Kings 20:4 it says that Isaiah had just reached the middle court of the palace when the Lord instructed him to return to the king. The Lord said he had heard Hezekiah's prayer and seen his tears and had determined to add 15 years to his life.

6. And I will deliver thee and this city out of the hand of the king of Assyria: and I will defend this city.

Then the Lord added the comforting prophecy we discussed in the previous chapter; namely, that Jerusalem would be delivered out of the hands of the Assyrians through God's divine intervention.

7. And this shall be a sign unto thee from the LORD,

Before considering these two verses we should remind ourselves of an interesting detail which appears

that the LORD will do this thing that he hath spoken;

8. Behold, I will bring again the shadow of the degrees, which is gone down in the sun dial of Ahaz, ten degrees backward. So the sun returned ten degrees, by which degrees it was gone down.

in 2 Kings 20:7–11. It states that a poultice of figs was placed upon the abscess with which Hezekiah was plagued and it began to have a healing effect. Nevertheless, Hezekiah was doubtful that he could be permanently healed. He asked how he could know with certainty that God intended to let him live another 15 years and make him well enough in three days to go up to the temple. Isaiah replied that the Lord would give him a sign. He would perform a great miracle by altering the sun dial ten degrees. Isaiah asked Hezekiah whether he wanted to see the dial go forward or backward. Hezekiah replied, "It is a light thing for the shadow to go down ten degrees: nay, but let the shadow return BACKWARD ten degrees" (2 Kings 20:10; emphasis added).

This brings us to our present text, which says, "So the sun returned ten degrees, by which degrees it was gone down."

We are not advised how the Lord accomplished this amazing phenomenon. Whether it was accomplished by astronomical means or by a refraction of the light, we are not told. He could have done it either way, and some-day we will know exactly what happened.

9. The writing of Hezekiah king of Judah, when he had been sick, and was recovered of his sickness:

As soon as Hezekiah was assured that he would indeed be allowed to live, he wrote down his feelings. Whoever assembled these particular scriptures felt this writing of Hezekiah should be included in the record. It specifically says he wrote this when he "was recovered of his sickness."

10. I said in the cutting off of my days, I shall go to the gates of the grave: I am deprived of the residue of my years.

Hezekiah begins with his original sense of grief when he thought he was going to die. He was overwhelmed with the thought of going to his grave prematurely and being "deprived of the residue of [his] years."

11. I said, I shall not see the LORD, even the LORD, in the land of the living: I shall behold man no more with the inhabitants of the world.

Knowing scarcely anything about the afterlife in the spirit world, Hezekiah states that he felt particularly sorrowful that he would not have the opportunity of seeing the Lord in this life and mingling among the children of men.

12. Mine age is departed, and is removed from me as a shepherd's tent: I have cut off like a weaver my life: he will cut me off with pining sickness: from day even to night wilt thou make an end of me.

He felt that suddenly his "age" had departed or his allotted years had run their course. It was as though his prospect of living had collapsed upon him like a shepherd's tent. He was like a weaver with an unfinished article. He was being cut off before he had finished what he wanted to do. What was especially repugnant to Hezekiah was the prospect of slowly pining away with a prolonged illness. If such were the case, he knew his suffering would extend ceaselessly by day and by night.

13. I reckoned till morning, that, as a lion, so will he break all my bones: from day even to night wilt thou make an end of me.

During the night he would lie awake thinking how his illness would destroy his physical body. It was like having a lion leap upon his frail body, breaking all his bones. Once again he repeats his fear that he might suffer endlessly, by day and by night.

14. Like a crane or a swallow, so did I chatter: I did mourn as a dove: mine eyes fail with looking upward: O LORD, I am oppressed; undertake for me.

But now Hezekiah admits that he has not been exhibiting very much faith. In his worry and anguish he has chattered away like a crane or a swallow. He has been in a constant state of mourning, like a cooing dove. He has sometimes fallen asleep while looking upward trying to petition the Lord for relief.

15. What shall I say? he hath both spoken unto me, and

Finally, the good news came—Hezekiah would be allowed 15 more years of life, the city of Jerusalem

himself hath done it: I shall go softly all my years in the bitterness of my soul.

would not be taken, and the Lord would serve as a protector of the people against the king of Assyria. The original text of this verse as it appears in the Joseph Smith Translation describes the feelings of Hezekiah more clearly than the King James Version. Here is what he said after receiving the good news: "What shall I say? he hath both spoken unto me, and himself hath HEALED ME. I shall go softly all my years, THAT I MAY NOT WALK in the bitterness of my soul." (JST, Isaiah 38:15; emphasis added.)

16. O Lord, by these things men live, and in all these things is the life of my spirit: so wilt thou recover me, and make me to live.

This verse is also given more clearly in the Joseph Smith Translation: "Oh Lord, THOU WHO ART THE LIFE OF MY SPIRIT, IN WHOM I LIVE; so wilt thou recover me, and make me to live; AND IN ALL THESE THINGS I WILL PRAISE THEE" JST, Isaiah 38:16; emphasis added).

17. Behold, for peace I had great bitterness: but thou hast in love to my soul delivered it from the pit of corruption: for thou hast cast all my sins behind thy back.

The Joseph Smith Translation renders this verse as follows: "Behold, I had great bitterness INSTEAD OF PEACE, but thou hast in love to my soul, SAVED ME from the pit of corruption, for thou hast cast all my sins behind thy back." (JST, Isaiah 38:17; emphasis added).

18. For the grave cannot praise thee, death can not celebrate thee: they that go down into the pit cannot hope for thy truth.

After this triumphant psalm of praise, Hezekiah could not help mentioning the fact that if he were dead he could not sing out these praises in this world. Furthermore, if he were sleeping in the grave his mind and body could not be instructed in the truth.

19. The living, the living, he shall praise thee, as I do this day: the father to the children shall make known thy truth.

In contrast to such a prospect, Hezekiah sings out in rejoicing that he is alive and can praise the Lord. As king and father of the people, he intends to teach them the truth.

20. **The LORD was ready to save me: therefore we will sing my songs to the stringed instruments all the days of our life in the house of the LORD.**

Since the Lord has said he is ready to save Hezekiah, surely it is time for rejoicing and praise.

21. **For Isaiah had said, Let them take a lump of figs, and lay it for a plaister upon the boil, and he shall recover.**

22. **Hezekiah also had said, What is the sign that I shall go up to the house of the LORD?**

Now the historian adds a postscript which he forgot to put in earlier, where it belonged. He mentions the poultice of figs and the fact that Hezekiah had asked for a sign to assure him he would indeed live.

Isaiah, Chapter 39

INTRODUCTION:

In order to appreciate the full significance of this chapter we have to refer to several historical details which are mentioned in 2 Kings, chapter 20, and 2 Chronicles, chapter 32.

As we have mentioned before, Sennacherib, the king of Assyria, threatened to destroy Jerusalem, but the Lord destroyed 185,000 of his troops in a single night. We have reason to believe that the sight of this vast host of dead soldiers so terrorized Sennacherib that he fled back to his homeland without even gathering up the personal treasures which these warriors had brought into the field of battle to prove to the king that they intended to fight valiantly. No doubt Hezekiah's people would have immediately gathered up this vast store of wealth and turned over much of it to the king. It will be recalled that earlier King Hezekiah had been forced to strip himself (and even the temple) of all the available wealth in an effort to pay the required tribute to the Assyrians. However, these latest developments made him one of the richest monarchs in the whole region. The scripture says:

"And Hezekiah had exceeding much riches and honour: and he made himself treasuries for silver, and for gold, and for precious stones, and for spices, and for shields, and for all manner of pleasant jewels;

"Storehouses also for the increase of corn, and wine, and oil; and stalls for all manner of beasts, and cotes for flocks." (2 Chronicles 32:27–28.)

Some of this wealth also came in the form of gifts from admiring followers throughout the kingdom and, no doubt, from the monarchs ot surrounding nations. The scripture says, "And many brought gifts unto the Lord to Jerusalem, and presents to Hezekiah king of Judah: so that he was magnified in the sight of all nations from thenceforth" (2 Chronicles 32:23).

But the good fortune of being healed of his deadly illness and then suddenly becoming wealthy had an unfortunate psychological effect on the king. The scripture implies that he forgot to pay tithes on this newly acquired wealth. Furthermore, he allowed himself to become rather proud of his new status. The Bible says, "But Hezekiah rendered not again according to the benefit done unto him; for his heart was lifted up" (2 Chronicles 32:25).

This seems to have been the situation as this chapter opens.

1. At that time Merodach-baladan, the son of Baladan, king of Babylon, sent letters and a present to Hezekiah: for he had heard that he had been sick, and was recovered.

There suddenly appeared in Jerusalem a royal delegation of ambassadors from the king of Babylon. At this time Babylon was a tributary of Assyria. Nevertheless they had unsuccessfully revolted in 721, 710, and 704 B.C. (*Interpreter's Bible,* p. 379) trying to get their freedom. Now they were getting ready to revolt again. (Notice that the king of Babylon is referred to as Merodach-baladan in Isaiah, but as Berodach-baladan in 2 Kings 20:12.) This embassy from Babylon brought presents to King Hezekiah, and also a letter from the Babylonian king congratulating him on his recovery from the dreadful disease which had afflicted him.

2. And Hezekiah was glad of them, and shewed them the house of his precious things, the silver, and the gold, and the spices, and the precious

King Hezekiah felt very complimented that the mighty king of Babylon would do him this great honor, and he therefore treated these ambassadors with the utmost courtesy. He even took the Babylonian

ointment, and all the house of his armour, and all that was found in his treasures: there was nothing in his house, nor in all his dominion, that Hezekiah shewed them not.

dignitaries into the royal treasury. This allowed them to see the vast wealth which the king had recently accumulated. They also saw the king's "armour" (probably referring to the shields and swords in the royal armory, but sometimes referring to precious jewels, see Clarke, *Commentary,* p. 155). King Hezekiah was in a proud and expansive mood. It says, "There was nothing in his house, nor in all his dominion, that Hezekiah shewed them not." The Babylonians never forgot what they saw.

3. Then came Isaiah the prophet unto king Hezekiah, and said unto him, What said these men? and from whence came they unto thee? And Hezekiah said, They are come from a far country unto me, even from Babylon.

Suddenly the prophet Isaiah appeared on the scene. From his words to the king it is apparent that he had already received a revelation in which the Lord had said he was very displeased with the proud and boastful way King Hezekiah was behaving with these strangers. Isaiah had even been told what Hezekiah's punishment would be. No doubt Isaiah must have wondered what the king had done that was considered by the Lord to be such a foolish and imprudent thing. He therefore asked the king, "What said these men? and from whence came they unto thee?" It was obvious that Isaiah was anxious to know what the king had done in his relationship with these visitors that had offended the Lord. Hezekiah simply replied that they were visiting dignitaries from a far-distant land—Babylon.

4. Then said he, What have they seen in thine house? And Hezekiah answered, All that is in mine house have they seen: there is nothing among my treasures that I have not shewed them.

Isaiah was still puzzled. Ordinarily there was nothing reprehensible about the king receiving visitors from distant kingdoms. It happened all the time. So he inquired further, "What have they seen in thine house?" In other words, what had the king shown these strangers that would offend the Lord? The king was very open and frank about what he had done as a cordial host. Said he, "All that is in mine house have they seen: there is nothing among my treasures that I have not shewed them."

5. Then said Isaiah to Hezekiah, Hear the word of the LORD of hosts:

6. Behold, the days come, that all that is in thine house, and that which thy fathers have laid up in store until this day, shall be carried to Babylon: nothing shall be left, saith the LORD.

Isaiah had his answer. Surely the king had been most unwise and imprudent to tempt these lustful people of the east with the disclosure of these abundant riches with which the Lord had blessed him. Therefore, Isaiah delivered the message which the Lord had given him. He said that because of the foolish thing which Hezekiah had done, the time would come when all of these treasures would be carried off to Babylon. Isaiah said there would be a complete desolating and looting of the king's possessions. He prophesies that "nothing shall be left."

7. And of thy sons that shall issue from thee, which thou shalt beget, shall they take away; and they shall be eunuchs in the palace of the king of Babylon.

But there was even more. Isaiah said that Hezekiah's descendants would also be carried off to Babylon as prisoners. Some of them would be subjected to the cruel indignity of being emasculated and made into eunuchs to serve in the Babylonian king's harem or palace.

Apparently this shocking disclosure greatly humbled Hezekiah. In 2 Chronicles 32:26 it says that "notwithstanding [his highmindedness in the recent past] Hezekiah humbled himself for the pride of his heart, both he and the inhabitants of Jerusalem, so that the wrath of the Lord came not upon them in the days of Hezekiah."

8. Then said Hezekiah to Isaiah, Good is the word of the LORD which thou hast spoken. He said moreover, For there shall be peace and truth in my days.

Hezekiah already knew from the words of Isaiah that this great Babylonian affliction would come upon his descendants at some time in the future. No doubt he sorrowed that his pride and imprudent foolishness had laid the foundation for this future invasion by the

Babylonians, but at least he knew that it would come in another generation. He therefore assured Isaiah that in spite of his recent folly and the tragedy it would bring to his children, he was relieved that "there shall be peace and truth in my days."

Hezekiah lived out the duration of his reign, which lasted 29 years. When he died he was buried in "the chiefest of the sepulchres of the sons of David" (2 Chronicles 32:33).

We are told that the details of Hezekiah's reign are contained in the book called "the vision of Isaiah the prophet, the son of Amoz" but we no longer have that sacred scripture (2 Chronicles 32:32).

In 2 Kings 20:20 it says that Hezekiah was always honored for having "made a pool, and a conduit, and brought water into the city." It says in 2 Chronicles 32:30 that he had "stopped the upper watercourse of Gihon, and brought it straight down to the west side of the city of David." This watercourse still exists. It runs from a pool of water dug out of solid rock to form a cave at the foot of the ancient city of David just below the temple mount. It flows down Hezekiah's tunnel to the pool of Siloam. A modern tourist may take a guide and traverse this tunnel from one end to the other.

In 1880 two Arab boys were going along this tunnel when their candlelight disclosed an inscription on the wall. Scholars later translated the words and found that they gave a history of the excavation from the days of Hezekiah. The slab of stone containing this inscription was cut from the wall and taken to Istanbul, the capital of the Turks, who ruled the entire region at that time.

The Gihon Spring is famous in Bible history. It was apparently named after one of the rivers that flowed through the Garden of Eden (see Genesis 2:13). It was the underground spring from which King David's nephew, Joab, gained entrance to the ancient city of the Jebusites and opened up the city so it could be conquered and made the new capital of Israel (see 2 Samuel 5:6-9; 1 Chronicles 11:4-6). It was the place where Solomon was crowned king (1 Kings 1:38-39), and this was where Isaiah met King Ahaz to announce to him that one day a virgin would conceive and bring forth a son whose name would be Immanuel (see Isaiah 7:3-14).

Isaiah, Chapter 40

INTRODUCTION:

Many scholars have speculated that chapters 40 to 66 are not the work of Isaiah but were written by one or more individuals at a later date. However, the Book of Mormon quotes from a number of these chapters as they appeared on the brass plates. The brass plates not only contained the entire book of Isaiah but were recorded during Isaiah's ministry or shortly thereafter. This would definitely indicate that all of these chapters were part of Isaiah's original writing.

1. Comfort ye, comfort ye my people, saith your God.

This chapter is devoted primarily to the last days when the Messiah will come in glory. The first verse is a proclamation from the Lord that in that great last day his people will finally enjoy their rest from all the afflictions of the past.

2. Speak ye comfortably to Jerusalem, and cry unto her, that her warfare is accomplished, that her iniquity is pardoned: for she hath received of the LORD's hand double for all her sins.

Jerusalem has been destroyed and rebuilt several times. Her people have been pillaged, imprisoned, scattered, and slaughtered. But Jerusalem has a day of destiny in the not-too-distant future. It will be a day when the prophets can assure Jerusalem that all her inhabitants will be able to relax and enjoy this mighty metropolis of the Lord. But that will not happen until she has passed through her "furnace of affliction" (Isaiah 48:10) and paid due penance for her sins against the Lord. Her penalty is all the more severe because her inhabitants were one of the Lord's chosen tribes of

Israel. As such, they were supposed to be the defenders of the Gospel and the representatives of the Lord among the nations. Having apostatized, Judah lost many blessings, as did the other tribes, but after paying double for their sins, they will be embraced and given full fellowship with the Lord.

3. The voice of him that crieth in the wilderness, Prepare ye the way of the LORD, make straight in the desert a highway for our God.

Here is the well-known verse referring to the mission of John the Baptist. As early as 600 B.C., the prophet Lehi identified this passage as referring to the prophet who would baptize the Savior and bear witness that he is indeed the Christ (see 1 Nephi 10:7–10). Luke also referred to this passage and said it was fulfilled by John the Baptist (see Luke 3:2–6). But this creates a problem because verses 4 and 5 of Isaiah 40 clearly refer to the time of the SECOND coming. How can this be?

The entire matter is clearly explained in the Joseph Smith Translation of the Bible. We find the Bible has FIVE VERSES MISSING between verses 4 and 5 of the third chapter of Luke. These five verses cover the period from the FIRST coming of Christ to the SECOND coming.

We assume these same five verses were in the original text of Isaiah which Luke is quoting. Joseph Smith did not have time prior to his martyrdom to complete the revision of the Old Testament, so the correction made in Luke is not made in Isaiah. It is obvious, however, that Joseph Smith knew what Isaiah had originally written, otherwise Joseph Smith would not have inserted these five verses in Luke, chapter 3, and attributed them to Isaiah, chapter 40.

Here is the way these eight important verses in Luke (including the five which are missing from our modern Bible text) read in the Inspired Version:

"4. As it is written in the book of the prophet Esaias; and these are the words, saying, The voice of one crying in the wilderness, Prepare ye the way of the Lord, and make his paths straight.

"5. For behold, and lo, he shall come, as it is written in the book of the prophets, to take away the sins of the world, and to bring salvation unto the heathen nations, to gather together those who are lost, who are of the sheepfold of Israel;

"6. Yea, even the dispersed and afflicted; and also to prepare the way, and make possible the preaching of the gospel unto the Gentiles;

"7. And to be a light unto all who sit in darkness, unto the uttermost parts of the earth; to bring to pass the resurrection from the dead, and to ascend up on high, to dwell on the right hand of the Father,

"8. Until the fulness of time, and the law and the testimony shall be sealed, and the keys of the kingdom shall be delivered up again unto the Father;

"9. To administer justice unto all; to come down in judgment upon all, and to convince all the ungodly of their ungodly deeds, which they have committed; and all this in the day that he shall come;

"10. For it is a day of power; yea, every valley shall be filled, and every mountain and hill shall be brought low; the crooked shall be made straight, and the rough ways made smooth;

"11. And all flesh shall see the salvation of God." JST, Luke 3:4–11.)

Note what these verses are saying:

Verse 4: Quotes Isaiah declaring that a certain "one" will come out of the wilderness proclaiming, "Prepare ye the way of the Lord." All of the prophets interpret this verse as being a reference to John the Baptist and his mission.

Verse 5: This verse states that Isaiah is talking about the time when the Savior will come to the earth to be crucified and "to take away the sins of the world."

Verse 6: The Gospel will then spread from the Israelites to the Gentiles.

Verse 7: Eventually it will spread over the whole earth, carrying its message of salvation and redemption for the dead.

Verse 8: This program of preaching the true Gospel will culminate in "the fulness of time" when the keys of the ministry will be returned to "the Father" (in this case, Jesus Christ, who is the Father of the Church, the Father of salvation, and the Father of creation under the direction of the great Elohim).

Verse 9: In the fulness of time, "he shall come" to administer justice and "to convince all the ungodly of their ungodly deeds."

Verse 10: It will be "a day of power" when the Savior will restructure the surface of the earth.

Verse 11: Then the Savior will make his appearance, and every person left alive on the earth will see him return in glory.

Now we can see how the ORIGINAL text of Isaiah led the reader from the days of John the Baptist in chapter 40, verse 3, to the cleansing of the earth and the Second Coming in verses 4 and 5. Somehow, FIVE INTERVENING VERSES WERE LEFT OUT! Now let us take a closer look at verses 4 and 5.

4. Every valley shall be exalted, and every mountain and hill shall be made low: and the crooked shall be made straight, and the rough places plain:

Just before the appearance of the Savior there will be tremendous changes on the surface of the earth. This is described in more detail in the Doctrine and Covenants:

"And he shall utter his voice out of Zion, and he shall speak from Jerusalem, and his voice shall be heard among all people;

"And it shall be a voice as the voice of many waters, and as the voice of a great thunder, which shall break down the mountains, and the valleys shall not be found.

"He shall command the great deep, and it shall be driven back into the north countries, and the islands shall become one land;

"And the land of Jerusalem and the land of Zion shall be turned back into their own place, and the earth shall be like as it was in the days before it was divided." (D&C 133:21-24.)

Notice that the whole surface of the earth is to be restructured for the Millennium in order to make it more verdant and productive, just as it was in the days of the Garden of Eden. Not only will the continents and islands become "one land," but the rugged barriers of mountain ranges will be lowered, and deep canyons and valleys will be raised so that the earth's crust will be more or less level. The surface of the earth will provide vast regions of luxurious fields and meadows with beautiful rolling hills, which are easy to beautify and cultivate.

5. And the glory of the LORD shall be revealed, and all flesh shall see it together: for the mouth of the LORD hath spoken it.

This will be the glorious moment when the Lord will appear with the resurrected host of heaven and those who were righteous enough to be "caught up" (D&C 88:95-98; 1 Thessalonians 16-17) so that they would not be killed during the terrestrial convulsions on the surface of the earth. Here is the way the Lord describes it in the Doctrine and Covenants:

"And there shall be silence in heaven for the space of half an hour; and immediately after shall the curtain of heaven be unfolded, as a scroll is unfolded after it is rolled up, and the face of the Lord shall be unveiled;

"And the saints that are upon the earth, who are alive, shall be quickened and be caught up to meet him.

"And they who have slept in their graves shall come forth, for their graves shall be opened; and they also shall be caught up to meet him in the midst of the pillar of heaven—

"They are Christ's, the first fruits, they who shall descend with him first, and they who are on the earth and in their graves, who are first caught up to meet him; and all this by the voice of the sounding of the trump of the angel of God." (D&C 88:95-98.)

6. The voice said, Cry. And he said, What shall I cry? All flesh is grass, and all the goodliness thereof is as the flower of the field:

7. The grass withereth, the flower fadeth: because the spirit of the LORD bloweth upon it: surely the people is grass.

8. The grass withereth, the flower fadeth: but the word of our God shall stand for ever.

Never before in human history will it have been more dramatically demonstrated that the present mortal existence is comparable to luxurious grass that easily withers away, or to the beautiful flowers that readily fade away into dust. Nothing is of enduring certainty during the second estate except the word of the Lord. The apostle Peter used these verses to emphasize the importance of living by the word of the Lord for security rather than trusting in the fragile elements of human flesh and earthly things. In his first epistle, Peter wrote:

"Being born again, not of corruptible seed, but of incorruptible, by the word of God, which liveth and abideth for ever.

"For all flesh is as grass, and all the glory of man as the flower of grass. The grass withereth, and the flower thereof falleth away:

"But the word of the Lord endureth for ever. And this is the word which by the gospel is preached unto you." (1 Peter 1:23-25.)

9. O Zion, that bringest good tidings, get thee up into the high mountain; O Jerusalem, that bringest good tidings, lift up thy voice

Here is the Lord's clarion call to the righteous in the latter days. First, there is the call to the righteous who will gather to the American Zion. The Lord tells them to establish their headquarters in the "high mountain."

with strength; lift it up, be not afraid; say unto the cities of Judah, Behold your God!

It is interesting that those who became the custodians of the restored Gospel or "good tidings" in our day were not allowed to set up the foundation of Zion in New York, Ohio, Missouri, or Illinois. They were forced to flee to the tops of the high mountains. On the way they endured much suffering, and buried several thousand of their loved ones on the plains. Nevertheless, they did what this passage in Isaiah said they would do.

Commenting on this achievement, Elder Orson Pratt declared: "Did you come up into these high mountains, you people of the latter-day Zion?... He foretold it, and you have fulfilled it.... What tidings have you been declaring the last forty-five years to the nations and kingdoms of the earth?... Is not the everlasting Gospel glad tidings to the children of men?" (*Journal of Discourses,* 18:150.)

On October 24, 1841, a modern apostle dedicated the land of Jerusalem for the return of the Jews. The glad tidings then gradually went forth among them, "Return to the land of your fathers!" In due time they also will be prepared to hear the fulness of the Gospel. When that time comes, the children of Judah will lift up their voices in great strength. They will no longer have need to be afraid. Their great cities will be securely rebuilt. Their beautiful temple will be rebuilt. When all is prepared, the Savior will appear on the Mount of Olives and the angels will proclaim, "Judah, Behold your God!" This will occur at the conclusion of the great battle of Armageddon. Here is the way the Lord describes it in the Doctrine and Covenants:

"Then shall the arm of the Lord fall upon the nations.

"And then shall the Lord set his foot upon this mount, and it shall cleave in twain, and the earth shall tremble, and reel to and fro, and the heavens also shall shake....

"And then shall the Jews look upon me and say: What are these wounds in thine hands and in thy feet?

"Then shall they know that I am the Lord; for I will say unto them: These wounds are the wounds with which I was wounded in the house of my friends. I am he who was lifted up. I am Jesus that was crucified. I am the Son of God.

"And then shall they weep because of their iniquities; then shall they lament because they persecuted their king." (D&C 45:47–48, 51–53.)

10. Behold, the Lord GOD will come with strong hand, and his arm shall rule for him: behold, his reward is with him, and his work before him.

The appearance of the Savior to the Jews will be a momentous event, but the subsequent appearance of the Savior in power and glory TO ALL THE WORLD will be even greater. The scripture says he will be seen by all flesh, and the glory of his appearance will be so overwhelming that "every knee shall bow, every tongue shall swear" that Jesus is the Christ (Isaiah 45:23; see also Romans 14:11; Philippians 2:10–11; and D&C 88:104). After this glorious "second coming" there will be a great revelation of world history followed by a day of judgment. This is not the final judgment, but it determines who can be resurrected during the Millennium and who must wait until the end (D&C 88:100–101). It is in connection with this judgment that the Lord will reveal the history of the world, 1,000 years at a time. The life of every person will be shown, except those parts which have been blotted out by the Atonement. In the Doctrine and Covenants the Lord says:

"And then shall the first angel again sound his trump in the ears of all living, and reveal the secret acts of men, and the mighty works of God in the first thousand years.

"And then shall the second angel sound his trump, and reveal the secret acts of men, and the thoughts and intents of their hearts, and the mighty works of God in the second thousand years—

"And so on, until the seventh angel shall sound his trump." (D&C 88:108–10.)

Surely it will not be difficult to get each person to accept whatever judgment is meted out to him after each person's private life has been revealed for all to see. Many who were first in popular acclaim during earth life will turn out to be last after their secret lives have been shown. On the other hand, many who were counted as humble and insignificant will be shown in this vision to be among God's choicest spirits. So Isaiah declared that after all of this is projected for everyone to see it can be truly said that the Savior has brought the "reward" which each one deserved, and all mankind can see in the vision the great "work" which the Lord has done for the children of men from the beginning.

11. He shall feed his flock like a shepherd: he shall gather the lambs with his arm, and carry them in his bosom, and shall gently lead those that are with young.

During the Millennium, the Savior will minister to his people like a kind and gracious shepherd. He will gather them, organize them, and provide for their every need so that the work which must be done during the Millennium can be accelerated.

12. Who hath measured the waters in the hollow of his hand, and meted out heaven with the span, and comprehended the dust of the earth in a measure, and weighed the mountains in scales, and the hills in a balance?

As Isaiah contemplated the vast dominions of the seas which God controls, he could not help but praise the manifest power of God. Who can even contemplate the vast depths of the mighty oceans which the Lord holds, as it were, in the palm of his hand? And what about the wonders of the heavens where the giant stars wheel their way through the night sky? Or who can consider with full understanding the dust of the earth which obeys the Lord's command; or the huge chains of mountains that can be raised up, lowered, or even moved out of their places by a word from their Creator?

13. Who hath directed the Spirit of the LORD, or being his counsellor hath taught him?

14. With whom took he counsel, and who instructed him, and taught him in the path of judgment, and taught him knowledge, and shewed to him the way of understanding?

Isaiah now asks the most profound of all philosophical questions. From whence came the wisdom and knowledge of God? Who guided and instructed him in the science of the universe? There is an answer to these questions, but it is beyond the scope of man's comprehension in this life. The schooling provided in the family of the Gods must indeed be marvelous. One day the righteous children of the Father will be told all of these things (see D&C 76:94; 88:49, 67; 93:28; 101:32-35; 2 Nephi 9:13).

15. Behold, the nations are as a drop of a bucket, and are counted as the small dust of the balance: behold, he taketh up the isles as a very little thing.

Certain nations have risen to great power and dominion, but Isaiah declares that in the eye of the Lord they are merely "a drop of a bucket," and are no more than "the small dust" on the spectrum of eternal reality. Even the strongholds on the secluded isles of the sea are "a very little thing" to God.

16. And Lebanon is not sufficient to burn, nor the beasts thereof sufficient for a burnt offering.

When it comes to making a worthy offering before the Lord, the beauty and richness of mighty Lebanon would not be sufficient as an offering. Nor would the beasts of that whole land be an adequate sacrifice to express the thanksgiving and praise that the Lord deserves from his children.

17. All nations before him are as nothing; and they are counted to him less than nothing, and vanity.

When one contemplates that great expanse of the universe which God rules, surely the pride of individual nations, which consider themselves so great, is nothing. Their self-esteem and pride are pure vanity.

18. To whom then will ye liken God? or what likeness will ye compare unto him?

Now the prophet takes after those who have the audacity to think they can capture the beauty or power of God in a statue or image of wood and stone. Isaiah wants to know where one might find a proper model for such a being as God. How can the artist or worshipper find a "likeness" on earth which will compare with God?

19. The workman melteth a graven image, and the goldsmith spreadeth it over with gold, and casteth silver chains.

Wealthy people have their workmen model an image of God out of various kinds of metal, and then try to glorify its beauty by overlaying it with gold and by decorating it with chains of silver.

20. He that is so impoverished that he hath no oblation chooseth a tree that will not rot; he seeketh unto him a cunning workman to prepare a graven image, that shall not be moved.

The poor, on the other hand, who cannot afford a molten image or even an "oblation," go out and try to find a hardwood tree that will not easily rot. They then seek out some clever person who can carve the tree into a permanent graven image of wood that cannot be moved.

21. Have ye not known? have ye not heard? hath it not been told you from the beginning? have ye not understood from the foundations of the earth?

Isaiah chastises these idolaters, both rich and poor. They have no excuse for their foolish endeavors to portray God in either molten images or sculptured wood. After all, have they not been told over and over again about the one true God? Has not this great knowledge concerning the Lord been known from the beginning, from the very foundations of the earth?

22. It is he that sitteth upon the circle of the earth, and the inhabitants thereof are as grasshoppers; that stretcheth out the heavens as a curtain, and spreadeth them out as a tent to dwell in:

Isaiah declares that God is the Almighty who "sitteth upon the circle of the earth." Here is an interesting scriptural reference written around 700 B.C. describing the earth as a sphere. It is part of the traditional mythology of some people to believe that ancient men thought the earth was flat. As a matter of fact, the true nature of the earth as a sphere has been shown to the prophets of God from the beginning. Abraham says the patriarchs before the great flood had extensive knowledge of astronomy, and the nature of the earth and the planets (see Abraham 1:31). Abraham was actually given an open vision of the entire galaxy in which the earth has been placed (Abraham 3:1–13). The Book of Mormon prophets also knew the true nature of the earth and the planets (Helaman 12:15). Ancient men not only knew the earth was round, but Eratosthenes, a Greek scholar, rather accurately calculated the actual circumference of the earth. (See Samuel Eliot Morison, *Admiral of the Ocean Sea: A Life of Columbus* [Boston: Little, Brown and Company, 1942], p. 65.) Washington Irving somehow gained the impression that people thought the earth was flat at the time of Columbus, but his source turned out to be completely erroneous. Concerning this myth which crept into the American history books, the late Dr. Morison wrote: "Of all the vulgar errors connected with Columbus, the most persistent and the most absurd is that he had to convince people 'the world was round.' Every educated man in his day believed the world to be a sphere, every European university so taught geography." (Morison, *Admiral of the Ocean Sea*, p. 33; see also p. 89.)

Isaiah wanted the people to remind themselves that God is not only the supremely intelligent being who governs above "the circle of the earth," but that from his vantage point the inhabitants of this planet are like "grasshoppers." After all, he operates in a cosmic expanse where the heavens stretch out before him and constitute a great canopy, or tent. In the midst of this vast domain he dwells in glory.

23. That bringeth the princes to nothing; he maketh the judges of the earth as vanity.

The rise and fall of princes who govern on the earth for a brief moment in history are as nothing. The mighty judges with their power over life and death are likewise mere instruments of private pride and empty vanity.

24. Yea, they shall not be planted; yea, they shall not be sown: yea, their stock shall not take root in the earth: and he shall also blow upon them, and they shall wither, and the whirlwind shall take them away as stubble.

All these haughty and proud magistrates among men will not endure. None of them have permanent roots in the earth; nor will their children survive to perpetuate their names in later generations. Their wickedness and pride will cause them to wither away and disappear from off the face of the earth. It will be as though they had been swept up and carried away in a whirlwind.

25. To whom then will ye liken me, or shall I be equal? saith the Holy One.

Isaiah now quotes the Lord, who challenges his children to find anyone or anything on the face of the earth which could be likened unto God.

26. Lift up your eyes on high, and behold who hath created these things, that bringeth out their host by number: he calleth them all by names by the greatness of his might, for that he is strong in power; not one faileth.

Isaiah then seizes upon this same theme and challenges the children of men to lift their eyes toward the heavens and behold the wonders of the skies, where literally millions of stars and planets move in their majestic order through the cosmos. God knows each of these creations by name. He governs them with "the greatness of his might." Each one fulfills the measure of its creation, and none of them fail.

27. Why sayest thou, O Jacob, and speakest, O Israel, My way is hid from the LORD, and my judgment is passed over from my God?

Isaiah challenges the Israelites. They think their sins are hidden from the Lord and his judgment has passed over them without punishing them.

28. Hast thou not known? hast thou not heard, that the

Isaiah declares that they cannot say they have not been told the nature of the everlasting God. He is

everlasting God, the LORD, the Creator of the ends of the earth, fainteth not, neither is weary? there is no searching of his understanding.

omniscient and omnipotent, the Creator of all that exists in the earth. He has reached a state of perfection where he neither needs rest nor is subject to weakness. In fact, his greatness is so all-encompassing that it is beyond the comprehension and understanding of man.

29. He giveth power to the faint; and to them that have no might he increaseth strength.

Not only is God omnipotent himself, but he gives power to the righteous when they are faint. When his children have no power to accomplish the tremendous tasks assigned to them, God increases their strength.

30. Even the youths shall faint and be weary, and the young men shall utterly fall:

31. But they that wait upon the LORD shall renew their strength; they shall mount up with wings as eagles; they shall run, and not be weary; and they shall walk, and not faint.

It is commonplace for the youth to feel they are virtually immortal and capable of any task, but eventually they discover their limitations and often they falter. Some of them fall. Nevertheless, the Lord wants those who humbly wait for him and obey his commandments to know that they will be supported so as to accomplish more than they ever dreamed. They will not be overcome by the weaknesses which can be seen in others. The Lord says he will actually "renew their strength; they shall mount up with wings as eagles; THEY SHALL RUN, AND NOT BE WEARY; AND THEY SHALL WALK, AND NOT FAINT." These words constitute a promise which the Lord reiterated in the latter days concerning those who would resist the temptation of addictive drugs, tobacco, alcohol, and kindred excesses. The Lord said these health-destroying poisons would be promoted "in consequence of evils and designs which do and will exist in the hearts of conspiring men in the last days" (D&C 89:4). He then gave this promise to all those who follow his revealed Word of Wisdom:

"And all saints who remember to keep and do these sayings, walking in obedience to the commandments, shall receive health in their navel and marrow to their bones;

"And shall find wisdom and great treasures of knowledge, even hidden treasures;

"AND SHALL RUN AND NOT BE WEARY, AND SHALL WALK AND NOT FAINT.

"And I, the Lord, give unto them a promise, that the destroying angel shall pass by them, as the children of Israel, and not slay them." (D&C 89:18–21; emphasis added.)

The Lord makes a similar promise in the Old Testament where he says:

"Trust in the Lord with all thine heart; and lean not unto thine own understanding.

"In all thy ways acknowledge him, and he shall direct thy paths.

"Be not wise in thine own eyes: fear the Lord, and depart from evil.

"IT SHALL BE HEALTH TO THY NAVEL, AND MARROW TO THY BONES." (Proverbs 3:5–8; emphasis added.)

Isaiah, Chapter 41

INTRODUCTION:

This chapter is addressed primarily to the seed of Abraham who will be gathered in the latter days on the "islands," which means the distant lands of America and the isles of the Pacific. Isaiah knew they would be persecuted and afflicted. Nevertheless, he also knew they would have true prophets among them whereas their persecutors would have deceptive leaders who would misguide and confuse them.

1. Keep silence before me, O islands; and let the people renew their strength: let them come near; then let them speak: let us come near together to judgment.

Whenever Isaiah speaks to the "islands" we always pay particular attention because the Book of Mormon prophets knew that the islands included the great Western Hemisphere (see 2 Nephi 10:20). The Lord's command that the islands "keep silence before me" no doubt refers to the fact that God intended to keep them hidden from Europe and Asia until it was time for the great work of the latter days to come forth (2 Nephi 1:8-9). Isaiah was shown that America would become the headquarters for launching God's premillennial campaign to spread the Gospel message to every nation, kindred, tongue, and people. Eventually the people of the "islands" would be renewed in strength because they would come near unto the Lord. This also might have reference to the raising up and establishment of the first free people in modern times on the American continent, where the Gospel could be restored (3 Nephi 21:4). Once this free nation becomes established, the Lord can say "let them come near" so that they can hear the great message of the restored

Gospel. After they have been taught the Lord can say "then let them speak" and declare the Gospel to the whole world. All of this is to prepare mankind for God's premillenial judgment that will occur shortly after the Savior comes in glory. Meanwhile, the peoples of the earth will either respond to the Gospel message and be blessed, or they will reject the message and receive the judgment that goes with it (D&C 43:23–30).

2. Who raised up the righteous man from the east, called him to his foot, gave the nations before him, and made him rule over kings? he gave them as the dust to his sword, and as driven stubble to his bow.

3. He pursued them, and passed safely; even by the way that he had not gone with his feet.

4. Who hath wrought and done it, calling the generations from the beginning? I the LORD, the first, and with the last; I am he.

Who is this "righteous man from the east" whom God raised up? Some thought it meant Abraham. Others thought it meant Cyrus, the famous Persian king. The points in favor of Abraham include the fact that the phrase "called him to his foot" is now said to be more accurately deciphered as being "called him to follow." This would apply to Abraham, but not to Cyrus.

Dr. Monte Nyman of Brigham Young University states that if verses 2 to 4 are taken in context, they clearly point to Abraham: "Abraham was called by the Lord to leave Ur of the Chaldees and go to the land of Canaan (see Genesis 11:31; 12:1; Abraham 2:1–6). He was given 'the nations before him' extending from 'the river of Egypt unto the great river, the river Euphrates' (Genesis 15:18).... A more positive identification of Abraham comes from verse 4, wherein the Lord makes reference to 'calling the generations from the beginning.' Abraham was chosen in the premortal life to be a ruler (see Abraham 3:22–23; Genesis 18:19) and was blessed that through the literal seed of his body the Lord would bless all the nations of the earth (Genesis 12:2–3; Abraham 2:8–11). These verses in Isaiah proclaim that the Lord was the one who had so ordained these things." (Nyman, *"Great Are the Words of Isaiah,"* p. 152.)

5. The isles saw it, and feared; the ends of the earth were afraid, drew near, and came.

6. They helped every one his neighbour; and every one said to his brother, Be of good courage.

7. So the carpenter encouraged the goldsmith, and he that smootheth with the hammer him that smote the anvil, saying, It is ready for the sodering: and he fastened it with nails, that it should not be moved.

Dr. Nyman continues: "Verse 5 describes the gathering of the nations to the Americas, as prophesied in verse 1. 'The isles saw it, and feared,' meaning they responded to Jehovah's call and, in the fear (love) of the Lord, 'drew near, and came,' and built up a mighty Gentile nation in the land of America (see 1 Nephi 22:7). Verses 6 and 7 describe the cooperation required of the people from many lands who firmly established a nation 'that it should not be moved.' Actually, this could be a dual prophecy of the establishment of the nation and of the Church upon that land." (Nyman, *"Great Are the Words of Isaiah,"* pp. 152–53.)

8. But thou, Israel, art my servant, Jacob whom I have chosen, the seed of Abraham my friend.

9. Thou whom I have taken from the ends of the earth, and called thee from the chief men thereof, and said unto thee, Thou art my servant; I have chosen thee, and not cast thee away.

"These verses," Dr. Nyman writes, "identify the servant who is to speak. The Lord promised Abraham that his literal seed would bless the nations of the earth (Abraham 2:11). He now calls Israel, the literal seed of Abraham, whom he has gathered from the nations of the earth to the islands (America), to be his servant in bringing judgment upon all the nations of the earth. The Doctrine and Covenants identifies the Latter-day Saints who had gathered as the literal seed of Abraham (see D&C 103:17; 132:30–31) and as the Lord's servants (see D&C 93:46; 133:30–32). Thus, chapter 41 is a prophecy of latter-day Israel, called initially to gather upon the isles of the sea (America) to be servants in the hand of the Lord to fulfill the covenant he made with Abraham to bear the ministry and the priesthood to the nations of the earth." (Nyman, *"Great Are the Words of Isaiah,"* p. 153.)

10. Fear thou not; for I am with thee: be not dismayed; for I

Anyone who is familiar with the great hymn "How Firm a Foundation" (*Hymns,* nos. 66, 313) will recognize words and phrases from this verse in Isaiah, which

**am thy God: I will strength-
en thee; yea, I will help
thee; yea, I will uphold thee
with the right hand of my
righteousness.**

became the inspiration for this beloved song. The Lord
knew the Saints of the latter days would necessarily
have to endure great trials in order to spread the
fulness of the restored Gospel to all mankind. This
admonition recorded by Isaiah was for their encouragement. They were to "fear...not" and "be not
dismayed," for the Lord would strengthen them and
help them. These words were sung by the Latter-day
Saints thousands of times during their travails and
tribulations as they found themselves being driven
from their homes four times and were finally forced to
flee to the mountains, just as Isaiah prophesied they
would (see Isaiah 40:9).

**11. Behold, all they that were
incensed against thee shall
be ashamed and confound-
ed: they shall be as nothing;
and they that strive with
thee shall perish.**

This is to assure God's servants of the latter days
that all those who would become angry and "incensed
against thee" shall become ashamed. They will be
confounded and "shall be as nothing." The Lord
promised that those who would diligently seek to
destroy his servants would perish themselves. An
interesting thing occurred on June 25, 1844, when a
group of militia officers came to visit Joseph Smith in
Carthage Jail. The latter-day prophet was only two
days away from martyrdom. As he looked at these men
who were persecuting the Saints, Joseph Smith said:

"I can see what is in your hearts, and [I] will tell you
what I see. I can see that you thirst for blood, and
nothing but my blood will satisfy you. It is not for
crime of any description that I and my brethren are
thus continually persecuted and harassed by our
enemies; but there are other motives,...and inasmuch
as you and the people thirst for blood, I prophesy, in
the name of the Lord, that you shall witness scenes of
blood and sorrow to your entire satisfaction. Your
souls shall be perfectly satiated with blood, and many
of you who are now present shall have an opportunity

to face the cannon's mouth from sources you think not of; and those people that desire this great evil upon me and my brethren, shall be filled with regret and sorrow because of the scenes of desolation and distress that await them. They shall seek for peace, and shall not be able to find it. Gentlemen, you will find what I have told you to be true." (*History of the Church*, 6:566.)

Joseph Smith prophesied the Civil War as early as 1832, and this prophecy appeared in a number of Church publications during the following three decades. On Christmas Day, 1832, Joseph Smith wrote:

"Verily, thus saith the Lord concerning the wars that will shortly come to pass, beginning at the rebellion of South Carolina, which will eventually terminate in the death and misery of many souls; ...

"For behold, the Southern States shall be divided against the Northern States, and the Southern States will call on other nations, even the nation of Great Britain, as it is called, ... in order to defend themselves. ...

"And it shall come to pass, after many days, slaves shall rise up against their masters, who shall be marshaled and disciplined for war." (D&C 87:1, 3-4.)

12. Thou shalt seek them, and shalt not find them, even them that contended with thee: they that war against thee shall be as nothing, and as a thing of nought.

In this verse Isaiah is referring to the humble efforts of the elders of Israel who went among their enemies to share with them the restored Gospel but found themselves rejected and sometimes mobbed by those they wanted to help. At the height of the persecution of the Saints in Ohio and Missouri, the Lord told his modern prophet to send missionaries to England. The work began in 1837. Over the next few years thousands were converted. Many of these new converts migrated to America and formed the bulwark of the Church during its migration to the mountains and early years of settlement in the West.

13. For I the LORD thy God will hold thy right hand, saying unto thee, Fear not; I will help thee.

Looking back, it is marvelous to contemplate the numerous ways in which the gathering Israelites of the latter days were blessed, and finally became a mighty commonwealth in the tops of the mountains.

14. Fear not, thou worm Jacob, and ye men of Israel; I will help thee, saith the LORD, and thy redeemer, the Holy One of Israel.

The Lord knew the Saints of the latter days would be ground into the dust under the heels of their oppressors but that out of this dust the "worm Jacob" (the humble, lowly servants of God) would come forth as mighty "men of Israel" because the Redeemer, the Holy One of Israel, would help them. Isaiah knew that Jehovah of the Old Testament was none other than the premortal Jesus Christ. He had seen the Savior and knew of his great mission as the Redeemer of the world (see 2 Nephi 11:2). He therefore referred to Jehovah on 13 occasions as the Redeemer, and on 8 occasions as the Savior. (These are listed in James Strong, *The Exhaustive Concordance of the Bible* [New York: Abingdon Press, 1890].)

15. Behold, I will make thee a new sharp threshing instrument having teeth: thou shalt thresh the mountains, and beat them small, and shalt make the hills as chaff.

16. Thou shalt fan them, and the wind shall carry them away, and the whirlwind shall scatter them: and thou shalt rejoice in the LORD, and shalt glory in the Holy One of Israel.

The Lord looks upon the missionary work in the latter days as a great threshing machine. The "teeth" are the missionaries who go in among the multitudes to seek out the good grain and to separate it from the chaff. In ancient times the threshed wheat was thrown into the air so that the wind could carry away the chaff and leave the golden grain on the threshing floor. This is what the Lord said he intended to do in the latter days. There is a great whirlwind coming for the unrighteous who will not accept the call of the Lord. On the other hand, those who realize what the restoration of the Gospel represents will "rejoice in the Lord, and [will] glory in the Holy One of Israel," whom Isaiah identifies in verse 14 as the Redeemer.

17. When the poor and needy seek water, and there is none, and their tongue faileth for thirst, I the LORD will hear them, I the God of Israel will not forsake them.

18. I will open rivers in high places, and fountains in the midst of the valleys: I will make the wilderness a pool of water, and the dry land springs of water.

19. I will plant in the wilderness the cedar, the shittah tree, and the myrtle, and the oil tree; I will set in the desert the fir tree, and the pine, and the box tree together:

In these three verses the Lord predicts that in the latter days the "poor and needy" Saints of God will be driven to lands where there is practically no water. They will pray to the Lord for help in making the land fertile. The Lord says he will hear them. Here are Brigham Young's descriptions of "the poor and needy" as they arrived in the Salt Lake Valley:

"[The Saints were badly off] when they came into this valley, twenty-five years ago. They picked up a few buckskins, antelope skins, sheepskins, buffalo skins, and made leggings and moccasins of them, and wrapped the buffalo robes around them. Some had blankets and some had not; some had shirts, and I guess some had not. One man told me that he had not a shirt for himself or family." (*Journal of Discourses,* 15:158.)

"I will venture to say that not one of four out of my family had shoes to their feet when we came to this valley." (Ibid., 11:288.)

"We came here penniless in old wagons, our friends back [east] telling us to 'take all the provisions you can, for you can get no more!'... We did this, and in addition to all this we have gathered all the poor we could, and the Lord has planted us in these valleys, promising that He would hide us up for a little season until His wrath and indignation passed over the nations." (Ibid. 13:217.)

When the Saints arrived in the Great Salt Lake Valley in 1847 it was a panorama of sagebrush, alkali flats, a dead sea, and one stunted tree to welcome them. When Horace Greeley saw it twelve years later he described it using words like: "Parched, glistening, blistering, blinding, sterility!" He declared that if the Mormons had paid the government a penny an acre for it they would have been swindled (William R. Palmer, "The Pioneering Mormon," *Improvement Era,* August 1942, p. 493).

To plant crops, the pioneers dammed up the tiny streams flowing from the mountains and forced the precious water out across the valley floor to soften the parched ground for their plows. Some of the pioneers planted their seed corn and potatoes the afternoon they arrived, and would not eat until they had finished. By the end of the Civil War, the Salt Lake Valley had 277 canals irrigating over 150,000 acres of what would otherwise have been arid, unusable land. (Susa Young Gates, *The Life Story of Brigham Young* [New York: Macmillan Co., 1930], p. 130.)

Not only was this done in the valleys of the mountains, but in the deserts and vast regions of wilderness which Isaiah no doubt saw in his vision. He saw them planting all kinds of trees and orchards. As they dug wells he saw that from the "dry land" came "springs of water."

20. That they may see, and know, and consider, and understand together, that the hand of the LORD hath done this, and the Holy One of Israel hath created it.

Isaiah saw that the blessings of the Lord would be so spectacular that there would be no doubt in the minds of the people that the Lord had intervened in their behalf. Brigham Young stated:

"We made and broke the road from Nauvoo to this place. Some of the time we followed Indian trails; some of the time we ran by the compass; when we left the Missouri river we followed the Platte. And we killed rattlesnakes by the cord in some places; and made roads and built bridges till our backs ached. Where we could not build bridges across rivers we ferried our people across, until we arrived here, where we found a few naked Indians, a few wolves and rabbits, and any amount of crickets; but as for a green tree or a fruit tree, or any green fields, we found nothing of the kind, with the exception of a few cottonwoods and willows on the edge of City Creek. For some 1200 or 1300 miles we carried every particle of provision we had when we arrived here. When we left our homes we picked up what the mob did not steal of our horses, oxen and calves, and some women drove their own teams here. Instead of 365 pounds of breadstuff when they started from the Missouri river, there was not half of them had half of it. We had to bring our seed grain, our farming utensils, bureaus, secretaries, sideboards, sofas, pianos, large looking glasses, fine chairs, carpets, nice shovels and tongs, and other fine furniture, with all the parlor, cook stoves, etc.; and we had to bring these things piled together with the women and children, helter skelter, topsy turvy, with broken down horses, ringboned, spavined, pole evil, fistula and hipped; oxen with three legs, and cows with one tit. This was our only means of transportation, and if we had not brought our goods in this manner we should not have had them, for there was nothing here. You may say this is a burlesque. Well, I mean it as such, for we, comparatively speaking, really came here naked and barefoot." (Brigham Young, in *Journal of Discourses,* 12:286–287.)

"We had to have faith to come here. When we met Mr. [Jim] Bridger on the Big Sandy River, said he, 'Mr. Young, I would give a thousand dollars if I knew an ear of corn could be ripened in the Great Basin.' Said I, 'Wait eighteen months and I will show you many of them.' Did I say this from knowledge? No, it was my faith; but we had not the least encouragement—from natural reasoning and all that we could learn of this country—of its sterility, its cold and frost, to believe that we could ever raise anything. But we travelled on, breaking the road through the mountains and building bridges until we arrived here, and then we did everything we could to sustain ourselves. We had faith that we could raise grain." (Ibid., 13:173.)

21. Produce your cause, saith the LORD; bring forth your

If all of these predictions concerning the future seem incredible, let those who are skeptics produce their

strong reasons, saith the King of Jacob.

arguments why they believe the God of Israel cannot do these things for his people.

22. Let them bring them forth, and shew us what shall happen: let them shew the former things, what they be, that we may consider them, and know the latter end of them; or declare us things for to come.

Let these doubters see if they can accurately predict such marvelous things which are yet to come. Let THEM prove their credibility. Let them demonstrate how they have predicted things of the past which literally came to pass.

23. Shew the things that are to come hereafter, that we may know that ye are gods: yea, do good, or do evil, that we may be dismayed, and behold it together.

Again the Lord challenges these doubters and worshippers of idols to produce their prophecies which have been fulfilled in the past. Their priests claim to have power from their deities of wood and stone. Very well, let us see them do something remarkably good, or even something remarkably evil, so that everyone will know that they are gods of power. Then the people can see it together and be "dismayed" by so spectacular an achievement.

24. Behold, ye are of nothing, and your work of nought: an abomination is he that chooseth you.

But, of course, this will never happen because these gods are nothing but wood and stone. They will never do anything. It is an abomination for anyone to believe in them and to use them as an excuse to deny the great powers of the one true God.

25. I have raised up one from the north, and he shall come: from the rising of the sun shall he call upon my name: and he shall come upon princes as upon morter, and as the potter treadeth clay.

The Lord declares to the unbelieving that he has already raised up a great prophet from the north who came out of the east. This is probably making further reference to Abraham, who came to the land of Canaan from Haran in the north, but had previously come from Ur in the east. Unlike those who doubt the Lord, this great servant of God called upon the Almighty in humble prayer from the rising of the sun. Consequently, he is chosen of God to overcome all princes and powers. They will be subject to him, and to his posterity, as clay under the feet of a potter who mixes it by treading upon it.

26. Who hath declared from the beginning, that we may know? and beforetime, that we may say, He is righteous? yea, there is none that sheweth, yea, there is none that declareth, yea, there is none that heareth your words.

The Lord once more challenges those who doubt his words and who worship idols. He asks if there have been any among them who have been able to describe all things from the beginning, or prophesy of things yet future, so that the people could plainly perceive that they were men of righteousness sent from God. They and their idols have had no such persons rise up to tell them of these great things of the past. Neither have there been any among them who could declare the future with accuracy as the prophets of God are able to do. Therefore, nobody can have confidence in anything the wretched, idolatrous prophets have to say.

27. The first shall say to Zion, Behold, behold them: and I will give to Jerusalem one that bringeth good tidings.

This verse is given more clearly in the Anchor Bible, where it says, "In the beginning I spoke to Zion, and to Jerusalem I will send a messenger" (58 vols. [Garden City, N.Y.: Doubleday & Co., 1968], 20:34). This would be a messenger who would bring good tidings and truthfully prophesy of great things to come.

28. For I beheld, and there was no man; even among them, and there was no counsellor, that, when I asked of them, could answer a word.

But among the unbelievers there will be no such messenger, nor will there be any "counsellor" who can give the people advice concerning the future. When the wicked are challenged to produce their great prophets and leaders with spiritual powers, they will not be able to "answer a word."

29. **Behold, they are all vanity; their works are nothing: their molten images are wind and confusion.**

The reason they will not be able to answer is because they are false prophets. They are the product of pride and vanity. They will pretend to be great prophets when they are not. They will amount to nothing of significance. The phony prophets of molten images will pontificate nothing but stomach wind and confusion.

Isaiah, Chapter 42

INTRODUCTION:

This portion of the book of Isaiah is almost like a continuous revelation sweeping along from chapter to chapter. Isaiah is looking into the future. There is no reference to any historical event or circumstance belonging to Isaiah's day that identifies the time or place where the revelation was given.

1. Behold my servant, whom I uphold; mine elect, in whom my soul delighteth; I have put my spirit upon him: he shall bring forth judgment to the Gentiles.

Beginning with the first part of this chapter, Isaiah makes four references to God's special "servant." The other three are in Isaiah 49:1-6; 50:1-11; and 52:13-53:12. In verses 1 to 4 of this chapter, Isaiah is speaking of the Christ. The words of Matthew give a better rendition of this first verse by saying:

"Behold my servant, whom I HAVE CHOSEN; my BELOVED, in whom my soul is WELL PLEASED: I will put my spirit upon him, and he shall SHEW judgment to the Gentiles." (Matthew 12:18; emphasis added.)

Notice that in the beginning of chapter 40 there was a clear reference to the coming of John the Baptist. At the beginning of this chapter Isaiah seems to be referring to the events which would transpire when John baptized the Savior "to fulfil all righteousness" (2 Nephi 31:5). Notice how much of Isaiah 42:1 is fulfilled in the third chapter of Matthew:

"And Jesus, when he was baptized, went up straightway out of the water: and, lo, the heavens were opened unto him, and he saw the Spirit of God descending like a dove, and lighting upon him:

"And lo a voice from heaven, saying, This is my beloved Son, in whom I AM WELL PLEASED." (Matthew 3:16–17; emphasis added.)

Isaiah adds that this "servant" of the Lord would show "judgment" to the Gentiles. In the end Jesus will proclaim a judgment upon all mankind.

2. He shall not cry, nor lift up, nor cause his voice to be heard in the street.

Matthew gives this verse as follows: "He shall not strive, nor cry; neither shall any man hear his voice in the streets" (Matthew 12:19). Jesus was not a rabble-rouser. He never gathered crowds in the street to harangue them.

3. A bruised reed shall he not break, and the smoking flax shall he not quench: he shall bring forth judgment unto truth.

This verse is also given more completely in the writings of Matthew: "A bruised reed shall he not break, and smoking flax shall he not quench, TILL HE SEND FORTH JUDGMENT unto VICTORY." (Matthew 12:20; emphasis added.)

Jesus made no attempt to exercise his mighty power against false teachers, the spiritually weak, or even against the smoking flax of the depraved and wicked rulers whose unrighteousness later brought down a conflagration of destruction on the people. All of these were endured by Jesus during his ministry. He knew they would come to judgment in the day of Christ's great victory just before his millennial reign is ushered in.

4. He shall not fail nor be discouraged, till he have set judgment in the earth: and the isles shall wait for his law.

During all the centuries of apostasy following the Savior's ministry, he did not falter or fail to dispense whatever light the Gentiles were willing to receive from his hand. Meanwhile, the inhabitants of the isles waited for the restoration of the Gospel, when God's law would be revealed in its fulness. As we have already seen, "the isles" refer to the Western Hemisphere (the American continents, 2 Nephi 10:20) and the islands where the scattered people of Israel are dwelling.

As we saw in chapter 29, Isaiah knew all about the restoration of the Gospel in America. He knew some of the most intimate details about the coming forth of the Book of Mormon. He also knew that the children of Lehi (the Indian nations) would be waiting for the reappearance of the "Great White God" who had appeared among their ancestors as a glorious resurrected being and had promised to return again with his law. These people on the "isles" were waiting for all of this when America was first discovered. In fact, the natives mistook the Spanish invaders for the return of the "Great White God." This happened not only in Mexico and Peru, but among the Hawaiians and Polynesians (see Mark E. Petersen, "The Great White God Was a Reality," *Improvement Era*, Sept. 1969, pp. 6-9; or "Christ in America," [pamphlet, n.d.]). In 1831 the law of the Gospel first began to be preached among the Indian tribes in fulfillment of Isaiah's prophecy.

5. Thus saith God the LORD, he that created the heavens, and stretched them out; he that spread forth the earth, and that which cometh out of it; he that giveth breath unto the people upon it, and spirit to them that walk therein:

Although the creation was actually carried out by the Savior as "the Word" (John 1:1-3), or the administrator of the Father's power, yet it was Elohim, the "Father of all," who provided the supreme guiding power through which the Savior carried out the creative work. In this verse the attributes of the Father are described although they were administered through his Son. It was the Father's power by which the heavens and the earth were brought into being, and everything that was produced from the dust of the earth and made to grow and flourish was by that same power. It was this same Supreme Being who gave life to mankind and placed spirits in all creatures that walk or move upon the face of the earth. This is the Being who declared what we read in the next verse.

6. I the LORD have called thee in righteousness, and will hold thine hand, and will keep thee, and give thee for a covenant of the people, for a light of the Gentiles;

The Father called Jesus Christ to be the Savior of the world because of his righteousness in the premortal existence. From the beginning, the Father intended to bless his Beloved Son and hold his hand to guide him through the dark corridors of earthly life through which his mission would take him. The Father intended to offer his Beloved Son in order to fulfill the promise or covenant that he had made during the Grand Council in Heaven. The Father promised to send his Son to redeem all mankind from death and exalt those who accepted God's plan to eternal salvation. He also promised to send his Beloved Son to give light and hope to the Gentiles as well as to Israel. As it turned out, the "light of Christ" was carried to the Gentiles by the apostles, especially Paul (see Acts 22:21; Romans 11:13).

7. To open the blind eyes, to bring out the prisoners from the prison, and them that sit in darkness out of the prison house.

The real meaning of this verse would be very obscure if it were not for the words of the apostle Peter, who said: "For Christ also hath once suffered for sins, the just for the unjust, that he might bring us to God, being put to death in the flesh, but quickened by the Spirit: by which also he went and PREACHED UNTO THE SPIRITS IN PRISON; which sometime were disobedient, when once the longsuffering of God waited in the days of Noah, while the ark was a preparing, wherein few, that is, eight souls were saved by water." (1 Peter 3:18–20; emphasis added.)

Isaiah knew that Jesus would preach to the spirits of the dead who had heard the Gospel before the Great Flood but had rejected it and died in wickedness. Consequently, when they passed over into the spirit world they were held in custody or imprisonment until they could be taught the Gospel again. Jesus initiated this ministry to those in the spirit world following his crucifixion. Joseph Smith commented on the seventh verse, saying, "It is very evident from this that He not only went to preach to them, but to deliver, or bring them out of the prison house" (Smith, *Teachings*, p. 219).

---

8. I am the LORD: that is my name: and my glory will I not give to another, neither my praise to graven images.

The very name of God, or Lord, refers to his complete supremacy in the heavens and on the earth. The glory and power of that supremacy will never be given to graven images of wood, stone, gold, or silver. Mankind instinctively longs to worship something it can see, but during our second estate God has purposely hidden himself from us. This is not because he no longer loves us, but because we are passing through a testing period, a probationary estate, where we are learning the difference between good and evil (see Abraham 3:24–26; 2 Nephi 2:5, 18, 26). Nevertheless, it is the inclination of all of humanity to want something tangible to remind them of God, hence they make graven images. Before long, however, they begin offering to the images the praise and glory which should be addressed only to God.

---

9. Behold, the former things are come to pass, and new things do I declare: before they spring forth I tell you of them.

All the former things which God has inspired his prophets to declare to the people have come to pass. They have come to pass literally in every instance. Now the coming of Christ and many new things are being declared, and these also will be fulfilled literally.

---

10. Sing unto the LORD a new song, and his praise from the end of the earth, ye that go down to the sea, and all that is therein; the isles, and the inhabitants thereof.

Isaiah invites the whole earth to sing a song of praise to God concerning these great things that the Lord will do for mankind. This song should be sung by all the inhabitants of the earth, those who are on the ships at sea, and those who are separated from the major continents, those who dwell upon the islands of the ocean seas.

11. Let the wilderness and the cities therof lift up their voice, the villages that Kedar doth inhabit: let the inhabitants of the rock sing, let them shout from the top of the mountains.

12. Let them give glory unto the LORD, and declare his praise in the islands.

Isaiah invites those who inhabit the wilderness, as well as those who are in the cities, to join in this great song of adoration and triumph to the Lord. Isaiah wants the villages of Kedar (the Arabian inhabitants of the desert named after the second son of Ishmael) to join in the song. He further invites "the inhabitants of the rock" to shout their praises from the tops of the mountains. He also wants to hear this praise from the inhabitants in the islands of the sea.

"The inhabitants of the rock" may have a more profound meaning than merely people living in the caves of the rocks. Isaiah may have known the same profound principles of God-science that Abraham, Jacob, Mormon, and other prophets have known; namely, that the elements exemplified in the rocks are INHABITED by innumerable intelligences that are organized and obey God by following the pattern that he has given them in their various kingdoms or levels of existence. Abraham described how the physical elements "obeyed" as God commanded them during the creation process (see Abraham 4:10, 18). Jacob described how those holding the Priesthood of God were able to command the trees, mountains, and the sea; and testified that the elements did obey (Jacob 4:6). Mormon described how the dust, even the planet on which we live, moves and obeys according to the commandment of God (see Helaman 12:8–14).

As Brigham Young said: "There is life [intelligence] in all matter, throughout the vast extent of all the eternities; it is in the rock, the sand, the dust, in water, air, the gases, and, in short, in every description and organization of matter, whether it be solid, liquid, or gaseous, particle operating with particle" (*Journal of Discourses,* 3:277).

These intelligences which "inhabit" the elements, or the rocks, also rejoice and honor God. That is why they "obey" him. They also can praise him. Isaiah very well may have known this doctrine which was revealed when the Gospel was restored.

13. The LORD shall go forth as a mighty man, he shall stir up jealousy like a man of war: he shall cry, yea, roar; he shall prevail against his enemies.

In the great day of the Lord's power he will go forth in strength like "a mighty man." Men will envy such a display of power even as they envy great and valiant men of war. During his earthly ministry Jesus was meek and relatively quiet. This will not be the case when he comes in judgment. He will denounce the wickedness of the world. His mighty judgment will roar through the earth to destroy those who have been the deliberate and defiant enemies of righteousness.

14. I have long time holden my peace; I have been still, and refrained myself: now will I cry like a travailing woman; I will destroy and devour at once.

Not only during his ministry, but down through the centuries of apostasy and wickedness that followed, the Lord has held his peace and refrained from exercising his great power. But in his day of judgment it will be different. He will cry out against those who have performed their wicked debaucheries on the earth. Like a whirlwind, the judgments of God will sweep down upon the wicked so that there will be few men left (see Isaiah 24:6).

15. I will make waste mountains and hills, and dry up all their herbs; and I will make the rivers islands, and I will dry up the pools.

This verse is a further elaboration on the catastrophic consequences that will accompany the unveiling of God's manifest power. It will sweep like a tidal wave of destruction over the whole earth. Mountains will be laid waste; forests and fields will be denuded of their foliage; rivers will become dry streambeds and sandbars; and the thousands of lakes which originally dotted the land will become bone dry.

16. And I will bring the blind by a way that they knew not; I will lead them in paths that they have not known: I will make darkness light before them, and crooked things straight. These things will I do unto them, and not forsake them.

The Lord now promises that those who were blind to the truth and had no knowledge of the true and only way to happiness and salvation will be shown the way. He will lead them into paths of righteousness that they did not know existed. Suddenly the way before them will cease to be dark and frightening. It will become illuminated. The crooked thoroughfare will be made straight. The Lord assures his people that he will do all of these things in the great last days.

17. They shall be turned back, they shall be greatly ashamed, that trust in graven images, that say to the molten images, Ye are our gods.

But as for those who remain caught up in their mythological idolatry, they will be turned back upon themselves. Nothing will save them, not even their cries of anguish to their dumb idols, saying: "Ye are our gods."

It is interesting that in modern times the instinct to worship in an idolatrous manner is no longer manifest in temples built to graven images, but rather in temples built to enshrine the elements of wealth and power. Some worship in temples where massive depositories of political power have been established. Others worship in 100-story skyscrapers, where their lust for greed and power sometimes leads them to make momentous decisions that adversely affect the lives and welfare of millions of people. In all of these temples it is not uncommon to hear the adulation, "Ye are our gods!" But in the end, Isaiah warned, these gods of power and wealth will find themselves enmeshed in a shambles of destruction. They will look upon the ruins of their temples and "be greatly ashamed."

18. Hear, ye deaf; and look, ye blind, that ye may see.

The Lord does not want to see his children ashamed, nor dependent on forces that will fail them. Therefore, he pleads with all humanity, saying: "Hear, ye deaf; and look, ye blind, that ye may see."

19. Who is blind, but my servant? or deaf, as my messenger that I sent? who is blind as he that is perfect, and blind as the LORD's servant?

In the King James Version this particular verse is puzzling. The Joseph Smith Translation gives us the correct text as Isaiah originally wrote it: "For I will send my servant unto you who are blind; yea, a messenger to open the eyes of the blind, and unstop the ears of the deaf; and they shall be made perfect notwithstanding their blindness, if they will hearken unto the messenger, the Lord's servant." (JST, Isaiah 42:19–20.)

20. Seeing many things, but thou observest not; opening the ears, but he heareth not.

The Inspired Version also gives this verse a more complete and comprehensible meaning: "Thou art a people, seeing many things, but thou observest not; opening the ears to hear, but thou hearest not." (JST, Isaiah 42:21.)

21. The LORD is well pleased for his righteousness' sake; he will magnify the law, and make it honourable.

In the King James Version, this verse is also seriously scrambled. Here is the way it originally read: "The Lord is NOT well pleased with such a people, but for his righteousness' sake he will magnify the law and make it honorable." (JST, Isaiah 42:22; emphasis added.)

22. But this is a people robbed and spoiled; they are all of them snared in holes, and they are hid in prison houses: they are for a prey, and none delivereth; for a spoil, and none saith, Restore.

Here is another verse which is rendered much more accurately in the Joseph Smith Translation: "Thou art a people robbed and spoiled; THINE ENEMIES, all of them, have snared THEE in holes, and they have hid THEE in prison houses; they have taken THEE for a prey, and none delivereth; for a spoil, and none saith, Restore." (JST, Isaiah 42:23; emphasis added.)

The Lord is not well pleased with such a people. It is not the Lord or his servants who do not see or hear. It is the people. They have been ensnared by their enemies.

23. Who among you will give
ear to this? who will hearken
and hear for the time to
come?

24. Who gave Jacob for a spoil,
and Israel to the robbers?

24. Who gave Jacob for a spoil,
and Israel to the robbers?
did not the LORD, he against
whom we have sinned? for
they would not walk in his
ways, neither were they
obedient unto his law.

25. Therefore he hath poured
upon him the fury of his
anger, and the strength of
battle: and it hath set him
on fire round about, yet he
knew not; and it burned
him, yet he laid it not to
heart.

These verses are arranged somewhat differently in
the Joseph Smith Translation. They are also given in a
different context: "Who among them will give ear unto
THEE, or hearken and hear THEE for the time to come?
and who gave Jacob for a spoil, and Israel to the
robbers? did not the Lord, he against whom THEY have
sinned?

"For THEY would not walk in his ways, neither were
they obedient unto his law; therefore he hath poured
upon them the fury of his anger, and the strength of
battle; and they have set them on fire round about, yet
THEY know not, and it burned them, yet they laid it not
to heart." (JST, Isaiah 42:24–25; emphasis added.)

It is tragic that those who were foreordained in the
premortal existence to be God's chosen leaders here on
earth (see Deuteronomy 32:6–9) will often ignore the
call of the Lord. Those who will not walk in the light of
Christ, and who will not allow the Lord to help them
straighten out their crooked pathways of life, will find
themselves reaping the same judgment of destruction
as the wicked. In the past it was this same stiff-necked
and rebellious spirit that brought about the sacking and
scattering of Israel. These calamities were permitted by
the Almighty, against whom they had sinned. In the
latter days pride and rebellion will produce similar
consequences. A fire will be set all about those
Israelites who remain disdainful when the Lord calls,
but they will be so blinded by indifference that they will
not know what caused it. And even though it burns
them, they will not lay it to heart, or care,

Isaiah, Chapter 43

INTRODUCTION:

In this chapter the Lord identifies the role of Elohim, the Father; the role of Jehovah, the Son; and the role of Israel, the Lord's chosen people. The Lord pleads with his people to draw near to him and recognize the great honor God has bestowed upon them.

1. But now thus saith the LORD that created thee, O Jacob, and he that formed thee, O Israel, Fear not: for I have redeemed thee, I have called thee by thy name; thou art mine.

In the last chapter the emphasis was on the Lord's great judgment and REAPING DOWN of the earth just before the Millennium. Now the Lord says he is going to talk about the redemption of Israel. He is the God and Creator of Jacob, father of the Twelve Tribes, and from these tribes he formed the great nation of Israel (Israel means "soldier of God"). The Lord tells them, "Fear not: for I have redeemed thee." The next phrase is acknowledged by most authorities to be an error. It says, "I have called thee by THY name; thou art mine." Dr. Adam Clarke wrote that this phrase appears nowhere else in scripture. What does appear repeatedly is, "I have called thee by MY name." (See, for example, verse 7.) It is believed that this was the original idea. (Clarke, *Commentary*, 4:170.)

2. When thou passest through the waters, I will be with thee; and through the rivers, they shall not overflow thee: when thou walkest through the fire, thou shalt

The people need not fear, for they will recall that when they passed through the great waters of the Red Sea it was the Lord who revealed his great power so that they would know he was with them. When they crossed the river Jordan on the way to the promised

not be burned; neither shall the flame kindle upon thee.

land, it was the Lord who held back the flowing river in a gigantic wall of water at floodtide so that they could cross over on dry land (see Joshua 3:14–17). By the same token, the people can be made to endure fire of the greatest intensity, even as the companions of Daniel in Babylon (see Daniel 3:19–27).

3. For I am the LORD thy God, the Holy One of Israel, thy Saviour: I gave Egypt for thy ransom, Ethiopia and Seba for thee.

The Great Jehovah now identifies himself. He is "the Holy One of Israel, thy Saviour." As we pointed out earlier, Isaiah had seen the Savior in vision (see 2 Nephi 11:2). He knew that this Holy Being who spoke to him from time to time was none other than "the Word," who was with the Father from the beginning (John 1:1–5). It was he who would come among men and dwell with them in the flesh (John 1:14). Isaiah knew that Immanuel was the one who would die for the sins of the world. In fact, he describes it in chapter 53 of his writings. Isaiah repeatedly referred to Jehovah of the Old Testament as his Redeemer and Savior.

As we mentioned earlier, some Christian sects preach that Jehovah is the Father; but Isaiah knew that after the Fall it was Jehovah, the Son, who ministered directly to the Father's children here on earth. The Father is supportive but it is the Son who carries the burden of leading, directing, and redeeming the children of men. All this was thoroughly understood by early Christians. Let us repeat what Eusebius, the great Christian historian, wrote: "But they [the ancient prophets] also clearly knew the very Christ of God; for it has already been shown that he appeared unto Abraham, that he imparted revelations to Isaac, that he talked with Jacob, that he held converse with Moses and with the prophets that came after" (Eusebius, "Church History," chapter 4, paragraph 8, in *A Select Library of Nicene and Post-Nicene Fathers of the Christian*

Church, Second series, 14 vols. [Grand Rapids, Mich: Wm. B. Eerdman's Publishing Company, 1952], 1:87).

On a number of occasions, both before and after the life of Isaiah, the Lord intervened to save his people from the great and powerful nations of Egypt, Ethiopia, and Seba. All of these were African nations. The nation of Seba was named for Seba, the oldest son of Cush and therefore a grandson of Ham. The people of Seba are believed to have lived adjacent to Egypt and Ethiopia.

4. Since thou wast precious in my sight, thou hast been honourable, and I have loved thee: therefore will I give men for thee, and people for thy life.

This verse describes what the Lord had done for Israel in the past when she had been honorable and righteous. On those occasions, the people of Israel were most precious in the sight of God. For their honorable and righteous lives, the Lord loved them. When they were threatened, he bestowed great blessings upon them, even when it required the destruction of the people that threatened Israel. Sometimes whole nations fell because they threatened Israel at a time when her people were relatively righteous.

5. Fear not: for I am with thee: I will bring thy seed from the east, and gather thee from the west;

6. I will say to the north, Give up; and to the south, Keep not back: bring my sons from far, and my daughters from the ends of the earth;

Isaiah had already prophesied that because of wickedness the northern Ten Tribes of Israel would be scattered. He knew that eventually the same thing would happen to Judah and Levi. However, he also knew that in the day of their redemption their "seed," or descendants, would be gathered from the east and from the west. Isaiah knew that there would be nations, like the Soviet Union of today, that have stubbornly resisted the pleas of the Israelites seeking to escape from their borders. But the Lord told Isaiah that the day would come when neither the north nor the south would be able to restrain the chosen children of the Lord from assembling in Jerusalem and the cities of Zion.

7. Even every one that is called by my name: for I have created him for my glory, I have formed him; yea, I have made him.

This great call in the latter days is to go to all who are "called by my name." Israel was created to preserve the honor and glory of God among the hosts of rebellious and wicked men.

8. Bring forth the blind people that have eyes, and the deaf that have ears.

As for those who reject the call, the Lord has a special challenge. Let these blind people who have eyes, but will not see, come forth. Let those who are deaf, because they have ears that will not hear, also come forth.

9. Let all the nations be gathered together, and let the people be assembled: who among them can declare this, and shew us former things? let them bring forth their witnesses, that they may be justified: or let them hear, and say, It is truth.

The Lord now challenges them to gather their hosts together in one great assembly. Among these doubters who reject the Lord of heaven and earth may be some who consider themselves gifted in the powers of their dumb idols. Let them step forth and declare, or describe, what this great redemption will be that the Lord has promised Israel. Or let them try to disclose and explain the great things that happened in the past which are well known to the Lord and his prophets. Let them declare what they claim to know and certify what they believe to be the truth.

Today there are some "learned" men who attempt to do this same thing. They have their own pet theories and deny the great events of the past such as the Universal Flood. They deny other miracles in the Bible and reject the witness of those who say they saw them happen. They use the most strenuous imagination to explain, by some natural phenomenon, what the prophets of old called the miraculous handiwork of

God. An ancient American prophet named Jacob (the brother of Nephi) warned those who profess to know more than God and his prophets. Jacob said:

"O the vainness, and the frailties, and the foolishness of men! When they are learned they think they are wise, AND THEY HEARKEN NOT UNTO THE COUNSEL OF GOD, for they set it aside, supposing they know of themselves, wherefore, their wisdom is foolishness and it profiteth them not. And they shall perish.

"BUT TO BE LEARNED IS GOOD IF THEY HEARKEN UNTO THE COUNSELS OF GOD." (2 Nephi 9:28-29; emphasis added.)

10. Ye are my witnesses, saith the LORD, and my servant whom I have chosen: that ye may know and believe me, and understand that I am he: before me there was no God formed, neither shall there be after me.

The Lord now addresses those who are "called by my name" (verse 7), even the children of Israel. The Lord says, "Ye are my witnesses." He calls Israel his great servant whom he has chosen to go forth and bear witness to every nation, kindred, tongue, and people concerning the nature of God and the plan of salvation. To be good witnesses they must know for themselves that the Lord is God and that he who speaks to them is the Savior of the world.

The Lord then adds this interesting statement: "Before me there was no God formed, neither shall there be after me." This statement emphasizes the stewardship principle in the family of the Gods. Until the Gospel was restored, scriptural scholars did not have a very good understanding of God. Most of the churches were teaching that God is some mysterious teleological force which was the "first great cause," and which made everything out of nothing.

Since the restoration of the Gospel we have gained a more correct knowledge of God. In fact, Jesus emphasized the importance of knowing the true nature of Deity when he said, "And this is life eternal, that they might know thee the only true God, and Jesus Christ, whom thou hast sent" (John 17:3). In order for his children to be able to know him, our Heavenly Father has revealed some amazing and wonderful things about himself, such as:

1. It has been revealed that our Heavenly Father was not always a God. Joseph Smith stated: "I am going to tell you how God came to be God. We have imagined and supposed that God was God from all eternity. I will refute that idea, and take away the veil, so that you may see." (Smith, *Teachings*, p. 345.)

2. Our Heavenly Father became God "by going from one small degree to another, and from a small capacity to a great one; from grace to grace, from exaltation to exaltation" (Ibid. p. 346–47).

3. His training included the experience of passing through a mortal or earthly probation, just as we are now doing. Joseph Smith described it as follows: "*God himself was once as we are now, and is an exalted man, and sits enthroned in yonder heavens! That is the great secret. . . . If you were to see him today, you would see him like a man in form—like yourselves in all the person, image, and very form as a man; for Adam was created in the very fashion, image and likeness of God.*" Ibid., *Teachings*, p. 345.)

4. It was revealed to the prophets that one of the names of our Heavenly Father is "MAN of Holiness" (Moses 6:57; 7:35). He is an exalted and glorified being with a resurrected "body of flesh and bones as tangible as man's" (D&C 130:22). His children are called MANkind, meaning that they belong to the family of this glorified being whose name is MAN. This is why Jesus is specifically called "the Son of MAN" (Moses 6:57).

5. Our Heavenly Father has a father who tutored him just as our Heavenly Father is tutoring us. As Joseph Smith said of the great Elohim: "He had a father also. Where was there ever a son without a father?" (Smith, *Teachings*, p. 373.)

6. At a certain point in his eternal progression, our Heavenly Father was "ordained to organize matter" (Brigham Young, in *Journal of Discourses*, 15:137; quoted by Spencer W. Kimball, in Conference Report, Apr. 1977, p. 70, or *Ensign*, May 1977, p. 50). In other words, he was made a steward in the family of the Gods. He was authorized to take from the masses of unorganized intelligences and unorganized matter the two ingredients spoken of by the prophet Lehi that are necessary to build planetary systems and embellish them with all forms of life (see 2 Nephi 2:14; D&C 93:30–33). While addressing the Priesthood in General Conference, President Spencer W. Kimball referred to this great moment in the plan of eternal progression when those who are qualified receive the ordination that authorizes them to begin to "organize matter." President Kimball stated, "This is a power available to us as we reach perfection and receive the experience and power to create, to organize, to control native elements" (Spencer W. Kimball, in Conference Report, Apr. 1977, p. 69; or *Ensign*, May 1977, p. 49).

This was the point of perfection which our Heavenly Father attained aeons ago. He was ordained to "organize matter" and to bring into being a veritable universe of new creations. Of course, these new creations had never had any other God to preside over them "before," and they will not have another assigned to them in the future. This is why our Heavenly Father is able to say in the most literal sense, "Before me there was no God formed [for you], neither shall there be after me." We who belong to our Heavenly Father's creations will have him as our Supreme Head forever.

11. I, even I, am the LORD; and beside me there is no saviour.

In the previous verse we were talking about the supreme and eternal stewardship of the Father, but in this verse we are being told of the high office which is the exclusive role of the Father's Beloved Son, Jesus Christ. Speaking of himself now, the great Jehovah, who was the premortal spirit of Jesus Christ, declares, "I, even I, am the Lord; and BESIDE ME THERE IS NO SAVIOUR."

Before discussing the significance of this statement we need to comment briefly on the fact that both verses 10 and 11 are being delivered to Isaiah by the same person. In verse 10 the words make it sound as though it is the Father speaking. In verse 11 the words clearly refer to the Savior. This problem is resolved when it is realized that the Beloved Son is allowed to deliver a message from the Father in the first person and speak as though he were the Father. He did this when he delivered the Father's message to Moses (see Moses 1:3-7, 31–33). However, in Isaiah 43:11 the Savior is referring to himself. He wants us to understand that he has been designated to be the Lord over this earth and has been assigned the office of being the Savior for the entire human family if they will follow him.

It is profoundly significant that the scriptures plainly teach that no other person in heaven or earth was in a position fo fulfill this assignment as "Savior" except Jehovah, or Jesus Christ. Not even the Father is able to save us without this atoning sacrifice by his Beloved Son. As Peter declared, "Neither is there salvation in any other: for there is none other name under heaven given among men, whereby we must be saved" (Acts 4:12).

It is also interesting that when Jesus came into mortality there was a time in the Garden of Gethsemane when he seems to have felt that his Father could have somehow worked out the plan of salvation without requiring him to go through the agonies of the crucifixion. He therefore prayed to the Father, "All things are possible unto thee: take away this cup from me" (Mark 14:36; see also Matthew 26:39).

The Father had to send an angel to explain to the Savior the nature of his mission (Luke 22:43). This was not something the Father could do himself. It was not in his power to save his fallen children except through the atoning sacrifice of his Beloved Son. When Jesus understood, he said, "Thy will be done" (Matthew 26:42). Then he sweat great drops of blood (see Luke 22:44).

This is why the Father's Beloved Son said to Isaiah, "Beside me there is no saviour."

Note that Doctrine and Covenants 76:1 also says, "The Lord is God, and beside him there is no Savior." Jacob explained what would happen to us if there were no atonement:

"Save it should be an infinite atonement this corruption could not put on incorruption [in other words, there would have been no resurrection]. Wherefore, the first judgment [whereby mankind was cut off from the presence of the Lord] . . . must needs have remained to an endless duration. And if so, this flesh must have laid down to rot and to crumble to its mother earth, to rise no more. . . .

" . . . If the flesh should rise no more our spirits must become subject to that angel who fell from before the presence of the Eternal God, and became the devil, to rise no more.

"And our spirits must have become like unto him, and we become devils, angels to a devil, to be shut out from the presence of our God, and to remain with the father of lies, in misery, like unto himself." (2 Nephi 9:7-9.)

12. I have declared, and have saved, and I have shewed, when there was no strange god among you: therefore ye are my witnesses, saith the LORD, that I am God.

The Lord reminds Israel that he has declared the things of the past and the things of the future, something their false gods and false prophets could not do. Furthermore, he has intervened and saved Israel on numerous occasions, and he can also save them from their sins and weaknesses if they repent. He has told them about these things from the days "when there was no strange god among you." Now, therefore, he wants Israel to go forth among the children of men as his "witnesses," declaring that God lives, that he rules in the universe, and that his plan of salvation is available to all who will believe, repent, enter into a covenant with God, and endure to the end.

13. Yea, before the day was I am he; and there is none that can deliver out of my hand: I will work, and who shall let it?

The Lord reminds Israel that before the first day of creation he existed. He is the Almighty, the Omnipotent Being to whom all things are subject. None can "deliver out of [his] hand." When he determines to do a work, "who shall let it?" This is a Hebrew phrase which means "who will turn it back?"

14. Thus saith the LORD, your redeemer, the Holy One of Israel; For your sake I have sent to Babylon, and have brought down all their nobles, and the Chaldeans, whose cry is in the ships.

In this verse the Lord once more identifies himself as the "redeemer, the Holy One of Israel." Verse 25 goes on to say he is the one "that blotteth out thy transgressions." This is clearly the premortal spirit of Jesus Christ speaking.

Now the Lord speaks of a future event. The Babylonians would capture Jerusalem (587 B.C.) and haul the Jews off to Babylon. But the Lord says that "for your sake" he will allow invading forces to conquer

Babylon sometime later. The invaders would bring down all the nobles of Babylon, and the Chaldeans, their leaders, who would be depending upon their ships to save them.

It is quite evident that this passage is a reference to the invasion of Babylon in 539 B.C. Cyrus, a Persian, invaded Babylon, conquered the Chaldean leaders, and impeded the famous seafaring activities of Babylon by building obstructions across the Euphrates River, which was Babylon's thoroughfare to the Persian Gulf. At one time, according to the Greek geographer Strabo, the Babylonians had a fleet of 3,000 galleys (Clarke, *Commentary*, 4:171). No wonder the Babylonians would "cry" or rely on their ships!

15. I am the LORD, your Holy One, the creator of Israel, your King.

16. Thus saith the LORD, which maketh a way in the sea, and a path in the mighty waters;

17. Which bringeth forth the chariot and horse, the army and the power; they shall lie down together, they shall not rise: they are extinct, they are quenched as tow.

The Lord reminds his chosen people of Israel who he is and what he has done for them. He is the Lord, the Holy One who created Israel, and he is their king. He is the Lord who made a way in the Red Sea when Moses brought Israel up out of Egypt. He made a pathway for them in those mighty waters so that they were able to cross on dry land. Into this same channel, with walls of water standing up on either side, came the Egyptian Pharaoh with his chariots and horses. Pharaoh also brought his army in order to conquer Israel and lead them back to the brick pits as slaves. But it never happened. The miraculous walls of water were suddenly released by the Lord, and they came thundering down on the Pharaoh and his military forces. The Egyptians suddenly went down to their death all together. They became extinct, never to rise again. They were snuffed out like an extinguished torch, or tow of hemp.

18. Remember ye not the former things, neither consider the things of old.

But the Lord says they can forget about all those wonders of the past. He is going to do something even

19. Behold, I will do a new thing; now it shall spring forth; shall ye not know it? I will even make a way in the wilderness, and rivers in the desert.

more spectacular. It will be something new—a marvelous work and a wonder. This will take place in the latter days when Israel has been gathered together from the ends of the earth. The Lord will make a way for them in the wilderness, and rivers will begin to flow in the desert. It is interesting that the modern Jews returned to a wilderness and had to make it blossom as a rose. The Saints in the Zion of America also faced the same task in the Great Basin of the Rocky Mountains and the deserts of the nearby states where they settled.

20. The beast of the field shall honor me, the dragons and the owls: because I give waters in the wilderness, and rivers in the desert, to give drink to my people, my chosen.

The Lord knew that as these desolate lands of rocks and deserts were gradually brought under cultivation—by digging wells, diverting rivers, and building a network of canals—the animal life would be as grateful as God's chosen people for these "rivers in the desert."

21. This people have I formed for myself; they shall shew forth my praise.

The Lord said that in this great day of gathering he would show forth his power by forming them into a mighty people, and that they would praise the Lord for all he had done for them.

22. But thou hast not called upon me, O Jacob; but thou hast been weary of me, O Israel.

But, with all of these wonders of the future in mind, the Lord has cause to be deeply offended by the wickedness of the people in Isaiah's day. They have ceased to make their prayers and petititons to the Lord. They seem to have become weary of their God!

23. Thou hast not brought me the small cattle of thy burnt offerings, neither hast thou honoured me with thy sacrifices. I have

The burnt offerings which were supposed to be made each night and morning have been neglected. Even so, the Lord has patiently endured all of this. He has not caused them to serve with their regular offerings, nor

not caused thee to serve with an offering, nor wearied thee with incense.

24. Thou hast bought me no sweet cane with money, neither hast thou filled me with the fat of thy sacrifices: but thou hast made me to serve with thy sins, thou hast wearied me with thine iniquities.

has he wearied them with demands for prayers and incense.

They have not bought any sweet cane and delivered it to the temple. This is the cane which provided certain spices used in the anointing oil. Neither have they brought the sacrifices of their domestic flocks to the temple as the Lord had commanded.

And while the Lord has not wearied them with demands for these many different oblations and sacrifices, they have certainly wearied him with their sins and iniquities. The Lord says they have made him "serve with [their] sins," probably meaning that they have been using God's altars and sacred temple to honor their idols and pagan deities rather than the one true God of Israel.

25. I, even I, am he that blotteth out thy transgressions for mine own sake, and will not remember thy sins.

26. Put me in remembrance: let us plead together: declare thou, that thou mayest be justified.

Now the Lord makes the same kind of plea that he made in the first chapter of Isaiah. He reminds the people that their Lord and Savior is the one who can blot out their sins so that they will no longer be remembered. He pleads with them to "put me in rememberance." He wants them to join him that they might "plead together"—the Lord pleading with his chosen people to repent, and the people pleading with the Lord for forgiveness. He wants them to declare their sins and transgressions openly, that his children may be justified and forgiven.

The Lord says that at the beginning of the Millennium he will hold a great conference. Every person who has lived on the earth will be assembled there. Then the Lord will show a vision of the world's history as it has been permanently recorded in heaven. The life and even the thoughts of every individual will be shown (see D&C 88:108-10). However, the Saints of every age will find that all of their mistakes which were brought under the atonement through repentance, reform, and endurance to the end will be blotted out. What a marvelous blessing it will be to avoid having those blunders of life revealed for all to see. No doubt all those who have gained this great blessing will be especially thankful and will praise the Lord for literally blotting out their sins from the heavenly "computer."

27. Thy first father hath sinned, and thy teachers have transgressed against me.

28. Therefore I have profaned the princes of the sanctuary, and have given Jacob to the curse, and Israel to reproaches.

The Lord reminds them that their "first father" (meaning either their leaders or their ancestors) had sinned and their teachers had become transgressors against the Lord instead of exemplary instructors in righteousness. The Lord says that it is for this reason that he has considered the priests, or "the princes of the sanctuary," profaned, unclean, and unacceptable to him. Furthermore, it has become necessary to allow the children of Israel to come under condemnation and suffer many severe afflictions before they can be redeemed.

Isaiah, Chapter 44

INTRODUCTION:

This chapter is virtually a continuation of chapter 43.

1. Yet now hear, O Jacob my servant; and Israel, whom I have chosen:

The first verse raises a very important philosophical question: How can a just God, who is supposed to treat everyone equally, have a "chosen" people? By 1830 scarcely anyone knew the answer because both Christians and Jews had almost completely lost the doctrine of pre-earth life or premortal existence. They did not know that we had been extensively tested before we came into our present life here on earth. The Lord speaks of our testing in the spirit world as our "first estate" (Abraham 3:26). Our testing in this life is called our "second estate."

Those who proved valiant and obedient in the first estate were selected as a special vanguard that God could depend on to be his leaders in the second estate. Moses tells us that even in the spirit world these valiant ones were called "Israel," or "soldiers of God." In fact, God sorted out the rest of his children and assigned them to their respective nations here on earth according to the number of chosen or proven leaders that he had available (see Deuteronomy 32:7–9).

Abraham was told that he was one of those who was chosen to be a "ruler" because of his righteousness in the pre-earth life (Abraham 3:23).

Jeremiah was told that he had been chosen to be a prophet before he was born (Jeremiah 1:4–5).

Paul says that those whom God foreknew to be righteous in the pre-earth life he did "predestinate," or foreordain, to have special blessings during this present earth life (Romans 8:29–30).

Alma describes how the Lord selected those in the premortal life who would be called to Priesthood service during our present existence. He says it was based on God's foreknowledge of their "faith and good works" (Alma 13:3-4), which obviously would have to be during their pre-earth life.

Nevertheless, God is no respecter of persons (Romans 2:9–11). Therefore, ANYBODY can become one of God's chosen people in THIS life by accepting the Gospel and obeying God's commandments.

A person who was not considered worthy to be of Abraham's seed in this life because of slothfulness in the premortal existence can become "adopted" into the chosen lineage by obedience to the Gospel here on earth (Abraham 2:9–10; Romans 8:14–15).

By the same token, those born under the covenant of Abraham who rebel against God in this life are no longer considered to be of Abraham's seed, but are pruned out of the vineyard of God (John 8:39–44; Jacob 5:7).

So in this first verse, the Lord issues a clarion call to all those who are descendants of Jacob and are the house of "Israel," whom God has "chosen" to be his leaders, missionaries, and special servants.

2. Thus saith the LORD that made thee, and formed thee from the womb, which will help thee; Fear not, O Jacob, my servant; and thou, Jesurun, whom I have chosen.

The person speaking to Isaiah in this verse is Jehovah, or the premortal spirit of Jesus Christ. Nevertheless, as we pointed out in the previous chapter, the name of the Father is in him and he can therefore speak as though he were the Father. He does this on a number of occasions, just as he did to Moses (see Moses 1:3-7, 31–33). The Father wants those who read the commitments of the Lord in these writings to know that these promises originated with the very Eternal Father, the Creator of us all. The Father will help Israel. The children of Jacob need not fear. The Lord says to Jesurun (which means the upright ones, alternate translation from the Hebrew; see also McConkie, *Mormon Doctrine*, p. 323) that they have been "chosen" to be God's people.

3. For I will pour water upon him that is thirsty, and floods upon the dry ground: I will pour my spirit upon thy seed, and my blessing upon thine offspring:

In a desert land the most precious of all resources is water. The Lord promises that Israel will have it in abundance. Furthermore, he will pour out his spirit upon them to provide comfort, knowledge, and revelations for the children of Israel from generation to generation.

4. And they shall spring up as among the grass, as willows by the water courses.

As a result of these blessings, Israel will be able to thrive, flourish, and blossom in places where other nations would never have believed it possible.

5. One shall say, I am the LORD's; and another shall call himself by the name of Jacob; and another shall subscribe with his hand unto the LORD, and surname himself by the name of Israel.

The great conversion process will bring together many different kinds of people. Some shall come confessing the name of the Lord. Some shall appear who are of the Twelve Tribes of Jacob. Yet others will be of Gentile origin. Nevertheless, they will come forth and ask to be adopted into the ranks of Israel. All of this will fulfill the promise of the Lord to Abraham when he said: "For as many as receive this Gospel shall be called after thy name, and shall be accounted thy seed" (Abraham 2:10). To be counted as a convert to the Gospel automatically makes a person an heir in Israel and of the seed of Abraham.

6. Thus saith the LORD the King of Israel, and his re-

In verse 2 the person speaking to Isaiah, and through him to the people, identified himself as "the Lord that

deemer the LORD of hosts; I am the first, and I am the last; and beside me there is no God.

made thee." This power of creation originates with the Father but is administered through the Son. Both are creators. But now, Jehovah identifies himself more specifically as the member of the Godhead who has been assigned by the Father to be king of Israel, the redeemer and the lord of all the hosts assigned to this segment of the Father's eternal family. For us, then, he is "the first" and "the last." There is no other name whereby mankind can be saved. In his role as our redeemer he is supreme and stands alone. Above him is the Father, but beside him there is no God, no other way, no other door, by which mankind can be redeemed. Notice that this is the same kind of language which Jesus used in referring to himself in Revelation 1:8, 17.

7. And who, as I, shall call, and shall declare it, and set it in order for me, since I appointed the ancient people? and the things that are coming, and shall come, let them shew unto them.

Beginning with this verse, the Lord challenges the false prophets and apostates who have become idolaters among his chosen people. He asks which of all these pretended priests who speak for their gods of wood and stone were ever able to call the people together and predict with exactness precisely what was going to happen in the future? In the early histories of Israel it can be demonstrated that it was only the one true Lord who could tell the people what was going to happen. Who else ever did this?

8. Fear ye not, neither be afraid: have not I told thee from that time, and have declared it? ye are even my witnesses. Is there a God beside me? yea, there is no God; I know not any.

The Lord wants the people to know that they can trust him and not be afraid. He calls upon the people to witness for themselves that he is indeed the one who has revealed the future to them and blessed them down through the centuries. Has any other source of such supreme power ever been manifest to them? The Lord says he knows of none.

9. They that make a graven image are all of them vanity; and their delectable things shall not profit; and they are their own witnesses; they see not, nor know; that they may be ashamed.

Now the Lord addresses himself to those who worship the workmanship of their own hands. They carve out images of wood or stone and point with pride to the object of their adoration. The Lord says it is pure vanity. No profitable or worthwhile thing shall ever come from these "delectable" things (the Hebrew word means "beloved," see alternate translation) to which they direct their devotions. They can see for themselves, as personal witnesses, that these idolatrous objects of wood and stone cannot see or hear or know. The stupidity of worshipping such senseless things should make the people feel ashamed.

10. Who hath formed a god, or molten a graven image that is profitable for nothing?

11. Behold, all his fellows shall be ashamed: and the workmen, they are of men: let them all be gathered together, let them stand up; yet they shall fear, and they shall be ashamed together.

The Lord then asks those who have formed these idols of wood, metal, and stone to make their presence known. He wants them to stand up together. In their vanity they consider themselves great artists and creators of graven images which the people should bow down and worship; nevertheless, in the end they will all be totally ashamed of what they have done. They will all be rejected together.

12. The smith with the tongs both worketh in the coals, and fashioneth it with hammers, and worketh it with the strength of his arms: yea; he is hungry, and his strength faileth: he drinketh no water, and is faint.

Who are these men who carve out objects of wood and stone and then give them to the people to worship? Take the artisans of metal, for example. The smith uses fire, bellows, and tongs to fashion an image, but he cannot imbue it with power and godlike qualities. He himself is a frail human being, subject to hunger, thirst, and physical weakness.

13. The carpenter stretcheth out his rule; he marketh it out with a line; he fitteth it

The same is true of the carpenter who uses all his skill and tools to carefully carve out the figure of a man for the people to worship.

with planes, and he marketh it out with the compass, and maketh it after the figure of a man, according to the beauty of a man; that it may remain in the house.

14. He heweth him down cedars, and taketh the cypress and the oak, which he strengtheneth for himself among the trees of the forest: he planteth an ash, and the rain doth nourish it.

15. Then shall it be for a man to burn: for he will take thereof, and warm himself; yea, he kindleth it, and baketh bread; yea, he maketh a god, and worshippeth it; he maketh it a graven image, and falleth down thereto.

The Lord asks the people to consider the following ridiculous situation: A man goes out into the forest to cut down various kinds of strong trees or perhaps even one he has planted himself. There is nothing unusual about these trees. They will burn like any other kind of wood, and might be used for heating or baking bread. But, nevertheless, the man will take this ordinary tree trunk, carve it into an image, and call it a god. What is worse, he will worship it and fall down before it in prayer and supplication.

16. He burneth part thereof in the fire: with part thereof he eateth flesh; he roasteth roast, and is satisfied: yea, he warmeth himself, and saith, Aha, I am warm, I have seen the fire:

17. And the residue thereof he maketh a god, even his graven image: he falleth down unto it, and worshippeth it, and prayeth unto it, and saith, Deliver me; for thou art my god.

The irony of it all is that part of this tree will be used to make an ordinary fire for heating or for cooking while the main part is used to carve into a graven image. Actually, the whole tree could have been used for fuel, for it is nothing more than a common tree. Nevertheless, the part which he has carved into an image is looked upon as something divine and supremely powerful. He pleads with this blind and dumb stump of a tree and cries out: "Deliver me; for thou art my god!"

18. They have not known nor understood: for he hath

Having lost the spirit of the Lord, and having filled their minds with superstition and darkness, such

shut their eyes, that they cannot see; and their hearts, that they cannot understand.

people are blind and without understanding. They cannot seem to comprehend how foolish they are.

19. **And none considereth in his heart, neither is there knowledge nor understanding to say, I have burned part of it in the fire; yea, also I have baked bread upon the coals thereof; I have roasted flesh, and eaten it: and shall I make the residue thereof an abomination? shall I fall down to the stock of a tree?**

The idolater seems to lack the ability to realize how irrational he is to take a tree, burn part of it for heat or for cooking meat or bread, and then take the remainder and think that by carving it into a graven image it becomes a god which can hear his prayers and respond to his devotions. He doesn't stop to realize how senseless it is to bow down to the stump of a tree.

20. **He feedeth on ashes: a deceived heart hath turned him aside, that he cannot deliver his soul, nor say, Is there not a lie in my right hand?**

Instead of worshipping the one true God, the idolater is feeding his spirit on ashes. He is allowing his self-deception to prevent him from realizing that the stump of a tree can never deliver his soul. He is unable to perceive that he is upholding in his right hand that which is a lie.

21. **Remember these, O Jacob and Israel; for thou art my servant: I have formed thee; thou art my servant: O Israel, thou shalt not be forgotten of me.**

In contrast to all of this intellectual and spiritual depravity, the Lord calls upon the people to turn to him. He wants Israel to remember that they have a special calling given to them before the earth was formed. They were chosen to be God's servants and called "Israel," or "soldiers of God," before they were born (see Deuteronomy 32:7-9). God not only created them and called them to be his servants, but he will never forget them nor forsake them.

22. **I have blotted out, as a thick cloud, thy transgres-**

It is true that the Israelites have sinned greatly against the God of their fathers; nevertheless the Lord

sions, and, as a cloud, thy sins: return unto me; for I have redeemed thee.

is willing to put a cloud of obscurity over all their past transgressions and say unto Israel, "Return unto me; for I have redeemed thee."

23. Sing, O ye heavens; for the LORD hath done it: shout, ye lower parts of the earth: break forth into singing, ye mountains, O forest, and every tree therein: for the LORD hath redeemed Jacob, and glorified himself in Israel.

The Lord invites those in heaven to sing aloud with rejoicing and anthems of praise, for the Lord is now going to bless Israel. The Lord speaks to all the earth to shout for joy and happiness, for the Lord has redeemed Jacob and glorified himself in Israel.

24. Thus saith the LORD, thy redeemer, and he that formed thee from the womb, I am the LORD that maketh all things; that stretcheth forth the heavens alone; that spreadeth abroad the earth by myself;

The Lord is about to make a great prophecy. He says that their Lord and Redeemer, who is about to make this prediction, is the Lord Almighty who formed mankind from the womb. He made all things, including the heavens, the earth, and everything which exists therein.

25. That frustrateth the tokens of the liars, and maketh diviners mad; that turneth wise men backward, and maketh their knowledge foolish;

He is also the one who ultimately frustrates all those who go up and down the earth filling the minds and hearts of the people with lies. The Lord is the one who will eventually make the false diviners mad with frustration and shame. Men who thought they were so wise and intellectually superior will find things turning out to be the opposite of that which they had predicted. What they called their "knowledge" will turn out to be nothing more than pompous foolishness.

26. That confirmeth the word of his servant, and performeth the counsel of his messengers; that saith to

It is the Lord God of Israel who will bring to pass those things which his servants (such as Isaiah) have proclaimed among the people. Even though the

Jerusalem, Thou shalt be inhabited; and to the cities of Judah, Ye shall be built, and I will raise up the decayed places thereof:

prophets predicted that the wicked would be destroyed and Jerusalem would fall, nevertheless, this same God declares that ultimately Jerusalem will be inhabited once more, and the cities of Judah will be rebuilt. The whole land will be revived and the decayed places made to flourish.

27. That saith to the deep, Be dry, and I will dry up thy rivers:

This is the God of the earth who has complete power over the elements. He can tell the sea to dry up, and it is done. He can dry up mighty rivers if he so desires.

28. That saith of Cyrus, He is my shepherd, and shall perform all my pleasure: even saying to Jerusalem, Thou shalt be built; and to the temple, Thy foundation shall be laid.

At this point the Lord addresses himself to Cyrus, a great future king of Persia who will not be born for another 175 years or so. The Lord tells Cyrus that he will be like a shepherd to the children of Israel. (Cyrus lived from approximately 600 B.C. to 529 B.C., first becoming ruler of the Medes and then the conqueror of Persia. In 539 B.C. his conquest of Babylon made it possible for the liberation of the Jews. They were allowed to return to Jerusalem in 538 B.C.) The Lord says Cyrus will be their protector and shepherd. He will tell them to occupy their ancient city of Jerusalem and rebuild their temple. (It was dedicated in 516 B.C., almost two centuries after this chapter of Isaiah was recorded!)

INTRODUCTION:

From God's point of view, Cyrus was a benevolent pagan who would live from approximately 600 to 529 B.C. and administer his kingdom in a way that would be a blessing to the Persian Empire. He would also be a special blessing to the Jews, who would need to be liberated from the Babylonians. The historical setting for all of this is as follows:

During the latter part of the seventh century B.C., the young king of Persia was named Cambyses. However, Persia was under the domination of a kingdom to the north called Media. The king of the Medes was named Astyages. To cement relations between the two countries, Astyages gave his daughter Mandane to be the wife of Cambyses. Around 600 B.C., a son was born to this royal couple named CYRUS. There had been an earlier Cyrus, so this one is called Cyrus II, or Cyrus "the Great."

By 550 B.C., the kingdom of the Medes had become so dissolute that the people encouraged Cyrus (who by then had inherited the throne of Persia) to come up and conquer his grandfather, King Astyages, and put things in order. As a matter of fact, the Medes themselves actually took Astyages prisoner. This allowed Cyrus to unite Media and Persia into one kingdom without extensive bloodshed or resistance.

Cyrus moved out across the northern region of the old Assyrian Empire and entered Asia Minor. He conquered the Lydian kingdom in 546 B.C. He also conquered the Greek colonies along the coast. Cyrus then returned to his home base in Persia greatly

strengthened. By 539 B.C., Cyrus thought he was
strong enough to conquer Nabonidus, king of Babylon,
as well as his son and co-regent named Belshazzar.

According to the Chronicle of Nabonidus, the king of
Babylon was out of circulation from the eleventh to the
seventeenth year of his reign. However, he returned to
take control of his kingdom in 539, just as Cyrus
invaded the Babylonian borders with his forces from
the east. King Nabonidus was defeated by Cyrus at
Opis but managed to escape. (After the fall of Babylon,
Cyrus made Nabonidus a governor over one of the
Persian provinces.)

The conquest of the great city of Babylon was
considered by the Babylonians to be impossible. Even
though King Nabonidus had been defeated, it was
thought the great capital city would stand up against
any attack because of its mighty walls and brass gates.

The walls of Babylon enclosed the entire city. Each
side was a little over 13 miles long, making a total of 56
miles of gigantic walls. Archaeologists have found that
the height and width of these walls almost defy the
imagination. They were 336 feet high and 136½ feet
wide. There were houses built along each side on the
top of the wall which still left a street between the
houses wide enough to permit four chariots to drive
abreast. (Samuel Fallows, ed., *The Popular and Critical
Bible Encyclopedia and Scriptural Dictionary*, s.v. "Babylon,"
pp. 208–9; as quoted in *Old Testament: 1 Kings—Malachi*
[Church Educational System, Rel. 302 student manual,
1981], p. 231.)

When Cyrus came to Babylon, the city was sealed
tightly against him. It is said it contained enough
supplies for many years. From the top of the wall the
Babylonians watched with curiosity as Cyrus dug a
deep trench around the city walls. It was thought that
this was part of a siege strategy. But Cyrus had

planned a tactic the Babylonians had never thought possible. During the night he diverted the river which flowed through the city and ran it down the new trench. This permitted the armies of Cyrus to march along the old riverbed as it passed under the walls and thus gain entrance to the city.

This happened the very night that the co-regent, Belshazzar, was feasting with his royal court and a hand wrote on the wall, "MENE, MENE, TEKEL, UPHARSIN" (see Daniel, chapter 5). The wise men of the king could not figure out the meaning of these words, so the king sent for the aged prophet Daniel, who had been in Babylon ever since he was a young man. The Hebrew prophet declared that the people of Babylon had been weighed in the balance and found wanting. Daniel predicted that the great city of Babylon was about to be conquered by the Medes and Persians. Daniel then went his way. During the night Belshazzar was murdered by two members of his own court, and before dawn Cyrus and his hosts were within the walls of the city. What they saw must have amazed them. In the center of the city was a huge artificial mountain that rose high above the walls of the city. This mountain was covered with "hanging gardens" which were so magnificent they were called one of the eight wonders of the ancient world.

1. Thus saith the LORD to his anointed, to Cyrus, whose right hand I have holden, to subdue nations before him; and I will loose the loins of kings, to open before him the two leaved gates; and the gates shall not be shut;

Now the Lord addresses this great Cyrus of the future and refers to him as "anointed," or selected by the Lord to be a benevolent ruler over his kingdom. The Lord indicated that he would hold Cyrus by the right hand and sustain him. He declared that Cyrus would go forth and "subdue nations." These turned out to be the Syrians, Assyrians, Arabians, Cappadocians, Phrygians, Lydians, Carians, Phoenicians, and Babylonians. He also brought under control the Bactrians, the Indians, the Cilicians, the Sacae Paphlagones, and the Mariandyni. (Clarke, *Commentary,* 4:177.)

Loosening "the loins of kings" probably refers to the fact that both king Nabonidus and his son Belshazzar would be conquered. The Lord said the mighty "two leaved" gates of Babylon would never be closed against Cyrus again.

2. I will go before thee, and make the crooked places straight: I will break in pieces the gates of brass, and cut in sunder the bars of iron:

The Lord truly did go before Cyrus to announce through Daniel that Belshazzar and his Babylonians would be overthrown by the Medes and Persians. The king, in fact, had been slain by his own courtiers, and the entry into the city through the streambed which ran under the walls certainly made the conquest of Babylon, which was the most heavily fortified city in the world, a remarkable feat.

3. And I will give thee the treasures of darkness, and hidden riches of secret places, that thou mayest know that I, the LORD, which call thee by thy name, am the God of Israel.

The records of the Persians indicate that Cyrus obtained vast quantities of gold, silver, and other precious materials wherever his armies conquered their foes. The Lord wanted Cyrus to know that these successes were not to be taken for granted or treated casually because over a century before Cyrus was born the Lord announced his name, his mission, and his military successes.

4. For Jacob my servant's sake, and Israel mine elect, I have even called thee by thy name: I have surnamed thee, though thou hast not known me.

Now the Lord discloses why he needed to have a benevolent pagan such as Cyrus over the leading nations of the earth and sublimate their policies of cruelty and brutality. It was so that the children of Jacob (who would be captured by the Babylonians) could be rescued and liberated. The Lord had Isaiah record the fact that it was for the sake of "Israel mine elect" that Cyrus had been anointed (selected) and identified by name several generations before he was born so that he could perform this great mission. Nevertheless, all of this was to be accomplished without Cyrus really knowing the true source of his strength. As the Lord said: "I have surnamed thee, THOUGH THOU HAST NOT KNOWN ME."

5. I am the LORD, and there is none else, there is no God beside me: I girded thee, though thou hast not known me:

Because Cyrus would be a pagan (but not a barbarian), the Lord knew he would be worshipping a pantheon of strange deities. The Lord wants Cyrus to know that there is only one supreme authority: "THERE IS NO GOD BESIDE ME." (See commentary on Isaiah 43:10.) He also wants Cyrus to know that it would be the Lord who "girded" him and helped him become the leader of a great new empire, even though "thou hast not known me."

6. That they may know from the rising of the sun, and from the west, that there is none beside me. I am the LORD, and there is none else.

It is important for all mankind to keep in mind that from the moment they awaken with "the rising of the sun" to the end of the day, when it disappears in the west, the earth and everything in it is under the dominion of the Lord. Beside him there is no one else.

7. I form the light, and create darkness: I make peace, and create evil: I the LORD do all these things.

The Lord has arranged all things which move in their majesty and power throughout the cosmic universe. He has established the light, and withdraws it at will to make darkness prevail. He can establish conditions of peaceful tranquility, or he can show forth the power of his mighty arm to bring a great judgment of evil and destruction upon the wicked. The Lord wants his children to remember that "I the Lord do all these things."

It is interesting that the scriptures say the Lord cannot act unjustly or he would "cease to be God" (Alma 42:13, 22, 25; Mormon 9:19). Therefore God does not *literally* "create evil" or do anything unjust. When his arm of destruction sweeps down upon a person, a people, or a nation, it is always because of the evil they have done. The punishment is therefore a righteous judgment. Nevertheless, it may be counted a great "evil" by the person, people, or nation upon whom God's judgment falls.

8. Drop down, ye heavens, from above, and let the skies pour down righteousness: let the earth open, and let them bring forth salvation, and let righteousness spring up together; I the LORD have created it.

In this verse Isaiah may have been referring to a famous passage of scripture from the writings of Enoch when he said: "And righteousness will I send down out of heaven; and truth will I send forth out of the earth, TO BEAR TESTIMONY OF MINE ONLY BEGOTTEN; HIS RESURRECTION FROM THE DEAD; yea, and also the resurrection of all men; and righteousness and truth will I cause to sweep the earth as with a flood, to gather out mine elect from the four quarters of the earth, unto a place which I shall prepare, an Holy City, that my people may gird up their loins, AND BE LOOKING FORTH FOR THE TIME OF MY COMING; for there shall be my tabernacle, and it shall be called Zion, a New Jerusalem." (Moses 7:62; emphasis added.)

Obviously Enoch was referring to the restoration of the Gospel in the latter days through the ministering of angels from heaven and the revealing of the Book of Mormon plates which would be buried in the earth. In those plates would be found recorded the fulness of the Gospel for the salvation of all mankind. In due time, after Israel had been gathered, there also would be a holy city established which would be called the New Jerusalem.

The role of the Book of Mormon in speaking from the dust to proclaim the fulness of the Gospel was referred to by Joseph who was sold into Egypt (see 2 Nephi 3:19-20) and by Nephi (see 2 Nephi 26:16; 33:13), and also by Moroni (Moroni 10:27). It had been previously mentioned by Isaiah when he said of those who would flee from Jerusalem:

"And thou shalt be brought down, and shalt speak out of the ground, and thy speech shall be low out of the dust, and thy voice shall be, as of one that hath a familiar spirit, out of the ground, and thy speech shall whisper out of the dust." (Isaiah 29:4.)

In this verse the Lord is saying that righteousness will "spring up together" as it comes down from heaven by revelation and springs up from the earth through the bringing forth of the hidden scripture of the American prophets.

King David seems to have known all about this glorious day as he sang forth in his psalm:

"Surely his salvation is nigh them that fear him; that glory may dwell in our land.

"Mercy and truth are met together; righteousness and peace have kissed each other.

"TRUTH SHALL SPRING OUT OF THE EARTH; AND RIGHTEOUSNESS SHALL LOOK DOWN FROM HEAVEN." (Psalms 85:9-11; emphasis added.)

9. Woe unto him that striveth with his Maker! Let the potsherd strive with the potsherds of the earth. Shall the clay say to him that fashioneth it, What makest thou? or thy work, He hath no hands?

The Lord pronounces a woe upon his children whom he created, but who strive against their Maker. He said it is like a piece of pottery protesting against the pottery maker, or pretending that the pottery maker could fashion nothing because he has no hands.

10. Woe unto him that saith unto his father, What be-

A rebel against God is like a rebellious child who rebukes his father concerning his own offspring; or

gettest thou? or to the woman, What hast thou brought forth?

sneeringly says to his mother, "What hast thou brought forth?"

11. Thus saith the LORD, the Holy One of Israel, and his Maker, Ask me of things to come concerning my sons, and concerning the work of my hands command ye me.

Even so, the Lord is willing to have his children ask him about his creations, both in heaven and earth; also concerning his children who dwell upon the earth.

12. I have made the earth, and created man upon it: I, even my hands, have stretched out the heavens, and all their host have I commanded.

The Lord declares again that he is the one who made the earth and created man to inhabit it. He is the Supreme Being who controls the cosmic universe and keeps all the hosts of heavenly bodies in their proper order.

13. I have raised him up in righteousness, and I will direct all his ways: he shall build my city, and he shall let go my captives, not for price nor reward, saith the LORD of hosts.

Now the Lord addresses Cyrus once more. It will be recalled that in the first verse of this chapter the Lord said, "Thus saith the Lord to his anointed, to Cyrus." The Lord states that Cyrus would not be raised up to hate and revel in cruel bloodshed. Rather, he would be raised up to show compassion on the nations he conquered. He treated his conquests with a certain spirit of benevolent restraint, compared to the tyrants of other nations. The Lord also inspired Cyrus to do the things that needed to be done. He liberated the Jews from Babylon and told them to go back to Jerusalem and rebuild the temple. He did this through the generosity of his heart and not "for price nor reward." As we have previously indicated, this was literally fulfilled in 538 B.C.

14. Thus saith the LORD, The labour of Egypt, and mer-

The Lord says that because of the benevolence of Cyrus he will become famous. The Lord promises that

chandise of Ethiopia and of the Sabeans, men of stature, shall come over unto thee, and they shall be thine: they shall come after thee; in chains they shall come over, and they shall fall down unto thee, they shall make supplication unto thee, saying, Surely God is in thee; and there is none else, there is no God.

the labor or wealth of Egypt and the commerce of Egypt, as well as that of Ethiopia and the Sabeans, will be channeled through the Persian empire. (The Sabeans occupied the land of Seba, which is believed to have been adjacent to Egypt; Smith, *Bible Dictionary*, s.v. "Seba.") The Lord says these people will come in chains, as it were, or in deepest submission in order to gain the favor of the Persian king. And because he is so blessed they will say that God is with him and that there is no other god as great.

15. Verily thou art a God that hidest thyself, O God of Israel, the Saviour.

Now Isaiah inserts his own tribute to the Lord. He declares his firm testimony that the God who will bless Cyrus is in reality the God of Israel, even Jehovah, who, when he comes in the flesh (as described in Isaiah in chapter 53), will be the Savior of the world.

16. They shall be ashamed, and also confounded, all of them: they shall go to confusion together that are makers of idols.

Isaiah continues his personal commentary that while God blesses Israel through the good offices of Cyrus, the opposite will occur among the heathen nations who render their devotions to idols. They will be confounded and ultimately ashamed. Their gods will do none of the things which the idolaters will be expecting of them. This will leave them utterly confused.

17. But Israel shall be saved in the LORD with an everlasting salvation: ye shall not be ashamed nor confounded world without end.

Meanwhile, Israel shall be saved, not only temporally but also spiritually. Israel will enjoy an everlasting salvation, and therefore need not be ashamed nor confounded either in this world or in the world to come.

18. For thus saith the LORD that created the heavens;

This passage refutes the speculation of those who have suggested that the earth came about as the result

God himself that formed the earth and made it; he hath established it, he created it not in vain, he formed it to be inhabited: I am the LORD; and there is none else.

of accident or happenstance. The Lord says he created this earth according to design. It was established and structured to BE INHABITED, and the Lord carefully superintended its creation so that it would be "created...not in vain."

19. I have not spoken in secret, in a dark place of the earth: I said not unto the seed of Jacob, Seek ye me in vain: I the LORD speak righteousness, I declare things that are right.

In this verse the Lord points out the difference between the way he reveals himself and the methods used by the false oracles of the pagan deities. For example, the mysterious oracles of Delphi and other pagan mystics received their messages in caverns or deep caves. On the other hand, the Lord converses with his servants by direct revelation and sometimes in open vision. The Lord talks to his prophets "as a man speaketh unto his friend" (Exodus 33:11). Never has the Lord told the children of Jacob (Israel) that they seek him in vain. Furthermore, when the Lord speaks it is always to do some great thing which is RIGHTEOUS in nature. The Lord says, "I declare things that are right!" The pretended revelations of the pagan priests were often to do evil. They would require the sacrifice of children or young virgins. They would proclaim sensuous rites and immorality as pleasing to the gods. They would require drunkenness as a tribute to the god of wine. They would hypocritically prophesy the things their listeners wanted to hear.

20. Assemble yourselves and come; draw near together, ye that are escaped of the nations: they have no knowledge that set up the wood of their graven image, and pray unto a god that cannot save.

In this verse the Lord invites all who survive the judgments that are coming upon the earth to assemble themselves together and hear the word of the Lord. These people will need instruction. They are without knowledge concerning God's great plan of salvation. They have been praying to images made with their own hands and worshipping dumb stumps of wood or clumsy images of metal which have no ability to save anyone.

21. Tell ye, and bring them near; yea, let them take counsel together: who hath declared this from ancient time? who hath told it from that time? have not I the LORD? and there is no God else beside me; a just God and a Saviour; there is none beside me.

The Lord now drives home once again the importance of recognizing who it is that has the power to reveal the future. The Lord says that it has been he alone who has told them of coming events which no man knew. In this connection the Lord emphasizes once again that he is the only God of this world. He is "a just God and a Saviour." He says, "There is none beside me!" (See commentary on Isaiah 43:11.)

22. Look unto me, and be ye saved, all the ends of the earth: for I am God, and there is none else.

Finally, here is the message of the Savior to all the world in every age. He says, "Look unto me, and be ye saved!" This call is not just to Israel but to "the ends of the earth." In the end people will know the truth of the matter. He is our Savior, and the only name given under heaven by which redemption can be obtained (see Acts 4:12).

23. I have sworn by myself, the word is gone out of my mouth in righteousness, and shall not return, That unto me every knee shall bow, every tongue shall swear.

The Lord has made an eternal decree in an oath to himself that the time must come when every knee shall bow and every tongue confess that Jesus is the Christ, the King of Kings, the Lord of Lords over the whole earth. This event to which Isaiah is referring in this verse is mentioned in Romans 14:11; Philippians 2:10-11; D&C 88:104.

It should be noted, of course, that just because these vast multitudes confess the sovereignty of Jesus Christ over the earth, this does not mean that they are necessarily converted to the fulness of the Gospel with its divine call of dedicated service in the kingdom. As Brigham Young explained: "Now when Zion is built up and reigns, the question may arise with some, will all be

Latter-day Saints? No.... In the Millennium men will have the privilege of [their own beliefs], but they will not have the privilege of treating the name and character of Deity as they have done heretofore. No, but every knee shall bow and every tongue confess to the glory of God the Father that Jesus is the Christ." (*Journal of Discourses,* 12:274.)

24. Surely, shall one say, in the LORD have I righteousness and strength: even to him shall men come; and all that are incensed against him shall be ashamed.

In that day, when a prophet or Priesthood leader shall rise up and say that he comes in righteousness and strength to proclaim the word of the Lord, the people will see the need to humble themselves and listen to his message. Those who have been incensed at the Lord's messengers in the past will become ashamed as they commence to realize who the Savior is and who his prophets are.

25. In the LORD shall all the seed of Israel be justified, and shall glory.

These cynical, unbelieving people who have had such disdain for Israel will finally commence to get the great vision of the future from the Lord's viewpoint. When they see how God has blessed the righteous of Israel, they will praise those who they formerly persecuted. In their eyes Israel will become thoroughly justified, and the popularity and wisdom of the Israelites will bring "glory" to both Israel and the Lord.

Isaiah, Chapter 46

INTRODUCTION:

This chapter lays a foundation for chapter 47, which describes the conquest and fall of Babylon. The main thrust of this chapter is the foolishness and vanity of those who rely upon idols to save them from the coming hour of crisis.

1. Bel boweth down, Nebo stoopeth, their idols were upon the beasts, and upon the cattle: your carriages were heavy loaden; they are a burden to the weary beast.

Isaiah opens this chapter as though he were viewing a procession led by the two principal gods of the Babylonians, which are being carted along on the backs of beasts at one of the Babylonian festivals. It seems completely ridiculous that these huge idols should be considered divine when they can't even sit steadily on the beasts of burden which carry them. Bel, also known by the name Marduk, was the chief Babylonian god (*Interpreter's Bible*, pp. 535-36). Nebo was considered to be his son. The images of these two gods were seen swaying precariously back and forth as they were hauled along by the weary draft animals.

2. They stoop, they bow down together, they could not deliver the burden, but themselves are gone into captivity.

Isaiah contemplates the sheer stupidity of a people worshipping these idols which can barely sit on their pedestals of transport. They could not deliver the people from anything, let alone the oppressive threat of captivity which Babylon would encounter from Persia.

3. Hearken unto me, O house of Jacob, and all the rem-

The Lord invites the children of Jacob (Israel) to observe the difference between the helpless gods of the

nant of the house of Israel, which are borne by me from the belly, which are carried from the womb.

4. And even to your old age I am he; and even to hoar hairs will I carry you: I have made, and I will bear; even I will carry, and will deliver you.

Babylonians and the God of Jacob, who has supported, intervened, and carried Israel as his burden through the centuries. Each Israelite has been sustained from the time he was born until he departed from his earthly life. Not only has the Lord done this in the past, but he wants Israel to know that he will do it in the future.

5. To whom will ye liken me, and make me equal, and compare me, that we may be like?

The Lord continues his comparison between himself and the helpless, man-made gods of the Babylonians. In what way can there be any real comparison? How can these idols be considered equal in the most minute way with the loving and mighty Lord God Jehovah of Israel?

6. They lavish gold out of the bag, and weigh silver in the balance, and hire a goldsmith; and he maketh it a god: they fall down, yea, they worship.

7. They bear him upon the shoulder, they carry him, and set him in his place, and he standeth; from his place shall he not remove: yea, one shall cry unto him, yet can he not answer, nor save him out of his trouble.

In these two verses the Lord outlines the construction of a golden idol. First there is the purchase of the gold from a bag, which is done by weighing out the price in silver. Then a goldsmith is employed to melt down the gold and mold or form it into a human image in the likeness of an idolatrous god. At this point the person who has paid to have all of this done falls down before the image in worshipful adoration.

But what can this man-made idol do? Nothing. Its disciples must carry it around on their shoulders and set it on a pedestal. Once this is accomplished the poor, dumb idol must sit there, incapable of moving, and incapable of answering when a worshipper comes to it crying out for assistance or seeking succor from his calamities.

8. Remember this, and shew yourselves men: bring it

The Lord calls upon Israel to remember the greatness of their own God and not be snared into thinking there

again to mind, O ye transgressors.

is some mysterious power in a dumb idol. He commands them to remember who they are and stand up like men instead of becoming transgressors by bowing down to graven images as did the idolatrous Babylonians.

9. **Remember the former things of old: for I am God, and there is none else; I am God, and there is none like me,**

The Lord wants the Israelites to come to their senses and remember all that he has done for them from the beginning. There has never been anything or anyone like him to help them, carry them, bless them, and provide for them.

10. **Declaring the end from the beginning, and from ancient times the things that are not yet done, saying, My counsel shall stand, and I will do all my pleasure:**

He has been able to tell their prophets "the end from the beginning." Even in the days of Adam the Lord disclosed the entire panorama of prophetic history through which the children of men would pass during their second estate (see D&C 107:56; Moses 5:10). Enoch had the same privilege (see Moses 7:67). Other prophets have been shown this same marvelous vision of future world history from generation to generation.

11. **Calling a ravenous bird from the east, the man that executeth my counsel from a far country: yea, I have spoken it, I will also bring it to pass; I have purposed it, I will also do it.**

The Lord is going to allow "a ravenous bird" to sweep down on Babylon. To the Babylonians this invading force from the east will be like a powerful bird of prey. As we have mentioned previously, this turned out to be Cyrus, who came down from the "far country" of the Medes and the Persians, which was located directly east of Babylon. With a spirit of fixed finality, the Lord declares: "I HAVE PURPOSED IT, I WILL ALSO DO IT"! The man-made gods of the Babylonians could do nothing to prevent it.

12. Hearken unto me, ye stout-hearted, that are far from righteousness:

God now calls out to the "stouthearted" (stubborn hearted) among the children of Israel who have been seduced by the idolatrous practices of the Babylonians. They have strayed far away from righteousness and obedience to the commandments of God.

13. I bring near my righteousness; it shall not be far off, and my salvation shall not tarry: and I will place salvation in Zion for Israel my glory.

The Lord wants them to know that he has a great plan for Israel. He wishes to surround the Israelites with a mantle of righteousness. Furthermore, he desires to do it soon so that they can see for themselves that the God of Abraham, Isaac, and Jacob is not far off, nor are his salvation and blessings to be long delayed. He desires to make Zion a place of salvation and lift up Israel so that the world can see that they are blessed because they glorify God.

Isaiah, Chapter 47

INTRODUCTION:

Now we come to Isaiah's prophecy concerning the conquest and fall of mighty Babylon. That historical spectacle has already been described in the introduction to chapter 45. This chapter is like a solemn dirge as Isaiah contemplates the subjugation of the once mighty pinnacle of power called Babylon.

1. **Come down, and sit in the dust, O virgin daughter of Babylon, sit on the ground: there is no throne, O daughter of the Chaldeans: for thou shalt no more be called tender and delicate.**

Isaiah invites mighty Babylon to prepare to come down from her proud throne and sit in the dust. Having never tasted captivity or defeat for several generations, she is like a virgin daughter who will now be forced to suffer the indignities which the Babylonian kings (of the proud Chaldean families) have inflicted on other nations. In her afflictions, she will be humbled to the ground and will no longer be called either tender or delicate.

2. **Take the millstones, and grind meal: uncover thy locks, make bare the leg, uncover the thigh, pass over the rivers.**

She will be treated like the most ordinary slave girls who are assigned the most tedious of all tasks—the grinding of meal between heavy stones. And as so often happens with slave girls, she will be subjected to the indignities of those who are sold in the slave market. She must uncover her locks, expose her body to the rude gaze of prospective buyers, and be transported across the Tigris River if it suits the fancy of her new Persian lords.

3. Thy nakedness shall be uncovered, yea, thy shame
shall be seen: I will take
vengeance, and I will not
meet thee as a man.

In this verse we seem to have a poor translation. Not only will Babylon be humiliated and left naked or open to conquest but Dr. Adam Clarke suggests that the phrase "I will not meet thee as a man" should read "NEITHER WILL I SUFFER MAN TO INTERCEDE WITH ME." (Clarke, *Commentary*, 4:184; emphasis added.)

4. As for our redeemer, the
LORD of hosts is his name,
the Holy One of Israel.

Isaiah then acclaims the one who will rescue the Israelites from the Babylonians and says, "As for OUR redeemer, the Lord of hosts is his name, the Holy One of Israel."

5. Sit thou silent, and get thee
into darkness, O daughter
of the Chaldeans: for thou
shalt no more be called,
The lady of kingdoms.

As for Babylon, she will be left silent and weeping in some dark place of mourning. For many years her rulers were the wealthy and powerful families from the province of Chaldea to the south. Babylon, the "daughter of the Chaldeans", shall no longer be called "The lady of kingdoms."

6. I was wroth with my people, I have polluted mine
inheritance, and given them
into thine hand: thou didst
shew them no mercy; upon
the ancient hast thou very
heavily laid thy yoke.

Speaking almost as though the fall of Jerusalem and the captivity of the Jews had already taken place, the Lord says he is angry with his chosen people, and that is why he has allowed the Babylonians to conquer them. Nevertheless, the Lord is also angry with the Babylonians. They mistreated the Israelites and showed them no mercy. They yoked down the elderly with burdens too hard to bear.

7. And thou saidst, I shall be a
lady for ever: so that thou
didst not lay these things to
thy heart, neither didst remember the latter end of it.

Babylon assumed that she would be the mistress of the civilized world forever. She did not hearken to the prophecies of warning such as the one given to Nebuchadnezzar by Daniel (see Daniel 2:37–40). It was assumed that the power of Babylon was eternally invincible, and no consideration was given to the final consequences which could result from the cruel and despotic policies that Babylon imposed on other nations.

8. Therefore hear now this, thou that art given to pleasures, that dwellest carelessly, that sayest in thine heart, I am, and none else beside me; I shall not sit as a widow, neither shall I know the loss of children:

Babylon wanted only sensuous pleasures and careless indulgences in the dissipations of the day. She said that nothing could threaten her because there was no power that came even close to being equal with her own. She had never dreamed that the kingdom could become a widow without a king or that she could lose her children by a foreign invasion and total conquest.

9. But these two things shall come to thee in a moment in one day, the loss of children, and widowhood: they shall come upon thee in their perfection for the multitude of thy sorceries, and for the great abundance of thine enchantments.

Isaiah tells Babylon that in the day of her greatest glory and power two things will happen in a single day:
1. She will lose her king (thus becoming a political widow); and
2. She will lose her children since they will be taken into captivity.

10. For thou hast trusted in thy wickedness: thou hast said, None seeth me. Thy wisdom and thy knowledge, it hath perverted thee; and thou hast said in thine heart, I am, and none else beside me.

The Lord said all of this will come to pass because Babylon will feel so secure in her wickedness. She will be taken unawares. She will feel that she can indulge herself in that which she knows is evil, for she will feel that there is none who can see her or judge her or punish her. The very wisdom and knowledge that she used to make herself so great will be used to corrupt her. She will feel that nothing can challenge her supreme position of power, either in heaven or on earth.

11. **Therefore shall evil come upon thee; thou shalt not know from whence it riseth: and mischief shall fall upon thee; thou shalt not be able to put it off: and desolation shall come upon thee suddenly, which thou shalt not know.**

Nevertheless, the day of God's judgment will descend upon her, and a flood of evil will sweep down upon her from a source she never would have suspected. It will be so overwhelming in its dimensions that nothing will be able to stay its power.

It is interesting that the cruel destruction described in this chapter did not come under Cyrus but under Darius, who reigned later. It is said that he crucified 3,000 of her principal inhabitants while he was king (Clarke, *Commentary*, 4:185).

12. **Stand now with thine enchantments, and with the multitude of thy sorceries, wherein thou hast laboured from thy youth; if so be thou shalt be able to profit, if so be thou mayest prevail.**

From the nation's infancy, even in the days of Abraham, the Chaldeans and the Babylonians had rejected the counsel of the Lord. They had trusted in their enchantments, their sorceries, and their phony diviners. Therefore the Lord now challenges them and says that in their hour of calamity let them see if any of these things will save them.

13. **Thou art wearied in the multitude of thy counsels. Let now the astrologers, the stargazers, the monthly prognosticators, stand up, and save thee from these things that shall come upon thee.**

The Lord knew that in their hour of desperation the Babylonians would be confused by the multitude of contradicting signals which would pour out of their mystic babblers who claimed to have powers of divination. The Lord reiterates his great challenge. In that hour of travail let all those stargazers, astrologers, and monthly prognosticators take over the leadership and see if they can save the mighty Babylon from captivity.

14. **Behold, they shall be as stubble; the fire shall burn them; they shall not deliver themselves from the power of the flame: there shall not**

The Lord assures them that this vast mystical resource of power on which the nation has always depended for guidance will be no better than stubble in the field, fit to be burned. They will not be able to save

be a coal to warm at, nor fire to sit before it.

themselves or the people. Neither will they be able to provide fuel for culinary needs, or even for household warmth.

15. Thus shall they be unto thee with whom thou hast laboured, even thy merchants, from thy youth: they shall wander every one to his quarter; none shall save thee.

The Lord says this is what the people of Babylon will receive from those in whom they have trusted so implicitly. This pattern of failure and helplessness will not only characterize their mystical soothsayers, but it will be equally true of their merchants, who have always been among the leaders of the city in the past. These scions of wealth will wander off to their homes, not knowing how to save the city any more than will the frightened people themselves.

INTRODUCTION:

Now we come to the first chapter of the book of Isaiah to be quoted by Nephi in the Book of Mormon. Nephi felt this chapter held particular significance for those who had been scattered abroad on the isles of the sea. He wanted them to know that in spite of Israel's rebellion in the past, there was a ray of hope for Israel in the far distant future.

Ordinarily Joseph Smith followed the King James translation whenever he was translating Book of Mormon passages which were quoted from the Bible. However, he made changes whenever it was indicated to him that the King James Version was not completely correct. It is significant that in Isaiah chapter 48, every verse in the Book of Mormon is somewhat different from its counterpart in the Bible. Some of these changes are not particularly significant, but others are extremely important. Altogether, Joseph Smith changed or modified 234 of the 433 verses of Isaiah that are quoted in the Book of Mormon (Sidney B. Sperry, *Our Book of Mormon,* 4th ed. [Salt Lake City: Bookcraft, 1947], p. 172).

As we shall see, a most important change appears in the first verse of this chapter.

1. **Hear ye this, O house of Jacob, which are called by the name of Israel, and are come forth out of the waters of Judah, which swear by**

This chapter is addressed to the whole house of Israel. These are they who are supposed to be known by the name of Jesus Christ, the very one whom Isaiah continually addresses as the "Saviour" and "Redeemer."

**the name of the LORD, and
make mention of the God
of Israel, but not in truth,
nor in righteousness.**

These are they who have come forth from "the waters of Judah," which are defined in the Book of Mormon text as "THE WATERS OF BAPTISM" (1 Nephi 20:1; emphasis added). Through the waters of baptism, Israel has entered into a covenant to always remember the Lord and keep his commandments. Unfortunately, they have not made this covenant with truth in their hearts, nor have they done it in a spirit of righteousness.

It is interesting that the excavations around the temple site in Jerusalem have revealed numerous baptismal fonts which archaeologists refer to as "ceremonial baths." Today, the Jewish people have virtually abandoned the rite of baptism, although they have carefully preserved the ritual of circumcision. Significantly, circumcision was given to God's people in the days of Abraham to remind them of baptism! The Lord said:

"My people have gone astray from my precepts, and have not kept mine ordinances, which I gave unto their fathers;

"And they have not observed mine anointing, and the burial, OR BAPTISM wherewith I commanded them;

"But have turned from the commandment, and taken unto themselves the washing of children, and the blood of sprinkling." (JST, Genesis 17:4–6; emphasis added.)

This would suggest that the people were participating in infant baptism and sprinkling their children with blood after the manner of the heathens. The Lord said the ordinance of circumcision was being introduced so that when male children were circumcised on the eighth day it would remind them that their children were to be baptized in their eighth YEAR. The Lord said that "children are not accountable before me [or eligible for baptism] until they are eight years old" (JST, Genesis 17:11).

The procedure for going down into "the waters of Judah" or baptism is described by James Hastings as follows: Each candidate was taken "to a pool, in which he stood up to his neck in water, while the great commandments of the Law were recited to him. These he promised to keep. Then a benediction was pronounced, and he plunged beneath the water, taking care to be entirely submerged." (James Hastings, ed., *A Dictionary of the Bible*, 4 vols with index [Edinburgh: T. & T. Clark, 1898], 1:239, s.v. "Baptism.")

Before leaving this verse we should also point out that the original text of Isaiah did not clarify "the waters of Judah" as meaning "the waters of baptism." Since that is what it meant to the people in ancient times Isaiah did not feel it was necessary to further clarify it. As a matter of fact, in the first edition of the Book of Mormon Joseph Smith left it in its original form. However, since modern readers of the Bible do not interpret "the waters of Judah" as "the waters of baptism," he decided to spell out its true significance when the second edition of the Book of Mormon was published. (See Hugh W. Nibley, *Since Cumorah* [Salt Lake City: Deseret Book Company, 1967], p. 151.) The clarifying words, "or of the waters of baptism," have been included in 1 Nephi 20:1 ever since.

2. For they call themselves of the holy city, and stay themselves upon the God of Israel; The LORD of hosts is his name.

Isaiah points out that the tribes of Israel, including the Jews, take pride in identifying themselves with the holy city of Jerusalem. However, the Book of Mormon version then goes on to say, "but they do NOT stay themselves upon the God of Israel, who is the Lord of Hosts" (1 Nephi 20:2; emphasis added). Notice that the absence of the word "not" in the King James translation almost makes the verse meaningless. The Book of Mormon corrects this error.

3. I have declared the former things from the beginning; and they went forth out of my mouth, and I shewed them; I did them suddenly, and they came to pass.

The Lord says in this verse that the Israelites have no excuse for not recognizing the integrity of the message which he has been giving the people from earliest times. The Lord has revealed with unerring accuracy those things which were going to come to pass long before the events transpired. The Lord did not wait until circumstances would suggest that those events were about to take place. The Lord revealed it "suddenly," long before anyone would have guessed it. (Examples of this would be the translation of the City of Enoch; the cleansing of the earth by a universal flood; the escape of Israel from slavery in Egypt; the captivity and transmigration of the northern Ten Tribes to Assyria, etc. God often revealed these events to his prophets centuries before they occurred.)

4. Because I knew that thou art obstinate, and thy neck is an iron sinew, and thy brow brass;

The Lord says he went out of his way to deliberately do this because the children of Israel have been such a strong-willed and "obstinate" people. Their necks have been so stiff and arrogant that sometimes it reminded the Lord of "an iron sinew." It has been so hard to get some things through their thick heads that the Lord refers to them as having a brow [of] brass.

5. I have even from the beginning declared it to thee; before it came to pass I shewed it thee: lest thou shouldest say, Mine idol hath done them, and my graven image, and my molten image, hath commanded them.

The Lord points out that those who have turned to making idolatrous images are so anxious to attribute divine powers to them that they will use the slightest coincidence as proof that their gods of gold or wood have provided SIGNS portending some great future event. That is why it has been necessary for the Lord to persuade his stubborn children of his own divine integrity by predicting events literally thousands of years before they happened. It had to be something spectacular (such as naming Cyrus 100 years before he was born) or these foolish idolaters would attribute a great event to the COMMAND of their graven idol or molten image.

6. Thou hast heard, see all this; and will not ye declare it? I have shewed thee new things from this time, even hidden things, and thou didst not know them.

The Lord longs to have his chosen people recognize what he is trying to do for them. He wants them to bear testimony that he has always told them what to expect. He has revealed "new things" and "hidden things," things which not even the wisest among them could have anticipated.

7. They are created now, and not from the beginning; even before the day when thou heardest them not; lest thou shouldest say, Behold, I knew them.

The Lord asks these stubborn Israelites to look about them and see what has happened. Things being "created now" are the very things which he said would happen. They are events and circumstances which no one among them could have guessed. Prophecy has been fulfilled in such a "sudden" and unexpected way that if someone had claimed that he had known it in advance, it would have been plain to everyone that he was lying.

8. Yea, thou heardest not; yea, thou knewest not; yea, from that time that thine ear was not opened: for I knew that thou wouldest deal very treacherously, and wast called a transgressor from the womb.

The Lord wants the people to confess that they did not know these things in advance. They had no way of speculating that such events would transpire in the amazing and marvelous way they did. The Lord then adds a note that reflects the frustrations and sorrow that a loving Heavenly Father feels when he must resort to such measures in order to get his children to give him at least some credence as their God and Creator. The Lord says that in spite of his love for his children he knew that during their second estate most of them would "deal very treacherously" with him and be counted transgressors with rebellious hearts from the day they were born.

9. For my name's sake will I defer mine anger, and for my praise will I refrain for thee, that I cut thee not off.

Nevertheless, the Lord now declares that he will not allow his anger and sense of justice to completely cut them off even though their abominable behavior deserves it. The Lord says he will "defer" his judgment so that his calling as a Savior may not be nullified. His name is Jesus the Christ (the latter word is Greek for Savior). Therefore, he will be their Savior for his name's sake, and he will put Israel through an extended course of training and discipline rather than cut them off.

10. Behold, I have refined thee, but not with silver; I have chosen thee in the furnace of affliction.

From generation to generation the Lord has had to put Israel through a continuous process of refining to save them from their own proud and wicked tendencies to rebel and lose their calling. The Lord says it is literally true that they have qualified as his CHOSEN people only after going through "the furnace of affliction." It is interesting that some ancient scribe apparently added the phrase, "but not with silver," or as some translations have it, "but not AS silver" (*Interpreter's Bible*, 5:557; emphasis added). The Book of Mormon text of Isaiah, the oldest in existence, does not contain this phrase. The intense heat required for the refining of silver was well known to the ancient Israelites, and it is likely that some scribe included this phrase to make it more impressive.

11. For mine own sake, even for mine own sake, will I do it: for how should my name be polluted? and I will not give my glory unto another.

The Lord repeats that he determined not to allow the rebellion and wickedness of the Israelites to rob the Savior of his calling as the Messiah. He is determined to persist in his endurance of their stiff-necked waywardness and continue the refining process. Otherwise his name, which means Savior, would be polluted or lose its significance. People would say he had not SAVED anyone.

12. Hearken unto me, O Jacob and Israel, my called; I am he; I am the first, I also am the last.

Now comes the Lord's clarion call to his people. He pleads with them to rally around their Lord and Savior. He reminds them that they were "called" from before the foundations of the world (Deuteronomy 32:7-9) to be his chosen witnesses, his Priesthood, his prophets, apostles, and leaders of mankind, so as to establish principles of righteousness in the earth. The Lord reminds them who it is that is calling them. He is the great Jehovah, their Savior, the first and the last.

13. Mine hand also hath laid the foundation of the earth, and my right hand hath spanned the heavens: when I call unto them, they stand up together.

The Savior is none other than the "Word" (John 1:1-5) who spoke in the name of the Father and laid the foundations of both the heavens and the earth. He organized the myriads of intelligences with vast quantities of element to come together according to certain patterns and designs. When he spoke to them and commanded them, they literally "[stood] up" in their places according to his word and became the marvels of the cosmic universe that we now see all about us. God's organizing genius of speaking to the intelligences in matter and having them "obey" is all through the scriptures. (See, for example, Abraham 4:9-10, 12, 18; Helaman 12:8-17; Jacob 4:6.)

14. All ye, assemble yourselves, and hear; which among them hath declared these things? The LORD hath loved him: he will do his pleasure on Babylon, and his arm shall be on the Chaldeans.

Now Isaiah discontinues quoting the Lord and tells the people to assemble themselves together. He asks who it is that has been declaring all these things to them. The answer, of course, is that Isaiah himself has been proclaiming these great prophecies to the people. Isaiah wants the people to know that "the Lord hath loved him" (Isaiah), "AND HE WILL FULFILL HIS WORD WHICH HE HATH DECLARED BY THEM," (or through Isaiah's prophecies). This phrase is missing from the Bible, but, it appears in the Book of Mormon version (1

Nephi 20:14; emphasis added). Isaiah says it will be the Lord's "pleasure" to fulfill all that has been predicted concerning Babylon and her Chaldean rulers.

15. **I, even I, have spoken; yea, I have called him: I have brought him, and he shall make his way prosperous.**

Isaiah now quotes the Lord as having endorsed his work. The Lord has said that he called Isaiah to perform this great mission and "TO DECLARE," says the Book of Mormon (1 Nephi 20:15; emphasis added), these things to the people. The Lord has promised to prosper Isaiah in his work.

16. **Come ye near unto me, hear ye this; I have not spoken in secret from the beginning; from the time that it was, there am I: and now the Lord GOD, and his Spirit, hath sent me.**

Isaiah invites the people of Israel to come near to him. He reminds them that he has not been teaching the people in secret, but openly, so that all might hear the message from the Lord. He says that from the very beginning he has passed on the word of the Lord to them as fast as he received it. He wants them to know that his message is no idle tale. He says that "the Lord God, and his Spirit, hath sent me." It is the mission of the Spirit or Holy Ghost to confirm the truthfulness of the message which Isaiah has delivered to them from the Lord (see 1 John 5:6; Moroni 10:3-5).

17. **Thus saith the LORD, thy Redeemer, the Holy One of Israel; I am the LORD thy God which teacheth thee to profit, which leadeth thee by the way that thou shouldest go.**

Isaiah wants the people to know that the person who dispatched him on this mission was none other than the "Redeemer, the Holy One of Israel." Then Isaiah quotes the Savior as saying, "I [the Lord] have sent him [Isaiah], the Lord thy God who teacheth thee to profit, who leadeth thee by the way thou shouldst go, hath done it" (1 Nephi 20:17). As we shall see in the next chapter, Isaiah had suffered great persecution and had been largely rejected by the people. He wants them to know that God, who loves Israel and is constantly seeking to make life profitable and happy for them, is the one who called Isaiah to deliver this great message to the people.

18. O that thou hadst hearkened to my commandments! then had thy peace been as a river, and thy righteousness as the waves of the sea:

The Lord's lamentation concerning Israel is that they have not been obedient to his commandments. If they had been obedient they would have enjoyed tremendous blessings. Their peace would have been like the quiet dignity of a great river flowing toward the sea and their righteousness would have made them strong like the waves of the sea.

19. Thy seed also had been as the sand, and the offspring of thy bowels like the gravel thereof; his name should not have been cut off nor destroyed from before me.

They would also have grown to be a much larger population if they had been more obedient to the Lord's commandments. Furthermore, they and their seed would not have forgotten the name of Jesus Christ, their Lord and Savior, which they had been commanded to always remember (see Mosiah 5:11).

20. Go ye forth of Babylon, flee ye from the Chaldeans, with a voice of singing declare ye, tell this, utter it even to the end of the earth; say ye, The LORD hath redeemed his servant Jacob.

In anticipation of the rescue of the Jews from their Babylonian captors in 538 B.C., the Lord tells them to go forth out of Babylon and declare to all the world that, "The Lord hath redeemed his servant Jacob."

21. And they thirsted not when he led them through the deserts: he caused the waters to flow out of the rock for them: he clave the rock also, and the waters gushed out.

It is important for Israel to remember that the Lord is mighty to save. He has continually blessed Israel and saved them from their oppressors. He led them out of Egypt and brought them across the great desert. They did not die of thirst because he brought water gushing out of the bare rock on two separate occasions (see Exodus 17:6; Numbers 20:11).

22. There is no peace, saith the LORD, unto the wicked.

The Book of Mormon gives the original text for this verse as follows: "AND NOTWITHSTANDING HE HATH DONE ALL THIS, AND GREATER ALSO, there is no peace, saith the Lord, unto the wicked" (1 Nephi 20:22; emphasis added).

Even when the Lord saves his people and showers blessings upon them, those who rebel and revel in wickedness will not have peace, happiness, or self-fulfillment even in the midst of such blessings. The Lord has declared it, and the experiences of life bitterly confirm it: "There is no peace, saith the Lord, unto the wicked!"

INTRODUCTION:

Isaiah was not the only prophet who was shown visions of events far in the future. In 600 B.C., when the prophet Nephi was approximately 16 years of age, he was shown a panoramic vision of approximately 2,600 years of prophetic history. Later, when he had a chance to study the scriptures of the Old Testament as contained in the brass plates of Laban, he realized that many of the writings of the prophets were related to the scenes and events which he himself had been allowed to see. He says:

"For behold, I have workings in the spirit, which doth weary me even that all my joints are weak, for those who are at Jerusalem; for had not the Lord been merciful, TO SHOW UNTO ME CONCERNING THEM, EVEN AS HE HAD PROPHETS OF OLD, I should have perished also.

"AND HE SURELY DID SHOW UNTO THE PROPHETS OF OLD ALL THINGS CONCERNING THEM [in Jerusalem]; and also he did show unto many [prophets] CONCERNING US;...they are written upon the plates of brass." (1 Nephi 19:20-21; emphasis added.)

Both Nephi and his brother, Jacob, spent considerable time and energy carefully copying into the Book of Mormon record many chapters of Isaiah. In a number of places the Book of Mormon version of Isaiah is more accurate than is the King James translation. This is an important advantage to the modern Bible student.

It is particularly interesting that Nephi was prevented from recording many of the scenes which he

saw concerning our own day. He was told that these
events would be recorded by John the Revelator (see 1
Nephi 14:18–28), who lived around 600 years after
Nephi. He even felt restricted in commenting on Isaiah
where it related to our day (see 1 Nephi 22:29). In fact,
toward the latter part of his life Nephi was forbidden
by the Spirit to tell some of the most exciting things
which he was anxious to relate concerning modern
times. It appears that he wanted to tell us how it will all
turn out, but the Lord wanted us to work it out for
ourselves (see 2 Nephi 32:7). However, there is no
restriction on Nephi's interpretation of Isaiah chapter
49. He recorded this chapter from the brass plates, thus
providing a more accurate text than we have in our
modern Bible.

**1. Listen, O isles, unto me;
and hearken, ye people,
from far; The LORD hath
called me from the womb;
from the bowels of my
mother hath he made men-
tion of my name.**

About half of this verse is missing from the Bible.
Here is the way it appears in the Book of Mormon:
"AND AGAIN: HEARKEN, O YE HOUSE OF ISRAEL,
ALL YE THAT ARE BROKEN OFF AND ARE DRIVEN
OUT BECAUSE OF THE WICKEDNESS OF THE PAS-
TORS OF MY PEOPLE; YEA, ALL YE THAT ARE
BROKEN OFF, THAT ARE SCATTERED ABROAD, WHO
ARE OF MY PEOPLE, O HOUSE OF ISRAEL. Listen, O
isles, unto me, and hearken ye people from far; the
Lord hath called me from the womb; from the bowels
of my mother hath he made mention of my name." (1
Nephi 21:1; emphasis added.)

This chapter is Isaiah's mighty proclamation to all the
hosts of Israel who have been scattered to every
continent of the earth and to the isles of the sea. Isaiah
says their scattering abroad has been the result of "the
wickedness of the pastors." These were the spiritual
and temporal leaders among those whom Isaiah (and
the Lord) refers to as "my people." In a sense, all
Israelites are relatives of Isaiah, and he wants them to

listen to the message of hope which he is about to present to them. He is not talking just to the people of Jerusalem but to "ye people from far."

Isaiah then presents his credentials. He wants the people who receive this message to know that he was called from the time of his birth to be a prophet and a messenger to Israel. Apparently, though the details are not related, Isaiah was prophetically known by name before he was born. Similarly, Jeremiah, the great prophet whose mission followed that of Isaiah, says that the Lord disclosed to him that he was called to be a prophet before he was born (see Jeremiah 1:4-5). This was also true of Abraham (see Abraham 3:23). In fact, the writings of Abraham would suggest that this was true of all the prophets. They were all chosen because of their valiancy in the premortal existence.

2. And he hath made my mouth like a sharp sword; in the shadow of his hand hath he hid me, and made me a polished shaft; in his quiver hath he hid me;

Isaiah was a highly educated citizen of Jerusalem. He wrote the entire book of Isaiah in poetic form. He also had an unusual gift of eloquence and spoke with great clarity, which all of the people who heard him understood (see 2 Nephi 25:5). Isaiah knew that he had a power of expression which was like a sharp sword, and he attributed this great gift to God. So far as we can tell, Isaiah was a mature man before the Lord called him to go forth among the people to declare his message. During his earlier years (of which we have no record), the Lord kept him hidden from the people while the Lord developed Isaiah into a "polished shaft" in the quiver of the Lord. Then he sent him forth like a spiritual battering ram to penetrate the stony hearts of the people with his great message.

It is interesting how the Lord begins revealing himself to many of his prophets long before he allows them to begin their mission. The Lord puts his servants through a period of training and refining to make them polished ambassadors of the truth. This happened to Moses, Jeremiah, Ezekiel, John the Baptist, and even the Savior. Jesus went through a long period of preparation before his mission began at the age of 30. Even by the age of 12 he knew he was on his "Father's business" (see Luke 2:41-49).

3. And said unto me, Thou art my servant, O Israel, in whom I will be glorified.

As a further credential, Isaiah relates that the Lord said to him, "Thou art my servant, O Israel [soldier of God], in whom I will be glorified." Note that the word "Israel" is a title as well as a name. It means "soldier of God," or "one who has prevailed with God." When this word is used in connection with an individual, it is a salutation of honor and should be translated as a salutation rather than left as "Israel." Otherwise it would seem to refer to the people as a whole, when it was originally intended to apply to Isaiah himself. Adam Clarke points this out in his commentary on the Bible (Clarke, *Commentary,* 4:190).

4. Then I said, I have laboured in vain, I have spent my strength for nought, and in vain: yet surely my judgment is with the LORD, and my work with my God.

In verse 3 the Lord had told Isaiah that through his mission the Lord would "be glorified," but Isaiah says he told the Lord that, so far his labor had been "in vain." He had labored with great diligence, but the people were not converted, neither were they giving him a respectful hearing. In verses 5 and 6 of chapter 50 Isaiah describes how he has been beaten with sticks, his beard has been pulled, and his face spat upon. He says it seems as though he has "spent [his] strength for nought, and in vain." Nevertheless, Isaiah makes his firm commitment that he will let the Lord judge the merits of his efforts and leave the fruit of his work with God.

Of all the assignments a servant of God can receive, the most discouraging kind is a mission which seems to be "in vain." Noah had such a mission. To a large extent the mission of Jeremiah was of this discouraging kind. So was the mission of John the Beloved, who was exiled to the Isle of Patmos. In each case these great prophets had to do their best, leave a powerful witness with the people, and then depend on the justice and understanding of the Lord to evaluate their work.

5. **And now, saith the LORD that formed me from the womb to be his servant, to bring Jacob again to him, Though Israel be not gathered, yet shall I be glorious in the eyes of the LORD, and my God shall be my strength.**

In this verse the prophet Isaiah states that the Lord has revealed something to him that has provided great comfort and encouragement in spite of the persecution he has suffered. He says the Lord has told him that even though Israel will not repent and gather together in righteousness during Isaiah's day, yet the time will come when the words of Isaiah will be completely vindicated and he will "be glorious in the eyes of the Lord." In the next verse the Lord describes how this will come about.

6. **And he said, It is a light thing that thou shouldest be my servant to raise up the tribes of Jacob, and to restore the preserved of Israel: I will also give thee for a light to the Gentiles, that thou mayest be my salvation unto the end of the earth.**

In response to Isaiah's complaint that his labor had been in vain, the Lord assures him that his words are designed for the Israelites of a later day. His burden is "light" and his assignment enjoyable when it is realized that his words will serve as a clarion call to gather the Twelve Tribes of Jacob in the latter days, and will also serve as a light to the great Gentile nations. Isaiah had already seen those great events in vision, and therefore he had no difficulty appreciating the significance of this thrilling promise. The Lord told him that the things which he was recording would be the means of converting the Israelites in the latter days. His words would help them understand the restored Gospel and would draw them into the net of the Lord's kingdom from the uttermost ends of the earth.

7. **Thus saith the LORD, the Redeemer of Israel, and his Holy One, to him whom man despiseth, to him whom the nation abhorreth, to a servant of rulers, Kings shall see and arise, princes also shall worship, because of the LORD that is faithful, and the Holy One of Israel, and he shall choose thee.**

The Lord further comforted Isaiah so that the prophet could quote the Savior and Redeemer, the Holy One of Israel, as saying to him that in the latter days he would be honored by kings. Isaiah's words would be the means by which they would be led to believe that the Lord had been faithful in fulfilling all his promises. They would come to realize that Isaiah was chosen of the Lord to write of the latter days and describe what the Twelve Tribes of Israel as well as the Gentiles must do in order to enjoy the blessings of salvation.

8. **Thus saith the LORD, In an acceptable time have I heard thee, and in a day of salvation have I helped thee: and I will preserve thee, and give thee for a covenant of the people, to establish the earth, to cause to inherit the desolate heritages;**

The Book of Mormon gives a more perfect rendition of this verse as follows: "Thus saith the Lord: In an acceptable time have I heard thee, O ISLES OF THE SEA, and in a day of salvation have I helped thee; and I will preserve thee, and give thee MY SERVANT for a covenant of the people, to establish the earth, to cause to inherit the desolate heritages." (1 Nephi 21:8; emphasis added.)

In the context of this chapter the Lord seems to be saying that Isaiah, "my servant," will comfort the scattered Israelites in the latter days, for his writings contain God's covenant or promise that they will be gathered to the lands of their inheritance. In a larger context it could also be said that God would send his "servant," even Jesus Christ, who is the messenger of the covenant, and he would set things right in the earth and establish the Israelites in their promised lands of inheritance. Both interpretations could be accurately applied to this verse. However, from Isaiah's point of view this chapter was given to assure him that his words were not being recorded in vain. God had designated him to be his servant, his "soldier of God" (see author's commentary on verse 3), to comfort Israel by assuring them of the covenant and promise which Isaiah had recorded, namely, that they would be gathered back to their desolated lands of inheritance in the latter days.

9. That thou mayest say to the prisoners, Go forth; to them that are in darkness, Shew yourselves. They shall feed in the ways, and their pastures shall be in all high places.

In the writings of Isaiah, the latter-day children of Israel are told that it is their calling to escape from the captivity of the Gentiles and go forth to the designated places of their inheritances. The Lord is going to intervene for them so that they can "feed in the ways," and have rich pastures in high and fertile places far removed from the scorching deserts where many of them were held captives.

10. They shall not hunger nor thirst; neither shall the heat nor sun smite them: for he that hath mercy on them shall lead them, even by the springs of water shall he guide them.

To further emphasize this theme, the Lord promises that the gathering Israelites will not hunger or thirst. Neither will they succumb to the heat of a blazing sun. Their gathering will be under the direction of the Lord, who will guide them to life-giving springs of refreshing water.

11. And I will make all my mountains a way, and my highways shall be exalted.

This verse is talking about something far more exciting than these simple words would seem to imply. The details of how the children of Israel will use the mountains for their thoroughfare, and have a mighty highway "exalted" (or lifted up) for them are described by the Lord in a modern revelation as follows:

"And they who are in the north countries shall come in remembrance before the Lord; . . . and they shall smite the rocks, and the ice shall flow down at their presence.

"And an highway shall be cast up in the midst of the great deep. . . .

"And they shall bring forth their rich treasures unto the children of Ephraim. . . .

"And there shall they fall down and be crowned with glory, even in Zion, by the hands of the servants of the

Lord, even the children of Ephraim." (D&C 133:26-27; 30, 32.)

This is describing the return of the lost Ten Tribes of Israel. They will come out of the north on a mighty highway which will be raised up in the deep so that they can come with their multitudes and their treasures to receive their endowments from the Ephraimite Saints in America. Jeremiah says the raising up of this highway "in the midst of the great deep" will be so spectacular that people will no longer talk about the miracle of dividing the Red Sea for Israel (see Jeremiah 16:14-15). That will seem insignificant compared to the latter-day highway in the great deep.

12. Behold, these shall come from far: and, lo, these from the north and from the west; and these from the land of Sinim.

Isaiah says these remnants of Israel will "come from FAR." Just how far is impossible to say, but there is a hint scattered throughout the scripture that some of them may come from another planetary home where God transplanted them. If such is the case, then they will have to reach the earth by a highway from the depths of space. Note the strange way in which Jesus described to his disciples the manner in which the great latter-day gathering would take place. Jesus said he would bring together his people "from one end of heaven to the other" (Joseph Smith—Matthew 1:37). We also note that Isaiah speaks of Judah being DISPERSED among the nations of the earth, but the main body of Israel being OUTCASTS (Isaiah 11:12; or 2 Nephi 21:12) It may turn out that these Israelites who come down "from the north" will have come from very far indeed. And their highway in the "great deep" may turn out to be a highway to the earth from the depths of the heavens.

As far as the gathering from among the nations of the earth is concerned, Isaiah says they will assemble from the north and the west, and also from "Sinim."

Hastings's *Dictionary of the Bible,* suggests that early scholars felt that "Sinim" meant China or the lands of the far east. Later scholars are less certain (Hastings, *Dictionary of the Bible,* rev. ed., s.v. "Sinim").

13. Sing, O heavens; and be joyful, O earth; and break forth into singing, O mountains: for the LORD hath comforted his people, and will have mercy upon his afflicted.

When these great events occur, the Lord says the whole earth will be able to break forth in singing because the Lord will comfort his people and bring mercy to them at a time when they will be sorely afflicted.

A more complete version of this text is given in the Book of Mormon as follows: "Sing, O heavens; and be joyful, O earth; for THE FEET OF THOSE WHO ARE IN THE EAST SHALL BE ESTABLISHED; and break forth into singing, O mountains; FOR THEY SHALL BE SMITTEN NO MORE; for the Lord hath comforted his people, and will have mercy upon his afflicted." (1 Nephi 21:13; emphasis added.) Those who are established in the east are probably the children of Judah at Jerusalem, while those who will be rescued from affliction in the mountains are probably the Lord's people on the Western Hemisphere. This is borne out by the next verse.

14. But Zion said, The LORD hath forsaken me, and my LORD hath forgotten me.

The full text in the Book of Mormon is as follows: "But, BEHOLD, Zion HATH said: The Lord hath forsaken me, and my Lord hath forgotten me—BUT HE WILL SHOW THAT HE HATH NOT." (1 Nephi 21:14; emphasis added.)

Apparently the righteous will suffer great afflictions in America before a Zion society is firmly established, and the people will feel that the Lord has forsaken them. Nevertheless, his people will find in their hour of ultimate crisis that God will intervene and succor them. Then they will know that he has not forgotten them.

When the prophets distinguish "Zion" from Jerusalem (which they often do), they are talking about North and South America. Joseph Smith said, *"The whole of America is Zion itself from north to south, and is described by the Prophets, who declare that it is the Zion where the mountain of the Lord should be, and that it should be in the center of the land"* (Smith, *Teachings*, p. 362; italics in original).

15. Can a woman forget her sucking child, that she should not have compassion on the son of her womb? yea, they may forget, yet will I not forget thee.

The Lord's response to the afflicted Saints in America, when they think they have been forgotten, will be a question: "For can a woman forget her sucking [unweaned and helpless] child, that she should not have compassion on the son of her womb? Yea, they may forget, yet will I not forget thee, O HOUSE OF ISRAEL" (1 Nephi 21:15; emphasis added).

16. Behold, I have graven thee upon the palms of my hands; thy walls are continually before me.

The Lord says he will never forget his people because they are "graven" or inscribed upon the palms of his hands. Dr. Monte S. Nyman has pointed out that the most profound "engravings" in the palms of the Savior are the marks left by the spikes at the time of his crucifixion. He retained these engravings even in his resurrected body. These engraven wounds will forever be the symbols of Christ's great sacrifice for all mankind, but especially for those who accept the Gospel and are numbered among God's chosen people of Israel (Nyman, *"Great Are the Words of Isaiah,"* p. 181).

17. Thy children shall make haste; thy destroyers and they that made thee waste shall go forth of thee.

The Book of Mormon gives this verse as follows: "Thy children shall make haste AGAINST thy destroyers; and they that made thee waste shall go forth of thee" (1 Nephi 21:17; emphasis added).

The Lord wanted the Israelites of the latter days to know that in spite of their persecutors they would prevail. He said their children (youth) should hasten forth to stand against the destroyers of Zion because those who spread waste and destruction across the land will be forced to retreat and leave God's people alone.

18. Lift up thine eyes round about, and behold: all these gather themselves together, and come to thee. As I live, saith the LORD, thou shalt surely clothe thee with them all, as with an ornament, and bind them on thee, as a bride doeth.

Then a great multitude will come in upon the land. This probably refers to the coming of the Ten Tribes from the north. Suddenly, as it were, those who were a persecuted minority of the Lord's people will become an overwhelming majority. These newcomers will bring great honor and prestige to the afflicted Saints. They will suddenly be honored as a new bride, and these vast multitudes will be to the Church as an ornament or a rich garment.

19. For thy waste and thy desolate places, and the land of thy destruction, shall even now be too narrow by reason of the inhabitants, and they that swallowed thee up shall be far away.

These multitudes of returning Israelites will be so numerous that they will occupy many cities which have been destroyed, and also the desolated places which have been laid waste. But even these vast regions will not be sufficient to accommodate them because of their great numbers. Furthermore, there will be no one to resist them as they spread over the land because, by this time, their enemies will "be far away."

20. The children which thou shalt have, after thou hast lost the other, shall say again in thine ears, The place is too strait for me: give place to me that I may dwell.

These vast numbers of newcomers will fill up the desolated cities and settled part of the land. Then they will need even more room as they continue pouring down from the north. They will ask the Israelites who are already dwelling in America to help them find a place to live.

21. Then shalt thou say in thine heart, Who hath begotten me these, seeing I have lost my children, and am desolate, a captive, and removing to and fro? and who hath brought up these? Behold, I was left alone; these, where had they been?

The members of the Church who will be so few when compared to the rest of the earth, will be astonished when they see their number multiplied so enormously. Of course, the Saints will have read in the scriptures how the ancient Israelites were carried off by the Assyrians and finally became lost. They will also know that those who remained behind became the captives of various nations which drove them to and fro. All through the centuries they will have wondered, "What ever happened to the lost Ten Tribes?" When these multitudes suddenly put in their appearance in the latter days and come swarming down from the north as a great nation, the Saints will feel compelled to ask, "Where have they been?"

22. Thus saith the Lord GOD, Behold, I will lift up mine hand to the Gentiles, and set up my standard to the people: and they shall bring thy sons in their arms, and thy daughters shall be carried upon their shoulders.

Now Isaiah begins a whole new theme. He is going to explain how the Lord intends to commence his work in the latter days to prepare for the ushering in of the Millennium. Amazingly, the work is going to begin with the Gentiles. It will be among them that a mighty standard will be raised up to which the Israelites from all over the world can rally. We now know that the Gentiles have had among them a large contingent of Ephraimites who didn't even know they were Israelites. They considered themselves Gentiles. The Lord had to reveal to them who they really are. Isaiah saw that in the latter days these Ephraimites would be gathered, the Jews would be gathered, and the Lamanites would be gathered. To accomplish this the Lord said that a great spirit would sweep over the Gentiles. It would cause them to reach out and help the Israelites by carrying them, as it were, on their shoulders and in their arms.

Nephi interpreted this verse, after he had seen the same vision, as follows: "And it meaneth that...after all the house of Israel have been scattered and confounded, that the Lord God will raise up a mighty nation among the Gentiles, yea, even upon the face of this land.... The Lord God will proceed to do a marvelous work among the Gentiles, which shall be of great worth unto our seed; wherefore, it is likened unto their being nourished by the Gentiles and being carried in their arms and upon their shoulders." (1 Nephi 22:7-8.)

23. And kings shall be thy nursing fathers, and their queens thy nursing mothers: they shall bow down to thee with their face toward the earth, and lick up the dust of thy feet; and thou shalt know that I am the LORD: for they shall not be ashamed that wait for me.

It will be an amazing situation. The Israelites of the latter days who will have been spurned, persecuted, deprived of their rights, and locked up in ghettos will suddenly be elevated to a position where kings and queens will seek to nourish them and support them. Royal families will bow before them and honor them almost as though they were the subjects of the Israelites. The Lord assures Israel that in that remarkable day they will realize the truth of the statement that the faithful Saints will not be ashamed if they patiently wait for the Lord to manifest himself.

24. Shall the prey be taken from the mighty, or the lawful captive delivered?

But before this prediction becomes a reality it will seem impossible to fulfill. For centuries the Jews, native American Indians, Polynesians, and other remnants of Israel will have been suppressed and virtually serving as captives of the Gentiles. Under these adverse circumstances they will read the prophecy in Isaiah and exclaim: "[How] shall the prey be taken from the mighty [Gentiles], or the lawful captive delivered?"

25. But thus saith the LORD, Even the captives of the mighty shall be taken away,

The Lord says it will all come to pass just as he has promised. The humble captives of Israelite descent who have been trodden down for many centuries by their

and the prey of the terrible shall be delivered: for I will contend with him that contendeth with thee, and I will save thy children.

Gentile overlords will be delivered from their power. They will become a great and delightsome people, and they who contend against them will find the Lord intervening in many remarkable ways to "save" the children of Israel.

Nephi comments on these passages and says that the standard which will be raised up among the Gentiles will be the restoration of the Gospel and the renewal of God's covenant with all who will repent and join God's kingdom. He says:

"Wherefore, the Lord God will proceed to make bare his arm in the eyes of all the nations, in bringing about [through direct revelation] his covenants and his gospel unto those who are of the house of Israel.

"Wherefore, he will bring them again out of captivity, and they shall be gathered together to the lands of their inheritance; and they shall be brought out of obscurity and out of darkness; and they shall know that the Lord is their Savior and their Redeemer, the Mighty One of Israel." (1 Nephi 22: 11-12.)

It is interesting how Israel has been brought out of obscurity and captivity. Many who were scattered among the Gentiles responded to the message of the restored Gospel and learned through their patriarchal blessings that they were actually of the Tribe of Ephraim (something they never would have guessed). These converts were used to form the nucleus of the Church so that the blessings of the restored Gospel could be taught to the Gentiles, the Lamanites, the Jews, and eventually to every nation, kindred, tongue, and people. Israelites have been found scattered all over the world—in Japan, India, Africa, the islands of the sea, and especially in Europe. However, the only Tribes which have been identified in any quantity so far have been Ephraim, Manassah, Judah, and Levi. The rest are still "lost."

26. And I will feed them that oppress thee with their own flesh; and they shall be drunken with their own blood, as with sweet wine: and all flesh shall know that I the LORD am thy Saviour and thy Redeemer, the mighty One of Jacob.

The scriptures indicate that the wicked Gentiles who will not respond to the Gospel message will seek to overthrow the Lord's headquarters on the American continent and will be especially determined to suppress the work of the restored Gospel. At some point in time this threat is going to be so ominous that it will be terrifying to contemplate. But the Lord promises in verse 26 that an astonishing thing will occur. Instead of annihilating the free nations on the Western Hemisphere, the wicked Gentiles will begin a great fratricidal war among themselves. They will slaughter one another until they become "drunken with their own blood." When it is all over the whole world will know that the hand of the Lord has been over his people to save them in their hour of peril.

CONCLUSION:

Having examined the tremendous promises contained in this chapter, it is obvious why Nephi would select it, along with chapter 48, to use as a frame of reference in discussing the great events of the latter days. His commentary on these two chapters will be found in 1 Nephi, chapters 21 and 22. It is interesting to note that while Nephi was unfolding the meaning of these two chapters he became anxious lest he might be revealing too much. He therefore concluded his commentary with the statement, "And now I, Nephi, make an end; for I durst not speak further as yet concerning these things" (1 Nephi 22:29). The Lord had warned him earlier not to record some of the things he was shown (see 1 Nephi 14:25, 28).

Isaiah, Chapter 50

INTRODUCTION:

This chapter is a continuation of the theme in chapter 49. It will be recalled that the Lord assured Isaiah that even though Israel had rejected him in his own day, the Lord would make him glorious in the eyes of Israel in the latter days. His prophecies concerning the final redemption of Israel would all be fulfilled. Nephi, who had seen the same vision, commented on chapter 49 by saying that a mighty nation would be raised up in America, and that out of this "Gentile" nation a "marvelous work" would come forth which would greatly assist the children of Israel in gathering to Jerusalem and Zion or America (see 1 Nephi 22:7-9). Chapter 49 also said there will be a terrible destruction of the wicked, but "the righteous shall not perish" (1 Nephi 22:19).

In chapter 50 Isaiah is contending with those who cannot believe that the Ten Tribes (who had already been carried away by the Assyrians) will be gathered again. The Jews of Jerusalem knew those tribes had been a wicked people and God had divorced them. Many thought he had divorced the Jews as well. In Isaiah's day the Jews were constantly badgered by Sennacherib, the Assyrian ruler, who wanted to conquer the whole civilized world.

1. Thus saith the LORD, Where is the bill of your mother's divorcement, whom I have put away? or which of my creditors is it to whom I

The Lord challenges these unbelieving Israelites. The Lord says he has never issued any bill of divorcement or cut off the children of Israel. It is true that the main body of the Israelites has been carried off, but their fate

have sold you? Behold, for your iniquities have ye sold yourselves, and for your transgressions is your mother put away.

is in consequence of their own wicked transgressions. God did not sell them into bondage to satisfy his creditors, for he has no creditors. If the Jews feel that they have been sold into bondage and the main body of Israel abandoned by the Lord, he has an answer for them: "Behold, for your iniquities have ye sold yourselves, and for your transgressions is your mother put away."

2. Wherefore, when I came, was there no man? when I called, was there none to answer? Is my hand shortened at all, that it cannot redeem? or have I no power to deliver? behold, at my rebuke I dry up the sea, I make the rivers a wilderness: their fish stinketh, because there is no water, and dieth for thirst.

The whole problem is simply this, that when the Lord came to the people and called upon them to repent, they ignored him. From generation to generation the Lord raised up prophets to plead with this stiff-necked people. They continually ran braying off into the wilderness. If they wanted to enjoy God's blessings, why didn't they answer the Lord when he called? Whatever made them think he could not pour out blessings upon them if they would prove themselves worthy? He is the Holy One of Israel who has delivered Israel in the past. He has dried up the sea (so Israel could cross safely). He even stopped the river Jordan so that the hosts of Israel could cross dry-shod. The miracle was so great that it left the fish stranded on the dry river bottom and they died because the water had been suddenly taken away.

3. I clothe the heavens with blackness, and I make sackcloth their covering.

He is the mighty Jehovah, who can intervene at any time to make the heavens foreboding with blackness as though they had been covered with heavy sackcloth.

4. The Lord GOD hath given me the tongue of the learned, that I should know how to speak a word in season to

At this point, Isaiah turns on those who have been his critics and persecutors. Why have they not believed his words? The Book of Mormon text is more complete

him that is weary: he wakeneth morning by morning, he wakeneth mine ear to hear as the learned.

as Isaiah says: "The Lord God hath given me the tongue of the learned, that I should know how to speak a word in season UNTO THEE, O HOUSE OF ISRAEL. When ye are weary [from being righteous] he waketh [me] morning by morning. He waketh mine ear to hear as the learned." (2 Nephi 7:4; emphasis added.)

In this verse Isaiah is simply saying that he did not come to them as some bumbling rustic to mumble out an unintelligible or incoherent message. God had given him a tongue which was skilled in oral expression so that none could misunderstand. He said the Lord has done this so that he might speak to the people according to their needs of the time and tell them the will of the Lord. He wants them to know what it is like to fill the role of a prophet. He has been awakened in the early morning hours by the Spirit, which has urged him to speak to the people. Furthermore, the message has been given to him in a clear, concise, and comprehensible way so that he could speak as one who is "learned."

5. The Lord GOD hath opened mine ear, and I was not rebellious, neither turned away back.

In the Joseph Smith Translation this verse reads, "The Lord God hath APPOINTED MINE EARS" (emphasis added). In other words, this calling as a spokesman for God is not something Isaiah undertook on his own initiative. God spoke to his ears in an audible manner. Therefore, he is only doing what God has commanded him to do. He did not rebel against this calling, neither did he turn away from its many hardships and difficulties.

6. I gave my back to the smiters, and my cheeks to them that plucked off the

Isaiah describes what it has been like to serve the Lord in this capacity. He has had to endure being beaten over the back with sticks or whips. He has had

hair: I hid not my face from shame and spitting.

to suffer the indignity of ruffians grabbing him by the beard and spitting in his face.

7. For the Lord GOD will help me; therefore shall I not be confounded: therefore have I set my face like a flint, and I know that I shall not be ashamed.

But in spite of all they have done to him, Isaiah says that he knows the Lord God will continue to help and sustain him, and he will not be confounded. In fact, Isaiah says he is determined to "set [his] face like a flint" and perform his great mission regardless of the consequences. In the end, he says, "I know that I shall not be ashamed."

8. He is near that justifieth me; who will contend with me? let us stand together: who is mine adversary? let him come near to me.

Isaiah calls upon those who want to contend with him. He says he knows the Lord will support him and justify what he is doing. He calls upon his opposition to make themselves known and come forth in order that they might dialogue together.

9. Behold, the Lord GOD will help me; who is he that shall condemn me? lo, they all shall wax old as a garment; the moth shall eat them up.

Isaiah says that no matter who might contend against what he is saying, he knows the Lord will help him in defending all that God has revealed to him. He also declares that any who condemn him and reject this important message will soon fade away like a worn-out piece of clothing that is moth-eaten and good for nothing.

10. Who is among you that feareth the LORD, that obeyeth the voice of his servant, that walketh in darkness, and hath no light? let him trust in the name of the LORD, and stay upon his God.

In this verse Isaiah is addressing any individuals in his audience who might be humble followers of Jehovah. He asks if any of them who have obeyed the voice of Isaiah and listened to the message from the Lord are still wandering in darkness without any light or understanding. The answer, of course, is that they are not. They are animated and enlightened by what has been given them. Isaiah wants all such persons to continue in their faithfulness. He says, "Let him trust in the name of the Lord, and stay upon his God."

11. Behold, all ye that kindle a fire, that compass yourselves about with sparks: walk in the light of your fire, and in the sparks that ye have kindled. This shall ye have of mine hand; ye shall lie down in sorrow.

Finally, Isaiah addresses himself to those arrogant sycophants who feel no need for any revelation or instruction from God because they kindle their own fire and try to light their way through life with their own sparks or torches. Isaiah predicts a coming calamity for such persons. He says, "This shall ye have of mine hand—ye shall lie down in sorrow!"

Isaiah, Chapter 51

INTRODUCTION:

Now Isaiah wants to describe what he has seen in the latter days when the Gospel will be restored and the glory of God's blessings to modern Israel will be made manifest.

1. **Hearken to me, ye that follow after righteousness, ye that seek the LORD: look unto the rock whence ye are hewn, and to the hole of the pit whence ye are digged.**

Notice that this chapter is addressed to those "that follow after righteousness" and "seek the Lord." Isaiah challenges them to consider who they are. He wants them to contemplate the mighty stone from which they were hewn and "the pit" from which they were dug.

2. **Look unto Abraham your father, and unto Sarah that bare you: for I called him alone, and blessed him, and increased him.**

Isaiah says the solid stone from which they were hewn was Abraham, and the sacred pit from which they were gestated and brought forth was the beautiful Sarah. Among all the multitudes who inhabited the earth around 2000 B.C., the Lord called upon Abraham and his wife Sarah to be his choice servants. The Lord promised them great blessings and said their posterity would be as numerous as the sands of the seashore. From these two notable and worthy ancestors the children of Israel in modern times have descended.

3. **For the LORD shall comfort Zion: he will comfort all her waste places; and he will make her wilderness**

The restoration of the Gospel is a process, and Isaiah had seen that there would be times when the modern Israelites would wonder whether or not they would

like Eden, and her desert like the garden of the LORD; joy and gladness shall be found therein, thanksgiving, and the voice of melody.

ever make it. This verse was a great comfort to the Saints when they were driven out of Missouri and later out of Illinois. The Lord assured the Saints that eventually he would pour out comfort and blessings upon his people in America. He said her wilderness areas would become as the Garden of Eden. Her deserts and barren regions would become like a "garden of the Lord." There would be a time of joy and gladness, and the thanksgiving of the Saints would pour forth in "the voice of melody." The moment the Gospel began to be restored in these latter days, the Lord commanded the people to gather their hymns and sing their praises to the Lord (see D&C 25:11–12; 136:28). Later their choirs became famous worldwide.

4. Hearken unto me, my people; and give ear unto me, O my nation: for a law shall proceed from me, and I will make my judgment to rest for a light of the people.

Isaiah quotes the Lord directly throughout the remainder of this chapter. In this verse the Lord calls upon the people to hearken to his commandments and look forward to the day when he will establish a divine law among them which will provide righteous judgment. One of the most disheartening aspects of most man-made governments is their low quality of justice and their lack of efficiency in administering the affairs of the people. As a result, the people often feel exploited rather than served, and those who have been the victims of fraud or crime seldom feel that genuine justice and equity have been meted out. The inauguration of God's law will change this. It will become the "light" and the hope of the people.

5. My righteousness is near; my salvation is gone forth, and mine arms shall judge the people; the isles shall wait upon me, and on mine arm shall they trust.

Since this chapter is addressed to the "righteous" (verse 1), the Lord wants to assure his people that his "righteousness" under divine law is near. His salvation, both temporally and spiritually, has gone forth to be available to any and every generation of his children who will seek after it. They do not have to wait for the Millennium to enjoy it. The people of Enoch found it and lived under it for 365 years before the city was translated. The people of Melchizedek found it. So did the Nephites following the Savior's ministry among them. They were able to enjoy its blessings for over a century. Only when they began to wander away from God's law did their society degenerate back to the ordinary level of man-made government with its internal corruption and low level of true justice.

6. **Lift up your eyes to the heavens, and look upon the earth beneath: for the heavens shall vanish away like smoke, and the earth shall wax old like a garment, and they that dwell therein shall die in like manner: but my salvation shall be for ever, and my righteousness shall not be abolished.**

In this verse the Lord seems to be looking forward to that period when his justice and divine law will be in full force and effect among his people. It will be a time when the "isles" shall wait upon him and serve him. This has specific reference to America, which is the major "isle" that is separated from the land mass of Europe, Africa, and Asia. Eventually, the whole human race must learn to trust the Lord and lean upon him for good government and divine guidance.

In this verse the vision of eternity presses even further into the future. The Lord is contemplating the time when the earth will have fulfilled its assignment as the abode for the second estate of the human family. It will be ready for its death and resurrection into a celestialized planet of brilliant glory. This will come at a time when there has been a great rebellion against the Lord, and Satan will have been loosed for a little season (see D&C 88:111-15). There will be a great battle between the forces of good and evil. As in the premortal existence, Michael or Adam will lead the forces of good, and when the victory is won the two great capitals of the righteous, Old and New Jerusalem, will be caught up, and the earth will go into a cosmic convulsion of total elemental destruction. When it is over there will be a new heaven and a new earth, and the great cities of the Old and New Jerusalem will be brought back like jewels to embellish it. All of the wicked will have been consumed, while God's glory and righteousness shall prevail on the earth forever (see Ether 13:8-12; Revelation 21:1-5).

7. Hearken unto me, ye that know righteousness, the people in whose heart is my law; fear ye not the reproach of men, neither be ye afraid of their revilings.

In contemplation of these great events the Lord addresses all those who have tasted of the sweetness of righteousness and have learned to live under God's law. He pleads with them not to become discouraged or intimidated by the reproaches of the unconverted. They have ridiculed the sacred things of God from the beginning. The Lord calls upon his people to ignore their revilings. This is not easy to do. Revilings and persecution are bitter to bear. In fact, the Lord says that one of the qualities of the beatification of a human being who has matured in the Gospel is the ability to endure revilings and persecution (see 3 Nephi 12:10-12; Inspired Version, Matthew 5:12-13).

8. For the moth shall eat them up like a garment, and the worm shall eat them like wool: but my righteousness shall be for ever, and my salvation from generation to generation.

Those who revile against the righteous are not a permanent fixture in the earth. History will catch up with them, and they will fade away like an old garment which is eaten up by moths or like a piece of wool devoured by worms.

9. Awake, awake, put on strength, O arm of the LORD; awake, as in the ancient days, in the generations of old. Art thou not it that hath cut Rahab, and wounded the dragon?

The Lord now recites the plea that Israel will make in the latter days as her people ask the Lord to awake and show forth his power as he did in ancient times. Even in our own day we find many of the Saints wondering why the miraculous powers of God are not turned loose on the wicked warmongers and debauchers of mankind as in earlier dispensations. It is almost as though they are saying, "Art thou not [that great God] that hath cut Rahab [believed to be Egypt; see Psalms 87:4], and wounded the dragon [Satan; see Revelation 12:9]?"

10. Art thou not it which hath dried the sea, the waters of the great deep; that hath made the depths of the sea a way for the ransomed to pass over?

After all, he is the Almighty God who dried up the Red Sea and piled the waters of the great deep into high walls on either side so that the ransomed children of Israel could pass over safely and escape from the Egyptians.

11. Therefore the redeemed of the LORD shall return, and come with singing unto Zion; and everlasting joy shall be upon their head: they shall obtain gladness and joy; and sorrow and mourning shall flee away.

This is why the redeemed of the Lord can have confidence that Israel of the latter days will indeed return and come with singing unto Zion. It will be a time of great gladness and rejoicing so that the sorrow and mourning for the afflictions which they previously endured will depart out of their minds. Modern revelations indicate that this verse is referring to modern times (see D&C 45:71; 66:11).

12. I, even I, am he that comforteth you: who art thou, that thou shouldest be afraid of a man that shall die, and of the son of man which shall be made as grass;

The Lord assures the hosts of Israel of the latter days that he is the same God who did great things for Israel in the past. They can be assured that he will come to comfort and bless them as he has blessed and comforted his people in former times. The Lord challenges those among his people of the latter days who find themselves trembling because of the reviling and persecution of those who despise them. The Lord says, "Who art thou, that thou shouldest be afraid of a man that shall die, and of the son of man which shall be made as grass"!

13. And forgettest the LORD thy maker, that hath stretch-

Those of God's people who are afraid of man and fearful of controversy or becoming unpopular even for

ed forth the heavens, and laid the foundations of the earth; and hast feared continually every day because of the fury of the oppressor, as if he were ready to destroy? and where is the fury of the oppressor?

a good cause are those who seem to forget that the Lord their God is he who stretched forth the canopy of the heavens and laid the foundation of the earth. These timid Saints are they who have feared continually because of the fury of their oppressors. They behave as though they felt their oppressors might even succeed in their evil campaign to destroy God's work. But with the passing of time these arrogant and noxious antagonists will have faded into nothing, and the Lord will ask, "Where is the fury of the oppressor?" No doubt many will be ashamed in that day because of their lack of courage and failure to demonstrate their faith.

14. The captive exile hasteneth that he may be loosed, and that he should not die in the pit, nor that his bread should fail.

Isaiah saw in vision that many of the Israelites would be captive exiles in Gentile lands. He saw the struggle and haste which many would employ to get free from their captivity so that they could return to the land of their inheritance and not die of starvation in the concentration camps or PITS of their captors.

15. But I am the LORD thy God, that divided the sea, whose waves roared: The LORD of hosts is his name.

16. And I have put my words in thy mouth, and have covered thee in the shadow of mine hand, that I may plant the heavens, and lay the foundations of the earth, and say unto Zion, Thou art my people.

These two verses appear to be addressed to Isaiah himself. The Lord first reminds his prophet (Isaiah had done a little complaining in verse 4 of chapter 49) that it is the Lord God Jehovah who divided the Red Sea for Israel. And he is the same Supreme Being who has been revealing his words to Isaiah. The Lord reminds Isaiah how he has protected him during his ministry almost as though he had hidden Isaiah in the shadow of his hand. The Lord says he has done all this in order to "plant the heavens." This may very well have reference to planting the Gospel among those who must be gathered "from one end of heaven to the other" (Joseph Smith—Matthew 1:37). And the Lord also intends to prepare the foundations of the whole earth so that the

Israelites of Europe, Africa, and Asia, as well as the Lamanites of the Americas and the Polynesians from the islands of the sea, can hear the message of the Lord in the latter days and establish the New Jerusalem (see 3 Nephi 21:23). He will say to Zion and the Israelites everywhere, "Thou art my people!"

17. Awake, awake, stand up, O Jerusalem, which hast drunk at the hand of the LORD the cup of his fury; thou hast drunken the dregs of the cup of trembling, and wrung them out.

Now Isaiah addresses these gathering Israelites of the latter days. His first message is to those who will gather in great multitudes around the precincts of ancient Jerusalem. This great body of Israelites will require a cleansing, as will the Saints in Zion. Isaiah seemed to be looking at the 3½-year siege of Jerusalem by Gog and Magog during the battle of Armageddon. He saw the Jews reduced to virtual starvation. He saw the forces of the Gentile armies preparing for the big push that would finally overrun the ramparts of Jerusalem. Isaiah wants them to know that when this crisis occurs their travail will soon be over. They will have drunk the cup of fury and the dregs of terror and trembling sufficient to cleanse them.

18. There is none to guide her among all the sons whom she hath brought forth; neither is there any that taketh her by the hand of all the sons that she hath brought up.

Of course, Isaiah could see in the vision that the people would be almost destitute of any responsible leadership. There would be none whom they would trust or follow. Of all her sons who had been raised and trained for leadership in Jerusalem, there would not be one who would dare to rise up and take charge of affairs in this terrible crisis. This would suggest that they might even reject the leadership of the righteous Prince David (or the Branch) who will direct them in building the new temple (see Zechariah 6:12–13).

19. These two things are come unto thee; who shall be sorry for thee? desolation, and destruction, and the famine, and the sword: by whom shall I comfort thee?

Nevertheless, in this most critical and terrifying moment of threatening destruction, the Lord will send two of his sons who are Priesthood holders to "comfort" them. The King James translation has been mutilated so it does not tell the whole story. The Book of Mormon version reads as follows: "These two SONS are come unto thee, who shall be sorry for thee—thy desolation and destruction, and the famine and the sword—and by whom shall I comfort thee?" (2 Nephi 8:19; emphasis added.) The Lord answers his own question in the next verse.

20. Thy sons have fainted, they lie at the head of all the streets, as a wild bull in a net: they are full of the fury of the LORD, the rebuke of thy God.

Once more we turn to the Book of Mormon for the correct translation. It says, "Thy sons have fainted, SAVE THESE TWO; they lie at the head of all the streets; as a wild bull in a net, they are full of the fury of the Lord, the rebuke of thy God" (2 Nephi 8:20; emphasis added). Since these two sons or prophets are included among the sons of Jerusalem, it would suggest that they are of the Tribe of Judah or the Tribe of Levi. These two prophets will be endowed with Priesthood power over the elements. John the Revelator saw them and was told:

"And I will give power unto my two witnesses, and they shall prophesy....

"And if any man will hurt them, fire proceedeth out of their mouth, and devoureth their enemies: and if any man will hurt them, he must in this manner be killed.

"These have power to shut heaven, that it rain not in the days of their prophecy: and have power over waters to turn them to blood, and to smite the earth with all plagues, as often as they will" (Revelation 11:3, 5–6).

Zechariah also talks about these two prophets (see Zechariah 4:1–3, 11–14). So does the Prophet Joseph Smith (see D&C 77:15).

These two prophets will be so filled with righteous indignation as they see the suffering of the people under the lethal onslaught of the Gentile armies that they will be "as a wild bull in a net" and "full of the fury of the Lord, the rebuke of thy God."

21. Therefore hear now this, thou afflicted, and drunken, but not with wine:

22. Thus saith thy Lord the LORD, and thy God that pleadeth the cause of his people, Behold, I have taken out of thine hand the cup of trembling, even the dregs of the cup of my fury; thou shalt no more drink it again:

Isaiah trumpets a message to the inhabitants of Jerusalem in that future day and says, "Hear now..., thou afflicted, and drunken, but not with wine." They will be drunken with their own rebellion and wickedness. Isaiah says he has a message from the Lord: "Behold, I have taken out of thine hand the cup of trembling, even the dregs of the cup of my fury; thou shalt no more drink it again." This simply says that this is the last travail which the inhabitants of Jerusalem will have to endure.

23. But I will put it into the hand of them that afflict thee; which have said to thy soul, Bow down, that we may go over: and thou hast laid thy body as the ground, and as the street, to them that went over.

The Lord says he will take "the cup of trembling, even the dregs of the cup of my fury," and put it into the hands of those who will be afflicting the Jews and Levites in that distant day. They will be the Gentile armies of Gog and Magog who will threaten the very soul of the people with total conquest so that they can be forced to prostrate themselves on the ground before their cruel conquerors and allow themselves to be trodden under foot. The extent of this overwhelming invasion of the land is described in Ezekiel 38:14-18.

The Lord wanted Isaiah to record this comforting message for the people of Jerusalem in the latter days because he had already anticipated what he would do to Gog and Magog when they make their attack. John the Revelator said these two witnesses or prophets will hold back the mighty war machine of the Gentile armies for "a thousand two hundred and threescore days" (Revelation 11:3). They will do it by the power of the Priesthood, and by that power they will bring down curtains of fire on the enemy. They will have power to afflict them with thirst by withholding the rain. They will even have power over water to turn it into blood and afflict this terrible enemy with great plagues and diseases (see Revelation 11:5–6).

Then John tells us something amazing. He states that "when they shall have finished their testimony, the beast...shall make war against them, and shall overcome them, and kill them. And their dead bodies shall lie in the street of the great city...three days and an half, and [Gog and Magog] shall not suffer their dead bodies to be put in graves." (Revelation 11:7–9). But as John looks upon that prophetic scene he describes a marvelous event: "And after three days and an half the Spirit of life from God entered into them, and they stood upon their feet; and great fear fell upon them which saw them. And they heard a great voice from heaven saying unto them, Come up hither. And they ascended up to heaven in a cloud; and their enemies beheld them." (Revelation 11:11–12.)

However, that is about the last thing the hosts of Gog and Magog will have a chance to see. For them it is literally the end of the world. Ezekiel describes the consuming conflagration of fire that will suddenly sweep down and destroy all but one-sixth of the Gentile hosts (see Ezekiel 39:2). Joel saw that this one-sixth would flee to the "east sea" trying to escape (see Joel 2:20).

Meanwhile the Mount of Olives will be divided into two parts, and the people of Jerusalem will frantically flee through this great canyon into the valley lying beyond, called Jehoshaphat (see Joel 3:2, 12). Jesus will then appear among them and the astonished people will ask, "What are these wounds in thine hands and in thy feet?" Jesus will then reveal his identity, and the Jews will finally know their true Messiah and Redeemer (see D&C 45:48–53).

Isaiah, Chapter 52

INTRODUCTION:

This chapter is the Lord's call to his people in the latter days. It is addressed to the Jews who are to assemble in Old Jerusalem and to the Saints who will be assembling in Zion or America. Some of the most famous passages quoted from Isaiah are in this chapter.

1. **Awake, awake; put on thy strength, O Zion; put on thy beautiful garments, O Jerusalem, the holy city: for henceforth there shall no more come into thee the uncircumcised and the unclean.**

When Jesus quoted this verse to the Nephites he said, "Awake, awake AGAIN, and put on thy strength, O Zion" (3 Nephi 20:36; emphasis added). The first half of the verse is addressed to the Saints of the latter days who will be gathering to America. What does the Lord mean when he says to "put on thy strength"? Joseph Smith said: "He [the Lord] had reference to those whom God should call in the last days, who should hold the power of priesthood to bring again Zion, and the redemption of Israel; and to put on her strength is TO PUT ON THE AUTHORITY OF THE PRIESTHOOD, which she, Zion, has a right to by lineage; also to return to that power which she had lost." (D&C 113:8; emphasis added.)

The Lord also instructs Jerusalem to put on her "beautiful garments." This no doubt refers to the rebuilding of Jerusalem and the beautifying of all her suburbs. At the present time the fulfillment of this prediction has almost become an obsession with the Jews. Even though they have been in a state of virtual war or siege ever since Israel became a nation in 1948, the Jews have spent great sums of money and tremendous energy rebuilding Jerusalem. The buildings are constructed out of "Jerusalem stone," which is white limestone with a pink or beige hue. It is becoming one of the most beautiful cities in the world. However, in this verse the Lord is referring to a yet future time when it will have become sanctified following the great battle of Armageddon and after the sudden appearance of the Savior. It is in that day that it will indeed be a "holy city," and the Lord declares that "henceforth there shall no more come into thee the uncircumcised and the unclean." Those sublime circumstances are far from the situation today. There are many people now treading the streets of that famous city (including Jews, Arabs, and Christians) who live unclean lives and violate the commandments of God continually. These are the uncircumcised of heart whom the Lord has declared he will one day cleanse from the city of Jerusalem in order that it might be prepared for the coming Messiah, who will no longer permit the uncircumcised to pollute its sacred precincts.

2. Shake thyself from the dust; arise, and sit down, O Jerusalem: loose thyself from the bands of thy neck, O captive daughter of Zion.

Here the Lord commands the Jews who occupy Jerusalem to rise from the dust in which many of them have been groveling and to sit in the seats of honor and dignity which the Lord has prepared for them. In ancient times, when it was customary for people to sit on the ground, it was a gesture of honor and distinction for the host to invite a person to rise and sit on a chair or cushioned couch. This is the invitation which the Lord is extending to Jerusalem of the latter days.

In this verse the Lord commands the captive daughters of Zion to "loose thyself from the bands of thy neck." Joseph Smith stated that the significance of this phrase is as follows: "We are to understand that the scattered remnants are exhorted to return to the

Lord from whence they have fallen; which if they do, the promise of the Lord is that he will speak to them, or give them revelation.... The bands of her neck are the curses of God upon her, or the remants of Israel in their scattered condition among the Gentiles." (D&C 113:10.) In other words, the Lord is commanding the Israelites of the latter days to do what is necessary to get out from under the bondage of poverty, debt, and affliction to which they have subjected themselves by ignoring the commandments of God.

3. For thus saith the LORD, Ye have sold yourselves for nought; and ye shall be redeemed without money.

Apostasy is usually justified on the basis that the Saints who are strictly obedient are "missing something." Physical pleasures, dissipation, and indulgences among the Gentiles become objects of lust and envy in the hearts of Israelites who take to the low road of apostasy. This is what happened to the ancient Israelites as they abandoned the "straight way" of God's commandments and went reeling after the lifestyle of the pagans. The next thing they knew they were in bondage to Satan and their lustful appetites had cut them off from the Spirit of the Lord, which brings true happiness. They literally "sold [themselves] for nought." Nevertheless, the Lord has a plan to bring his wayward children back to their lands of inheritance and out of the bondage which they have imposed upon themselves. Those who have held the Israelites in captivity will release them, and "not for price or reward" (Isaiah 45:13).

4. For thus saith the Lord GOD, My people went down aforetime into Egypt to sojourn there; and the Assyrian oppressed them without cause.

The Lord reminds the Israelites that he rescued them from the Egyptians by the show of his power (and therefore not for price or reward), and that he wiped out the oppression of the Assyrians by slaying 185,000 of Sennacherib's armed men in a single night (see Isaiah 37:36). When he is ready, he can do it again.

5. Now therefore, what have I here, saith the LORD, that my people is taken away for nought? they that rule over them make them to howl, saith the LORD; and my name continually every day is blasphemed.

In contemplation of that future day (which Isaiah was shown in vision), the Lord says, "What have I here?" Actually, it was identical with what ancient Israel had done. The latter days would find millions of Israelites subject to all kinds of bondage and oppression. In every part of the earth they would be weighed down in ignorance, poverty, and exploitation to the point where they would howl out in anguish and even blaspheme the name of God.

6. Therefore my people shall know my name: therefore they shall know in that day that I am he that doth speak: behold, it is I.

The Lord says that he is determined that the wayward children of Israel who live in the latter days shall once more know his name. It will be a time when mankind, even Christians, will be worshipping a strange concept of God which is neither accurate nor acceptable to the Lord. But the Lord is determined to reveal his true self to mankind again. As he has stated in a modern revelation, "I give unto you these sayings that you may understand and know how to worship, AND KNOW WHAT YOU WORSHIP, that you may come unto the Father in my name, and in due time receive of his fulness." (D&C 93:19; emphasis added.)

With the restoration of the Gospel, the Lord revealed himself anew. In one revelation after another he declared: "I am he that doth speak: behold, it is I!"

7. How beautiful upon the mountains are the feet of him that bringeth good tidings, that publisheth peace; that bringeth good tidings

Now we come to those triumphant verses which were made famous by George Frederick Handel in his magnificent oratorio, *Messiah*. "How beautiful upon the mountains are the feet of him that bringeth good

of good, that publisheth salvation; that saith unto Zion, Thy God reigneth!

tidings." This is the literal fulfillment of Daniel's vision when he saw the little stone cut out of the mountain without human intervention, which rolled forth until it filled the whole earth (see Daniel 2:44–45). This is a description of the establishment of the kingdom of God in the latter days. The missionaries who descend from the mountains to bring the good tidings of great joy are indeed beautiful to those who accept their message and enter into the covenants of obedience which will rescue them from the oppression and spiritual captivity of the adversary which has ensnared them. The Lord said these messengers from the mountains would be beautiful to the lonely Israelites of the latter days because their message will bring peace to their souls; it will be joyful and exciting news concerning the kind of good life which leads to salvation; their message will trumpet the welcome news to all the pure in heart: Behold, "Thy God reigneth!"

A great Nephite prophet named Abinadi, who lived around 148 B.C., referred to these passages in Isaiah and said that the feet of all the prophets from earliest times have been "beautiful upon the mountains" (Mosiah 15:13–18). And the most beautiful of all is the Savior himself, who stands upon the mountains and sends his messengers forth to spread the good tidings of great joy.

Paul applies these passages of Isaiah to the preaching of the Gospel by the missionaries (Romans 10:13–15), and in modern times the Lord has described the preaching of the Gospel by the missionaries as the "glad tidings of great joy" (D&C 19:29; 31:3; 79:1).

8. Thy watchmen shall lift up the voice; with the voice together shall they sing: for they shall see eye to eye,

Jesus told the Nephites that even though the Gospel would first be revealed to the Gentiles in the latter days, the Gentiles would have to repent or they would

when the LORD shall bring again Zion.

not be able to enjoy the blessings reserved for the righteous Israelites. He is not going to allow the Gentiles (in their wickedness) to have power over those who accept the Gospel. If the Gentiles attempt to do so, they will ultimately be destroyed. On the other hand, if they accept the Gospel they will be numbered with Israel (see 3 Nephi 16: 9–15). In either event, the Savior said, there will come a time when the watchmen of Israel (the Priesthood leadership) will proclaim with joy and satisfaction that at last the people are united and well governed. They will see their important role in life and the teachings of the Gospel "eye to eye," and they will know for a certainty that the Lord is ready to establish "Zion" or the New Jerusalem in their midst (see Smith, *Teachings,* pp. 79–80).

Jesus also taught the Nephites that just as Zion will be established in America, so the Jews will eventually become well established in Jerusalem. Jesus said: "I have covenanted with them that I would gather them together in mine own due time, that I would give unto them again the land of their fathers for their inheritance, which is the land of Jerusalem. . . .

"And it shall come to pass that the time cometh, when the fulness of my gospel shall be preached unto them;

"And they shall believe in me, that I am Jesus Christ, the Son of God, and shall pray unto the Father in my name.

"Then shall their watchmen lift up their voice, and with the voice together shall they sing; for they shall see eye to eye." (3 Nephi 20:29–32.)

9. Break forth into joy, sing together, ye waste places of Jerusalem: for the LORD hath comforted his people,

So the Jews in Jerusalem as well as the gathering Israelites in Zion (or America) will "break forth into joy." Then it says they will begin to sing their anthems

he hath redeemed Jerusalem.

to the Lord. Isaiah does not set forth the full text of this song, but it will be found in the Doctrine and Covenants (see D&C 84:99–102).

10. **The LORD hath made bare his holy arm in the eyes of all the nations; and all the ends of the earth shall see the salvation of our God.**

All of this will come to pass after the "Lord hath made bare his holy arm [of revelation and power over the elements] in the eyes of all the nations." In that day there will be no atheists nor agnostics. Every human being will have seen with his or her own eyes. This will be a time when every knee shall bow and every tongue confess that Jesus is the Christ (see Isaiah 45:23; Romans 14:11; Philippians 2:10–11; D&C 88:104).

11. **Depart ye, depart ye, go ye out from thence, touch no unclean thing; go ye out of the midst of her; be ye clean, that bear the vessels of the LORD.**

The missionary work of the latter days was to occur in three phases. The first phase was to gather the converts to the central stakes of Zion so that the kingdom could be established in strength. The second phase (which is the one we are now in) is to send forth the missionaries to establish stakes all over the world. Then there is the third phase, when all of the Saints will be gathered "for the last time" (D&C 88:84). This will be just prior to the reaping down of the wicked. The Lord says this last gathering is so that "their souls may escape the wrath of God, the desolation of abomination which awaits the wicked" (D&C 88:85). Jeremiah says the Lord's servants will go forth from "the mount Ephraim" (Zion in America) and "shall cry: Arise ye, and let us go up to Zion unto the Lord our God" (Jeremiah 31:6).

This will be a time of great urgency. The Saints must be sought out wherever they are—in distant lands, in the high mountains, and out on the desert. Jeremiah quoted the Lord as saying: "Behold, I will send for many fishers, saith the Lord, and they shall fish them [the first and second phases of missionary work]; and

AFTER will I send for many hunters, and they shall hunt them from every mountain, and from every hill, and out of the holes of the rocks." (Jeremiah 16:16; emphasis added.) That is when they shall cry: "Arise ye, and let us go up to Zion" (Jeremiah 31:6). Otherwise, any who tarry might be destroyed when the abomination of desolation sweeps down upon the wicked.

In the light of what we have just read, notice that the Lord says this last gathering is to be a pilgrimage of righteous dedication. The Saints are to gather out of the world and leave behind them anything which is "unclean." There are many things in the Gentile world which tend to taint the lives of those who are called to be God's servants. The Lord reminds his Priesthood bearers that they are to be sacred vessels of Priesthood power. They are literally "vessels of the Lord." This gives special significance to the last line of this verse, which says, "BE YE CLEAN, THAT BEAR THE VESSELS OF THE LORD." This is a royal mandate to the Priesthood of God.

12. For ye shall not go out with haste, nor go by flight: for the LORD will go before you; and the God of Israel will be your rereward.

Notice that this great last gathering of the Saints is to be done in a very orderly manner. The first gathering of the Saints was accomplished at tremendous risk and with much suffering. People came in the most abject poverty. Many had neither time nor opportunity for adequate preparation. Some literally came with not much more than the clothes on their backs. Several thousand died of disease or exhaustion and were buried on the plains between the Missouri River and the Rocky Mountains. It was a time of desperate and urgent struggle. However, the great last gathering will be different. The Saints will have adequate time if they hearken promptly to the leaders of the Church when the call first goes out to them. They will be specifically told not to leave their homes "with haste." It is not an emergency situation where they must "go by flight." The Lord and his servants will prepare the way so that everything can be done carefully and in proper order. They will also be protected so that they cannot be attacked from behind after they have left the security of their homes.

13. Behold, my servant shall deal prudently, he shall be exalted and extolled, and be very high.

In a modern revelation the Lord quotes this verse from Isaiah, but emphasizes with even stronger language that he wants this gathering to be done a certain way. The Lord says, "Let not your flight be in haste, BUT LET ALL THINGS BE PREPARED BEFORE YOU; AND HE THAT GOETH, LET HIM NOT LOOK BACK LEST SUDDEN DESTRUCTION SHALL COME UPON HIM" (D&C 133:15; emphasis added). In other words, this will not be a time to dally or to be faint-hearted. It will be a time to rise up, get prepared, and move to Zion.

Some of the Saints have wanted to gather prematurely. In 1933 when an earthquake hit California a lot of Saints became frightened and wanted to return to Utah. This writer recalls the message from President Heber J. Grant, which said in effect: "Your mission is in California. If you return to Utah you will not be blessed."

14. As many were astonied at thee; his visage was so marred more than any man, and his form more than the sons of men:

Now the Lord talks about "my servant." This servant is to be a wise and prudent person who "shall be exalted and extolled" for the great work he will do. He will be very high in the estimation of both God and man. Nevertheless, his work will not be accomplished without much suffering and travail. People will be astonished when they see what happens to him, for his visage or appearance will be marred and so will his physical body. It will be worse for him than is generally the case with most other men.

All commentaries universally agree that this must be referring to the Savior. Certainly all of these things are precisely what happened to him when he filled his mission in his second estate and was afterwards resurrected and exalted by the Father. However when the Savior appeared among the Nephites following his resurrection, he gave a different interpretation to this passage. He said this was referring to his great servant who would be raised up to restore the Gospel and begin the gathering of Israel in the latter days. The quotation from Isaiah by the Savior appears in 3 Nephi 20:43–44; the commentary appears in the following chapter, 3 Nephi 21:9–11. Here is what Jesus said concerning "my servant" to which Isaiah had referred:

"For in that day, for my sake shall the Father work a work, which shall be a great and a marvelous work among them; and there shall be among them those who will not believe it, ALTHOUGH A MAN SHALL DECLARE IT UNTO THEM.

"But behold, the life of my servant shall be in my hand; therefore they shall not hurt him, ALTHOUGH HE SHALL BE MARRED BECAUSE OF THEM. Yet I will heal him, for I will show unto them that my wisdom is greater than the cunning of the devil.

"Therefore it shall come to pass that whosoever will not believe in my words, who am Jesus Christ, which the Father shall cause HIM [the latter-day prophet] to bring forth unto the Gentiles, . . . shall be cut off from among my people who are of the covenant." (3 Nephi 21:9–11; emphasis added.)

From all of this we conclude that even though Isaiah's words were literally fulfilled in the life of the Savior, the Savior himself applied these verses to "my servant" who would be raised up in the latter days.

Joseph Smith was marred when he was assassinated on June 27, 1844, but he was not permanently hurt, nor was the work of the kingdom hurt. The Lord said he would heal his servant, which the resurrection certainly accomplishes, and he said the work would go on to prove to Joseph Smith's arrogant assassins and to all the world that the Savior's wisdom is greater than the cunning of the devil.

15. So shall he sprinkle many nations; the kings shall shut their mouths at him: for that which had not been told them shall they see; and that which they had not heard shall they consider.

When Joseph Smith was translating this verse for the Book of Mormon, he left the word "sprinkle" in the text just as it appears in the King James translation. However, when he was doing the inspired revision of the Bible, he was given to understand that the original Hebrew text meant that the Spirit of the Lord would "sprinkle" itself upon the scattered children of Israel and cause them to gather together again. He therefore inserted the word "gather" (Inspired Version, Isaiah 52:15) instead of "sprinkle" so that the full implication of the term would be understood by the modern reader.

Jesus explained to the Nephites that the last portion of this verse refers to the restoration of the Gospel in the latter days. He said that when the Lord's work begins to unfold, kings will shut their mouths in wonderment, for something will begin to appear before their eyes which they had never anticipated, and things which they had never been taught will begin to attract their thoughtful consideration.

The Lord said that his work in the latter days would begin by first establishing in "this land [America] . . . a free people" (3 Nephi 21:4) so that the Gospel could be revealed among them. No wonder kings began to look with astonishment as they saw the rise of the first free people in modern times. They saw something happening which they never would have believed possible—especially those who had thought it was the DIVINE RIGHT OF KINGS to rule autocratically and often tyrannically over the children of men. The Savior revealed that the thing which would astonish them most profoundly would be the fact that this free people would develop until they became "lifted up by the power of God above all other nations" (1 Nephi 13:30). As it turned out, the kings of the east were astonished indeed, not the least of whom was King George III of England. Other kings have been astonished ever since.

Isaiah, Chapter 53

INTRODUCTION:

Now we come to the famous chapter of Isaiah which refers to the life and death of Jesus Christ. It also refers to his resurrection and the efficacy of his atoning sacrifice as the means of redeeming the human family.

It is unfortunate that we do not yet have all of the writings of the prophets in ancient times, but if we did we undoubtedly would find that every one of those prophets testified to the people concerning the life and mission of Jesus Christ (see Mosiah 13:33-35). With the restoration of the Gospel we have received some additional scriptures, and in them we read of the knowledge and understanding which Adam had concerning the mission of the Savior (Moses 5:6-8). We also learn that Enoch proclaimed the coming of the Savior among all nations in his day (Moses 6:47-57). This same scripture says that for 120 years Noah told the people about the Gospel of Jesus Christ (Moses 8:17, 19-20, 23-24). Furthermore, Abraham not only knew about the mission of Jesus Christ, but taught it to the Egyptians (James R. Clark, *Before Ye Go into Egypt*, 2 vols. [n.p., 1952], 1:2; 2:2). We also learn that Moses was told about the great work of the Savior even before he rescued the Israelites from Pharaoh (Moses 1:17, 21, 32-33; 4:1-3). The Book of Mormon scripture says that Isaiah not only knew about the mission of Christ but had personally seen the Savior in vision (2 Nephi 11:2).

One would have thought that after so many witnesses concerning the life, death, and resurrection of the Savior, the people of Israel would have been fully persuaded by this vast array of testimonies down through the centuries. But they were not. Therefore, Isaiah begins chapter 53 with the following questions for the people of his day:

1. Who hath believed our report? and to whom is the arm of the LORD revealed?

Isaiah knew that the people rejoiced when they contemplated the coming of the Messiah in glory and power just before the Millennium, because that was a "report" they loved to hear over and over again. But there was another report—the story of the Savior's earthly mission as a mortal being—which they counted a myth. After all, who could ever believe a wild tale about the people slaying their own beloved Messiah? It was preposterous. Yet Isaiah knew it would happen. And he knew that all of the prophets who had testified from generation to generation concerning the earthly mission and crucifixion of Jesus Christ had told the truth. So he shot out at the people, "Who hath believed OUR report?" Practically none of them had! And yet, to whom was the Savior going to come? He would be born among the descendants of those very people Isaiah was addressing.

It is almost miraculous that this one chapter of all the prophecies concerning the coming of the Savior should have been preserved in the Jewish scripture. All others which the scribes could identify as referring to Christ's earthly mission were stricken out. No doubt that is why it was so difficult for the Jews in the days of Jesus to identify him as their promised Messiah. They knew about the "coming in glory," the destroying of their enemies, and the elevating of the Jews to a place of respect and renown (e.g., see Zechariah 8:22-23). Down through the centuries, the learned men of the Jews had rejected the "myth" about the earthly mission of the Savior. Furthermore, they vigorously persecuted any who tried to "report" or tell them this "abominable myth" was really going to happen. In the case of Isaiah, the people spurned him. They beat him with sticks, pulled his beard, and spit in his face (Isaiah 50:5-6). With the prophet Zenoch, who preceded Isaiah, it was even worse. They stoned him to death for making this "report" (Alma 33:15-17). They also killed Zenos (Helaman 8:19). They appear to have destroyed all the prophetic writings concerning Christ which were written by Neum (1 Nephi 19:10), as well as the writings of Ezias (Helaman 8:20). When Lehi came a century after Isaiah, the people tried to kill him for telling them of the coming Savior (1 Nephi 1:18-20). To save his life the Lord told Lehi to flee from Jerusalem with his family (1 Nephi 2:1-2; Helaman 8:22).

2. For he shall grow up before him as a tender plant, and as a root out of a dry ground: he hath no form nor comeliness; and when we shall see him, there is no beauty that we should desire him.

We know that many of the prophets were shown the principal highlights of the Savior's life. They were shown to Enoch (Moses 7:47-59). They were shown to Nephi (1 Nephi 11:18-34). They were shown to father Lehi (1 Nephi 10:1-17). They were shown to Nephi's brother, Jacob (2 Nephi 2:3-4).

In this chapter, it is clear that they had been shown to Isaiah. He knew that the Savior would grow up before his Father like "a tender plant," carefully nourished and protected. Nevertheless, his environment would be of the most common kind. He would be raised as a carpenter's son in the rustic Galilean village of Nazareth, like a root growing out of dry, barren ground. In physical appearance, Isaiah said the Savior would be very much like other men. He wouldn't be a mighty Samson or a Saul who was "head and shoulders" above his fellows. Neither would he be so handsome and charismatic that people would run after him. The question therefore arises, "How will they know him?" Isaiah seems to be saying that the people must be truly alert when the Savior comes or they will miss him and never know that the Son of God has dwelt among them.

3. He is despised and rejected of men; a man of sorrows, and acquainted with grief: and we hid as it were our faces from him; he was despised, and we esteemed him not.

It is almost as though Isaiah were seeing the vision of the Savior's life unfolding before him as he says, "He is despised and rejected of men." Isaiah called him "a man of sorrows" as he beheld the people turning against him in spite of the Savior's hundreds of miracles, including the feeding of the multitudes; the healing of the lame, the blind, and the deaf; even the raising of the dead. There were also other kinds of sorrow. There were the manifest frailties of the Twelve when they all fled in his hour of greatest crisis (see Mark 14:50). Later, Peter, the chief of the apostles, denied him three times (see Mark 14:66–72). There was the sorrow of having a Judas in the midst of his disciples. There was the sorrow of looking down from the cross and seeing the suffering of his mother as she watched him in agony through her streaming tears. Truly, Jesus was "acquainted with grief."

In his vision of the Savior's life, Isaiah watched the people rejecting the Savior. He recognized the collective responsibility of all mankind for the universal tendency to rebel against the Lord and reject the teachings of the Father's Beloved Son. Isaiah says, "WE [as a human family] hid as it were our faces from him; he was despised, and WE esteemed him not."

4. Surely he hath borne our griefs, and carried our sorrows: yet we did esteem him stricken, smitten of God, and afflicted.

Now Isaiah seems to be looking at the crucifixion scene itself. He cannot help but exclaim, "Surely he hath borne OUR griefs, and carried OUR sorrows." Once again he is referring to all mankind. Nevertheless, at the time of the crucifixion those members of the human family who were closest to the scene (Romans and Jews) considered the crucifixion a just punishment. He was condemned and punished precisely as were the two thieves on either side of him. It was thought that he, like them, should die for his crimes. The offense which Jesus was believed to have committed was blasphemy. He had claimed to be the very Son of God. It was this for which he was pronounced guilty and therefore "stricken" and "afflicted."

5. But he was wounded for our transgressions, he was bruised for our iniquities: the chastisement of our peace was upon him; and with his stripes we are healed.

Isaiah saw in vision that Jesus was terribly wounded, bruised, and subjected to cruel "chastisement" in connection with his several trials and final crucifixion. He went approximately 33 hours without any sleep. At his preliminary hearing he was struck across the face by an officer of the Sanhedrin (see John 18:22). After that he was tormented by his guards. They blindfolded him and then abused him by striking him with their hands and fists, beating him with sticks, spurting spittle into his face. Then they would mock him and say, "Prophesy, who is it that smote thee?" (Luke 22:63–64; Matthew 26:67–68.) Pilate sought to satisfy the vengeful hostility of the Sanhedrin by severely punishing Jesus and proposing that this should be sufficient to justify his release. But they were not persuaded. The "punishment" meted out by Pilate's soldiers was brutal. Jesus was first stripped and scourged. A crown of cruel thorns was pressed down upon his skull. The soldiers beat him with sticks and mocked him. He was such a pitiful sight when the soldiers brought him forth that Pilate said to the Sanhedrin, "Behold the man!" It was like saying, "Aren't you satisfied?" Their only response was a united shout, "Crucify him!" (John 19:5–6.)

The final agony of torment for Jesus was when the Roman soldiers drove spikes through his hands and wrists, and then through his feet. They left him hanging on this tree of torture for six terrible hours.

Isaiah does not want any member of the human family who might read his words to miss the profound significance of all this suffering. It was a role the Son of God was required to fulfill if he were to become the great Mediator in the Father's plan to insure the resurrection of all his children and redeem all of those who would take upon themselves the name of Christ. Isaiah knew that in a very literal sense Jesus was "bruised" for the iniquities of mankind and wounded for their transgressions. For all of those who would repent and obey his commandments, by his "stripes" they would be healed.

6. All we like sheep have gone astray; we have turned every one to his own way; and the LORD hath laid on him the iniquity of us all.

Human beings are in the earth to learn the difference between good and evil. They are also here to be tested. Each person receives a glory in the next world commensurate with the quality and promptness of obedience in this life. But no one goes through this learning process or probationary estate without a lot of detours and behavioral aberrations. It is the very nature of life to make mistakes, and the Father knew this from the beginning. That is why he provided an atonement so that as fast as we overcame our weaknesses and turned to the Lord, the mistakes of the past could be blotted out. This is what Isaiah meant when he said that all of us, like sheep, have wandered off from time to time as we stubbornly followed our own inclinations instead of the way of the Lord. But when we turn back, a loving Savior welcomes us into his fold. Through his suffering and death a way is provided so that there can be "laid on him the iniquity of us all" as rapidly as we repent.

To better appreciate the manner in which the suffering of the Savior makes it possible for him to fulfill this role as our Mediator and Redeemer, see the appendix entry in W. Cleon Skousen, *The First 2,000 Years*, under the title "Why Was the Atonement Necessary?"

7. He was oppressed, and he was afflicted, yet he opened not his mouth: he is brought as a lamb to the slaughter, and as a sheep before her shearers is dumb, so he openeth not his mouth.

To fulfill his mediator role, Jesus allowed himself to be "oppressed" and "afflicted." In the Garden of Gethsemane he would not allow Peter to use his sword to prevent the Savior's arrest (see John 18:10–11). At his trial he would not make a defense before his accusers in the Sanhedrin (Matthew 27:12). Neither would he plead his cause when his accusers brought him before Herod (Luke 23:8–9) and Pilate (John 19:9–10). Therefore, Isaiah could say that in a very literal sense Jesus was led like a helpless lamb to the slaughter. He so completely surrendered to whatever his persecutors wished to do to him that he was like "a sheep before her shearers." Though they abused him and scourged him (Mark 15:15–20), "he openeth not his mouth."

8. He was taken from prison and from judgment: and who shall declare his generation? for he was cut off out of the land of the living: for the transgression of my people was he stricken.

Isaiah predicted that Jesus would not be lynched or killed by a mob, but that he would be taken from "prison" following a formal conviction and judgment. He would be cut down in the prime of his life and taken from "the land of the living." Therefore, "who shall declare his generation?" Is this not a life only partially fulfilled? Isaiah answered his own question by saying that all this was necessary. It was part of the plan. Quoting the Father, Isaiah wrote, "For the transgression of my people was he stricken." The Septuagint version and the older manuscripts say, "stricken TO DEATH" (Clarke, *Commentary*, 4:205; emphasis added).

This verse makes it obvious that Isaiah was talking about the death of a specific person and not the fall of the people of Israel, as the Jewish scholars so often insisted. Origen and other early Christians used the 53rd chapter of Isaiah to convince the Jews that Jesus literally fulfilled all of the prophecies contained in this chapter. He pointed out that it referred to the Messiah and not the rise and fall of the PEOPLE of ISRAEL (Clark, *Commentary*, 4:205).

9. And he made his grave with the wicked, and with the rich in his death; because he had done no violence, neither was any deceit in his mouth.

This verse is not entirely coherent in its present form. Perhaps a clearer translation was given by Bishop Robert Lowth when he wrote that this phrase should read, "And his grave was APPOINTED with the wicked; BUT with the rich man was his TOMB" (emphasis added). Dr. Adam Clarke analyzed the original Hebrew to show why Bishop Lowth was correct (see Clarke, *Commentary*, 4:205–6). Because Jesus was crucified as a malefactor between two thieves, his body undoubtedly would have been disposed of with those of the two thieves in a common grave. This was the customary or "appointed" way the authorities usually did it. However, a rich man—Joseph of Arimathaea—secured permission from Pilate to place the body of Jesus in his own new tomb, so "with the rich man was his tomb." Why would the rich man feel compelled to do this? Isaiah said it was because he would know that the Savior had done no "violence." (The Book of Mormon says "no EVIL" in Mosiah 14:9; emphasis added.) He also knew that there had been no "deceit" in the Savior's declarations concerning himself. He had spoken the truth. As an honest member of the Sanhedrin who had not voted to condemn Jesus, Joseph of Arimathaea felt that his colleagues had done a great injustice to this innocent man. In fact, the scripture says that this rich man of Arimathaea had actually become a disciple of Jesus (see Matthew 27:57).

10. Yet it pleased the LORD to bruise him; he hath put him to grief: when thou shalt make his soul an offering for sin, he shall see his seed, he shall prolong his days, and the pleasure of the LORD shall prosper in his hand.

Here Isaiah says that it "pleased" the Lord (meaning the Lord God, or the Father) to "bruise him" and "put him to grief." We have enough modern scripture to help us understand what this means. Since the atoning sacrifice of the Savior was ABSOLUTELY ESSENTIAL to the plan of salvation, it pleased the Father that Jesus would volunteer for the assignment. Jesus did this, knowing beforehand that it would entail great suffering and ultimately his death. The scripture is plain that this was the "will" of the Father (Moses 4:2; Matthew 26:42). Had there been no Atonement, there could have been no redemption. The entire human family would have been consigned to the same miserable existence in "outer darkness" as that which Satan and his angels will inherit (2 Nephi 9:8–9).

This verse says that after Jesus has made himself an "offering for sin," he shall "see his seed." This refers to those who accept the Gospel and become the "sons and daughters" of Christ (D&C 25:1; 39:4; 50:41). So the Savior will not be "cut off" from the living after all. Nor will he lose any blessings of the living. Isaiah says the Father will "prolong his days" (into all eternity!), and it will be the pleasure of the Father to "prosper" and bless him in everything which his Beloved Son has set his hand to accomplish.

11. He shall see of the travail of his soul, and shall be satisfied: by his knowledge shall my righteous servant justify many; for he shall bear their iniquities.

Isaiah says the Father will see the travail of the Savior's "soul" and know that it will be sufficiently intense to satisfy the requirements for an atonement in behalf of all mankind. Jesus understood what had to be done to fulfill this role. Isaiah quotes the Father as saying that his "righteous servant" had "knowledge" of how to "justify many," and thereby "bear their iniquities." This may seem like a complex and roundabout way to solve the problem, but it was terribly real. In fact, he was the only qualified person and this was the only available way to overcome the inflexible demands of absolute justice. This is why the scripture speaks of the "demands of justice" being overcome by the principle of "mercy" which was generated by the suffering of the Savior (see Alma 34:15–16).

We should add, of course, that mercy cannot "rob justice" (Alma 42:25). Mercy can be pressed only to its legitimate limits. Therefore, although Jesus can stretch the Atonement to cover ALL mankind for the purpose of getting them resurrected (see John 5:28–29), the Atonement will not allow a person to be forgiven of his sins and be exalted unless that person will do all he can to repent and obey the commandments of God. That is why Nephi says we can be saved by the free gift of grace through the Savior's atoning sacrifice, but ONLY "AFTER ALL WE CAN DO" (2 Nephi 25:23).

12. Therefore will I divide him a portion with the great, and he shall divide the spoil with the strong; because he hath poured out his soul unto death: and he was numbered with the transgressors; and he bare the sin of many, and made intercession for the transgressors.

The Father continues by saying that he will reward his "righteous servant" by giving him "a portion with the great" and a division of "the spoil" (the Father's legacy) with those who prove themselves "strong" and are worthy to receive so great a blessing. The Father says he will do this because his "righteous servant" has "poured out his soul unto death" in order to fulfill the role which the Father had assigned to him. As we read this verse it is difficult to explain how the Jewish scholars could have decided that this chapter is talking about the people of Israel and not a specific person, their Messiah.

This chapter closes with the assurance that the Savior will be glorified and rewarded in spite of the fact that he was at one time numbered among the "transgressors." He valiantly endured his awful agony that he might bear the sins "of many" and be the means of making "intercession for the transgressors." In a modern revelation the Savior describes how this is done. Jesus goes before the Father and says:

"Father, behold the sufferings and death of him who did no sin, in whom thou wast well pleased; behold the blood of thy Son which was shed, the blood of him whom thou gavest that thyself might be glorified;

"Wherefore, Father, SPARE THESE MY BRETHREN THAT BELIEVE ON MY NAME, that they may come unto me and have everlasting life." (D&C 45:4-5; emphasis added.)

CONCLUSION:

Thus we conclude the famous Messianic chapter of Isaiah. It was designed to help the Jews recognize their Savior when he came the first time; but only a few of them perceived it. Nevertheless, we should not forget the mighty work which those few Jews (who were converted) did indeed achieve. In the beginning the Jews constituted the ENTIRE Christian Church. The first Quorum of Twelve Apostles were all Jews. It was these Jewish disciples who took the Gospel to the Gentiles, and "to all the world." They were the first to be beaten, imprisoned, persecuted, and pilloried. They were the first to lay the foundation for the kingdom of God in the meridian of time.

Isaiah, Chapter 54

INTRODUCTION:

It will be recalled that in chapter 52 Isaiah was writing at full stride as he described the glorious redemption of Israel in the latter days. Then he came to chapter 53 and suddenly interrupted himself to remind the reader that this same Jesus who would appear in such glory and power in the latter days is the same person as the one who would come in the meridian of time. Isaiah said he would be rejected by his own people because they would not believe the "report" of the prophets. Having completed this task in chapter 53, Isaiah now commences chapter 54 by returning to the earlier theme concerning the restoration of Israel in the latter days. It is interesting that this chapter was quoted in its entirety by the Savior when he appeared among the Nephites following his resurrection (see 3 Nephi, chapter 22). However, before quoting it the Savior outlined what would precede it (3 Nephi, chapter 21). There would be a free nation raised up in America where the Gospel would be restored among the Gentiles. The Lord's servant who restored the Gospel would be "marred because of them," but the Lord would heal him (3 Nephi 21:10; see also Isaiah 52:14). Eventually there would be a cleansing of the land, leaving many of the Gentile cities in America "desolate." Then the Lord would prepare to destroy the wicked in other parts of the earth. However, before doing so, he would gather out all the members of the Church and as many Gentiles as would repent. This is the great final gathering spoken of by Jesus when he said:

"Yea, the work shall commence among ALL THE DISPERSED OF MY PEOPLE, with the Father, to prepare the way whereby they may come unto me....

"Yea, and then shall the work commence, with the Father among all nations in preparing the way whereby his people may be gathered home to the land of their inheritance.

"And they shall GO OUT FROM ALL NATIONS; and they shall not go out in haste, nor go by flight, for I will go before them, saith the Father, and I will be their rearward." (3 Nephi 21:27-29; emphasis added.)

Jesus then introduces Isaiah chapter 54 by saying, "AND THEN SHALL THAT WHICH IS WRITTEN COME TO PASS" (3 Nephi 22:1; emphasis added).

1. Sing, O barren, thou that didst not bear; break forth into singing, and cry aloud, thou that didst not travail with child: for more are the children of the desolate than the children of the married wife, saith the LORD.

Isaiah knew that there would be great cause for rejoicing among the Saints of the latter days when they saw these millions of Israelites gathering together and becoming the dominant influence in the land. In our own day, the members of the Church find themselves lamenting that they are so few compared to the several billion people presently inhabiting the planet earth. Nevertheless, the time will come when the Gentile nations will have spent their strength, and their empty and desolated lands will vividly demonstrate the fallacy of war and the fruits of unrighteous dominion which they have exercised. Not only will the members of the Church have been gathered out of their midst to ZION, but it will be in that day that the vast hosts of the Ten Tribes will suddenly appear to inhabit the desolate cities of America. All these will add millions to the membership of the Church. Because the Ten Tribes have been lost from the knowledge of both Jews and Christians for around 2,500 years, it has been assumed that they are like an abandoned wife which has remained "desolate" and without children. However, Isaiah said that when the Ten Tribes put in their appearance in the latter days the members of the Church (the married wife) will look upon these multitudes and say, "More are the children of the desolate [abandoned wife] than the children of the married wife."

2. Enlarge the place of thy tent, and let them stretch forth the curtains of thine habitations: spare not, lengthen thy cords, and strengthen thy stakes;

In anticipation of this great event, Isaiah sends out a clarion call to the Saints of the latter days to "enlarge the place of thy tent." This means the kingdom of God in Zion or America. The millions of newcomers will need room in which to dwell. Now notice how the Lord wants this to be achieved. The Church is to "stretch forth the curtains of thine habitations." The Church must be willing to "lengthen" the cords of administration to the various stakes of the Church and "strengthen" them by letting them have an increasing amount of authority and responsibility. Even today, one can observe this gradually occurring. The stakes are doing many things which were done by the General Authorities just a few years ago.

The concept of Zion being a tent which must be "enlarged" is where the "stakes" of the Church get their name. It is expected that someday Zion with its vast encirclement of "stakes" will extend up and down the entire Western Hemisphere. As Joseph Smith said, *"The whole of America is Zion itself from north to south"* (Smith, *Teachings,* p. 362; italics in original). The "tent" of the Lord is like the sacred tabernacle of Moses, with strong cords attached to stakes so as to hold it firmly upright. It is also interesting that territorial organizations called "stakes" seem to be particularly adapted to the expansion of the Church in the latter days. The early Christian churches set up by the apostles did not seem to extend much beyond the development of wards operating under their respective bishoprics. Isaiah knew that the vast network of Church units in the latter days would involve a more complex arrangement. Isaiah 33:20 is the first reference to "stakes" in the scriptures.

3. For thou shalt break forth on the right hand and on the left; and thy seed shall inherit the Gentiles, and make the desolate cities to be inhabited.

In the day of their final gathering, the Saints will break forth on the right hand and on the left. The Israelites will not only occupy the mountains, valleys, desert, and plains, but they will invade the "desolate" and abandoned cities of the Gentiles. This would suggest that a certain amount of domestic warfare will have cleansed the land of Gentile wickedness. After each of the world wars ended, it was amazing how the people were able to clean up the rubble and erect magnificent modern cities in a relatively short time. The gathering Saints will do the same in America. They will take over the desolate cities of the Gentiles and cause them to be inhabited.

4. Fear not; for thou shalt not be ashamed: neither be thou confounded; for thou shalt not be put to shame: for thou shalt forget the shame of thy youth, and shalt not remember the reproach of thy widowhood any more.

For the next several verses the Lord addresses himself to the Israelites (the lost Ten Tribes) who were cut off. They were assumed by both Christians and Jews to have wandered away and lost their identity like an abandoned wife with no children. In this verse the Lord is assuring this segment of his people that they will not be ashamed in the day of their gathering and sanctification. It will be so wonderful that they will practically forget the hundreds of years when they were cut off as a people and consigned to the status of a widow without a husband or children.

5. For thy Maker is thine husband; the LORD of hosts is his name; and thy Redeemer the Holy One of Israel; The God of the whole earth shall he be called.

The Lord identifies himself as the husband of this forlorn widow who has been desolate and seemingly left alone for so many years. The Lord assures this body of Israelites that they will be so blessed they will soon forget "the shame of thy youth, and shalt not remember the reproach of thy widowhood any more."

6. For the LORD hath called thee as a woman forsaken and grieved in spirit, and a wife of youth, when thou wast refused, saith thy God.

In the latter days the Lord will call on these lost Israelites to return to him. Even though they felt forsaken and were grieving in their hearts because they were "refused," yet will the Lord call for the bride of his youth to return to him.

7. For a small moment have I forsaken thee; but with great mercies will I gather thee.

In terms of heavenly time, it was but a small moment that the Lord turned away from this body of "lost" Israelites. In the latter days he will make it up to them. With great mercies and an abundance of blessings, he will gather them together.

8. In a little wrath I hid my face from thee for a moment; but with everlasting kindness will I have mercy on thee, saith the LORD thy Redeemer.

The Lord confesses that the ancestors of these Israelites were so wicked that he felt compelled to hide his face from them. Nevertheless, it was but a small moment, and now he will shower everlasting kindness and mercy on their descendants.

9. For this is as the waters of Noah unto me: for as I have sworn that the waters of Noah should no more go over the earth; so have I sworn that I would not be wroth with thee, nor rebuke thee.

The Lord states that this promise which he is making to the returning tribes of Israel is as sacred as the covenant which he made with Noah. It will be recalled that after the ark had landed, following the great deluge, the Lord said, "And I will establish my covenant with you; neither shall all flesh be cut off any more by the waters of a flood; neither shall there any more be a flood to destroy the earth" (Genesis 9:11). However, it will be noted that when the Lord quoted this covenant to Isaiah he used somewhat different words, that "the waters of Noah SHOULD NO MORE GO OVER THE EARTH." Scientists have found it difficult to believe that the Great Flood literally covered the whole planet, but the Lord here declares that they did indeed "go over the earth." Of course, as we shall see in the next verse, as well as in the Doctrine and Covenants 133:22-24, the surface of the earth was apparently much more uniform than it is today. Here is the way Moses recorded the literal covering of the earth by the Great Flood in Genesis:

"And the waters prevailed exceedingly upon the earth; and all the high hills, that were under the whole heaven, were covered.

"Fifteen cubits upward did the waters prevail; and the mountains were covered.

"And all flesh died that moved upon the earth, both of fowl, and of cattle, and of beast, and of every creeping thing that creepeth upon the earth, and every man:

"All in whose nostrils was the breath of life, of all that was in the dry land, died." (Genesis 7:19-22.)

Moses said the Great Flood commenced in the second month (Genesis 7:11), and after the hills and mountains were covered with water they were not seen again until the tenth month (Genesis 8:5). There are a number of other factors confirming that the flood-waters of Noah did indeed "go over the earth."

First, the Lord declared that "all [creatures] in whose nostrils was the breath of life, of all that was in the dry land, died" (Genesis 7:22). No local flood would have fulfilled this description of what the Lord says actually happened.

Second, we know from modern scriptures that the ark was launched from what is now called the Western Hemisphere and landed on a high peak of the Eastern Hemisphere. This would require a worldwide flood.

Third, the Lord has verified that the Flood included the part of the earth which is now America. He said to Ether, "After the waters had receded from off the face of THIS LAND it became a choice land above all other lands, a chosen land of the Lord" (Ether 13:2; emphasis added). Notice also that after the Flood it was necessary for the Jaredites to replenish America with domestic animal life by bringing in the barges "their flocks and herds, and whatsoever beast or animal or fowl that they should carry with them" (Ether 6:4).

Fourth, the Great Flood is spoken of as the "baptism" of the earth. As Brigham Young declared, "The earth . . . has been baptized with water, and will, in the future, be baptized with fire and the Holy Ghost, to be prepared to go back into the celestial presence of God" (*Discourses of Brigham Young*, sel. John A. Widtsoe [Salt Lake City: Deseret Book Company, 1954], p. 393). The symbolism of baptism for the earth would require a universal flood. John A. Widtsoe declared: "Latter-day Saints . . . look upon the flood as a baptism of the earth, symbolizing a cleansing of the impurities of the past, and the beginning of a new life. This has been repeatedly taught by the leaders of the Church. The deluge was an immersion of the earth in water." *Evidences and Reconciliations*, 3 vols. in 1 [Salt Lake City: Bookcraft, 1960], p. 127.)

10. For the mountains shall depart, and the hills be removed; but my kindness shall not depart from thee, neither shall the covenant

One of the remarkable phenomena which is to occur just prior to the Millennium is the Lord's prediction that "every valley shall be exalted, and every mountain and hill shall be made low" (Isaiah 40:4; see

of my peace be removed, saith the LORD that hath mercy on thee.

also D&C 49:23). In other words, the Lord is going to level out the surface of the earth before he returns to reign over it during the final 1,000 years of the second estate. In this present verse the Lord is assuring Israel that the certainty of this coming event is already established as a prophetic reality, and it is with equal certainty that he is promising the Israelites that, once he has begun gathering them together in the latter days, his kindness and blessings of peace will never depart from Israel again.

11. O thou afflicted, tossed with tempest, and not comforted, behold, I will lay thy stones with fair colours, and lay thy foundations with sapphires.

12. And I will make thy windows of agates, and thy gates of carbuncles, and all thy borders of pleasant stones.

In contemplation of the restoration of the Old Jerusalem and the building up of the New Jerusalem, the Lord says that his people who were afflicted and tossed so violently in the storm of life will find their cities laid with the finest stones of beautiful colors. Their gates will be ornamented with precious jewels.

13. And all thy children shall be taught of the LORD; and great shall be the peace of thy children.

What a glorious day it will be when Zion and her children "shall be taught of the Lord." It will indeed be a time of peace for all the Israelites and their young ones. In a modern revelation the Lord speaks of this same period that Isaiah is talking about: "And the earth shall be given unto them for an inheritance; and they shall multiply and wax strong, and their children shall grow up without sin unto salvation. FOR THE LORD SHALL BE IN THEIR MIDST, and his glory shall be upon them, and he will be their king and their lawgiver." (D&C 45:58–59; emphasis added.) As Isaiah says, "And all thy children shall be taught of the Lord."

14. In righteousness shalt thou be established: thou shalt be far from oppression; for thou shalt not fear: and from terror; for it shall not come near thee.

The fundamental key to survival in the day of God's judgment will be RIGHTEOUSNESS. It means keeping God's commandments, diligently serving one another, being generous to the poor, remaining virtuous and clean. These are they who will remain "established" in the land. God delights to intervene on behalf of his worthy Saints, therefore those who become established in righteousness will find that any who seek to oppress and destroy will be kept far away. This means that the people who are righteous will be protected from the terrifying destruction which will descend upon the wicked, and consequently they need not fear (see D&C 38:30).

Referring to these same circumstances, a modern revelation states, "For they that are wise and have received the truth, and have taken the Holy Spirit for their guide, and have not been deceived—verily I say unto you, THEY SHALL NOT BE HEWN DOWN AND CAST INTO THE FIRE, BUT SHALL ABIDE THE DAY" (D&C 45:57; emphasis added).

15. Behold, they shall surely gather together, but not by me: whosoever shall gather together against thee shall fall for thy sake.

Isaiah saw that the survival of the righteous will not be due to the fact that they have no enemies. The Book of Mormon version of this passage makes the point that "they shall surely gather together AGAINST THEE, [but] not by me; whosoever shall gather together against thee shall fall for thy sake" (3 Nephi 22:15; emphasis added).

16. Behold, I have created the smith that bloweth the coals in the fire, and that bringeth forth an instrument for his work; and I

In the day of their great peril, the Lord wants the righteous to remember that mankind is under the dominion of the Creator. He has made the smith who forges weapons and also those who prepare themselves

have created the waster to destroy.

to go forth and lay waste. He can protect his people against all such enemies of the righteous.

17. **No weapon that is formed against thee shall prosper; and every tongue that shall rise against thee in judgment thou shalt condemn. This is the heritage of the servants of the LORD, and their righteousness is of me, saith the LORD.**

Isaiah closes with the Lord's promise that Israel will be protected by the Lord and "no weapon that is formed against thee shall prosper." Those who revile the Lord's servants in the latter days will be "confounded" (D&C 71:10). And so will their armies. Apparently the enemy hosts will be so overwhelming and threatening that it will be as though they had dug a great pit into which the righteous could be buried alive. But the prophet Nephi saw in vision what would happen and wrote, "And every nation which shall war against thee, O house of Israel, shall be turned one against another, and they shall fall into the pit which they digged to ensnare the people of the Lord" (1 Nephi 22:14).

When that hour of peril comes, great will be the display of God's power on behalf of the righteous. And this passage will be a tremendous comfort to the people. In their most perilous moment they will know that eventually these warring nations will commence fighting among themselves and fill the pit with their own bodies.

Isaiah, Chapter 55

INTRODUCTION:

In the last chapter the Lord declared that Zion and her stakes would be established and the Israelites would be gathered back to the lands of their inheritance. The Lord promised that they would never again be confounded or driven from their homelands. He assured them that, though they had been cut off in the day of their apostasy, they would finally be taken back into full fellowship with the Lord.

Now we come to chapter 55 and the Lord's special message to the people of the earth after the Gospel is restored.

1. Ho, every one that thirsteth, come ye to the waters, and he that hath no money; come ye, buy, and eat; yea, come, buy wine and milk without money and without price.

In the writings of the prophets the Gospel is often likened unto water or bread. Jesus did the same thing during his ministry. When he went to Samaria he invited the woman at the well of Jacob to drink of the "living water" and said: "Whosoever drinketh of this water [from the well] shall thirst again: but whosoever drinketh of the water that I shall give him shall never thirst; but the water that I shall give him shall be in him a well of water springing up into everlasting life." (John 4:13–14.)

Through the words of Isaiah the Lord is saying the same thing to the human family in the latter days. He knew they would run to and fro upon the earth seeking peace and happiness but would not find it. He therefore extends an invitation to all those who thirst for genuine joy, peace, and happiness to come and drink at the fountain of eternal life. He says it is free. It will cost no money. It is like milk and wine that can be had without price. When Jesus sent out his Twelve Apostles he said, "Freely ye have received, freely give" (Matthew 10:8). Micah said it was a great iniquity when "the priests...teach for hire, and the prophets...divine for money" (Micah 3:11–12). Peter instructed the elders of the Church in his day to "feed the flock of God...not for filthy lucre, but of a ready mind" (1 Peter 5:2). Paul wrote to the Saints in Corinth, saying: "What is my reward then? Verily that, when I preach the gospel, I may make the gospel of Christ without charge, that I abuse not my power in the gospel" (1 Corinthians 9:18).

It is interesting that the word "Ho" in Isaiah is written more explicitly in the Book of Mormon as "COME, MY BRETHREN" (2 Nephi 9:50; emphasis added). Jesus is indeed our brother, having been the "Firstborn" of all the Father's family to which we belong (D&C 93:21–23).

2. Wherefore do ye spend money for that which is not bread? and your labour for that which satisfieth not? hearken diligently unto me, and eat ye that which is good, and let your soul delight itself in fatness.

The Book of Mormon gives this verse in its more complete form: "Wherefore, do NOT spend money for that which is of NO WORTH, nor your labor for that which cannot satisfy. Hearken diligently unto me, and REMEMBER THE WORDS WHICH I HAVE SPOKEN; AND COME UNTO THE HOLY ONE OF ISRAEL, AND FEAST UPON THAT WHICH PERISHETH NOT, NEITHER CAN BE CORRUPTED, AND LET YOUR SOUL DELIGHT IN FATNESS." (2 Nephi 9:51; emphasis added.)

Every year billions of dollars are expended by the human family for things which are of "no worth." Many find that not only have these expenditures gone for things which are soon forgotten, but in many cases they themselves have been corrupted by the things their money bought. The most magnificent aspect of the Gospel of Jesus Christ is the fact that it is of eternal value. It never ceases to be of continuing significance in the lives of those who seek after it. It provides the deepest sense of satisfaction and a knowledge of being one with the universe and its Creator.

3. Incline your ear, and come unto me: hear, and your soul shall live; and I will make an everlasting covenant with you, even the sure mercies of David.

The greatest obstacle to the spreading of the Gospel of peace and happiness is indifference or apathy. The Lord pleads with the people to "incline" their ears. All they have to do is listen with interest and prayerful intent, and the Spirit will confirm to them that this is the truth and the means by which the soul can acquire eternal life. It is amazing how few people are intellectually curious or spiritually sensitive to the great Gospel message. Sometimes the Lord has to put whole nations through a shock treatment before they will humble themselves and listen.

The Lord says he wants to make an "everlasting covenant" with any who will listen and follow his instructions. He identifies this covenant with the "mercies of David." When David asked if he could build a temple to the Lord, he was told, through the prophet Nathan, that he was to let this honor fall upon his son, Solomon. Nevertheless, the Lord assured David that "my mercy shall not depart away from him [Solomon], as I took it from Saul, whom I put away before thee. And thine house and thy kingdom shall be established for ever before thee: thy throne shall be established for ever." (2 Samuel 7:15-16.) Of course, it was the fact that the Savior would be a descendant of David that made this promise truly meaningful. Through the lineage of David the Savior would be born, and he would reign over mankind forever. The everlasting covenant of the latter days is when the Savior will come and take over the government of the earth in a very literal sense. Daniel saw these events in vision (see Daniel 7:13–14). When these events transpire, they will completely fulfill God's merciful (or compassionate) promise to David that his throne (through Christ) would rule over the earth forever.

4. Behold, I have given him for a witness to the people, a leader and commander to the people.

The Lord now quotes his own Father, who said, "I have given him [David's descendant, the Savior] for a witness to the people." He will be their great leader and he will be the commander of the people.

5. Behold, thou shalt call a nation that thou knowest not, and nations that knew not thee shall run unto thee because of the LORD thy God, and for the Holy One of Israel; for he hath glorified thee.

To lay the foundation for the Savior's reign on earth, there had to be a great nation raised up which the people of Isaiah's day had never heard of. Isaiah knew that it would be the principal means by which the Israelites would be gathered and protected in the latter days. When Jesus visited the Nephites he spoke of this nation which he intended to raise up. It would be the first free nation in modern times, and it would be established so that the Gospel could be safely restored there and "the covenant of the Father . . . fulfilled which he hath covenanted with his people, O house of Israel" (3 Nephi 21:4).

The Lord said that in due time he would glorify Israel and her people to the point that nations which had never known the greatness or destiny of Israel before would seek after her and want to be identified with her.

6. Seek ye the LORD while he may be found, call ye upon him while he is near:

Many people do not realize that the Lord is working on a timetable with a predetermined deadline. There is an allotted time during which mankind can repent and call upon the Lord and receive of his blessings. But that opportunity does not last forever. If they wait until the very end to repent it will be too late and they will be sealed up unto judgment. In that hour of desperate anguish they will find they have waited too long. The Lord says: "And this shall be your lamentation in the day of visitation, and of judgment, and of indignation: The harvest is past, the summer is ended, and my soul is not saved!" (D&C 56:16.)

Amulek, who was Alma's convert and missionary companion, cried out to the wicked Zoramites: "This life is the time for men to prepare to meet God....

"Do not procrastinate the day of your repentance ...; if we do not improve our time while in this life, then cometh the night of darkness wherein there can be no labor performed.

"Ye cannot say, when ye are brought to that awful crisis, that I will repent, that I will return to my God....

"For behold, if ye have procrastinated the day of your repentance even until death, behold, ye have become subjected to the spirit of the devil, and he doth seal you his." (Alma 34:32–35.)

So this is what Isaiah was talking about when he quoted the Lord as saying: "Seek ye the Lord while he may be found," for there will come a day when he cannot be found; and "call ye upon him while he is near," because there will be a day when the judgment will be set and he will not be near.

7. Let the wicked forsake his way, and the unrighteous man his thoughts: and let him return unto the LORD, and he will have mercy upon him; and to our God,

God's call is not only to the apostate and confused children of Israel, but it is to all those throughout the world who are reveling in wickedness and snaring themselves in the devices of the devil. As the Lord would later say to Jeremiah, "They are wise to do evil,

for he will abundantly pardon.

but to do good they have no knowledge" (Jeremiah 4:22). Their thoughts are continually concentrated on clever schemes to deceive and defraud the unsuspecting, to debauch the innocent, to indulge their passions and appetites. They are often cruel, brutal, and ruthless. But so was Nineveh. And the Lord suspended his judgment on that wicked city when they asked forgiveness. It is interesting that the people of Nineveh were so wicked that it angered Jonah that the Lord would not punish them in spite of their repentance! (See Jonah, chapter 4.) But that is the way God is. He is a being of tremendous compassion when he sees the spirit of repentance manifest itself. He will indeed have mercy on the wicked and "will abundantly pardon."

8. For my thoughts are not your thoughts, neither are your ways my ways, saith the LORD.

9. For as the heavens are higher than the earth, so are my ways higher than your ways, and my thoughts than your thoughts.

God's infinite capacity for mercy and compassion is not the only way in which he differs from the proclivities of his earthly children. In this verse he is reminding us that his thoughts are not operating on the same plane as our thoughts, neither are his "ways" of doing things like our ways. That is why he goes on to say that if we are to understand the mind and operations of our Heavenly Father, we must think in terms of heavenly things or God-science. These principles are discovered by two means. One is by careful investigation into the things of nature which God has so carefully organized. This is the task of the physical scientists. The other means is through direct revelation. This is the most exciting of all. It gives us a direct exposure to the principles of God-science from the great architect of the universe himself. But to comprehend him, we must think big—as big as eternity. Physical scientists have to do this in order to make their discoveries. So do spiritual scientists. It is amazing how many people find it virtually impossible to believe, and therefore comprehend, what the Lord is willing to reveal concerning himself and the wonders he has wrought. In this present text the Lord is warning us that if we think of the earth and the cosmic universe in terms of our own reasoning we will make erroneous judgments. For example, the reasoning of modern man says there never was a universal flood (Genesis, chapters 6–8). They also say that the story of Jonah and the whale (Jonah, chapters 1 and 2) could not possibly have happened. They also refuse to believe that the continents could have been suddenly divided in the days of Peleg (Genesis 10:25). But this is man's thinking, not God's. All kinds of things are possible to God which would totally baffle the mind of lowly man here on earth. That is why we must remain humble and teachable. Concerning the Great Flood, Peter could hardly comprehend how men could doubt it. He said:

"There shall come in the last days scoffers, walking after their own lusts,

"And saying,... since the fathers fell asleep, all things continue as they were from the beginning of creation.

"For this they willingly are ignorant of, that by the word of God the heavens were of old, and the earth standing out of the water and in the water:

"Whereby the world that then was, BEING OVER-FLOWED WITH WATER, perished." (2 Peter 3:3–6; emphasis added.)

As for Jonah and the whale, the fact that a modern man had a somewhat similar experience should cause the "scoffers" mentioned by Peter to give this subject further consideration. (See W. Cleon Skousen, *The Fourth Thousand Years,* pp. 458–63.)

10. For as the rain cometh down, and the snow from

The Lord wants to remind us that just as the rain and the snow fall to the earth to provide essential moisture

heaven, and returneth not thither, but watereth the earth, and maketh it bring forth and bud, that it may give seed to the sower, and bread to the eater:

11. So shall my word be that goeth forth out of my mouth: it shall not return unto me void, but it shall accomplish that which I please, and it shall prosper in the thing whereto I sent it.

to all living things, even so his words are sent forth to be literally fulfilled, and none can prevent it. Regardless of how incomprehensible some of his predictions may be to mankind, the scientific fact of heaven is that what he has declared "blessed" will be blessed, and what he has said will "prosper" will prosper.

12. For ye shall go out with joy, and be led forth with peace: the mountains and the hills shall break forth before you into singing, and all the trees of the field shall clap their hands.

The Lord promises that those who will hearken to his message, no matter how wicked they may have been, can be pardoned "abundantly" (verse 7) and go out from their wilderness of wickedness into the land of promise with joy. In the day of the Lord's reign, not only will mankind rejoice, but even the elements and the plants of the earth. They have intelligences in them which are capable of expressing their joy when the Lord reigns.

13. Instead of the thorn shall come up the fir tree, and instead of the brier shall come up the myrtle tree: and it shall be to the LORD for a name, for an everlasting sign that shall not be cut off.

This verse would seem to imply that during the Millennium the noxious thorns and thistles which came with the Fall (see Genesis 3:18) will no longer be present on the planet to plague mankind. What a blessing to farmers!

The land will be so abundant and joyful for all who dwell there that these fortunate circumstances will be represented in its name. The Lord has given similar names to choice lands before. A name such as "Bountiful" will be a sign to all mankind that the Lord will never cut off his people from their blessings again.

INTRODUCTION:

In chapter 55 the Lord was directing his remarks primarily to scattered Israel and the "wicked" among the nations. The Lord wanted to extend a gracious invitation to all of them to come and drink at the fountain of eternal life.

In chapter 56 the Lord expresses concern over the converts who join the Church.

1. Thus saith the LORD, Keep ye judgment, and do justice: for my salvation is near to come, and my righteousness to be revealed.

This verse sets forth the Lord's injunction to keep a judicious eye on the things we do. We should ask if our business dealings operate according to the Golden Rule or if we practice the popular doctrine of *caveat emptor* ("let the buyer beware"). This means a customer buys at his own risk. If he gets cheated that's his bad luck. Obviously there is no justice in a crooked deal. The Lord wants his children to know that he holds them accountable. They are expected to mete out "justice" in everything they do. This message will carry particular significance in the times of the Gentiles because the Lord's day of judgment will be near, and his administration of righteousness will ferret out those who have used corrupt judgment and betrayed the principles of justice.

2. Blessed is the man that doeth this, and the son of man that layeth hold on it; that keepeth the sabbath

At the same time the Lord will have an abundance of blessings for those who have kept themselves accountable in their personal and public life. There will

from polluting it, and keepeth his hand from doing any evil.

also be blessings for those who have carefully kept the Sabbath and performed necessary services to both God and man. The Lord is also respectful of all his children who have resisted temptation and kept their hands from evil acts of any kind.

3. Neither let the son of the stranger, that hath joined himself to the LORD, speak, saying, The LORD hath utterly separated me from his people: neither let the eunuch say, Behold, I am a dry tree.

The Lord comforts the converts who are sons of strangers (Gentiles means "strangers"). The Lord does not want them to feel as though they were not part of Israel, because they are. The prophet Mormon quotes the Lord as saying to the Gentiles, "Come unto me, and be baptized in my name, that ye may receive a remission of your sins, and be filled with the Holy Ghost, THAT YE MAY BE NUMBERED WITH MY PEOPLE WHO ARE OF THE HOUSE OF ISRAEL" (3 Nephi 30:2; emphasis added).

The Lord also encourages the eunuchs to refrain from thinking of themselves as a "dry tree." A dry tree is one which flourishes with leaves but never produces buds, blossoms, and fruit. Among the Gentile nations it was very common to cut out the genitals of house servants, particularly if they were assigned to the women's quarters. In modern times many become like eunuchs by making themselves sterile or infertile. However, after they join the Church they learn how important the Lord considers family life. Since this has become impossible for them, they feel greatly deprived because they can beget no children.

4. For thus saith the LORD unto the eunuchs that keep my sabbaths, and choose the things that please me, and take hold of my covenant;

The Lord wants them to know that the Gospel plan still provides a place for them in the kingdom of God. Those who cannot have children in this life will be given the power to beget children in the next life if they are righteous (D&C 132:22-24, 55). Furthermore, the

5. Even unto them will I give in mine house and within my walls a place and a name better than of sons and of daughters: I will give them an everlasting name, that shall not be cut off.

righteous, no matter how they may have been handicapped in this life, will receive a name of renown and a place of distinction in the house of God's kingdom which will endure forever and never be "cut off."

6. Also the sons of the stranger, that join themselves to the LORD, to serve him, and to love the name of the LORD, to be his servants, every one that keepeth the sabbath from polluting it, and taketh hold of my covenant;

Now the Lord wishes to comment further on the children of the "stranger," or the Gentiles "that join themselves to the Lord" and who demonstrate that they love the Lord by obeying him and keeping his commandments. The Lord describes how they can become his acceptable "servants." He wants his kingdom made up of those who keep the Sabbath day holy and do not pollute it with routine labor or holiday activities. His choice servants are those who honor the covenants which they have made with the Lord. They will seek to diligently do the things they have promised to do—pay their tithes, assist the poor in helping themselves, teach the Gospel both at home and abroad, study the scriptures, bear testimony, be honest, work hard, be kind, raise up a righteous family to the Lord, and be willing to keep themselves unspotted from the world by avoiding intoxicants, drugs, immorality, or any form of debauchery.

7. Even them will I bring to my holy mountain, and make them joyful in my house of prayer; their burnt offerings and their sacrifices shall be accepted upon mine altar; for mine house shall be called an house of prayer for all people.

The Lord says that all these—whether they be strangers or eunuchs or anyone else—if they are righteous, the Lord will bring them to the holy mountain where the temple is located. He will accept their sacrifices and oblations and listen to their prayers and supplications. The Lord says the temple is a "house of prayer for all people," and Jesus quoted this verse to the money changers when he cleansed the Jerusalem temple the second time. Jesus told them, "It is written, My house shall be called the house of prayer; but ye have made it a den of thieves" (Matthew 21:13).

8. The Lord GOD which gathereth the outcasts of Israel saith, Yet will I gather others to him, beside those that are gathered unto him.

In this verse the Lord emphasizes that when he brings the "outcasts" of Israel back to the lands of their inheritance, he will also gather "others," even as many as will hearken to the Gospel call. It is the purpose of God to make his plan of salvation as inclusive as possible. There is a tendency among men to set up organizations that are exclusive, but not the Lord. He wants to include all who are willing to live under the higher law of the Gospel whether they be Israelites, strangers, or eunuchs. They are all his children and he loves them.

9. All ye beasts of the field, come to devour, yea, all ye beasts in the forest.

Suddenly the Lord seems to turn from that glorious vision of the future to the ugly situation in Isaiah's day. The Lord sees the whole House of Israel in a pitiful state. Israel, like a huge flock of sheep, is surrounded by ferocious enemy nations which are about to sweep in upon them. As with a flock of sheep, the "beasts of the field" are ready to devour them up, and the "beasts in the forest" are about to come out for their prey.

10. His watchmen are blind: they are all ignorant, they are all dumb dogs, they cannot bark; sleeping, lying down, loving to slumber.

The Lord continues to compare Israel with a flock of sheep and says their "watchmen" or shepherds are blind. The leaders of the Jews in Isaiah's day seemed oblivious to the destruction which was gathering like wild beasts of the forest all around them. They were "blind" to the danger and refused to repent so the Lord could save them. Furthermore, the guardians of the people (soldiers and political leaders) were like shepherd dogs who seemed "ignorant" of the impending danger; or perhaps they were "dumb" and could not bark; or else they were stretched out sleeping and therefore not watching over the flock.

11. Yea, they are greedy dogs which can never have enough, and they are shepherds that cannot understand: they all look to their own way, every one for his gain, from his quarter.

Now the Lord comes right out and proclaims what their situation actually is. The guardians or "dogs" are "greedy," and the "shepherds" are without comprehension of what is going on. They are completely distracted from the task of watching over the sheep because their entire passion is to get gain for themselves. They do not go out among the flock or survey the terrain for any lurking danger. They stay in their own "quarter" and use their high offices to accumulate personal wealth.

12. Come ye, say they, I will fetch wine, and we will fill ourselves with strong drink; and to morrow shall be as this day, and much more abundant.

Furthermore, these shepherds of the flock are a bunch of drunken sots. They are continually feasting and drinking. And in spite of the debauchery and drunkenness of each day, they promise themselves the prospect of an even greater binge on the morrow.

Isaiah, Chapter 57

INTRODUCTION:

This chapter is a continuation of the theme in chapter 56. The Lord wants those who are "eunuchs," or strangers, or the righteous who feel they have been treated indifferently by their brethren to know that God is mindful of them, and in the next life they shall receive the reward which was lacking in this one.

1. **The righteous perisheth, and no man layeth it to heart: and merciful men are taken away, none considering that the righteous is taken away from the evil to come.**

It is rather amazing that throughout history it has usually been the most ruthless, the most heartless, and the most depraved who have been honored with the greatest popular acclaim. When they have died the public has gone into massive demonstrations of lamentation and mourning. Huge public funerals mark the event. With the death of the humble and the righteous, however, there is seldom any kind of demonstration at all. As far as the public is concerned, the righteous usually pass from this life unknown, unhonored, and unmourned except among their immediate family and friends. But they are honored of God, and sometimes he takes them in death as a special blessing so that they can be spared the suffering and evil which is about to be unleashed upon the land.

2. **He shall enter into peace: they shall rest in their beds, each one walking in his uprightness.**

Alma describes what happens to the righteous when they die (see Alma 40:11-12). Their spirits enter into a state of peace and happiness. Their bodies lie sleeping, as it were, in the "beds" of their graves, while their spirits walk among those who are entitled to enjoy the "paradise" of God. They inherit this great blessing because of their "uprightness" during earth life. Here is the way Alma described it to his inquiring son: "The spirits of those who are righteous are received into a state of happiness, which is called paradise, a state of rest, a state of peace, where they shall rest from all their troubles and from all care, and sorrow" (Alma 40:12).

3. But draw near hither, ye sons of the sorceress, the seed of the adulterer and the whore.

But now the Lord turns on those who have been reveling in their wickedness. The Lord calls them children of witches, or those having familiar spirits who parade about the land claiming to have supernatural powers. They practice the immorality and vices of Satan so that the children they beget are often conceived in adultery or as a result of whoredoms.

4. Against whom do ye sport yourselves? against whom make ye a wide mouth, and draw out the tongue? are ye not children of transgression, a seed of falsehood,

The Lord wants these wicked children of the covenant to stop for a moment and consider the identity of the one whom they continually ridicule and of whom they make "sport." (It is none other than the Lord God Jehovah, to whom they owe their very existence!) They open their mouths, stick out their tongues, and profane the name of their Heavenly Father and his Son. As Jesus would later say to the apostate people of his own day: "Ye are of your father the devil, and the lusts of your father ye will do. He was a murderer from the beginning, and abode not in the truth, because there is no truth in him. When he speaketh a lie, he speaketh of his own: for he is a liar, and the father of it" (John 8:44). In the days of Isaiah, the Lord said virtually the same thing: "Are ye not children of transgression, a seed of falsehood?"

5. Enflaming yourselves with idols under every green tree, slaying the children in the valleys under the clifts of the rocks?

The ancients often carved the images of their male and female "gods" as though they were engaging in all kinds of sexual depravity. Similar obscenities carved in elaborate displays of the most bizarre orgies of immoral perversion exist today in the Hindu temples of Khajuraho, India. The Israelites copied these pagan practices by placing obscene images in groves of trees. They used these to inflame their passions and provide a gathering place for the licentious and wanton sexual indulgences which modern textbooks politely refer to as "fertility rites." Throughout the Old Testament the Lord repeatedly commanded his servants to "cut down" these groves, destroy the pagan altars, and break the pagan images (see Exodus 34:13; Deuteronomy 7:5; 2 Kings 18:4; 2 Chronicles 31:1; Micah 5:13-14). These practices were so abhorrent to the Lord that he had Elijah command the people to slay all 450 of the degenerate "prophets" of Baal who had been promoting these rites among the Israelites during the reign of King Ahab (see 1 Kings 18:22, 40).

The false prophets also induced the people to bring their infants to be burned "under the clifts of the rocks." These sacrifices of children to the fire gods, particularly Molech, are believed to have taken place in the extremely deep valley just south of Jerusalem which is called Hinnom today.

6. Among the smooth stones of the stream is thy portion; they, they are thy lot: even to them hast thou poured a drink offering, thou hast offered a meat offering. Should I receive comfort in these?

It was the pagan priests who used smooth stones cemented neatly together for their altars. The Lord said to the Israelites: "Build an altar unto the Lord thy God, an altar of stones: thou SHALT NOT LIFT UP ANY IRON TOOL UPON THEM. Thou shalt build the altar of the Lord thy God of WHOLE STONES." (Deuteronomy 27:5-6; emphasis added. See also Exodus 20:25; Joshua 8:31.) In this verse the Lord accuses his people of identifying themselves with the gods whose altars are

Isaiah Speaks to Modern Times

of smooth stone. On these polluted sanctuaries the people have offered their oblations. The Lord asks his people, "Should I receive comfort in these?"

7. Upon a lofty and high mountain hast thou set thy bed: even thither wentest thou up to offer sacrifice.

The people in Isaiah's day had available in Jerusalem a holy temple dedicated to God where they could worship and offer sacrifices. Instead, they had gone up to a lofty mountain to make their beds with the false gods of the pagans. There they had taken their sacrifices to offer them up to idolatrous deities whom the devil had put it in their hearts to worship.

8. Behind the doors also and the posts hast thou set up thy remembrance: for thou hast discovered thyself to another than me, and art gone up; thou hast enlarged thy bed, and made thee a covenant with them; thou lovedst their bed where thou sawest it.

Into the pagan shrines on the high mountain the Lord's people had taken their sacrifices and made their vows. The phrase "thou hast discovered thyself to another" has reference to the intimacies of the marriage bed. The Lord accuses his people of making a covenant with these pagan deities and taking to their lustful beds the debaucheries of their fertility rites.

9. And thou wentest to the king with ointment, and didst increase thy perfumes, and didst send thy messengers far off, and didst debase thyself even unto hell.

They had joined with the pagan king in these sentient indulgences. They had taken ointments and perfumes to add pleasure to those participating in these rites. They had sent their "messengers" or personal servants far away (probably back home) so they would not witness their depraved activities. When these servants had gone, these apostates Israelites indulged themselves so repulsively that the scripture says they debased themselves "even unto hell."

10. Thou art wearied in the greatness of thy way; yet

In this verse the Lord is saying that the people have set their feet on a great highway which wearies them,

saidst thou not, There is no hope: thou hast found the life of thine hand; therefore thou wast not grieved.

and they cannot escape from it. Nor can they reach any kind of satisfying destination. But they will not admit it. The double negative "yet saidst thou not, There is no hope" means that, as of yet, the people traveling this highway refuse to admit that it offers no hope. They have set their hand to the task of following this evil pathway and are not yet sufficiently "grieved" with their blundering mistake to abandon it.

11. And of whom hast thou been afraid or feared, that thou hast lied, and hast not remembered me, nor laid it to thy heart? have not I held my peace even of old, and thou fearest me not?

The Lord asks his people who it was that intimidated them into following such an evil course. Who was it that made them afraid and induced them to LIE by violating their covenants with God and turning their hearts away from him? The Lord says he has held his peace and demonstrated his long-suffering toward his apostate children. Perhaps this is why they have not respected their God and FEARED to offend him.

12. I will declare thy righteousness, and thy works; for they shall not profit thee.

The Septuagint version says, "I will declare MY righteousness, and thy works; for they shall not profit thee" (emphasis added). This would appear to be the correct rendition. The Lord is going to proclaim to all the world what he has done to help his children, and at the same time he is going to completely expose the wickedness of those who were called to be the Lord's chosen people. They were supposed to set an example to the rest of the world!

13. When thou criest, let thy companies deliver thee; but the wind shall carry them all away; vanity shall take them: but he that putteth his trust in me shall pos-

The Lord challenges these Israelites to consider what they will do when the coming calamity sweeps down upon them. They will cry out to have the Lord save them, but he will tell them to go to their pagan friends for help. Of course, it will do them no good for they

**sess the land, and shall in-
herit my holy mountain;**

will all be swept away like leaves before the wind. Only those who put their trust in the Lord will be allowed to inherit the land and dwell within the precincts of the "holy mountain" where the Lord's temple and the headquarters are located.

14. And shall say, Cast ye up, cast ye up, prepare the way, take up the stumblingblock out of the way of my people.

As the righteous return to their respective lands of inheritance, They will utter a cry to go forth unto Zion in America and to "cast ye up," or ascend unto Jerusalem. They will ask the Lord to remove all of the stumbling blocks that might hinder their return. It is interesting that the modern Jews refer to their gathering back to Jerusalem as the "Aliyah"—the "ascent" to the Holy City.

15. For thus saith the high and lofty One that inhabiteth eternity, whose name is Holy; I dwell in the high and holy place, with him also that is of a contrite and humble spirit, to revive the spirit of the humble, and to revive the heart of the contrite ones.

The Lord will respond with a declaration that he is indeed the Almighty, who presides over the infinite expanse of eternity. He dwells on high (near Kolob; see Abraham 3:2–3), and those who are allowed to dwell with him are the contrite and humble. It is in these heavenly mansions that the Lord says he will "revive the spirit of the humble," and "revive the heart of the contrite ones."

16. For I will not contend for ever, neither will I be always wroth: for the spirit should fail before me, and the souls which I have made.

The Lord wants to assure all mankind that he is a God of love as well as a God of justice. He sorrows for the elements of wickedness among the children of men, but he rejoices in those who are humble, contrite, and seeking to obey God's commandments the best they can. The Lord says in this verse that he will not always be wroth against his children. Were he angry continuously, the hearts of mankind would sink into despair.

17. **For the iniquity of his covetousness was I wroth, and smote him: I hid me, and was wroth, and he went on frowardly in the way of his heart.**

The Lord wants his people to understand that it was because of their greed and covetousness that he was wroth. That is why the Lord hid himself from Israel and let her wicked children go their stubborn way.

18. **I have seen his ways, and will heal him: I will lead him also, and restore comforts unto him and to his mourners.**

But the Lord has been watching. He has always had a plan to ultimately recover Israel and heal her children from their afflictions. He says their mourners will be comforted when the Israelites once more return to the glorious prosperity and happiness which awaits them.

19. **I create the fruit of the lips; Peace, peace to him that is far off, and to him that is near, saith the LORD; and I will heal him.**

God creates "the fruit of the lips," which means that he creates the blessings which cause mankind to praise their Creator. As Paul says, "By him therefore let us offer the sacrifice of praise to God continually, that is, THE FRUIT OF OUR LIPS giving thanks to his name" (Hebrews 13:15; emphasis added). To all those who accept the Gospel and obey God's commandments, there is a satisfying spirit of peace. Whether his people are far or near, he plans to bless them and heal them.

20. **But the wicked are like the troubled sea, when it cannot rest, whose waters cast up mire and dirt.**

21. **There is no peace, saith my God, to the wicked.**

But the wicked will always be tossed about on the sea of life in restless confusion. Their circumstances will continually be like a sea casting up mire and dirt. Isaiah closes this chapter with his personal witness, "THERE IS NO PEACE, SAITH MY GOD, TO THE WICKED."

INTRODUCTION:

Chapters 58 to 60 seem to go together. They describe the sins of Israel just prior to the time when the Gospel will be restored in the latter days. Some of these events were also fulfilled to a certain extent during earlier periods of Israel's history.

1. Cry aloud, spare not, lift up thy voice like a trumpet, and shew my people their transgression, and the house of Jacob their sins.

The most difficult assignment given to a prophet by the Lord is the command to cry out against the people concerning their sins. It is so much more pleasant to speak of their good qualities and their achievements. However, at frequent intervals the Lord insists that his prophets and Church leaders raise their voices like a mighty trumpet and tell the people they are violating the law of God and committing serious sins or transgressions against the Lord.

2. Yet they seek me daily, and delight to know my ways, as a nation that did righteousness, and forsook not the ordinance of their God: they ask of me the ordinances of justice; they take delight in approaching to God.

But how can they be so sinful when they attend church regularly and call upon the Lord as though they were a nation seeking to be righteous? They even perform "the ordinance of their God" and pray for God's just reward to be meted out to them. From their multitude of prayers and professions of faith one would assume that they took "delight in approaching to God."

3. Wherefore have we fasted, say they, and thou seest not?

However, in spite of all the ritual and formal ceremonies, the people continually complain. They

wherefore have we afflicted our soul, and thou takest no knowledge? Behold, in the day of your fast ye find pleasure, and exact all your labours.

wonder why there are no special blessings as a result of all their fasting and ostentatious religious rites. The Lord never seems to manifest himself to them. In response to this the Lord says he has a complaint of his own. Their day of fasting is supposed to be a holy day, but they have made it a holiday. They use it as a day of celebrating and pleasure. Meanwhile, on the Sabbath they exact a full measure of labor from their servants, who must cook great feasts which usually mark the end of the fast.

4. Behold, ye fast for strife and debate, and to smite with the fist of wickedness: ye shall not fast as ye do this day, to make your voice to be heard on high.

When people fast for the wrong reason they find themselves miserable and highly irritable. They are easily aroused to engage in quarreling and debate. Instead of fasting to share with the poor, the poor are shunted aside and abused when they come seeking help. It is interesting that the Septuagint version gives the last part of this verse as follows: "To smite with the fist the POOR. Wherefore fast ye unto me in this manner?" (Clarke, *Commentary*, 4:217; emphasis added.) The people fast and pray to get the attention of God, but abuse the poor, whom God loves as much as those who have plenty.

5. Is it such a fast that I have chosen? a day for a man to afflict his soul? is it to bow down his head as a bulrush, and to spread sackcloth and ashes under him? wilt thou call this a fast, and an acceptable day to the LORD?

The Lord asks Israel in the days of their apostasy whether they are fasting in the manner prescribed by him. Did the Lord ask them to "afflict" the soul in great lamentation, and "bow down" in mock humility like a bulrush? Did he ask the people to go about in sackcloth and ashes? Do they think this is the kind of fast which is expected by the Lord?

6. Is not this the fast that I have chosen? to loose the

In contrast to the manner of fasting which the people are following, the Lord describes what he expects on bands of wickedness, to undo the heavy burdens, and to let the oppressed go free, and that ye break every yoke?

these sacred occasions. It is a time for people to disengage themselves from the bands of wickedness and worldly preoccupations which have cluttered up their lives. It is a time to forgive debts where possible and to succor the oppressed with the bounties of life so that they are liberated from the gnawing anxiety of want and poverty. It is a time to break off the yoke of sin and self-centered pleasures which the people are dragging after them like a burden on a cart rope.

7. Is it not to deal thy bread to the hungry, and that thou bring the poor that are cast out to thy house? when thou seest the naked, that thou cover him; and that thou hide not thyself from thine own flesh?

The Lord asks if this is not a time to place bread in the hands of the hungry and call back to their houses those who came begging but were driven away? Is this not a time to get out some of that extra, unused clothing to cover the nakedness of the poverty stricken? Furthermore, is this not a time to look to the needs of one's own relatives who may be in desperate need? Charity should always begin at home.

Bishop John H. Vandenberg commented on verses 6 and 7 by stating:

"Certainly, it takes no imagination to understand what is meant when he says, '...that thou bring the poor that are cast out to thy house? when thou seest the naked, that thou cover him; and that thou hide not thyself from thine own flesh?'

"He meant that in addition to taking care of the poor, that we should watch over our own kin and be responsible for our father, mother, brother, and sister when they are in need.

"It is here that I would like to state that the Lord has caused a day of fasting and prayer to be set up in this day so that collectively the Church might join together to fulfil the purposes of fasting.

"In the general letter from the Council of the Twelve to the Church under date of May 17, 1845, which Orson Pratt read to the Saints, these words appear:

" 'Let this be an ensample to all saints, and there will never be any lack for bread: When the poor are starving, let those who have, fast one day and give what they otherwise would have eaten to the bishops for the poor, and every one will abound for a long time; and this is one great and important principle of fasts, approved of the Lord. And so long as the saints will all live to this principle with glad hearts and cheerful countenances they will always have an abundance. (*History of the Church*, 7:413.)'

"The bishop should frequently encourage the members of his ward to observe the fast day and voluntarily contribute a generous offering. The Lord knows in his wisdom that individually we are generally not prone to seek out the poor, the hungry, and those in need, and individually attend to their needs on a continuing basis. By fasting collectively there is no end to the good that can be done; that no one need suffer; that such assistance as might be given is rendered through the bishop in love and mercy and that full dollar value is rendered without any administrative cost." (John H. Vandenberg, in Conference Report, April 1963, p. 28; also in *Improvement Era*, June 1963, p. 478.)

8. Then shall thy light break forth as the morning, and thine health shall spring forth speedily: and thy righteousness shall go before thee; the glory of the LORD shall be thy rereward.

To those who will follow these instructions there is a great reward awaiting them. They will find themselves awakening to each new day with zest and joy. They will find that fasting improves the health of those who give their bodies a rest. Such people become known for their generosity and righteousness. The Lord also rejoices in their obedience to the true law of the fast, and he will smile upon them in glorious approbation. He will also watch over them to prevent an unexpected attack from the adversary sneaking up behind them unawares.

9. **Then shalt thou call, and the LORD shall answer; thou shalt cry, and he shall say, Here I am. If thou take away from the midst of thee the yoke, the putting forth of the finger, and speaking vanity;**

The Lord has a great blessing for those who humble themselves and participate in regular fasting and prayer. In response to the prayers of those who accompany their petitions with fasting the Lord promises he will answer their pleas. All the Lord requires is that the people take away the yoke or bondage of sin under which they are laboring and stop pointing the finger of scorn at others.

10. **And if thou draw out thy soul to the hungry, and satisfy the afflicted soul; then shall thy light rise in obscurity, and thy darkness be as the noonday:**

Those who "draw out" their souls in compassion by sacrificing to help the poor will not go without their reward from the Lord. They will be like a light in obscure darkness which suddenly shines forth. That which was formerly dark and depressing shall suddenly take on the brightness of the sun at noonday.

11. **And the LORD shall guide thee continually, and satisfy thy soul in drought, and make fat thy bones: and thou shalt be like a watered garden, and like a spring of water, whose waters fail not.**

Bishop Vandenberg commented on this verse as follows:

"And the Lord shall guide thee continually, (or the Holy Ghost will direct your daily life) and satisfy thy soul in drought, (This is your personal security in times of need and difficulty.) and make fat thy bones: (I believe this has to do with health. In the bone there is marrow, and marrow manufactures the blood that is vital to the strength and well-being of the body.) and thou shalt be like a watered garden, and like a spring of water, whose waters fail not (or inspiration and wisdom will flow from you continually)." (John H. Vandenberg, in Conference Report, April 1963, p. 29; also in *Improvement Era*, June 1963, p. 479.)

12. **And they that shall be of thee shall build the old waste places: thou shalt raise up the foundations of**

Continuing, Bishop Vandenberg stated:

"To me this is a promise to those working with the members of the Church who are in need physically and

many generations; and thou shalt be called, The repairer of the breach, The restorer of paths to dwell in.

spiritually, 'they that shall be of thee,' or that you may be able to help them—to do what? 'Build the old waste places,' and as you help them to build 'thou shalt raise up the foundations of (their) many generations (to follow); and then thou shalt be called, The repairer of the breach.' In other words, you have helped them overcome their weaknesses, to restore their souls, to bridge the gap through reactivating, rehabilitation, and 'restoring' the path for them to walk in.

"To those responsible for the leadership of the Saints in every unit of the Church, I say, teach the people the principle of fasting, in love, in gentleness, in firmness, and in humility. Fasting will give them spiritual strength and help them to develop self-control." (Ibid.)

13. If thou turn away thy foot from the sabbath, from doing thy pleasure on my holy day; and call the sabbath a delight, the holy of the LORD, honourable; and shalt honour him, not doing thine own ways, nor finding thine own pleasure, nor speaking thine own words:

To "turn away thy foot" from the routine labors of the regular work week and cease from personal pleasures or recreation in order to make the Sabbath meaningful is very pleasing to the Lord. The Lord wishes to have his people make the Sabbath a delightful day, a day of rest, a day of service to the needy, the shut-ins, and the downhearted. It is also a time to renew our covenants by honoring the Lord, partaking of the sacrament, studying the scriptures and meditating on the great blessings which come to us when we are obedient to the commandments of the Lord.

14. Then shalt thou delight thyself in the LORD; and I will cause thee to ride upon the high places of the earth, and feed thee with the heritage of Jacob thy father: for the mouth of the LORD hath spoken it.

When the servants of the Lord celebrate the Sabbath in this manner and make it a "delight," then the people themselves become a "delight" to the Lord. The Lord will bless them so that they will travel the high road through life and enjoy all the blessings which were promised to Jacob, the great high priest and patriarch of Israel. The Saints can rely upon these promises because they come directly from the Lord, himself.

Isaiah, Chapter 59

INTRODUCTION:

In this chapter Isaiah expresses his reaction to the things which he has both seen and heard. He reasons with the apostate children of Israel and emphasizes God's promise that he will renew his covenant with Israel in the latter days.

1. Behold, the LORD's hand is not shortened, that it cannot save; neither his ear heavy, that it cannot hear:

During a period of apostasy, it has always been characteristic of Israel to complain that God is no longer able to save his people from a threatening calamity. They say he does not intervene to destroy their enemies as in days gone by. They also say he does not seem to hear their prayers, which are sent to heaven periodically in between their debaucheries.

2. But your iniquities have separated between you and your God, and your sins have hid his face from you, that he will not hear.

Isaiah wants the people to take the shock treatment, a sort of reality therapy. He wants them to realize that it is not God who has changed or broken his promises or refused to hear any worthy petitions. Rather, it is the violent wickedness of the people which has separated them from their God. And it is because of their ugly crimes against heaven that the Lord has shut his eyes and his ears to their occasional prayers in between their riotous iniquities.

3. For your hands are defiled with blood, and your fingers

Now Isaiah sets forth a bill of particulars against Israel just as he did in chapter 1. He states that the

with iniquity; your lips have spoken lies, your tongue hath muttered perverseness.

people are continually indulging in murder to get gain. Their hands are full of blood. Their hands are continually picking the pockets of their neighbors or the unwary so that their fingers are tainted with iniquity. They perpetrate frauds by getting people to trust them at a time when their lips are full of lies and their tongues are entangled in corruption and deceit.

4. None calleth for justice, nor any pleadeth for truth: they trust in vanity, and speak lies; they conceive mischief, and bring forth iniquity.

Among this people it does not appear that any inspired leaders will rise up to succor the weak victims of all the crimes and frauds which are continually being perpetrated. No one seems to stand up and demand justice for those who are being wronged. They don't even seem anxious to have the truth of all these predatory evils brought to light. Instead, each man goes about like a proud, self-righteous peacock, massaging his own vanity and speaking lies just like all the rest. Each one seems bent on contriving evil continually and reveling in the fruits of his own iniquity.

5. They hatch cockatrice' eggs, and weave the spider's web: he that eateth of their eggs dieth, and that which is crushed breaketh out into a viper.

Isaiah says that this whole consortium of evil is producing nothing but the eggs of a poisonous serpent which will hatch out and sting them to death. Their daily lives are spent in weaving conspiracies against one another like spiders' webs. Those who gather the eggs of the poisonous cockatrice and attempt to devour them will die. When these eggs are broken open, vipers (poisonous snakes) will crawl out of them.

6. Their webs shall not become garments; neither shall they cover themselves with their works: their works are works of iniq-

Isaiah predicts that all their intrigue and spinning of deceptive webs will not clothe them in robes of riches as they are expecting. Instead they will find themselves attired in the vestments they deserve, the wretched

uity, and the act of violence is in their hands.

rags of their own evil works. Their clothing will display the iniquities they have practiced, and the tools or devices of violence and fraud will be discovered in their hands.

7. Their feet run to evil, and they make haste to shed innocent blood: their thoughts are thoughts of iniquity; wasting and destruction are in their paths.

The people are found to be fleet-footed when it comes to running toward the slightest opportunity to cheat, lie, rob, or even kill for gain. Always their thoughts are monopolized with a complete preoccupation to hurt or destroy. Their pathway through life always carries in its wake the mangled remnants of waste and destruction.

8. The way of peace they know not; and there is no judgment in their goings: they have made them crooked paths: whosoever goeth therein shall not know peace.

Among the wicked, the well-nigh universal excuse for all their criminal conniving is to gain peace and security. Isaiah says they will never find it. There is no peace along the crooked paths they are pursuing. They make reckless decisions without applying the most elementary aspects of sound judgment based on moral principles. Consequently, they are constantly reaping a whirlwind of trouble, contempt, distrust, and rejection. Those who follow such crooked paths will never know peace.

9. Therefore is judgment far from us, neither doth justice overtake us: we wait for light, but behold obscurity; for brightness, but we walk in darkness.

Isaiah now quotes the lamentation of those who suddenly become aware of what they are doing to themselves. They realize they are exercising catastrophic judgment in nearly everything they do. There is no justice in their personal dealings with others. Deceit is a characteristic of their lifestyle both personally and professionally. They keep thinking the light will break through and their lives will become brighter and more satisfying. Instead, they continue to see things in a panorama of blurred obscurity. They continually walk in darkness.

10. We grope for the wall like the blind, and we grope as if we had no eyes: we stumble at noonday as in the night; we are in desolate places as dead men.

It is true that when those who are righteous and walking by the light of the Holy Spirit look upon those who have rejected the Lord's way it seems as though the wicked literally have no eyes. They appear to be groping along the wall in blindness. Even when the right way is pointed out to them, or those who love them try to show them the light, they continue to walk in darkness at noonday. They are surrounded by the wreckage of their own self-made desolation. Instead of being alert, intelligent, and responsible human beings, they follow a course which is irresponsible, irrational, and indifferent to the realities around them. It is almost as though they were walking "dead men."

11. We roar all like bears, and mourn sore like doves: we look for judgment, but there is none; for salvation, but it is far off from us.

In the hour of their lamentation, the wicked recognize their awful situation and begin wailing against the gates of heaven for relief. But it doesn't seem to come. Though their lamentation becomes boisterous like the roar of a bear or they sob quietly to themselves like the cooing of lonely doves, the Lord will not respond. They seek for wisdom and judgment to struggle out of their dilemma, but it eludes them. It seems as though the search for salvation and an escape from the hell-hole which they have dug for themselves is impossible.

12. For our transgressions are multiplied before thee, and our sins testify against us: for our transgressions are

In this hour of distress, the wicked and rebellious cannot help but exclaim, "Our transgressions are multiplied [stretched out] before thee [O Lord], and our

with us; and as for our iniquities, we know them;

sins testify against us: for our transgressions are with us; and as for our iniquities, we know [and acknowledge] them."

13. In transgressing and lying against the LORD, and departing away from our God, speaking oppression and revolt, conceiving and uttering from the heart words of falsehood.

There is a final recognition that all of their rebellion and wickedness has been "lying against the Lord." They have ridiculed his commandments and pretended they were of no account. They not only departed from the way of the Lord but tried to get others to do likewise. They became advocates of oppression and exploitation of the poor and the weak. They plotted in their hearts how they would get people to believe their lies and thereby defraud them.

14. And judgment is turned away backward, and justice standeth afar off: for truth is fallen in the street, and equity cannot enter.

What judgment they exercised was backwards and upside-down. There was no justice or equity in their schemes. Literally, truth was trodden underfoot in the streets, and not even a small degree of pity or equity was allowed to enter into their decisions.

15. Yea, truth faileth; and he that departeth from evil maketh himself a prey: and the LORD saw it, and it displeased him that there was no judgment.

Because truth is replaced with error and deceit and there is no justice or equity, any person who tries to depart from evil becomes the prey of those who still want to lie, rob, and commit murder to get gain. But all of this is abhorrent to the Lord. The situation cries out for justice and judgment, but there is none.

16. And he saw that there was no man, and wondered that there was no intercessor: therefore his arm brought salvation unto him; and his righteousness, it sustained him.

Isaiah therefore predicted that in the latter days, when the Lord can see that there is no leadership to right these wrongs and no human agency to act as intercessor for the weak and the exploited, he will provide a new dispensation for Israel. God's righteous arm will be extended, and he will be sustained with complete success as he sets forth to restore the Gospel for the last time. (It becomes clear that this is what Isaiah is leading up to when we read verse 20.)

17. For he put on righteous-ness as a breastplate, and an helmet of salvation up-on his head; and he put on the garments of vengeance for clothing, and was clad with zeal as a cloke.

When Isaiah saw the vision of the Lord's power which would be made manifest in the latter days, he could not help but see the sacred symbols of a mighty armor protecting the Lord and the things he intended to do. Isaiah says righteousness was his "breastplate," and salvation was like a magnificent "helmet" on his head. For "clothing," he wore vestments of righteous indignation and judgment to avenge the wrongs of the weak and the oppressed. His royal cloak was symbolic of the zeal and determination with which he would carry out this rescue mission.

18. According to their deeds, accordingly he will repay, fury to his adversaries, recompence to his enemies; to the islands he will repay recompence.

The Lord's sword of righteous judgment will sweep across the wicked nations of the earth according to their deeds. Those who have defied the Lord, and desecrated the heritage which God gave them as a stewardship, will feel the Lord's fury as he recom-penses them for their wickedness in rebelling against God and his plan for human happiness. This will not only be in Europe, Asia, and Africa, but it will include "the islands" of the sea, a term which Isaiah often used to designate America and the islands of the Pacific.

19. So shall they fear the name of the LORD from the west, and his glory from the ris-ing of the sun. When the enemy shall come in like a flood, the Spirit of the LORD shall lift up a standard against him.

This reaping down of the wicked will cause the people of the earth who survive the judgments of that day to fear and respect the name of the Lord, who has manifested such power in righteous judgment. His name shall be honored from the east to the west. All those who try to resist the Lord by coming up like a flood to overwhelm his righteous servants will find the Lord himself raising up a standard against them.

20. And the Redeemer shall come to Zion, and unto them that turn from transgression in Jacob, saith the LORD.

The Lord will reveal himself and come to Zion and rescue all of the seed of Jacob who are willing to turn from their sins and support the work of the Lord.

21. As for me, this is my covenant with them, saith the LORD; My spirit that is upon thee, and my words which I have put in thy mouth, shall not depart out of thy mouth, nor out of the mouth of thy seed, nor out of the mouth of thy seed's seed, saith the LORD, from henceforth and for ever.

In contemplation of that great day, the Lord says he will renew his everlasting covenant with Israel of the latter days just as he has revealed it to his servant Isaiah. The Lord assures Isaiah that the spirit of revelation and the prophetic words which he has recorded will all be fulfilled. This will also be true of the words which are uttered under the inspiration of the Lord by those who follow Isaiah. When Jesus appeared among the Nephites he referred to the writings of Isaiah and said, "Search these things diligently; for great are the words of Isaiah" (3 Nephi 23:1).

INTRODUCTION:

The previous chapter ended with the Lord's promise that in the latter days the wicked would be destroyed and the Lord's covenant established among the righteous forever. However, these events were not designed to sweep in upon the earth in one spectacular display of splendor. Instead, the Lord designed to bring these things to pass in carefully planned stages. The scriptures indicate that these events were planned to occur approximately as follows:

1. The restoration of the Gospel, which is to be preached to every nation, kindred, tongue, and people.
2. The return of the Jews to Jerusalem and the rebuilding of their temple.
3. The cleansing of America so that it can become the principal refuge for the righteous when war and destruction sweep across the rest of the earth.
4. The final gathering of the righteous to America, where they will fill up the land and rebuild all the "waste" places.
5. The isolation of the Western Hemisphere from the rest of the world so that it can become the only safe place where there will be peace.
6. The building of the New Jerusalem in America and the structuring of a Zion society in North America, Central America, and South America.
7. The return of the lost Ten Tribes, who will come to America to receive their endowments. Eventually they receive their inheritance in the

promised land of ancient Israel, but Ephraim and Manasseh retain their inheritance in America.

8. The seventh seal is opened, and all of the plagues and wars seen by John the Revelator are poured out upon the wicked.

9. In the midst of these afflictions the great battle of Armageddon takes place and Jerusalem is besieged by the Gentiles for three and one-half years. The Jews are eventually rescued by the Savior and finally recognize and accept him as their true Messiah. Shortly afterwards the Arab nations are also converted.

10. At a time when it appears that the wicked are about to destroy all flesh from off the face of the earth, the Lord will quicken the righteous and take them up from the earth for their safety. He will then change the surface of the planet. Mountains will be leveled and valleys raised. The seas will be driven into the north, and the continents will come together as they were before the days of Peleg. The earth will stagger in its orbit around the sun and finally whirl out of the solar system completely. As it races back toward Kolob the stars will appear to be falling from heaven. Once the earth is established in its new environment it will be surrounded by light. There will be no more day or night, no more weeks, months, or change of seasons. All these devices for measuring time will be gone. It will seem as though there is "time no longer."

11. The worthy dead are resurrected, and the Savior takes away the veil so that all can see him together.

12. The Lord then calls together a great conference of all who have lived upon the earth whether resurrected or not. He then reveals the history of

mankind 1,000 years at a time, and a preliminary judgment is held.

13. The millennial reign is finally ushered in.

This chapter now introduces the theme that in the latter days the darkness which shrouds the human race will be shattered by the bursting forth of the brilliant new dispensation of the fulness of times, in which the splendor of the Savior's ministry will be unveiled.

1. Arise, shine; for thy light is come, and the glory of the LORD is risen upon thee.

Isaiah seems to have been in a state of sublime rapture as he contemplated the vision of our own day when the Gospel would be restored and Zion would put on her beautiful garments. It was shown to Isaiah that the glory of the Lord would be bestowed upon his people.

2. For, behold, the darkness shall cover the earth, and gross darkness the people: but the LORD shall arise upon thee, and his glory shall be seen upon thee.

Isaiah saw that the Restoration would come when there was gross darkness across the whole face of the earth, and the minds of the people would be clouded with the obscurity that comes from apostasy and wickedness. In 1837, when the restored Church was only seven years old, the Lord quoted this verse from Isaiah and made an interesting comment concerning it:

"Verily, verily, I say unto you, darkness covereth the earth, and gross darkness the minds of the people, and all flesh has become corrupt before my face.

"Behold, vengeance cometh speedily upon the inhabitants of the earth, a day of wrath, a day of burning, a day of desolation, of weeping, of mourning, and of lamentation; and as a whirlwind it shall come upon all the face of the earth, saith the Lord.

"And upon my house shall it begin, and from my house shall it go forth, saith the Lord;

"First among those among you, saith the Lord, who have professed to know my name and have not known me, and have blasphemed against me in the midst of my house, saith the Lord." (D&C 112:23-26.)

Joseph Smith had this to say concerning verse 2:

"Consider for a moment, brethren, the fulfillment of the words of the prophet; for we behold that darkness covers the earth, and gross darkness the minds of the inhabitants thereof—that crimes of every description are increasing among men—vices of great enormity are practiced—the rising generation growing up in the fullness of pride and arrogance—the aged losing every sense of conviction, and seemingly banishing every thought of a day of retribution—intemperance, immorality, extravagance, pride, blindness of heart, idolatry, the loss of natural affection; the love of this world, and indifference toward the things of eternity increasing among those who profess a belief in the religion of heaven, and infidelity spreading itself in consequence of the same—men giving themselves up to commit acts of the foulest kind, and deeds of the blackest dye, blaspheming, defrauding, blasting the reputation of neighbors, stealing, robbing, murdering; advocating error and opposing the truth, forsaking the covenant of heaven, and denying the faith of Jesus— and in the midst of all this, the day of the Lord fast approaching when none except those who have won the wedding garment will be permitted to eat and drink in the presence of the Bridegroom, the Prince of Peace!" (Smith, *Teachings*, p. 47.)

Since the days of Joseph Smith, the evil in the world has continued to increase. The young modern prophet knew the Gospel would have to be preached in every nation; nevertheless, he also knew that ultimately Zion in America would be the only available refuge for the righteous. Joseph Smith taught that "Zion" included both North and South America, and he stated that the day would come when the whole world would be in a state of war except the American continent. Here is what he said about it:

"We ought to have the building up of Zion as our greatest object. When wars come, we shall have to flee to Zion. The cry is to make haste. The last revelation says, Ye shall not have time to have gone over the earth, until these things come. It will come as did the cholera, war, fires, and earthquakes; one pestilence after another, until the Ancient of Days comes, then judgment will be given to the Saints....

"Look to the Presidency and receive instruction. Every man who is afraid, covetous, will be taken in a snare. The time is soon coming, when no man will have any peace but in Zion and her stakes.

"I saw men hunting the lives of their own sons, and brother murdering brother, women killing their own daughters, and daughters seeking the lives of their mothers. I saw armies arrayed against armies. I saw blood, desolation, fires. The Son of Man has said that the mother shall be against the daughter, and the daughter against the mother. These things are at our doors. They will follow the Saints of God from city to city. Satan will rage, and the spirit of the devil is now enraged. I know not how soon these things will take place; but with a view of them, shall I cry peace? No; I will lift up my voice and testify of them. How long you will have good crops, and the famine be kept off, I do not know; when the fig tree leaves, know then that the summer is nigh at hand." (Smith, *Teachings*, pp. 160–61.)

Elder Orson Pratt adds an additional dimension to this verse by stating: "What condition do you suppose the wicked will be in in those days, even all the inhabitants of the earth except Zion? 'For behold darkness shall cover the earth and gross darkness the people; but the Lord shall arise upon thee [O Zion!], and his glory shall be seen upon thee.' What a difference between Zion and the rest of mankind! Darkness covering the whole four quarters of the globe. Why darkness? Because the salt of the earth is gathered out; the children of light are gathered together to Zion, and those who are left behind are in darkness, that is, a great many of them. No doubt there will be honest ones, and vast numbers who will come to Zion, notwithstanding the darkness that covers the earth." (Orson Pratt, in *Journal of Discourses*, 14:355.)

3. And the Gentiles shall come to thy light, and kings to the brightness of thy rising.

No doubt Isaiah is emphasizing in this verse the very point referred to by Elder Pratt. There will be those among the Gentiles who will be righteous, and they will want to come to Zion to enjoy its security, the blessings of a righteous lifestyle, and also to be taught.

4. Lift up thine eyes round about, and see: all they gather themselves together, they come to thee: thy sons shall come from far, and thy daughters shall be nursed at thy side.

As Isaiah beheld the vision of all the righteous being gathered out of the precincts of the wicked, he could not help but invite us to see what he was seeing. There were multitudes of the sons and daughters of Israel coming from all directions to enjoy the bounties and blessings of Zion.

5. Then thou shalt see, and flow together, and thine heart shall fear, and be enlarged; because the abundance of the sea shall be converted unto thee, the forces of the Gentiles shall come unto thee.

In that day the people shall flow to Zion in such multitudes that it will cause the native Saints to fear lest they cannot accommodate the waves of immigrants who come swarming into their land. Many of these shall be from the islands of the sea, and others will come with their wealth (mistranslated "forces") from the lands of the Gentiles (Clarke, *Commentary*, 4:223).

6. The multitude of camels shall cover thee, the dromedaries of Midian and Ephah; all they from Sheba shall come: they shall bring gold and incense; and they shall shew forth the praises of the LORD.

Many of these people will not come to Zion in poverty but will bring with them their accumulated fortunes. It will be like the great caravans of the past when camels and dromedaries from Africa and Arabia brought their heavy burdens of precious things to the Lord's sanctuary.

7. All the flocks of Kedar shall be gathered together unto thee, the rams of Nebaioth shall minister unto thee: they shall come up with acceptance on mine altar, and I will glorify the house of my glory.

There will also be an abundance of flocks similar to those of Kedar the second son of Ishmael, who was so famous for his rich herds. At the same time there will be rams like those of Nebaioth, the eldest son of Ishmael, whose herds and flocks were of the finest breed. All these will be brought as an offering to the work of the Lord and the glorification of his holy house.

8. Who are these that fly as a cloud, and as the doves to their windows?

Isaiah inquires as to the identity of all of these multitudes who come to Zion like doves to the windows of their birdhouse. The Lord revealed that they are the gathering Israelites. Although this chapter is speaking primarily of the gathering of the tribes to America when the missionaries give their final rallying call, the gathering of the Jews to Jerusalem is a comparable fulfillment as far as they are concerned. That is why the great Apostle to the Jews, Orson Hyde, declared in his dedicatory prayer on the Mount of Olives: "Incline them [the Jews] to gather in upon this land according to Thy word. Let them come like clouds and like doves to their windows. Let the large ships of the nations bring them from the distant isles; and let kings become their nursing fathers, and queens with motherly fondness wipe the tear of sorrow from their eye." (*History of the Church*, 4:457.)

9. Surely the isles shall wait for me, and the ships of Tarshish first, to bring thy sons from far, their silver and their gold with them, unto the name of the LORD thy God, and to the Holy One of Israel, because he hath glorified thee.

Because Isaiah had no way of identifying America by name, he referred to it as part of the "isles" to which remnants of the children of Israel had been scattered (see 2 Nephi 10:20). He knew that in the latter days it would be the region which would wait upon the Lord. It would also be to America that the gathering Israelites and righteous Gentiles would come. The largest ships in the days of Isaiah were the Phoenician ships that sailed to Tarshish (probably Tartessus, an ancient Phoenician city in southern Spain) for tin (Smith, *Bible Dictionary,* p. 674).They were therefore called the ships of Tarshish. Isaiah saw that in the latter days the largest vessels would be needed to transport the gathering Israelites to Zion. He also saw that they would not come in haste or as refugees, but they would have time to gather together their wealth and bring it to Zion to offer to the Lord for the building up of his kingdom.

10. And the sons of strangers shall build up thy walls, and their kings shall minister unto thee: for in my wrath I smote thee, but in my favour have I had mercy on thee.

Isaiah also saw that the waste places of America would be rebuilt by the children or sons of the Gentiles (Gentiles means "strangers"), and even their kings and most distinguished leaders would be among those who would elect to leave their homelands and come to America in that day. In the past the Lord felt compelled to punish the tribes of Israel for their apostasy and wickedness, but in this new age he will show forth his mercy and blessings upon them.

11. Therefore thy gates shall be open continually; they shall not be shut day nor night; that men may bring unto thee the forces of the Gentiles, and that their kings may be brought.

The cities of the Saints will be open day and night to welcome the hosts coming to Zion. There will be vast numbers to be accommodated, but they will not come to beg, but rather to offer their wealth (mistranslated "forces") from the land of the Gentiles and will introduce to the Lord's people their most distinguished leaders, including their kings.

12. For the nation and kingdom that will not serve
thee shall perish; yea, those
nations shall be utterly
wasted.

Zion will be the only place on the face of the earth where there will be peace. All other nations which revel in wickedness shall perish. Their fate is sealed. Once the judgment is set, there is no turning back. Their time for repentance has passed, and they shall perish. As nations, they shall be "wasted."

13. The glory of Lebanon shall
come unto thee, the fir tree,
the pine tree, and the box
together, to beautify the
place of my sanctuary; and I
will make the place of my
feet glorious.

As Zion is to be built up in both North and South America she will become a land of beautiful cities. Her buildings will be of the finest wood, which in Isaiah's day came from Lebanon.

14. The sons also of them that
afflicted thee shall come
bending unto thee; and all
they that despised thee shall
bow themselves down at
the soles of thy feet; and
they shall call thee, The city
of the LORD, The Zion of
the Holy One of Israel.

The prophets have indicated that just prior to the redemption of Zion, the Saints will suffer bitter persecution so that only the most faithful will survive as members of the Church. However, when Zion is redeemed and the work of the Lord begins to blossom forth in all its beauty and power, many of those who ridiculed and persecuted the Saints will come to plead for their forgiveness and ask to join them. There are some who do not recognize the truth until history catches up with them. That is why those who know the truth can afford to be patient. The Lord has promised that some of those who persecuted them with the greatest bitterness will one day bow in deepest humility and ask the Saints to accept them in fellowship.

15. Whereas thou hast been
forsaken and hated, so that
no man went through thee,
I will make thee an eternal

By way of comfort to the Saints during their time of persecution, Isaiah promises that if they will endure these hardships valiantly, the day will come when the

excellency, a joy of many generations.

Lord will reward them in "eternal excellency," and they will become the pride and "joy of many generations."

16. Thou shalt also suck the milk of the Gentiles, and shalt suck the breast of kings: and thou shalt know that I the LORD am thy Saviour and thy Redeemer, the mighty One of Jacob.

During their days of sorrow it will be difficult for the Saints to believe that respite is near, but the Lord provides the assurance through the words of Isaiah that one day they will be feeding upon the breasts of their persecutors. The Gentiles and their kings will bring their wealth to Zion to nourish and embellish the people whom they formerly treated with disdain.

17. For brass I will bring gold, and for iron I will bring silver, and for wood brass, and for stones iron: I will also make thy officers peace, and thine exactors righteousness.

The redemption of Zion will usher in an era of great prosperity. Where brass would be the usual ornament, there will be gold. Objects of utility where iron has served in the past will be replaced by items of polished silver. Iron and steel will replace the rough stones of the past in building beautiful structures. Best of all, those who govern will be public servants who are peacemakers, and those who are assigned to collect needed revenue for public service will be righteous administrators.

18. Violence shall no more be heard in thy land, wasting nor destruction within thy borders; but thou shalt call thy walls Salvation, and thy gates Praise.

The most significant thing about the Zion society will be the fact that there will be no more violence anywhere in the whole land. There will no longer be any destruction by war or civil strife. It will be a time of prosperous and productive peace. It will provide security and hope for all who dwell there. The people will therefore call the walls of their precincts, "salvation," and people will enter the gates of Zion's cities with praise in their hearts for the blessings which are to be had in these great communities of righteousness.

19. The sun shall be no more thy light by day; neither for brightness shall the moon give light unto thee: but the LORD shall be unto thee an everlasting light, and thy God thy glory.

Now the vision of Isaiah seems to extend even further into the future, when the earth will have returned to its sanctuary near Kolob. There the Lord's creations form a collection of stellar giants which are so bright that they outshine all the other stars of the Milky Way combined. It was in the vicinity of Kolob and its related satellites that the earth was first formed prior to the Fall (see Abraham 5:13). In that environment there was continuous radiance. There was no sun or moon, no day or night, no months or years. In other words, there were no times and seasons. At the beginning of the Millennium Isaiah had seen the earth hurling back toward Kolob like "a chased roe" (Isaiah 13:14). Isaiah saw the earth "remove out of her place" (Isaiah 13:13)," and scientists have described what it would be like for people living on a planet near the center of our galaxy where there are over two million stars radiating light in every direction. (See Bart J. Bok, "The Milky Way Galaxy," *Scientific American*, March 1981, pp. 92ff.; also Thomas R. Geballe, "The Central Parsec of the Galaxy," *Scientific American*, July 1979, pp. 60–70.)

Isaiah also knew what it would be like, for he had seen it in vision. No longer would there be a sun to give light to the earth by day, nor a moon to provide its light at night. Instead, the glory of the Lord will be there with the radiance of Kolob and the stars of the central system to give continuous "brightness" to the whole face of the earth.

20. Thy sun shall no more go down; neither shall thy moon withdraw itself: for the LORD shall be thine everlasting light, and the days of thy mourning shall be ended.

Having left the present solar system, the earth will no longer have a sun to go down or a moon to give or withhold its light. In its new environment the earth will have the Lord and his creations to be the everlasting light for those living in that day. Isaiah

wants all of the children of Israel to know that when all
of this happens it will be such a time of rejoicing and
thanksgiving that it will be said, "The days of thy
mourning shall be ended."

**21. Thy people also shall be all
righteous: they shall in-
herit the land for ever, the
branch of my planting, the
work of my hands, that I
may be glorified.**

The people of the whole earth will be inclined toward
righteousness and peace. Every knee shall bow and
every tongue confess that Jesus is the Christ (see D&C
88:104). In this manner, says Isaiah, the people will
become heirs of the land forever, never again to be
driven out of their possessions.

**22. A little one shall become a
thousand, and a small one a
strong nation: I the LORD
will hasten it in his time.**

During the great winding-up scene the Lord says he
will bless his people so that "a little one shall become a
thousand, and a small one a strong nation." The Lord
promises to hasten the work of the kingdom so that all
those marvelous things that must be accomplished in
order to perform God's purposes will be accomplished
"in his time."

Isaiah, Chapter 61

INTRODUCTION:

This chapter is a continuation of the theme relating to the redemption of Zion. It also pertains to the coming of the Savior, both in the meridian of time and in the latter days.

1. The Spirit of the Lord GOD is upon me; because the LORD hath anointed me to preach good tidings unto the meek; he hath sent me to bind up the brokenhearted, to proclaim liberty to the captives, and the opening of the prison to them that are bound;

2. To proclaim the acceptable year of the LORD, and the day of vengeance of our God; to comfort all that mourn;

After opening his ministry in Jerusalem, Jesus came back to his home in Nazareth and attended the worship services at the synagogue on the Sabbath. When it came his turn to read the scripture he turned to this passage. Everyone knew it pertained to the future coming of the "anointed" one. (The Hebrew word "Messiah" means "anointed." It is the equivalent of the Greek word "Christ" [Peloubet, *Bible Dictionary*, s.v. "Messiah"].) As he sat down, everyone waited for him to comment on the scripture as he was supposed to do. His comment almost caused a riot. He said, "This day is this scripture fulfilled in your ears" (Luke 4:21). In other words, "What you have heard me read today is fulfilled. I am he." The scripture continues:

"And all they in the synagogue, when they heard these things, were filled with wrath,

"And rose up, and thrust him out of the city, and led him unto the brow of the hill whereon their city was built, that they might cast him down headlong.

"But he passing through the midst of them [unperceived] went his way." (Luke 4:28-30.)

It is interesting that Jesus did not quote all of verse 2 to the men of the synagogue. He quoted only that which would be fulfilled during his earthly mission in the meridian of time. He left out the part which spoke of the "day of vengeance of our God," since that pertained to his Second Coming.

3. To appoint unto them that mourn in Zion, to give unto them beauty for ashes, the oil of joy for mourning, the garment of praise for the spirit of heaviness; that they might be called trees of righteousness, the planting of the LORD, that he might be glorified.

In this verse the theme continues to treat the redemption of Zion in the latter days. The Lord promises that he will bring comfort to those who mourn in Zion. Their sackcloth and ashes will be replaced with perfume and ointments, reflecting a time of renewed gladness and joy. There will be vestments of happiness and praise for the Lord instead of the bedraggled raiment of persecuted and hated outcasts. When Zion is redeemed and the Lord comes to praise the integrity of the valiant, they will be considered trees or monuments of righteousness established or planted by the Lord.

4. And they shall build the old wastes, they shall raise up the former desolations, and they shall repair the waste cities, the desolations of many generations.

In 3rd Nephi, chapter 21, the Savior described to the Nephites how completely the Gentile nations in America will be destroyed if they reject the work of the Lord in the latter days. Should this be the case, the Lord told Isaiah that the waste places and the gutted cities would be rebuilt. There are also many rich regions in Mexico as well as Central and South America where the ruins of many ancient cities lie buried in the tangled verdure of tropical jungles. The Lord declares that even these areas which have been desolate for so many generations will be refurbished and rebuilt.

5. And strangers shall stand and feed your flocks, and

Because of the vast numbers of people migrating from other nations and needing employment, the

the sons of the alien shall be your plowmen and your vinedressers.

Saints will have their flocks fed and tended by the strangers or Gentiles who have come into their midst. Much of the work in the vineyards and on the farms will be performed by these new arrivals from distant places.

6. But ye shall be named the Priests of the LORD: men shall call you the Ministers of our God: ye shall eat the riches of the Gentiles, and in their glory shall ye boast yourselves.

Meanwhile, the established members of the kingdom will find themselves deeply involved in the minstry of the kingdom. Teaching the newcomers and ministering the ordinances in the temples will be a tremendous task which the Priesthood will have to perform. Instead of devoting most of their time to horticulture and industry as in the past, the Priesthood will be performing their much-needed service while the Gentiles provide their necessities and receive the blessings of their Priesthood ordinances (D&C 133:32).

7. For your shame ye shall have double; and for confusion they shall rejoice in their portion: therefore in their land they shall possess the double: everlasting joy shall be unto them.

In the past the Israelites were shamed by the Gentiles and sometimes bitterly persecuted. However, when Zion is redeemed the children of Israel will receive a double portion of blessings for all they have suffered in the past. They also endured great confusion, persecution, and dislocation in the past. However, they will now rejoice in the stewardship which God will bestow upon them. They will own double portions of land and other property. They will have it within their means to enjoy everlasting happiness both during this life and in eternity.

8. For I the LORD love judgment, I hate robbery for burnt offering; and I will direct their work in truth,

The Lord loves equity and justice. He despises those who rob and steal and then try to enjoy the confidence of God with fatlings or tithes brought to the altar as a

and I will make an everlasting covenant with them.

sacrifice. The wicked robbed the Israelites in the past, but now the Lord will direct the work among his chosen children and make an everlasting covenant with them. He will also do the same for the many converts who come to receive their blessings under the restored Gospel of Jesus Christ.

9. And their seed shall be known among the Gentiles, and their offspring among the people: all that see them shall acknowledge them, that they are the seed which the LORD hath blessed.

The children of Israel will become known as a great and righteous people. Everyone will continually comment on how greatly they have been blessed.

10. I will greatly rejoice in the LORD, my soul shall be joyful in my God; for he hath clothed me with the garments of salvation, he hath covered me with the robe of righteousness, as a bridegroom decketh himself with ornaments, and as a bride adorneth herself with her jewels.

Now Isaiah speaks for himself. Prior to this time, Isaiah has been quoting the word of the Lord and describing the visions he has seen. He is so animated to behold the final redemption of Zion that he rejoices in the Lord. He feels that he will have a part in this great final triumph of the righteous so that he will be clothed in the "garments of salvation," which may mean the garment of the Priesthood. He will also be dressed in the robes of righteousness, which could mean the holy robes of the temple. With the righteous hosts of Israel, he will await the Bridegroom of the Church.

11. For as the earth bringeth forth her bud, and as the garden causeth the things that are sown in it to spring forth; so the Lord GOD will cause righteousness and praise to spring forth before all the nations.

When Zion is redeemed, it will be as natural for righteousness and praise to emanate from God's people as it is for trees to bud, flowers to blossom, and the well-cultivated garden to bring forth its abundance.

Chapter 62

INTRODUCTION:

The last chapter was addressed primarily to the Zion in America of the latter days. Now the Lord anticipates the glorious day when BOTH Zion in America and Jerusalem in Palestine will be renewed and redeemed.

1. For Zion's sake will I not hold my peace, and for Jerusalem's sake I will not rest, until the righteousness thereof go forth as brightness, and the salvation thereof as a lamp that burneth.

We sometimes think that because "the Lord knoweth all things from the beginning" (1 Nephi 9:6), he waits indifferently until all things are fulfilled. But this is not the case. The Lord plans, works, and organizes with the greatest anxiety and anticipation until all of those things come to pass for the children of men which constitute his "work" and his "glory" (Moses 1:39). In this verse the Lord expresses the great anxiety which he feels for the ultimate redemption of BOTH Zion (in America) and ancient Jerusalem in Palestine. He declares that he is not going to wait indifferently for their ultimate day of triumph. Rather than quietly holding his peace, the Lord is going to have every one of his prophets triumphantly proclaim it. He wants his prophets to declare that future glorious day to every generation. And he will do the same concerning the redemption of Jerusalem. He wants all humanity to rejoice in the fact that the supreme righteousness of these two great capitals will someday be so famous that it will be the "brightness" of the world, and the temporal and spiritual salvation which they will offer mankind will shine out into the darkness of evil and human confusion like a burning lamp.

2. And the Gentiles shall see thy righteousness, and all kings thy glory: and thou shalt be called by a new name, which the mouth of the LORD shall name.

The Gentiles (those who are not of Israel) will see the righteousness of Zion and Jerusalem. Kings will admire their quality of life and the refinement of their culture. Each of these great capitals will be called by a new name in the hour of their power. Ezekiel says that after Armageddon the city of old Jerusalem will be called "Jehovah-shammah," which is interpreted to mean "The Lord is there" (Ezekiel 48:35). When Jesus was among the Nephites he said the great capital city of Zion in the latter days would be called "the New Jerusalem" (3 Nephi 21:23).

3. Thou shalt also be a crown of glory in the hand of the LORD, and a royal diadem in the hand of thy God.

The Lord says each of these great cities will be like a crown of glory in the hand of the Savior and like a diadem in the hand of our Heavenly Father.

4. Thou shalt no more be termed Forsaken; neither shall thy land any more be termed Desolate: but thou shalt be called Hephzi-bah, and thy land Beulah: for the LORD delighteth in thee, and thy land shall be married.

We know how "desolate" the land of old Jerusalem became for many hundreds of years, and there are modern prophecies which indicate that the New Jerusalem will also be built on territory that has been desolated. (See the prophecy of Heber C. Kimball, for example, in W. Cleon Skousen, *Prophecy and Modern Times*, 5th ed. [Salt Lake City: Deseret Book, 1954], pp. 31–33.) However, neither of these great cities will any longer be called desolate after the day of their redemption.

Neither will they be called forsaken any longer. Instead they will be called Hephzibah (which means "my delight is in her"), and the land on which each of them is located will be called Beulah (which means "married" or "united").

In a modern revelation the Lord explains that this verse carries far greater implications than many might have supposed. It is referring to a series of events mentioned by Isaiah much earlier (see Isaiah 40:4) when the crust of the earth will be radically changed. Mountains will be lowered, deep canyons and valleys will be raised, and whole continents will shift back into their original position as they existed prior to the days of Peleg (see Genesis 10:25).

A modern revelation describes these events in more detail than any other scripture: "And he [the Lord] shall utter his voice out of Zion, and he shall speak from Jerusalem, and his voice shall be heard among all people;

"And it shall be a voice as the voice of many waters, and as the voice of a great thunder, which shall break down the mountains, and the valleys shall not be found.

"He shall command the great deep, and it shall be driven back into the north countries, and the islands shall become one land;

"And the land of Jerusalem and the land of Zion shall be turned back into their own place, and the earth shall be like as it was in the days before it was divided." (D&C 133:21-24.)

If the shelves that protrude out from the Western Hemisphere were joined with the shelves protruding from Europe and Africa, it would make them "one land" but still leave a "sea east" of relatively shallow dimensions like the one which existed in the days of Enoch (see Moses 6:42). It would also leave the Mediterranean Sea intact. But what about the regions of the Pacific? If the massive continental plates of Europe, Africa, and America came together again, what could we expect to happen between Asia and America? Since the Lord states that "the great deep...shall be driven back into the north countries," this would suggest that a great Pacific continent will rise up out of the deep to force the water back toward the poles. The

Lord also says that the surface of the earth will then be "like as it was in the days before it was divided." Scientists are now finding evidence of sunken continents in the ocean depths; if these were raised up to join Asia with America, there would be a belt of land circumscribing the whole earth and the major body of seawater would be driven toward the poles. (See Drs. Amos Nur and Zvi Ben Avraham, "Extra Continent May Have Existed," *Science News,* 18 June 1977, p. 389; also Avraham, "The Movement of Continents," *American Scientist,* May–June 1981, pp. 291 ff., especially the section entitled "Continental Fragments in the Ocean.")

5. For as a young man marrieth a virgin, so shall thy sons marry thee: and as the bridegroom rejoiceth over the bride, so shall thy God rejoice over thee.

Not only will the land be MARRIED or brought together again, but the Lord will marry his Church and be one with the people of Israel again. When Joseph Smith was translating this verse he found that it originally said, "For as a young man marrieth a virgin, so shall thy GOD MARRY THEE" (JST, Isaiah 62:5; emphasis added). Then the verse concludes, "as the bridegroom rejoiceth over the bride, so shall thy God rejoice over thee."

6. I have set watchmen upon thy walls, O Jerusalem, which shall never hold their peace day nor night: ye that make mention of the LORD, keep not silence,

The Lord commences to give a special message of comfort and assurance to the tribe of Judah and the inhabitants of ancient Jerusalem. From its earliest history the Lord has set up prophets and "watchmen" over Jerusalem. In fact, the people of Judah often grew weary of the constant preaching and warning from these special messengers of the Lord. But the Lord does not want his watchmen to be intimidated into silence. He wants them to continue preaching, to continue warning the people, and to continue petitioning heaven for the redemption of Jerusalem.

7. And give him no rest, till he establish, and till he make Jerusalem a praise in the earth.

The Lord wants these faithful spokesmen to "give him no rest" until he makes Jerusalem a monument of beauty, justice, and righteousness so as to attract the praise of the whole earth. Of course, the Lord was planning to perform this great work anyway, but he wants the people of Jerusalem involved. He wants them to make themselves worthy and look forward to the day when this great work will be accomplished. By constantly petitioning the Lord, they cannot help but be mindful of this great day and endeavor to prepare themselves so they will be worthy of it.

8. The LORD hath sworn by his right hand, and by the arm of his strength, Surely I will no more give thy corn to be meat for thine enemies; and the sons of the stranger shall not drink thy wine, for the which thou hast laboured:

The Lord has sworn that once the Jews begin gathering again to Jerusalem in the latter days they shall "no more be confounded" (1 Nephi 15:20). This means that no nation will conquer them again or put them under tribute. In the past the Jews have been continually robbed of their labor because predatory nations around them would come at the time of harvest and take their grain, their wine, and their flocks. The Lord is saying in this verse that he has sworn that in the latter days this shall no longer occur.

9. But they that have gathered it shall eat it, and praise the LORD; and they that have brought it together shall drink it in the courts of my holiness.

The Jews have always been a diligent, hard-working people, and the Lord promises that when they gather in the latter days they will be able to eat what they have raised, and with the rebuilding of their temple they will be able to drink the consecrated wine in the "courts of my holiness," which is the temple.

10. Go through, go through the gates; prepare ye the way of the people; cast up, cast up the highway; gather

In these last three verses of this chapter the Lord seems to be speaking to both Jerusalem and Zion. He urges the gathering Israelites to enter through the

out the stones; lift up a standard for the people.

gates or portals into these two chosen gathering places. They are to go through and not let anything hinder them. They are to facilitate the gathering by raising up the means for the gathering Saints and casting out any stone or roadblock that might get in their way. This will be a great moment when a standard or ensign is lifted up in Zion and in Jerusalem, calling upon the Israelites and the righteous to gather for the last time.

11. Behold, the LORD hath proclaimed unto the end of the world, Say ye to the daughter of Zion, Behold, thy salvation cometh; behold, his reward is with him, and his work before him.

The great clarion call which shall go forth into every nation, kindred, tongue, and people will carry the message that the Lord has decreed that Zion and Jerusalem will now be redeemed. The Lord assures his people that he has the power to do it, and as they draw near to him and he draws nearer to them, all these great blessings will be fulfilled on their heads.

12. And they shall call them, The holy people, The redeemed of the LORD: and thou shalt be called, Sought out, A city not forsaken.

As the people of the world contemplate the wonders of the two Zion societies which will be built in America and Jerusalem, they will feel compelled to declare that they are indeed a "holy people." They will not only see that they have been "redeemed of the Lord," but they will call them the blessed people who have been gathered or "sought out" by the Lord and have built unto themselves these great municipalities of righteous government which will never again be called "forsaken."

Isaiah, Chapter 63

INTRODUCTION:

After Jerusalem and Zion are both redeemed there will be a considerable period of time for the great last missionary thrust, particularly among the heathen nations. Meanwhile, the depravity and wickedness among the majority of mankind in the Gentile world will greatly multiply. It will finally become as evil as the degenerate debauchery which the people attained in the days of Noah, when the Lord felt compelled to destroy them in the Great Flood. Jesus predicted the same degree of wickedness in this particular period of the latter days as that which existed just before the Great Flood (see Matthew 24:37–39; Joseph Smith—Matthew 1:41-43). However, the destruction in the latter days will not be by water. It will be by fire. It will be so devastating and universal that it will be necessary for the righteous to be caught up into heaven until the cleansing is completed. The coming of the Lord to avenge the offenses of the wicked against both God and humanity is the major theme as this chapter opens.

1. **Who is this that cometh from Edom, with dyed garments from Bozrah? this that is glorious in his apparel, travelling in the greatness of his strength? I that speak in righteousness, mighty to save.**

In a modern revelation the Lord quoted from this chapter of Isaiah but gave a much improved version over the text that appears in our King James Version. This verse should read: "AND IT SHALL BE SAID: Who is this that cometh DOWN FROM GOD IN HEAVEN with dyed garments; YEA, FROM THE REGIONS WHICH ARE NOT KNOWN, clothed in his glorious apparel, traveling in the greatness of his strength?

AND HE SHALL SAY: I AM HE who spake in righteousness, mighty to save." (D&C 133:46–47; emphasis added.)

2. Wherefore art thou red in thine apparel, and thy garments like him that treadeth in the winefat?

This verse is also given somewhat differently: "AND THE LORD SHALL BE red in his apparel, and his garments like him that treadeth in the wine-vat" (D&C 133:48; emphasis added).

The red apparel of the Savior is the badge of his atoning sacrifice. It symbolizes that he washed his garments in "the blood of grapes" (Genesis 49:10–11), the wine of the grapes thereafter representing his great sacrifice (see 3 Nephi 18:8–11).

3. I have trodden the winepress alone; and of the people there was none with me: for I will tread them in mine anger, and trample them in my fury; and their blood shall be sprinkled upon my garments, and I will stain all my raiment.

This verse appeared as follows when the Lord quoted it in modern times: "AND HIS VOICE SHALL BE HEARD: I have trodden the wine-press alone, AND HAVE BROUGHT JUDGMENT UPON ALL PEOPLE; and none were with me" (D&C 133:50; emphasis added). This assignment required that the Savior fulfill this atoning sacrifice without help or assistance. Even the Father had to withdraw his sustaining spirit in order to make the infinite atonement perfect (see Matthew 27:46; Mark 15:34). Having thus fulfilled his mission, the Savior invites all mankind to partake of its blessings.

If they do not, each unrepentant person must suffer for his or her own sins. The Savior assures mankind that their suffering will be much more severe than they may have imagined (see D&C 19:15–20). They who have defiantly rejected the Lord and indulged in cheating, robbing, killing, fornication, adultery, and other forms of disobedience to his commandments will find the arm of justice reaching out over their heads when the Savior comes. They and their wickedness will be wiped off the face of the earth. They will be destroyed by the shedding of THEIR blood because they rejected the blood of the Savior's sacrifice. This will be done to cleanse wickedness from the earth, but so that the Savior might fulfill his role as a God of justice as well as a God of love. He says his apparel will be sprinkled with the blood of those who deserve to die.

4. For the day of vengeance is in mine heart, and the year of my redeemed is come.

In these verses the person who is speaking is the very Son of God, who had to watch humanity through several thousand years as the vast majority of mankind elected to debase themselves, plunder the weak, debauch the innocent, murder the defenseless, and rob the poor. How the Savior longed for the day when the earth could be cleansed of all this human corruption. Down through the centuries, this was in his heart.

5. And I looked, and there was none to help; and I wondered that there was none to uphold: therefore mine own arm brought salvation unto me; and my fury, it upheld me.

In the Garden of Gethsemane the Savior asked the Father to redeem mankind without requiring him to endure the terrifying and excruciating suffering on the cross (see Matthew 26:39; Mark 14:36). The Father had to send an angel to explain to him that there was no other way (Luke 22:42-43). He was the only one who could perform this great mission (Acts 4:10-12). Jesus finally told the Father, "Thy will be done" (Matthew 26:42). And the anguish of that hour caused him to sweat great drops of blood (Luke 22:44). All of this provides the background for this statement in verse 5, where the Savior says there was none who could do what he did. Now that he has performed this great service for mankind, he is justified in his anger when he finds the rebellious and unregenerate sons of evil spreading terror and bloodshed across the face of the earth and refusing to accept his sacrifice and the forgiveness which their repentance could bring.

6. And I will tread down the people in mine anger, and make them drunk in my fury, and I will bring down their strength to the earth.

So this is why the Lord will feel totally justified in using his omnipotent powers to impose a righteous judgment on the wicked and execute the penalty that goes with that judgment. The Lord says he will tread them down, and when they see the realities of God's judgment sweeping down upon them, the unrighteous men and women will go into a state of panic. It will be as though they were DRUNKEN with terror as they see the prospect of God's judgment engulfing them. God is determined to "bring down their strength to the earth" when he finally undertakes to cleanse their wicked way of life from off the face of this planet.

7. I will mention the loving-kindnesses of the LORD, and the praises of the LORD, according to all that the LORD hath bestowed on us, and the great goodness toward the house of Israel, which he hath bestowed on them according to his mercies, and according to the multitude of his loving-kindnesses.

At this point, Isaiah does not want the reader to misunderstand. The Lord is not a God of hate. The previous verses, which refer to the day when the righteous indignation of the Lord will be poured out upon the wicked, do not mean that it is done in a spirit of vindictive wrath. Rather, it is the role of the righteous judge executing judgment in the name of true justice. Isaiah says he wants to "mention the loving-kindnesses of the Lord" so that his anger with the wicked will not be misconstrued. Isaiah then goes on to remind the reader of the "great goodness [of the Lord] toward the house of Israel." He says this has been a dramatic demonstration of the loving-kindness of the Lord, even when Israel did not deserve it.

8. For he said, Surely they are my people, children that

He had chosen them to be his people. They entered into covenants with him. This was done in good faith.

will not lie: so he was their Saviour.

"Surely they . . . will not lie," he said. Thus he agreed to be their Savior.

9. In all their affliction he was afflicted, and the angel of his presence saved them: in his love and in his pity he redeemed them; and he bare them, and carried them all the days of old.

Isaiah reminds the reader that when Israel was afflicted, the Savior felt the pangs of their sufferings. He sent ministering angels to help and protect them. He undertook to redeem them. He carried them in his arms as though they were little children. All of this reflected his patience and lovingkindness toward them.

10. But they rebelled, and vexed his holy Spirit: therefore he was turned to be their enemy, and he fought against them.

When Israel became apostate and rebellious, the people not only violated their covenants with the Lord, but they began adopting the worst elements of the pagan practices around them. It "vexed" the Spirit of the Lord so that he turned away from them and treated them as enemies of righteousness. Instead of blessing them and caring for them, he raised up opposition and resistance in their way.

11. Then he remembered the days of old, Moses, and his people, saying, Where is he that brought them up out of the sea with the shepherd of his flock? where is he that put his holy Spirit within him?

12. That led them by the right hand of Moses with his glorious arm, dividing the water before them, to make himself an everlasting name?

13. That led them through the deep, as an horse in the wilderness, that they should not stumble?

Nevertheless, the Lord recalls with satisfaction the ancient times when he commanded Moses to bring Israel up out of Egypt. He put his spiritual power in Moses to divide the Red Sea and made Moses the Lord's shepherd to bring Israel out of captivity. These mighty miracles made the name of the Lord God Jehovah a glorious symbol of love and guidance among the Israelites. It gave them the assurance that, like the shepherd's flocks, they would be brought to a safe haven in the valley to rest if they would but follow the guidance of God.

14. As a beast goeth down into the valley, the Spirit of the LORD caused him to rest: so didst thou lead thy people, to make thyself a glorious name.

15. Look down from heaven, and behold from the habitation of thy holiness and of thy glory: where is thy zeal and thy strength, the sounding of thy bowels and of thy mercies toward me? are they restrained?

At this point Isaiah launches into a prayer of supplication to the Lord. He pleads with the Lord to look down on Israel with mercy and show forth his strength.

12. Doubtless thou art our father, though Abraham be ignorant of us, and Israel acknowledge us not: thou, O LORD, art our father, our redeemer; thy name is from everlasting.

Isaiah is saying that no doubt the Lord will continue to consider himself the Father of this people even though the Twelve Tribes of Israel came into existence long after Abraham, who received the original covenant, had passed away. Moses had admonished Israel to look upon the Lord as the "Father" of Israel. He said to them: "Do ye thus requite the Lord, O foolish people and unwise? is not he thy father that hath bought thee? hath he not made thee, and established thee?" (Deuteronomy 32:6.)

Notice that Isaiah says that "Israel acknowledge us not." In Isaiah's day, the northern Ten Tribes were usually referred to as "Israel." In this verse Isaiah is lamenting that the Ten Tribes had been taken far away by Assyria and they made no attempt to even acknowledge or contact Judah anymore.

17. O LORD, why hast thou made us to err from thy

Modern revelation has provided us with the text of this verse as Isaiah originally wrote it: "O Lord, why

ways, and hardened our heart from thy fear? Return for thy servants' sake, the tribes of thine inheritance.

hast thou SUFFERED us to err from thy ways, and TO HARDEN our heart from thy fear? Return for thy servants' sake, the tribes of thine inheritance." (Joseph Smith Translation, Isaiah 63:17; emphasis added.)

The Ten Tribes who had been taken away were in an extreme state of apostasy long before they were conquered and made captive of the Assyrians. Isaiah prays that for the sake of the Lord's spiritual leaders, or "servants," he will make it possible for the tribes to return.

18. The people of thy holiness have possessed it but a little while: our adversaries have trodden down thy sanctuary.

It is believed this verse should read, "The people of thy holy house [the temple] have possessed it but a little while." Then the last part makes better sense as Isaiah complains that "our adversaries have trodden down thy sanctuary," which is the temple.

19. We are thine: thou never barest rule over them; they were not called by thy name.

Isaiah emphasizes that he and his people are the Lord's chosen servants, and those who have trodden down the sanctuary have never been the subjects of the Lord's righteous government. Nor have they ever been known by his name. For this reason they should be driven from God's holy place.

INTRODUCTION:

This chapter continues the theme of the first six verses of the previous chapter—the Second Coming of Christ. This is referring to his sudden appearance just before the Millennium to cleanse the earth. All mankind will see him together, and the Saints will be caught up in order to escape the terrible destruction which will be loosed upon the earth. The Savior will come in red apparel to signify that he is the one who had "[trodden] the winepress alone" (Isaiah 63:3; D&C 133:50) and redeemed all who would repent and obey the commandments of God which lead to salvation.

Now we know that this chapter apparently had several introductory verses which are missing from the King James Version. Here is the way the Lord introduced Isaiah, chapter 64, in a modern revelation (D&C 133:37–40):

"And this gospel shall be preached unto every nation, and kindred, and tongue, and people.

"And the servants of God shall go forth, saying with a loud voice: Fear God and give glory to him, for the hour of his judgment is come;

"And worship him that made heaven, and earth, and the sea, and the fountains of waters—

"Calling upon the name of the Lord day and night, saying:" (At this point the revelation continues with the first verse of Isaiah, chapter 64.)

1. Oh that thou wouldest rend the heavens, that thou

Down through the centuries the prophets have known that when the Lord comes in glory there will be

wouldest come down, that the mountains might flow down at thy presence,

devastating convulsions in the earth. The destruction will be so terrible that the Saints will have to be caught up to escape. The great mountain ranges of the earth will seem to melt into their surrounding continental terrain and the valleys will come up to meet them. The symmetry of the earth's surface will be changed, and the Western Hemisphere will be once more joined with that of Europe and Africa. The seas will be driven back toward the poles, indicating that sunken continents in the Pacific will rise to push back the seas.

2. As when the melting fire burneth, the fire causeth the waters to boil, to make thy name known to thine adversaries, that the nations may tremble at thy presence!

Modern revelation gives this verse as follows:

"And it shall be answered upon their heads; for the presence of the Lord shall be as the melting fire that burneth, and as the fire which causeth the waters to boil.

"O Lord, thou shalt come down to make thy name known to thine adversaries, and all nations shall tremble at thy presence." (D&C 133:41-42.)

This is the time spoken of by Malachi when he said: "For, behold, the day cometh, that shall burn as an oven; and all the proud, yea, and all that do wickedly, shall be stubble: and the day that cometh shall burn them up, saith the Lord of hosts, that it shall leave them neither root nor branch." (Malachi 4:1.) The terror of this hour will cause the wicked to call upon the rocks to fall upon them and blot out their lives (Isaiah 2:19). They will yearn to escape the judgment which they had disdainfully ridiculed and claimed would never happen.

3. When thou didst terrible things which we looked not for, thou camest down, the mountains flowed down at thy presence.

As Isaiah contemplated what he had seen in vision, he could not help but express his amazement concerning the terrible destruction which is scheduled for the wicked at the time of the Second Coming. Who would have anticipated that the very mountains would FLOW DOWN at the presence of the Savior when he reveals himself in power and glory?

4. **For since the beginning of the world men have not heard, nor perceived by the ear, neither hath the eye seen, O God, beside thee, what he hath prepared for him that waiteth for him.**

On the other hand, Isaiah said that it was equally astonishing to learn what God had prepared by way of a blessing for those who had patiently waited for him, and who had lived out their earthly sojourn in faithful obedience to his commandments. Isaiah said it would never enter into the imagination of the human heart what great things the Lord has prepared for his righteous Saints.

5. **Thou meetest him that rejoiceth and worketh righteousness, those that remember thee in thy ways: behold, thou art wroth; for we have sinned: in those is continuance, and we shall be saved.**

In a modern revelation this verse is rendered more clearly: "Thou meetest him that worketh righteousness, and rejoiceth him that remembereth thee in thy ways; IN RIGHTEOUSNESS there is continuance, and SUCH shall be saved." (Joseph Smith Translation, Isaiah 64:5; emphasis added.)

In other words, he that accepts the gospel AND ENDURES TO THE END shall be saved.

6. **But we are all as an unclean thing, and all our righteousnesses are as filthy rags; and we all do fade as a leaf; and our iniquities, like the wind, have taken us away.**

This verse is also given with greater clarity by Joseph Smith: "But WE have sinned; we are all as an unclean thing, and all our righteousnesses are as filthy rags; and we all do fade as a leaf; and our iniquities, like the wind, have taken us away." (JST, Isaiah 64:6; emphasis added.)

The true prophets of God have never been self-righteous. They have recognized the frailties of both themselves and their fellowmen. They have been quick to confess these weaknesses and ask God to give them strength to overcome them.

7. And there is none that calleth upon thy name, that
stirreth up himself to take
hold of thee: for thou hast
hid thy face from us, and
hast consumed us, because
of our iniquities.

As Isaiah contemplated the suffering and wickedness among his own people, he could not help but confess that the people had ceased to call upon the Lord or stir themselves into activity as far as the Lord's work was concerned. Isaiah acknowledged that the Lord is justified in hiding his face from the people because of their sins and iniquities.

8. But now, O LORD, thou art
our Father; we are the clay,
and thou our potter; and we
all are the work of thy hand.

Isaiah makes the same plea that he did in the previous chapter. He reaffirms that the Lord is the "father" of this people. Isaiah says the people are like clay and the Lord is like the potter. Since the people are the work of the potter's hands, they should not be abandoned.

9. Be not wroth very sore,
O LORD, neither remem-
ber iniquity for ever: behold, see, we beseech thee,
we are all thy people.

Isaiah pleads with the Lord not to cast them off. He also asks him not to remember their blunders and iniquity forever. He emphasizes once again that he and his fellow Israelites are "all thy people."

10. Thy holy cities are a wilderness, Zion is a wilderness,
Jerusalem a desolation.

In his visions Isaiah had seen what would happen to Zion (the Western Hemisphere) and to the ancient city of Jerusalem. He saw the grandeur which existed under the Nephite civilization become a wilderness of ruins. He saw Jerusalem become a desolation.

11. Our holy and our beautiful
house, where our fathers
praised thee, is burned up
with fire: and all our pleasant things are laid waste.

He knew that the "beautiful house" of the Lord would be burned with fire, and all of her courts and surrounding precincts of vineyards, orchards, and "pleasant things" would become a desolate waste.

12. Wilt thou refrain thyself for these things, O LORD? wilt thou hold thy peace, and afflict us very sore?

Isaiah was led to ask questions just as the prophets before him had asked. In fact, most of his visions probably came in response to questions. In this instance he wants to know if the people can ever be restored to God's favor. Can they eventually have peace? Can they someday live without these afflictions?

Isaiah, Chapter 65

INTRODUCTION:

Isaiah concluded chapter 64 by asking if there would ever be a time when the Saints would no longer have to endure affliction. As Isaiah saw the vision of all the destruction which would come upon the wicked Israelites, he could not help but wonder how the Lord would bring about all of his wonderful promises concerning the redemption of his people and the ultimate establishment of righteousness in the earth. This present chapter contains the Lord's answer. Many of the verses are very similar to the Lord's answer to the modern Saints when they were driven from Jackson County, Missouri, and were wondering why such a great affliction had fallen upon them. They also wondered if Zion would ever be redeemed, seeing that they had been driven from its outermost boundaries. The Lord's answer is in the Doctrine and Covenants, section 101.

1. I am sought of them that asked not for me; I am found of them that sought me not: I said, Behold me, behold me, unto a nation that was not called by my name.

Down through the centuries of transcribing this verse many times, the copiers changed the words and accidentally distorted its true meaning. Here is the way it was given to Joseph Smith: "I am FOUND of them who SEEK AFTER ME, I GIVE UNTO ALL THEM THAT ASK OF ME; I am NOT found of them that sought me not, OR THAT INQUIRETH NOT AFTER ME" (JST, Isaiah 65:1; emphasis added).

In other words, the Lord is answering Isaiah by saying that he has never forsaken those who humbly sought him out. He has always given to them that asked for the sweet water of eternal life. On the other hand, he will not be discovered by those who turn disdainfully aside, nor will he pour out the blessings of the Gospel on the heads of those who do not seek after him.

The Joseph Smith Translation continues, "I SAID UNTO MY SERVANT, Behold me, LOOK UPON ME; I WILL SEND YOU unto a nation that is not called after my name" (JST, Isaiah 65:2; emphasis added).

The Lord is anticipating the day when the Gospel will be taken from Israel and preached among the Gentiles, a great body of people who were not originally called after the Lord's name, but who are entitled to hear the Gospel because it is to be preached to every nation, kindred, tongue, and people. Had Israel been obedient she could have built another City of Enoch and attracted the Gentiles to her, but since Israel apostatized, the Lord knew he would have to send the Gospel to the Gentiles.

2. I have spread out my hands all the day unto a rebellious people, which walketh in a way that was not good, after their own thoughts;

Here is the Lord's lamentation, but once again this verse is stated more completely in the restored version: "FOR I have spread out my hands all the day to a people who walketh not in my ways, AND THEIR WORKS ARE EVIL AND not good, AND THEY WALK after their own thoughts." (JST, Isaiah 65:2; emphasis added.) This is the Lord's explanation for the sorrow and darkness that will befall Israel because of her wickedness, and the reason why the Lord will send his messengers to another people (the Gentiles) who were not originally called his chosen ones. (This is the meaning of being "called by my name" [Isaiah 65:1]. This term refers to those who were chosen in the beginning, before the world was, to be the Lord's leaders for the rest of mankind. This is described in Deuteronomy 32:7-9.)

3. A people that provoketh me to anger continually to my face; that sacrificeth in gardens, and burneth incense upon altars of brick;

The Lord says that Israel has provoked him to indignation and anger continually. They have desecrated his ordinances and lived lives of such wickedness that it became an insult to his face. They did not go to the altars of unhewn stones which the priests of the Lord had consecrated for sacrifice, but they built their own private shrines of burned brick in their private gardens and burned idolatrous incense there.

4. Which remain among the graves, and lodge in the monuments, which eat swine's flesh, and broth of abominable things is in their vessels;

They also indulged in the worship of the dead. They set up their lodgings among the monuments which had been raised up to memorialize those who had passed away. This was a heathen practice. Today in Cairo, and many cities of the East, will be found a "city of the dead." There many of the people live with their dead and lodge among their monuments. The Lord said the Israelites had not only copied these practices from the heathen nations but also followed their practice of eating swine's flesh and broth of abominable "beasts" (JST, Isaiah 65:4) which the Lord had forbidden them to eat.

5. Which say, Stand by thyself, come not near to me; for I am holier than thou. These are a smoke in my nose, a fire that burneth all the day.

The Lord says that those Israelites who thus indulged themselves assumed that their lifestyle was greatly superior to others. They would say to all others, "Stand by thyself, come not near to me; for I am holier than thou." In their utter and contemptible self-righteousness, the Lord says they condemned themselves to hell. He says they are like smoke in his nostrils which causes one to choke and strangle in disgust. And it is not smoke from an occasional offense. It comes from a fire of abominable practices which burns offensively all the day long.

6. Behold, it is written before me: I will not keep silence, but will recompense, even recompense into their bosom,

God is a God of love, but, as we have previously mentioned, he is also a God of justice. He must therefore warn the wicked and rebellious Israelites of all ages that just as blessings are predicated on obedience to certain laws (see D&C 130:20-21), it is equally true that lives of pernicious evil have their "recompense." It is measured in the "bosom" of the offender, or according to the intents of his heart.

7. Your iniquities, and the iniquities of your fathers together, saith the LORD, which have burned incense upon the mountains, and blasphemed me upon the hills: therefore will I measure their former work into their bosom.

As the Lord contemplates the wickedness of Israel from generation to generation, his sense of justice calls for severe judgment. They have gone after licentious practices in the mountains where temples were built to the goddess of illicit love, and where incense was burned in her honor prior to indulging in the wild debaucheries connected with her rites.

8. Thus saith the LORD, As the new wine is found in the cluster, and one saith, Destroy it not; for a blessing is in it: so will I do for my servants' sakes, that I may not destroy them all.

Nevertheless, in spite of all these offenses against the Lord, he does not intend to destroy Israel and all her roots. True, there will be a great cleansing, but just as a vineyard is spared because of the occasional cluster of sweet fruit, so likewise the Lord intends to cleanse his vineyard—but he will "not destroy them all."

9. And I will bring forth a seed out of Jacob, and out of Judah an inheritor of my mountains: and mine elect shall inherit it, and my servants shall dwell there.

The Lord says there is going to be a remnant out of the seed of Jacob which will be preserved, and there will also be a few heirs of the tribe of Judah who will survive and inhabit God's holy mountain in Jerusalem. However, it will only be the "elect," those who are righteous and deserve an inheritance, who will receive the Lord's blessings. One of the greatest blessings will be the presence of the servants of the Lord, his prophets and apostles, who will eventually preside in these places to govern and guide the people.

10. And Sharon shall be a fold of flocks, and the valley of Achor a place for the herds to lie down in, for my people that have sought me.

In those days when the remnant of the Jews return to rehabilitate the land of Jerusalem, the plains of Sharon along the coast will be a place of marvelous abundance. It is interesting that after the destruction of the Jews by the Romans, the plains of Sharon were neglected. Sand dunes accumulated along the beaches from the tides, and this cut off the drainage from the mountains. They therefore became malarial swamps. When the remnants of the tribe of Judah began to return in modern times they purchased these swamplands and drained them. Today they are some of the richest producers of citrus, truck gardening, and various kinds of fruit and flocks that exist in the entire Mediterranean basin. Great blessings will also come to "Achor." This is believed to be the "valley of trouble" where Achan was stoned because of his disobedience to the Lord by attempting to preserve some idolatrous artifacts consisting of "a goodly Babylonish garment," which was an "accursed thing," and gold and silver, which apparently belonged to the idol's treasury (see Joshua 7:1, 6–26). This region is believed to be the area not far from Jericho on the West Bank of the Jordan. For many years it was so barren that even donkeys and goats could barely survive there. Today, however, it is beginning to flourish again. The Lord promises in this verse that the baren wastes of the West Bank will some day be inhabited by abundant flocks and herds.

11. But ye are they that forsake the LORD, that forget my holy mountain, that prepare a table for that troop,

Nevertheless, the Lord wants to make it clear that just because a person has been allowed to inhabit this choice part of the earth, it does not mean that he can take it for granted. If the people who are thus blessed in

and that furnish the drink offering unto that number.

the latter days forsake the Lord, they can expect to suffer destruction along with the wicked Gentiles. It will be noted that the Joseph Smith Translation emphasizes this very point by rendering the first part of this verse as follows: "But you who forsake the Lord, who forget my holy mountain..." should know that the sword of justice is hanging over you. This is especially true for those who no longer listen to the prophets or believe in the divine destiny of this choice land. He warns that those who surrender themselves to Gad (the pagan god of fortune, mistranslated "troop") and depend upon Meni (the god of fate, mistranslated "number") will find themselves in the eye of the hurricane of destruction referred to by the Lord in a modern revelation, where he said:

"Behold, vengeance cometh speedily upon the inhabitants of the earth, a day of wrath, a day of burning, a day of desolation, of weeping, of mourning, and of lamentation; and as a whirlwind it shall come upon all the face of the earth, saith the Lord.

"AND UPON MY HOUSE SHALL IT BEGIN, AND FROM MY HOUSE SHALL IT GO FORTH, SAITH THE LORD;

"First among those among YOU, saith the Lord, who have professed to know my name and have not known me, and have blasphemed against me in the midst of my house [the Lord's temple], saith the Lord." (D&C 112:24–26.)

12. Therefore will I number you to the sword, and ye shall all bow down to the slaughter: because when I called, ye did not answer; when I spake, ye did not hear; but did evil before mine eyes, and did choose

The Lord declares that all of those who called themselves Saints and heirs of the kingdom will find that their going to God's temple unworthily, and literally blaspheming his name by lying to get their recommends, will reap a terrible recompense in God's hour of judgment. They will not find themselves and their wicked families being protected and rescued from

that wherein I delighted not.

destruction by the Lord. Rather, they will find themselves being put to the sword and will go down in the wave of "slaughter" which will sweep over the land. The Lord says all of this will happen because these wicked people in both Jerusalem and Zion did not heed the call of God when his prophets commanded that they repent. They did not answer the call with godly sorrow and good works. Instead they revelled in their secret wickedness. They chose to do that which is repugnant to the Lord and participate in those things in which he finds no delight whatsoever.

13. Therefore thus saith the Lord GOD, Behold, my servants shall eat, but ye shall be hungry: behold, my servants shall drink, but ye shall be thirsty: behold, my servants shall rejoice, but ye shall be ashamed:

In contrast to this, the Lord says his righteous and obedient Saints in both Jerusalem and Zion will be rescued. Those who serve God in righteousness during the latter days will have food when the wicked among them who did not take the welfare program seriously will go hungry. The righteous will have nourishment and be able to quench their thirst when the wicked will not. It will be a time when the righteous who patiently waited on the Lord will rejoice mightily, but the wicked will stand condemned and ashamed.

14. Behold, my servants shall sing for joy of heart, but ye shall cry for sorrow of heart, and shall howl for vexation of spirit.

When the Lord finally divides the wheat from the tares, it will be very plain to everyone what is about to happen. Those who have conscientiously served the Lord, performed missions, paid their tithes, helped to build temples, and kept themselves unspotted from the sins of the world will see the hand of the Lord revealed to rescue them from the terrors of destruction which will begin sweeping across the earth. They will sing songs of praise and thanksgiving as they see themselves preserved and blessed. On the other hand, Isaiah saw that those who had betrayed their callings and were not valiant would cry out in the anguish of their hearts and the vexation of their spirits. It would cause them to "howl" as they saw the hour of destruction sweeping down upon them.

15. And ye shall leave your name for a curse unto my chosen: for the Lord GOD shall slay thee, and call his servants by another name:

Those who only pretended to be Saints will be remembered with abhorrence when it is finally revealed how much damage they did to the cause of Zion. Their fate will be sealed up with the rest of the wicked in the conflagration of destruction which will sweep the earth. Meanwhile, the servants of the Lord will be called by another name. From time to time the Lord has changed the name of his chosen people. In the days of Enoch they were referred to by the Lord as Zion (see Moses 7:18-19). In the days of Moses, God's people were called Israel (Exodus 3:16 and the Old Testament thereafter), which means "soldiers of God," or those who overcome with God (see McConkie, *Mormon Doctrine,* p. 389). In the days of the Savior's ministry they were called the Church of Christ (3 Nephi 26:21; 28:23; 4 Nephi 1:1). In modern times, those who respond to the fulness of the restored Gospel are called The Church of Jesus Christ of Latter-day Saints (D&C 115:4). However, the Lord says that those "who overcome by faith, and are sealed by the Holy Spirit of promise" (D&C 76:53), and who are considered worthy to be caught up "in the clouds" (D&C 76:63) at the time of the great judgment, will be referred to as "the church of the Firstborn" (D&C 76:54). This appears to be the new name by which God will call his people during the Millennium (see D&C 76:54, 102; 78:21; and many similar references in the index under "Church of the Firstborn").

16. That he who blesseth himself in the earth shall bless

It is the very nature of mankind to seek self-improvement or blessings. However, some seek

himself in the God of truth; and he that sweareth in the earth shall swear by the God of truth; because the former troubles are forgotten, and because they are hid from mine eyes.

personal advantages by becoming a law unto themselves. The Lord wants mankind to know that "there is a law, irrevocably decreed in heaven before the foundations of this world, upon which all blessings are predicated—and when we obtain any blessing from God, it is by obedience to that law upon which it is predicated" (D&C 130:20-21). During the Millennium those who live upon the earth and seek to be blessed will do so by obedience to those laws which bring such blessings, and when they make their oaths or covenants they will swear "by the God of truth," and then abide by their sacred oaths in order to receive his blessings. Because of this, the Lord says that all the "former troubles"—the wars, famines, concentration camps, tortures, executions, degradation, poverty, and debauchery—will all be forgotten, for they will no longer exist anywhere on the face of the earth to offend the righteous eyes of God.

17. **For, behold, I create new heavens and a new earth: and the former shall not be remembered, nor come into mind.**

Everything will be changed when the earth graduates from its present "telestial" state of its mortal existence (the lowest through which it passes) and moves up to the "paradisiacal" or intermediate stage similar to the one which existed before the Fall. Eventually, there will be the third stage when the earth is resurrected into its final, celestial glory. However, this verse is referring to the renewing of the heavens and the earth at the beginning of the Millennium, which is the intermediate stage. The changes will be so great that the Lord says there will be "new heavens and a new earth," and the paradisiacal glory of the earth will be so marvelous that the terrible, wicked conditions through which we are now passing "shall not be remembered, nor come into mind."

The term "new heavens" mentioned in this verse no doubt refers to the new cosmic environment in which the earth will exist after "the earth shall remove out of her place" (Isaiah 13:13). Isaiah says the earth will be like a "chased roe" as it goes racing back toward the precincts of Kolob (Isaiah 13:14). Because astronomers say the earth is approximately 30,000 light years away from the center of our galaxy, the speed with which the earth is taken back will be of almost incomprehensible swiftness—faster than the speed of light. It will appear as though the stars are falling from heaven (see Matthew 24:29; Joseph Smith—Matthew 1:33). The light of the sun and the moon will be hidden from sight (ibid.). When Isaiah saw the vision of this catastrophic transition, he said: "And all the host [stars] of heaven shall be dissolved, and the heavens shall be rolled together as a scroll: and all their host [of stars] shall fall down, as the leaf falleth off from the vine, and as a falling fig from the fig tree." (Isaiah 34:4.) Those who are still alive on the earth will undoubtedly think the clusters of stars whirling past the speeding earth are falling from heaven.

The "new earth" refers to the cleansing of the earth by fire (see Malachi 4:1), the driving back of the seas to the poles (D&C 133:23), and the restoring of all the continents and islands to the places they occupied before the days of Peleg (D&C 133:24). The Lord also says the mountains will be broken down and the deep valleys "shall not be found" (D&C 133:22).

The Lord says that the new, paradisiacal earth will be so marvelous that the sights and scenes of the old earth will "not be remembered, nor come into mind."

18. **But be ye glad and rejoice for ever in that which I create: for, behold, I create Jerusalem a rejoicing, and her people a joy.**

The Lord wants his people to be "glad and rejoice for ever in that which [he has created]." He assures the Israelites of Isaiah's day that during the Millennium the ancient city of Jerusalem will be exalted and her people will be filled with rejoicing.

19. And I will rejoice in Jerusalem, and joy in my people: and the voice of weeping shall be no more heard in her, nor the voice of crying.

Furthermore, the Lord will be there to rejoice with his people. It will be an age of peace, happiness, and accomplishment. There will be no occasion for weeping or crying out in anguish as happened so frequently during the history of Jerusalem in the past.

20. There shall be no more thence an infant of days, nor an old man that hath not filled his days: for the child shall die an hundred years old; but the sinner being an hundred years old shall be accursed.

This verse is clarified somewhat in the Joseph Smith Translation: "IN THOSE DAYS there shall be no more thence an infant of days, nor an old man that hath not filled his days; for the child shall NOT die, but shall LIVE to be an hundred years old; but the sinner, living to be an hundred years old, shall be accursed." (JST, Isaiah 65:20; emphasis added.)

The Lord refers to this same theme in a modern revelation where he says: "And there shall be no sorrow because there is no death.

"In that day an infant shall not die until he is old; and his life shall be as the age of a tree;

"And when he dies he shall not sleep, that is to say in the earth, but shall be changed in the twinkling of an eye, and shall be caught up, and his rest shall be glorious." (D&C 101:29-31.)

From this we learn that there will be no infant mortality during the Millennium. The righteous will live to the age of 100 and then be resurrected in the twinkling of an eye. However, those who are less than valiant will not receive this blessing. They will be "accursed," which suggests that they will have to sleep in the grave and await their resurrection at a later time.

21. And they shall build houses, and inhabit them; and they shall plant vineyards, and eat the fruit of them.

Now comes the promise of peace and security which mankind has been seeking since the days of Adam. One of the greatest blessings in earth life is to build homes and be able to possess them without disturbance or molestation. Equally gratifying is the sense of security which comes with the planting of crops and vineyards, knowing that the fruits of the harvest will not be stolen, destroyed, or taken away by a predatory ruler.

22. **They shall not build, and another inhabit; they shall not plant, and another eat: for as the days of a tree are the days of my people, and mine elect shall long enjoy the work of their hands.**

In this verse the Lord confirms that war, theft, vandalism, and predatory government will no longer take away that which a person has built, or the fruits of the crops he has planted. In fact, the Lord says that since the life of human beings and that of a tree will be the same (100 years), the planter of orchards will live as long as the trees which he has cultivated and preserved as part of his earthly estate.

23. **They shall not labour in vain, nor bring forth for trouble; for they are the seed of the blessed of the LORD, and their offspring with them.**

So often in man's present condition, he often labors "in vain" and has the fruits of his labor snatched away. But this will not be the case during the Millennium. The righteous Saints will be called "the seed of the blessed of the Lord," and their children shall be of the covenant so that they will receive the same blessings.

24. **And it shall come to pass, that before they call, I will answer; and while they are yet speaking, I will hear.**

Throughout the Millennium, the Lord will have a very close association with the Saints. He will read their hearts and know their feelings. Therefore he says, "Before they call, I will answer; and while they are yet speaking, I will hear."

25. **The wolf and the lamb shall feed together, and the lion shall eat straw like the bullock: and dust shall be the serpent's meat. They**

Now the Lord makes a declaration which is almost incredible to mankind in our own day. The Lord says that during the Millennium all creatures will be able to survive without destroying one another. Carnivorous

shall not hurt nor destroy in all my holy mountain, saith the LORD.

animals in our own day thrive on the meat of weaker prey. During the Millennium they will feed on plants. Even serpents will thrive without devouring small animals as many of them do now. Not only will all enmity cease among the animals of the earth, but it appears that mankind will also cease to be hunters and butchers to feed on the flesh of animals. The Lord says that nothing shall "hurt nor destroy in all my holy mountain." As the Lord says in a modern revelation, "And in that day the enmity of MAN, and the enmity of beasts, yea, the enmity of all flesh, shall cease from before my face" (D&C 101:26).

Isaiah, Chapter 66

INTRODUCTION:

This chapter has three themes which more or less summarize the most important aspects of Isaiah's prophetic message concerning the latter days:

1. Israel, as a nation, shall be "born" in one day.

2. The wicked shall be destroyed.

3. The Gentiles will hear the Gospel.

1. Thus saith the LORD, The heaven is my throne, and the earth is my footstool: where is the house that ye build unto me? and where is the place of my rest?

This verse introduces the theme that when the great Millennium is ushered in, the Lord will make the earth his dwelling place. It is his footstool, meaning the place where his feet shall rest. He therefore asks about his house in which he can dwell and the place where he can call his place of rest or a place of dwelling. No doubt this is referring to a temple, which the Lord says "my people are always commanded to build unto my holy name" (D&C 124:39).

2. For all those things hath mine hand made, and all those things have been, saith the LORD: but to this man will I look, even to him that is poor and of a contrite spirit, and trembleth at my word.

The Lord reminds us here that all things we behold in the earth and in the heavens are things which in their original state "[his] hand made." And when the Lord comes to minister upon the earth, there will be one type of humanity on whom he will look with kindness and approbation. It will be "him that is poor and of a contrite spirit." The proud and the haughty, the stubborn and the unteachable, are not those to whom the Lord will entrust his great revelations or with whom he will carry on "conversations" (D&C

124:39). Rather, his conversations will be with "him that ... trembleth at my word," who appreciates the magnificence, the excitement, and the responsibility of receiving so much light and knowledge.

3. He that killeth an ox is as if he slew a man; he that sacrificeth a lamb, as if he cut off a dog's neck; he that offereth an oblation, as if he offered swine's blood; he that burneth incense, as if he blessed an idol. Yea, they have chosen their own ways, and their soul delighteth in their abominations.

There were those who came to the temple in Isaiah's day whose sacrifices and oblations were in vain. The same is true of those who seek an endowment in the temple in our own day but who enter its sacred premises unworthily. Speaking of such people in the days of blood sacrifices, the Lord says some came to his altars to slay an ox and did it in the spirit of killing a man (i.e., to rob or get gain). They sacrificed a lamb with no more thought of the true meaning of this sacred ceremony than if they were cutting off the head of a dog. The wine or water oblation was poured out on the altar or sacred place with no more sense of godly worship than if they were pouring out swine's blood— something completely forbidden to the Israelites. The incense, which was supposed to represent their prayers ascending to heaven, was offered with no more consideration than if it were being offered in adoration of an idol. God pronounces his strongest indictment against all of these unworthy exercises at his sacred altars. It is not God's way of worship. Those guilty of such sacrilegious insults to the Lord's house "have chosen their own ways, and their soul delighteth in their abominations."

This same lesson could be applied to our own day, when some thoughtlessly partake of the sacrament with unclean hands and impure hearts. The sacrament is to renew covenants after a person has repented of his wrongdoing, repaired the wrong to the best of his ability, and presented himself before the Lord with a broken heart and a contrite spirit.

4. I also will choose their delusions, and will bring their fears upon them; because when I called, none did answer; when I spake, they did not hear: but they did evil before mine eyes, and chose that in which I delighted not.

Those who claim to be the people of the Lord but offer sacrifices unworthily (because their hearts and minds are unworthy) will reap such a whirlwind of delusions and destruction that it will cause their hearts to fail them for fear. The Lord says this condemnation will come upon those who were "called" but did not hear or respond. They ignored calls to serve on missions, to accept callings of responsibility, or to contribute their tithes and offerings and build up the kingdom. Instead, they went their own way, violating the Sabbath, indulging in a worldly lifestyle, and doing those things in which God takes no delight.

5. Hear the word of the LORD, ye that tremble at his word; Your brethren that hated you, that cast you out for my name's sake, said, Let the LORD be glorified: but he shall appear to your joy, and they shall be ashamed.

Now the Lord speaks a word of comfort to those who are anxious to hear the message of the Lord and "tremble at his word." He assures them that he fully recognizes that those haughty members of the Church who looked down on their more humble brethren with disdain, and even despised them by casting them out from their more exclusive circles, will claim that they were doing this to improve the quality of the Lord's kingdom and thereby honor God's name. But the Lord says he can easily perceive what was really in their hearts. When he comes to make up his jewels, the humble and contrite members of the Church who continuously moved forward in quiet obedience to all the commandments will be the ones who will have great joy as the Lord honors and acclaims them. The others will be denounced and rejected. They will be ashamed to face their Maker.

6. A voice of noise from the city, a voice from the temple, a voice of the LORD that

When the Lord comes there will be a mighty voice of judgment uttered from his holy city. It will emanate from the temple where he has come to dwell. He will

rendereth recompence to his enemies.

pronounce a judgment of justice upon the wicked to recompense them according to their works.

---

7. Before she travailed, she brought forth; before her pain came, she was delivered of a man child.

On the other hand, from out of obscurity a humble people who were treated indifferently by the world will suddenly emerge as a mighty nation of righteousness, purity, strength, and virtue. Almost like a child born without travail, this nation of loyal sons and daughters of God will suddenly come into being.

---

8. Who hath heard such a thing? who hath seen such things? Shall the earth be made to bring forth in one day? or shall a nation be born at once? for as soon as Zion travailed, she brought forth her children.

There will have been nothing like it before in all human history. How can a humble people who were scattered abroad in the earth suddenly gather together in a mighty throng of righteous, well-organized humanity and become, as it were, a nation in one day? But this is what will happen. The great last gathering of the people of God to Zion will raise up a commonwealth of the pure in heart that will become an astonishment to the whole earth.

---

9. Shall I bring to the birth, and not cause to bring forth? saith the LORD: shall I cause to bring forth, and shut the womb? saith thy God.

To any who might doubt this sudden accomplishment, the Lord extends a point of inquiry. Do they believe that after all the preparation and careful gestation of his kingdom he cannot bring it into full term and have it come forth a mighty nation in one day? The Lord assures the doubter he is able to do it. The travail and preparation for birth will not be frustrated. His kingdom shall come forth.

---

10. Rejoice ye with Jerusalem, and be glad with her, all ye

Not only will this be true of Zion (mentioned in verse 8), but it will also be true of Jerusalem, where the Jews

that love her: rejoice for joy with her, all ye that mourn for her:

will be gathered. The Lord wants the people of Zion in America to rejoice as well as his children in Jerusalem. He invites those who loved Jerusalem and mourned for her long period of suffering and persecution to now rejoice as she becomes liberated from her enemies and is rebuilt into a beautiful metropolis of godly glory.

11. That ye may suck, and be satisfied with the breasts of her consolations; that ye may milk out, and be delighted with the abundance of her glory.

When the people of Zion see how completely the Lord will fulfill every promise he made to the prophets concerning Jerusalem's final beautification, it will nourish their souls with the deepest satisfaction and pleasure. They will be "delighted with the abundance of her glory."

12. For thus saith the LORD, Behold, I will extend peace to her like a river, and the glory of the Gentiles like a flowing stream: then shall ye suck, ye shall be borne upon her sides, and be dandled upon her knees.

The name "Jerusalem" comes from a Hebrew word which means place of peace, and that is what it will eventually be. The Lord says, "I will extend peace to her like a river." The Gentiles will come to hear the Gospel from her teachers and drink of the living waters of the Gospel, which will be ministered from Jerusalem "like a flowing stream." Those who come to be taught will partake like suckling children held in the laps of their mother.

13. As one whom his mother comforteth, so will I comfort you; and ye shall be comforted in Jerusalem.

The Lord declares that just as a mother nourishes and comforts her children, so will he comfort all who come to Jerusalem to hear the Gospel and receive the ministration of the Lord's servants.

14. And when ye see this, your heart shall rejoice, and your

This hour of power in righteousness will be a great source of joy and satisfaction for those who have

bones shall flourish like an herb: and the hand of the LORD shall be known toward his servants, and his indignation toward his enemies.

patiently waited for the day of the Lord's redemption and judgment. The Lord assures his children that the great day of his power is coming. It will be apparent to all mankind that "the hand of the Lord shall be known toward his servants," and those who have been wicked and done violence to God's people will feel the wrath of his indignation.

15. For, behold, the LORD will come with fire, and with his chariots like a whirlwind, to render his anger with fury, and his rebuke with flames of fire.

The Lord is a Savior of love and compassion, but he is also a mighty judge who is required to restore equity and justice among mankind so that the innocent who have suffered so much affliction will see the scales of recompense fully balanced by God's mighty hand of judgment. Therefore, the earth will seem to be visited in the day of his coming with a conflagration of consuming cremation as the Lord's chariots of fire sweep through the earth.

16. For by fire and by his sword will the LORD plead with all flesh: and the slain of the LORD shall be many.

This terrible day of judgment will be just as frightening and just as devastating as the prophets predicted. The abomination of desolation of war by fire and sword will devour whole nations so that those who will be slain in that day will be "many."

17. They that sanctify themselves, and purify themselves in the gardens behind one tree in the midst, eating swine's flesh, and the abomination, and the mouse, shall be consumed together, saith the LORD.

The destruction will sweep down those who have been trying to sanctify themselves with the ancient heathen indulgences of sex worship, seeking peace and pleasure by going into their gardens and extending their adoration to their false god of seductive passion, their fertility god. Anciently, the Israelites worshipped before "one tree," which was usually carved into a phallic symbol, in the midst of their garden. They indulged themselves in everything which was unclean and an abomination before the Lord. All of these wicked practices brought destruction to the apostates of ancient Israel. The Lord declares that those who follow this same trail of the serpent in the latter days will be "consumed together."

18. For I know their works and their thoughts: it shall come, that I will gather all nations and tongues; and they shall come, and see my glory.

The Lord also assures mankind that he knows their works and their thoughts, whether they be good or evil. He will therefore know how to gather out the righteous from every nation, kindred, tongue, and people; and he will also know how to gather the wicked into bundles by themselves so that they may be burned. Those who survive will see the glory of God as he makes bare his mighty arm in judgment. They will rejoice to see the time of his promised coming fulfilled.

19. And I will set a sign among them, and I will send those that escape of them unto the nations, to Tarshish, Pul, and Lud, that draw the bow, to Tubal, and Javan, to the isles afar off, that have not heard my fame, neither have seen my glory; and they shall declare my glory among the Gentiles.

Among those who escape this terrible destruction, there will be a mighty ensign raised up. In ancient times an ensign was raised up near the tent of the king so that wherever the ensign appeared they knew their leader was in that place. In the day of God's judgment, there will be a mighty ensign so that the people of the earth will know where they can rally to receive guidance and direction from the Lord and his officers. Perhaps this is the time when the 144,000 high priests will be sent forth as described in a modern revelation: "They are they who are ordained out of every nation, kindred, tongue, and people, by the angels to whom is given power over the nations of the earth, to bring as many as will come to the church of the Firstborn." (D&C 77:11; see also Revelation 7:4.)

The Lord says these messengers will go to the various Gentile nations represented by Tarshish (Spain), Pul (Lybia), Lud (Lydia, which was famous for its mighty bowmen); and also Tubal and Javan, two Gentile nations of the north. These messengers will also go "to the isles afar off," to people that have never heard the message of the Gospel nor the glory and fame of the Lord Jesus Christ. All these "Gentiles" will finally get to hear the message.

20. And they shall bring all your brethren for an offering unto the LORD out of all nations upon horses, and in chariots, and in litters, and upon mules, and upon swift beasts, to my holy mountain Jerusalem, saith the LORD, as the children of Israel bring an offering in a clean vessel into the house of the LORD.

The thousands of converts who will be harvested from this mighty missionary effort will be gathered to the "holy mountain Jerusalem" (no doubt including a similar gathering to the New Jerusalem as well), and they will be like a gift offering which these mighty high priests will make in righteousness to the Lord.

21. And I will also take of them for priests and for Levites, saith the LORD.

The Lord says he will take from among these worthy and valiant servants those who will be his "priests" and his "Levites" over the people. In ancient Israel it was the "priests" who attended to the spiritual ordinances and the "Levites" who ministered to their temporal needs. It will therefore be from among these worthy and proven missionary quorums of the latter days that the Lord will choose his presiding authorities for the whole earth.

22. For as the new heavens and the new earth, which I will make, shall remain before me, saith the LORD, so shall your seed and your name remain.

The Lord wants these members of his ministry to know that this is no temporary arrangement. Just as the new heavens and the new earth will abide before the Lord, so also shall the Priesthood holders and their children after them be honored by the Lord in these great callings of righteous service.

23. And it shall come to pass, that from one new moon to another, and from one sabbath to another, shall all flesh come to worship before me, saith the LORD.

The day of which the Lord is speaking will be far different from the days of wickedness which preceded it. Instead of the multitudes of mankind largely ignoring or defying God and reveling in their wicked indulgences, the whole inhabited earth will come up regularly to their designated places of worship to express their adoration for the Lord and seek instructions from his servants.

24. And they shall go forth, and look upon the carcases of the men that have transgressed against me: for their worm shall not die, neither shall their fire be quenched; and they shall be an abhorring unto all flesh.

It will not be difficult to remember the Lord in that day, for during the season of God's judgment the masses of humanity that have been slain will be a terrible torment to the living. The carcasses of the slain will be scattered across the face of the land. The odor of death and decay will be an offense to all the living until their bodies have either been devoured by the worm or cremated in fires of cleansing. The burning or disposing of these decaying bodies will continue until the entire face of the earth has been cleared of this human debris which will be so abhorrent to all of the survivors. Thus will the earth be purified so that mankind can enter into the great new era of peace on earth, good will toward men.

Bibliography

Clarke, Adam. *The Holy Bible . . . with a Commentary and Critical Notes.* 6 vols. Nashville: Abingdon Press, n.d.

Conference Report.

Dummelow, J.R. *A Commentary on the Holy Bible.* New York: Macmillan Publishing Co., 1949.

Hastings, James, ed. *Dictionary of the Bible.* Rev. ed. New York: Charles Scribner's Sons, 1963.

Herrmann, Paul. *Conquest by Man.* Translated by Michael Bullock. New York: Harper & Brothers, 1954.

Interpreter's Bible. 12 vols. Nashville: Abingdon, 1956.

Josephus, Flavius. *Josephus: Complete Works.* Translated by William Whiston. Grand Rapids, Mich.: Kregel Publications, 1960.

Journal of Discourses. 26 vols.

Keyes, Nelson Beecher. *Story of the Bible World.* Pleasantville, N.Y.: Reader's Digest Association, 1962.

Lundwall, N. B. *Temples of the Most High.* Salt Lake City: Bookcraft, 1968.

McConkie, Bruce R. *Mormon Doctrine.* 2d ed. Salt Lake City: Bookcraft, 1966.

Nibley, Hugh. *Since Cumorah.* Salt Lake City: Deseret Book Co., 1967.

Nyman, Monte S. *Great Are the Words of Isaiah.* Salt Lake City: Bookcraft, 1980.

Old Testament: 1 Kings–Malachi [Religion 302 student manual]. Salt Lake City: The Church of Jesus Christ of Latter-day Saints, 1981.

Peloubet, Francis N., ed. *Peloubet's Bible Dictionary.* Philadelphia: John C. Winston Co., 1925.

Reynolds, George, and Sjodahl, Janne M. *Commentary on the Book of Mormon.* 7 vols. Salt Lake City: Deseret Book Co. 1958.

Roberts, Brigham H. *A Comprehensive History of the Church.* 6 vols. with index.

Skousen, W. Cleon. *Fantastic Victory: Israel's Rendezvous with Destiny.* Salt Lake City: Bookcraft, 1967.

———. *Prophecy and Modern Times.* Salt Lake City: Deseret Book Co., 1948.

———. *The First 2,000 Years.* Salt Lake City: Bookcraft, 1953.

———. *The Fourth Thousand Years.* Salt Lake City: Bookcraft, 1966.

———. *The Third Thousand Years.* Salt Lake City: Bookcraft, 1964.

Smith, Joseph. *History of the Church of Jesus Christ of Latter-day Saints.* 7 vols. with index, 2d ed. rev. Salt Lake City: Deseret Book Co., 1978. (Commonly known as *Documentary History of the Church.*)

————. *Teachings of the Prophet Joseph Smith.* Selected by Joseph Fielding Smith. Salt Lake City: Deseret Book Co., 1938.

Smith, William. *A Dictionary of the Bible.* Rev. ed. Grand Rapids, Mich.: Zondervan Publishing House, 1967.

Sperry, Sidney B. *Book of Mormon Compendium.* Salt Lake City: Bookcraft, 1968.

————. *Our Book of Mormon.* 4th ed. Salt Lake City: Bookcraft, 1947.

————. *The Old Testament Prophets.* Salt Lake City: Deseret Sunday School Union, 1965.

————. *The Voice of Israel's Prophets.* Salt Lake City: Deseret Book Co., 1952.

Strong, James. *The Exhaustive Concordance of the Bible.* Nashville: Abingdon, 1980.

Young, Brigham. *Discourses of Brigham Young.* Compiled by John A. Widtsoe. Salt Lake City: Deseret Book Co., 1954.

Index

A

Abraham, writings of, translated by Joseph Smith, 105; marries Sarai, 289; descendants of, to bless all nations, 534-35; ancestor of God's chosen people, 633; knew and testified of Jesus Christ, 655

Adam, saw in vision the future history of the world, 3; knew and testified of Christ, 655

Agnostics, absence of, during Millennium, 141

Ahaz (king of Judah), Isaiah's encounter with, 19-20; death of, 25, 230, 285; Isaiah ministers during reign of, 145; wickedness of, 199; Isaiah prophesies to, 200-207; invited to ask for a sign from God, 203

Alcoholism, in ancient Israel, denounced by Isaiah, 20, 21, 181, 186, 384, 385, 386, 689

Aliyah (Jewish migration to Palestine), the First, 123; the Second, 124; the Third, 124

Amaziah (king of Judah), Isaiah may have been a nephew of, 145

America, its early history foreseen by Isaiah and Nephi, 80; to be preserved as a land of liberty, 80-81; the latter-day "Mount Zion," 81; discovery by Columbus foretold, 81-82; conquered and inhabited by European Gentiles, 82-83, 399; wars for independence foretold, 83; latter-day restoration of the Gospel in, 85, 119; Israelites in, addressed by Isaiah, 88-89; North and South, referred to as "Zion," 111, 286, 620, 669; Gentiles to inhabit, as a free people, 119; New Jerusalem to be built in, 120-21, 313; world's largest Jewish population in, 124; Isaiah's visions and prophecies of, 309-13, 397-422, 464-66, 533-41; to be protected during destruction of last days, 362-63; remnant from Jerusalem escapes to, in 600 B.C., 501-2; Spanish invaders in, mistaken for Jesus Christ, 547; God to comfort and bless his people in, 634; kings astonished at establishment of a free people in, 653-54; latter-day gathering to, 667-70; coming domestic warfare among Gentiles in, 670; desolate cities of, to be inhabited by Ten Tribes of Israel, 670; free nation established in, so that Gospel could be safely restored, 680; the only refuge of peace in last days, 717. *See also* New Jerusalem; Rocky Mountains; Zion

Amil-Marduk (king of Babylon), reign of, 273

Amoz, father of Isaiah, 145

Animals, enmity of, to cease during Millennium, 140-41, 244-46, 760-61. *See also* Creatures

Anthon, Charles, examines transcript from Book of Mormon plates, 99-100, 417; noted American classicist, 413, 414

Anti-Semitism, Latter-day Saints not to harbor feelings of, 250; condemned by Heber J. Grant, 251

Arabia, conquered by Assyria, 336-38

Arabs, to be united with Jews as God's people in last days, 127-29; similarities to the Jews, 128

Ariel, meaning of, 397-98

Ark of the Covenant, described, 497-98

Armageddon, battle of, 161, 169, 322-23, 523-24, 639-42

Ashdod (Canaanite city), conquered by Assyria, 327, 328

Assyria, conquers northern Ten Tribes of Israel, 24-25, 33, 181-82, 229-30, 271, 284, 304-5, 327-28, 385; destruction of, foreseen by Isaiah, 25, 49-50, 234-35, 498-503; conquers 46 cities of Judah and threatens Jerusalem, 33-37, 40-42, 147, 212-13, 271, 434, 445, 457, 485, 486-92; 185,000 soldiers of, slain by God, 41, 446, 457, 458, 459, 503-4; to be converted to restored Gospel in last days, 129, 382; Isaiah prophesies conquest of Syria and Ten Tribes by, 201, 202, 209, 211-14, 225-27; Isaiah prophesies invasion of Judah by, 205-7; brutality of its military policy, 211; seeks to conquer Egypt, 219, 220, 221, 229, 495; kings of, 229-30, 329; not allowed to conquer Judah, 236-37, 444-45; destroyed by Babylon in 605 B.C., 260, 272, 284, 306-7, 331-35; conquers Philistines, 285-86; conquers Moab, 292-301; conquers Syria, 303-6; conquers Egypt, 328-30, conquers Arabia, 336-38; conquest of, 491, 496-97. *See also* Nineveh; Sennacherib

Humanism. *See* Secular humanism

Hyde, Orson, dedicates Palestine for return of the Jews, 121–22, 719

Hypocrites, God's judgments on, 462–63

I

Idolatry, practiced in ancient Israel, 152, 156; reproved by God, 152, 526–27, 552, 573–75, 587, 591–92, 693–94; modern forms of, 552; sexual depravity of ancient "fertility rites," 693

Idumea, meaning of the term, 472; to remain a desert during Millennium, 474–76

Immanuel, a name for Jesus Christ, 66, 204

Indians. *See* Lamanites

Intelligence, found in all matter, 550–51

Iran, to fight against Israel in battle of Armageddon, 323

Iraq, to be converted to the Gospel in last days, 324–25

Isaiah (the prophet), recorded more prophecy than other Old Testament prophets, 3, 4; his brilliance and poetic style, 6; his literary skill, 7; his writings endorsed by the Savior, 11, 110–11; born about 780 B.C., 13; family of, 13–14, 145; length of his ministry, 14, 145; his humility and resolution, 14–15; discouraging nature of his calling, 15–16, 614–15; importance of his writings, 16–17, 107, 615–16; a resident of Jerusalem, 17, 25; sees the Lord in vision, 17–18, 191–98, 538, 655; receives his prophetic calling, 18–19, 191–98; his encounter with King Ahaz, 19–20, 200–207; consulted by King Hezekiah about Assyrian threat, 37, 493–95, 498–503; promises Hezekiah an extension of life, 38–40, 505–10; overview of his ministry, 45; tradition of his martyrdom at hands of King Manasseh, 46; ministers during reigns of four kings of Judah, 145; sons of, 200, 210–11; wife of, a prophetess, 210; goes among people of Judah "naked and barefoot," 328; his personal reaction to visions of God's judgments, 333–34, 363; lost writings of, 485, 515; on his calling as a prophet, 607–8; foreordained as a prophet before his birth, 612–13; his preparation for his ministry, 613; to be honored by kings, 616; challenges his adversaries, 628–31; suffers persecution during his ministry, 629–30; prophecies of, will all be fulfilled, 711

Isaiah (the book), longest prophetic book in the Bible, 3; its meaning deliberately obscured, 4–5; difficulty of its poetic expressions, 6; frequently jumps from one time period to another, 6, 268–69; included in Nephites' brass plates, 8, 17, 79; Nephi's prophetic commentary on, 8–9, 79–80, 89–95, 404–21; fragmented by modern scholars, 9–10; written by a single author, 10–11, 517; endorsed by the Savior, 11, 110–11; importance of, 16–17, 107, 615–16; fulfillment of prophecies in, 96–107, 711; original title of, 145; source of historical chapters, 485; clarified by the Book of Mormon, 601, 611–12

Israel, a remnant of, to be preserved, 19, 379–80; Isaiah denounces sins of, 20–23, 29–30, 33, 145–47, 155–56, 179–87, 225, 385–86, 566–67, 568, 604, 605, 627–28, 692–95, 699–700, 705–7, 739, 750–52; latter-day gathering of, 113–14, 249–54, 275–76, 477–84, 557–58, 616–25, 667–70, 696; creation of the modern state of, 125; God rejects sacrifices of ancient, 148; meaning of the name, 177; foreordained to provide spiritual leadership on earth, 177–78, 238–39, 554; God's judgments on, 179–87, 197, 380–82, 553–54; to be redeemed and returned to land of their inheritance in last days, 235–36, 239–40, 255–57, 373–78, 555–56, 643–46, 670–71, 697, 711, 739–41, 752–53; Egypt's military losses to modern state of, 320; Egypt's President Anwar Sadat visits, 321; Ten Tribes revolt against Judah about 922 B.C., 383; remnants of several tribes remain with Judah, 383; to be upheld and blessed by God, 427–28, 587, 590, 592, 594, 608–9; called as God's "witnesses," 564; reason for their calling as a chosen people, 569–70; rebellious among, rejected as Abraham's seed, 570; Gentiles can be adopted into, 570, 686, 687; refined by affliction, 606; Gentiles to "nourish" gathering, 622–24; scattered all over the world, 624; ancient, rejected earthly ministry and crucifixion of Christ as a myth, 656; to be protected from all enemies in last days, 675–76; to be glorified, 680; sinful leaders of, reproved

Last days, Isaiah's prophecies of the, 109-42; summary of events in the, 713-15. *See also* Armageddon; Earth; Gathering; Millennium; Second Coming; Wicked

Law of Moses, King Hezekiah asks the Lord to overlook irregularities in observance of, 31; added because of Israel's transgressions, 62; purpose of, to bring the people to Christ, 62; sacrifices and rituals meaningless without obedience, 62-64

Leadership, dearth of, in ancient Jerusalem, 161-62, 164; descendants of Jacob to provide spiritual, 177-78

League of Nations, gives England a mandate over Palestine, 124

Lebanon, to be converted to the Gospel in last days, 324-25; latter-day restoration of, 425

Lehi, foretells preservation of America as a land of liberty, 80-81; possible ancestral home of, destroyed in 701 B.C., 213; sees Isaiah's vision of America, 397; family of, escapes from Jerusalem, 502; foresees events in the Savior's earthly ministry, 657

Levites, charged to renew temple service by King Hezekiah, 26-29; persecuted by Jeroboam, 384; flee northern Ten Tribes and join with Judah, 384

Libya, to fight against Israel in battle of Armageddon, 323; to be converted to the Gospel in last days, 324-25

Lost tribes. *See* Ten Tribes of Israel

Lot (nephew of Abraham), ancestor of Moabites, 289; flees valley of Sodom and Gomorrah, 289; death of his wife, 289; begets children by his daughters, 289-90

"Lovers of Zion," early Zionist organization among Russian Jews, 123

Lucifer, "son of the morning," 279; means "light bearer," 279; premortal rebellion of, 280-81. *See also* Satan

M

Magog. *See* Gog and Magog

Maher-shalal-hash-baz (son of Isaiah), meaning of his name, 211

Mahonri Moriancumer. *See* Brother of Jared

Malachi, on burning of the wicked at Second Coming, 133

Manasseh (king of Judah), succeeds his father, Hezekiah, 44; wickedness of, 46; tradition of his murder of Isaiah, 46

"Marvelous work and a wonder," performed by God in latter days, 421-22

Mary (mother of Christ), prophetically named by Nephite prophets, 58, 65n

Matter, intelligence found in all, 550-51; God ordained to organize, 561

Medes, Babylon conquered by Persians and, 260, 331-35; Cyrus becomes king of, 269, 273, 577, 579

Messiah. *See* Jehovah; Jesus Christ

Messiah (oratorio by Handel), based on Isaiah's writings, 646

Micah, on the temple in modern Jerusalem, 126

Millennium, conditions to exist during the, 137-42, 151, 224, 447-50, 452-55, 465-66, 684, 757-61; enmity of animals to cease during, 140-41, 244-46, 760-61; peace to prevail during, 154-55, 244-47, 759-60; Zion and Jerusalem to enjoy God's presence during, 173-74; universal knowledge of God during, 246; increase of knowledge in, 246-47; earth to be cleansed in preparation for, 358-62; sun and moon not needed to illuminate earth during, 366-67, 723; two world capitals during, 465-66; Christ to minister to his people during, 525; no infant mortality during, 759; the Lord to dwell in his temple during, 763; all to worship God during, 771. *See also* Last days; Second Coming

Missionary work, in latter days, 534, 535, 537, 538, 646-47; three phases of latter-day, 649; final great mission by 144,000 high priests, 769-70. *See also* Gathering

Mitchill, Samuel Latham, examines transcript from Book of Mormon plates, 99, 100, 417-18

Moab, history of, 289-92; conquered by Assyria, 292-301; Judah provides refuge for besieged people of, 297-99; rebuilt but later destroyed by Babylon, 302

Moon, to be turned into blood, 264-65, 357, 471; not needed to illuminate earth during Millennium, 366-67, 723

Sarah (wife of Abraham), ancestor of God's chosen people, 633; originally called Sarai, Genesis 17:15

Sargon II (king of Assyria), conquers Ten Tribes of Israel, 24–25, 33, 213, 327–28; accedes to Assyrian throne, 229; not a mythical figure, 229–30; death of, 230, 328, 329, 339, 434

Satan, cast out of heaven, 278–81; to be loosed at end of Millennium, 635. *See also* Lucifer

Saudi Arabia, to be converted to the Gospel in last days, 324–25

Scriptures, importance of regular study of the, 217; references to Christ's earthly ministry stricken from ancient, 656

Second Coming, the righteous caught up to meet Christ at his, 131–32, 521–22; events related to the, 132–36, 156–60, 371–72, 471, 518–25, 735–38, 743–44; earth to be cleansed by fire at the, 133–34, 172–73, 223, 264, 360, 440, 441, 442, 461, 474, 735, 758, 768, 771; resurrection of the just at the, 134–35, 371, 522; disappearance of rainbow a sign of the, 175; veil separating spirit world from temporal world to be removed at the, 371. *See also* Last days; Millennium; Mount of Olives

Secret combinations, condemned by God, 389–90, 391–92, 422–23, 424–25; God's coming judgments against, 392–94; introduced by Satan through Cain, 423; a modern example, 423–24

Secular humanism, creed of, 185–86

Sennacherib (king of Assyria), destroys 46 cities of Judah and threatens Jerusalem, 33–37, 40, 147, 213, 434, 445, 457, 485, 486, 495–97; his death foretold by Isaiah, 37, 495; flees to Nineveh after destruction of his army, 41, 446, 457–58, 459, 504; murdered by two of his sons, 42, 329, 504; accedes to Assyrian throne, 230, 328, 339; fulfills God's purposes in attacking Judah, 232–34; to be humbled by God, 233–34; battles Egyptians, 495

Seraphim, God worshipped by, 192–93, 194–95

"Servant" of God, identified as Christ, 651–52; also refers to Joseph Smith, 652

Shalmaneser V (king of Assyria), conquers Ten Tribes of Israel, 213; accedes to Assyrian throne, 229; death of, 229

Sharon, plains of, reclaimed in modern times, 478, 753

Shear-jashub (son of Isaiah), meaning of his name, 200

Shebna (treasurer to king of Judah), corrupts his office, 344–45

Singing. *See* Music

Smith, Emma, her testimony of the Book of Mormon, 98; on "unlearned" status of Joseph Smith, 418–19

Smith, George A., rededicates Palestine in 1873 for return of the Jews, 122–23

Smith, George Albert, prays for advance of freedom and Constitutional principles, 154

Smith, Joseph, his mission foretold by Isaiah and other prophets, 85–87; "root of Jesse" identified as, 85–86, 247–48; "unlearned," yet translates the Book of Mormon, 98, 102 and *n*, 418–19; warned to keep Book of Mormon plates and artifacts hidden from the world, 103; First Vision of, 104–5; many revelations given to, 105–6; raised up in latter days to restore the Gospel, 119; on the rebuilding of Jerusalem and its temple, 126; delayed recording of his First Vision, 191; instructed to make transcripts of Book of Mormon characters, 406, 415–16; prophesies to his captors in Carthage Jail, 536–37; prophesies Civil War, 537; on the true nature of God, 560; called God's "servant" by Isaiah, 651–52; assassinated, 652–53; on wickedness of the last days, 716

Smith, Joseph F., on Christ's mission to the spirit world, 76–77*n*

Socialism, inimical to law of consecration and stewardship, 180

Sodom and Gomorrah, annihilated by fire from heaven, 289

Solomon's Temple. *See* Temple of Solomon

Sperry, Sidney B., on single authorship of Isaiah's writings, 10–11

Spirit prison, the wicked consigned to, 365–66

Spirit world, Isaiah foretells Christ's mission to the, 73–77, 548–49; veil separating temporal world from, to be removed at Second Coming, 371; state of the righteous in, 691–92

Spiritualism, condemned by God, 216–17, 598

Y

Z